MODERNIZING REPRESSION

A volume in the series
Culture, Politics, and the Cold War
Edited by Christian G. Appy

Other titles in the Series

Modernizing Repression

Police Training and Nation-Building
in the American Century

JEREMY KUZMAROV

University of Massachusetts Press • Amherst and Boston

Copyright © 2012 by University of Massachusetts Press
All rights reserved
Printed in the United States of America
LC 2012007996
ISBN 978-1-55849-917-1 (paper); 916-4 (hardcover)

Designed by Jack Harrison
Set in Adobe Minion Pro with Formata display
Printed and bound by Thomson-Shore, Inc.

Library of Congress Cataloging-in-Publication Data
Kuzmarov, Jeremy, 1979–
Modernizing repression : police training and nation building in the American century /
Jeremy Kuzmarov.
    p. cm. — (Culture, politics, and the cold war)
Includes bibliographical references and index.
ISBN 978-1-55849-917-1 (pbk. : alk. paper) — ISBN 978-1-55849-916-4 (library cloth : alk. paper)
1. Police—Political aspects—History.   2. Police training—Developing countries—History.
3. Military planning—United States—History.   4. United States—Foreign relations—Developing countries.
5. Developing countries—Foreign relations—United States.   6. Imperialism.
I. Title.
HV7903.K89 2012
363.2'2—dc23
                    2012007996

British Library Cataloguing in Publication data are available.

To Ngosa and Chanda

Contents

Part III
The Cold War on the Periphery
Police Training and the Hunt for Subversives in Africa, Latin America, and the Middle East   163

Acknowledgments

Many people have assisted me over the years in writing this book. First, I thank the archivists and staff of the libraries I visited, including the National Archives; Michigan State University archives; the Truman, Eisenhower, Kennedy, and Johnson presidential libraries; and Carlisle Barracks Military Archives; and at the National Archives in Lusaka, Zambia, where I found some interesting material on U.S.-Zambian relations during a visit to the country not primarily related to the research. Second, I thank Sergeant Tony Sanders of the Kansas City Police Department for providing me with documents on Byron Engle's tenure with the department; Gary Wilkinson of the Indiana State Police for providing documents on a number of the Indiana troopers who served with the Office of Public Safety; and Patricia Harrington of Richmond, Virginia, for taking the time to put together materials for me about her father, Jeter Williamson, who served for over a decade in the global police programs.

I also wish to thank to the University of Tulsa and the Oklahoma Council of Humanities for supporting my research with a number of grants and Dean Tom Benediktson and department chair Tom Buoye for their encouragement and for assisting me to obtain a subvention to help cover production costs. My colleagues in the history department also deserve thanks, as do Andy Lupardus, Tamra Stansfield, and staffs at the University of Tulsa library and the Bucknell University library, who assisted me in tracking down rare documents and books.

Brett Reilly, who went on to become a Ph.D. student at the University of Wisconsin–Madison, served as my research assistant while I was at Bucknell and was very helpful in locating materials at the Kennedy Library, National Archives, and Carlisle Barracks. Sam Redmond and Matthew Pembleton provided valuable research assistance in Berkeley and in College Park, Maryland, and Jared Eberle and Michael Juen assisted me in going through WikiLeaks documents. Kirsten Weld and Sinae Hyun assisted me with material from their own research on Guatemala and Thailand. Georgina Sinclair provided material on Afghanistan, and Marieke Bloembergen provided information on Indonesia. She also invited me to a panel at the Association of Asian Studies conference in Hawaii in 2011, which stimulated a number of the ideas expressed in the book.

Sam Brawand and Jill Oglesbee assisted with the manuscript preparation. Clark Dougan, senior editor at the University of Massachusetts Press, helped to shepherd the book from its infancy and provided valuable comments on rough drafts. I am grateful for his support for my work. Carol Betsch and the staff at the University of Massachusetts Press were as usual a great pleasure to work with. Amanda Heller did yeoman's work as copyeditor, helping to improve the writing and catching many small errors. The peer reviewers for this study, Jennifer Fronc, Alfred W. McCoy, and Martha K. Huggins, offered extremely valuable insights that helped me broaden my analysis and improve the book. Christian G. Appy was an additional reader who provided excellent feedback. I am very grateful to have had the assistance of such a gifted group. I give extra thanks to McCoy for reiterating his advice in various conversations. His richly detailed and pathbreaking scholarship is a seminal influence.

Many other outstanding scholars, including Mark Selden and Michael Schwartz, took an interest in my book and provided invaluable commentary on articles and chapters which led to its improvement. Further thanks go to David C. Engerman, Michael Willrich, Kyle Longley, Jerry Lembcke, Hannah Gurman, Murray Polner, Brad Simpson, Richard Waller, Leslie Patrick, Fred Branfman, Noam Chomsky (who promptly answered several e-mail inquiries and made detailed and insightful comments on articles of mine related to this book), and Jack Tobin, who provided valuable editing at an early stage.

Finally, I thank Margaret Kalufianya for her warm hospitality during my extended visits to Silver Springs, Maryland, to work at the National Archives, and my family for their support, including my parents and wife, Ngosa, and daughter Chanda.

Abbreviations Used in Text

AMG	American Military Government, South Korea
ANC	Congolese Army
ANP	Afghan National Police
ARVN	Army of the Republic of Vietnam
BPP	Border Patrol Police, Thailand
CIC	Counter-Intelligence Corps, U.S. Army
COINTELPRO	Counter Intelligence Program, FBI
CPA	Coalition Provisional Authority, Iraq
DAS	Departamento Administrativo de Seguridad, Colombia
DEA	Drug Enforcement Administration
EAM	National Liberation Front of Greece
ELF	Eritrean Liberation Front
ELN	Ejército de Liberacion Nacional, Colombia
FAR	Rebel Armed Forces, Guatemala
FARC	Fuerzas Armadas Revolucionarias de Colombia
FBN	Federal Bureau of Narcotics
FMLN	Farabundo Martí National Liberation Front, El Salvador
FSLN	Sandinista Liberation Front
GHQ	General Headquarters
GMD	Guomindang, China
GVN	Government of Vietnam
ICA	International Cooperation Administration
ICITAP	International Criminal Investigative Training Assistance Program
INP	Iraqi National Police
IPA	International Police Academy
IPS	Internal Defense and Public Safety
ISI	Inter-Services Intelligence, Pakistan
JCP	Japanese Communist Party
KKE	Communist Party of Greece
KNP	Korean National Police
LDP	Liberal Democratic Party, Japan

LNP	Lao National Police
MAAG	Military Assistance Advisory Group
MSU	Michigan State University
MSUG	Michigan State University Vietnam Advisory Group
NLF	National Liberation Front, Vietnam
OISP	Overseas Internal Security Program (formerly 1290-d)
OPS	Office of Public Safety
OSS	Office of Strategic Services
PAVN	People's Army of Vietnam
PGT	Communist Party of Guatemala
PKI	Indonesian Communist Party
PLO	Palestine Liberation Organization
PRU	Provincial Reconnaissance Units, Vietnam
PSD	Public Safety Division
RLA	Royal Lao Army
RLG	Royal Lao Government
ROK	Republic of Korea
ROKA	Republic of Korea Army
SAVAK	National Security and Intelligence Unit, Iran
SCAP	Supreme Command of the Allied Powers
SKLP	South Korean Labor Party
TNP	Thai National Police
USAID	U.S. Agency for International Development
USMAGIK	United States Military Advisory Group in Korea
USOM	United States Operations Mission
VBI	Vietnamese Bureau of Investigation
VC	Vietcong
VCI	Vietcong infrastructure

MODERNIZING REPRESSION

Introduction

Through the activities of the OPS, the notion of the US as world policeman is transformed from a metaphor to a reality.
—Joe Stork, "World Cop: How America Builds the Global Police State," 1970

In history, the man in the ruffled shirt and gold-laced waistcoat somehow levitates above the blood he has ordered to be spilled by dirty-handed underlings.
—Francis Jennings, *Empire of Fortune*, 1988

In a March 19, 2010, cover story, "The Gang That Couldn't Shoot Straight," *Newsweek* reported that although the United States had spent $6 billion trying to create an effective police force in Afghanistan, officers could barely shoot a rifle or hit a target fifty meters away, and much of the ammunition wound up being used by insurgents. Mohammed Moqim, an eight-year veteran of the force, was quoted as saying: "We are still at zero. [Recruits] don't listen, are undisciplined, and will never be real policemen." Tracy Jeansonne, a sheriff from Louisiana who worked as a police trainer for the defense contractor DynCorp from 2006 to 2008, added: "A lot of the police officers wanted to be able to extort money from locals. If we caught them, we'd suggest they be removed. But we couldn't fire anybody. We could only make suggestions."[1]

While critical of U.S. policy, the *Newsweek* article, as these comments suggest, conveyed the impression that more sustained American managerial oversight could rectify the shortcomings of the police programs and help overcome local cultural impediments to success. Historically, however, persistent oversight by the United States has often been catastrophic for the subject society, largely because of the repressive function for which the police programs were designed. What is ignored in much mainstream commentary is the fact that American strategy in the Middle East and Central Asia today is consistent with practices honed over more than a century in the poor nations of the global periphery. Presented to the public as humanitarian initiatives designed to strengthen democratic development and public security, police training programs achieved neither, but were critical to securing the power base of local elites amenable to U.S. economic and political interests. These programs helped to facilitate the rise of antidemocratic forces, which operated with impunity and above the law, contributing to endemic violence and state terrorism.[2]

In his essay "Shooting an Elephant," George Orwell recounts his experiences as a young man serving with the British colonial police in Burma. He felt despised everywhere he went. Toward the end of his tenure, he was called on to shoot a stray elephant that had encroached on public space. Although he felt guilty for doing so, he wanted to uphold the manly public image that the colonialists were trying to convey. And so, against his better conscience, he performed the deed. Summing up the episode, Orwell comments that, in the police, "you see the dirty work of Empire at close quarters. The wretched prisoners huddling in the stinking cages of the lock-ups, the grey cowed faces of the long-term convicts, the scarred buttocks of the men who had been bogged [flogged] with bamboos."[3]

Orwell's observations contain a large measure of universality and could have been echoed by Americans stationed in colonial enclaves such as the Philippines and Haiti, or in the Cold War era in South Vietnam, or in the Middle East today. Compared to its European counterparts, the American empire, especially since World War II, is unique in its reliance on indirect mechanisms of social control and the use of native proxies to promote its strategic interests. Accordingly, its elephant killers have been predominantly native to their region but no less hated.

Over the years, as U.S. imperial attention has shifted from one trouble spot to another, police training and financing have remained an unobserved constant, evolving with new strategies and weapons innovations but always retaining the same strategic goals and tactical elements. The programs have been valued as a cost-effective, covert mechanism for suppressing radical and nationalist movements, precluding the need for military intervention, which was more likely to arouse public opposition, or enabling the drawdown of troops. With remarkable continuity, the United States has trained police not just to target criminals but to develop elaborate intelligence networks oriented toward internal defense, which allowed the suppression of dissident groups across a wide range and in a more surgical and often brutal way. The United States in effect helped to modernize intelligence-gathering and political-policing operations in its far-flung empire, thus magnifying their impact. The programs helped to militarize the police and fostered, through rigorous ideological conditioning, the dehumanization of political adversaries and a sense of suspicion toward grassroots mobilization. The result has been a reign of torture and terror as part of police practice in many countries subject to U.S. influence and an increase in corruption levels pushing regimes toward kleptocracy.[4]

The Progressive Era was a watershed in the evolution of American imperial policing strategies. Progressivism as an ideology was concerned with regulating the excesses of market capitalism and creating a centralized state bureaucracy to manage social change and, in theory, break down parochial prejudice, privilege, and local power by expanding the reach of the federal government.

Its proponents viewed the reform of the criminal justice system, including the creation of juvenile courts, uniform sentencing, and humane prisons, as integral to the state-building process and the realization of a more just society. Professionalism in policing institutions was seen as especially vital to the task of restraining the anarchy of a rapidly expanding capitalism and establishing internal security and order in an age of increasing social agitation and unrest.[5]

As William E. Leuchtenburg noted over a half century ago, imperialism was a logical extension of progressivism. The new technocratic elite that it fostered believed in their own capacity not only to regulate social life within the United States but also to apply the same techniques of governance to American colonial enclaves abroad. In their view, Third World peoples could be uplifted through the importation of modern technology and Western administrative systems, of which policing was seen as a cornerstone.[6] Local hostility and resistance, however, and a political context unlike that of the United States, thwarted their designs. Officials appropriated American assistance for their own purposes and held different visions of how to manage society. The United States was fixated, furthermore, on stamping out resistance groups and thus mobilized police along political and military lines, which resulted in the spread of ample violence and terror. Ideological imperatives ultimately combined with an imperial drive for hegemony and control to encourage the growth of highly coercive policing and surveillance networks, which were later reimported back home to similarly repressive effect.[7]

Liberal commentators have often heralded the Progressive Era reforms and rise of the "administrative state" as a positive step in the evolution of democratic governance in the United States. With regard to criminal justice, these claims are not totally misplaced. During the Gilded Age, police were notoriously corrupt and beholden to wealthy industrialists and political machines. Instead of going on patrol, officers often spent their shifts drinking in a local bar.[8] They intimidated voters during elections, spied on radical social organizations, and viciously broke up worker demonstrations and strikes, often in conjunction with the antiunion Pinkerton Detective Agency. Police were further prone to excessive force, including the use of billy clubs to bludgeon suspects, a proclivity magnified by rampant nativism and anti-immigrant sentiment.[9] Lincoln Steffens, the famous muckraker, and a former police reporter, recalled in his autobiography, "Many a morning when I had nothing else to do I stood and saw the police bring in and kick out their bandaged, bloody prisoners, not only strikers and foreigners, but thieves too, and others of the miserable, friendless, troublesome poor."[10]

Progressive reformers, including Theodore Roosevelt, head of the New York City Police Commission from 1895 to 1897, emphasized that police should be committed to an ideal of public service. They sought to increase administrative efficiency according to the principles of the managerial revolution, standardize weapons, and promote due process, speedy sentencing, and the protection of civil liberties. To minimize corruption, pay was increased, and chiefs were promoted on the basis of their record of service rather than political connections. Training was systematized through the use of textbooks and the development of police academies. Progressives conceived of modern policing as a science and took pains to incorporate new technologies. The automobile and two-way radio helped transform the nature of police work, allowing for wider patrol networks and coordination between units. Advances in photography led to the famed mug shot and wanted posters. The advent of the Bertillon procedure, using physical measurements and fingerprinting, enhanced the efficiency of record-gathering systems, vital to modern policing.[11]

Diplomatic officials sought to reproduce these innovations globally as part of the attempt to internationalize the American criminal justice system and promote "nation-building" and progress through the importation of Western institutions and governing systems. A commitment to legal procedure and due process was perceived as a defining feature of Western societies and a marker of their civility, to be replicated in colonial enclaves. Paradoxically, the Progressive Era reforms were decidedly limited in their effect and bore damaging consequences in the effort to stabilize the existing political and economic structure. Police brutality continued to proliferate, especially against working-class immigrants and African Americans. "Red squads" used sophisticated surveillance technologies to monitor and harass union activists and leftists.[12] The 1931 Wickersham report, coauthored by August Vollmer, the "father of modern law enforcement," known for his innovations as police chief in Berkeley, California, pointed to the perpetuation of "flagrant corruption" and "third degree" methods of torture, concluding that "law enforcement agencies are usually held in contempt and law enforcement is one of our national jokes." Over time, an accelerating emphasis on training and paramilitary policing led many departments to become "powerful, independent political entities," in the words of Los Angeles Police Department historian Joe Domanick, and helped transform the criminal justice system into a vast "criminal justice industry."[13]

The modernization of police institutions in the United States during the Progressive and New Deal eras was accompanied by attempts to upgrade the prison system, including efforts to improve sanitation and promote rehabilitation, which policymakers again sought to duplicate worldwide. Convict leasing was outlawed, and literacy, recreation, and vocational training programs were established, along with juvenile facilities and a parole system, in part in response to inmate activism. There were even experiments in self-governance.[14] As with the police, the reforms were restrictive in their effects and not uniformly implemented. A continued emphasis on order and discipline took precedence over the idealistic vision of progressive penologists. The conditions in most prisons remained harsh and, according to leading sociological studies, created breeding grounds for crime. Beatings by guards and draconian solitary confinement practices remained commonplace. Reading material was usually restricted, labor regimens remained exploitative, and racial segregation was the norm.[15] The criminologist John L. Gillin wrote in a 1931 study: "Monuments to stupidity are these institutions we have built. . . . How silly of us to think that we can prepare men for social life by reversing the ordinary process of socialization—silence for the only animal with speech; repressive regimentation of men . . . outward conformity to rules which repress all efforts at constructive expression; work without the operation of economic motives; motivation by fear of punishment rather than by hope of reward or appeal to their higher motives."[16]

The most flagrant abuses occurred in southern prisons such as Parchman Farm in Mississippi, where mostly black inmates were forced to labor from dawn to dusk in the hot sun, fed wretched food, and subjected to electroshocks and whippings by trusties, privileged inmates responsible for discipline.[17] Conditions in the rest of the country were often not much better. In her 1923 memoir, the socialist Kate O'Hare, who was incarcerated in Missouri for speaking out against U.S. entry in World War I, recounted being ordered to bathe after a woman infected with syphilis and open sores, who had dripping pus and maggots streaming out of filthy bandages. She wrote that cell areas were "very dirty . . . shabby and unsanitary" and "every crack and crevice of the cellhouse was full of vermin. . . . Rats overran the place in swarms, scampered over the dining tables, nibbled [at the food] . . . and crept into bed with us."[18]

In spite of repeated efforts at reform, injustices continued through the ensuing decades. George Jackson's memoir *Soledad Brother* sheds light on the systematic racial discrimination in California prisons leading to violence and rebellion during the 1960s.[19] In 1970 Attorney General John A. Mitchell described the penal system to a *Washington Post* reporter as a "national shame." The reporter editorialized that prisoners in the United States were "more carelessly handled than animals in our zoos. . . . Guards aren't even paid as much as zookeepers."[20] Conditions only worsened thereafter with the abandonment of the goal of rehabilitation and rampant overcrowding spawned by tough-on-crime policies such as the "War on Drugs." In June 2008, 2,310,984 prisoners were being held in federal or state prisons or local jails, by far the highest incarceration rate in the world. Supermax facilities have become increasingly prevalent, in which inmates are locked up for twenty-three hours a day under intense electronic surveillance, with almost no social interaction. Mumia Abu-Jamal wrote in *Live from Death Row* of the "profound horror . . . in the day-to-day banal occurrences in prison . . . a second-by-second assault on the soul."[21] The harsh reality cuts deep into myths of national exceptionalism and virtue embraced by those who have sought to remake other countries in the American image and export the model of American criminal justice. The United States' system has never been ideal.

The abuses spawned by international training programs therefore did not evolve as some kind of aberration but were rather an extension of domestic practice. Anthony Russo of the RAND Corporation, indicted with Daniel Ellsberg in the Pentagon Papers case, remarked in a 1972 *Harper's* magazine interview that he finally understood "why we torture people in Vietnam— because we torture people *here*. The American advisers to the people who run the prisons in Vietnam are retired wardens, retired policemen, retired highway patrolmen, people who work in the so-called law and order field here in the United States." Russo went on:

> I knew a man who worked for USAID public safety who had been a warden here in the United States. I used to try and talk to him and try to get some reason out of him concerning the conditions of prisons in Vietnam. He used to always come back to his experience with prisons here in the United States. . . . He was trying to get across to me that convicts are scum. He said, "We go to all this trouble to keep them in prison when we should take them out in a ship and drop them out at sea, just throw them overboard. They're worthless human beings. There's no reason to keep them alive. They're no good to anybody."[22]

These comments convey the attitudes that many advisers brought with them from the United States, which led to abuse. The political context in which they operated and the racist sentiments they exhibited toward Third World peoples brought out their most repressive qualities. Many subscribed to the worldview of the New Right, which was dedicated to America's international preeminence through superior armaments and intervention and saw peace and reform movements as fronts for communist subversion, a viewpoint that resulted in intolerance for dissent of any kind.[23]

Embodying a U.S. imperial style grounded in short-term duty and the quest for serviceable information but not deep knowledge of the subject society, police advisers took pride in their ability to serve as "missionaries of modernization," as one historian termed it, and sought to bolster organizational efficiency and police professionalism in targeting both criminals and "subversives." While there were some soldiers of fortune among them, many had experience with political intelligence units ("red squads"), were skilled technicians, or had compiled distinguished records promoting progressive reforms in domestic police institutions which they sought to extend internationally.[24] Language and cultural barriers, however, hampered these efforts. Their labor was directed, furthermore, toward larger geostrategic ends, including the fortification of client regimes, which prevented the development of genuinely democratic policing standards characterized by a respect for due process and a commitment to abolishing torture and other forms of brutality.[25]

Under the banner of the anticommunist crusade, radical leftist and nationalist organizations were demonized to such an extent that their proponents were considered not to have any rights, even when engaging in lawful activity, and were subjected to surveillance, arrest, and torture. The architects of the police programs believed the suppression of left-wing groups, including through paramilitary police raids, to be legitimate in preserving the government's authority and maintaining law and order, as internal security was thought to be a primary responsibility of the police. Many of the violent excesses that ensued were tacitly sanctioned or covered up as part of a counterterror doctrine which held that since insurgents did not typically abide by Western legal norms, neither should the United States or its proxies in dealing with them.[26]

During the 1950s and 1960s, police from around the world were sent to observe the workings of the FBI, whose methods it was hoped they would emulate. Given the agency's checkered past, this boded ill for civil liberties. Founded in 1908 within the Department of Justice, the Federal Bureau of Investigation was a quintessentially progressive institution designed to expand the government's social control capabilities and centralize antiradical and anti-union pursuits. Though it became involved in combating organized crime and prostitution, its overriding focus was in the realm of political intelligence and the suppression of groups that threatened the existing power structure, such as the anarcho-syndicalist Industrial Workers of the World. In August 1919, after the bombing of his home, Attorney General A. Mitchell Palmer created a Radical Division headed by a young J. Edgar Hoover, who saw in the unrest of the period a "vast and monstrous conspiracy" to destroy the "religions, governments, and institutions of the Judeo-Christian world."[27] With Hoover's support, Palmer initiated a series of raids leading to the beating and arrest of over ten thousand suspected radicals, the ransacking of offices and homes, and the deportation of 556 people, including the anarchist Emma Goldman.[28]

Beginning in the late 1930s, the FBI undertook its first international operations, training the secret police of the Chinese Guomindang in the use of lie detectors, police dogs, weaponry, and electronic surveillance, and during World War II worked with police agencies in Latin America to track down Axis power sympathizers. Owing to faulty intelligence and paranoid fears of subversion, many rounded up in these campaigns were rivals of U.S.-backed dictators or German Jewish refugees forcibly interned alongside a few genuine Nazis in the Texas desert. In spite of its flaws, as the sociologists Cecilia Menjívar and Néstor Rodríguez point out, the program was significant in the evolution of the Bureau's practices. It put in place a "new science and technology of surveillance and social control, a bureaucratic method of following 'suspects,' gathering information from 'informants' or 'interrogations,' keeping files, constructing 'lists,' and centralizing 'data' at high administrative levels," which was foundational to the global police programs.[29]

The FBI experienced its most explosive growth in the 1950s during the McCarthy era, when it was called upon to enforce loyalty oaths, carry out security checks, and employ investigative techniques such as wiretapping, break-ins, and mail intercepts. Building on World War I–era and colonial policing practices in the Philippines and the Caribbean, much of its surveillance was carried out under the auspices of COINTELPRO (Counter Intelligence Program), established in 1956 with the aim of "disrupting, harassing, and discrediting" the American Communist Party and other "subversive" organizations through "creative" and "aggressive" methods, including the dissemination of "black" propaganda (misinformation).[30] The targets of COINTELPRO came to include a wide spectrum of the American left, including civil rights activists such as Paul Robeson and Martin Luther King Jr., the antiwar and student movements, the Black Panther Party, and the American Indian Movement. The FBI was particularly effective at using saboteurs to infiltrate and foment dissension within the New Left and encouraged counterproductive forms of protest, contributing to its eventual implosion. Robert Hardy, an FBI informant, testified that he led thirty antiwar activists in a raid on a Camden, New Jersey, draft board in 1971, teaching them "how to cut glass and open windows without making a noise . . . how to open file cabinets without a key."[31]

As these actions illustrate, COINTELPRO resulted in myriad constitutional violations, including illegal surveillance, blackmail, and collusion with police, as in the murder of Chicago Black Panther activists Fred Hampton and Mark Clark. The American Indian Movement and the Panthers were subjected to the greatest repression, and many of their members were imprisoned or killed.[32] COINTELPRO was exposed in 1971 after a break-in at FBI offices in Pennsylvania and was repudiated by the American public. The report of the investigating committee headed by Senator Frank Church, an Idaho Democrat, characterized it as a "vigilante operation" involving fundamentally undemocratic techniques. Nevertheless, it provided a model for political policing operations in the developing world.[33] Because of inadequate judicial oversight and constitutional checks owing to a different political climate, the human costs of these operations were usually far worse. The United States created vast policing apparatuses where none had existed before and strengthened local powerbrokers, who used police aid to repress their political opposition. Highly damaging was the militarization of the police and the inculcation of a national security ideology that allowed for the rationalization of gross human rights violations and cruelties, as police torturers and murderers have themselves acknowledged.[34]

Operating under the premise that good policing is a pivotal characteristic of a modern nation, American training programs introduced technical innovations and sought to provide foreign police with skills in management, fingerprinting, intelligence gathering, counter-narcotics, and counterterrorism, as well as more mundane tasks like traffic control. They promoted penal reform and set up training academies to institutionalize professional standards. Internalizing broader societal norms in viewing technology as a marker of advancement and a pathway to social progress, American advisers were committed to importing the scientific policing model prevalent in the United States and to modernizing police administration. They stressed the importance of record keeping as a means of elevating arrest and prosecution rates and provided funds to upgrade police pay and benefits in order to limit corruption. They further supplied state-of-the-art equipment, including radios and telecommunication gear, fingerprint kits, revolvers, handcuffs, and laboratory materials, in addition to police cruisers and vehicles, hand grenades, gas masks, and shields for riot control.[35]

It was not police modernization in itself, however, but the political context in which the programs were implemented that resulted in the spread of major human rights abuses. Because police trained by the United States frequently served as the enforcement arm of undemocratic regimes valued by the Americans for promoting free trade and anticommunism and oriented toward internal security and social control, the new equipment frequently aided an intensification of state repression, in effect modernizing it. The creation of elaborate intelligence infrastructures allowing for better coordination in tracking down "subversives," who often represented popular aspirations for social justice and change, accelerated this development.

Although in theory trainees were supposed to be apolitical, when "all the chips were down," reports conceded, they were militantly anticommunist and conservative, owing in part to the ideological conditioning they underwent. An internal blueprint stated that "political orientation should be subtly included in the overall instruction" and that "the United States has something to sell: a favorable impression of democracy." Coming from a social sector described by Los Angeles police chief Willie Parker in the early 1960s as "conservative, ultra-conservative and very right-wing," police advisers were influential in helping to impart an obsession with security, resulting in the creation of mass surveillance states and the devaluing of personal liberties. American police were themselves organized along authoritarian and predominantly military lines, in part because leading proponents of police professionalism were military veterans, which was not conducive to the spread of enlightened practice.[36]

After World War II, police programs emerged as a crucial dimension of the U.S. occupation of South Korea and in Japan, where they were designed to consolidate the power of the pro-West Liberal Democratic Party and crack down on the Japanese Communist Party and labor movement. During the Eisenhower presidency, police training was institutionalized under what was known as the 1290-d program (later the Overseas Internal Security Program, OISP), run out of the State Department, whose central mission was to develop local police and security forces to "provide internal security in countries vulnerable to communist subversion" and to "aid in the detection of communist agents and fellow travelers" and "suppress local dissidence before military-type action was necessary." The planning board included hard-liners from the Pentagon and

CIA who were obsessed with "the techniques of international communism." It was initially headed by Douglas MacArthur II, a former OSS (Office of Strategic Services) operative and nephew of the famous general, who later served as the ambassador to Japan and Iran. He was succeeded by Henry Villard (a onetime silent movie actor and grandson of the abolitionist William Lloyd Garrison), who had been the first chief of the State Department's African Affairs Division during World War II and ambassador to Libya in the early 1950s.[37]

An internal outline of the 1290-d program written by Colonel Albert R. Haney, CIA station chief in Seoul during the Korean War and an architect of the 1954 Guatemalan coup, states, "An efficient internal security system is a fundamental aspect of any growing society and contributes substantially to its orderly progress and development." In Haney's view, American support for distasteful political regimes, including dictatorships and juntas, was necessary to prevent the loss of an ally to neutralism or communist control:

> Confronted as we are against a deadly enemy who is highly disciplined and organized and dedicated to our capitulation, the U.S. cannot afford the moral luxury of helping only those regimes in the free-world that meet our ideals of self-government. . . . For those who decry efforts to make over others in our likeness and those who oppose helping undemocratic regimes to entrench themselves in power, let it be said that American methods *are in fact superior* to most others in the world and if we are to help them combat communism we can contribute greatly to the adoption of American democratic ways in achieving this end.[38]

These comments exemplify the extreme nationalism and anticommunism characteristic of the postwar era and the kind of moral logic used to rationalize support for wide-scale repression. Staffed with men of like mind, the Kennedy administration expanded the police programs to new heights in a larger infatuation with unconventional warfare. Contrary to the humanitarian image promoted in popular culture and fawning memoirs written by former aides, Kennedy was a Cold Warrior who embraced violence as a means of expanding American global hegemony.[39] Opposed to Eisenhower's commitment to a nuclear arms buildup, he promoted a flexible response doctrine calling for new counterinsurgency strategies in the face of radical nationalist movements in the developing world.

In 1961, in the aftermath of the Bay of Pigs debacle, Kennedy convened a cabinet-level Special Group on Counter-Insurgency, headed by his brother Robert and five-star general Maxwell Taylor, which championed the training of indigenous security forces in unconventional warfare and the creation of "hunter-killer" teams. Robert W. Komer of the National Security Council advised colleagues that "while treaty arrangements and international law" were to be given careful consideration, there was "no overriding bar to [clandestine] action when overriding national interests prevail. . . . [W]hen a government that is inimical to U.S. interests emerges, risks should be evaluated in encouraging and supporting the overthrow of that government."[40]

These remarks reveal the embrace of terrorist methods by Washington's "best and the brightest," who argued the need to maximize police training without damaging the public image of the United States, "with due recognition that specific country programs will often fall short of this ideal" owing to "local limitations."[41] In 1962 Kennedy established the Office of Public Safety (OPS) within the United States Agency for International Development (USAID) to "develop the civilian police component of internal security forces in underdeveloped states . . . identify early the symptoms of an incipient subversive situation," and "maintain law and order without unnecessary bloodshed and an obtrusive display of the bayonet."[42] Until it was disbanded in 1974, the OPS supplied approximately half a billion dollars' worth of equipment, advisers, and training toward these ends. The Philippines constabulary developed at the turn of the twentieth century was one model, owing to its proficiency in jungle warfare and its role in combating messianic peasant revolts that threatened American colonial domination.

The OPS director, Byron Engle, was a Kansas City police captain and a CIA operative who ran police operations in Japan and Turkey after World War II. Described by colleagues as a "masterful bureaucrat" and "compulsive modernizer," he was committed to improving police administration, communications, surveillance, and record keeping in the countries in which he operated worldwide. Influenced by a training course he took at the FBI, Engle sat in on the meetings of the Special Group and established a close connection between the OPS and the CIA, which were effectively merged. The Kennedy administration saw in him, according to the political scientist Thomas Lobe, a "perfect blend of deep commitment to civilian police work as an important and worthwhile occupation in society and an appreciation for the darker areas of political police intelligence."[43]

Under Engle's oversight, hundreds of foreign police were brought each year for training to the International Police Academy (IPA) in Washington, D.C., considered the West Point of law enforcement. Headed by Michael McCann, an FBI agent and Indiana state trooper who trained the Shah's security apparatus in Iran and was an adviser in Vietnam, Saudi Arabia, and Brazil, the IPA provided instruction in police administration, scientific methods, counterintelligence, and anticommunist ideology. One of its trademarks was a two-story pistol range with cardboard targets dressed as "subversives." The culmination was a mock counterinsurgency operation in which students had to suppress a disturbance and protect the ruling government from being swept from power. Observers noted that the simulation was harder than real life and that officers returned home with a certain "swagger," ready to engage in the fight against communism—at whatever human cost.

Most controversial was a secret bomb-making course in Los Fresnos, Texas, where police were taught not only how to defuse but also how to make bombs. McCann told Engle in a private meeting that "the offensive use of explosives would be vital in order to inculcate an understanding of the capabilities characteristic of various types of ordnance prior to training in disarmament techniques." As with military academies such as the School of the Americas, a primary aim of the IPA was to cultivate "assets" who, it was hoped, would rise in the national security apparatus of their home countries and provide information and assistance to American intelligence, paving the way for greater U.S. political influence and control. Occasionally an overseas corporation would send a private security officer to the IPA, as did Gulf Oil, Firestone Rubber of Liberia, and the Arabian American Oil Company.[44]

Robert Komer, a CIA veteran who served as director of pacification in Vietnam and was known as "Blowtorch" for his fiery temper, was a driving figure behind the expansion of the police programs. In May 1961 the Harvard Business School graduate conducted a study of the Eisenhower administration's police operations, which he termed "an orphan child that nobody seems to be paying any attention to. The 30 million that we give is small potatoes," he wrote in a memo to the Special Group. "The police are in many cases a far more effective and immediately useful counter-subversive instrument than the military. . . . The Indonesian mobile brigade, for example, is generally regarded as the most effective force in Indonesia."[45] In another memo to Taylor and McGeorge Bundy, the president's special assistant for national security affairs, Komer stressed that the police were "more valuable than Special Forces in our global counter-insurgency efforts" and particularly useful in fighting urban insurrections. "We get more from the police in terms of preventative medicine than from any single U.S. program," he said. "They are cost effective, while not going for fancy military hardware. . . . They provide the first line of defense against demonstrations, riots, and local insurrections. Only when the situation gets out of hand (as in South Vietnam) does the military have to be called in."[46]

Mirroring the thinking of British imperial strategists such as Winston Churchill, who wrote in 1954 that an "efficient police force and intelligence service are the best way of smelling out subversive movements at an early stage, and may save heavy expenditures on military reinforcements," these comments illuminate the underlying geostrategic imperatives shaping the growth of the programs and the mobilization of police for political and military ends, which accounted for the spread of human rights abuses. Charles Maechling Jr., staff director of the Special Group on Counter-Insurgency, acknowledged years later that in failing to insist on "even rudimentary standards of criminal justice and civil rights, the United States provided regimes having only a facade of constitutional safeguards with up-dated law-enforcement machinery readily adaptable to political intimidation and state terrorism. Record keeping in particular was immediately put to use in tracking down student radicals and union organizers."[47]

Maechling's remarks constitute a striking admission and underscore the vapidity of academic modernization theorists who championed military and police training programs as a means of providing the security deemed necessary for economic "take-off," which could then undercut support for left-wing movements.[48] A key aspect for Walt W. Rostow, the most prominent of the modernization theorists and a Special Group member, was that communism was a "disease of the transition"; it prospered when the need for savings reduced standards of living before natural economic growth could take hold. Counterinsurgency was thus necessary to maintain order and stability as a precondition for development and for attracting foreign investment.[49]

George F. Kennan, the influential State Department planner whose views resembled the modernization theorists', told a group of Latin American ambassadors in 1950: "It may be unpleasant but we should not hesitate before police repression by the local government. . . . It is better to have a strong regime in power than a liberal government if it is indulgent and relaxed and penetrated by communists."[50] These remarks help explain the strategic calculations underlying American support for right-wing dictators during the Cold War and the importance attached to police training in bolstering their power. Kennan referred to human rights in the Far East as an unrealistic objective to pursue, owing to the region's perceived backwardness and need to deal in "straight power concepts." The State Department attributed human rights abuses in Latin America, meanwhile, to "pervasive cultural and legal attitudes typical of lesser developed countries," which, it predicted, would "be overcome as the country gradually modernizes."[51]

Not coincidentally, given such attitudes, Amnesty International documented widespread physical and psychological torture by police in twenty-four of the forty-nine nations that hosted police training teams. Declassified interrogation manuals used at the International Police Academy show a particular emphasis on sensory deprivation and other psychological torture techniques derived from CIA-funded mind-control experiments, which were widely adopted across the so-called Third World. Special Forces officer Donald Duncan testified before the International War Crimes Tribunal, organized in 1966 by the philosopher Bertrand Russell, that American advisers rarely participated themselves in torture sessions, deferring to their protégés largely for tactical reasons. They did not want the United States to be identified with political repression and could claim plausible deniability when abuses got of hand, as with the covert Phoenix program, which aimed to wipe out the leadership of the revolutionary movement in South Vietnam through coordinated policing and targeted assassination.[52]

The police programs ultimately exemplify the dangers of social engineering efforts by the United States and the hidden and coercive aspects of American power. Unlike the spectacular but ephemeral pyrotechnics of the battlefield, these training programs usually had long-term consequences for the subject society—fostering new elites, creating a lasting apparatus of social control, and often introducing a potent mechanism for the suppression of social reform. In this last respect, they proved effective in advancing American imperial ambitions, which were rooted in part in the desire to integrate countries of the developing world into the global capitalist economy and create a stable environment for investment and trade.[53] The police programs could also backfire, however, and breed uncontrollable violence, instability, and resistance in a "blowback effect." In numerous cases they fueled the rise of rogue operators who used the policing apparatus built up by the United States to carve out personal fiefs and wipe out rivals, warping democratic development.

Owing to cultural barriers and an underlying paternalism, police commanders often had little respect for U.S. advisers but accepted weaponry out of self-interest. A large degree of cynicism consequently accompanied the programs. Engle grumbled to colleagues that what "all these countries wanted was an 'equipment drop' and not our advice." But as a USAID official recognized, "to have a former desk sergeant in some two-bit town where he was responsible for twenty policemen give advice to a well-educated police general who comes from the social elite of his country and commands literally thousands of men is an insult."[54]

While differing political contexts have ensured different results historically, there are some patterns that emerge as universal, in particular the role of the United States in providing sophisticated policing equipment and trying to professionalize the internal security apparatus of client regimes as a means of fortifying their power. New technologies were developed in an attempt to advance the efficiency of this latter task, though the overriding goal remained the same, from the Philippines occupation on down.

This book breaks new ground in providing a comparative analysis of the police programs sponsored by the United States and their link to the spread of political repression. The topic has been ignored in most standard histories. Martha K. Huggins's *Political Policing* offers a notable exception in detailing the history of police training and the link to major human rights violations in Brazil. A. J. Langguth's *Hidden Terrors* is a revealing journalistic exposé of police training and state-sponsored terrorism in Latin America during the Cold War. Thomas Lobe's dissertation covers the impact of the programs in Thailand. Michael T. Klare's *War without End* and Michael McClintock's *Instruments of Statecraft* and *The American Connection* show the centrality of the programs to global counterinsurgency strategies. Noam Chomsky and Edward S. Herman in *The Washington Connection and Third World Fascism* and Gabriel Kolko in *Confronting the Third World* contextualize them as part of a larger pattern of subversion in the Third World, driven by economic and other imperialist motives, while Alfred W. McCoy in *A Question of Torture* shows their contribution to the spread of torture. More recently, in *Policing America's Empire*,

McCoy chronicles the history of the Philippines constabulary and its adoption of advanced methods of surveillance, intimidation, and violence to secure imperial domination. These methods were later appropriated by policing institutions in the United States, contributing to an erosion of civil liberties.[55]

Building on these invaluable works, *Modernizing Repression* incorporates newly declassified documents, including the field reports of police advisers, to provide a comparative analysis of the police training programs and their harmful effects. In my view, the programs encapsulate how the United States resembles other empires in being sustained by violence and coercion.[56] Much recent scholarship in American diplomatic history has focused on modernization theory and anticommunist "nation-building" as the key motivating factors driving American foreign policy during the Cold War.[57] Police training can be seen as central to both processes. It served key political and ideological functions in establishing the internal security deemed necessary for liberal capitalist development; and it was crucial as well in upgrading the surveillance capacity of states in the developing world, thus allowing for more extensive social control—the ultimate marker of modernity in the post-Enlightenment era.[58] Therein lay its dark side.

The first section of the book, "Taking Up the 'White Man's Burden,'" discusses the pioneering efforts by the U.S. military to create police constabularies in the Philippines and the Caribbean in order to solidify colonial occupations in the first half of the twentieth century. Drawing on the domestic innovations of the Progressive Era, American commanders imparted sophisticated police technologies and psychological warfare techniques with the aim of suppressing nationalist and messianic peasant movements. The United States in turn helped to establish some of the first modern police states, which provided a model for subsequent interventions.

The second section, "Under the Facade of Benevolence," examines the evolution of the police programs during the Cold War period and their centrality to operations meant to "roll back" the progress of communism in Southeast Asia. The "reverse course" in Japan was a watershed in that, fearing the loss of a beachhead in the Asian Pacific with the triumph of the Chinese revolution, the Supreme Command of the Allied Powers abandoned efforts to promote civil liberties and mobilized police to crack down harshly on the left. American advisers led by a young Byron Engle taught novel techniques of population control, including the use of tear gas to quell urban demonstrations, which became a feature of the programs. In South Vietnam, where it had the largest budget, the OPS laid the groundwork for Operation Phoenix, though it spiraled out of control, breeding indiscriminate violence.

The third section, "The Cold War on the Periphery," examines the police programs on the edges of the Cold War, where many of the same methods were incorporated as in Southeast Asia, by many of the same personnel, and with a similar outcome. In Latin America, the traditional workshop of empire, public safety advisers refined techniques that were trademarks of the OPS, such as the development of databanks on subversives, and trained forces that became implicated in systematic human rights violations. In the Middle East, police training was designed to fortify client regimes that ensured American access to the region's oil, such as that of the Shah of Iran. In Africa, meanwhile, it helped to dash early hopes of liberation by contributing to the empowerment of right-wing dictators and the exacerbation of ethnic conflict.

The final chapter analyzes the legacy of the OPS and the continuity of policy in Afghanistan and Iraq, where the United States again promoted police training as a cost-effective means of pacifying insurgent movements. The discourse paid little attention to historical precedent, and, predictably, history repeated itself. Problems were aggravated by a reliance on private security corporations and police advisers caught up in domestic human rights and corruption scandals.

The covert manner in which police operations have been historically carried out underscores the contradiction between America's republican self-identity and its global ambitions, which can usually be achieved only through force or the threat of it. Framed in a benevolent rhetoric, the programs helped to modernize repression across much of the so-called Third World. They exemplify the coercive underpinnings of American power, which policymakers have repeatedly tried to conceal in the attempt to preserve the myth of American exceptionalism, the notion that the United States is a uniquely selfless nation. In reality, American conduct abroad resembles that of past imperial powers in the propensity to manipulate political developments in weaker nations, seize control over strategic resources, and crush those not obedient to America's whims, frequently by proxy in order to preserve an anti-imperialist facade. Despite its preponderant power, the United States has often failed to assert its will effectively and bred disastrous unforeseen consequences in the countries in which it has intervened. How the police programs fit this paradigm and contributed to the spread of political violence during an era of American global hegemony is the subject of this book.

Part I

Taking Up the "White Man's Burden"

Imperial Policing in the Philippines and the Caribbean

Do his orders come at one a.m.,
He's on his way by two.
Tho' lacking rations for his men,
He'll stay till he gets through.
He may be gone a week or month.
To Samar or to—well,
The daily papers never learn
What this young man could tell.
—"Constabulary Man," popular song

We were all imbued with the fact that we were trustees of a huge estate that belonged to minors.
—GENERAL SMEDLEY BUTLER, Haiti, 1917

From the Philippine Islands in 1901 to Afghanistan in 2012, police training, through a cadre of technical specialists, has been a central facet of Washington's foreign interventions. The programs evolved in distinctive ways and have been carried out by different bureaucratic agencies, including the military, the State Department, the Central Intelligence Agency, and, more recently, private mercenary firms such as DynCorp and Xe (formerly Blackwater). The primary motive, consistent across time and space, has been to fortify and gain leverage over the internal security apparatus of client regimes and to root out groups resisting U.S. power. In addition, the programs have provided an opportunity for exporting new policing technologies and administrative techniques, as well as modern weaponry and equipment which has all too often been used for repressive ends.

American imperialism has been driven by a yearning for commercial trade and growth as well as a missionary-like zeal to export American institutions and ideologies abroad. The Progressive Era was a watershed moment, owing to the maturation of an industrial economy with a productive capacity outstripping domestic demand, the flowering of social Darwinian philosophies, and the development of a modern military and government bureaucracy. The new American empire required an infrastructure of shipping lanes, naval bases, treaty ports, and coaling stations, which fueled the conquest of the Philippines, and that of Haiti and Nicaragua following the construction of the Panama Canal.[1]

The creation of indigenous constabularies provided a key, cost-effective mechanism for projecting American power. The organizations were conceived in the belief that the centralization of state authority and regulation of social life were conducive to the development of a modern nation-state, and that a professional police force could ensure the domestic stability needed to spur foreign investment and allow for economic development. In the eyes of policymakers, the United States was at once helping to uplift the native population by aiding in the creation of a modern administrative state while advancing American strategic interests. The architects of the programs could thus always feel good about what they were doing, even if the forces under their command acted cruelly.

Local elites welcomed the programs because they shared a similar worldview, and they used the technical aid and weapons to strengthen their authority. Trained in counter-guerrilla warfare and espionage, the constabularies assisted the U.S. Marines in pacification and sought to ensure a smooth transition from direct to indirect colonial rule. Many of the tactics developed, including training academies, the novel data management and fingerprinting techniques, penal reforms, and psychological warfare, were foundational to the global police programs. They contributed to the growth of modern surveillance states, supple in their omnipresence, as the historian Alfred W. McCoy notes, yet suffocating in their omniscience.[2]

Like their European counterparts, the first wave of U.S. advisers came from military backgrounds and endured harsh jungle conditions while carrying out clandestine intelligence operations. Many devoted years of service and learned local languages, which helped them in recruiting native forces, penetrating enemy encampments, and winning over sectors of the population. Colorful figures such as "Black Jack" Pershing, Lewis "Chesty" Puller, and Smedley Butler earned public fame through their exploits and went on to decorated military careers. Constabulary officers saw themselves as contributing to the advancement of civilization through the spread of Western technology and were endowed with enormous powers compared to their successors, becoming district and provincial governors. The opportunities for private enrichment and corruption were consequently rife, and many took advantage. Wide-scale violence was rationalized by demonizing opponents, who were characterized as "bandits," "savages," "ladrones," and "gugus," among other refrains.

True to Orwell's observations, American police officials embodied the repressive underpinnings of the American empire. In taking the call of Rudyard Kipling's "White Man's Burden" to heart, they tortured those who did not acquiesce to their whims, provided intelligence for bombing attacks, oversaw forced labor projects, and were implicated in massacres, such as the slaughter of over six hundred *people in the Moro province of the Philippines. After American troops were with-drawn, the police institutions they created remained the all-powerful instrument of authoritarian leaders. The United States left not only a legacy of violence and social division but also sophisticated apparatuses of social control, which paved the way for continued governmental repression over the long term.*

Chapter 1

The First Operation Phoenix
U.S. Colonial Policing in the Philippines and the Blood of Empire

To be outnumbered, always, to be outfought, never.
— Philippines constabulary slogan, early 1900s

The history of the American occupation of the Philippines is in large measure the history of the Philippines constabulary—for it was this force of native infantry that applied the finishing touches of civilization to a jungle land that had known no law.
—VIC HURLEY, *Jungle Patrol*, 1938

"Let any critic try the nerve-racking sport of hunting well-armed *babaylanes, pulajanes*, Moros or . . . *ladrones* [euphemisms for guerrilla bandits] before he censures the constabulary for firing quickly—and to kill."[1] So wrote the soldier of fortune John R. White in *Bullets and Bolos: Fifteen Years in the Philippine Islands*, his 1928 account of his tenure with the Philippines constabulary. Written as an adventure tale and a homily on the gallantry of American fighting forces, White's book was characteristic of its time in its favorable reference to Kipling and the "white man's burden." Furthermore, it exemplifies the importance of the police constabulary to U.S. imperial strategy.

After invading the islands in 1899 shortly after the Philippines declared itself an independent republic, the American military engaged in a systematic campaign to wipe out the nationalist movement, culminating in orders by General Jacob Smith to turn the rebellious Samar province into a "howling wilderness."[2] Foreshadowing by nearly seventy years the Nixon doctrine strategy of "using Asian boys to fight Asian boys," the governing commission created an indigenous constabulary to complete the pacification. Modern weaponry and equipment were provided, training academies were established, penal reforms were initiated, and a surveillance apparatus was developed, using new technologies that were a product of the information revolution. Building on the model of the British police in India and American practice toward the Native Americans, the subcontracting of counterinsurgency enabled policymakers to fulfill their imperial ambitions at minimal cost and to quell public dissent spearheaded by the Anti-Imperialist League. Since its constabulary operations were kept secret, the identity of the United States as an anti-imperialist power was furthermore preserved.[3]

During the Vietnam War, over a half century after the Philippines constabulary took shape, Pentagon analysts were still heralding its accomplishments.[4] Roger Hilsman, assistant secretary of state for Far Eastern affairs in the early 1960s, characterized it as crucial in the waging of "one of the most successful counterguerrilla campaigns in history" and a prototype for ongoing efforts to contain the spread of revolutionary nationalism across the developing world. Prior to the formation of the constabulary, "the army tried to fight the guerrillas, but with little success," he wrote, "the enemy faded into the jungle, and the unwieldy regular units were too burdened with equipment, too slow.... Finally, the United States found the solution... recruiting native Filipinos, men wise to jungle ways who knew the mountains and trails like their own back yard."[5] These comments provide a clear explanation of the purpose behind the police programs, which remained unchanged across the decades. They also suggest a selective memory in ignoring the violence associated with the constabulary's exploits, replicated again and again among its offspring.

Creating a Modern Surveillance State: Police Training, Nation-Building, and the "Civilizing Mission" in the Philippines

Although the United States had been an expansionist empire from its founding, the colonization of the Philippines at the turn of the twentieth century was a pivotal point, marking the beginning of the nation's rise to global dominance. Building on the foundation of its seizure of Hawaii, the conquest of the Philippines was to provide a beachhead in the Asia-Pacific and a steppingstone to the fabled China market. Senator Albert Beveridge asserted before Congress: "The power that rules the Pacific . . . is the power that rules the world. And, with the Philippines, that power is and will forever be the American Republic."[6]

Relying on the collaboration of Westernized elites (the *illustrados*), the governing commission, headed by future president William Howard Taft, presided over a grand nation-building experiment designed to legitimate colonial rule. Technical advisers worked to extend Western technology, built roads, infrastructure, and schools, and promoted better hygienic standards and public health. By supporting free trade and removing legal barriers to corporate land-ownership, the commission also sought to stimulate foreign investment. The ultimate aim was to lift the Filipinos up from their "primitiveness" through the import of Western mores and Christianization.[7]

While influenced by progressivism and its emphasis on technical efficiency, and viewing the Philippines as a laboratory of reform, commission members, as the historian Glen May notes, were politically conservative. They sought to restrict suffrage and attract foreign investors without concern for corporate regulation or the poor. Few antipoverty programs were ever contemplated.[8] The heavy emphasis on policing accorded with the conservative philosophy and shows that the major aim of the occupation was to secure American interests and power on the islands.

On August 8, 1901, upon the urging of Vice Governor Luke E. Wright, a Confederate war hero and designer of an electric streetcar system in Memphis, the constabulary was established with the goal of stabilizing the country to allow for economic development. Taft complained that under General Arthur MacArthur (father of Douglas) the U.S. military lacked "discretion" in arresting people suspected of disloyalty, which could be better accomplished by indigenous police. William Cameron Forbes (a grandson of the philosopher Ralph Waldo Emerson), who was commissioner of commerce and police in the Philippines from 1904 to 1908 and governor-general from 1909 to 1913, stated that four Filipinos could be maintained for less than the price of one American soldier.[9] The constabulary grew to six thousand in the first few years. Many recruits had served in the Spanish colonial Guardia Civil or as native scouts. The commission reported, "The calls upon them for the suppression of ladronism [banditry] and other disturbances have been so numerous that there has not been time or opportunity [to focus on improving their civil function]. . . . [S]ix years of war has created a restless class of men lacking in the habits of industry" and prone to disrupt occupational initiatives.[10] The police thus developed into an overtly politicized force, which accounted for their repressive character.

Setting an important benchmark, the United States organized a secret service bureau whose primary aim was to detect and frustrate plots against the government and capture the records and munitions of insurgents. Military intelligence officers imparted new methods of data management and surveillance. The recruitment of ex-insurgents and others loyal to exiled leader Emilio Aguinaldo was pivotal in penetrating private space and co-opting the nationalist movement.[11] In 1907, after Harry H. Bandholtz, a West Point graduate responsible for crushing a coal miners' strike in West Virginia, took over the constabulary, members of the secret service adopted novel psychological warfare techniques, such as wearing disguises, fabricating disinformation, and recruiting paid informants and saboteurs in their efforts to "break up bands of political plotters." They monitored the press, broke up radicals' street rallies, carried out periodic assassinations, and compiled dossiers on thousands of individuals as well as information on the corruption of key government leaders, which was used as leverage to keep them loyal to the occupation. The declaration of martial law enabled the secret service to carry out surveillance and make arrests without the application of due process.[12]

The efficiency of the internal security apparatus was enhanced by the importation of the most advanced crime control technology, including a centralized telephone network, electric streetlights, and the Bertillon photo identification and later fingerprinting system, which enabled police to establish an "all-embracing index file" on the political beliefs of nearly 70 percent of Manila's population. Through these initiatives the United States helped to create one of the first modern surveillance states, a feature of colonial rule seen as a marker of its modernity.[13] The reach of the constabulary was so deep that it was able to infiltrate and sow dissension within radical organizations, including an incipient labor movement, and even played a role in apostolic succession by undermining Bishop Gregorio Aglipay through the spread of disinformation. Aglipay was a nationalist with socialist sympathies whose services were attended by thousands of the urban poor.[14]

One of the crowning technical achievements was the installation of a Gamewell police and fire alarm system in Manila to curb dependency on the public telephone system. The Philippines commission proudly reported that this "put the city on equal footing with any in the United States."[15] In 1902 the commission passed a sedition law which imposed the death penalty or a long prison term on those advocating independence and a brigandage act classifying guerrilla resistance as banditry. The constabulary was given the task of enforcing these laws. Wielding immense powers, far greater than those of police forces in the United States, it also oversaw forced labor codes designed to build the country's road infrastructure, ran tax collection and quarantine programs, helped develop health clinics and schools, and had its officers appointed as governors in districts inhabited by rural people such as the Bontoc, Ifugao, and Kalinga whose head-hunting practices they sought to curtail. In addition, constabulary officers protected telegraph lines used to coordinate military operations and commercial development and enforced laws against vagrancy, gambling, and opium promoted by Protestant missionaries.[16] Owing to deep-rooted cultural acceptance, the reception of kickbacks by police, and the ingenuity of Chinese smugglers, these laws were predominantly unsuccessful and contributed to the growth of organized criminal networks. Despite the seizure of large amounts of contraband in raids, as late as 1930 American investigators found that opium was easily obtainable and that the trade was so lucrative that it had corrupted elements of the political elite. The historian Alfred W. McCoy concluded that in Manila, "police in effect became partners in crime, accepting bribes to protect opium dens and gambling houses" as well as brothels which sprang up to service Americans. Periodic exposure served to undermine the legitimacy of the colonial order, sparking several highly publicized though ultimately limited efforts at reform.[17]

In 1906 the governing commission approved the creation of a national police school at Baguio, where courses were offered in marksmanship, police administration, and guerrilla warfare. Constabulary officers were required to wear new uniforms in khaki and red and were equipped with modern weaponry, including Remington and Colt revolvers and Springfield carbines. Police headquarters were repaired and new ones built to encourage a more professional atmosphere. Officers were required to take four hours of weekly instruction in the law related to arrests, search warrants, and processing evidence. Medical care was provided, and physical fitness was emphasized in training. Attempts were made to standardize pay and ensure that upper-level appointments were made from within the ranks. A pension and retirement fund was established to promote loyalty and allow constabulary members to view policing as a career.[18]

These measures were all consistent with progressive-style reforms implemented as part of the managerial revolution in the United States. They exemplified the desire of American colonial officials to remake the Philippines in the American image and to promote progress through the importation of Western institutions and governing systems.[19] As McCoy documents, innovations pioneered in the Philippines further contributed to the evolution of policing practices in the United States, including the advent of a formidable surveillance apparatus set in place during the first Red Scare. Constabulary veterans such as Ralph Van Deman, known as the "father of U.S. military intelligence" and of the "American blacklist," played a crucial role in applying their expertise in the clandestine arts to spy on and repress radical organizations such as the American Communist Party and the Industrial Workers of the World, contributing to their demise. American Civil Liberties Union attorney Frank Donner characterized Van Deman as "one of the giants of anticommunism, a super-hawk . . . a phobic nativist red-hunter" whose "undercover network penetrated not only the Communist Party but a whole spectrum of liberal targets, including religious, civil rights, and labor organizations."[20]

Most constabulary officers came from military backgrounds and were soldiers of fortune and/or veterans of the Indian Wars. The historian Thomas A. Reppetto characterized them as a "wild bunch," epitomized by Winfield Scott Grove, chief of detectives in Manila, who beat up the governor of Laguna outside an official reception, and Jesse Garwood, a western gunfighter who seduced local officers' wives, shot apples off the head of his houseboy, and offered bounties for cutting off enemy heads. Hardened by their time on the frontier, they claimed to "understand the ways of wild people," and felt it was their responsibility to "mend a country wracked by war and now subject to raids, pirates, plunderers, and murderers." One member of the constabulary, Harold H. Elarth, later commented, "We began to live Kipling for ourselves."[21]

A number of the officers learned local dialects and devoted years of service, gaining a sense of attachment to the country that was lacking among their heirs in later interventions. Some built schools and fostered agricultural development, though many abused their power, imposing forced labor regimens to expand the highland trail network and compiling fortunes in shady business dealings and speculation in mining and gold. When someone complained that Walter F. Hale, lieutenant governor in the Kalinga sub-province, was "monopolizing the rice trade" and undermining local production, Hale responded: "Up here I am God. You do what I tell you."[22]

Until 1917, when Colonel Rafael Crame, Bandholtz's protégé, became chief of the constabulary, Filipinos could not be named to command positions. Forbes, an investment banker who coached the Harvard football team, wrote in his diary that American leadership was crucial in "making the police observe the rules of civilized warfare. . . . The native, when given authority, is very brutal to his own people and would treat them to a little Spanish deviltry if unchecked." If the United States withdrew, he added, the country would become enmeshed in "hopeless anarchy," and every valley would become "red with blood."[23] Epitomizing the ethnocentrism underlying U.S. policy, Vic Hurley included in his memoir *Jungle Patrol* the photo of a longhaired Filipino wearing nothing but a string around his waist. Next to this was a more recent picture of the man dressed in his constabulary uniform. He was now cleanly shaven and had short hair. The caption reads, "Exposed to civilization."[24]

With Us or Against Us: Misperceptions of a Dehumanized Enemy

The first chief of the constabulary, Henry T. Allen, embodied the dominant martial and imperialist spirit of the age. Born into an antebellum Kentucky household with eleven slaves, Allen graduated from West Point in 1882, led an exploration mission in Alaska, and then joined the military's new information division in St. Petersburg as a spy on behalf of the tsarist regime. His superiors faulted his reports for being "too political." Allen went on to serve in the Spanish-American War in Cuba and with the Forty-third Infantry division in the Philippines campaign in Samar, where he condemned General Jacob Smith's scorched earth policy as a "disgrace." He urged his subordinates to master the local language and understand the natives in order to gain "the confidence of the people," or as his successors would put it, win their "hearts and minds." Allen at the same time sanctioned merciless tactics against resistant Filipinos, whom he characterized as suffering from "intense ignorance" and the "fanatical" characteristics of "semi-savagery."[25] After his appointment as constabulary chief, he wrote to General Robert P. Hughes: "Considerable killing still remains to be done. I suspect that we will have a lot of trouble in Negros before all the *ladrones* and others equally deserving are killed there."[26] In a subsequent letter to Taft, Allen remarked: "Education and roads will effect what is desired, but while awaiting these, drastic measures are obligatory. . . . The only remedy is killing and for the same reason that a rabid dog must be disposed of."[27]

These comments reveal the dehumanizing language used to rationalize wide-scale violence. Writing to the secretary of the province of Leyte, Allen commented: "It is absolutely important that the bands of *ladrones* infesting certain parts of the province be exterminated. The future of Leyte . . . [including] the needed capital to construct railways and start up other enterprises . . . depends on this."[28] Presaging the outlook of modernization theorists during the Cold War, Allen saw the opponents of the United States as a barrier to the progressive social change that the import of new technologies ostensibly offered. He portrayed them as relics of an earlier phase of civilization whose removal would clear the way for national development. The logic is not dissimilar to that of others who have committed genocide or seen the killing of large groups as fitting into a broader social or humanitarian design. It also fit the pattern of racial violence characteristic of Western imperialism and American life in the early twentieth century.[29]

Most individuals pursued by the constabulary were nationalists who served in the liberation armies. Allen acknowledged in 1902 that "four years of fighting aided by the loss of life by cholera and [the] plague of animals by rinderpest and of crops in many places by locusts has been demoralizing to the people and favorable to the development of ladronism."[30] San Miguel was declared an outlaw after he helped to revive the anticolonial Katipunan Party. He had ties with the labor movement, a constant target of constabulary surveillance and harassment, which was eventually co-opted from within.[31] General Macario Sakay was president of the New Katipunan movement, which Allen referred to as a "disease of the Tagalog mind." Greeted as a hero in Manila, he promoted class consciousness and sought to establish a breakaway Tagalog republic. In 1907 his second-in-command, Cornelio Felizardo, was ambushed and hacked to death while urinating, and Sakay was betrayed by informants. Standing on the execution platform in the Bilibid prison plaza, Sakay declared: "Death comes to all of us sooner or later, so I will face the lord Almighty calmly. But I want to tell you that we are not bandits and robbers, as the Americans have accused us, but members of the revolutionary force that defended our mother country, the Philippines! Farewell! Long live the Republic and may our independence be born in the future!"[32]

Many constabulary targets such as the socialist Felipe Salvador promoted a messianic ideology mixing folk religion and populist nationalism. In Negros province, Dionisio Sigobela (known as "Papa Isio"), a displaced sugar laborer, preached a doctrine of free love and promised followers immunity from diseases bred by the ravages of war. He was arrested by Colonel John R. White, a veteran of the Greek Foreign Legion, who gained great repute through his exploits. Forbes referred in his journals to Papa Isio's death in February 1905 at sixty-seven as untimely because "it should have occurred 16 years ago!"[33] Violent scorched earth campaigns against rebel forces, which in some cases resulted in the taking of human flesh as a trophy, continued through much of the

1910s. Elarth wrote in his memoirs that after the last embers of the insurrection died down in 1911, it took another ten years of "strenuous patrolling" by the constabulary before "peace conditions" emerged.[34]

Pacification in the Moro provinces of Mindanao and Sulu took even longer and was never fully achieved. In 1903 the United States abrogated the agreement promising autonomy to the Moros, Muslims who had never acquiesced to Spanish rule either, and appointed General Leonard Wood head of the province. A former colonial governor of Cuba and decorated veteran of the campaign against Geronimo's Apaches, Wood and his associates showed little respect for Moro traditions and culture and believed, like twenty-first-century neoconservatives, that Muslims could only understand force. Central to their strategy was the creation of a native constabulary to "tame" those who resisted American hegemony and, as one of Wood's biographers put it, help "plant the seeds of civilization in their mind."[35]

Much blood was spilled in the attempt to achieve these aims. Peasants were driven into government-controlled enclaves overseen by the constabulary, where thin children with bloated abdomens reminded observers of "the pictures of re-concentration in Cuba and famine in India."[36] John White, who served in France in World War I, recounts how men under his command burned houses, loaded themselves down with loot, and destroyed sugar and other foodstuffs in the attempt to isolate and starve the enemy. They left "the pretty plateau a burned and scarred sore." This "was hard," he wrote, "but necessary, for we did not want the job of taking Mansalanao [Mindanao] again."[37]

In 1906 U.S. Army and constabulary units massacred over six hundred Moros, including women and children, at a volcanic crater in Bud Dajo after they refused to pay a head tax. Theodore Roosevelt congratulated Wood for "upholding the honor of the American flag." According to the anthropologist Dean Worcester, it "was no more possible to avoid killing women and children [there] than it was . . . in the Wounded Knee fight."[38] In another atrocity seven years later on Mount Bagsak, constabulary men under John J. Pershing, a veteran of the Sioux and Apache campaigns, "exterminated all the Moros who had taken their stand," as Forbes put it favorably. According to Pershing, who was promoted from captain to brigadier general, a "severe though well-deserved punishment" was administered.[39] Warfare continued until as late as 1935. Much as they would with the "Vietcong" decades later, Americans developed a grudging respect for the fighting capability of the Moros, but referred to them in racist terms as "Mohammedan fanatics," "medieval savages," and akin to a "swarm of hornets."[40]

Rebel commanders often imposed especially harsh penalties for collaboration with the occupying forces, including the cutting of tendons and feet, and extorted food from villagers when popular support waned.[41] One realistic aspect of White's *Bullets and Bolos* is the hardship experienced by constabulary officers facing the threat of spike-filled pits and surprise bolo (spear) attacks while trekking through harsh jungle terrain. White was himself shot in the knee by Moro rebels in Sulu. Many of his colleagues died in the field from dysentery, malaria, and typhoid as well as from crocodile attacks and drowning.[42]

"Capturing and Destroying Ladrones": The Constabulary and the First Operation Phoenix

The militarization of the policing programs was a major factor accounting for the high levels of abuse. Setting the precedent for the anti-Huk campaign of the 1950s in the Philippines (to be discussed in chapter 5) and the Phoenix program, which aimed to wipe out the leadership of the Vietnamese revolutionary movement, constabulary units measured their success by the number of enemy captured or killed. The objective was laid out in the training manual: "Capture or destroy ladrones." Another passage recommended: "Once a ladrone camp is located, there must be no hesitancy in attacking vigorously. The best time for attack is at or before daylight and during rainy weather."[43]

Field reports provide a good indication of the high casualty rates. Henry Knauber reported, for example, on June 11, 1903, that his unit had "killed 8 outlaws" and seized "3 rifles, 1 revolver, several bolos and one trumpet while losing only one horse."[44] Henry Allen boasted to the Philippines commission that on a harrowing expedition his men "killed 2 ladrones, captured 23 including 1 Commandante," adding that "93 surrendered unconditionally, 69 conditionally, and that 96 rifles and 36 revolvers were captured." One month later Allen wrote to Senator Albert Beveridge that because of recent successes, he believed "within a couple of years practically every band of ladrones in the island (Moro country not included) could be exterminated."[45]

White's memoir *Bullets and Bolos* is replete with stories, many of them embellished, of his prowess in capturing and killing outlaw forces. He wrote, "While living the sheltered life, it seems a rather awful thing to find sport in taking human life . . . yet . . . it was either kill or be killed and it must be emphasized that the enemy had every advantage."[46] These comments demonstrate the mindset of soldiers in the field, who, in the face of constant danger and a hostile population, did what they felt was necessary to protect their own lives. Furthermore, they were seeking to uphold an ideal of masculinity that was deeply rooted in American culture and contingent on the achievement of military prowess and the ability to project strength in the face of adversity.[47]

White and his contemporaries were honored with medals of valor for killing insurgents, and they rose in the military hierarchy. Harry Bandholtz became provost marshal and went on to found the U.S. Military Police during World War I. "Black Jack" Pershing led the punitive expedition against the Mexican revolutionary Francisco "Pancho" Villa alongside Henry Allen and became commanding general at the end of the Great War.[48] James Harbord, the constabulary's third commander, served as Pershing's chief of staff and then president of the Radio Corporation of America (RCA) from 1923 to 1947. Other veterans went on to have distinguished law enforcement careers in the United States and to head constabulary forces in the Caribbean, imparting the skills they had developed while chasing Filipino rebels. Rough Rider George R. Shanton headed the Insular Police in Puerto Rico and oversaw policing of the Panama Canal Zone, where he organized the plainclothes surveillance of workers and the blacklisting and deportation of radicals.[49]

The abuses of the Philippines constabulary, like those of its numerous spin-offs, were synonymous with its social control function. In a 1933 study, Major Emmanuel Baja reported that it repeatedly carried out the "water torture" and other harsh interrogation methods, including beating suspects with snakes to extract information. "Get your man" was the slogan of patrols, resulting in excessive force and brutality. Officers engaged in blackmail, terrorism, and extortion and stole food from the peasantry. They sexually assaulted women, and in Mindanao were authorized to take them as concubines (ironic, given that Muslim slavery was adopted as moral justification for the conquest of the Moro).[50] Violent political policing operations were generally seen as compatible with democratization in view of the need for order and stability as a precondition for development. After the suspension of the writ of habeas corpus in Cavite and Batangas due to heavy guerrilla activity, Forbes noted in his journal that the constabulary was now "free to run in the suspects. . . . A lot of innocent people will be put in jail for a while, but it will also mean that some guilty ones will catch it and the whole cancer will be cut out."[51] This comment exemplifies the philosophy of "the end justifies the means" which underlay the violation of human rights, setting the standard for the "American century."

"Total Institutions": The Philippine Penal Apparatus as an Instrument of Social Control

In an important precedent, American colonial officials built up the Philippines penal apparatus alongside the police as an important mechanism of state-building and social control. The prison was seen as a pivotal institution not just for punishing offenders but for molding them into disciplined colonial subjects and industrious citizens. Ignacio Villamor, the first Filipino director of prisons, commented in 1910: "The penitentiary system of the Philippines follows the latest reforms adopted by the most civilized countries of Europe and America in the sense of securing the protection of society by correction as well as the reformation of the criminal. . . . The principle of such a system is summarized as follows: isolation, work, and education."[52]

Studies on colonial prisons have generally shown that regardless of the professed ideals, racism on the part of colonial officials and rampant overcrowding caused by heightened policing led to the breakdown of reform and the proliferation of barbaric abuses.[53] The American experience in the Philippines and later interventions such as in Vietnam fit with this norm. Because of the persistence of war and high crime rates bred by the ravages of the occupation, Philippine prisons became filled to overcapacity, resulting in "hellish conditions," as eyewitnesses described them. Many prisoners died of undernourishment, cholera, or beriberi (caused by a deficiency of vitamin B).

In Manila's Bilibid prison, built by Spain in 1866 as a model Benthamite panopticon with a central tower from which guards could see inside all radiating cell blocks, the death rate rose from 72 per 1,000 in 1902 to 438 per 1,000 in 1905. Hospital facilities were inadequate. The food was usually rotten and, according to one commission report, "too aged to be palatable."[54] The dilapidated buildings had holes in the roofing and walls, which left inmates unprotected from bad weather but also enabled some to escape. The death penalty was widely applied, particularly for political offenders. Colonial officials introduced the gruesome apparatus of the electric chair, typifying the U.S. role in modernizing repression through the importation of new technologies.[55]

On December 7, 1904, a riot broke out in which nineteen prisoners were killed and forty wounded before order was restored. Forbes boasted that "prompt use of a gatling gun in the tower and the riot guns with which the guards on the walls were armed ended the trouble in eight minutes." After another rebellion at the convict labor camp at Albay, Forbes put armed scouts in the thickly planted hemp fields to keep inmates fearful and obedient.[56]

Over time, the Philippines commission attempted to improve prison conditions, largely to advance political reeducation efforts. In an extension of the progressive reforms in the United States, facilities were renovated, juveniles and the insane were removed to separate institutions, and a leper colony was established on the island of Culion. Prison records were systematized, and wardens were trained in administrative methods. A rewards system was initiated, a library was established, and classes were offered in reading, writing, and mathematics. Religious services and recreational programs were also organized, including baseball games and theatrical performances on weekends, some led by an inmate band. Fly-proof hospital facilities were built on prison grounds, and sick prisoners were given access to medical care and drug treatment and cleansed of intestinal parasites.[57] These practices resulted in a decline in overall mortality rates, though in adopting public health innovations, officials sometimes treated prisoners as objects of scientific study and guinea pigs for new vaccines. In 1906, ten prisoners died from the bubonic plague when Dr. Richard P. Strong injected subjects with the virulent plague bacillus.[58]

Beyond such medical experimentation, the penal reforms were limited by the corruption of guards, who smuggled in drugs and syringes for morphine injections, and by chronic overcrowding resulting from the roundup of political prisoners. In 1923, Bilibid housed 7,986 inmates when it was intended for 3,400. Detainees were crammed into poorly ventilated cells lacking proper toilets, and they endured food shortages and flooding. In 1923, the Philippines commission recorded that over three dozen prisoners had died from tuberculosis and another thirty-seven from pneumonia. The rates increased significantly over the next four years. The 1928 annual report of the director of prisons acknowledged that the spread of diseases was "the natural sequence of the congested conditions of the prison."[59]

A central aim of the new penology was to inculcate an industrious spirit among inmates without allowing their labor to be exploited by private interests, as under the convict-leasing system in the Jim Crow South. Prisoners were treated like soldiers, living in barracks and forced to undergo drill formations. They worked on labor projects; were instructed in trades such as woodworking, carpentry, plumbing, and blacksmithing; and produced furniture of apparently high quality. Instructors were also sent into women's prisons to teach handicrafts, including needlework and sewing, as well as stenography. Repair of automobiles and machinery was performed on-site for a small remuneration.[60]

Colonial officials took pride in the latest innovations and sought to portray them as a marker of progress. The State Department sponsored a motion picture travelogue by Burton Holmes, a pioneer of the genre, titled *Going to Jail in Manila,* which featured inmates being trained at Bilibid in silversmithing and wicker-working. The advent of a Taylorized routine resulted in the efficient production of goods. The director of the prison stated, "Our objective is to transform the human being into a man—to change weak shiftlessness into active responsibility."[61] This comment summed up the ideology of the new penology, which affirmed a faith in individualism and achievement through work and discipline.

In actuality, however, abusive practices continued. Recalcitrant inmates were thrown into solitary confinement and forced to wear leg irons joined by a chain, a method condemned by Western penologists as resembling medieval torture. When questioned about their use by a visiting academic observer, John L. Gillin, the director of Bilibid responded, "We have to deal here with a people in a different stage of social development than those you deal with in the United States."[62] The adoption of racist stereotypes to rationalize draconian measures exemplified the continuity from the Spanish era, from which some of the torture artifacts were ironically kept on display in an on-site museum.

Part of the problem was the attempt to emulate American penal practice, which was marred by racial violence, overcrowding, and harsh punitive policies. According to Gillin, the conditions in Bilibid were comparable to those in "nine-tenths of American prisons in terms of the discipline carried out," a powerful commentary on the repressive character of the American penal system.[63]

In spite of the lofty rhetoric, Filipino prisons ultimately served as a more effective instrument of social control than in the United States. They emerged as a powerful "total institution," in the analogy of the sociologist Erving Goffman, designed to inculcate conformity with hegemonic societal norms promoted by colonial elites, while marginalizing traditional practices and quashing dissent.[64]

Some of the worst conditions were in provincially run facilities operating beyond the control of central government administrators. Inspection tours revealed maladministration, corruption, "woeful health care," the lack of adequate air and food, and torture with whips and heavy chains. One prisoner, forced to climb a tall coconut tree while in chains, fell off and had to have a leg amputated. Inmates awaited trial for long periods, and some were driven insane (with care of the insane generally considered to be medieval). Women were placed in the same cells as men, leaving them susceptible to sexual abuse.[65] While an edict outlawing torture was issued prior to 1910, it was not until 1926 that the Bureau of Prisons took any steps to enforce it. At the same time, it organized a convention for provincial wardens where, in accord with the new professional standards in the United States, lectures were given on recordkeeping, compiling monthly reports, and instilling a tightly disciplined structure.

During a 1928 inspection tour colonial officials nevertheless found prisons to be badly run (including an instance in which the gun rack was within reach of the inmates) and lacking in sanitation. Wardens were incompetent political appointees who took vengeance upon prisoners belonging to a rival party. Guards were poorly trained and did not have "the slightest conception of prison management or penology."[66] In the province of Rizal, a seedbed of resistance, conditions were "entirely unsatisfactory," inspector Edmund Fritz wrote to the Bureau of Prisons. The cells were "dirty . . . those of the women prisoners have a particularly obnoxious smell. . . . Discipline is poor and inmates complain about the quality, quantity, and character of the food furnished." In Batanagas, Fritz and two Filipino inspectors compared a municipal jail to a "chicken roost." In Cavite, they lamented that inmates sat around smoking cigarettes and cigars all day without being forced to work. In addition, "the cells have obnoxious smells and are filled with cigar and cigarette stubs and dirty clothes. The dining room smelled like a stable!"[67]

These comments capture the fixation of colonial officials with order and discipline and shed light on the oppressive environment pervading the prison system. After reading the reports, Forbes recommended a crackdown on political patronage and the construction of new facilities to relieve congestion. There is little indication, however, of much follow-through or improvement, in part because under the Filipinization program, the governing commission supported many of the same corrupt officials criticized in the reports and, at the end of the day, did not care enough about the well-being of inmates lacking in political capital.[68]

The most ambitious penal initiative was an agricultural cooperative on the island of Palawan at Iwahig and at San Ramon in the province of Zamboanga, where prisoners engaged in self-management and policing and grew their own food on over 100,000 acres of land. They also participated in lumbering and fishing, had a pig and poultry house, and produced handicrafts for sale, including hats, raincoats, and furniture.[69] If they behaved well, prisoners could own little farms and live in a hut with their families. The next step was a full pardon. The institutions were modeled after the George Junior Republic, a reformatory school in upstate New York where delinquent children lived in family cottages and were taught to become productive, self-governing citizens.[70]

Iwahig in particular was heralded as a model of progressive reform and influenced the development of American penal farms. White, who was appointed warden, wrote in his memoirs that Forbes was "an idealist" who believed that "men in the penal colonies were redeemable". . . . His vision was to "apply to Filipino outlaws . . . and fanatics, murderers and cattle thieves, insurgents and political intriguers the same medicine that had cured [delinquent] American boys."[71] When Iwahig was first established in 1904, White noted that the death rate was over 250 per 1,000; "men died like flies of beriberi, malaria, and dysentery, and wallowed in their own filth until the remainder rose in revolt, nearly killing the neglectful superintendent. Many of the convicts fled to the wild mountain interior of the island where they lived with the pagan Tagbanua tribes."[72]

Eventually the inmates cleared the land and developed the necessary infrastructure to allow for its sustainability, although malaria remained endemic and cases of beriberi were still recorded. Progressives took pride in the fact that while Bastille-type prisons were being built in the United States, Iwahig was born without prison walls or guards and gave inmates the opportunity to regain their self-respect. The Wood-Forbes mission in 1921 characterized it as among the most successful institutions created by the colonial occupation as a result of the adoption of "advanced reformatory methods," which yielded low recidivism rates.[73] Vice Governor Newton W. Gilbert was quoted in the *Manila Times* as saying that he had observed convicts living and working together in harmony as practically free men with the absence of violence and "not a single gun on the island. . . . The humanitarian spirit which engendered the idea of a penal colony may now be said to have been fully justified. The success of the experiment is wonderful!"[74]

In 1931, after visiting penitentiaries throughout the United States and the world, the criminologist John Gillin found Iwahig to be the most remarkable experiment in penal reform then in existence.[75] While Iwahig was indeed innovative in many of its ideals, conditions were nevertheless far from utopian. Many of the inmates were political prisoners, including captured leaders of the messianic peasant movements and the Moro resistance. Discipline could be severe, and White, who had overseen the massacre at Bud Dajo, referred to himself as a "czar." His successor Carroll H. Lamb was forced to resign for allegedly misappropriating public funds in fraudulent cattle purchases. Later Filipino administrators also stood trial for graft and corruption.[76] The death rate remained high. Fifteen inmates died from tuberculosis, for example, in 1928. Scattered violence and rebellions were further recorded. In 1914, twenty-one escapees committed robbery and murdered an American schoolteacher in defiance of the occupation.[77] Public officials tellingly referred to Iwahig not as a penal farm but as a "plantation" or "reservation." These analogies, as the historian Michael Salman has pointed out, underscore parallels with the treatment of African Americans and Native Americans in the United States. Colonialists saw penal reform as a benevolent means of uplifting those of a supposedly inferior race through the inculcation of a spirit of industriousness. Seen from a different vantage point, however, it was part of a racist and authoritarian structure centered on economic exploitation.[78]

In response to the wave of neoconservative pundits extolling the virtues of colonialism on the eve of the 2002 Iraq war, the historian Eric Foner commented that "the benevolence of benevolent imperialism lies in the eyes of the beholder." The political scientist Chalmers Johnson observed in *Nemesis: The Last Days of the American Republic*, "The idea of forcing thousands of people to be free by slaughtering them—with Maxim machine guns in the nineteenth century, with 'precision munitions' today—seems to reflect a deeply felt need as well as a striking inability to imagine the lives and viewpoints of others." Johnson asserted further that "all empires require myths of divine right, racial preeminence, manifest destiny, or a 'civilizing mission' to cover their often barbarous behavior in other people's countries."[79] These comments are clearly relevant to the United States' colonization efforts in the Philippines. In the face of popular resistance, American officials responded with savage repression, carried out largely through the formidable policing apparatus they developed, exemplifying the coercive underpinnings of American power.

In *Policing America's Empire*, Alfred W. McCoy concluded that the army's "application of military science to municipal administration created something of a revolution in policing. Combining militarized coercion, information management, and covert operations, the army created a police force far more advanced than either its Spanish antecedents or its American contemporaries." As a consequence, the nationalist movement was suppressed, and the Philippines evolved as an American neo-colony, plagued by rampant inequality, political repression, and corruption. Over the coming decades, the constabulary and its successor organizations continued to receive lavish subsidies, particularly in periods when armed insurgencies developed among marginalized social groups against the Westernized elite.[80] American constabulary veterans meanwhile received career promotions and were contracted to develop counterpart organizations in Central America and the United States. Many of the techniques that they pioneered, including the importation of fingerprinting and communications equipment, the establishment of training academies, and the advent of psychological warfare methods became a staple of the global police programs. During the Vietnam War, the Pentagon studied the history of the constabulary and sought to emulate its exploits in combating a determined nationalist movement skilled in the art of jungle warfare. The continuity in policies was thus explicit, as the violence of empire came full circle.

Chapter **2**

"Popping Off" Sandinistas and Cacos
Police Training in Occupied Haiti, the Dominican Republic, and Nicaragua

Who are We?
We are Tigers!
What do Tigers eat?
Blood!
Whose Blood?
The Blood of the People!
—Nicaraguan Guardia chant, 1970s

It seems funny as hell to me, every once in a while some misguided fool up in the States, who knows nothing of the trouble here sets up a howl over a few black bandits being knocked off.
—Lewis B. "Chesty" Puller, 1921, letter to fellow marine John Pullen

I know of no inhumane action and crimes greater than those committed by the U.S. against the defenseless peoples of Latin America through its legally authorized agents and representatives.
—H. H. Knowles, former minister of Nicaragua, early 1930s

In 1917, two years after the marines landed in Haiti to protect American business interests there, General Smedley D. Butler, one of the most decorated marines in American history, was sent to Haiti to create a police Gendarmerie that would serve the same purpose. Much like his counterparts in the Philippines, where he had spent a year battling nationalist forces in Cavite, Butler and his men sought to mold the force in the leatherneck image. He declared in his autobiography that "with shoes and buttons shining and hats cocked over one eye, they strutted with a swagger and basked in the admiring glances of strapping Negro women."[1] In reality, the Gendarmerie committed numerous atrocities in suppressing the resistance of the rebels known as Cacos (for the type of clothing worn by peasants in the northern mountains), as Haiti under U.S. occupation was turned into a laboratory for the development of new policing technologies and methods of coercion. Butler acknowledged years later while barnstorming around the United States that he had been a "high-class muscle man for big business and the bankers" and that men under his command "were made to regard murder as the order of the day. . . . We used them for a couple of years and trained them to think nothing at all of killing or being killed."[2]

U.S. foreign policy in Latin America during the early twentieth century was guided by the Roosevelt Corollary to the Monroe Doctrine, which asserted that the United States had the right to function as a police power to "protect" nations in the hemisphere from encroachment by European powers. A main impetus was the desire to secure a stable investment climate and access to the Panama Canal. In 1905, Secretary of State Elihu Root argued that the United States' trading partners needed professional police forces that could "repress subversive disorder and preserve the public peace."[3] Dana G. Munro, U.S. chargé d'affaires in Nicaragua and minister to Haiti, commented:

> The establishment of non-partisan constabularies in the Caribbean states was one of the chief objectives of our policy. . . . The old armies were or seemed to be one of the principal causes of disorder and financial disorganization. They consumed most of the government's revenue, chiefly in graft, and they gave nothing but disorder and oppression in return. We thought that a disciplined force, trained by Americans, would do away with the petty local oppression that was responsible for much of the disorder that occurred and would be an important step towards better financial administration and economic progress generally.[4]

These remarks suggest the importance attributed to police training programs in engendering stability, economic development, and more efficient government administration. They also display a confidence in the ability of Americans to remake foreign societies and solve deeply rooted social problems without considering cultural barriers, the political context, or local reaction. In practice, the American-trained constabularies evolved into instruments of repression and vehicles for the rise of dictators who upheld American regional interests. Police training in turn laid an important foundation for Cold War–era programs that were similarly designed to suppress radical nationalist movements threatening U.S. power.

Progeny of FDR and Smedley Butler: The Haitian Gendarmerie and the U.S. Occupation, 1915–1934

Since the 1804 revolution overthrowing French domination, the United States had hoped to incorporate Haiti into the American orbit and tame the country's radical and defiant spirit. In July 1915, the Wilson administration invaded under the pretext of restoring stability after several coups d'état. American corporations took control of the banking system, and the marines blocked Dr. Rosalvo Bobo, an "idealist" and "dreamer" known for treating the poor without charge, from taking power. In his place, they inserted Philip Sudre Duartiginave, whom Butler characterized as an "old rogue," and then Louis Borno, an admirer of Benito Mussolini whom William Cameron Forbes described as "thin, tall, toothy and most disagreeable. . . . It just did not seem possible that any man should be so patent a stage villain."[5]

In December 1915, Secretary of the Navy Franklin D. Roosevelt transmitted a plan for a Gendarmerie whose function was to enable the drawdown of American troops while preserving U.S. strategic interests in Haiti. The sum of $508,234 was appropriated for the force, headed by Butler, which consisted of 2,400 Haitians and 100 white marines, a number of whom would go on to storied military careers. Lewis M. "Chesty" Puller, for example, would earn decorations in Nicaragua and the Pacific, while Lemuel C. Shepherd Jr., who served in Haiti after World War I and was assistant chief of staff from 1928 to 1931, would lead the Sixth Marine Division to victory in Okinawa and become commandant of the Marine Corps from 1952 to 1955. Likening the war against the Cacos rebels to "frontier fighting," Shepherd commented retrospectively: "We did a great deal to, I think, bring Haiti up from what it had been to a good country. It didn't last too long after we left, but still that's another story."[6]

Equipped with Springfield rifles and carbines, the Gendarmerie was modeled after the Philippines constabulary and the New Jersey and Pennsylvania state constabularies, which were developed by Philippines constabulary veterans (including Sergeant Jesse Garwood) and were known for suppressing strikes and "beating down foreigners." Following the model of progressive reforms, American officers instituted a platoon system and traffic police and encouraged the systemization of records and the adoption of an index card filing system on arrested persons to improve administrative efficiency.[7] These innovations were consistent with the prevailing viewpoint that a professional police organization should play a vital function in regulating social life, thus laying the foundation of a modern nation.

In what would become a familiar cycle of exportation and reimportation, initiatives pioneered in Haiti and other colonial enclaves helped to transform domestic policing in the United States, reflected in the militarization of police institutions and foreshadowing the era of SWAT (Special Weapons and Tactics) teams. Exemplifying this trend, while on leave from the army in 1924, Butler served a stint as police chief in Philadelphia, appointed by Republican mayor W. Freeland Kendrick, who promised an administration of sound business principles and law and order. The wiry Butler took the oath of office in his marine uniform. He sought to instill discipline in his men in the manner in which he had trained the Haitian Gendarmerie. Known for his fiery temper and blunt speech, Butler cracked down on corruption, promoted the use of high-speed cars and new radio technology, set up an iron ring of semi-military posts around the city, and followed what he called a "pound policy"—ordering his men, armed with sawed-off shotguns, to raid speakeasies and suspected bootlegging institutions suddenly and repeatedly if necessary. During his tenure, police closed 2,566 speakeasies in Philadelphia, in comparison with only 220 in the preceding year, though the conviction rate was low, in part because of police carelessness in securing evidence. Claiming that the best way to stop crime was to shoot criminals and make jails unbearable, Butler was replaced after he stormed the Ritz-Carlton hotel, shutting down a debutante ball. One angry citizen compared him to a military dictator, while another complained that "military tactics which might do in Mexico and other places . . . has no place in the administration of civil affairs."[8]

In Haiti, given the colonial context and the lack of constitutional safeguards, the Gendarmerie was even more brutal. A critic noted that the gendarmes were a "menace . . . recruited from the lowest elements. . . . The training they are giving makes soldiers, not police." They committed many excesses in directing the internment of resident Germans during World War I and enforcing an ill-advised anti-voodoo campaign in which people were arrested for such crimes as "preparing food for the saints." The journalist Samuel G. Inman observed that the Gendarmerie enjoyed practically "unlimited power" in the districts where it served, creating opportunities for extortion and kickbacks. "He [the Gendarmerie officer] is the judge of practically all civil and criminal cases . . . the paymaster for all funds from the central government . . . and ex-officio director of the schools inasmuch as he pays the teachers. He controls the mayor and city council, since they cannot spend funds without his ok. As collector of taxes, he exercises a strong influence on all individuals in the community."[9]

Lieutenant Faustin E. Wirkus, who enlisted in the marines at seventeen to escape the Pittstown, Pennsylvania, coal mines, was even crowned the "white King" of La Gonave, an island three hours from Port-au-Prince, which he ruled as a personal fief. His story was popularized in William Seabrook's 1929 book *The Magic Island,* which portrayed him as an embodiment of the benevolent paternalism of the U.S. occupation. Embracing voodoo rituals and native dress and dance, the blond-haired Wirkus lived in a concrete house overlooking the sea, which Seabrook described as a "Kiplingesque outpost on the edge of the jungle." He was considered a god by many locals because of his importation of quinine and other modern medicines and because he helped farmers irrigate their land. At the same time, Wirkus meted out brutal justice to those who were not obedient to his whims, recalling in his memoirs how killing rebels was like playing "hit the nigger and get a cigar games" at amusement parks back home. A lot of killing, he said, was necessary before one could start reasoning with the peasant whose hunger and poverty drove him to join the Cacos.[10]

Wirkus's career recalls Joseph Conrad's observation in *Heart of Darkness* that "the conquest of the earth, which mostly means taking it away from those who have a different complexion or slightly flatter noses than ourselves, is not a pretty thing when you look into it much." Terrible abuses took place within the prison system overseen by the Gendarmerie. Under the watch of "Chesty" Puller, who told a visiting officer that he "may go to hell for this," inmates at

St. Marc's prison in Port-au-Prince labored under severe conditions quarrying stone to make new barracks for the Gendarmerie, causing some to break down and die. L. Ton Evans, a Baptist missionary jailed at St. Marc's for criticizing American policy, reported that he could hear the "groaning of prisoners who were being cruelly pounded and beaten" by gendarme officers and that dead bodies covered with vermin remained exposed in the prison yard.[11] Even after reforms were enacted, the prisons remained exploitative. Butler's successor, Lieutenant Alexander S. Williams, reported that the prison at Jacmel, heralded as a model of progressive penology, was "too hard," adding, "It is one of our best—it is sanitary, comfortable and the food ample—but [as at all prisons] the prisoners are required to work and to work hard."[12]

A career soldier who served under Jacob Smith in Samar and with the Philippines constabulary, Williams was the son of Alexander S. "Clubber" Williams, a notoriously cruel cop in New York's vice district, which he coined "the Tenderloin" after telling a friend that he had eaten "chuck [steak] for a long time" and was now "going to eat tenderloin." Characterized by the *New York Times* as a "bully," Clubber Williams once told a reporter that "there is more law in the end of a nightstick than in a decision of the Supreme Court." During the 1894 Lexow Committee investigations, a New York State Senate probe into police corruption in New York City, he admitted to owning extensive property and a yacht, which he'd bought with the proceeds from gambling and prostitution payoffs. Although there is no evidence that Alexander Junior was corrupt like his father, he was undoubtedly influenced by him in his hard-edged approach toward policing and his nativist and antiradical views. He met a sad demise, driving his car off the pier in San Francisco in 1926 after having been court-martialed for pressing cocktails on his mentor, Butler, at a dinner party which he hosted in violation of army Prohibition statutes.[13]

A critical function of the police programs in Haiti was to enhance American intelligence-gathering capabilities through close collaboration with local policing agents. In August 1920 the United States established an intelligence branch under Major W. G. Emery which developed organized files on insurgents and mapped out enemy territory, allowing for better battlefield planning. Psychological warfare tactics were widely promoted.[14] The Gendarmerie cultivated informants by presiding over community development and cockfighting events, creating centers for local gossip and information exchange. Sharing information on Bolshevik agents and radicals from other countries, it tried to censor the Haitian press, which, according to a February 1921 intelligence report, "poisoned inhabitants by circulating anti-occupation propaganda to all parts of Haiti which is read to ignorant Haitians who cannot read."[15] The editor of the *Courieur* newspaper was characteristically imprisoned over ten times in five years, though he was brought to court for trial only twice. Sometimes as many as seven editors were in jail at the same time.[16]

In 1924, as a marker of pride, two gendarmes won silver medals in rifle shooting at the Olympics. Williams reported, however, that trainees generally fared poorly on firing tests. "In hunting bandits, the failure to shoot straight results in the escape of many."[17] Colonel Frederic M. Wise, who took charge after Williams, noted that marines deliberately "discouraged target practice on the theory that it was dangerous to teach the native how to shoot. Some day they might possibly turn against us!"[18] In riot control training, gendarmes were taught the Progressive Era approach of using "fists and clubs" rather than firearms so as to lessen casualties. Americans did not usually object, though, when demonstrators were beaten and clubbed, sometimes to death.

Racism undermined any effort to promote humane standards. On rural search and destroy missions, "popping off" Cacos was likened to a sport, much as with the "pulajanes" and "ladrones" in the Philippines, and later the "gooks" in Vietnam.[19] The Gendarmerie adopted as its anthem an adaptation of the racist tune "Damn the Filipino, civilize him with a krag," in which they referred to Cacos as "voodoo-dancing drones." Marine Colonel Robert Denig noted in his diary that "life to them is cheap, murder is nothing." The marine John H. Craige believed that 90 percent of the Haitian peasantry possessed a "semi ape's brain," a remnant from the "Stone Age."[20]

Exemplifying the progressive fixation with statistical data and quantification, monthly reports from Haiti resemble those from the Philippines in judging success on the basis of the number of enemy captured, "neutralized," or killed. Williams's report of November 6, 1918, was typical in praising the Gendarmerie for dispersing rebels and killing six "bandits" in the Hinche district. A subsequent dispatch reported the killing of eighty-five bandits, the capture of ninety-two, and the seizure of 579 rifles, forty-five bayonets, and forty-one machetes.[21] Pressure for results led to the employment of excessive firepower and civilian casualties. A $2,000 bounty was offered for Caco commander Charlemagne Peralte, an ally of the deposed leader Bobo who had attacked a police post in Hinche in retaliation for the imprisonment of a local chief.[22] After an ambush of Peralte's forces near the town of Grande Rivière, marine Captain Herman H. Hanneken, blackened his skin, disguised himself as a Caco, and bribed one of Peralte's bodyguards to gain access to the rebel camp. He then shot Peralte at point-blank range, earning a commendation from President Wilson for "one of the most singularly important acts of heroism in my time."[23]

The marines subsequently disseminated a photo of Peralte's body that resembled Christ hanging from the cross, inspiring continued resistance. Minister of Revolution Benoît Batraville captured and decapitated the American general Lawrence Murth, telling him beforehand: "Your politicians say that you came to bring us civilization. We do not want civilization. Your chiefs say that we must stop fighting. We do not want to stop. We Cacos have been fighting since *longtemps, longtemps* [a long time]. There is nothing else that we want to do. We do not believe your politicians. Our own politicians have lied to us. We think you have come to take our country and make us your slaves. We want to keep our country and our freedom. We intend to drive the *blancs* [whites] into the sea."[24] These comments provide insight into the motives of the Caco movement in view of their long history of oppression by whites.

Making use of captured documents and spies, the Gendarmerie eventually tracked down Batraville, killing him and dozens of his men, dealing a deathblow to the insurgency. Jungle patrols continued into the early 1920s to suppress "malcontents who did not surrender," most notably the Caco chiefs Estraville, Jean-Jacques Albert, and Alcius Jean, who vowed to resist until the end. Monthly intelligence reports in 1921 noted that Estraville was sick with smallpox and Alcius's followers were surviving "mainly on fruit" and wore "poorly provided clothes," demonstrating their weakened state. Though "bandits still roamed the countryside[,] all are exhausted and in poor health. . . . They engage in few depredations except the illegal procurement of food by occasional foraging." The July report recorded the death of one of Alcius's men who had been "severely macheted by a native guide" after his capture near the border of the Dominican Republic. By October, most of the remaining chiefs had been captured and killed. Anti-occupation sentiment remained pervasive nevertheless, and U.S. intelligence feared the return of Dr. Bobo from exile in Jamaica.[25]

The Gendarmerie's "success" at pacification was aided by improvements in radio technology and communications. In a task later performed by USAID, army engineers constructed and oversaw the repair of telegraph lines, allowing for better coordination in pursuit of guerrillas. Introducing the use of airplanes in searching out remote mountain camps was another turning point. On August 4, 1920, Williams reported that two Gendarmerie planes had fired 1,200 machine gun rounds at a bandit camp, contributing to its destruction. In a radiogram to the State Department, Colonel J. J. Meade stated: "The planes maneuvered excellently and directed their fire with apparently good effect, taking bandits from their hiding places. . . . This demonstrates that airplanes are a success in such affairs. Bandits thought they were safe but found out there is no place that will protect them."[26] The adoption of aerial technology helped to usher in a new age of "total war" in which people could be killed without ever seeing the face of their attacker. For Haitians on the ground, the consequences were terrifying.

"Like Being Back in the Days of Boss Tweed": Further Misconduct and the McCormick Commission

A lack of legal regulations broadened the scope of police abuses throughout the occupation. Torture, or the "third degree," was considered "justifiable under field conditions" and because of the "uncivilized" nature of the Haitian people.[27] The court system was notoriously inefficient and marred by patronage and graft, problems that consular officials did not try to confront. Unless they had political connections, prisoners were usually held for long periods without trial. Speaking from personal knowledge, Williams testified before Congress that "the administration of justice in Haiti would be a farce if it were not a tragedy. . . . It was like being back in the days of Boss Tweed in New York."[28] Most gendarmes could neither read nor write and were ill-acquainted with the law. Williams, whose military service included tours in Panama, Cuba, and Mexico, complained to Secretary of State Robert Lansing that "the [Gendarmerie] cannot present their case in court, which is a major hindrance to the proper policing of the country." He added that most gendarmes were "lacking in ethical or civil standards and lacked sympathy for the people."[29]

In 1921, amidst an outcry by remnants of the Anti-Imperialist League and the National Association for the Advancement of Colored People, Senator Joseph Medill McCormick, an Illinois Republican, chaired hearings that revealed sickening cruelty by the Gendarmerie, including the burning of huts and the rape and shooting of prisoners.[30] Butler testified that officers were intoxicated by their newfound authority and given to excessive drinking of native liquor (taffia), which led to "unnecessarily harsh and brutal" conduct. He rationalized their behavior on the grounds that while 99 percent of the people of Haiti are the "most kindly, generous, hospitable, and pleasure loving people," the other 1 percent, when stirred up by liquor and voodoo, were "capable of the most horrible atrocities; they are cannibals."[31]

These views paralleled racial attitudes in the United States, where paternalistic affection was often displayed toward African Americans as long as they "stayed in their place."[32] The institution of forced labor (corvée) brought out the worst qualities of the Gendarmerie and harked back to the abuses of French colonialism. L. Ton Evans noted that the gendarme functioned as "an instrument of oppression and torture" in enforcing the "barbaric" marching of men "like a pack of slaves" under the corvée system, which reminded him of "the brutal slavery and savage treatment" meted out by the Belgians a "few years ago in Africa." One witness before the commission, the sociologist Carl Kelsey of the University of Pennsylvania, had observed severely malnourished men "manacled under the charge of the Gendarmerie several days' journey on foot from their home." He and others testifying at the hearings nevertheless argued in favor of continuing the occupation, claiming that it was having a civilizing effect. Senator McCormick ultimately recommended that the occupation be sustained for twenty more years and that the Gendarmerie continue to receive choice funding lest Haiti be thrust into anarchy and revolution, which was what American officials feared the most.[33]

"Pursuing an Active Campaign of Harassment": The Duvalier Era and Legacies of Colonialism

American colonial rule was on the whole a disaster for Haiti. The United States failed to develop viable social institutions, including in public health and education, and the road infrastructure was primarily designed to improve army transportation and expedite trade to the benefit of American corporations. The police constabulary served as one of the few enduring institutions, and its legacy was overwhelmingly negative. Emily Balch, a professor of economics at Wellesley College who traveled to Haiti in 1927 with a peace delegation, warned about "self-maintenance in power of whomsoever has control of this force, subject only to the development of a situation where, like the Pretorian guard, the soldiers sell themselves to the highest bidder."[34] This is exactly what transpired.

Prior to the withdrawal of the marines in 1934, the administration of Franklin Roosevelt stepped up riot control training and selected pro-American Colonel Demosthène Calixte to head the Gendarmerie. He used his position to launch a coup, which was suppressed by Stenio Vincent, a moderate nationalist who, along with his corrupt and autocratic successor Elie Lescot, intensified the politicization of the force, placing it firmly under his control.[35] Then, after ascending to power in 1957 following a period of military rule, François "Papa Doc" Duvalier used the policing apparatus built by the United States to brutalize opponents of his regime. His Tonton Macoutes, or secret police, were described as "thugs, thieves and murderers." A May 1959 State Department report mentioned a typical incident in which a student who criticized the government was kidnapped by Tonton Macoutes, who burned off his beard with a lighter. The report concluded that the "regular and secret police pursue an active campaign of harassment and terrorism all over the country."[36]

The United States tolerated these methods because of Duvalier's anticommunism and openness to foreign investment. As *Time* magazine editorialized, "With communist Cuba only 50 miles away, the U.S. cannot cut flat-broke Haiti off the dole without risking a red takeover."[37] The bulk of police aid was provided through a military assistance program headed by Colonel Robert Heinl Jr., whose own son was arrested, allegedly for asking why peasants had nothing to eat. Retaining old contacts, including army chief of staff Antonio Kébreau, who looked upon him as a father figure, Lemuel Shepherd Jr., former commandant of the Marine Corps, was influential in advocating for the continuation of police training for internal security purposes. American advisers worked with the presidential guard, who in turn trained the Tonton Macoutes in order to "keep Duvalier in power so he could fulfill his full term in office and maybe longer," as Heinl put it.[38] The U.S. ambassador argued, "Though critics would charge we are abetting repression, the embassy feels that any reasonable person, even if critical of the Duvalier regime, would admit to the necessity of the police being adequately equipped."[39] These comments illustrate the mindset of many in the State Department, bent on modernizing institutions such as the police regardless of the human implications. In the end, the United States helped to prolong the agonies of the occupation and inhibited the growth of political liberty. The seeds were being planted all the while for the global expansion of police training programs.

"If He Has Political Aspirations They Are Not Apparent": The Dominican Guardia and the Ascendancy of Trujillo

Police aid in the Dominican Republic, Haiti's neighbor on the island of Hispaniola, yielded a similar outcome to that in Haiti. In April 1917, a year after the marines invaded (an operation designed to shore up America's regional power and protect its sugar interests), governor Harry S. Knapp issued an executive order appropriating $500,000 for "organizing, equipping, and maintaining a national Dominican police force," the Guardia Nacional, which was considered by the State Department the "most solemn obligation we have assumed within this republic." A main purpose was to fight insurgents in the eastern provinces, who were a product of the disempowerment of local caudillos and the uprooting of the peasantry caused by the economic reorientation toward cash crop exports.[40]

Arguing that intervention was necessary to teach the Dominicans the advantages of industry and provide education, which was lacking in even "rudimentary form," minister William W. Russell recruited Puerto Rican officers experienced in enforcing colonial occupation. Dominicans, he believed, "would not be as efficient as American officers whose places they will take."[41] The force was commanded by Colonel George R. Shanton, chief of the Insular Police of Puerto Rico and a former Rough Rider who was said to "know the natives well." It was plagued, however, by poor discipline and low morale, having an abnormally high rate of courts-martial. A visitor observed that officers had a "cocky and insolent air," and their numbers "included some of the worst rascals, thieves, and assassins in the country," who used their position to "vent private hates."[42]

In December 1924, after the withdrawal of the marines, Russell lamented that "politics is fast destroying the efficacy of the Dominican police." The second-in-command was forced to resign because he failed to back President Horacio Vásquez enthusiastically. His replacement, Rafael L. Trujillo, a faithful Horacista, rose to lieutenant colonel owing to his expertise as an interrogator and informant.[43] Trujillo's alleged mentor, Captain Charles Merkel, committed suicide on the eve of his trial for what the diplomat Sumner Welles referred to as "the most revolting acts of barbarism charged against the forces of occupation in the Eastern Provinces." Trujillo himself had been indicted in 1920 on charges of holding a man for ransom and raping a seventeen-year-old girl. He was nevertheless seen as a loyal soldier capable of avoiding the pitfalls of factional politics. An intelligence report noted in 1927, in a remarkably poor judgment, that "if he has political aspirations, they are not apparent."[44]

In fact, Trujillo used his control over the Guardia to unseat Vásquez in 1930, establishing a thirty-one-year dictatorship. Sadistic tortures, including screwing electrical devices into people's skulls, were carried out under his oversight. In October 1937, Guardia units massacred 15,000 to 20,000 Haitian migrant workers.[45] The scale of violence was made possible by the influx of modern weapons and information technologies, a cornerstone of the police training programs which contributed significantly to Trujillo's rise.

Imperial Gendarmes: The Guardia Nacional in Nicaragua

Like those in Haiti and the Dominican Republic, the police training programs in Nicaragua aimed to institute progressive-style innovations and modernize police institutions, though they led to many excesses as a result of their militarization and the larger geopolitical designs to which they were attached. In 1909 the administration of Theodore Roosevelt toppled modernizer José Santos Zelaya after he resisted overtures to build a canal, installing as president Adolfo Díaz, former secretary of the American-owned La Luz mining company. Díaz sold the country's banks, customs office, and railroads to American investors and pushed through the Bryan-Chamorro Treaty, which gave the United States the right in perpetuity to build a canal on Nicaraguan territory. When a rebellion led by the liberal general Benjamin Zeledón broke out, Butler and the marines were called upon to put it down.[46]

Writing to his wife about the crass economic motives underlying American policy (views he made public after retiring from the army), Butler proposed creating a police constabulary to ensure law and order after the departure of the marines. In 1912 the Bureau of Insular Affairs appointed as inspector of the Managua police Guy Scull, a thirty-six-year-old Harvard graduate and former Rough Rider who had previously served with the New York Police Department and the Department of Justice secret police along the Mexican border. Scull surveyed the police stations and aimed to establish more professional standards. His tenure did not last long, as the brother of the minister of police took sides against him when he attempted to close down a café that was a base of political agitation.[47] This incident exemplifies the deep mistrust among local officials for the motives of Americans, which was not unique to Nicaragua.

From 1912 to 1933, the United States kept a contingent military force in Nicaragua to safeguard its economic interests in banking and the banana and coffee industries and to ensure the election of pro-American candidates.[48] In December 1924, after an eight-month study, Major Ralph Keyser, director of intelligence with the army's Second Division in World War I, outlined a plan for a Nicaraguan constabulary incorporating the national police, customs, and prison guard, which functioned as a "tool to gain political advantage by partisan and oppressive measures against those who differ in their politics from the government." Building on Butler's earlier proposal, Keyser aimed to professionalize training, improve pay, and equip the new force with top-of-the-line weapons. The Guardia Nacional was to become "the sole agency for the enforcement of internal law and order and the main reliance for national defense." Secretary of State Robert Olds envisioned that it would be the "cornerstone of stability for the whole country for years to come."[49]

These comments epitomize the emphasis placed by policy elites on social stability (on American terms, of course), which was seen as a precondition for development. The Coolidge administration supported the program largely on economic grounds, feeling that a foreign-controlled constabulary was the only means of giving capital sufficient assurance to undertake a large and permanent investment in Nicaragua, an underlying motive behind all the training programs.[50] In May 1925, just before the revival of civil war, the Nicaraguan Congress approved the creation of a Guardia at a budget of $689,132. The United States provided training and weapons (Krag and Jorgenson rifles and Lewis machine guns) and recruited Spanish-speaking officers with experience in the Philippines, the Panama Canal Zone, and Haiti.[51] Major Calvin Carter, a veteran of the Philippines constabulary from Elgin, Texas, reported that the locals of different party affiliations were providing the Americans "with valuable information on the plans and movement within their former parties." A number had been employed as security contractors for American companies such as Vaccaro Brothers Fruit. J. Antonio Lopez, former Managua chief of police, was heralded by U.S. intelligence for "looking like an American as a white and blond" and "saving a banana plantation during the revolution."[52]

According to the army's G-2 intelligence section, the Guardia acted "with great arrogance and even injustice towards the population," committing "serious crimes," such as beating the president of the Supreme Court, resulting "from the abuse of liquor." In 1930, when the visiting pacifist Charles Thomson was arrested, a North American official declared, "The National Guard is the constitution of this country," implying that it operated above the law. The State Department protested liberal president José Maria Moncada's use of the police to "arrest and deport for political reasons members of the conservative party," which went against the pledge of nonpartisanship.[53]

The historian Michel Gobat notes that many enlistees were from the lower class, and they subjected landowning elites to humiliating arrests for petty offenses, earning their enmity. Local judges showed their opposition to the police by refusing to sentence suspects, or even to arraign them; during 1931–32, police in Managua arrested 1,097 people, of whom only three were convicted.

These numbers suggest the contempt with which the Guardia was held, cutting across the class spectrum.[54]

In an attempt to bolster the image of the police, American officers implemented "civic action" programs, such as building rural schools, offering smallpox vaccinations, and presenting movie festivals and baseball games, whose primary purpose was to cultivate informants through close contact with the population.[55] Surveillance was enhanced by modernizing transport and radio communication and improving coordination with security forces in Honduras, which were partially financed by the U.S. War Department. An intelligence report signed by military attaché Fred T. Cruse noted that "[Honduran chief of detectives] Francisco Moran was a young Cuban, capable in carrying out investigations[,] who watched over the activities of [rebel leaders] Sandino [Augusto Cèsar] and Turcios [Froylan] in Tegucigulpa." He added approvingly that the city was "full of under-cover agents of Cuyamel and United Fruit Company," who worked with local police.[56]

Based in the Nueva Segovia district of Nicaragua, rich in coffee, bananas, lumber, and gold, Sandino emerged at the forefront of the resistance to the American occupation, promoting land reform, territorial sovereignty, and native rights. Inspired by Emiliano Zapata and the Mexican revolution, his forces sabotaged American businesses, such as La Luz Mining Company, of which Secretary of State Philander Knox was a shareholder.[57] The journalist Carleton Beals profiled Sandino admiringly in *The Nation* magazine, and Senator Thomas J. Heflin, an Alabama Democrat, likened him to the American founding fathers.[58] The State Department, however, denounced him as a "bandit who preached communism and death to Americans" and "used the stealthy and ruthless tactics which characterized the savages who fell upon American settlers in our country 150 years ago."[59] The Guardia was deployed to hunt him down, adopting search and destroy tactics which, in the words of the historian Walter LaFeber, "provided a remarkable preview of the sixties in Vietnam and early 1980s in Central America."[60]

The Sandinista campaign was headed by "Chesty" Puller, by now a veteran of the Caco war in Haiti. As commander of Company M, which was subsidized by rich Segovian merchants and coffee growers, Puller recruited Indians as police because of their remarkable endurance and knowledge of the jungle terrain.[61] Puller himself narrowly escaped death on several occasions and cemented his reputation as a skillful jungle fighter, winning the Navy Cross and a Presidential Order of Merit from Nicaraguan leader José Moncada for securing the capture of Pedro Altamirano, one of Sandino's key generals. General Julian Smith later wrote: "Puller was probably the bravest man I ever knew. His was a cool courage, never desperation. He would go anywhere without support, knowing that if he got in a jam, he had to get himself out. . . . He never hesitated, he invited that kind of work."[62]

Distinguished by his barrel chest, gruff voice, and propensity to speak his mind, Puller was a product of the same militarized culture in the United States during the Progressive Era which produced Theodore Roosevelt as president. His grandfather had served in the Confederate army, and while growing up, he had wanted nothing more than to emulate him. According to his biographer, the young "Chesty" was fascinated by the stories of old Civil War veterans in his hometown of West Point, Virginia, and once asked a sergeant who befriended him: "Why did we [the Confederacy] lose the war when there were so many of them [Confederate soldiers] left alive? Why didn't we fight until everybody was dead? I wouldn't have given up." The sergeant responded: "You definitely are John Puller's grandson. Flesh and blood. It's neck or nothing with you Pullers." This anecdote reveals the win-at-all costs mentality that Puller brought with him in fighting the rebel movements in Haiti and Nicaragua and sought to instill in his men. Puller returned to the United States a conquering hero and went on to gain great fame for his exploits against the Japanese in World War II at the battle of Guadalcanal, where he served alongside several former Guardia and Gendarme officers, including Herman Hanneken. Respected by his men for his fearlessness in battle and his lack of pretense, Puller ended his decorated career by winning his fifth Navy Cross at the age of fifty-two as a lieutenant general during the Korean War. His last public act, fittingly, was to testify in 1956 in defense of Sergeant Matthew McKeon, a Marine Corps drill instructor at Parris Island, South Carolina, who had led a platoon on a disciplinary night march through the swamps in which six young men drowned. Though he regretted the deaths, Puller claimed that harsh methods were necessary to prepare troops for combat. In the late 1960s, Puller's son, Lewis Jr., paralyzed while fighting in Vietnam, turned against a war that "Chesty" had advocated expanding into the North. Reflective at the end of his life, the general told his wife ironically that if he had to live again, he would "like to be an engineer and get a chance to build something, rather than having to wreck things."[63]

These comments notwithstanding, Puller's career demonstrates how the "anti-bandit" campaigns in Haiti and Nicaragua were formative in the development of both the American police programs and the U.S. military and served as a workshop for honing the methods that would be adopted in later conflicts. The men under Puller's command were known for their aggressive determination and ruthlessness. Characterizing the enemy as savage, Puller offered bounties for cutting off enemy ears. Taking few prisoners alive, his company boasted an estimated kill ratio of sixteen to one during decisive battles near the town of Jinotega. The discrepancies testify to the superior technology of the Guardia and its lack of restraint in the field.

Puller's unit played a key role in identifying targets for dive-bombing attacks, or what one historian has termed "aerial terrorism." In spite of claims of pinpoint accuracy, a village in Honduras was bombed by mistake. In a battle at Ocata, strafing by American planes killed hundreds of civilians, prompting demands by Governor Edward Dunne of Illinois that General Logan Feland, who ordered the attacks, be fired. Instead Feland was decorated by the Coolidge administration. The historian Neill Macaulay writes, "Why much of the world should excuse the excesses of the partisans when condemning the countermeasures taken by the occupying forces was as incomprehensible to the Marine aviators as it was to the German High Command."[64]

For all the firepower at its disposal, the Guardia struggled to break the back of the insurgency, which was given sanctuary in the communities where it operated and developed an effective espionage system. According to an official Marine Corps history, villages filled with Sandino sympathizers were "only too glad to report on the movements of Guardia patrols," making them susceptible to ambush.[65] In June 1930 Sandino sustained a leg wound from a bomb fragment. He was kidnapped and assassinated four years later while on his way to the president's palace after agreeing to a truce. The following day, the Guardia descended on the Sandinista cooperatives and massacred their inhabitants, the reprisals lasting for several months.[66]

The orders for Sandino's murder were given by Anastasio "Tacho" Somoza García, a liberal revolutionary commander and the first native director (jefe) of the Guardia, who came to rule Nicaragua like a personal fief. A graduate of Philadelphia's Pierce Commercial College, he was appointed by Minister Matthew Hannah, who considered him most capable of "laboring intelligently to maintain the non-partisan character" of the Guardia. Henry Stimson, special emissary and later secretary of state, referred to Somoza as "a . . . friendly, likeable young liberal whose attitude impresses me more favorably than any other."[67] Once in power, he doubled the revenues accorded to the Guardia and made it an instrument of his control, using it to spy on opponents, systemize graft, and suppress dissent, shooting officers at the slightest hint of insubordination.

In June 1941 J. Edgar Hoover warned Assistant Secretary of State Adolf Berle Jr. about the prevalence of Nazi sympathizers within the Guardia, including the former chief of staff. U.S. minister Arthur Bliss Lane commented in 1935 that the Guardia represented "the biggest stumbling block to progress in Nicaragua and an instrument that blasted constitutional procedure off the map," adding, "In my opinion it is one of the sorriest examples on our part of our inability to understand that we should not meddle in other people's affairs."[68]

Unfortunately for Nicaraguans, the meddling would continue through the ensuing decades. The United States provided a total of over $20 million to the Guardia and $350 million to Somoza and his sons, who were valued for their staunch anticommunism, acquiescence to American economic interests, and support for CIA operations in Guatemala and Cuba.[69] As head of the Guardia in the 1950s, Somoza's son Anastasio Jr., a West Point graduate, jailed thousands of suspected enemies, whom he screened with American lie detectors. Luis Napoli, a political attaché to the U.S. embassy, which sat on a ridge overlooking Somoza's palace, reported in 1958 that Luis Somoza, another son who succeeded

Anastasio Sr. in 1956 after the latter's assassination by a young poet, "rules with an iron grip and makes flagrant use of the police to maintain the status quo. If the police are not enough, he uses the army and also has goon squads to disrupt the opposition."[70] These comments provide a fitting epitaph for decades of American foreign policy, which helped create and sustain a repressive police state similar to its counterparts on Hispaniola.

In a pioneering two-volume study, the historians David Anderson and David Killingray show how police were developed into critical mechanisms for upholding the power of European colonial regimes. In country after country, officers were trained in information technologies and organized for counter-intelligence and along paramilitary lines, especially as anticolonial movements became more organized. Over the long term, the repressive apparatus proved difficult to expunge and was in many cases appropriated by postcolonial leaders to root out their political rivals.[71]

Though the United States fashions itself as exceptional, American interventions fit this general pattern. Laying the foundation for subsequent training programs, the United States developed police constabularies as critical instruments of social control. These institutions, as we have seen, were a product of the dominant progressive belief that centralized state power and the regulation of social life were vital to the construction of a modern state and could provide the stability necessary for capitalist development. The architects of American policy, however, did not foresee the long-term danger associated with creating militarized police forces in nations without an established legal structure or a judicial system capable of reigning in abuses. The political scientist Marvin Goldwert notes with regard to Nicaragua: "What the United States failed to see was that partisanship was based not on party principle but opportunism. When the third force, led by the rising young politician Somoza, came to power on the back of a strong National Guard, the historical parties were political midgets at its side."[72]

These comments encapsulate the importance of the police programs in giving rise to a new breed of authoritarian leader who supplanted the old oligarchies and used the modern policing apparatus built up by the United States as a political instrument. In the early 1960s, government officials with a short historical memory attributed the widening scope of police repression and civil strife in Latin America to "deeply ingrained cultural, economic, and political characteristics," which seemingly inhibited the spread of law and order and basic standards of human rights.[73] Police adviser Herbert Hardin commented, with reference to Nicaraguans, that "they are real uncivilized . . . in a backwards state of development, and settle disputes by force."[74] In reality, however, the violence was a product of deep-rooted sociopolitical and historical contingencies and a legacy of American colonialism. The fateful decisions of that era cast a long and dark shadow that still haunts the region today.

Part II

Under the Facade of Benevolence
Police Training and the Cold War in Southeast Asia from the "Reverse Course" to Operation Phoenix

Humanitarianism is laudable if one can afford it. The greatest act on behalf of all humanity however is for the U.S. to help others from falling under the control of communism.

—COLONEL ALBERT R. HANEY, Overseas Internal Security Program planning document, 1957

They called me a red bitch. Any red was not considered human. . . . They looked at me as if I was a beast or a bug. . . . Because we weren't human, we had no rights.

—PAK WAN-SO, South Korean writer who faced imprisonment and torture by U.S.-trained police

Though separated by less than fifteen years from the withdrawal of U.S. troops from the Caribbean, the post–World War II American occupation of Japan and the onset of the Cold War marked the opening of an entirely new era, one in which the United States emerged as the preeminent global power. Amidst a flowering of nationalist sentiment—what Tom Engelhardt referred to as the postwar "victory culture"—the United States was bent more than ever before on projecting its power and exporting its institutions to all corners of the globe, partly as a means of countering the influence of its Cold War rivals, the Soviet Union and China. The United States intensified its pursuit, furthermore, of a coherent global strategy designed, in the words of Noam Chomsky, to carve out a system of "open societies" in which American capital could operate more or less freely.[1] While the scope of American interventions consequently increased, they changed in character and became, with some exceptions, more informal than in the past and reliant on indirect mechanisms of social control. The old approach toward colonialism had become discredited as a result of the dying of the British and French empires and the waning of social Darwinian philosophies in the wake of the Nazi holocaust. No longer could policymakers rationalize their actions by claiming to be "taking up the white man's burden." Nor could they justify the long-term administration of colonies. Instead they focused on developing pliable proxy regimes that ruled in accord with U.S. interests.

Police training became especially important in this context. Kept largely hidden from the public, it was designed to promote the social stability deemed necessary for liberal capitalist development and to suppress radical nationalist and communist movements, which had become increasingly popular and well organized as a result of sociohistorical circumstances.[2] A new generation of police advisers, now culled from the Office of Strategic Service, the FBI, and state police organizations, embraced the Cold War mission and worked to professionalize the police and improve their capacity to serve as the "first line of defense" against subversion. Believing in the universality of American institutions, they operated predominantly in the shadows from one Cold War trouble spot to the next, providing technical advice and equipment and lectures at American-financed police academies, usually by translation. They received little public acclaim; few Americans even knew that they existed. Many of the police whom they trained, however, rose to positions of prominence in their own countries, owing in part to the stockpiles of weapons they received from their generous patron.[3]

Throughout the Cold War, the budget for police programs was highest in Southeast Asia. The United States had always prized the region as one of the richest and most strategically located in the world, hoping to convert it into what General Douglas MacArthur characterized as an "Anglo-Saxon lake." In a March 1955 Foreign Affairs article, William Henderson of the Council on American Foreign Relations (which Laurence Shoup and William Minter aptly termed the "imperial brain trust") wrote: "As one of the earth's great storehouses of natural resources Southeast Asia is a prize worth fighting for. Five-sixths of the world's natural rubber, and more than half of its tin are produced here. . . . [It] accounts for two-thirds of the world output of coconut, one-third of the palm oil, and significant proportions of tungsten and chromium. . . . No less important than the natural wealth is Southeast Asia's key strategic position astride the main lines of communication between Europe and the Far East."[3]

Envisioning Chinese Guomindang leader Jiang Jieshi (Chiang Kai-shek) as one of the four great policemen of the postwar order, American advisers from the OSS, FBI, Federal Bureau of Narcotics (FBN), and the New York Police Department began instructing his secret police, commanded by Dai Li, in the late 1930s. The focus, OSS agent Milton Miles wrote, was on "political crimes and means of effective repression" against the communist movement, adding that the Americans were never able to "separate police activities from guerrilla activities." Tied to the Green Gang underworld, Dai Li's forces developed a reputation as a "Chinese Gestapo," running mass surveillance and a network of concentration camps in which Jiang's opponents faced torture, starvation, or death by firing squad. A museum of one of the sites contains a photograph of a pit in which ninety-four dead bodies were found bound with handcuffs made in Springfield, Massachu-setts, a testament to the complicity of the United States in the reign of terror.[4]

The brutality of the secret police contributed to the triumph of the Chinese revolution, which aimed to extract China from dependency on Western trade and promote rapid industrialization and land reform for poor peasants. According to the historian William Neumann, the Maoist victory represented "an even greater disaster for American policy than Pearl Harbor. For proponents of the Open Door—a program of state-supported penetration of world markets by U.S. businesses—the loss of the fabled China market nullified the purpose of the Pacific War."[5] The United States subsequently intensified efforts to "roll back" left-leaning and communist regimes, relying on clandestine police programs in an attempt to avoid military entanglement in the wake of the Korean War, which had been waged at a high price in terms of blood and treasure. Police advisers provided training in riot control, set up modern communications and record-collection systems, and trained paramilitary units in jungle warfare. They helped amass thousands of dossiers on alleged communists, weaving information into a dark tapestry of "threat" where sober analysis might have found none.[6]

Many advisers in these later programs, including Byron Engle, first gained international experience during the postwar occupation of Japan, where they inaugurated techniques honed on the periphery of the Cold War. Following World War II, the Supreme Command of the Allied Powers (SCAP) adopted a new con-stitution in Japan with provisions to protect civil liberties. Nevertheless, under the "reverse course," aimed at rolling back the progress of the left, police were orga-nized to monitor and suppress the labor movement and the Japanese Communist Party, resulting in human rights violations, including torture, which set the pat-tern for the Cold War, an era in which the use of torture by American-backed forces was systematic and the United States repeatedly violated international law.[7]

During the Vietnam War, which saw the "cresting of America's westward drive," the State Department spent close to half a billion dollars on police training in the attempt to subdue the Southern-based National Liberation Front (NLF). Sir Robert Thompson, a RAND Corporation analyst who helped Britain sup-press a Chinese-backed uprising in Malaya, was influential in arguing that police were effective at gathering intelligence and guarding strategic hamlets and more capable than the military in implementing public works projects designed to win the political war for "hearts and minds."[8] Michigan State University and USAID advisers developed a far-reaching surveillance apparatus and expanded the prison system, in which torture and other abuses proliferated. Operation Phoenix used advanced computer data management systems in the attempt to "neutralize" the NLF leadership, breeding wide-scale violence in the absence of institutional correctives for false identification and inflated statistics. The government of Nguyen Van Thieu and the U.S. war effort were in turn undermined, having lost a monopoly on the legitimate use of force.

Operation Phoenix represents a fitting symbol of the excesses associated with the police programs, which contributed to significant human rights violations through the importation of advanced weapons and social control mechanisms. Under the facade of benevolence, the Office of Public Safety (OPS) and its predecessors were instrumental in creating modern policing apparatuses designed to fortify client regimes and root out oppositionist movements, with varying yet frequently deadly consequences.

Chapter **3**

"Their Goal Was Nothing Less than Total Knowledge"

Policing in Occupied Japan and the Rise of the National Security Doctrine

Despite the fact that SCAP has ordered the . . . Home Ministry to democratize its police force . . . the average Japanese lives today in just as great a fear of the police as he did before the occupation. He knows that the police are supported by the occupation troops.

—ARTHUR D. BOUTERSE, chief public welfare sub-section GHQ, Supreme Commander for the Allied Powers, Lt. Col. Philip H. Taylor, G-2 War Department, and Arthur Maass, Military Government post liaison officer for Kanagawa prefecture, 1948

You Americans are very difficult. We had all the Communists in jail when you occupied the country in 1945. Then you told us to release them. Now you ask us to find them and put them in jail again. A very cumbersome process.

—Japanese leader YOSHIDA SHIGERU to an American reporter following the "reverse course," 1951

If we do not stop the communist hordes in this area now, it is quite possible for them to be in the USA a few years hence.

—COLONEL HOWARD E. PULLIAM to Chairman of the Board, Police Commission, Kansas City, Missouri, September 12, 1950

In the late 1940s, police recruits at a training academy established by the United States in Osaka were required to watch a feature-length film on democratic policing standards titled *Midnight in a Great City*. The story centered on a generational conflict between a father, a veteran of the police force who clung to traditional methods, and his son, who was schooled in modern scientific techniques. The two got into frequent arguments about the best way to track down criminals, and each followed his own approach. At the climax of the film, the father is wounded by a gangster. Through the incorporation of new technologies and forensic science, the son is able to bring the culprit to justice. The father comes to recognize defects in the old system and after his recovery becomes a major proponent of new scientific methods.[1]

This film captured the ideological underpinnings of the American police programs in Japan, which were designed to inculcate new technologies and professional standards to heighten police efficiency. U.S. officials envisioned that the police would be the bulwark of a new democratic society and provide the security necessary for liberal capitalist development. As the historian John Dower notes, Japan was considered the "super-domino" of the containment doctrine in Southeast Asia, which policymakers desperately hoped to incorporate into the Western orbit. The Pacific War had been fought and atomic bomb dropped, in part to prevent Japan's accommodation to a mainland communist bloc and its becoming the industrial heartland of a new order from which the United States might be excluded.[2]

The police programs took on special importance in this context. New Dealers within the Supreme Command of the Allied Powers (SCAP) initially pressed for police decentralization, the purging of militarists, and the protection of civil liberties; the possibility of a more progressive foreign policy, however, was blighted by the entrenchment of the Cold War. Following the "reverse course" policy aimed at undermining leftist advances, police advisers focused more exclusively on counterintelligence and riot control training, mobilizing police to crack down on the Japanese Communist Party (JCP) and the political left, which promoted independent development outside American control.[3] Novel techniques in population control became institutionalized. By the early 1950s, the Truman administration was providing flamethrowers and tanks to the police reserve, causing people to question whether the United States was abandoning its pledge to bring about demilitarization. But police modernization was on the whole tied to a larger strategic design centered on advancing U.S. hegemony in Southeast Asia, which precluded support for human rights.

Exporting the New Deal? Police Modernization and the Limits of Reform

The history of modern policing in Japan dates to the 1868 Meiji restoration, when a national police bureau was established and samurai from the warrior class were trained as urban constables. Meiji reformers traveled abroad to survey Western police systems, which they sought to emulate as the country underwent a process of modernization and urbanization. Many of the innovations were later exported to Japan's colonies in the attempt to increase internal security. During World War II, Japanese police were indoctrinated in the belief that "all communists, socialists, and liberals as well as those opposed to the war should be regarded as a national enemy." The Special Higher Police (Tokkô) presided over a vast surveillance apparatus, tortured suspects, and purged members of the Home Ministry thought to be disloyal.[4]

After the war, the United States initiated police reform as an integral dimension of its democratization program and with the goal of establishing law and order in the wake of Japan's demilitarization. These twin aims often existed at odds with each other. American officials were divided between liberal reformers in the civilian branches who were committed to upholding human rights, and conservatives concentrated in the military and intelligence sections who championed the police as an instrument of social control. State Department planners, committed to rebuilding Japan's economy so as to prevent the spread of communism and foster the country's reemergence as a regional power, sought to revive the Open Door policy in the Far East, guaranteeing U.S. and Japanese access to the resources and markets of other Asian countries, a key motive underlying the Korean and Vietnam wars.[5]

The New Deal lawyer Charles Kades was representative of the liberal idealists who viewed Japan as a laboratory of progressive reform, warning about the dangers posed by a strong, centralized police force—namely, the "ruthless liquidation of opposing elements." General Charles Willoughby, head of the U.S. Army's G-2 intelligence unit, was an opponent of police reform and an admirer of Benito Mussolini and Francisco Franco; in the words of the historian Michael Schaller, Willoughby "saw communists and Jewish conspiracies at home, abroad, and especially in SCAP's ranks."[6]

Committed to promoting democracy "from above"—in other words, without input from the Japanese people, whom he likened to a "boy of twelve" compared to Americans' forty-five—General Douglas MacArthur viewed the rebuilding of police institutions as crucial to larger state-building efforts and the consolidation of a stable proxy regime. He requested that six police administrators be assigned to the G-2 Public Safety Division (PSD), headed by Colonel H. E. Pulliam, a veteran of the Berkeley, California, police department known for progressive innovations such as using bicycle and motorized patrols and establishing a fingerprint filing system. Warning about turning over the nation to "pinks and reds," the anti-union Pulliam believed that just as "Ghengis Khan in China, the House of Hapsburg under Charles V[,] . . . Napoleon[,] . . . Lenin, Mussolini, and Hitler in their march to power relied upon a centralized police," Japan should do likewise. "Mawkish sentimentality over the individual rights of man" could not sit easily alongside practical considerations in a "world of eternal conflict."[7]

Pulliam's successor Byron Engle believed similarly in the necessity of a strong central state and police power as a bulwark against revolution. Born in 1910 in Buffalo, Missouri, Engle was one of the youngest police administrators in the United States. He was known for helping to stamp out corruption in the Kansas City Police Department, a vital cog in the political machine of "Boss Tom" Pendergast. Beginning his career as a patrolman during the depression, he served at nearly every level of law enforcement, including as director of recruitment and training after taking a three-month course at the FBI's police academy in 1943. He was mentored by Chief Lear Reed, a marine captain who warned in *Human Wolves: Seventeen Years of War on Crime* of the menace of communism, drugs, and racial integration and bragged about punching one of his subordinates in the face and knocking out his front teeth after being offered a bribe. A devotee of J. Edgar Hoover who became CIA station chief in the Dominican Republic, Reed advocated putting communists in concentration camps. He ran an internal security unit that shared information with the FBI on thousands of suspected radicals, many of them civil rights, human rights, and peace activists and labor organizers, whom Reed characterized as "alien minded mongrels" who "blaspheme Americanism."[8]

Described by a contemporary as a stickler for detail who seemed never to forget a face or a name (good qualities to have in his line of work), Engle considered the police a critical point of contact between the government and the people. He believed that its effectiveness could be augmented by developing skilled intelligence and paramilitary units, which he worked to do in Japan and then worldwide as director of 1290-d and the Office of Public Safety. It was from Reed and Hoover that Engle developed the idea that police should serve as the "first line of defense" against subversion, a principal slogan of the OPS.[9]

In 1950 Engle was recruited by the CIA to inaugurate police training in Turkey. His position was taken over by Captain Harold Mulbar, head of a police investigations unit ("red squad") with the Michigan State Police, which compiled dossiers on more than twelve thousand residents and infiltrated dozens of radical and labor organizations. Through the war years, Mulbar spoke each week on the radio in Michigan, enlisting voluntary reports on suspected foreign agents. During the 1937 sit-down strike at the General Motors plant in Flint, he led a team of plainclothes officers seeking to gain information on radical and communist elements in the United Auto Workers and Congress of Industrial Organizations and testified about their activities before the House Un-American Activities Committee. Influenced by the professional ethic of the Progressive Era, Mulbar was a proponent of scientific methods, including the use of lie detector tests, and wrote a book on the art of interrogation in which he condemned torture as "a futile, unethical, and barbarian practice."[10]

Mulbar and Engle exemplify the effort to apply the standards of Progressive Era policing internationally and to expand the role of police surveillance and espionage in the antiradical political agenda shared by both major parties.[11] From 1945 to 1952, SCAP provided over 80 billion yen (roughly $200 million) for police salaries, training, and equipment in Japan, from armored cars, radios, and teletype machines (for disseminating information) to flashlights, holsters, and Colt revolvers. Putting out detailed surveys and maps, the PSD sought to instill American concepts of policing, including organizational patterns and an emphasis on scientific investigation and community relations, and provided training in undercover work. In Hiroshima, where police were killed by the atomic attacks and police buildings were gutted, the PSD rebuilt a new force from scratch.[12] Reforms were slow to get off the ground, in part because of their implementation through conservative Japanese leaders, including the emperor. Alfred Oppler, head of the Courts and Law Division of SCAP, claimed that the calls for police decentralization were "ideologically sound but unrealistic."[13]

One important measure favored by MacArthur, who described Japan as the "westernmost outpost of our defense," was the substitution of wooden clubs for traditional short swords for Japanese police, in part for symbolic effect. On October 11, 1945, SCAP issued a directive authorizing a reduction of police strength to 93,935 from over 120,000. As part of the purging of ultranationalists, officers linked to past abuses were dismissed, including two prefectural chiefs and 4,900 members of the "thought control" section, which MacArthur saw as "the strongest weapon of the military clique." Forty-four percent of police officers left voluntarily. To keep watch over purged officials, MacArthur established a special investigations bureau, which evolved into a reincarnation of the Tokkô by maintaining surveillance over suspected communists.[14]

In June 1946, under Engle's leadership, the PSD established an academy in Osaka for 2,200 police, who in turn trained the rest of the force. The academy was equipped with an indoor rifle and pistol range; courses were taught in marksmanship, arrest techniques, "Anglo-Saxon" jurisprudence, judo, and scientific policing methods, including fingerprinting and forensics.[15] Instruction manuals from the United States written by leading police theorists such as August Vollmer, chief of police in Berkeley from 1905 to 1931 and founding dean of the Department of Criminology at the University of California at Berkeley, were translated into Japanese. The film *Midnight in a Great City*, promoting the use of modern scientific techniques, was a staple of the course. Over time, at least fifty training schools were established, and police executives were sent to study the American police system, including in Berkeley under Vollmer's successor John D. Holstrom, later a consultant to 1290-d. In retirement, Vollmer corresponded with members of the Metropolitan Police in Osaka and the reformer Yusai Takahashi, who wrote a textbook on patrolling which advocated the Berkeley system and its emphasis on community relations.[16]

Setting the standard for the training programs in Japan, Vollmer had been among the first American police chiefs to go abroad to promote police reform. In 1926, after being elected chairman of the International Association of Chiefs of Police, which sought to promote professional standards worldwide, he spent two months setting up a police training school and teletype communications system on behalf of Cuban dictator Gerardo Machado. In the early 1930s, at the request of the Chinese Nationalist government, Vollmer sent his deputy Arthur G. Woods to modernize the police under Generalissimo Jiang Jieshi (Chiang Kai-shek). Two of Vollmer's Chinese students at Berkeley (Feng Yukun and Frank Yee) went back to China after graduation to set up police academies, which incorporated his teachings on modern managerial and scientific techniques. The largest of these academies, at Zhejiang, trained the secret police of Dai Li, whom OSS operative Oliver J. Caldwell referred to in his memoirs as a "Chinese Himmler."[17]

The police programs in Japan built on these dubious precedents, with the government now institutionalizing the effort to export the American professional policing model. PSD advisers such as retired LAPD deputy chief Henry S. Eaton, Arthur Kimberling (police chief in Louisville, Kentucky, who later co-managed 1290-d), and Clyde Phelps (chief of police in Spokane, Washington, who went on to Iraq, Brazil, Somalia, and Peru) gave lectures at the police academy and set up a detective bureau, immigration agency, and licensing system for private detective agencies staffed primarily by former police officers who had been dishonorably discharged. They tried to recruit better-educated personnel (a hallmark of Vollmer's tenure in Berkeley), promoted higher wage standards, and aided in the systematization of records, providing new steel file cabinets.[18] The PSD further authorized the hiring of female police officers and set up a criminal investigations laboratory in Tokyo directed by Lieutenant Calvin H. Goddard, a firearms identification (ballistics) expert who was professor of police science and the first director of the Northwestern Scientific Crime Detection Laboratory, which brought together specialists in chemistry, toxicology, microscope identification, and photography.

A medical doctor by training who served with the Army Medical Corps in World War I, Goddard testified for the prosecution at the Sacco and Vanzetti trial and helped to locate two of the submachine guns used in the gangland St. Valentine's Day Massacre in Chicago.[19] His background was typical of the experience of many of the advisers, who were pioneers in the professionalization of American law enforcement and sought to extend their technical expertise abroad, largely to help consolidate America's strategic position in the Far East.

One of the central tasks of the PSD was to restore telecommunication networks ravaged during the war. At the beginning of the occupation, the phones worked only sporadically. By the early 1950s, reports boasted that technical advisers had established a radio network allowing for easy communication among police agencies across the country.[20]

In another important innovation, the PSD worked with lawyers to promote legislative and judicial reforms guaranteeing suspects the right to habeas corpus, speedy sentencing, and appeal. This was crucial in the attempt to ensure an institutional commitment to due process, lacking among past forces built up by the United States. To get around a reliance on forced confessions, instruction was provided in evidence collection. In 1946, coinciding with progressive labor reform, SCAP passed a law guaranteeing political rights of assembly and protest, and authorizing the release of communist and left-wing activists imprisoned during the war.[21]

A number of advisers expressed frustration that the police remained under-equipped and were unreceptive to learning new approaches. Pointing to the persistence of high crime rates and the violent suppression of riots in Osaka, one reported that "modernization of police methods must be preceded by a change in the mentality of police officers to a more scientific way of thinking. ... Police with old ideas handling machines are like monkeys riding bicycles."[22] These comments illustrate the fixation on technology and modernization as a pathway to progress, which was not always shared by the local people and police whom the United States worked with.

Overcoming the "Oriental Psychology": The Valentine and Olander Reports

In January 1946, as reorganization and reform were beginning to take root, General MacArthur requested that an eminent police expert come to Japan to oversee the process. The PSD chose Oscar G. Olander, commissioner of the Michigan State Police, who solicited the assistance of his former colleague Harold Mulbar, and Lewis Valentine, commissioner of the New York City Police Department, who brought with him several of his associates.

Both Olander and Valentine were among the top professionals in their field. Working his way up from assistant records clerk in the early 1920s, Olander developed an excellent reputation for reorganizing the Michigan detective bureau and constabulary, adopting new scientific innovations, keeping the police free from machine politics by promoting from within, and improving training, encouraging officers to take courses at Michigan State University, which was developing one of the best criminal justice programs in the country. Characterizing the Wobblies (Industrial Workers of the World, or IWW) as "enemies of the country and law and order," Olander also oversaw strikebreaking and kept a file of "dangerous and un-American residents" which he shared with the FBI. His organization was known for its close relationship with business elites and for the strength of its red squads.[23]

The son of a fruit store owner from Italy who began his career as a patrolman in 1903, Valentine was recognized for bringing discipline and professionalism to the New York Police Department and was hailed by the *New York Times* as the "best police commissioner in city history." Operating on the premise that residents have the right to "expect courtesy and service in return for their tax dollars," he dismissed more than three hundred corrupt officers and fined 8,500 in his first six years (1934–1940). A favorite of liberal mayor Fiorello La Guardia and a lifelong Democrat, he adopted a more tolerant policy toward strikes and public demonstrations than his predecessor, though as the historian Marilynn S. Johnson notes, he had little sympathy for communists and union "agitators" and relied on sophisticated forms of clandestine surveillance and repression and the undercover red squad. In his treatment of criminals, Valentine was known to be brutal, promising promotions to cops who "kicked the gorillas around." When a stickup man was brought in covered with bruises and died in custody, Valentine dismissed the affair as "just another dead criminal." Balking at the sight of a well-dressed suspect in a lineup, he at another time told one of his subordinates: "That velvet collar should be smeared with blood. . . . I don't want these hoodlums coming in looking as if they stepped out of a barber's chair. From now on, bring 'em in messed up."[24]

These comments typify the lack of regard for civil liberties in American police institutions, which extended into the international programs. (A New York City police officer working with Dai Li was no doubt sincere in commenting, "He does nothing [in interrogation] that the New York 'confession department' wouldn't do.") Supportive of U.S. foreign policy objectives, as were so many of their generation, Olander and Valentine concluded after visiting police precincts that the Japanese police system was organized not to serve the public but to advance the political ambitions of those in control and needed to be transformed. Olander suggested that a national rural police system be established under the direction of an appointed head who would be responsible to an elected government official. He advocated improving the physical facilities of police stations and jails and providing modern equipment and weaponry. In his view, change had to be accomplished gradually because of ingrained cultural traditions and the peculiar "oriental psychology," which was resistant to modernization.[25]

Valentine, who stepped down from a $45,000-a-year job as a commentator on the popular *Gang Busters* radio program to head the police reorganization (for which he was paid $10,000), recommended that working hours be reduced and pay systematized to improve professional standards and that SCAP supply patrol cars, radios, and technical assistance to upgrade communications. He called for better uniforms and speedier court procedures, the eradication of binding (a practice whereby arrested persons were bound with cord or rope before being taken to detention), and the elimination of police control of the health and welfare systems.

Referring to the current system as "medieval," Valentine further advocated for the enforcement of anti-vice laws, the standardization of training at police academies, and gradual decentralization through commissioners to ensure effective administrative control and fairer promotion standards. He saw the New York Police Department as a model for Japanese cities and recommended extensive oversight by American PSD officials. In his view, adapting an American police system to Japan had a dual purpose: to raise the morale and efficiency of the new police force and to secure the respect of the general public. "New Yorkers don't fear their policemen, they respect them and trust them and don't run from them," he told reporters. "There is no reason why the Japanese police can't be the same."[26]

On February 28, 1947, the Japanese cabinet presented a draft plan based on the recommendations of the Valentine and Olander reports, which codified existing reforms; it was put into effect a year later. The legal foundations for vicious police practices, including "third degree," methods were formally removed, and the right to habeas corpus was ensured. Pre-indictment detention was limited to a period of ten days, and arrests could be made only after the issuance of judicial warrants. In a break from previous interventions, police activities related to sanitation, subpoenas, public health, fires, census enumeration, economic controls, conservation of natural resources, and marine affairs were transferred to other agencies in order to limit the powers of the police. A public safety commission was also established at the national and municipal levels to ensure citizen control.[27]

The most controversial provision was the retention of the Rural Guard, which SCAP supplied with weapons and shortwave radio equipment. Working with G-2 intelligence, the Guard, which could be activated in the case of a national emergency, was considered "necessary in a country without experience in democracy."[28] This remark exemplifies the contradictions of U.S. policy, which promoted democracy in principle but did not trust the indigenous capacity for self-government. Order and stability took precedence over civil liberties, particularly as social unrest increased.

"There Comes a Time When Patience Ceases to Be a Virtue": Penal Reform and Its Limits

Olander and Valentine promoted a measure important to their recommendations: an overhaul of the prison system on the model of progressive reforms. Unbeknownst to many SCAP officials, who underestimated the ability of the Japanese to advance progressive social change on their own accord, Japanese officials had studied European prison systems during the Meiji era and embraced many aspects of Western penology, including the separate classification of male and female prisoners and juveniles, outlawing torture, the imposition of labor regimens and a rewards system, and support for rehabilitation through vocational training and education. After touring penal facilities in the late 1920s, the University of Wisconsin criminologist John L. Gillin wrote that Japan had something to teach Americans in "the care with which she selects her prison wardens, the training of prison officials, and in the treatment of offenders."[29]

Reflecting the deteriorating conditions during World War II, PSD inspections at the beginning of the occupation found "appalling privations" among detainees, many of whom were held for lengthy periods without trial. Children and pregnant women were confined with the general population, there was insufficient light and ventilation, and inmates were deprived of physical exercise and medical care. Sanitation standards were "undesirable," and "obnoxious smells" and "mustiness" were reported in many of the overcrowded cells, which resembled "dungeons." Prisoners with communicable diseases including scabies were mixed in with the others, corporal punishment was common, and death rates were excessive.[30]

The PSD prison branch, headed by Burdett Lewis, former commissioner of corrections in New York City and an admirer of the legendary prison reformers Zebulon Brockway and Thomas Mott Osborne, worked to rectify these problems as an integral aspect of the civil liberties directive. Influenced by social scientific research on the environmental roots of human behavior, Lewis in a 1921 book advocated "kind, firm, and intelligent" treatment of the criminal offender, whose "blood should not be contaminated, his body destroyed and his spirit broken and brutalized. . . . He should be trained as a child in school, treated as a patient in a hospital, molded as an apprentice in his trade so that he may be able to take his place as a self-supporting member of society."[31]

Following these principles, Lewis and his staff—including Admiral Lloyd W. McCorkle, a sociology professor with a Ph.D. from New York University; Wilbur Burke, an intelligence officer with a law degree from Indiana University; and George Fitzgibbon, a Harvard Ph.D.—promoted improved sanitation and health care, reorganized the prisoner classification procedure, set up a parole and indeterminate sentencing system, and separated women and juvenile inmates from the men. The professional training of guards in modern penology became obligatory. Bail was made a matter of law, and inmates were to be considered innocent until proven guilty. Schools were opened for inmates, and the PSD encouraged wardens to allow even recalcitrant prisoners daily exercise and regular baths.[32] Long-term solitary confinement was abolished, and psychologists were brought in to assist in rehabilitation. Recreational facilities were also established, and sporting teams, notably baseball, and sumo wrestling competitions were organized. The PSD additionally helped set up industrial training, shops, and penal farms modeled after the Iwahig colony in the Philippines and the George Junior Republic.[33]

Although Lewis acknowledged "limitations" because of the supposedly different Japanese attitude toward the "worth of the individual," PSD inspection reports show improvement in a number of the facilities targeted under the reforms. An inmate at the Amori prison commented in 1947 that "since the war, the food is worse but handling prisoners is much better with no military orders being given and psychological handling more considerate."[34] Public safety officials were especially impressed with the running of the Sapporo prison by J. Kusomoto. A prison report characterized the law school graduate as a highly intelligent and cultured man who liked to discuss philosophy and was in "sympathy with the spirit of rehabilitation which is the basis of the ordinance set up under the new 'progressive' system." According to the inspector, Kusomoto had worked vigorously to haul snow out of the prison yard to allow for recreation, initiated counseling programs, and kept the prisoners productive through work in various industries and on an adjacent farm that he helped develop.[35] The adulation for Kusomoto exemplifies the spirit of progressive-style reform promoted by American officials and their belief in the capacity of the penal system to rehabilitate inmates and mold them into productive citizens.

The Fuchu prison outside Tokyo, whose warden had been injured in the atomic blast, was heralded as another model of reform. Pointing to declining tuberculosis rates, a squeaky-clean mess hall, and the manufacture by prisoners of pins, bike parts, cigarette lighters, and locks, a laudatory article in *Japan News* proclaimed Fuchu "an institution of which any country could be justifiably proud. By no stretch of imagination could the prison be described as comfortable, yet the conditions under which prisoners live could hardly be improved while still keeping it a place of punishment. The atmosphere is that of a modern factory in which the workers are getting a fair deal from management."[36]

Beneath the radar of SCAP's public relations machine, however, problems lurked. A former guard at the prison, Murai Kazuo, complained about illegal food distribution, the appropriation of government supplies by guards for personal use, and the cruelty of the chief jailer, who drove at least one inmate to hang himself. A prisoner he interviewed stated, "It seems as if we have come to the prison not to be given moral training but to study how we can rationalize the methods of robbing the prisoners."[37]

These comments point to the persistence of serious abuses in even the best of Japan's prisons, which PSD officials tried to keep under wraps. Inspection reports detail continued poor sanitation and medical care as well as overcrowding in many facilities, which Lewis's team was unable to curb, owing in part to cultural and logistical barriers as well as indifference on the part of the Americans stemming from the racialized belief that Japanese did not value the "worth of the individual." In Hueno, where meals were provided by a local restaurant but only if inmates could pay, Lieutenant Colonel Robert F. Malburg, a Los Angeles police officer who would go on to become police chief in Las Vegas, reported that fifteen-year-olds were incarcerated with adults in a "dirty stinking condition of slovenliness with the cell so small that all [including semi-naked women] had to sleep body to body in a stifling heat." The Hiroshima prison meanwhile was never properly rebuilt after being ravaged by the atomic bomb. Lieutenant George Cornelius reported that rats pervaded the facility and that inmates could wash their underwear only once every ten days.[38]

In April 1949, PSD chief H. E. Pulliam expressed concern to Lewis about the poor morale and esprit de corps among the prison branch and complained that "the stars" were not pulling together, notably Fitzgibbon and McCorkle.[39] The "reverse course" and hardening anticommunist sentiments were leading to a general shift away from the goal of rehabilitation. Starting in 1949, reports show increased detention of communists and other social "agitators" due to police roundups. The problem of overcrowding, caused in part by high crime rates, became more acute, and suspects were held for lengthy periods without trial. Inmates designated as "commies" were segregated and treated in a dehumanizing and abusive way. Many were put in solitary confinement for long periods for causing "disturbances" and "ranting about their rights." Following the suppression of a rebellion in Kobe, a guard was reprimanded for bringing one suspect a law book and urging him to demand a legal hearing to clarify the reasons for his arrest.[40]

After the resignation of McCorkle, an advocate of education programs and group therapy, the PSD brought in Alfred Dowd, warden of the Indiana state prison in Michigan City, who was known for being "tough and square" and for his expertise in preventing and quelling prison riots.[41] A supporter of capital punishment, Dowd called for a separate penal facility at Hokkaido for "malcontents," writing to Pulliam in February 1949, "I appreciate that no-one wants publicity of an unfavorable nature but this is the kind of situation calling for strong [and realistic] measures." He added that some prisoners were as "stubborn as mules" who only understand a "piss elm club between the eyes." Although, he conceded, the "general trend nowadays is to conduct prisons in a humane fashion, there comes a time when patience ceases to be a virtue."[42]

These remarks embody the mindset, similar to that of law and order hawks in the United States, underpinning the retrenchment of reform. Because of the perceived threat of communism, Dowd and his colleagues abandoned the emphasis on civil liberties, which was light at times to begin with. This resulted in greater guard brutality and the restoration of a repressive penal order as realpolitik triumphed over progressive idealism.[43]

Going after the Reds: The "Reverse Course" and Revival of the Tokkô Spirit?

George F. Kennan, the architect of the containment doctrine, was a key figure spearheading the "reverse course." He argued that police and prison reforms went too far in weakening the state's ability to control the population and criticized the purging of "war criminals" and the adoption of "lenient policies" toward the Japanese communists, who, as he wrote in his memoirs, were "being given a free field for political activity and were increasing their strength rapidly." The lack of an effective counterintelligence force, army, and maritime police in his view created a "set-up ... favorable ... for a communist takeover."[44]

Kennan's counterparts in the State Department proclaimed the need to achieve a balance capable of avoiding "the excesses of the pre-surrender Japanese police system" and "yet not leave the police impotent to execute their responsibility for public order and safety." They feared that new laws were "swinging the pendulum to the other extreme," resulting in the need for revisions to "strengthen and not weaken the Japanese police," while allowing them to "maintain public peace and order without infringing upon civil liberties."[45]

Prime Minister Shigeru Yoshida (1948–1954), a former ambassador to Rome and proponent of expansion in China, complained that police decentralization prevented effective action against "communists in small towns and villages who took possession of police stations and occupied municipal offices. . . . Strikers occupied factories in the same way and began operating them for their own profit. The police had in truth ceased to mean much."[46] In Taira, in Fukushima prefecture, after the firing of 143 members of the Coal Mine Workers' Union, including the chairman and vice chairman, who belonged to the Communist Party, a mob occupied police headquarters for eight hours and hung red banners from the building. The scholar Chalmers Johnson characterized this incident as "the closest thing to actual insurrection that occurred in Japan in 1949." It demonstrated that the "dual police system was incapable of coping with organized subversive elements," as rightist citizens organized a body of 1,300 vigilantes.[47]

Fearing the dawn of revolution, Yoshida proposed a revision of police laws placing the police back under central government control. Socialists in parliament fervently opposed the idea, which they saw as a step toward reviving antidemocratic practices.[48] Many of the public felt similarly. In spite of the embrace of defeat by a war-weary population, Japan was rife with protest throughout the postwar occupation, owing largely to the social and economic dislocation and poverty gripping the country. Tokyo and other cities had been reduced to rubble by American bombing, which crippled the economic infrastructure. Corruption and graft among authorities and the siphoning off of relief aid on the black market only made things worse.[49] Police records refer to constant strikes and demonstrations among workers, peasants, and students, who called for larger food allocations, wage increases, job creation programs, punishment of war criminals, the resignation of the Yoshida government, and an end to the occupation.[50]

The labor movement, which in the words of the American journalist Robert Textor had a "record for orderly behavior that would put to shame similar movements in the history of many a 'democratic' Western country, including our own," was strong despite being subjected to surveillance, co-optation, and harassment by police counterintelligence units (eventually causing union membership to decline).[51] The JCP organized mass demonstrations in Tokyo and other big cities during May Day celebrations and on the anniversary of VJ Day. Membership peaked in spring 1949, following the imposition of economic austerity measures recommended by the Detroit banker Joseph Dodge to cut down on inflation. Endorsed by the Wall Street–connected Japan lobby, which sought to keep the Far East open to American goods and investment, the Dodge reforms resulted in mass layoffs and wage reductions, curtailment of workers' rights to strike and to bargain collectively, an increase in food costs because of the reduction of government subsidies, and the cutting of vital social services. Theodore Cohen of SCAP tellingly described the new policies as having been "ruthlessly" imposed "without regard for Japanese views."[52]

Despite American claims that it was Russian-dominated and a "conspiracy from within," the JCP worked independently of the Soviet Comintern and embraced nonviolent means of protest in challenging economic injustices and the political status quo. Leaders such as Nosaka Sanzō (Okano Susumu), Kyūichi Tokuda, and Yoshio Shiga were skilled organizers who had been exiled or imprisoned during World War II for their pacifism. Winning thirty-five Diet seats in the January 1949 elections, the JCP legislators were parliamentarians opposed to the reinstallation of the emperor, whom they viewed as a war criminal and despot. They sought a united front with the Socialist Party, pursuing a "democratic revolution" within a capitalist framework, including workers' control of factories. They called for the destruction not of capitalism per se but rather of the system of "monopolistic capitalism" dominated by the Zaibatsu, or corporate clique, which became entrenched as a result of the Dodge reforms and the "reverse course."[53]

As Henry Oinas-Kukkonen documents, American policy toward unrest in Japan changed from one of grudging toleration in 1945 to increasing suspicion in 1946 to outright hostility and repression by the end of the decade. In May 1946, MacArthur issued a warning against the "growing and dangerous movement towards organized group violence," and characterized public demonstrations as a "menace to the security of the occupation." At the same time that war criminals were being restored to positions of prominence, he pressed for the banning of communist literature and the expulsion of communists from universities, and enacted educational reforms to ensure that communism was portrayed in the classroom as the equivalent of fascism.[54]

On April 4, 1949, in response to the JCP's electoral gains, mounting protest against the Dodge reforms, and isolated acts of industrial sabotage (which government authorities tried to link to a coordinated plot), MacArthur extended Imperial Ordinance 101, providing a legal basis for the surveillance and investigation of communists, enabling police to gain a "thorough and intimate knowledge of party activities." Over twenty thousand communists and "fellow travelers" lost their jobs, including a number of police, who were forced to take loyalty oaths. JCP leaders were thrust "underground," imprisoned, or exiled, their homes subjected to pre-dawn raids. Prime Minister Yoshida helped pass a "subversive activities prevention law" and created an organization under the attorney general to enforce legislation against communists and assume control of the police in the event of a revolutionary insurrection.[55]

The "loss of China" and the outbreak of the Korean War in 1950 intensified fears about the waning of American hegemony and bolstered the movement toward expanded police authority. MacArthur told the *Nippon Times* that "the current conflict in Korea speaks to us of how terrible subversive activities and the planning of lawless minorities are. The augmentation of police strength is undoubtedly a desire of the majority of the people except the communists." He warned of the need to pay attention to the "slipping of rightists among them who have a hallucination to take the current international situation for the revival of a past golden age."[56] These comments convey MacArthur's desire to intimidate the JCP, which he characterized as the "satellite of an international predatory force," without giving the impression that he was accommodating right-wing ultranationalists. Nevertheless, he was committed to using the police to crack down on many of the same forces that opposed military rule and supported many of the same tactics.

The PSD worked increasingly to enhance police surveillance and espionage capabilities, which Mulbar and Engle were well equipped to do. With colleagues such as Arthur M. Thurston, an FBI agent with the national defense division who had headed the OSS counterespionage branch in China during World War II, and Lieutenant Lee Echols, a "dynamic, extroverted egotist," according to his OSS personality sketch, "possessing fearless courage and stamina but very little intellectual ability," they provided electronic bugging equipment and sound-recording machines first developed by a Chicago scientist in 1936 for eavesdropping. They also assisted the special investigations bureau headed by former Tokkô officer Mitsusada Yoshikawa in cultivating informants and compiling databanks on "communist agitators" and "subversives."[57] Orrin DeForest, a CIA counterintelligence specialist and national police liaison who later sought to apply Japanese procedure in Vietnam, wrote in his memoirs that the Japanese were "fanatic collectors of information, always exerting themselves to achieve a comprehensive understanding of a person and his activities before making any overt moves against him. . . . Their goal was nothing less than total knowledge."[58]

These comments raise questions about who was advising whom and point to the striving of American advisers for total information control, which was applied in later interventions (and at home under the FBI's COINTELPRO). A Z Special Unit attached to the PSD's Special Operations Branch kidnapped left-wing dissidents (such as the communist intellectual Wataru Kaji, who had been involved in efforts to reeducate Japanese Imperial Army POWs in China) and plotted secret operations against North Korea and possibly the Soviet Union. From Okinawa, where one of the administrators, Paul H. Skuse, later recruited Hmong tribal leaders for the CIA in Laos, some detained communists were shipped to Bolivia. At the behest of Charles Willoughby, who recruited Imperial Army generals later linked to a 1952 coup plot into G-2's historical branch, police spied on SCAP officials and Japanese politicians suspected of having communist sympathies, compiling voluminous dossiers to be used for potential blackmailing purposes. The dossiers later became the basis for sensational media exposés on the night life of high-placed occupation officials.[59]

Foreshadowing the CIA's legacy of ashes, counterintelligence operations were marred by considerable ineptitude. As one agent stated: "We were supporting every right-wing jerk who came along. It was so chaotic . . . that American agents were stumbling over each other. Five different guys were running one Japanese and the Japanese were collecting money from each of them. Most of them [Japanese rightists] had their own agendas anyways. It was hard to say who was running who."[60]

In June 1947, in one of its major successes, Willoughby's staff leaked secret information that high-ranking officials had taken bribes from Showa Denka, Japan's largest manufacturer of fertilizer, in return for channeling Reconstruction Finance Bank funds into company coffers. The scandal implicated Prime Minister Hitoshi Ashida and key members of his coalition of Democratic, Socialist, and People's Cooperative parties, helping to precipitate the downfall of the government, the last in which socialists would participate for over four decades.[61]

Besides surveillance and spy-ops, a central focus of American police training was riot control using the Progressive Era standard of fists and clubs rather than firearms so as to lessen casualties and avoid bad publicity. In an influential 1937 article which provided a blueprint for the Public Safety Division and later the Office of Public Safety, Lewis Valentine wrote that "brutal measures . . . tend to further intensify an already serious situation by sometimes making martyrs of professional agitators and trouble-makers."[62] Paradoxically, the PSD supplied police with tear gas, a weapon developed during World War I to clear crowds, which causes burning in the eyes, dizziness, and nausea. It was first widely used in the United States in 1932 by police and army units headed by Douglas MacArthur in suppressing the Bonus Army marchers, causing the asphyxiation death of two children and partial blinding of an eight-year-old boy. It became thereafter a staple of efforts to break up demonstrations and of the global police programs.[63] The PSD set another precedent by providing riot control pump shotguns capable of penetrating a three-quarter-inch pine board from sixty yards away. SCAP authorities invoked the clear and present danger rule in the U.S. Constitution to argue that liberties are not absolute under the First Amendment but subject to limited restraint amid threats to national security.[64]

During the suppression of 1952 May Day demonstrations, police attacked a crowd with tear gas and pistols and beat hundreds of people as they fled. A university student and a municipal employee were killed, and more than 2,300 people were injured. Engle claimed in a 1976 interview that the scope of violence would have been even worse if the tactics of the World War II era had been employed. In his view, American training had "paid off and a threat to internal order was righted with the minimal amount of casualties," demonstrating the importance of the police to internal defense.[65] This is the idea he would promote as head of the 1290-d program and OPS, which evolved in the same spirit as the programs in Japan and built on many of their initiatives.

Japanese police were far from a model of efficiency, however. The Matsukawa incident, involving a case of railway sabotage in Taira in which three people were killed, turned a national spotlight on their often slipshod methods. In a case equivalent to the Rosenberg and Hiss cases in the United States, twenty local communists were charged with a conspiracy to derail a train in response to the firing of workers under the Dodge reforms. In the course of the investigation, police repeatedly mishandled evidence, kept shoddy records, and forced confessions out of the defendants, who were all eventually acquitted. Speculation abounds as to whether they were framed as a means of discrediting the JCP.[66]

Overall, the police programs exacerbated human rights violations by providing advanced surveillance and crowd control technologies and instilling a fervent anticommunism that bred intolerance toward dissent of any kind. Under PSD oversight, police attacked youths protesting the dropping of the atomic bombs, shadowed intellectuals such as the physicist Shoichi Sakata who campaigned for the peaceful use of atomic energy, spied on students in Korean schools considered breeding grounds for communism, and raided university campuses.[67] As Robert Textor described it: "Groups of cops pounce down upon some hole-in-the-wall, shove the kids around with night-sticks, stuff their [police] trucks with party literature, pamphlets, etc., haul a few kids to jail. This is embarrassing to the occupation who can't give the police Hell for doing in their own way what [General Headquarters] wants done in its own way."[68]

Exemplifying the wide scale of brutality, Theodore Cohen, chief of SCAP's labor division and himself a target of G-2 surveillance, observed workers from Japan's third-largest newspaper, *Yomiuri Shinbun*, being subjected to "unnecessarily harsh treatment . . . held incommunicado for a week, one had a bad chest bruise and now they had shown up manacled like a chain gang." PSD administrator Paul Harrison, an FBI agent from Los Angeles, reported that warrants were often not issued. In Kyoto, police arrested speakers at an antifascist youth rally and beat up participants trying to take their pictures. Borrowing a page from the FBI playbook, the municipal police in Asahigawa even hired a professional burglar in an attempt to obtain evidence against a JCP member who allegedly made anti-occupation remarks.[69]

To protest police brutality, prisoners conducted hunger strikes, and young JCP adherents began throwing Molotov cocktail bombs at police boxes and organized "activist units" in select mountain villages that could be developed into guerrilla bases along the Chinese Yennan model.[70] In Tokyo, after police harassed labor leaders, beat demonstrators, and mistreated them in detention, the victims proclaimed: "We are human beings and not dogs. Is [sic] not such acts of violence undemocratic?"[71] American officials were unmoved. After the arrest of twenty-nine labor leaders for instigating a strike in Ikegami, Johnson F. Monroe, a PSD communications specialist who had handled public relations for the Nashville Police Department, wrote to Harold Mulbar that the police chief had been "strictly on the ball," adding, "I'd like to meet him soon to congratulate him on the good work he is doing."[72] In this way the PSD supported repressive methods, particularly when directed against those who were working to transform the existing social order.

In spring 1951, partly as a means of crippling a chief source of JCP income, police confiscated 125,000 copies of the leftist newspaper *Heiwa-no-kee* for its "subversive" content and arrested ten employees. Plainclothes officers raided the home of the editor, seizing more articles slated for publication.[73] Harold Mulbar urged police to conduct their investigations smoothly and to "pay special attention to persons going in and going out of the police stations where the suspects are examined lest the secrets be leaked out to the outside."[74] These comments reveal the PSD's oversight of clandestine interrogation undertaken in violation of constitutional statutes, which officials were careful to cover up.

To make room for political prisoners, Engle oversaw construction of police interrogation facilities where "third degree" methods decried by domestic reformers were routinely carried out. A customary practice was to force prisoners to sit cross-legged for days in concrete cells and periodically beat them to force a confession. Journalists found evidence of police assaulting suspects and breaking their legs. In the Ishikawa prefecture, a local paper reported that a forty-year-old farmer was abducted by the rural police and returned home several days later "half dead" after enduring barbarous beatings and torture. A towel that he carried was stained with blood. He subsequently committed suicide. In Saitama prefecture, a twenty-eight-year-old suspected communist was kidnapped, strapped to a chair naked, choked with a belt, and beaten with electroshock devices. The doctor of his village told him that only his strong constitution saved his life, for "an ordinary man would not have survived."[75]

In another instance, police humiliated a politician accused of communist sympathies by forcing him to "crawl into his cell like a dog on all fours and sit in a convoluted position for hours." The journalist Takeo Takagi wrote in the *Nippon Times*: "One could go on forever listing brutalities and injustices of this kind. Many incidents go unreported out of fear of reprisal. The Tokkô spirit remains very much alive in certain quarters of the democratized police force."[76] The PSD bore significant responsibility for this abuse, owing to its abandonment of the civil liberties directive and its remobilization of the police for political ends. Thus did the "reverse course" help to usher in a revival of draconian methods that were a remnant of Japan's darkest hour.

"In Bed with Racketeers": Police Corruption and the Failed War on Narcotics

Police corruption, fueled in part by meager pay, was another problem throughout the occupation. Postwar nouveaux riches with criminal backgrounds constructed dormitories and stations for the police in return for immunity from prosecution. In some cases, police used their authority to demand protection fees from local business owners and to compel them to vote for favored candidates in municipal or national elections. PSD reports point to fraud within the public safety commissions and to police being "in bed with racketeers" and *oyabun* gangsters who controlled the black-market economy.[77]

Periodic crackdowns were undermined by GHQ (General Headquarters) intelligence's hiring of gangsters such as Hisayuki ("the Violent Bull") Machii to fight communists and break labor strikes. Despite indictments for manslaughter (with his bare hands), extortion, and assault, the Korean-born Machii and other mafia bosses such as Ozu Kinosuke, "Tokyo's Al Capone," never served any prison time because of their political connections and support for rightwing causes. The Tokyo chief prosecutor commented: "Every time we tried to get him [Machii, who helped U.S. diplomats normalize Japanese relations with the Republic of Korea], we were always pulled back. We'd bring him in, but each time there were pressures from above and he'd wind up being released."[78]

SCAP's double standards helped to perpetuate a tide of lawlessness and corruption in Japan which survived the occupation. In one incident, gang members tried to intimidate JCP Diet member Katsumi Kikunami into calling off a strike by slashing his forehead with a dagger.[79] U.S. government officials and soldiers were themselves involved in criminal enterprises such as gambling, slot machine scams, prostitution, and the sale of pirated goods, for which they were investigated though rarely punished.[80] Further exposing the underside of the occupation, PSD reports document police abuse in enforcing public health edicts. In Kyoto, officers entered the homes of women suspected of transmitting venereal disease to American troops at night without warrants, and in Tokyo they subjected women arrested off the street to humiliating genital inspections. Some were raped.[81]

In line with the growing internationalization of American criminal justice, the PSD mobilized police to prevent the dealing in opiates, particularly near military installations. Heroin was sold as a colorless liquid for as little as five hundred yen ($3) per vial to GIs seeking an escape from the monotony of their daily existence, often by prostitutes who hung around the bases. SCAP authorities and the army brass considered drugs a threat to military preparedness and a weapon of communist agents.[82]

The anti-drug campaign, however, failed to reduce the supply while contributing to the violation of civil liberties by giving police greater powers of search and seizure. Although 5,500 arrests were made over a three-year period, fewer than five hundred offenders spent more than a couple of months in jail. In April 1951 complaints were lodged when police ordered 571 Chinese residents of Tokyo out of their beds and into the streets late at night during a raid. According to witnesses, the police were hostile and insulted and abused the women. Narcotics agent Wayland Speer claimed that valuable information was obtained about narcotics sales by Chinese communist agents and that one apartment that was raided was a hideout for peddlers who were selling opium to prostitutes, who in turn sold it to military personnel stationed at airbases in the vicinity.[83]

Many police officers refused to cooperate with the narcotics drive because American servicemen were the ones fueling the demand, and opium entering Japan was arriving by way of the CIA-subsidized airline Civil Air Transport (later nicknamed "Air America") at U.S. bases not open to Japanese customs inspections. The airline was known for hauling drugs for Chinese Guomindang rebels who occupied the opium-growing Golden Triangle region in Burma as they plotted to reinvade the People's Republic of China with CIA support.[84] America's regional allies were on the whole deeply implicated in the narcotics trade, and this hampered prohibition. After he bought his way out of prison in 1948, the CIA recruited Yoshio Kodama, a Class-A war criminal and Yakuza (Japanese mafia) godfather who traded opium and heroin on behalf of the Japanese navy for scarce raw materials. Nicknamed "Little Napoleon" for his short stature and ruthless qualities, he was valued by the Americans because of his influence within the dominant Liberal Democratic Party (LDP) and as co-founder of the Asian People's Anti-Communist League. He was paid $10 million by the Pentagon for smuggled tungsten, used for hardening missiles.[85]

"It Isn't a Tank, It's a Special Vehicle": Toward Full-Scale Remilitarization

Despite all the problems with the police, the Cold War and the outbreak of the Korean War convinced occupation leaders of the importance of maintaining a strong police presence. A bill was passed permitting towns and villages to integrate local forces into the National Police. G-2 intelligence continued its collaboration with the Rural Guard. In line with Kennan's recommendation, a maritime police force was developed. The National Public Safety Commission was eventually placed under the control of the prime minister, paving the way for gradual recentralization.

Most important, SCAP established a national police reserve of 75,000 men, stocked with over $1 million in weapons, including mortars, bazookas, flame-throwers, and tanks.[86] Over half of the enlisted men were Imperial Army veterans, including eight hundred unpurged officers of the Manchukuo army valued for their anticommunism. In order to maintain the fiction that the United

States was not violating constitutional provisions mandating demilitarization, American advisers, as Colonel Frank Kowalski noted in his memoirs, were told "not to call their men soldiers or officers by military ranks. If you ever see a tank, it isn't a tank, it's a special vehicle."[87] (Kowalski had played a major role in training the force.) Yoshida eventually raised the reserve to over 100,000 men, prompting the Communist Party to issue a leaflet that declared, "Having failed in their attempt to invade Korea, the United States intends to strengthen the police reserve and enact a conscription system to make the Japanese people into a shield to protect American soldiers and turn Japan into an American foothold and staging base for her aggression in Asia."[88]

Secretary of State John Foster Dulles, Vice President Richard M. Nixon, and five-star general Omar Bradley were influential in championing the reserve, which was trained in combat and riot control as a means of defending Japan from attack, though it was recognized that there was "no reliable information" to indicate that this might come to pass.[89] In 1954, after the occupation ended, the reserve became the Self-Defense Force, which has since grown into a formidable military organization (but has been used sparingly). Through the late 1950s, coinciding with illicit financing of LDP election campaigns, the State Department spent over $1 million on police training and military-type weapons under the 1290-d program, with a continued emphasis on counterintelligence and riot control.[90] After a stint in Turkey, Byron Engle came back as a police liaison. His presence underscores the importance of the police programs to CIA operations, whose aim was to keep tabs on the communist movement, control unrest, and solidify American ties with leading figures in the national security bureaucracy, run for many years by the convicted war criminal Okinori Kaya.[91]

In 1957 the Japanese scholar Suichi Sugai concluded that the "bureaucratic police mentality" and its "power complex" were much the same as before the war and that the police had nearly reverted to the prewar system in a "backswing of the pendulum."[92] These comments encapsulate the shortcomings of American reform efforts, which were subordinated to larger geostrategic goals. Japan was always a key to the informal empire that the United States sought to forge in Southeast Asia in the aftermath of World War II. Seeing them as a bulwark against communist China, American policymakers placed a premium on safeguarding the power of Yoshida and the LDP, which promoted export-driven economic growth and foreign investment and preserved the network of military bases on Okinawa, later used as a staging ground for bombing Vietnam. Remilitarization and the breech of constitutional guarantees of civil liberties were viewed as a small price to pay in keeping the political left in check and ensuring Japan's role as a junior partner in the Cold War. So was the revival of some of the vicious police practices from the imperial era.[93]

In a 2003 survey of "nation-building" programs since World War II, James Dobbins, a RAND Corporation analyst and special envoy to Afghanistan, heralded Japanese police reforms in contributing to a stable and prosperous democracy.[94] Barely glancing beneath the surface, his interpretation was used to legitimize military intervention in the Middle East and billion-dollar police training operations. A more critically oriented body of scholarship rooted in primary documents and Japanese sources tells a different story. John Dower's magisterial *Embracing Defeat* demonstrates how, while the war-weariness of the population limited dissent against MacArthur's imposition of "democracy from above," unrest existed below the surface but was curtailed through police repression. Christopher Aldous's work similarly shows how SCAP supported violations of civil liberties against leftists who threatened occupational authority.[95]

My own research confirms that although American policy spawned improvements after World War II, and Japan never evolved into a full-fledged police state, the police were still built up as an instrument of social control. SCAP initially encouraged progressive innovations, including in the realm of penology; the "reverse course," however, heralded the triumph of more anti-democratic ideals. Police programs came to play a key role in suppressing left-wing movements, ensuring the triumph of conservative hegemony and Japan's emergence as an American client state, exactly as planners such as George F. Kennan envisioned.[96]

After 1947, PSD advisers mobilized police primarily to ferret out subversion and emphasized political intelligence and military-style training, which set a precedent for future interventions. The carryover of personnel was significant, with Byron Engle serving as a key bridge figure. He went on to impart many of the techniques he honed in Japan as head of the 1290-d program and the OPS, drawing on lessons from his experience and the use of newly adapted technologies such as tear gas. The Japanese police were especially admired for their intelligence-gathering capabilities and provided a model for forces trained by Engle and his associates, including the South Vietnamese. During the 1950s, Japan's political stability, economic growth (contingent in large part on the supply of equipment for the Korean War), pro-Western orientation, and successful integration into the global capitalist economy crystallized the view for American Cold Warriors that a nation's police force was the critical factor needed to provide for its internal defense. From this realization, the public safety program evolved.

Chapter 4

"Law in Whose Name, Order for Whose Benefit?"

Police Training, "Nation-Building," and Political Repression in Postcolonial South Korea

Beautiful land, Korea our country,
covered with flowers of hibiscus in full bloom,
That's where our noble brethren live staunchly,
That's where the democratic police stand resolutely,
with a glorious mission on their shoulders.
—Korean National Police song, late 1940s

Are you not from the Korean nation? Have you not the same blood and bone? Why do you fire on Koreans?
—People's Committee pamphlet, Chinju, 1946

The tragedy of the liberation period and the depth of American responsibility are most evident in the history of the Korean National Police (KNP) during [the] occupation.
—BRUCE CUMINGS, *The Origins of the Korean War*, 1981

In July 1946, as part of an investigation by the American Military Government (AMG) in South Korea, an adviser asked the police chief in Kongju if he believed that left-wing leaders should be suppressed. The chief hesitated and asked, "As a policeman or echoing the opinion of the people?" After the adviser responded, "as a policeman," the chief replied with a wink: "I cannot say because we are ordered not to express any opinions. Ninety per cent of the people would like to eliminate leftists."[1] This conversation sheds light on the political function of the police, which was built up as an integral part of the American occupation (1945–1948) and efforts to stabilize the rule of Syngman Rhee, an OSS liaison exiled for almost forty years under the Japanese, and first president of the Republic of Korea (ROK).

Following World War II, Korea emerged as a crucial theater of competition with China and with the Soviet Union, which, after the three-year occupation, backed Rhee's rival Kim Il Sung, an anticolonial fighter who advocated sweeping land reform, state socialism, and economic self-sufficiency (*juche*).[2] Seeking to counter Kim's radical nationalism, U.S. policy aimed to open up Korea's economy, largely to enable Japan to extract raw materials capable of sustaining its economic recovery, thus preventing the rise of leftist movements there and keeping Japan in the Western orbit. In January 1947, Secretary of State George Marshall scribbled a note to Dean Acheson: "Please have plan drafted of policy to organize a definite government of So. Korea and *connect up* its economy with that of Japan."[3] To achieve this objective, the Truman administration promoted the construction of a police surveillance apparatus mobilized to protect Korea from "foreign aggression" and "internal subversion." Military advisers developed a 24,000-man constabulary whose record would prove little different from that of its Philippine and Haitian counterparts in suppressing popular revolts. Despite contributing to extensive human rights abuses, the police programs were seen as effective because the ROK remained pro-West and later experienced rapid economic development, considered in elite sectors as validation of Walt Rostow's influential modernization theory. The intervention thus entrenched the view that a modernized police force was crucial to a nation's internal security, setting the standard for the Cold War.

Conscience and Convenience: The Korean National Police and Consolidation of a U.S. Sphere

As Bruce Cumings notes in *The Origins of the Korean War*, the ROK was more of an American creation than any other postwar Asian regime. The CIA predicted that its economy would collapse in a matter of weeks if U.S. aid were terminated.[4] As with Jiang Jieshi in China and Ngo Dinh Diem in South Vietnam, U.S. diplomats tired of Rhee's obstinacy and unwillingness to promote basic land reform, though they stood by him as a bulwark against communism. The CIA considered the Princeton Ph.D. a "demagogue bent on autocratic rule" whose support was maintained by that "numerically small class which virtually monopolizes the native wealth."[5]

The American occupation was headed by General John Reed Hodge, an Illinois farmer known as the "Patton of the Pacific," who knew little about Korea. He worked to build a professional police force, which he believed to be pivotal to "nation-building" efforts; its central aim was to stamp out the political left and bolster Rhee's power. A secret history of the Korean National Police (KNP) argued, "No one can anticipate what insidious infiltration may develop, and [so] the police must be given latitude to carry out the desires of the new government; more so than would be necessary in normal times."[6] The KNP consequently evolved as a politicized and essentially counterrevolutionary force, placed in the hands of many who had served in the Japanese occupation of Korea (which lasted from 1910 to 1945) and saw almost all opposition as communist driven. The CIA bluntly noted that "extreme Rightists control the overt political structure in the U.S. zone mainly through the agency of the national police," which has been "ruthlessly brutal in suppressing disorder. . . . [T]he police generally regard the Communists as rebels and traitors who should be seized, imprisoned, and shot, sometimes on the slightest provocation."[7]

During the period of Japanese colonization, the national police presided over a sophisticated surveillance apparatus, dominating "every phase of daily activity," according to the State Department, through "terror, intimidation, and practices inconceivable to the American."[8] As much as the Americans considered their nation exceptional, U.S. rule was marred by colonial continuities, including a blatant carryover of personnel. In principle, occupation officials sought to purge collaborators and wipe out the vestiges of the old system by training police in democratic methods, instilling in them the maxim that they were "servants and not masters of the people." The new police slogan, according to the Americans, was "impartial and non-partisan."[9] In practice, however, political exigencies and the fear of a leftist takeover resulted in the abandonment of those ideals.

The AMG retained 80 percent of pro-Japanese officers above the rank of patrolman, including northern exiles experienced in suppressing the anticolonial underground. As Colonel William Maglin, the first director of the KNP, commented, "We felt that if the Korean element of the KNP did a good job for the Japanese, they would do a good job for us." A June 1947 survey determined that eight of ten provincial police chiefs and 60 percent of the lower-ranking lieutenants were Japanese-trained, a crucial factor triggering opposition to the police.[10] To head the organization, Hodge appointed Chang T'aek-Sang and Chough Pyong-Ok, known for their "harsh police methods directed ruthlessly against Korean leftists." Chang, a wealthy businessman with ties to the missionary community, had prospered under the Japanese. The Marine Corps historian Harold Larsen referred to him as "a ruthless and crass character with the face of Nero and the manners of Goering."[11]

In the first days of the U.S. occupation, chaos prevailed. Prison doors were thrown open, police records were destroyed, and Koreans confiscated Japanese property, which led to violence. In some places, leftists seized power and installed their own governments. The police were demoralized and had to be accompanied on rounds by American military officers.[12] A reorganization plan was drawn up by Major Arthur F. Brandstatter, who was flown in from Manila, where he had served with the military police. A bruising fullback with the Michigan State football team in the mid-1930s, known for single-handedly engineering a fourth-quarter comeback against an undefeated Temple team coached by Glenn "Pop" Warner, Brandstatter was a veteran of the Detroit (1938–1941) and East Lansing police (chief 1946) and professor of police administration at Michigan State University. He emphasized the importance of creating standard uniforms for the KNP, improving communications, and abolishing the thought-control police, who had amassed 900,000 fingerprint files and were known to inspect homes to see if the Japanese emperor's picture occupied a place of honor.

The United States Military Advisory Group in Korea (USMAGIK) responded to Brandstatter's report by providing sixty-three police advisers, who developed a network of thirty-nine radio stations and fourteen thousand miles of telephone lines, resulting in the upgrading of communications facilities from "fair" to "good." Manpower was stabilized at twenty thousand, and swords and clubs were replaced with machine guns and rifles. Americans were appointed police chiefs in every province, with the mandate of grooming a Korean successor. Typical was the background of Lieutenant Colonel Earle Miller, stationed in Kyonggi-do province, a twenty-six-year veteran of the Chicago police and supervisor of military police detachments and POW camps.[13] Brandstatter commented in a December 1945 interview that the Koreans were "fifty years behind us in their thinking on justice and police powers" and advocated a "huge, preposterous force of men," which he feared could lead to oppression. He added that high turnover among the American advisers was hampering the police program and predicted that, regardless of the amount of U.S. aid, the police bureau would become a "political plum" belonging to "a big shot in the new government" (a prediction that proved accurate).[14]

Starting at a budget of 1.5 billion won per annum (over $1 million U.S.), the Public Safety Division rebuilt police headquarters, adopted a uniform patterned after that of the New York Police Department, and eliminated the system whereby officers were on call for twenty-four hours. It improved record collection by importing filing cabinets and oversaw the opening of a modern crime laboratory in Seoul staffed by eight Korean technicians trained in ballistics, chemical analysis, and handwriting techniques. Police advisers recommended routine patrols to foster improved community relations, and established provincial training centers and, under Lewis Valentine's oversight, a national police academy, which opened on October 10, 1945. Many of the graduates, who included forty-five policewomen, reportedly went on to "distinguish themselves as guerrilla fighters." Chi Hwan Choi, a graduate of the academy, rose to become superintendent and chief of the uniformed police. He was reunited with Maglin in the mid-1950s on a tour of American police institutions.[15]

Staff at the academy provided training in firearms and riot control and lectures on anticommunism, and were supplied with over six thousand pistols and one thousand carbines and rifles. J. Edgar Hoover's G-men were solicited for instruction in surveillance, interrogation and wiretapping techniques, which they had also provided to Dai Li's secret police in China. In December 1945, USMAGIK opened a school for detectives in Seoul and established a special "subversive sub-section," which kept a blacklist of dissidents. American training generally emphasized the development of an effective police force in light of the threats of subversion and insurgency, creating a trend toward militarization.[16]

In January 1946, USMAGIK began developing the police constabulary, which provided the foundation for the Republic of Korea Army (ROKA). The chief adviser, Captain James Hausman, was a combat veteran who provided instruction in riot control and psychological warfare techniques such as dousing the corpses of executed people with gasoline so as to hide the manner of execution or to allow blame to be placed on the communists. Douglas MacArthur forestalled the delivery of .50-caliber machine guns and howitzers "in order to maintain [the] appearance [of the constabulary] . . . as a police-type reserve force." Most of the officers were Japanese army veterans. Although they were not authorized to make arrests, they consistently ignored "this lack of legal right." The constabulary gained valuable guerrilla experience suppressing rebellions in Cheju-do and Yosu, committing numerous atrocities in the process. It became infiltrated by leftists, who instigated several mutinies.[17] Characterizing Koreans as "brutal bastards, worse than the Japanese," Hausman worked to purge radical elements, impose discipline, and bolster intelligence gathering. At these tasks he was predominantly successful, especially in comparison to American advisory efforts in South Vietnam.[18] Like the Philippines constabulary, the ROKA developed into a formidable and technically competent force. It was also renowned for its brutality, however, and became a springboard to political power, thus hindering democratic development.

"The Gooks Only Understood Force": The Evolution of a Police State

Throughout the late 1940s, South Korea resembled what political adviser H. Merrell Benninghoff referred to as a "powder keg ready to explode." An AMG poll revealed that 49 percent of the population preferred the Japanese occupation to the American "liberation."[19] Korea had both a tradition of radicalism and the oldest Communist Party in Asia, with experienced leaders who had led the struggle against Japan. While food imports and public health initiatives brought some benefits, land inequalities, poverty, and the desire for unification with the North made circumstances ripe for revolution, as did official corruption and heavy-handed rice collection policies enforced by the KNP. Hodge wrote in a memo that "any talk of freedom was purely academic" and that the situation left "fertile ground for the spread of communism."[20]

In a February 1949 study the State Department noted, "Labor, social security, land reform, and sex equality laws have been popular in the North and appeal to South Koreans as well." Emphasizing that although increased regimentation, heavy taxes, and the elimination of individual entrepreneurship were sowing the seeds of discontent, the northern regime still enjoyed greater popularity than that of the South because it "gave a large segment of the population the feeling of participation in government" that was absent in the South.[21] This document acknowledged the lack of popular legitimacy of the southern regime, which could survive only through force.

Resistance was led by labor and farmers' associations and People's Committees, which organized democratic governance and social reform at the local level. The mass-based South Korean Labor Party (SKLP), headed by Pak Hon-Yong, a veteran of anti-Japanese protest with communist ties, led strikes and carried out acts of industrial sabotage, eventually becoming infiltrated by agents of the U.S. Army Counter-Intelligence corps (CIC).[22] Trained in sophisticated methods of information gathering and population control, the KNP maintained an "observation section" focused on political activity, which provided information to U.S. intelligence and at times even spied on Americans. (Ambassador John Muccio reported that the Pusan embassy was under constant surveillance by "little men with notebooks.") With government authorities accusing almost anyone opposed to their policies of being communists and traitors, police raided homes, arrested newspaper editors for printing "inflammatory articles," and intimidated voters during fraudulent elections, such as the one in May 1948 that brought Rhee to power. In the countryside, they extracted rice from the peasantry "the same way as under the Japanese except with worse treatment," and in cities jailed student and labor leaders and even schoolteachers for merely mentioning communism in their classrooms.[23]

Once in custody, suspects were tortured through such methods as kidney-punching, hanging by the thumbnails, forced eating of hot peppers, and electroshocks in the attempt to extract confessions. A standard entry in the police registry was "died under torture" and "died of heart failure." One prison report referred to a young girl whose face was covered because she had been struck with a rifle butt and another a man who had gone deaf from beatings. Some KNP units morphed into death squads (such as the "Black Tiger Gang," headed by Chang T'aek-sang) and assassinated opposition figures, including, it is alleged, Yo Un-Hyong, a nationalist who promoted reconciliation between North and South.[24] American military commanders often promoted brutal tactics. CIC agent Donald Nichol reported in his memoirs that the KNP were advised to "dump [untrustworthy agents] off the back of a boat, in the nude, at high speed or give him false information plants—and let the enemy do it for you."

Despite attempts to develop greater professionalism, salaries were so inadequate, according to one army report, that police were "forced to beg, buy, or steal other items besides rice which go with the making of a regular diet." Another report stated that the KNP "lacked enthusiasm" in cooperating with the army's Criminal Investigation Division in halting the illicit sale of scrap metal and other American products, as they "often took a share of the cut."[25]

The leverage of the Americans to curtail such problems was often limited, as relations with Korean officials were marred by mutual mistrust. Police adviser David Fay told General Albert Wedemeyer that in his province, "not one problem of police administration had been presented to the Americans for discussion."[26]

In July 1946, Captain Richard D. Robinson, assistant head of the AMG's Bureau of Public Opinion, conducted an investigation which found police methods to be "extremely harsh" and intimidation such that people were afraid to talk to Americans. Believing that oppressive methods were driving moderates into the communist camp, Robinson was outraged when he witnessed Wu Han Chai, a former machine gunner in the Japanese army, using the "water treatment" to get a suspected pickpocket to confess and had his arms forced back by means of a stock inserted behind his back and in the crooks of his elbow. When confronted, Wu said he did not believe he had done anything wrong, which appeared to Robinson to reflect a deficiency in his training. Robinson was later threatened with court-martial by Hodge's assistant, General Archer Lerch, and was harassed by the FBI, examples of the military's attempt to silence internal critics.[27]

In October 1946, at a conference to address public grievances, witnesses testified that the KNP was bayoneting students and extorting from peasants in the administration of grain collection. Due process, they said, was rarely abided by, and warrants were rarely issued. Police looted and robbed the homes of leftists and used money gained from shakedowns to entertain themselves in "Kaesong houses" and fancy drinking and eating establishments. The head of the youth section of the Farmers' Guild in Ka Pyung testified that he had been arrested in the middle of the night and held in a dirty cell for five days.

Other leftists, including juveniles and women, spoke about being beaten to the point where gangrene set in and pus seeped out of their legs. Cho Sing Chik of Sung-Ju recounted his experience under detention of seeing a room full of people who had been crippled by mistreatment. He stated that many of the worst abuses were committed by firemen organized into an emergency committee to support the police and collect money for them. "The police[,] not being able to themselves beat the people[,] turn them over to the firemen and the firemen work on them," he declared. Another witness testified that the police were "worse than under the Japanese[,] who were afraid to do such things [as torture]. . . . Now they have no respect for their superiors."[28]

Director Chough Pyong-Ok, a Columbia University Ph.D. who made an estimated 20 million yen (about $200,000) in bribes during the first two years of the occupation, admitted that the KNP were "partial to the ideas of the rightists," though he insisted that "all those arrested have committed actual crimes," a lie given that the CIA reported in 1948 that the police were taking action against known or suspected communists "without recourse to judicial process."

Stressing the importance of speedy court procedure and judicial reform in strengthening the legitimacy of the police, Robinson recommended to Hodge that he remove those who had held the rank of lieutenant under the Japanese and whose actions were "incompatible with the . . . principles of democracy in the police system."[29] Roger Baldwin, a founder of the American Civil Liberties Union, set up a branch in Korea in the attempt to abolish torture. The exigencies of maintaining power and destroying social subversion from below, however, took precedence. Those branded as communists were dehumanized to the extent that they were seen as unworthy of legal protection. Pak Wan-so, a South Korean writer who had been imprisoned and tortured by the police, charged: "They called me a red bitch. Any red was not considered human. . . . They looked at me as if I was a beast or a bug. . . . Because we weren't human, we had no rights."[30]

The KNP maintained a symbiotic relationship with right-wing vigilantes, whose headquarters were located next to or inside police stations. They were described by the journalist Mark Gayn as resembling "Hollywood underworld killers." Their ranks were swelled by an influx of Northern refugees bearing deep grievances against communism. Chang T'aek Sang, who became prime minister, was on the board of the National Youth Association, which the CIA characterized as a "terrorist group in support of extreme right-wing politicians." Its head, Yi Pom Sok, was a Dai Li protégé and OSS liaison recruited in 1945 by Paul Helliwell and William Donovan (discussed in the next chapter). Later appointed as defense minister, he received $333,000 in equipment and assistance from Colonel Ernest Voss of the internal security department to set up a "leadership academy" with courses in combating strikes and the history of the Hitler jugend (Hitler Youth), whom Yi admired.[31] Opposed to the very idea of a labor union, his men beat leftists and, in violation of United Nations provisions, conducted surveillance and forays across the Thirty-eighth Parallel, with CIC support. There were even attempts to assassinate Kim Il Sung, no doubt a factor accounting for the origins of the Korean War, which was not simply a matter of Northern aggression as the standard interpretation suggests.[32]

In the rare instances when right-wing paramilitaries were prosecuted, they were often given red carpet treatment. In May 1946 in Taejon, for example, fourteen rightists were arrested after attacking suspected communists and stealing rice from farmers. While taking them to court, KNP officers stopped at the house of one of the prisoners and, according to internal records, enjoyed a "drunken picnic" arranged by relatives of the prisoners. In another case, the rightist gangster Kim Tu-han got off with a small fine for torturing to death two leftist youth association members and seriously injuring eight others (one of whom was emasculated). At the trial, the judge refused to call as witnesses counterintelligence officers who had taken photographs and supervised the autopsies. Such double standards were predominantly supported by American authorities owing to larger power considerations.[33]

According to information officer John Caldwell, who was ardently anticommunist and pro-Rhee, a majority of the Americans in Korea operated under the premise that "the 'gooks' only understood force," a key factor accounting for the embrace of repressive methods.[34] A 1948 report by the lawyers Roy C. Stiles and Albert Lyman on the administration of justice asserted that "acts considered to be cruel by western standards were only part of the tested oriental modus operandi. Low evaluation of life results in the acceptance of human cruelty." Police adviser Robert Ferguson, a beat cop from St. Louis, commented, "Orientals are accustomed to brutality such as would disgust a white man." Yet another report remarked that "concepts of individual rights were incomprehensible to the oriental. It would take much vigorous training backed by prompt punishment to change their thinking."[35] Such comments reveal the racism that underlay the trampling of civil liberties and abandonment of the progressive policing model.

In February 1948 the State Department produced a report, "Southern Korea: A Police State?," acknowledging that the KNP had a well-known "rightist bias," which led police to assume the function of a political force for the suppression of leftist elements. Although the authors admitted that the "charges that the U.S. is maintaining a police state through its military government is not subject to flat refutation," they argued that American policy was not at fault and that the police programs sought to inculcate democratic principles, which are "the antithesis of a police state." Native agencies, however, were not able to "achieve a full understanding of these principles," owing to a "heritage of Japanese oppression" and "the fact of occupation—the excesses, disorders, and growing pains accompanying the development of a self-governing society."[36] These remarks provide a striking admission of the lack of democratic standards and demonstrate the kinds of arguments adopted by public officials to absolve themselves of responsibility for the unfolding violence in the ROK.

"We're Having a Civil War Down Here": The October 1946 Revolts and Prison Overcrowding

According to the U.S. Army's official history of the Korean occupation, the "public's ill feeling toward the police, which police abuse had engendered, became a potent factor in the riots and quasi-revolts which swept South Korea in October 1946."[37] In South Cholla province, after the KNP killed a labor leader, Njug Ju Myun, and jailed unemployed coal miners celebrating the first anniversary of Korea's liberation from Japan, angry peasants dynamited a police box and ambushed a prisoner convoy by throwing stones. Constabulary detachments hunted those deemed responsible with the assistance of American troops, firing into crowds. Hundreds died or were injured. An editorial proclaimed: "We cannot take the humiliation any longer and must fight against imperialism and the barbarity of the U.S. Army. . . . In North Korea, Japanese exploitation was abolished and land was given back to the people through the agrarian and labor laws. In South Korea, the property of the Japanese imperialists was taken over by the Americans and Korean reactionary elements. . . . The people are suffering from oppression and exploitation. This is democracy?"[38]

Such sentiments lay at the root of mounting civil strife across the country, to which authorities responded the only way they knew how—through further police repression and violence. In Taegu, martial law was declared after riots precipitated by police suppression of a railroad strike left thirty-nine civilians dead, hundreds wounded, and thirty-eight missing. Fifteen hundred were arrested, and forty were given death sentences, including SKLP leader Pak, who fled to the North. Over 100,000 students walked out in solidarity with the workers, while mobs ransacked police posts, buried officers alive, and slashed the face of the police chief, in a pattern replicated in neighboring cities and towns. (In Waegwon, rioters cut the police chief's eyes and tongue.)[39] Blaming the violence on "outside agitators" (none were ever found) and the "idiocy" of the peasants, the American military called in reinforcements to restore order. Colonel Raymond G. Peeke proclaimed, "We're having a civil war down here." The director of the army's Department of Transportation added: "We had a battle mentality. We didn't have to worry too much if innocent people got hurt. We set up concentration camps outside of town and held strikers there when the jails got too full. . . . It was war. We recognized it as war and fought it as such."[40]

By mid-1947, after the AMG passed a national security law expanding police powers, there were almost 22,000 people in jail, nearly twice as many as under the Japanese. KNP director William Maglin later acknowledged in a 1999 article that "in their retaliation for murders and indignities [during the 1946 riots] police went too far in arresting large numbers of communists, leftists, and leftist sympathizers." Many were sentenced by military tribunal, while others languished in prison without counsel. Thousands were held in outlying camps, including seven members of the National Assembly charged with leading a "communist conspiracy."[41]

During an inspection of Wanju jail, Captain Richard D. Robinson found six prisoners sharing a mosquito-infested twelve-foot-by-twelve-foot cell accessible only through a small trapdoor and tunnel. In other facilities, inmates were beaten and stripped naked to keep them from committing suicide. Blankets were shared and never cleaned, and washing facilities were nonexistent. The latrine was usually nothing but a hole in the floor. Food was inadequate, winter temperatures were sub-zero, and medical care was scant. Prisoners were not allowed to write letters or have outside communications and usually had to sleep standing up. In Suwan, inmates were forced to sleep in pit cells without heat. Their water was drawn from a well located next to a depository for raw sewage, causing rampant disease, including a scabies epidemic.[42]

In April 1948, to relieve overcrowding, Major William F. Dean, a onetime Berkeley patrolman, recommended the release of 3,140 political prisoners whose offense consisted only of "participation in illegal meetings and demonstrations and distributing handbills."[43] Authorities established work camps in order to "utilize the capabilities of the inmates in useful occupations," which often entailed performing duties for the American military. Enacting the ideals of the progressive movement, U.S. advisers introduced vocational training, a rewards system, prison industries, and movies and recreation. They brought in chaplains, constructed juvenile facilities, and established a guard training school with courses in modern penology, fingerprinting, and weapons.[44]

What effect the reforms had is unclear, as prisons remained riddled with abuse. According to the U.S. Army, guards displayed a "harshness that was repugnant to Department of Justice legal advisers." At the Inchon Boys' Prison, inmates were deprived of exercise and forced to work at making straw rope without sufficient light. Prisoners engaged in hunger strikes and led jailbreaks. In Kangju on August 31, 1947, 172 inmates overpowered guards, and seven drilled their way to freedom. Two years later in Mokpo, near Seoul, 237 guerrillas from Cheju-do Island were killed by police and U.S. Army soldiers after breaking free into the neighboring hills; another eighty-five were captured alive.[45] On the whole, the prison conditions contradict the myth that the American influence in South Korea was somehow benign. As in later interventions, the repressive climate catalyzed the opposition and hastened armed resistance.

"A Cloud of Terror": The Cheju-do Massacre and Korean War Atrocities

Some of the worst police crimes occurred in suppressing the uprising on the island of Cheju-do at the southern tip of the country. The source of the upheaval was unequal land distribution and police brutality, as the CIA acknowledged. Hodge ironically told a group of congressmen that Cheju-do was a truly "communal area . . . peacefully controlled by the People's Committee," who promoted a collectivist and socialist philosophy "without much Comintern influence."[46] In March 1947, as the AMG tried to assert its authority, the KNP fired into a crowd and killed eight peaceful demonstrators, then imprisoned another four hundred. Governor Pak Kyong-jun was dismissed for being "too red" and replaced by Yu Hae-jin, an extreme rightist described as "ruthless and dictatorial in his dealing with the opposing political parties."[47] KNP units and right-wing youth groups terrorized the People's Committee and cut off the flow of food and construction supplies, turning the island into an open-air prison.

In response, the Cheju-do branch of the SKLP, long known for its anticolonial defiance, established guerrilla units in the Halla Mountains supported by an estimated 80 percent of the population.[48] In April 1948 the rebellion spread to the west coast of the island, where guerrillas attacked twenty-four police stations. KNP and constabulary units operating under U.S. military command and aided by aerial reinforcements and spy planes swept the mountains, waging "an all-out guerrilla extermination campaign," as Everett Drumwright of the American embassy characterized it, massacring people with bamboo spears and torching homes. One report stated, "Frustrated by not knowing the identity of these elusive men [the guerrillas], the police in some cases carried out indiscriminate warfare against entire villages." Between 30,000 and 60,000 people were killed out of a population of 300,000, including the guerrilla leader Yi Tôk-ku, and another 40,000 were exiled. The ferocity of the violence was in part attributed to racism directed against Chejuns, who were seen as backward compared to the Korean mainlanders.[49]

Police atrocities were only slightly less marked in the suppression of the insurrection in Yosu, which left that port town in ashes. After the declaration of martial law on October 22, 1948, constabulary units under Captain James Hausman rounded up suspected rebels, stripped them to their underwear in schoolyards, and beat them with bars, iron chains, and rifle butts. Cursory screenings were undertaken, and several thousand were executed in plain sight of their wives and children in revenge for attacks on police stations. The corpses of many of the dead were placed in city streets with a red hammer and sickle insignia covering the chest for propaganda purposes. Order was restored only after purges were enacted in constabulary regiments that had mutinied in support of the rebel cause, and the perpetrators executed by firing squad.[50]

The Yosu and Cheju-do massacres contributed to the decimation of the leftist movements, which deprived Kim Il Sung's armies of the support they expected after crossing into South Korea on June 25, 1950, precipitating the Korean War. When fighting broke out, the KNP, expanded to seventy thousand men, joined in combat operations, later receiving decorations for "ruthless campaigns against guerrilla forces." Many officers were recruited for secret missions into North Korea by the CIA's Seoul station chief, Albert Haney, a key architect of the 1290-d program, and Hans Tofte, a hero of the Danish underground who later served under OPS cover in Colombia. A large number were killed, owing to the infiltration of the secret teams by double agents, though Haney doctored the intelligence reports to cover up their fate.[51]

In the summer of 1950, to keep Southern leftists from reinforcing the Northerners, KNP and ROKA units emptied the prisons and shot as many as 100,000 detainees, dumping the bodies into hastily dug trenches, abandoned mines, or the sea. According to archival revelations and the findings of a Truth and Reconciliation Commission, women and children were among those killed.[52] The British journalist James Cameron encountered prisoners on their way to execution only yards from U.S. Army headquarters and five minutes from the UN Commission building in Pusan. "They were skeletons and they cringed like dogs," he wrote. "They were manacled with chains and . . . compelled to crouch in the classical Oriental attitude of subjection. Sometimes they moved enough to scoop a handful of water from the black puddles around them. . . . Any deviation from [the Oriental attitude] brought a gun to their heads."[53]

The most concentrated killing occurred in the city of Taejon, where the KNP slaughtered thousands of leftists under American oversight. Official histories long tried to pin the atrocity on the communists. The conduct of the KNP was not an aberration, however, but the result of ideological conditioning, training in violent counterinsurgency methods by the Americans and Japanese, and the breakdown of social mores in the war. According to the historian Kim Dong-Choon, the police killings represented among the "most tragic and brutal chapters" of a conflict that claimed the lives of 3 million people and left millions more as refugees.[54]

Managing the Counterrevolution: Police Training and "Nation-Building" in South Korea in the War's Aftermath

The Korean War ended in stalemate in 1953. Syngman Rhee remained leader of the ROK until his death in 1960, when, after a brief power struggle, he was replaced by General Park Chung Hee. Throughout the 1950s and 1960s, American policy elites conceived of South Korea as a laboratory for the promotion of free-market capitalism and modernizing reforms. Strategic planners hoped that South Korea could surpass its Northern rival in achieving political stability and economic take-off and benefit Japan's economy by serving as its trading partner and source of raw materials, thus helping to keep it in the Western camp. The success of South Korea and Japan could then be used for propaganda purposes to undercut the appeal of the nonaligned movement and of socialist experiments in the developing world which Washington was working to subvert.[55]

Operating on a budget of $900,000 per year, police programs were designed to wipe out the last vestiges of guerrilla resistance and promote the stability on which economic development could take root. Concerned about police corruption and outdated technical equipment, the CIA noted that South Korea had emerged from the war with a "rigid anti-communist national attitude and vigilant . . . repressive internal security system . . . which has resulted in the virtual elimination of all but the most covert and clandestine communist operators."[56] Various revenge regiments were in existence, whose mission was to hunt down Northern collaborators. American training focused on building up espionage and "counter-subversive" capabilities, creating a central records system, and lecturing on the severity of the "communist threat."

U.S. military advisers oversaw police units carrying out "mop-up" (death squad) operations against "bandits" and spies, in which civilian deaths were widely reported. In a precursor to the Vietnam Phoenix program, efficiency was measured by the number of weapons seized and guerrillas captured and "annihilated," usually at least four times more than the number of police wounded or killed.[57] Typical was a report in February 1954 in which adviser Edward J. Classon lauded the discovery and destruction of an enemy hideout in Sonam in which thirty-one "bandits" were killed and fifty-four captured.[58] Another report referred to a police drive in December 1953, Operation Trample, which "reduced the number of 'bandits' from 691 to only 131 [in the Southern Security Command]," the remainder of whom were now "widely scattered" and "represented little danger to the population."[59]

In the face of repression and waning support among a war-weary population, guerrillas resorted to kidnapping and extortion in an attempt to survive. A police report dated May 1, 1954, noted that five "bandits" under the cover of darkness raided the homes of two farmers, tied up their families, and demanded millet, salt, potatoes, and clothing, which gives a good sense of their desperation.[60] In December 1956, public authorities announced the success of pacification efforts. They claimed to have arrested the last known "guerilla bandits" of the anti-American regiment, a seventeen-year-old girl, Koon Ja Kim, and eighteen-year-old Sam Jin Koh, in a mop-up campaign in Chullo-Pukto province. Seven subversives were shot, including commander Kaun Soo Pak, age thirty-three. The photos of Koon and Sam under police arrest were broadcast in the *Korea Times* in order to publicize the KNP's strength in reestablishing law and order.[61] The Korean War had been a long drawn-out affair, and as the images reveal, South Korean society remained bitterly divided in its aftermath and, like the North, subjected to continued state repression. The country could be stabilized only by force.

Throughout the duration of Rhee's rule, the police remained mobilized for paramilitary operations. Interference in elections and ballot stuffing remained prevalent, as did customary practices such as surveillance, black propaganda, and torture.[62] Police adviser William Maxfield complained about on-duty patrolmen found sleeping, drinking, or away from their post. According to State Department documents, the KNP was especially "brutal in exacting punishment and revenge" against those who had cooperated with the North Korean military, sometimes "slaughtering them." Rhee used the police to undertake "extralegal and violent tactics" against opponents. In April 1960, police opened fire on student demonstrators protesting the recent fraudulent elections, killing or wounding several hundred. Koreans in the United States picketed the White House, demanding that America take a stand against "the brutal, degrading butchery."[63]

The Korea Times reported on the arrest and beating of Kim Sun-Tae, an MP, after he protested staged elections in 1956. Lee Ik-Heung, minister of home affairs, and Kim Chong-Won, head of the public security bureau, who worked closely with Captain Warren S. Olin, a career army officer, ordered troopers to "nab the bastard" and kept him in detention for five days, during which time he was "treated like a dog." The newspaper editorialized, "There can never be a representative democracy with men like Lee and Kim in positions of power."[64]

Born to a poor Korean family in Japan, Kim was trained in the 1930s in Japanese military academies, whose rigorous ideological conditioning and harsh, dehumanizing methods set the course for his career. Known as the "Paektu Mountain Tiger," he decapitated suspected guerrilla collaborators during the suppression of the Yosu rebellion with a Japanese-style sword and machine-gunned thirty-one detainees in the Yongdok police station who were suspected of being "contaminated elements." In Yonghae myon, Kim's men arrested civilians after finding propaganda leaflets at a nearby school and shot them in front of villagers, opening fire on women and children who ran from the scene. Over five hundred were killed in the massacre, for which Kim was sentenced to three years in prison, though he was amnestied by Rhee.[65]

Driven by an obsessive anticommunism and the rapacious pursuit of power, "Tiger" Kim presided over further atrocities as vice commander of the military police in Pusan during the Korean War. His appointment as head of the public security bureau was a reward for his loyalty to Rhee and reflected the KNP's continued emphasis on counterinsurgency and utter disregard for human rights. Ambassador John Muccio, who later oversaw another dirty war in Guatemala, characterized Kim's methods as "ruthless yet effective," typifying U.S. support for brutal tactics, as long as they were directed against "communists."[66]

Viewing the police programs as a great success, the State Department sought to replicate them in Vietnam, where the United States and the French faced a similar problem of communist infiltration and an "inability to distinguish friend from foe." Colonel Albert Haney, in his internal outline of the 1290-d program, boasted that "U.S efforts behind the ROK in subduing communist guerrillas in South Korea, while not generally known, were exceptionally effective at a time when the French were spectacularly ineffective in Indochina." On May 27, 1954, Lieutenant Colonel Philippe Milon of the French army was briefed by American officials on KNP techniques of surveillance and population control. Milon was impressed by the effectiveness of police in anti-guerrilla campaigns, which he sought to incorporate as a model.[67]

In 1955, after transferring police training to the State Department under 1290-d, the Eisenhower administration provided over $1 million in commodities to the KNP, including radio transmitters, steel filing cabinets, a $500,000 switchboard, and fire trucks. Lauren "Jack" Goin, an air force officer with B.A. and M.S. degrees in criminology from the University of California at Berkeley and director of the Allegheny Crime Lab in Pittsburgh, set up a scientific crime lab equipped with fingerprinting powders and the latest forensic technology. (He later did the same in Vietnam, Indonesia, Dominican Republic, and Brazil.)[68] Advisers from Michigan State University's Vietnam project, including Jack Ryan, Ralph Turner, and Howard Hoyt (whose backgrounds are discussed in chapter 7), served as consultants and helped set up a communication system. They then went on to Taipei, where, on a visit sponsored by the CIA-fronted Asia Foundation, they instructed police led by the Generalissimo's son Chiang Ching-kuo in rooting out Maoist infiltration.[69]

The 1290-d police training program in South Korea was headed by Ray Foreaker, retired chief of police in Oakland, and a twenty-seven-year veteran of the Berkeley police force, where he had been mentored by August Vollmer, the "father of modern law enforcement." During his tenure as Berkeley chief, Vollmer pioneered many innovations, including the use of fingerprinting, patrol cars, and lie detector tests, illustrating, according to his biographers, his "love of gadgets, of scientific breakthroughs that he hoped could make the process of detecting and solving crimes enormously more efficient." A veteran of the Spanish-American War who cut his teeth training police in Manila, Vollmer was more liberal than many of his contemporaries in defending communists' right to free assembly and speech and in criticizing drug prohibition laws. He worked to curtail the "third degree" and embraced a social work approach to policing, visiting local jails each morning to talk to inmates and urging his officers to interact with members of the community on their beat.[70]

Apart from in his attitude toward communism, these are the kinds of ideals that Foreaker, a specialist in criminal and security investigations, sought to promote in South Korea, and later in Indonesia, Ethiopia, Guatemala, and Vietnam. He commented, "Our work here [in the 1290-d program] is in the total field of public safety rather than in police work alone."[71] Foreaker's successor as Oakland police chief, Wyman W. Vernon, was part of the advisory team, later serving in Vietnam and Pakistan. Like Foreaker, he had a reputation as an incorruptible reformer, having established a special planning and research unit in Oakland staffed by Berkeley students to analyze and address police problems, including poor relations with minorities. The Oakland police nevertheless continued to be viewed as an army of occupation in the black community, their brutalization of antiwar demonstrators and Black Panthers during the 1960s exemplifying the limits of the Berkeley professionalization model.[72] Shaped by the conservative, hierarchical, and lily-white institutional milieu from which they came, Foreaker and Vernon were generally ill-equipped to bring about enlightened police practice in South Korea, where they faced an alien cultural environment and a war climate that brought out the most violent tendencies of the police.

In the attempt to instill greater professionalism, the State Department sent twenty top-ranking KNP, including General Hak Sung Wang, head of the national police college, and Chi Hwan Choi, chief of the uniformed police, trained by the Americans in the 1940s, for courses at the FBI Academy and at leading criminology institutes such as at Berkeley, Michigan State University, and the Northwestern Traffic Institute.[73] A dozen more were sent to the Los Angeles Police Department, headed by Chief Willie Parker (1950–1966), who was known for cleaning up corruption and for his right-wing politics and insensitivity toward racial minorities and the poor. Subscribing to J. Edgar Hoover's brand of theological anticommunism, the CIA-connected Parker helped to set up American-style police systems in Frankfurt and Munich after World War II and, in a fitting gesture, was named an honorary chief of the KNP.[74]

Korean officers trained in prison management at George Washington University returned home to reform the ROK penal system. Drawing on the ideals of progressive penology, they revived efforts to establish rewards and parole, promoted industrial training, and created juvenile reformatories to address skyrocketing delinquency rates resulting from a profusion of war orphans. The PSD pledged $553,688 and assisted in developing a work farm outside Seoul based on the Boys Town juvenile detention center in Nebraska.[75]

Coinciding with the passage of mandatory minimum sentencing for drug offenses in the United States, the International Cooperation Administration established police counter-narcotics units, which raided opium dens and launched Operation Poppy, deploying army aviation units to detect and destroy poppy fields.[76] These campaigns were undermined by police and governmental corruption. A report from the U.S. Army's Criminal Investigation Division pointed to ties between Japanese gangster Hisayuki Machii (known in Korea as Ko Yung Mok) and ROK naval intelligence, stating that he was "too strong politically to be touched by the police," despite having murdered a Korean boxer. American troops also participated in the black market, working with their Korean girlfriends and local "slickie" boys to sell drugs, cigarettes, and pirated consumer goods such as watches, cameras, and radios.[77] Their involvement in crimes, including vehicular manslaughter, arson, rape, and murder, dominate police reports of the period.[78]

In the late 1950s, the State Department suspended the police programs, acknowledging their contribution to widespread human rights violations. The United States was integral in creating a repressive internal security apparatus that made even hardened Cold Warriors blanch. A 1961 cabinet-level report tellingly referred to the KNP as the "hated instrument of the Rhee regime."[79] The Kennedy administration nevertheless revived police training under Rhee's successor, Park Chung Hee, a master of political musical chairs who was once a member of the South Korean Communist Party and who had also hunted Korean resistance fighters in Manchuria during World War II with the Japanese Imperial Army. After mutinying during the 1948 Yosu rebellion, General Park escaped execution by informing on onetime associates, allegedly including his own brother, and subsequently rose through the military hierarchy with the assistance of Captain Hausman, who remained in country as a liaison with the ROKA. After the 1961 coup in which Park seized power, he presided over a period of spectacular economic growth, resulting from visionary state planning, technological development, war profiteering, and a massive interjection of foreign capital.[80]

The ROK Supreme Council meanwhile passed a law mandating the purification of political activities, creating a seven-man committee to identify persons holding "rotten politics" and dedicated to "anti-democratic acts." Living conditions remained difficult for the majority, as Park collaborated with the management of large *chaebol* (conglomerates) in using police and hired goons to suppress strikes, and in keeping wages low in order to attract foreign investment. *Forbes* magazine glowingly advertised South Korea in this period as a great place to do business because laborers worked sixty hours per week for very low pay.[81]

Characterized as a quasi-military force, the KNP retained a crucial role in suppressing working-class mobilization and monitoring political activity. Surveillance was coordinated with the Korean Central Intelligence Agency which was developed out of police intelligence units trained by the United States. OPS advisers in the CIA—including Arthur M. Thurston, who left his official job as chairman of the board of the Farmers National Bank in Shelbyville, Indiana, for months at a time, telling friends and family he was going to Europe—helped set up intelligence schools and a situation room facility equipped with maps and telecommunications equipment. By the mid-1960s, Korean Central Intelligence had 350,000 agents, out of a population of 30 million, dwarfing the Russian NKVD at its height. CIA attaché Peer De Silva rationalized its ruthless methods by claiming, "There are tigers roaming the world, and we must recognize this or perish."[82]

From 1967 to 1970 the OPS team in Korea was headed by Frank Jessup, a Republican appointee as superintendent of the Indiana State Police in the mid-1950s and veteran of police programs in Greece, Liberia, Guatemala, and Iran. A sergeant with the Marine Corps Third Division who served in counterintelligence during the Pacific war and as chief of civil defense with the U.S. federal police, Jessup was a national officer of the ultraconservative American Legion. He received the Gold Star for Valor after having been shot while apprehending the killer of an FBI agent. Lacking any real knowledge of Korean affairs, he subscribed to the worldview of the American New Right, with its commitment to social order, military preparedness, and counterrevolutionary activism at home and abroad. His politics were characteristic of the advisory group, which included William J. Simmler, chief of detectives in Philadelphia, with experience in the Philippines; Peter Costello, a twenty-four-year veteran of the New York Police Department, who helped run the dirty war in Guatemala; and Harold "Scotty" Caplan of the Pennsylvania State Police, who maintained contacts with the KNP until his death in 1998.

Peaking at a budget of $5.3 million in 1968, the OPS organized combat police brigades and village surveillance and oversaw the interrogation of captured agents and defectors. It also improved records management, trained industrial security guards, oversaw the delivery of 886 vehicles (35 percent of the KNP fleet), and provided polygraph machines and weaponry such as gas masks and grenade launchers.[83] The KNP claimed to have apprehended 80 percent of North Korean infiltrators as a result of American assistance. In 1990 Jessup, Caplan, and "Jack" Goin were invited back for a reception by the ROK minister of the interior, a graduate of the International Police Academy in Washington, D.C., in a rare public recognition of the police programs.[84]

Sweeping under the rug the tyrannical aspects of Park's rule, modernization theorists in Washington considered U.S. policy in South Korea to be a phenomenal success because of the scale of economic growth, which was contingent in part on manufacturing vital equipment for the American army in Vietnam. The United States was especially grateful to Park for sending 312,000 ROK soldiers to Vietnam, where they committed dozens of My Lai–style massacres and, according to a RAND Corporation study, burned, destroyed, and killed anyone who stood in their path.[85] The participation of police in domestic surveillance and acts of state terrorism was justified as creating a climate of stability, allowing for economic "take-off." Together with Japan, South Korea helped crystallize the view that a nation's police force was the critical factor needed to provide for its internal defense.[86]

In January 1974, President Park passed an emergency measure giving him untrammeled power to crack down on dissenters. Amnesty International subsequently reported an appalling record of police detentions, beatings, and torture of journalists, churchmen, academics, and other regime opponents. Leftists (dubbed *chwaiksu*) confined in overcrowded prisons were forced to wear red badges and received the harshest treatment.[87] In May 1980, KNP and ROKA officers, a number of them Vietnam War veterans, killed up to three thousand people in suppressing the Kwanju pro-democratic uprising—South Korea's equivalent to Tiananmen Square. Students were burned alive with flamethrowers as the officers laid siege to the city. A popular slogan from the period proclaimed, "Even the Japanese police officers and the communists during the Korean War weren't this cruel." These words provide a fitting epitaph to the American police programs, which, over a thirty-five-year period, trained some of the forces implicated in the massacre and provided the KNP with modern weaponry and equipment used for repressive ends.[88]

In a study of police torturers in the Southern Cone of Latin America, Martha K. Huggins and a team of researchers concluded that ideological conditioning and the political climate of the Cold War helped shape their behavior and allowed for the rationalization of actions that the perpetrators would normally have considered abhorrent, and now do in the clear light of day.[89] Their insights are equally applicable to South Korea, where police violence was justified as saving the country from a dangerous enemy. Conceiving of police as crucial to broader state-building efforts, the American programs were designed in theory to professionalize police standards and incorporate the kinds of progressive-style reforms that were prevalent in the United States. Owing to political circumstances, however, they became heavily militarized and focused on the suppression of left-wing activism, resulting in significant human rights violations. American intervention empowered authoritarian leaders and provided security forces with modern surveillance equipment, forensics technology, and weapons which heightened their social control capabilities. The vibrancy of the labor movement and political left was curtailed, thus contributing to a weakening of civil society. The working classes were largely left out of the Park-era economic boom, and North-South rapprochement was made impossible.

Throughout the Cold War, people who challenged the status quo were subjected to imprisonment, torture, and too often death. Their plight has largely been suppressed in the West, along with the buried history of U.S.-ROK atrocities in the Korean War. Undisturbed by all the bloodshed, the practitioners of realpolitik in Washington viewed the intervention in South Korea, like that in Japan, as an effective application of the containment doctrine. Police advisers were consequently called upon to pass along their technical expertise so as to fend off revolution in other locales, including South Vietnam, again with cataclysmic results.

Chapter **5**

"Free Government Cannot Exist without Safeguards against Subversion"
The Clandestine Cold War in Southeast Asia I

Local security forces must be trained in clandestine operations and sabotage techniques particularly for the penetration of enemy forces and the gaining of operational intelligence. Pinpointing of enemy concentrations and hideouts can permit effective use of trained "hunter-killer" teams. [In spite of] political inhibitions and UN or other control commissions and treaty arrangements, there should not be any long-standing iron-clad bar to such action when overriding national security interests prevail.
—ROBERT W. KOMER, national security adviser, 1961

If we had our druthers to relive bygone days, wouldn't we look for more Nelson Miles to replace George Custer, strengthen the cadre of civilian agencies with a more select group of men and train assigned personnel for the realities of the frontier?
—EDWARD G. LANSDALE to Walt W. Rostow, Special Group on Counter-Insurgency, 1961

From 1956 to 1959 Jeter Williamson, the police chief in Greensboro, North Carolina, spent much of his time in the Philippines jungles, training rural police and constabulary units to suppress remnants of the Huk guerrilla movement. Like the constabulary officers of yesteryear, Williamson was willing to endure difficult field conditions in an effort to export professional American standards and improve police efficiency, now in the service of the Cold War. No Ugly American, he took pains to learn Tagalog and other dialects in the countries where he served, and he ate local foods. In Thailand, where he went after leaving the Philippines, Williamson earned a commendation from the king for helping to secure the border through his work with the Border Patrol Police (BPP).[1]

A throwback to an earlier era of colonialists who believed deeply in the virtues of American capitalism and democracy, Williamson was a contemporary of CIA agent Edward Lansdale, a man fond of quoting Tom Paine's dictum "Where liberty dwells not, there is my country." Upon entering mainland China in 1955, Williamson commented that he was "standing at the end of the free world."[2] In spite of their romantic illusions, America's clandestine Cold Warriors in reality fought on the side of political reaction, opposing nationalist movements that were socialist or communist in orientation owing largely to historical circumstance and their role in spearheading opposition to Japanese colonialism.

Southeast Asia emerged as a key Cold War theater following the triumph of the Chinese revolution in 1949, which threatened the Open Door policy and America's foothold on the continent. The danger of the revolution for American planners, Noam Chomsky points out, was not the threat of military aggression, which was nonexistent, but what Walt Rostow writing in 1955 called the "ideological threat," specifically "the possibility that the Chinese Communists can prove to Asians by progress in China that Communist methods are better and faster than democratic methods."[3] Successive administrations consequently became committed to a continental rollback strategy, halting the progress of socialism across Asia, of which police training was a critical dimension. Advisers like Williamson trained security forces in riot control and counterintelligence, set up communications networks to aid in the tracking of subversives, and oversaw various destabilization campaigns.[4] These in turn contributed to a rising tide of violence and the stifling of democratic development. The cases of Indonesia, Thailand, and the Philippines are instructive in this respect. In these three countries, American programs were intermeshed almost completely with CIA operations and designed to prevent the rise of socialist or left-leaning regimes closely tied to China. They succeeded at this task, though at a terrible human cost.

An "Unorthodox Project": Police Aid in Indonesia and the Overthrow of Sukarno

Indonesia was the site of one of the largest and longest-running police programs. As George McT. Kahin documents in his groundbreaking study *Subversion as Foreign Policy*, American policymakers valued the country almost as much as Japan because of its oil and mineral wealth. Secretary of State Dean Acheson warned President Truman in January 1950 that "because of its great wealth and the dynamic character of its nationalist movement, [Indonesia's] political orientation has a profound effect on the political orientation of the rest of Asia. . . . It [also] lies athwart the principal lines of communication between the Pacific and Indian Oceans."[5]

After World War II, the United States supported the Dutch in retaining their colonial rule over Indonesia under the Marshall Plan. When the Dutch sent troops to crush the nationalist movement in 1948, the Truman administration changed its position, largely because the movement's key leaders, Mohammed Hatta and Achmed Sukarno, used their leverage over the police mobile brigade (mobrig) to put down a rebellion by the Indonesian Communist Party (PKI) in Central Java—the Madiun rebellion. Hoping to secure influence after independence, the CIA sent a senior agent to Yogyakarta to interview mobrig officers and made arrangements to fly the most promising through the Dutch blockade for training at American military facilities. Raden Saïd Soekanto, the "father" of the modern Indonesian police, whose statue stands outside the police history museum in Jakarta, was among those recruited. Instilled with fervently anticommunist views by the Dutch, he became a key CIA "asset," referred to in intelligence reports as a man of "high personal integrity."[6]

The United States' main goal was to create a pro-Western force to check the power of Tan Malaka, a nationalist communist leader who proposed a radical socioeconomic program stipulating the nationalization of key resources and high tariffs to foster local development.[7] Malaka was a rival to Prime Minister Mohammed Hatta, who, through CIA liaison Louise Page Morris—a fashion model from a Boston Brahmin family who ran secret operations for Jay Lovestone and James Jesus Angleton—requested technical advisers to solidify his power. William Lacey, Indonesian desk officer at the State Department, was skeptical, telling Morris that providing arms without the consent of Congress was "unworkable and undesirable."[8]

Matthew Fox, however, director of the American-Indonesian Corporation, a CIA front, cabled the embassy in May 1949: "We know that we cannot run any risks in Southeast Asia and have got to support this group around Hatta. . . . We have equipment in Malaya that can be sent to assist Soekanto [who also had ties with British intelligence and studied in Italy under the Carabinieri]. We have technical men whom we can put at his disposal immediately. While we are making up our mind, the communists are getting stronger."[9] Emphasizing Indonesia's importance as a producer of commodities vital to American industry and the seriousness of the communist threat, which was "internal rather than external," Acheson issued a directive to strengthen the twenty thousand–man mobrig constabulary and provide it with $12 million in equipment, including tear gas bombs, which could be used in "jungle country" and in commando operations against leftists.[10] Thousands of small arms, as well as cameras and mimeograph machines, were sent through a secret fund (of the Office of Policy Coordination) fronted through Fox's American-Indonesian Corporation and a dummy deposit in the Chase Manhattan Bank. Raymond E. Murphy, a CIA analyst hired to study the communist movement in Southeast Asia, had recommended that "since the project is unorthodox and unprecedented for the department it should have the appearance of sponsorship by private organizations or individuals."[11]

Livingstone Merchant, later undersecretary of state for political affairs, wrote to John Peurifoy, architect of the 1954 U.S. coup in Guatemala, that the training of an "elite corps of police in American methods," including counterintelligence, was essential because of the "importance of Indonesia to our overall plans in Southeast Asia." The mission of the police was to "recognize and liquidate communist infiltration" and "resist subversion efforts of communists to take over the country."[12] Six Indonesian policemen were sent for training at FBI headquarters in fingerprinting, photography, espionage, and explosives. Part of the aim was for them to see "more about the American way of life." The CIA even took them to local brothels to fulfill their fantasy of sleeping with a white woman. They returned home to provide the "nuclei," in Soekanto's words, for a paramilitary police force of seventy thousand men dedicated to waging the Cold War.[13]

In April 1950, Lieutenant Colonel Louis E. Kubler was hired as a technical adviser to the Indonesian police. He had experience as a ballistics and explosives specialist and a patrolman with the New York Police Department and New Jersey State Police and had won a Bronze Star for gallantry while with the OSS as a security officer in China. Higher-ups noted that Kubler's correct agency affiliation, the CIA, "should not be made known." Kubler set up his office at General Soekanto's house, working with him to create blacklists and expand training in advanced weaponry, counterinsurgency, and espionage.[14]

U.S. relations with Indonesia soured when President Sukarno took up leadership of the nonaligned movement and legalized the PKI, which garnered 7 million votes (18 percent of the total) in the 1955 elections. Though acknowledging his "outstanding oratorical ability" and status as a "national hero," the State Department criticized Sukarno for being "irresponsible in his financial management" and "taken in by revolutionary dogma," exemplified by his calls to nationalize foreign-owned industry; this was "lamentable" because "the country has "much national wealth . . . [particularly] oil resources . . . which the Indonesians believe belongs to Indonesia."[15] The popularity of the PKI was attributed to "widespread illiteracy and political and economic ignorance," which "left the masses subject to demagogic nationalist appeals."[16]

In order to keep the PKI under close watch (despite its legal status) and meet threats in the "pre-insurrection phase," in June 1955 Secretary of State John Foster Dulles increased the police budget to $6 million and ordered sound trucks and crowd-control devices for the use of the police, writing to Ambassador Hugh Cumming, Jr. that while the "current government does not support the police build-up, perhaps as a hedge against their present policy of cooperating with the PKI . . . the desirability of providing assistance to the . . . police as an important anticommunist force [is] well known."[17]

The International Cooperation Administration (ICA) provided riot control training, supplied jeeps, patrol boats, and aircraft, and set up training academies where CIA manuals such as *Covert Paramilitary Training Course* (1952) and *The Sabotage Manual* (1954) were used. Advisers with experience in Greece, the Philippines, and Korea constructed a communications center in Jakarta, a radio teletype system, and a secure message center and code room at the National Police headquarters to organize the flow of information on the PKI. Robert Janus, a Coast Guard adviser with experience in Japan, furnished advice to the sea police and maintained small patrol craft on loan from the U.S. Navy.[18]

1290-d planners complained that while the National Police had developed extensive knowledge of communist activities, thanks in large part to U.S. training, the "law abiding and united front tactics of the communists combined with the attitude of the government precluded repressive measures."[19] These comments typify the national security establishment's preference for repression over legal compromise. Police surveillance extended to Sukarno himself, whose womanizing tendencies the CIA tried to exploit by manufacturing a pornographic film starring an impersonator wearing a Sukarno facemask.[20]

ICA staffers inspecting Indonesia's prisons, including the Tjilatjap "devil's island," built amidst shark-infested waters, were ironically impressed with the emphasis on rehabilitation and the "lack of political prisoners, orderly physical appearance, success of agricultural and industrial endeavors, and the professional responsibility of prison service staff." Sukarno's human rights record was indeed far better than that of many American-backed regimes marred by brutal penal systems.[21]

A key component of the 1290-d program was to build up the mobile brigade as a counterweight to the military, which was considered to be "infiltrated with pinks and reds."[22] Major Melville "Buck" Fruit of the U.S. Air Force reported that having worked with a number of Asian police forces, he was "impressed beyond his expectation by the level of training, morale, effectiveness [of the mobrig]," which "had its own intelligence organization for the main purpose of identifying communists" and "could deal effectively with an attempted uprising or coup d'état." Fruit, who served with the Air Police during the Korean War and trained the paramilitary civil guard in Vietnam, was high on Soekanto, who, according to Fruit, had "threaded his way through various controversies to maintain a stable position politically." The school for paramilitary training at Surabaya, in his estimation, met the "highest standards of efficiency and produced the most democratic attitude among police yet seen in the Orient."[23]

Through the police programs, the Dulles brothers (Allen was then CIA director and John Foster secretary of state) funneled weapons to Islamic fundamentalists and dissident generals leading separatist revolts in the oil- and rubber-rich regions of Sumatra and Sulawesi, where Caltex and other U.S. firms had large investments. Soekanto aroused Sukarno's suspicions when he refused to lend sea vessels to the Indonesian army, which had been mobilized under General A. H. Nasution to suppress the rebellion.[24] The CIA cover was blown when Allen Pope, a Civil Air Transport pilot on contract with the agency, was shot down and taken prisoner after shelling an Indonesian village and allegedly bombing a church, causing the deaths of dozens of civilians.[25]

In December 1959 Sukarno placed General Soekanto on inactive duty for insubordination, replacing him with Soekarno Djojonegoro, commissioner of police in East Java, who had been trained in the United States with mobrig head Soetjipto Joedodihardjo. U.S. ambassador Howard P. Jones was dismayed by Soekanto's dismissal, writing in a memo that "the turnover ceremony in which Soekanto relinquished authority to Sukarno was a sad occasion as a result of the loss of a respected leader. It is too early to predict the ultimate outcome of the struggle for control of the police except it appears that Soekanto is definitely out."[26]

The Kennedy administration expanded the budget for the Indonesian police program to $10 million in 1962 and 1963, second only to that for South Vietnam. After a visit by Robert Kennedy, in which he made contact with future president Suharto, the administration's Special Group on Counter-Insurgency advocated ramping up training to the mobrig, which national security adviser Robert Komer hoped could "lay the groundwork for our returning and expanding influence in Indonesia in the years and decades to come."[27] Byron Engle received reassurance from the minister of police that in the event that the communists illegally tried to seize power, the mobrig would "fight to the last man." In the event of a legal takeover, he added, they would resist by "any means available, including underground operations."[28]

Building up its "counter-subversive" capabilities, the OPS provided armored cars, steel helmets, M-1 carbines with "excellent killing power," and three thousand tear gas canisters and set up a mobile brigade academy for training in ranger operations. Fifteen advisers worked full-time, including Robert Lowe, a former OSS agent from Tunica, Mississippi, who served in the Kunming station in China and with the police programs in Japan, Thailand, Liberia, and Vietnam; Paul H. Skuse, who went on to Vietnam and Laos; and Jack Goin, who would replace Engle as OPS director in 1972. Henry Samoriski, another Cold Warrior, recommended establishing "goon squads" consisting of uniformed civilians who could be "put into action at a moment's notice." Orders were given to deal firmly with pro-communist demonstrators and to protect U.S.-owned rubber plantations and oil companies, which it was feared Sukarno was bent on expropriating.[29]

The Anticommunist Bloodbath and Suharto's Long Reign of Terror

In October 1965, General Suharto, who had served in the police under the Japanese occupation of Indonesia during the Second World War, took power in a coup d'état under the pretext that he was saving the country from takeover by the PKI, which was allegedly behind the brief seizure of power by Colonel Untung, a member of Sukarno's palace guard. He formed army and police death squads to liquidate PKI members identified through lists produced by CIA and police intelligence. *Time* magazine reported that the killing was on "such a scale that the disposal of the corpses . . . created a serious sanitation problem in East Java and Northern Sumatra, where the humid air bears the reek of decaying flesh. Travelers from these areas tell of small rivers and streams that have been literally clogged with bodies."[30]

As the genocide was unfolding, Ambassador Jones wrote to Secretary of State Dean Rusk that "the [public safety] mission requires no further commodities be shipped to Jakarta because of the sensitivity of factors involved. Shipment of gas grenades brings the possibility of discovery in spite of precautions. Suggest return to military stocks."[31] These comments hint at direct American complicity, which the White House took pains to cover up. Robert Amory Jr., deputy director of the CIA from 1952 to 1962, commented that "the groundwork done there [with police training] in Indonesia may have been responsible for the speed with which [the Suharto coup] . . . was wrapped up."[32]

The police program also helped accelerate the scope of the killings, numbering in the hundreds of thousands. The blacklists it created were used to target dissidents, while improved communication allowed for better coordination among security forces. Police and mobrig officers ran prison camps, where over a million people suspected of communist sympathies were subjected to forced labor and torture.[33] A lack of legal constraints resulted in extraordinary judicial corruption, ensuring that many were detained indefinitely without charge and only those with political connections were freed. The anguish of inmates was captured in a popular song written by a political prisoner in Tangerrang prison near Jakarta: "Prison life's like self-torment, entering thick, leaving slim, forced labor and underfed, still alive but nearly dead."[34]

Impervious to the human suffering, State Department staffer Rob Barnett wrote to Charles Mann of USAID in April 1966 that since the coup, "the trend of Indonesian political development has been drastically altered in a direction favorable to United States interests in the Far East. The PKI has been eliminated as an effective political force. . . . The new leaders are trying to integrate the country into the international community. Investment should be encouraged. . . . Caltex is optimistic." Intelligence reports similarly gushed that the PKI had "suffered a massive defeat" and that "reverence for Sukarno" was finally "broken. . . . Suharto is now inviting the IMF [International Monetary Fund] to help develop policies and restoring to foreign owners some plantations and mines taken over by Sukarno."[35]

To help consolidate the new order, USAID gradually revived old police contacts. In January 1971, James McMahon, director of OPS technical services, wrote to Brigadier General "Benny" Soebianto, chief of police in Jakarta, agreeing to his request for assistance. In warm personal terms, McMahon asked about Soebianto's wife and told him that their recent meeting in Washington had brought back fond memories of their association in Indonesia in 1954.

McMahon then noted that the United States would ship a lock-picking gun and a supply of .38 Special revolvers through Fargo International and would help Soebianto locate arms dealers in western Europe and Japan.[36]

This revealing letter demonstrates how the CIA was continuing to arm police into the 1970s and how the programs paid dividends by creating loyal "assets" who achieved positions of power years after being trained by the United States. In another example, American-trained General Anton Sudjarwo, an adjutant to Soekanto in the mid-1950s and commander of the mobrig's ranger company and scout battalion, was appointed by Suharto as head of the Jakarta police, then as director of the National Police in the early 1980s, where he worked vigorously to ferret out subversives. In 1961 he had been sent to study policing operations in Athens, Georgia, and became thereafter a CIA "asset."[37] On the whole, the police programs contributed to the militarization of Indonesian society and the growth of a modern surveillance apparatus, which Suharto utilized to liquidate the PKI and any other threats to his power. From 1967 until 1998 he presided over one of the most brutal and corrupt dictatorships of the twentieth century, which likely would not have come to pass without the Washington connection.

Playground of the CIA: Police Training and the Militarization of Thailand

In Thailand, police programs were similarly intertwined with clandestine operations and created an infrastructure primed for political repression. The country was strategically important as a launching pad for covert warfare throughout Southeast Asia and a venue for the expansion of American oil interests and investment opportunities.[38] The United States began providing police aid in the late 1940s to undermine the left-leaning Pridi Phanomyong, head of the anti-Japanese Free Thai movement during World War II, and to prop up Phibun Songkhram, a Japanese collaborator who presided over a "government of force" led by "strong men" in the army and police.[39]

In 1948, two years before Harry Truman approved $5 million for the creation of a constabulary in Thailand, the CIA initiated a $35 million police program through a front corporation, Sea Supply, which specialized in importing fruit and dairy products as well as tear gas for the military and police. Based out of Miami, Sea Supply was headed by Lieutenant Colonel Willis Bird, deputy chief of OSS operations in China and an ordnance specialist characterized by colleagues as a "con man," and by Colonel Paul Helliwell, head of OSS special intelligence in China, who worked with the Guomindang (GMD) secret police. Helliwell allegedly bribed a Vietnamese nationalist with a pouch of opium to secure a dossier on Ho Chi Minh's revolutionary background.

Like Claire Chennault, famed World War II airman and original owner of the CIA-connected Civil Air Transport—known as the Flying Tigers—Bird and

Helliwell combined moneymaking of an often illegal variety with anticommunism. A Miami attorney and mover and shaker in the Republican Party later involved with the Bay of Pigs operation, Helliwell had connections with organized crime and helped Thai officials invest their drug profits in Florida land deals. Bird, a graduate of the Wharton School of Business and a top executive at Sears, Roebuck who helped establish the Thai stock exchange in 1961, was caught smuggling opium and was indicted by the attorney general's office for bribing ICA officials in Laos.[40]

The pair worked closely with Thai chief of police Phao Sinyanon, who used American aid to transform the police department into a quasi-military force over 35,000 strong with its own mounted, mechanized, tank, and seaborne divisions. In November 1951, chargé d'affaires William Turner complained to the State Department about Bird: "A character who handed over a lot of military equipment to the police without any authorization as far as I can determine and whose status in the CIA is ambiguous to say the least. . . . [W]hy is [he] allowed to deal with the police chief in such matters?"[41] There is no recorded answer to the query. As part of the quid pro quo, Phao established a "special operations unit" in Burma to transfer arms to GMD commander Li Mi for an invasion of Yunnan province in southern China. According to Ambassador David Key, who resigned in protest, the operation, codenamed Paper, brought "chaos to the Shan states" of Burma and was conducted in "flagrant disregard for Burmese sovereignty." It ended with the routing of Li Mi's forces by the Chinese Red Army, as few in southern China rallied to their cause.[42]

Operation Paper illustrates the intersection between American police training and covert operations in Southeast Asia. Heir to the heroic image of the OSS, the CIA possessed a mystique in Thailand that it would never entirely lose. According to the historian Daniel Fineman, "[it] had the power to turn to gold anyone it touched."[43] Solidly built with intense, unsmiling eyes, Phao was part of a younger generation of military officers who had helped orchestrate the 1947 coup that brought Phibun to power. He was characterized by Free Thai leader Seni Pramoj as the "worst man" in the history of the country and by C. L. Sulzberger of the New York Times as a "superlative crook."[44] Allied with the pro-GMD business elite, Phao commanded police to "take the sternest action against all persons suspected of aiding the communist cause." He was linked to the murder of the chief of detectives and four cabinet ministers who were accused of supporting an abortive coup against Phibun in February 1949. Taking advantage of draconian national security laws granting sweeping powers of detention, Phao's lieutenants arrested and tortured intellectuals, peace activists, and Free Thai veterans who supported Pridi, creating "terror and bitter resentment" among the public.[45]

Phao's power derived in part from his control of the rail, banking, and trucking industries and the gold exchange and opium trade, which made him one of the richest men in the world. In 1956 and 1957 the Bangkok press and the *Saturday Evening Post* published exposés on the police monopoly over smuggling under Phao.[46] The embassy reported that as a result of institutionalized corruption, Bangkok had become a major transshipment point for opium, which represented a danger to the "free world," but there was "little likelihood of the traffic being suppressed so long as officials in power like Phao continued to reap major financial reward."[47] Garland Williams of the army counterintelligence corps and Federal Bureau of Narcotics concluded in another secret report that Thailand was the "greatest source of illicit opium in the world" because of the "involvement" of GMD irregulars and "Thai officials . . . of great prominence," and that "some Americans [likely referring to Helliwell and Bird] were known to enter the clandestine opium business in Bangkok. . . . Public safety officers have much information, but little has been placed in written reports."[48]

The reason for the silence was that Phao was an important strategic asset and opium a means of funding rollback operations. American officials considered the police "more flexible and open to new roles . . . than the bureaucratically entrenched army," and Phao's way of dealing with opponents was "ruthless yet effective," much like "Tiger" Kim's in South Korea. Phao was awarded the U.S. Legion of Merit for "exceptionally meritorious service," one of two major opium dealers to receive the distinction. (General Li Mi of the GMD was the other. Bird and Helliwell won the award too.)[49]

Two hundred U.S. advisers trained Phao's men, providing them with bazookas, artillery, tanks, and helicopters. A paratrooper base was established at Lopburi (later moved to Hua Hin), where CIA operatives ate, slept, and marched with their protégés, training them in small-unit warfare. A few were killed in action.[50] In 1952 the Eisenhower administration sanctioned a top-secret program, PSB D-23, which engaged anthropologists to study Thailand's divergent ethnic groups, with the aim of recruiting them to "develop, expand, and accelerate sound programs for the creation and employment of indigenous guerrilla and paramilitary forces." Adopting sweeping generalizations about the Thai national character, an internal blueprint contended that the Thais were "incorrigible individualists, gentle and light-minded and not given to ponderous philosophic thought or warlike and military ambitions," traits that made them "better suited to guerrilla activities than to the development on a large-scale of conventional military forces."[51]

To implement PSB D-23, Eisenhower appointed OSS director William "Wild Bill" Donovan ambassador to Thailand in the summer of 1953. A Wall Street lawyer who first become involved in clandestine activities by funneling arms to pro-czarist generals during the Russian civil war, Donovan was an intimate of CIA director Allen Dulles and, according to his biographer, "a fanatic believer in the value of covert operations and guerrilla struggle."[52] By this time in his mid-seventies, he was given instructions to build up the "overt and covert" capabilities of Phao's police and "intensify . . . the efficiency of psychological warfare" against the communist political underground for the purpose of constructing "a bastion in Thailand from which various operations can be initiated into adjoining areas."[53]

During World War II, Donovan had made contacts with Ho Chi Minh and was impressed by the organizational capabilities of the Vietminh. He urged the United States to mold in their image guerrilla forces capable of ruthless action when necessary and of winning over the peasantry through civic engagement, infrastructure development, and health and education projects. During his ambassadorship, Donovan presided over the growth of an intelligence organization, the Krom Pramuan Ratchakan Phaen-din, which followed dissident activity (communist and noncommunist) in Thailand and neighboring countries, and encouraged the Pentagon to assume "increased responsibility for constabulary training" and to support an "unattributed program of similar nature for Cambodia."[54]

One of his central preoccupations was expanding the 4,500-man Border Patrol Police (BPP), which was given responsibility for refugee resettlement and security along Thailand's loosely policed frontiers, conducting area and population surveys, and eliciting information on communist activity. Modeled after the Philippines constabulary, the BPP was armed with machine guns and rocket launchers and trained in crowd control and jungle warfare.[55] The Police Aerial Reconnaissance Unit was another unconventional force built up under Donovan's oversight, which specialized in parachuting into isolated areas. Headed by James "Bill" Lair from Texas, a captain in the Thai police (he stated in a 2001 interview, "I'm not sure that Jesus Christ wasn't pretty close to a communist when you think about the fact that he said rich people ought to give all their money to the poor"), the unit was fashioned after commando units developed by the CIA in eastern Europe to carry out ill-fated rollback operations behind the Iron Curtain.[56]

Ironically, the 1290-d planning group concluded in 1955 that "communist pressures are small and do not seem to justify heavy handed police methods" and that the "ruling group does not face any significant challenge to its authority. . . . [T]he number and character of Thai internal security forces exceed the norms for effective maintenance of internal security against current and foreseeable requirements."[57] The cowboys in the Eisenhower administration had gone way overboard. Aging and in financial trouble, Donovan was recalled to Washington, where he was paid $100,000 as a lobbyist for the Thai government. (Helliwell served in the same capacity.) American policies during his tenure contributed, if anything, to the growth of armed insurgency, particularly in northern Thailand, where the hill tribes resented the violent disruption of their way of life and encroachment on their sovereignty bred by the expansion of state authority.[58]

In 1954, CIA operative Edward G. Lansdale was sent to northeast Thailand to organize hill tribespeople into paramilitary militias to serve as scouts for the BPP and mount armed incursions into North Vietnam and Laos. Financing was obtained in part through the sale of opium. The CIA encouraged the BPP to refrain from enforcing anti-opium edicts because it would deny the hill tribes, which the United States was trying to win over, their traditional source of income, and because opium was being used to purchase intelligence.[59]

Lansdale and his associates organized civic action teams which promoted political education, set up schools and medical clinics, and tried to improve village infrastructure as a means of "winning hearts and minds." A main purpose was to collect intelligence through close contact with the population.[60] Schools were supplied with radio equipment and staffed with BPP who spied on faculty and students. One CIA adviser commented that "schoolchildren are just about the best sources of information around." Another gushed to the ambassador that "students tell their teachers when their relatives are making trips to Burma to contest the communists."[61]

While yielding some benefit, the civic action programs were hampered by what one adviser characterized as the "historic clash between the people and officialdom," which was "hard to overcome." State Department officials characterized the hill tribesmen as a "primitive minority" equivalent to the American Indians and a "thorn in the side of broader modernization efforts," ordering napalm attacks and the burning of villages when they resisted resettlement.[62] Many schools were flimsily built because of underfunding and graft. The BPP took bribes, used drugs, enforced unpopular laws against brewing alcohol and woodcutting without a permit, and generally acted in an "arbitrary and authoritarian manner," doling out "violence to those not obedient to their wishes."[63]

A USAID official commented that through the civic action program,

> police were . . . required to perform all kinds of services no policeman would ever perform, be kind to dirty, smelly, inferior peasants [as they saw them] and maybe get killed by the communists. They were told by us not to steal a few chickens or rape a village girl now and again. . . . We told them to work hard, patrol the rice paddies, and be upright. But the Thais don't become policemen for these reasons: a cop is a guy who wants to . . . flaunt his power and status, to show off his uniform to the girls, and make lots of money by hook or by crook.[64]

These comments shed light on a central problem of the police programs, which empowered men of limited education prone to abusing their powers. The political thrust of the training and its molding of the police into a Cold War instrument further accelerated human rights violations.

"Keeping the Reds under Close Watch": Police Aid in the Era of Marshal Sarit and General Thanom

In 1957, Marshal Sarit Thanarat seized power in a coup, forcing Phao into exile in Switzerland. Forging an alliance with the king in an attempt to cement his legitimacy, Sarit looted Thailand's coffers of 3 billion baht—roughly $90 million. The Eisenhower and Kennedy administrations valued him, as they did many other Third World despots, as a staunch anticommunist and "military modernizer," and for his openness toward foreign investment, which increased fivefold during his tenure, largely because he kept wages low and suppressed dissent by arresting over two hundred labor leaders.[65]

Under the 1290-d program, twenty advisers, including CIA agent Albert DuBois, former police commissioner in Philadelphia, were sent to develop a scientific crime lab, establish modern fingerprinting methods, and deliver lamination machines for the initiation of an identity card system. They further created a Tactical Operations Center to collect data and analyze intelligence on communist organizational activities, beefed up the immigration division of the Thai National Police (TNP), constructed a twelve-channel communications system linking remote village areas to major towns, and built up the police special branch, which was responsible for "detecting and apprehending subversive elements who would destroy the freedom of Thailand."[66] A pamphlet from the United States Operations Mission (USOM) proclaimed that "farmers cannot till their land if an area is overrun by bandit groups; industrialists are reluctant to invest in property vulnerable to criminal attack . . . free government cannot exist without safeguards against subversion."[67]

These comments illustrate the essential link between security, foreign investment, and development forged by policymakers, which made police training a crucial component of global counterinsurgency efforts. Internal reports meanwhile pointed to the venality of public officials and cumbersome trial procedures, and criticized the TNP special branch for keeping an "unnecessarily large group of people in prison for political crimes which do not involve actual subversion."[68] As a key consequence of the police programs, the prison population increased from 16,555 in 1950 to 35,000 in 1959. Some of those arrested were executed outright by roving death squads. A USOM brochure revealingly depicted a special branch officer searching the small thatched home of a Thai man and discovering evidence of communist activity behind a trapdoor. The caption noted with approval that the man was later executed.[69]

From 1959 to 1966, the OPS in Thailand was headed by Jeter Williamson, chief of the Greensboro, North Carolina, police department, which evolved during his tenure (1951–1955) into one of the "most professional and best-run law enforcement agencies in the South—a model for other departments," according to the journalist Jerry Bledsoe. A graduate of the University of Richmond's T. C. Miller School of Law and the FBI's training academy, where he was class president (one of his classmates was the bodyguard of Egypt's King Farouk), Williamson introduced fixed pay grades and incentives for promotion as well as new uniforms and squad cars, raised administrative and training standards, and cultivated ties with business and community leaders to bolster the public image of the police. He also cleaned up corruption in the all-white organization by purging officers implicated in illegal gambling and lottery rackets, imposed strict regulations on the use of force, set up a separate juvenile division, and according to colleague Walter "Sticky" Burch, was known for his "honesty, integrity, and handling of the law as it was written."[70]

Tall and athletic with the looks of a movie star, Williamson was a self-made man of the depression era who came to Greensboro from Richmond, Virginia, where he had won three Golden Gloves boxing championships. He became known as a "Cinderella man" after being promoted from patrolman to captain in 1947 upon acing a merit exam. During World War II, he served with army intelligence in Berlin and earned a commendation for uncovering a black market ring stretching across three countries. Conservative politically and possessing an exceptional work ethic, Williamson was recruited into the Foreign Service by O. W. Wilson an authority on policing and an ICA consultant, who thought highly of Williamson's work. He was called upon to replicate the reforms he had introduced in Greensboro in Thailand and the Philippines, and later other Cold War "hot spots" such as the Congo, Saudi Arabia, Indonesia, South Korea, and Vietnam. He also coordinated paramilitary operations, for which the police were specially trained.

After Williamson's death in 2005, Burch told reporters, "Jeter said he wasn't involved in covert operations but . . . I think he was." Tellingly, while on leave in 1965, Williamson mentioned to the *Greensboro Daily News* an incident in which police under his oversight had "dispersed" a group of three hundred insurgents who had set up a base in southern Thailand complete with trenches, machine gun emplacements, and "a basketball court—that capitalistic game," capturing and killing a few. He stated, "We've managed to keep the reds off balance and disorganized." Williamson disclosed to another reporter that his job was to "work with police forces in combating communist activities," adding: "If the Chicoms [Chinese Communists] take all of Vietnam, then they will have an open door corridor to Thailand. If they capture Thailand, then Burma, Laos, Cambodia, and Malaysia will fall and the Reds will have Asia. I do not see how we can afford to get out of Asia."[71]

Williamson's career is instructive as to the motives of public safety officers, who sought to modernize police institutions in order to facilitate postcolonial "nation-building" and win the Cold War. His experience in turn demonstrates the difficulty of trying to export domestic innovations in a foreign cultural setting, particularly when these efforts are connected to an underlying political agenda that is antithetical to the flowering of democracy and human rights.

In January 1959 the State Department sent one of Williamson's contemporaries, James V. Bennett, the liberal director of the Federal Bureau of Prisons, to survey and overhaul Thai prisons. A veteran of the Army Air Corps and a graduate of George Washington Law School eager to advance the ideals of the new penology, Bennett had authored an influential report in 1928 proposing the centralization of the U.S. prison system. He created a corporation, Federal Prison Industries, Inc., to reduce inmate idleness. After being appointed director of the prison bureau in 1937, he strove to eliminate political patronage and corruption and implemented progressive reforms, including abolishing corporal punishment, improving inmate classification, and developing better educational and vocational training programs, new juvenile facilities, a prison hospital, and liberalized mail and grievance procedures, which the ICA sought to extend internationally.

Bennett was an admirer of the progressive reformer Thomas Mott Osborne, who spent a week undercover in the Auburn, Pennsylvania, penitentiary in the 1910s to gain a better understanding of the experience of inmates. He was a vigorous proponent of the rehabilitative ideal, though he also served as a "talent scout" for the notorious Alcatraz prison, where incorrigibles were sent.[72] After World War II, Bennett helped to reorganize the civil prisons in Germany and remained thereafter a consultant for the State Department. He found that facilities in Thailand were "overcrowded" and that inmates were held for "considerable amounts of time without charge," often confined in "leg chains."[73] He recommended expanding education and prison work, speeding up court procedures, and establishing a probation system. Because counterinsurgency came to assume top priority, there is scant evidence that these initiatives were ever implemented.

Beneath the progressive veneer, American prisons were themselves oppressive, characterized by harsh regimentation, racism, and violence. When the legendary activist David Dellinger, imprisoned in Danbury, Connecticut, as a conscientious objector during World War II, led a work stoppage in support of International Student Peace Day, Bennett came from Washington to tell him, "Dellinger, the American prison system is the most authoritarian institution in the world, and if you don't straighten up, the full weight of the system will come down on you." As these comments indicate, the abuses that ensued in the international programs were not an anomaly but an extension of domestic practice, made worse by the demands of the Cold War.[74]

In 1961 an ICA study recommended that the police programs be terminated because Thailand had evolved into a "police state." National security adviser Robert Komer, noting that the military and police served as "counterparts to each other in an internal balance of political power," warned, "Our aid programs have become unavoidably involved in the complexities of domestic politics," which went against official stipulations.[75] The Kennedy administration nevertheless expanded police aid to over $2 million in 1962 and $3 million in 1963, up from $500,000 in 1958 and $600,000 in 1959. The OPS provided weapons and equipment, including antipersonnel mines, and contracted a Pennsylvania cartridge company to supply over 800,000 rounds of ammunition. General Pote

Pekanand of the Thai National Police boasted to reporters that his men were "keeping the reds under close surveillance" and that "tracking, destruction, and apprehension" were being "perseveringly conducted."[76]

In 1964, following the accession of General Thanom Kittikachorn as prime minister, police aid was expanded to $12 million, peaking at $17 million in 1967. Over five hundred officers were sent to the International Police Academy in Washington, D.C., second only to the number from South Vietnam, and five new police counterinsurgency schools were established. Manpower rose from 51,000 to 74,000, and the BPP was increased by 70 percent. Mass arrests of dissidents were carried out, especially in the northeast, where a village alarm system was developed to improve communications.[77] The economist Peter Bell noted that Thailand had come to resemble an "occupied country," with tens of thousands of military and police officers trained in or receiving equipment from the United States, and fifty thousand U.S. troops stationed at seven major airbases: "There were U.S. advisers everywhere; they occupied choice residences in the best districts of Bangkok (usually with four or five servants), sat in high positions in Thai government ministries . . . [and] were seen at the best golf and country clubs."[78]

Police aid was geared in part toward forming defense perimeters around the airbases used for bombing raids into Indochina, to prevent attacks against them by insurgents, and to allow for the free movement of cargo. Assistant Police Chief General Vithoon Yasawasdi admitted that he ran paramilitary operations into Laos in cooperation with the CIA. Police were supplied with M-16 rifles, though the Special Group on Counter-Insurgency told USAID in March 1966 that they were "inappropriate as a police weapon" and should be procured through the military. In August 1967 the National Security Council approved shipment to the police aviation division of eleven Huey helicopters equipped with machine guns.[79] Their function was to aid the nine thousand–man BPP in surveillance and tracking down insurgents in remote villages not reached by road systems. The helicopters were seen as especially valuable during monsoon season, when ground mobility was limited. Pilots were among the hundreds of Thai police trained in the United States.[80]

In October 1976, following a democratic interlude, a coup led to the rise of General Kriangsak Chamanand, a GMD client heavily implicated in the drug trade. BPP units along with paramilitary Red Gaurs massacred at least forty-three pro-democracy advocates and arrested hundreds more after storming Thammasat University in Bangkok. Many of the weapons were supplied and police trained by the OPS, including General Vithoon, who controlled the Red Gaurs. BPP officers were contracted by wealthy landowners protected by local officials to assassinate radical students and members of the Farmers' Federation of Thailand, which organized against unjust land distribution practices.[81]

On September 28, 1971, Ambassador Leonard Ungar brokered a pact to send

Huey helicopters to bolster police drug enforcement. By 1974, the TNP were receiving upwards of $12 million per year for these purposes, though police corruption was so widespread, an army criminal investigation report concluded that efforts to cut the supply were like "trying to imprison the morning mist."[82] National Police director Pramual Vanigbandhu, who had studied police administration at the University of Tennessee (and who owned a luxurious Bangkok villa with manicured gardens and a swimming pool despite a salary of $250 a month), was sentenced to twenty-five years in prison for drug-related extortion. (He later bought his way out.) Another CIA "asset" in the police, Puttaporn Khramkhruan, who was arrested at JFK airport in New York with fifty-nine pounds of heroin, had his case dismissed.[83]

These incidents epitomize the failure of the War on Drugs and police programs, which empowered corrupt forces who contributed to the degradation of Thai society. According to the historian Alfred W. McCoy, American aid unwittingly aided the "modernization" of the drug industry as "modern aircraft replaced mules, naval vessels replaced sampans, and well-trained military organizations expropriated the traffic from bands of illiterate mountain traders." Thailand was left just another victim of the Cold War: a militarized yet underdeveloped state deeply polarized and marred by police repression and corruption.[84]

Reviving the Powers of the Constabulary: Police Aid and Neocolonialism in the Philippines

Police training bore a similar outcome in the Philippines, where the State Department reorganized the Manila police after World War II to keep tabs on the Hukbalahap, an amalgamation of unionists and radical parties advocating land reform and independence from neocolonial control. Lieutenant Calvin H. Goddard, police adviser in Tokyo and director of the Northwestern University scientific crime lab, provided lectures in forensics and technical investigations, while others focused on riot control. Corruption remained endemic, as police were beholden to "unscrupulous politicians," partook in gambling, and adopted "third degree" methods to extract confessions, prompting the *Manila Chronicle* to refer to them as a "local Gestapo."[85]

The Hukbalahap, or Huks, drew popular support from their resistance to the Japanese invasion in World War II and a historically inequitable land tenure system resulting in wide-scale poverty. They adopted the slogan "Bullets not Ballots" after leader Luis Taruc and nine others were prevented from taking their congressional seats. According to the CIA, the Huks were "champions of the people until 1950, when the armed forces seized the people's cause away from the enemy."[86] A hidden motive for the war was revealed in a 1953 State Department report expressing optimism over plans by Caltex to construct an oil refinery near Manila and the Import-Export Bank's financing a steel drum factory, which was made possible by the friendliness of the government of President Ramon Magsaysay toward foreign investment.[87]

To assist the anti-Huk campaign, the Truman administration revived training of the police constabulary, a holdover from the Japanese occupation during World War II, praised for its "long and distinguished fighting record."[88] The mission was led by Edward Lansdale, an advertising executive working under CIA cover, who was the inspiration for two Cold War novels, *The Ugly American* and *The Quiet American*. Comparing the Cold War to the "winning of the West," he developed a close relationship with Magsaysay and promoted civic action and psychological warfare methods reminiscent of the colonial era, including the dissemination of black propaganda (disinformation) and the exploitation of native superstitions.[89] In a precursor to the Phoenix program in Vietnam, Lansdale and associates such as Danish resistance hero Hans Tofte oversaw Nenita hunter-killer teams within the constabulary which sought to "neutralize" the Huk leadership. Headed by Napoleon Valeriano, who later served as a guest lecturer at the IPA, the Nenita practiced the "water cure," broke bones, cordoned off areas, and stacked Huk corpses along the highways beneath warning placards to intimidate the population. An internal study concluded that that they "inflicted terror and oppression on the people of Central Luzon."[90]

Several members of Lansdale's country team, including Robert Whitmer, a Berkeley police officer who held B.A. and M.A. degrees in criminology from the University of California at Berkeley, aided in the growth of the Philippine National Bureau of Investigation, which specialized in population control and intelligence.[91] At Magsaysay's request, the ICA acquired bloodhounds for apprehending Huk dissidents and trained Filipino officers in the use of the animals. Napalm strikes were called to reinforce violent sweeps, which culminated, according to an official history, with the "burning of barrio after barrio." Military intelligence noted that "civilians within the vicinity of the operations always suffered more than the dissidents."[92]

In a December 1955, working under a Michigan State University public administration contract, Jeter Williamson conducted a survey of the national police, visiting police precincts and going undercover in seedy bars and among organized criminals. He found that the budget was inadequate, there was a shortage of firearms, only 15 percent of officers had training, and patrolmen were forced to communicate via commercial long-distance telephones, which were frequently out of order. Williamson noted further that the military was used for civil police functions; that salaries were below the minimum wage, creating "the obvious necessity of income from other sources"; and that promotions were given as a reward for political servitude, paralleling the "most disgraceful period in American police history from the turn of the twentieth century through the 1920s."[93]

The State Department worked over the next decade and a half to try to rectify these problems, remnants from the colonial era. Williamson took police officers to Greensboro to study the administrative reforms he had put in place and to attend lectures at the FBI Academy and the Southern Police Institute, where he had been a part-time faculty member. Charles M. Wilson, director of the Wisconsin state criminal lab (and former director of the Los Angeles Police Department lab), was contracted to develop a replica facility in Manila.[94] USAID sent technicians to improve communications and riot control. An identity card program was initiated by Frank E. Walton, deputy chief of the Los Angeles Police Department, who taught police planning at Los Angeles State College and was an intelligence officer under Greg "Pappy" Boyington with the Black Sheep Aviation Squadron in the Solomon Islands in World War II and a Marine Corps staff officer in Korea.

A member of the 1948 Olympic water polo team, the red-haired Walton infused the Los Angeles Police Department's training with a military ethic during his twenty-year career, imposing boot camp drills. He headed the Department of Corrections and the patrol division and oversaw the political intelligence unit, which compiled thousands of dossiers on radicals and monitored the liberal-left sector in Hollywood. Recruited to go to Vietnam in 1959 at the age of fifty after a stint overhauling the Chicago Police Department, Walton worked closely with Los Angeles chief of police Willie Parker, who railed against the "flabbiness" and "permissiveness" of American society, which in his view was poised to be overtaken by "godless, disciplined communists." Sharing a similar worldview with Parker, the John Birch Society hero, Walton gained notoriety for overseeing the "tiger cages" in South Vietnam's Con Son prison, where inmates were shackled to the floor and fed starvation diets. According to Senator Augustus Hawkins, a California Democrat who knew him from his police days, Walton had a reputation for being "tough on minorities" and "unsympathetic to human rights and civil liberties," an attitude that carried over into his overseas service.[95]

Walton and his colleagues worked closely with the Manila police and constabulary, which were deployed to suppress regional rebellions that persisted long after the Huks were disbanded, owing to continued social inequalities and the marginalization of poor farmers.[96] One of the rebel leaders of the late 1950s, Pedro Borja, considered to be a "Philippines Castro," promoted land reform, while Leonardo Manecio (also called Nardong Putik) was more of a criminal bandit known as a "Robin Hood." He was killed in an ambush by the National Bureau of Investigation and the constabulary, as was populist Prudencio Opinianzo of Leyte, who carried on the Huk legacy by setting up an organization called The Philippines for Poor Farmers.[97]

The character of the people targeted illustrates how the technical expertise and professional standards promoted by American advisers were used for repressive political ends. The better they did their job, the worse off the population often was. The historian James C. Scott notes that any class system produces a "dissonant subculture" of subordinate groups that expresses itself not just in revolt but in deviant values, manifest in jokes, songs, or illicit activity such as narcotics and gambling, which the police were deployed to suppress all the same. Popular disaffection escalated during the presidency of Ferdinand Marcos (1965–1986), which was marred by authoritarianism and corruption.[98] Valued by the United States for allowing Philippine military bases to be used for bombing attacks on Vietnam and opening up the country to foreign investment, Marcos won a blatantly rigged election in 1969 and three years later suspended the writ of habeas corpus.[99]

Human rights organizations estimated that over 53,000 people were detained under draconian national security laws and upwards of 3,257 killed. The scarred remains of victims were dumped in city streets for purposes of intimidation.[100] Acknowledging that police were charged with murder, rape, robbery, and smuggling, and that firemen engaged in shakedowns and looting at the scene of fires, public safety reports nevertheless praised the martial law programs for contributing to an "abrupt halt in the crime rates," due to the surrender of over half a million loose firearms, and applauded Marcos for curbing "dangerous" demonstrations and weakening the Maoist New People's Army. "The images of barbed wire and tanks in the streets are untrue," one report declared. "Manila and its environment never appeared so peaceful, nor so clean and prosperous."[101]

From 1966 to 1973, the OPS provided over $3.9 million in police aid. American advisers such as Indiana state trooper Stanley Guth, James McGregor of the Kalamazoo police, "Scotty" Caplan, and Paul Katz, who worked with Montagnard units in South Vietnam, oversaw the refurbishing of police buildings, the development of crowd control units, and the systematization of records. They taught fingerprinting and telecommunications technology, including in Mindanao, where the Moro engaged in armed resistance in the face of state repression and the encroachment on their lands by agribusiness corporations. Hundreds of police were trained at the IPA and went back to head local police academies, where Williamson and colleagues provided lectures.[102]

According to declassified documents, the OPS encouraged "aggressive interrogation of suspects" and smuggled in electric transceivers used in torture sessions. In a 1976 report, *The Logistics of Repression*, a group of academics concluded that the OPS could take "credit for helping to institutionalize the most advanced techniques of information and confession extraction from political suspects, like the common use of electric shocks, subtle psychological torture, and selective beatings—methods remarkably similar to those employed in Brazil, Korea, Vietnam, Iran, and Uruguay, all of which have received significant amounts of OPS assistance and training."[103]

Between 1972 and 1976, owing in part to concerns about drug abuse among GIs at the Clark and Subic bases in the Philippines, USAID and the Drug Enforcement Administration provided over $1.28 million in narcotics control assistance, establishing a training course, anti-smuggling center, and anti-narcotics unit within the constabulary.[104] While contributing to the arrest and execution of heroin trafficker Lim Seng, the Government Accounting Office expressed concern that equipment was being diverted for non-narcotics-related purposes and that "narcotics advisers perform essentially the same function that public safety advisers used to perform" and were "training the same units." OPS reports also pointed to longstanding corruption in the army and police, accounting for the "tremendous volume of smuggling." Syndicate bosses such as Don José "Pepe" Oyson, a methamphetamine trafficker, were used by Marcos to control the poor.[105]

In 1973 the Constabulary Anti-Narcotics Unit raided the home of Liliosa Hilao, a suspected radical, and tortured her to death. Even Secretary of Defense Juan Ponce Enrile, who admitted to staging his own assassination attempt to provide Marcos with a final pretext for the declaration of martial law, felt obliged to dissociate himself from them. *The Logistics of Repression* concluded that under the narcotics program, "sophisticated police communications equipment, vehicles, and light weaponry have been channeled to such bodies as the Philippine constabulary," which were responsible for serial human rights abuses. These comments demonstrate the continuity of American programs that, while masked by a rhetoric of humanitarian reform, contributed the growth of a draconian national security apparatus, Orwellian in scale.[106]

Writing about America's support for the drug traffic in Thailand that it purported to be combating, *Ramparts* magazine editorialized in the late 1960s that "were [the story] to appear in an Ian Fleming plot, we would pass it off as torturing the credibility of thriller fiction."[107] This is no doubt true for all the police programs and the entire clandestine Cold War in Southeast Asia, which remains largely unknown to the American public. The effects, however, were all too real for the people of the region. Embodying the contradiction between America's republican self-identity and global ambitions, police training was pivotal in the efforts to suppress left-wing movements, recruit local "assets," and orchestrate regime change on the subcontinent, a key strategic prize.

In the three cases surveyed, the programs were effective in serving the interests of the American state, but they contributed to the consolidation of dictatorship. Modernization was promoted to enhance efficiency in carrying out political operations. Due process and civil liberties were little prioritized, which accounted for the lawless character of the forces operating under American oversight. The political stability valued by policy elites was eventually achieved, at least in Indonesia, but at the expense of major human rights violations and the decimation of civil society, which was of little consequence in Washington. Ralph McGehee, a senior CIA manager during the years of the coup, noted that Indonesia was viewed as a "model operation. . . . You can trace back all major, bloody events run from Washington to the way Suharto came to power. The success of that meant that it would be repeated, again and again."[108] Critical to the operation, the police programs were indeed repeated again and again across the globe, leading to much additional bloodshed. The outcome, however, was often less favorable for the United States, as the terror spiraled out of control and produced civil wars, failed states, or regimes dedicated to resisting American global hegemony.[109]

Chapter **6**

The Secret War in Laos and Other Vietnam Sideshows
The Clandestine Cold War in Southeast Asia II

No grand TV exposures, no detailed reporting on the scene by journalists and TV crews, none of the exposure in the media that has plagued the similar American effort in Vietnam. The murder and destruction [in Laos] have been carried out in delightful obscurity.
—NOAM CHOMSKY, *Laos: War and Revolution*, 1970

The Laotian people are killing each other—and the Americans are pulling the strings.
—BANNING GARRET, *Ramparts*, 1970

In the spring of 1959, Paul H. Skuse, a CIA operative working undercover in Laos as a police adviser with the State Department's International Cooperation Administration (ICA), invited two Hmong chiefs, Touby Lyfoung and Toulia Lyfong, to his French-style villa outside Vientiane for dinner with the aim of securing their cooperation in the escalating war against the Pathet Lao.[1] A deputy in the national assembly, Toulia was openly sympathetic to the Pathet Lao, and had urged the Hmong not to fight their fellow tribesmen. Touby was more fervently anticommunist and amenable to accepting aid from the United States, in part out of a desire to bolster the power of his clan against the rival Lo. Little did Touby realize at the time that in forging an alliance with the United States, he was sowing the seeds of disaster for the Hmong people as well as the country as a whole, which became enmeshed in a destructive civil war. In effect, he was handing his people over to a wolf in sheep's clothing. Skuse was employing a classic colonial strategy of manipulating tribal minorities to serve broader political ends.

Left out of previous scholarly accounts because the documents have only recently been declassified, Skuse's role in brokering the U.S. alliance with the Hmong exemplifies the centrality of police training programs to American anticommunist rollback operations, including their function in recruiting intelligence "assets." As Alfred W. McCoy has noted, the secret war in Laos represents one of the least understood yet most cataclysmic developments

121

of the Indochina wars. Many policymakers viewed it as a success because it was waged almost entirely by proxy and without cost to the United States. U. Alexis Johnson, undersecretary of state for Far Eastern Affairs, considered the operation "something of which we can be proud as Americans. It has involved virtually no American casualties. What we're getting for our money out there . . . is, I think[,] to use the old phrase, very cost effective."[2] The consequences, however, were devastating for the Lao population as an estimated 3,500 villages were destroyed, 350,000 people killed, and another million rendered refugees.

While local actors drove the conflict, the United States played an important role behind the scenes, pulling the strings. Triggering the onset of civil war, the United States provided modern weapons to security forces under the police programs with the goal of fortifying the Royal Lao Government (RLG) and trained Hmong militias implicated in significant human rights violations. In theory, counterinsurgency experts aimed to minimize "collateral damage" by cultivating effective intelligence networks and building local forces to pinpoint the location of the enemy. In practice, however, levels of violence are impossible to manage in a war zone. The campaign was waged beyond the reach of public scrutiny and international law and served as a laboratory for testing new weapons and psychological warfare techniques. A State Department official commented about Laos: "This is [the] end of nowhere. We can do anything we want here because Washington doesn't seem to know that it exists."[3] This attitude more than anything else accounted for the carnage on the ground.

Combating "Communist Subversion": Police Training and Foreign Assistance in Laos

America's involvement in Laos originated in the mid-1950s after the Pathet Lao, a nationalist and pro-communist organization headed by Prince Souphanouvong, aided the Vietminh in defeating the French at the battle of Dien Bien Phu. The Geneva Accords assigned it temporary control over the northern provinces of Sam Neua and Phong Saly until scheduled elections in 1958 and called for integration of Pathet Lao units into the Laotian armed forces. This worried the Eisenhower administration (which had refused to sign the accords). A blueprint for the 1290-d program warned that "through peaceful legal means, Pathet Lao dissidents will take positions within the Lao Cabinet, army, and civil service enabling them to subvert the entire country."[4]

On January 1, 1955, a United States Operations Mission headed by Daly Lavergne was established in the capital, Vientiane. Justified for "political purposes and not to assist Laos in long-range social and economic development," it was meant to prevent a Pathet Lao takeover and establish Laos as a stable pro-Western buffer between North Vietnam and China to the north and east and Thailand to the west. Policymakers feared the emergence of an independent socialist bloc in Southeast Asia capable of undercutting U.S. influence and investment in a region they hoped to convert into an "Anglo-Saxon lake." A successful socialist experiment in Laos could provide a model for surrounding countries, notably Indonesia and Japan, which U.S. planners were desperate to retain in the Western orbit in the wake of the Chinese revolution.[5]

In order to avert this possibility, the United States propped up the Royal Lao Government, which was dominated by a small clique of families who owned most of the country's major businesses and mostly collaborated with the French. According to the CIA, Prime Minister Katay Don Sasorith, president of the Lao-Thai Bank and owner of Air Laos, had his "fingers in every large pie in the country" and was an uncouth person, disliked for his rudeness and a habit of insulting people. A former leader of the Lao Issara (anti-French movement), he was a favorite of John Foster Dulles because of his book *Laos: Ideal Cornerstone in the Anticommunist Struggle in Southeast Asia.* Ambassador Graham Parsons, a loyal Dulles disciple, worked to undermine negotiations with the Pathet Lao, who promoted land redistribution, literacy, and public health programs and, according to a leading historian of Laos, worked with the people at the local level to "meet their needs."[6]

The State Department characterized Souphanouvong, who became interested in Marxism while studying civil engineering in France, as an "outstandingly able and energetic leader," much like the Vietnamese revolutionary Ho Chi Minh, whom OSS agent Frank White described as an "awfully sweet man" and the "least sort of megalomaniacal leader" he had ever met.[7] America's allies, by contrast, as *Newsweek* reported, represented "the traditional ruling class and had little interest in reform. The political methods they used—stuffing ballot boxes and intimidating neutralist voters—succeeded only in driving the moderates to the left."[8]

The influx of American aid coupled with an inflated currency exacerbated the climate of corruption. A congressional inquiry found mismanagement in customs, banking, and foreign trade, as well as bribery in the awarding of contracts to American construction firms, including the Virginia-based Vinnell Corporation and Universal Construction Company, a CIA front.[9] The United States spent over $140 million, or 80 percent of the foreign aid budget, creating a 25,000-man army designed to serve, in Dulles's words, as an "agent of modernization" and a "tripwire to halt communist aggression." Training was carried out by American Special Forces and the CIA, with the assistance of Thai translators, para-commandos, and support staff. Vientiane was swimming with "spooks," as Laos became the only country in the world where the United States underwrote the entire military budget.[10]

In spite of its being supplied with planes, tanks, helicopters, and guns, intelligence reports noted deficiencies in the Royal Lao Army (RLA), warning that it was "too weak to combat the well organized communist army," meaning the

Pathet Lao. Officers were corrupt and "up to their ears in the opium trade"; conscripts "refused to fight." CIA director Allen Dulles lamented that while the RLA employed "hit and run tactics against the communists, it was not clear whether there was more hit or run."[11] The *New York Times* mocked the pacifist tendencies of its soldiers, who "abhorred killing and moved to the front often with a plucked flower sticking out of the muzzle of their ill-kept rifle." Roger Hilsman, assistant secretary of state for Far Eastern affairs under President Kennedy, reported in his memoirs that the RLA was "more political than anything else—a focal point for graft, the principal lever for ambitious men plotting coups, and a symbol of government repression in those villages to which it did, intermittently, penetrate."[12]

Because of these tendencies, the USOM channeled aid to the Lao National Police (LNP), which appeared better equipped than the RLA to establish domestic security, collect intelligence, control arms smuggling, and win popular support through civic action. A 1961 cabinet-level report noted that "police were able to operate without interference in Pathet Lao–controlled areas and earned respect from the population through close contact. . . . The Laotian army [meanwhile] was ambushed in these areas because it lived off the land, burned villages, and had aroused widespread hatred."[13] Paul Skuse, a patrolman in the Boston Police Department who, after a stint in the navy, served as a police administrator in Okinawa, commented in another report that while "soldiers and police both wear uniforms and carry firearms... there the similarity stops. A soldier is indoctrinated and trained to . . . kill and destroy. The policeman's job is to protect life and property, prevent crime, instill in the people a respect for the law, and to assist those in need. Their basic training is entirely different. The first is concerned mainly with fighting and maintenance of his weapons . . . the latter... with learning the constitution and laws of the land, the rights of an individual[,] . . . and proper public relations."[14]

Laos was a peaceful, nonmaterialistic society, and crime rates were extraordinarily low.[15] Training was consequently designed for purely political objectives under the State Department's 1290-d program, which operated at a $3.9 million budget, among the highest in the world. Its central goal was to strengthen the internal security apparatus of the RLG while avoiding costly military intervention. Priority was given to the police Special Branch. The LNP were trained in modern records management and counterintelligence techniques designed to "facilitate the early detection of communist penetration of the civilian population."[16] U.S. advisers further worked to cultivate anticommunist solidarity among CIA "assets" in the police, who were kept on guard for a possible coup in case a political settlement was brokered allowing for Pathet Lao participation in government and the national army, which the Americans deemed unacceptable.[17]

The LNP, which had been established by the French in 1949 to control subversion, included a paramilitary wing. In contrast to the armed forces, recruits were mostly literate and had to pass a written exam. In April 1955, two American police experts with CIA connections, Byron Engle and Louise Page, conducted a survey of police organizations. In their report, they advocated establishing a U.S. assistance program based on the program in Indonesia. Drawing on Engle's experience in Japan, they asserted that "combating communist infiltration and subversion and the maintenance of public safety in Laos" were essentially a "police problem, and not a military one. . . . If the people are to have confidence in their government and give it their support, then it must be capable of establishing law and order and affording them protection." The report went on to recommend that the police and Gendarmerie be combined under a single ministry and that police intelligence should be bolstered and village patrols established in the countryside, where "small bandit gangs preyed on the population" and "communist agents engaged in propaganda and harassment activities." Engle and Morris stressed that the LNP were seriously handicapped by the lack of adequate facilities and equipment and that remedying this problem should be a central priority. Road building, too, was vital to improve transportation and communication, which were needed to identify and track down subversives.[18]

The RLG and the State Department responded favorably to Engle and Page's report. The Royal Gendarmerie (540 men strong) was merged with the LNP (580 men strong) in the Ministry of the Interior, and manpower was increased to 2,800. The ICA contracted nine police advisers, including Jack Ellis, superintendent of the Kansas City Police Department, and four third-country technicians and supplied the LNP with over 1,500 carbines, 1,000 revolvers, uniforms, boots, saddles, jeeps, and radios provisioned by airlift to the director-general of the Gendarmerie, Tiao Somsanith the brother of "red" Prince Souphanouvong.[19] A photo lab was constructed for improving classification of detainees, along with a modern radio communications system linking remote areas with Vientiane. Manufactured by Barrow and Brown, Ltd., of Bangkok, the system included thirty-seven transmitter stations and 187 operators and was considered one of the best means of "ensuring internal security."[20] These initiatives illustrate how modern information technology and communications techniques were being exported in order to heighten social control.

ICA staff nevertheless felt hampered by the lack of qualified personnel left over from the French colonial administration, as well as by dilapidated police stations, the reliance on vehicles of World War II vintage, and the absence of paved roads, which made communications difficult.[21] Starting in 1956, LNP being groomed for leadership positions, including Tiao Somsanith and his successor Soukan Vilayrsarn, a protégé of Katay Don Sasorith, were sent to take courses at Michigan State University, whose Department of Police Administration was among the best in the country.[22] Part of the aim was to cultivate their loyalty to the anticommunist cause. The State Department sent police for additional instruction in Malaya and Thailand, where they attended a radio technician school at Korat and studied under Colonel Chai Sevikul, chief of the fingerprint and central records office in the National Police headquarters in Bangkok. He was considered "more effective than American advisers because of his fluency in the Lao languages." LNP officers also trained with the CIA-subsidized Border Patrol Police in jungle warfare. In June 1957, ninety officers were sent to the constabulary school in Manila, where they were taught by veterans of the anti-Huk campaign.[23] The nature of the training reveals the political function of the police programs and the push for militarization, which resulted in a proliferation of human rights violations.

In order to foster increased professionalism, a police training center was set up at Done Noune, twelve kilometers from Vientiane, with the assistance of Jeter Williamson. Because of a lack of proper classroom equipment, water, and electricity, it never proved functional. Supplies intended for construction were resold on the black market. The living conditions were so poor that public safety officers feared the outbreak of diseases; they lamented that students had to hitchhike or walk twelve to fourteen kilometers (a trip of at least two to three hours) to the nearest river in order to bathe. The classroom had no blackboard, and students couldn't even hear their instructors' lectures. One short course in paramilitary tactics and criminal investigation was given at the center in early 1957. It was otherwise used as a storage depot for donated equipment.[24]

The academy provides a fitting symbol of the shortcomings of the police program. The General Accounting Office concluded in spring 1959 that "little progress" had been made and that there was a "serious lack of control over counterpart fund expenditures with evidence pointing to the possible diversion of substantial sums for unauthorized purposes."[25] The corruption resulted in part from the rising cost of living, owing to an influx of foreign capital on a hollow economic base and the new availability of luxury goods. Construction projects designed to improve police facilities never got off the ground because the materials were pilfered and sold on the black market. Reports complained that police wasted their gasoline rations taking their families on country picnics, rendering their vehicles unusable for part of the year.[26] Vincent Cillis, an army counterintelligence specialist with a degree from LaSalle University in Chicago, noted that provincial commanders were more interested in the "success of private enterprises in which they have investments than police work." An American missionary, George Tubbs, told the embassy that the GMD and local merchants were smuggling opium from Thailand and in Sayaboury province, where the police chief was a leading opium producer and his officers were "afraid to interfere" or were "themselves involved."[27]

The chain of corruption extended to top police executives who used their status to enrich themselves through extortion and by demanding kickbacks from Chinese merchants in return for work permits. ICA reports noted that

Major Vattah Phankham, head of the police Special Branch, built a mansion that cost over 2 million kip (the equivalent of $488, 400). Public safety advisers wondered where he got the money. Colonel Levan Vilayhon, commissioner of the provincial police, invested in commercial enterprises and bought a huge house next door to police chief Tiao Somsanith and a big Chevrolet Deluxe. Tiao's replacement, General Soukan Vilayrsarn, who had studied law in France and was valued for his strong anticommunism, used his position to pay off political candidates and to purchase three Mercedes-Benzes and five Renault Dauphines. He was subsequently promoted to secretary of state for veteran affairs. (Tiao became secretary of state for the interior.) According to Skuse, Soukan was a "good police officer but keeps bad company. . . . He is being misguided by [association with] Vattah, which will bring his ruin."[28]

Failing to acknowledge the roots of the problem, public safety advisers rationalized the lack of professionalism and graft as a product of cultural backwardness. Vincent Cillis commented in a report that the "Lao is by nature unambitious and indolent, perhaps due to the enervating climate, which reduces mental and physical vigor and produces a 'manna philosophy.'" Taking a page from the Portuguese theory of Lusotropicalism, these remarks typify the ethnocentrism underlying the American aid programs. Lao people were frequently disparaged by government officials and the media for being unambitious, unintelligent, lazy, and pacifist. CIA station chief Henry Hecksher attributed the failure of U.S. programs to the fact that "our propaganda is too sophisticated" to answer that of the Pathet Lao "in the mind of the villager."[29]

Owing to such attitudes, Lao police did not often respect their advisers and were suspected of being double agents. The ICA's Nikolas Perazic reported to the U.S. embassy that the police commissioner in Sam Neua "wears an old and shabby field outfit and not a police uniform," adding, "My sense is that he is not a man to be trusted."[30] The State Department continued to back forces they acknowledged to be corrupt out of geopolitical expediency, pressing for civic action, including the building and staffing of rural schools, to improve the LNP's image. In March 1959 the American ambassador urged Secretary of State for the Interior Khoranhok Souvannavong to tighten control over the police and fight corruption, which Souvannavong admitted had "taken root like a plague."[31] Little changed, however, because of the institutionalization of corruption at the highest levels and the weakness of the legal system and judiciary, and because the problem was partially a product of American foreign aid programs and the culture of materialism and greed that they fostered.

"A Youthful Prank": Subversion of Elections and Growth of a Dirty War

The police programs in Laos received added priority following the 1958 elections, in which the political arm of the Pathet Lao, the Neo Lao Hak Xat (Laotian Patriotic Front), encompassing a wide coalition of leftists, won nine of twenty-one contested seats. The State Department, though acknowledging that the Patriotic Front was a "well organized and disciplined legal political party" and "thoroughly pro-democratic and pro-Laotian at heart," sought to undermine it by enacting a rural development program, Operation Booster Shot, and by funding anticommunist candidates. Seizing upon the corruption bred by the American aid program, Prince Souphanouvong won the largest number of votes. Neutralist Souvanna Phouma, Souphanouvong's half-brother, emerged as the head of state. He supported a coalition government, which included the integration of Pathet Lao units into the RLA. Disappointed by the results, Ambassador Parsons backed the Laotian right wing in forming the Committee for the Defense of National Interests, which sponsored police surveillance and harassment of the elected Patriotic Front deputies and forced Souvanna to resign.[32]

A new cabinet was subsequently formed, headed by CIA "asset" Phoui Sananikone, who had previously served under the French and was implicated in a financial scandal while director of the Lao-Vieng Bank.[33] The Pathet Lao was criminalized and thrust underground, sparking the onset of civil war. To justify the initiation of search and destroy operations, the RLG claimed that North Vietnam had invaded the country in violation of the Geneva neutrality pledge (which the United States itself had repeatedly violated), a line the press swallowed. A United Nations investigation concluded, however, that while North Vietnam had provided material assistance, "there was no conclusive proof that North Vietnamese Army units had crossed the border," which would have been impossible anyway during the rainy season. Even Oudone Sananikone, a firmly anticommunist general related to Phoui, noted in his account of the conflict that the Laotian government had precipitated the crisis. William Lederer wrote in his book *A Nation of Sheep*: "The people of the United States were led to believe that Laos physically had been invaded by foreign Communist troops from across its northern border. . . . The entire affair was a fraud. No military invasion of Laos had taken place."[34] According to the Australian journalist Wilfred Burchett, once the war began, the repression directed against the Pathet Lao and its supporters was especially savage. Troops and police killed any cadre they could get their hands on, including some members of parliament. They allegedly stuck the decapitated heads of some victims up on stakes in district and provincial centers for purposes of intimidation.[35]

In spite of the virulence of the campaigns, American and RLG hard-liners sought the removal of Phoui because he did not "prosecute the war against the Pathet Lao with enough vigor" or take the advice of Ambassador Horace Smith and CIA station chief Henry Hecksher "to eliminate the leftist opposition entirely."[36] The CIA subsequently backed a coup d'état led by Colonel Phoumi Nosavan, a cousin of Thai dictator Marshal Sarit Thanarat who had studied at the École Supérieure de Guerre in France. Described by the CIA as "cocky regarding military action," the portly man, who had Thai and GMD troops operating under his command, used his power to amass a fortune of $137 million through control of casinos, a pork monopoly, and the traffic in gold and opium. Even anticommunist Lao referred to him as a "crook."[37]

After the coup, black-shirted soldiers loyal to Phoumi surrounded Phoui's home with tanks and joked about assassination if he "did not behave." Elections held in April 1960 were crudely rigged in Phoumi's favor, with "innumerable examples" of bribery, voter fraud, and intimidation. A U.S. embassy officer reported that he had seen CIA agents distribute bagsful of money to village headmen. The Pathet Lao officially recorded 1,927 votes, a figure arbitrarily derived from the year in which CIA agent Stuart Methven was born. CIA director Dulles considered the fraud a "youthful prank." All leftists were defeated, and even loyal moderates were excluded from the assembly.[38] The remaining Pathet Lao army units were disarmed, and Souphanouvong was condemned to death for treason. During the height of a rainstorm, however, he escaped from prison, where the wretched conditions were likened by one observer to those of a horse stable. According to a fellow prisoner, Souphanouvong won over the guards through political education and persuaded them to join the nationalist cause.[39]

The Pathet Lao forces, led by troops from the Thai-speaking Lao Loum majority, subsequently took to the mountains and recaptured much of the Plain of Jars, consisting of Sam Neua and Phong Saly provinces. They received assistance from the North Vietnamese, though the U.S. embassy reported after a comprehensive effort to accumulate evidence through photos, documents, and eyewitnesses, that "allegations of Vietminh activity" in Laos were "exaggerated."[40] U.S. Army Green Berets, under the code name Erawan, began training native forces in counter-guerrilla warfare as secret monies were dispensed to secure political loyalties.[41] Scorched earth tactics and relocation programs designed to isolate the guerrillas from their base were adopted, and Secretary of State Dean Rusk sanctioned the use of Royal Lao Air Force T-28s manned by employees of the CIA subsidiary Air America and Lao and Thai pilots for bombing missions along with the use of napalm at the discretion of the ambassador.[42]

Previously, in August 1959, Paul Skuse had cabled Daly Lavergne requesting an increase in police manpower and ammunition to address the "disturbed political situation and emergency that now exists." Recently, he noted, "a 12 man border patrol team was sent on a 14 day patrol with only two revolvers and five carbines."[43] At the behest of the National Security Council, Lavergne in turn contracted Civil Air Transport (later Air America) to fly in ammunition, revolvers, Motorola radios, generators, carbines, and rifles from Thailand and the Philippines. Patrol boats were sent for a marine branch to "control subversive infiltration through the river," and gasoline was provided for LNP vehicles through a local Caltex dealer.[44]

The ICA further earmarked over $600,000 to build a central interrogation center and new provincial headquarters, designed to "give prestige to the police and serve as a symbol of Royal Lao authority."[45] Advisers worked to improve record collection and accounting, set up a national registry and identity card system to monitor political activity, and trained border patrol officials to regulate the entry of Thai and Chinese immigrants suspected of communist sympathies. (Many were detained indiscriminately on these charges.)[46]

Several advisers with experience training Ngo Dinh Diem's police agents in South Vietnam, including Air Force captain Jack Ryan, who had been an FBI agent in East Lansing, Michigan, from 1948 to 1953, supplied instruction to the Special Branch, which received secret slush funds from the USOM to build up its intelligence-gathering capabilities under General Vattah Phankham. Ryan drafted a plan to create an elite civil police organization capable of efficiently handling "subversion, terrorism, and crime," and which commanded respect from the population so as to "permit the development of necessary sources of information."[47] Working with a French intelligence officer, Major Jean Deuve, he taught revolver training, weapons maintenance, and methods of counter-guerrilla warfare, including interrogation in which the aim was to try to "break" the suspect. These activities resulted in the spread of gross human rights violations and an intensification of the war.

"Brutal, Corrupt Activity": Arming Phoumi and His Hatchet Man, General Siho

In August 1960, Kong Le, a Laotian military officer characterized by the CIA as a "highly competent and professional soldier and born leader," launched a coup d'état with the aim of rooting out corruption and "suppressing those who were making their harvests off the back of people."[48] Paul Skuse, who had survived the war in the Pacific, was shot and wounded while coordinating public safety operations in Vientiane after several civilian advisers were taken hostage. The CIA and Graham Parsons, now assistant secretary of state for Far Eastern affairs, backed the strongman Phoumi, who reclaimed the capital. Though acknowledging his corruption and the fact that his son had caused public disturbances by throwing wild, drunken parties at his mansion in Savannakhet, they felt that "without him, the jealous, vicious, and ineffective bickering of lesser military figures in Vientiane would cause chaos," thus benefiting the Pathet Lao.[49]

With American backing, Phoumi set up a paramilitary organization known as the Directorate of National Coordination in the Ministry of Defense under the command of General Siho Lamphouthacoul, a CIA "asset" who played a vital role rigging the 1960 election on Phoumi's behalf. The Directorate was overseen by three full-time CIA officers and two South Vietnamese intelligence agents who worked closely with Siho. Viewing neutrality as synonymous with communism, it conducted surveillance operations in the capital of Vientiane, as well as sabotage, kidnappings, and commando-style raids. Six hundred neutralist politicians were among those detained, including Souvanna Phouma and former police chief Tiao Somsanith.[50]

A stocky man of mixed Chinese-Laotian parentage and humble background, the thirty-year-old Siho had spent a year in France and attended the General Staff School in Taiwan, where he fell under the influence of Chiang Ching-kuo, chief of Taiwan's secret police and son of dictator Chiang Kai-shek (Jiang Jieshi), who had close ties to American intelligence. A protégé of Dai Li, Chiang ran a ruthless internal security apparatus permeating all aspects of Taiwanese society. Described by the New York Times as "rough and tenacious" and by his CIA case officer as "vain" and "dangerous [like Phoumi] if in a flash of hot temper," Siho similarly headed a militarized force which adopted "gangster methods" to eliminate the opposition, according to U.S. reports, including the use of "twisted cord in interrogating recalcitrant subjects." His men abused their power, extorted money, were involved in gambling and prostitution, and conducted themselves, in the words of one of Phoumi's supporters, "in an absolutely irresponsible manner."[51]

In January 1961 the LNP was removed from the control of the Ministry of the Interior and its members absorbed by the Directorate of National Coordination.[52] Laotian politics were marred in this period by constant factionalism over the spoils of power. The Sananikone clan maintained its rivalry with Phoumi, while Siho's forces quarreled with General Kouprasith Abhay over control of medicine imports and fees from opium and gambling. Kong Le continued to resist with a supply of Soviet arms. Siho's police and Kouprasith's soldiers, led by his cousin Phao, fought and arrested each other, with the army and police engaged in a rivalry for power. Dead bodies were left to rot in the streets with their guts hanging out. Siho launched a coup and briefly controlled key parts of Vientiane, including the National Bank, causing considerable destruction.[53] His putsch exemplified the danger of the police programs in empowering far-right elements, which used the influx of weaponry to try to fulfill their ambitions for power.

A 1965 OPS report by Frank Walton, Paul Skuse, and telecommunications specialist Wendell Motter lamented that American aid had contributed to the police evolving into a "private army" of General Siho and Phoumi, who organized vice and the "considerable traffic in smuggling into Thailand" as a means of raising money for a "wave of repression against political opponents," including "mass jailing and executions."[54] Siho's men, according to the report, engaged in "Gestapo"-like tactics, carrying out operations that "rivaled anything ever heard of in terms of brutal, corrupt activity."[55]

On February 3, 1965, General Siho and Phoumi launched a failed coup d'état and fled to Thailand. Short of funds with which to "buy supporters" as a result of the death of Marshal Sarit, they were tried in absentia for corruption and misconduct in office. Siho decided to return after being told by a soothsayer that he could reenter Laos unharmed. Upon crossing the border, he was imprisoned and "shot while trying to escape" (legend has it that General Kouprasith threw him out of a helicopter without a parachute).[56] Colonel Soukan Vilayrsarn noted that Phoumi and Siho were like "idiotic children with no judgment and no foresight who acted without thought to international repercussions or the future of Laos." Though disassociating itself at the end, the United States had helped to spur them on. The CIA concluded that Phoumi and Siho were attempting to emulate General Nguyen Khanh's coup in South Vietnam and that the "politically unsophisticated" Siho had sought to win over the Americans by demonstrating his vigorous opposition to communism.[57] These comments again reveal the ideological influence of the American training programs, which was often just as powerful as their material influence.

After Siho's death, the LNP was returned to civilian control, and two hundred Siho loyalists were purged from key positions. The Kennedy and Johnson administrations backed Souvanna Phouma after he forged ties with right-wing generals and allowed for air strikes on zones controlled by the Pathet Lao. Souvanna was favored because, according to national security adviser Michael Forrestall, while "not a rock of Gibraltar, we do not think he is communist."[58] Above all else, he was seen to promote stability at the top, which had been lacking under the more flamboyant yet venal Phoumi. American leaders had seemingly found a reliable client, or so they thought.

"A Precious Collection of Killers": Auto-Defense Units and the Hmong Clandestine Army

As Machiavellian political intrigues played out in Vientiane, the USOM funneled military equipment under the 1290-d program to rural commandos, or auto-defense units, who served as an arm of the police Special Branch. First organized by Special Forces in 1954, they were viewed as crucial to the preservation of Royal Lao authority in the face of "serious armed threats" and the Pathet Lao rebellion aimed at "overthrowing the legally established administration by means of a general uprising of the Lao people," which would "take the form of a social and democratic revolution."[59]

Following a classic colonial strategy, the Special Group on Counter-Insurgency championed the training of "tribal groups with en exploitable paramilitary capability" throughout the developing world, including the Montagnards in South Vietnam and ethnic clans in Thailand, Colombia, Venezuela, and Iran.[60] Building upon the precedent established by Dean Worcester in the Philippines, anthropological studies were contracted to assist in these efforts. The auto-defense units were primarily drawn from the Hmong based in Xieng

Khouang province and other "primitive" minorities (as they were called), who joined because of grievances against the Pathet Lao or because their chiefs had been bought off through patronage.

The training was overseen by Adolphe Bonnefil, a Michigan State police officer who had served as an instructor at the Haitian military academy, and for a time by Ralph Johnson, a veteran of the Flying Tigers (American aviators who fought in China in World War II), described by colleagues as a "good-looking, fast-talking snake-oil salesman." The commandos carried out armed propaganda, served as scouts for the RLA, penetrated Pathet Lao encampments, and joined in combat missions. Operating on both sides of the Laotian-Vietnamese border in liaison with South Vietnamese units, they were instructed in spy-craft and sabotage, given sweeping powers of detainment, and authorized to assassinate Pathet Lao leaders, a pattern consistent with the designs of Western counterinsurgency theorists to fight terror with terror and emulate the methods of guerrillas who selectively assassinated hated government officials and police. Fitting a cultural tradition dating to the Indian Wars, the "savagery" of the enemy was used to justify parallel or even greater barbarity by U.S. troops and their proxies bringing "liberty" and "civilization" to all who would embrace it.[61]

Reminiscent of the Filipino constabulary and "Chesty" Puller's units in Nicaragua and Haiti, the auto-defense units dressed in black and were recruited on the basis of their knowledge of the local population and rugged mountain terrain. Equipped with carbines, grenade launchers, bolo knives, and antipersonnel mines, as well as ammunition belts, compasses, binoculars, and shovels, they were conceived as an alternative to the army, whose posts were being overpowered by the Pathet Lao, and whose officers rarely took the field with their men or even left the luxury of their expensive villas and air-conditioned offices. Ruben Tucker, head of the Military Advisory Assistance Group, referred to the RLA as "gutless." Bonnefil noted in a memo that the commandos, by contrast, would always "be in motion in the jungle. . . . Billeting or rest and recuperation in insecure or suspicious villages will be absolutely forbidden [to prevent defections]."[62]

Subsequent reports, however, noted a lack of ideological motivation and observed that in the face of battle the auto-defense units were prone to flee or "turn their weapons over to the Pathet Lao and Vietminh." Willard O. Brown, head of the USOM, complained that in a campaign on the Plain of Jars, the men never received their bonus money from their commander, who pocketed it, driving them to mutiny.[63] Apart from tactical concerns, a few American advisers were uneasy about the State Department's role in supporting military-style police organizations. In a memo to L. B. Swick, chair of the Overseas Internal Security Program (formerly the 1290-d program), Skuse voiced dismay that the broad powers of the auto-defense units were lending themselves to abuse, including the "arrest of anyone believed to be inimical to the RLG." Swick replied, "We need to ensure [that] police or constabulary units operate within a legal framework designed to safeguard the rights of individuals." Though he agreed with the program in principle, he recommended that the country team obtain assurances that persons arrested would be "turned over promptly to civil authorities for investigations and trial in accordance with the law."[64]

These suggestions accorded with the liberal Skuse's concern for civil liberties and due process. As a police administrator in Okinawa in the 1940s, he had criticized village raids by military police to confiscate U.S. properties as an "abuse of police powers" characteristic of the "NKVD, Kempe Tai, and other feared organizations of fascist and communistic states."[65] Paradoxically, the USOM in Laos strengthened hard-line elements within the RLG, fixed elections, and created mobile paramilitaries trained in violent psychological warfare tactics. The belief that these forces could operate within any sort of legal or humane framework given the context was naïve and reflected the moral contradictions common to liberal Cold Warriors, who failed to understand that human rights atrocities are inevitable in war. In practice, Swick's recommendations were not pursued, and American-backed forces continued to operate outside the law. Public safety reports referred to General Vattah Phankham's forces as a "merciless band of terrorists" trained in secret police methods. Wilfred Burchett characterized the commandos as a "precious collection of killers, thugs and bandits," owing to their expertise in the black clandestine arts. Among the victims of assassination was the son of Prince Souphanouvong.[66]

The auto-defense units served as the forerunner of the CIA's clandestine Hmong army, which was gradually integrated into the RLA and became the principal means by which the United States fought the Pathet Lao. The embassy and CIA sought to exploit splits within the Hmong between the Ly and Lo clans. Lo Faydang was a founding member of the Pathet Lao, while his cousin Touby Lyfoung had initiated resistance activities in the communist-controlled provinces of Sam Neua and Phong Saly starting in 1956, when the CIA began arming tribal elements under the cover of 1290-d.[67] With the escalation of civil war, the CIA sought to cement its alliance with Commandant Vang Pao, a Hmong chief who volunteered the services of four to five hundred Hmong as bodyguards for the auto-defense units. For him, alliance with the United States provided guns and food, which would enable him to solidify his power.

A skilled commander respected by his men, Vang Pao had served in the RLA in charge of a school for noncommissioned officers near Phonasavan and had fought with the French against the Vietminh. Because of an intimate knowledge of the jungle terrain and effective intelligence, his troops proved difficult to subdue deep inside Pathet Lao–controlled territory.[68] Known for his dedication to his people and ruthlessness toward his enemies, Vang had replaced the previous chief, Touby Lyfoung, the president of the national assembly, whose brother Toulia, a deputy, was pro-communist. Both were courted by Skuse, who invited them for dinner, where they recounted the history of the Hmong and their migrations from China's southern Yunnan province. Toulia had urged the Hmong not to fight their fellow tribesmen in the communist camp. He did not think that the RLG was strong enough to defend the country from the Vietminh. A Hmong informant subsequently went to the RLA general in command of the province and suggested that Toulia be arrested. Vang Pao, said the informant, was "capable of managing the Hmong. . . . He has the confidence of the tribesmen who are willing to fight under his leadership."[69] Vang Pao accepted the deal and became the head of the CIA's clandestine army.

The USOM established a close relationship with General Vang from this point forward. CIA agent Stuart Methven brought him a goodwill gift of blankets, sweaters, and radios.[70] In 1962 the United States signed the Geneva Accords, which called for an end to foreign interference and the formation of a coalition government including the Pathet Lao, though the Americans had no intention of abiding by it. The Kennedy administration subsequently expanded the training of guerrilla irregulars, relying on the CIA to allow for plausible deniability. Its cover was blown in September 1964, when Charles F. Klusman, an Air America pilot, was shot down over Route 7 in Laos. He spent fifty days in solitary confinement but was well treated by his captors, who gave him fresh food, regular medical checkups, and even vitamins.[71]

The CIA's alliance with the Hmong built on the precedent of the French and was designed to get around the "woeful performance" of the regular army, as CIA station chief Douglas Blaufarb noted in his memoirs, and to circumvent the Geneva Accords' prohibition on direct military assistance.[72] Since the Hmong were a tribe and not a nation, the CIA could negotiate with Hmong leaders without incurring any formal diplomatic obligations. Many of the CIA operatives and cabinet-level officials such as Roger "Tex" Hilsman had experience training tribal groups in Burma during World War II and, according to the official history of the CIA, entertained fantasies from their OSS days of rousing the tribal population to overthrow a communist regime. They wanted to defeat the guerrillas at their own game.[73]

The consequences were devastating for the Lao population. The CIA's official historian notes that in combat operations, Hmong guerrillas made use of walkie-talkies and Gatling guns supplied by public safety advisers to "obliterate everything in their path." Napalm was deployed by T-28 reinforcements and U.S. planes in clearing operations.[74] And while the Pathet Lao committed their share of atrocities, when the Hmong briefly conquered the Plain of Jars in 1969, they took revenge on the villagers and, according to the testimony of victims, "burned whatever shelters and belongings remained, and either stole or slaughtered their water buffalo, cows, pigs and chickens."[75]

Like OSS operations with the Kachin ethnic minority in Burma during World War II, the war in Laos was funded in part through the opium trade. The

Hmong had grown opium for centuries and used it for medicinal and spiritual purposes as well as to fund military campaigns. Vang Pao developed a pipeline for heroin with international connections. As Victor Marchetti, a fourteen-year CIA veteran, observed: "We were officially spending $27 million a year on the war in Laos. The war was costing ten times that amount. It was no secret how they were doing it: they financed it with drugs. They gave [CIA station chief Theodore] Shackley a medal for it."[76]

Opium-funded military campaigns were accompanied by the escalation of the air war. From launching pads in Thailand, the United States dropped over 2.1 million tons of bombs, including white phosphorus, predominantly along the Ho Chi Minh Trail and on the northern Plain of Jars, with the aim of interdicting supply routes and breaking enemy morale.[77] As one of their central functions, CIA-trained commando units provided intelligence for the bombing attacks and prepared lists of targets. Contradicting government claims of surgical precision, internal reports demonstrate that numerous strikes hit the wrong target. On May 13, 1964, in spite of "clear weather and brilliant sunshine," bombs dropped by U.S. planes struck two civilian buses west of Muang Phalane, killing fourteen people, mostly women and children, and wounding forty-one others. In January 1965, errant bombs hit a "friendly" Kha (Lao Thung) village, resulting in the wounding of five civilians, decimation of five houses, and killing of water buffalo; in November that year, U.S. bombs accidentally hit the town of Khang Khay, causing "considerable destruction."[78]

On the Plain of Jars, countless villages were leveled and thousands of civilians were wounded or killed. Their livestock and cattle depleted, peasants survived by living in underground caves and farming their fields at night. Over a quarter of the population was forced to flee to refugee camps, where malnutrition and disease were rampant.[79] Expressing himself in verse, one refugee lamented, "What terrible sadness, so many loved ones killed, because of the huge bombs the airplanes rained down upon us, so many loved ones forced to leave their native villages, leaving behind spacious rice fields and gardens now turned to dust."[80]

By the end of the war, much of the northeastern part of the countryside had been turned into a "wasteland" reminiscent of "the pocked, churned earth in storm-hit areas of the North African desert," according to the journalist T. D. Allman. Fred Branfman, an International Voluntary Service employee, whose book *Voices from the Plain of Jars* is one of the few written from the perspective of the Lao peasants, characterized it as a "lake of blood" where "after a recorded history of 700 years, civilized society had ceased to exist." He added that "a new type of warfare had been developed fought not by men but machines and which could erase distant and unseen societies clandestinely, unknown to and even unsuspected by the world outside."[81]

For all the devastation, the bombing attacks did little to diminish the strength of the revolutionary movement, whose cadres hid deep in the forest and made use of effective spying networks.[82] The CIA's clandestine army meanwhile was decimated and was forced to recruit child soldiers for a "one-way helicopter ride to death," as Allman characterized it. CIA operative Edgar "Pop" Buell told correspondent Robert Shaplen: "Here were these little kids in their camouflage uniforms . . . [who] looked real neat. . . . But V.P. [Vang Pao] and I knew better. They were too young and they weren't trained and in a few weeks 90 percent of them will be killed."[83]

Throughout the long years of fighting, police programs remained an important element of American strategy and a significant means of funneling arms to the RLA and Hmong. Many CIA agents used the programs as a cover, including Thomas L. Ahern Jr., who would later be detained in the Iranian hostage crisis; Major (not a military rank but an unusual first name) McBee, a California narcotics agent with experience in Ecuador, Vietnam, and Iran; and Gordon Young, a Lahu translator in Burma's Shan states who trained Thai BPP. From 1961 to 1965, police training was temporarily cut because of the chaos engulfing the country and because Phoumi and Siho were appropriating American aid to create private armies.[84] According to an OPS survey, the LNP was left in a state of "complete disorganization—stripped of its equipment, its records and facilities destroyed, preempted or deteriorated and having had practically no police training in four years." Walton, Skuse, and Motter suggested renewed technical and commodity assistance and a revival of the identity card program which had been instituted in the 1950s to monitor political activity.[85]

The embassy approved the recommendations, with the LNP now headed by General Vattah and Colonel Bounkhong Pradichit, a former staff officer of air force general Ouane Rattikone, the country's leading heroin trafficker, and liaison to the U.S. military mission in Saigon, who was considered "more aggressive and energetic than the usual Southeast Asian" and hence capable of revitalizing the force.[86] Operating on a budget of $900,000 in 1965 and $1.1 million in 1966, the OPS created antenna-based provincial stations and provided electronic surveillance equipment, including spy cameras, revolvers, Smith & Wesson handcuffs, and 63,600 rounds of carbine ammunition procured through a USAID warehouse in Bangkok. Advisers from Vietnam such as Delmar Spier of the Aurora County, Colorado, Police Department and Ray Landgren of LaGrange Park, Illinois, developed a scientific lab, assisted with mail intercepts, and tried to rebuild the training school, which was never in the end completed.[87] Eleven Laotian police were sent to the International Police Academy in Washington. In December 1968, Dean Rusk approved shipment of projectiles and tear gas "of the burning type," designed to quell urban riots. Again we see the repressive character of the training programs.[88]

The OPS operated until it was disbanded in 1974, providing several million dollars to police training programs in its last years under the War on Drugs. The programs were especially valued for creating agent networks, leading to intelligence breakthroughs such as forewarning of Pathet Lao sapper attacks on munitions dumps.[89] After the Pathet Lao victory, many LNP migrated to the United States alongside the Hmong to escape retribution. American intervention had played a key role in triggering the civil war and fueling violence by training and equipping paramilitary units with advanced weapons and communications. A fixation with stamping out "communist" subversion trumped any commitment to human rights. The greatest tragedy was that opportunities for peaceful rapprochement were not pursued. Had the United States accepted the 1958 election results and a neutralist government that included the Pathet Lao, the conflict likely could have been avoided and many lives saved.

"Pollyana Approach to Subversion": Police Aid in Another Secret War

Police aid contributed to deepening violence in another "sideshow" to Vietnam: Cambodia.[90] In the mid-1950s, Byron Engle and Louise Page surveyed the country's internal security forces and oversaw the development of a $2 million per year program headed by "Jack" Monroe and Roy Carlson, a veteran of the Washington State Police who went on to the Congo, Jordan, and Haiti. Acknowledging that in Cambodia as in Laos crime was minimal, Engle and Page observed that the main aim of police training was to develop paramilitary units capable of "effectively combating communist infiltration." A nationalist tilting toward China and the nonaligned movement, Prince Norodom Sihanouk oscillated between acceptance and repression of the Maoist Khmer Rouge, earning the condemnation of 1290-d planners for his "pollyana approach to subversion" and "lack of guts" in confronting the "communist threat."[91] (By contrast, the U.S. client in South Vietnam, Ngo Dinh Diem, was praised for "actually doing something" about it.)

In August 1963, after Sihanouk agreed to jail Khmer Rouge leaders, the OPS provided $807,000 for construction of a Royal Police Academy and a photography and scientific crime lab and sent a half-dozen police officers to Washington for courses at the IPA.[92] Some funds were channeled to General Ne Win of Burma, considered later the "Asian Noriega," to repress the Burmese Communist Party and assorted ethnic minorities. Valuing the country for its tungsten, a CIA report spoke favorably of the ability of the police to establish village surveillance, noting "in [Burma's] Tenasserim district, almost totally dominated by communists, a police detachment arrested and brought out three communist leaders. . . . In guard patrol duty, police units are now in daily armed conflict with communist insurgents."[93]

In the mid-1960s, Sihanouk halted police aid after learning that the CIA was organizing commandos led by Son Ngoc Thanh to overthrow him. Several

OPS advisers were CIA agents, including Raymond Babineau, who trained Diem's secret police in South Vietnam.[94] In 1970, the police training program was resuscitated after Sihanouk was toppled in a coup d'état by Prime Minister Lon Nol, a hard-liner who spoke favorably about the anticommunist blood-bath in Indonesia and signed an oil exploration agreement with Unocal and Chevron.[95] Some of the training was conducted under the pretext of narcotics control, owing to Cambodia's importance as a supply route for opium. In May 1972, with USAID funding, President Sirik Matak established a narcotics enforcement unit headed by Van Houth, which inspected aircraft departing Pochtong airport in Phnom Penh, engineered high-profile raids on opium dens, and shut down clandestine heroin labs. The corruption of high-level officials, however, including Lon Nol's brother, Lon Non, who ran paramilitary training camps along the Lao border used for smuggling purposes, limited the unit's effectiveness.[96]

On the whole, American intervention in the "sideshows" of Vietnam bore a heavy cost, resulting in an exacerbation of local conflict and immeasurable human suffering. The secret war in Laos was characterized by *New York Times* reporter Anthony Lewis as the "most appalling episode of lawless cruelty in American history."[97] The police programs were one component of a larger strategy to funnel in arms and train counterinsurgent forces in the attempt to create a client regime. In the face of concerted resistance, democratic policing standards were thrust aside and training was heavily militarized, accounting for widespread human rights abuses. The primary legacy was the creation of rogue paramilitary organizations beholden to unscrupulous warlords, notably General Siho and Vang Pao, who used control over criminal rackets like Phao in Thailand to consolidate their power ruthlessly, which proved unsustainable over the long term.

E. L. Godkin, editor of *The Nation*, wrote on the eve of the Spanish-American-Philippines War that "an immense democracy, mostly ignorant, and completely secluded from foreign influence[,] . . . with great contempt for history and experience, finds itself in possession of enormous power and is eager to use it in brutal fashion against anyone who comes along, *without knowing how to do it,* and is therefore constantly on the brink of some frightful catastrophe."[98] His comment is apropos in relation to the police programs in Laos and elsewhere in Southeast Asia. Eager to advance its interests and roll back the spread of communism, the United States provided sophisticated weapons and technologies and trained paramilitary forces without a proper understanding of the local political dynamic. This in turn helped to unleash violent social forces beyond its control, which tore apart the societal fabric. Disregarding the human costs, American imperial strategists viewed covert policing operations as a success because they were cost-effective, there were few American casualties, and limited protest was aroused (as even committed antiwar activists knew little of what was going on). In the 1983 PBS television history of the Vietnam War, William Colby, CIA director from 1973 to 1976, praised the tenacity of the Hmong in holding out against the Pathet Lao for over ten years. Accordingly, the strategy of molding client armies and training paramilitary police units in psychological warfare became a model for subsequent foreign policies, with continued deleterious effects for almost everyone involved.[99]

Chapter 7

"As I Recall the Many Tortures"

Michigan State University, Operation Phoenix, and the Making of a Police State in South Vietnam

... the dreary wall of the Vietnamese Sureté that seemed to smell of urine and injustice.
—Graham Greene, *The Quiet American*, 1955

As I recall the many tortures they tried on me, I remember the perverse inhuman joy in their shouts.
—Vietnamese prison detainee, 1970

The whole thing was a lie. We weren't preserving freedom in South Vietnam. There was no freedom to preserve. Opposition to the government meant jail or death.
—Master Sergeant Donald Duncan, U.S. Army, 1966

On April 19, 1965, a seventeen-year-old suicide bomber walked into the Flower nightclub in Dalat, Vietnam, seeking to emulate "heroes" who had given their lives for the anti-imperialist cause, including Nguyen Van Troi, a legendary guerrilla executed after attempting to assassinate Secretary of Defense Robert S. McNamara and Ambassador Henry Cabot Lodge. The teenager detonated a bomb that killed thirteen people, including himself, and injured forty-two. In a brief suicide note he condemned the war and Vietnamese who collaborated with the United States. The greatest tragedy, he wrote, was that "U.S. imperialism had made Vietnamese kill Vietnamese."[1] The young suicide bomber may very well have had the American police training programs in mind in composing his final words. Following the model of previous operations in Japan and South Korea, advisers from Michigan State University and USAID trained thousands of South Vietnamese police in riot control and counterinsurgency, contributing to extensive human rights violations. In importing new technologies and Western policing standards, they felt that they were helping to create a modern administrative state capable of controlling its population efficiently and fighting communism. In practice, they modernized repression by providing the mechanisms with which state security forces could coordinate their activities more systematically and on a wider scale in the service of an authoritarian regime. Worst of all, as the suicide bomber recognized, American training programs helped to stoke civil conflict and violence and turned Vietnamese against one another, forever transforming the country.

University on the Make: The Military-Academic Complex and Consolidation of the Diem Dictatorship

In April 1966, the left-wing magazine *Ramparts* published an exposé on the training of South Vietnam's police by Michigan State University professors and infiltration of the program by the CIA. Illustrated by a cover featuring South Vietnam's first lady, Madame Nhu, as a buxom MSU cheerleader, the article chronicled the role of political scientist Wesley Fishel as a key adviser to Premier Ngo Dinh Diem, describing how he and tweed-jacketed colleagues had worked to build up a repressive police apparatus to liquidate the pro-communist Vietminh. The authors, Warren Hinckle, Robert Scheer, and Sol Stern, felt that Fishel and his associates had sacrificed their integrity as academics and epitomized the growth of a dangerous military-academic complex in which the brainpower and resources of America's major universities were being put in the service of U.S. imperial interests.[2]

Although MSU president John Hannah denounced the article as "grossly inaccurate," the police training programs were indeed a bulwark of American efforts to create a client regime below the Seventeenth Parallel after the temporary division of Vietnam under the 1954 Geneva Accords.[3] Regarding the accords as a "disaster," the Eisenhower administration refused to allow elections to reunify the country, knowing that Ho Chi Minh, who had led the liberation movement against France, would win. Bent on stamping out the "virus" of independent nationalism, which it feared would spread throughout Southeast Asia, the Eisenhower administration instead attempted to consolidate Diem's rule in the South. Diem had little popular backing and was described by his own advisers as "egotistical... neurotically suspicious, stubborn, self-righteous, and a complete stranger to compromise." According to the CIA, Diem was so dependent on American support, "he would have fallen in a day without it."[4]

A Catholic anticommunist who refused a position in Ho Chi Minh's cabinet after the August 1946 revolution because the Vietminh had killed his brother, Diem was championed by Congress, academia, and the Catholic Church as a "third force" alternative to communism and colonialism because he had not collaborated with France.[5] In May 1955 the State Department contracted with the MSU School of Police Administration at a budget of $25 million to provide technical assistance and training to the South Vietnamese police, with the aim of "facilitating law and order so as to create the conditions necessary for economic and social development and the enlargement of freedom and prosperity."[6] Much like their forerunners in the Philippines and Haiti, Fishel and his cohorts stressed the need for mass surveillance capable of monitoring subversion and dismantling the political opposition to Diem (including Binh Xuyen gangsters and the Hoa-Hao and Cao Dai religious sects). New technologies expanded the scale of violence associated with these efforts, overseen by Diem's brother, Ngo Dinh Nhu, an opium addict who, according to the British ambassador, attached "every bit as much importance to the apparatus of a police state as the most enthusiastic advocate of the social order of '1984.'"[7]

The contract with MSU was unique, though it presented limitations from the vantage point of the State Department "because of the sensitive security aspects of the program." A precedent had been established six years earlier when, at the behest of Arthur Brandstatter, a public safety consultant to U.S. High Commissioner John J. McCloy, the MSU School of Police Administration brought German police, including ex-Nazi soldiers, and South Koreans onto campus for an eight-week course and arranged for them to observe local law enforcement. Vietnam became a logical next undertaking, in part because of the close relationship Fishel had developed with Diem dating from their meeting in Japan in 1950.[8]Brandstatter, a Legion of Merit winner and former MSU football star, commented that the MSU group was the "only one who could have provided the technical skills. . . . We never found worse conditions. The country had been sold out to gangster hoodlums," meaning the Binh Xuyen gang, which controlled the police for a period under French puppet Bao Dai.[9]

Taking charge of most of the administrative details, Brandstatter appointed Howard W. Hoyt, the chief of police in Kalamazoo, Michigan, and a visiting MSU lecturer, as the first in-country director of the Vietnam project. A former director of police training at Purdue and the University of Minnesota, Hoyt had worked with Brandstatter as a police consultant in Germany and spent the first eleven years of his career in Wichita, Kansas, where he was mentored by Orlando W. Wilson, a leading advocate of police professionalization, who succeeded August Vollmer as dean of the Berkeley School of Criminal Justice.[10]

The Michigan State University Group (MSUG) trained the Vietnamese Bureau of Investigation (VBI or Cong An), an off-shoot of the French Sureté commanded by General Nguyen Ngoc Le, a twenty-year French army veteran. His successors Pham Xuan Chieu and Nguyen Van La, "a rank novice in police work," according to Hoyt, were also military men trained by the French.[11] Cultivating networks of informants, the VBI operated in plainclothes and functioned principally as a "political police" and "political repression organization." Its mission was to "correlate information regarding the security of the state, manage political information services," and "discover plots and activities capable of compromising public order."[12] In 2005, Ngo Vinh Long, a leading Vietnamese scholar, testified that he had worked undercover for the VBI as a "public health specialist" in malaria eradication in order to enter people's homes and search for information on their political affiliations.[13]

The 1290-d planning group emphasized the necessity of bolstering the "counter-subversion" capabilities of the police and their proficiency in intelligence and pacification against the Vietminh, who resettled in the South after the victory over the French at Dien Bien Phu and established shadow governments in the villages, extending "their influence to many who are not communist party members through a substantial network of front organizations covering all sectors of the population," according to the CIA, which warned that "internal security was at present poor" and there appeared to be "little capability of opposition to Vietminh efforts to further internal chaos and eventually complete takeover probably through democratic means of free elections. . . . The government's survival will be determined in large measure by the degree of protection foreign sources will provide in guaranteeing its future."[14]

These comments provide a striking acknowledgment of the weakness of Diem and his reliance on foreigners, and of the strength of the Vietminh, which was targeted for liquidation.[15] Most of the MSU advisers were retired beat cops, including Gil Shelby, a Detroit police inspector; Robert Gollings of the California Highway Patrol; and Charles Sloane, chief of police in Cortland, New York, and at the U.S. Naval Training Station. CIA agents operating under MSU cover, such as George Boudrias, a Canadian with investigative experience in Washington, and army veteran Raymond Babineau, worked with the counterespionage section of the VBI.[16]

Jack Ryan, who ran covert operations in Laos, the Congo, and Indonesia and who succeeded Hoyt as project director, told reporters, "You need to develop pros to combat terrorism directed by pros," in other words, the so-called Vietcong. He and Boudrias, who was close to General Le, established an information clearinghouse equipped with a polygraph and microfilm and organized an espionage and jungle warfare course at an old French army installation near Saigon. With John Manopoli, a twenty-two-year veteran of the New York State Police who had "red squad" experience, Ryan also inspected interrogation facilities and coordinated construction of a VBI detention center next to the Chi Hoa prison.[17]

Richard W. Rogers, police chief in Midland, Michigan, who later served with the 1290-d program in Liberia and Iran, and Everett Updike, a New York state trooper who developed a serious drinking problem and was accused of falsifying reports, provided weapons training to the paramilitary Civil Guard (Bao An Doan), which was modeled after the Philippines constabulary and focused on guarding fortified villages and "rooting out dissident elements." Headed by officers of the Army of the Republic of Vietnam (ARVN), the Guard was built up in explicit violation of the Geneva agreements, which limited the strength of the armed forces to 150,000. Morale was poor and desertion rates high (2,870 in August 1957 alone). According to the Pentagon Papers, the Guard's "brutal-ity, petty thievery, and disorderliness induced innumerable villagers to join in open revolt against the GVN [government of Vietnam]." Training was even-tually taken over by "Buck" Fruit and by Frank Walton of the USOM's Public Safety Division, whom Brandstatter praised as an "aggressive leader."[18]

In November 1955 MSUG inaugurated a national police academy in Saigon, which provided courses in patrol techniques, disarming criminals, handcuff-ing, fingerprinting, undercover surveillance, and firearms. Top graduates were sent for further training in East Lansing and at Camp Crame near Manila. Lan-guage and cultural barriers were formidable. Only Boudrias and Ryan spoke even French. Advisers found it difficult to teach through interpreters: "One could not always tell from looking at their faces if they 'got the message.'"[19]

Correspondence between Brandstatter and project directors included much discussion about the Michigan State football team (which Art Jr. played for) but little of substance on political developments or Vietnam's history and culture. Few second thoughts were given to the moral implications of the program. Hoyt, a prototypical "ugly American," was most enthusiastic about weekend hunting expeditions and a trip to Bangkok hosted by General Phao, where he and his wife stayed in a five-story house with six servants and were wined and dined.[20]

Interacting mainly with government or police officials, most of the advisers displayed at best a paternalistic and at worst a contemptuous attitude toward the Vietnamese. One report noted that on road trips, Verne Dagen, a thirty-year veteran of the Michigan State Police who worked with the Civil Guard, refused to pay for meals if they were not to his liking, causing "poor relations with natives."[21] Infighting among the MSUG group was a problem. Hoyt ver-bally abused some of the men, including Carl Rumpf, the former chief of police in Roseburg, Oregon, whom he chastised as a "250 pound man with the brain of a 12-year old." His abrasive manner boded ill for efforts to promote any kind of humane policing system and led to his being denied an academic appoint-ment which he coveted.[22]

One of the central tasks of MSUG was to develop a communications system and provide radio and telegraph equipment to connect rural headquarters to Saigon and other cities. A scandal erupted when MSU adviser Lyman Rundlett was found to have worked for Motorola, which received bidding contracts. MSUG supplied the VBI with over $10 million in jeeps, revolvers, handcuffs, tear gas weapons, projectiles, crystal microphones used for wiretapping, sub-machine guns, and hand grenades. Internal reports lamented that many police conducted investigations on bicycle, foot, or horse cart and used "antique weapons" and ammunition predating World War II, which sometimes failed to fire. In one instance, they lacked enough paper to file reports, and in Ninh Tuan, police had to transport prisoners on the public bus.[23]

Seeking to rectify these shortcomings, American advisers upgraded office facilities, centralized records, and established scientific crime labs equipped with modern fingerprint powders and forensic technology. Traffic engineers with the Michigan State Police painted parking lines and crosswalks in an attempt to relieve congestion on Saigon's streets. Cory Dymond, a criminal records and identification specialist with twenty-five years' experience in Michigan, taught the Henry classification system and improved the filing system (many files had become moldy from bad ventilation).[24] He was succeeded by Elmer H. Adkins Jr., an identification specialist with the Miami Beach Police Department and the FBI who later served in Saudi Arabia, the Congo, and the Dominican Republic, and Ralph Turner, a professor of criminalistics at MSU who oversaw a scientific laboratory on Saigon's Philipini Street, the VBI's records division, and an identity card system to monitor political activity.

Trained as a chemist at the University of Wisconsin, Turner was a world-renowned forensic scientist who appeared regularly as a witness in criminal cases; after the assassination of Robert Kennedy, he was selected to review the firearms evidence. Turner began his career in the 1930s as a laboratory supervisor for the Kansas City Police Department, where he developed the "drunkometer," a forerunner of modern-day breathalyzer tests for intoxication. A chain- smoker of cigars with a love of Sherlock Holmes novels, he once got money from the university to purchase ninety bottles of Kentucky bourbon for a study on the effects of alcohol. Turner's involvement with MSUG is one example of the efforts made to export cutting-edge scientific techniques in order to professionalize the GVN police and internal security services. Pointing to the project's failure, he commented years later, "We had no experience dealing with Far-Eastern governments . . . didn't know anything about their culture and couldn't deal with guerrilla warfare."[25]

For all the outrage over acts of "terrorism" by the "Vietcong" (or "VC," as the Americans called NLF cadres), MSUG reports show that for every VBI or province chief assassinated, at least six suspected "VC" were killed by state security forces and hundreds more arrested "for breeches of security" and "purely political violations." (Later the kill discrepancy would be far higher.)[26] Relatives of "dissidents" and politicians opposed to Diem were among those imprisoned, tortured, and sometimes executed by roving guillotine. With no apparent objection, one MSU professor interviewed a local police chief in his headquarters, where a twenty-year-old peasant lay "curled up, his feet in manacles, the left side of his face swollen, and his eye and cheek badly bruised."[27] In the summer of 1956, an MSU official parked across from VBI headquarters in Saigon witnessed an escaped prisoner being shot. A report stated that there was often not enough food to feed prisoners or cells to hold them and so they were "therefore eliminated after interrogation."[28]

Thousands died in the anticommunist campaign, which, according to Paul

Harwood, head of covert action in the CIA's Saigon station, was infused with a "totalitarian spirit." Diem's chief of staff Tran Van Don derided the "Gestapo-like police raids and torture." Jack Ryan wrote privately about the "heavy-handed tactics of police and military units, rigged courts, stacked elections . . . and the virtual extinction of a free and nationalist opposition." Joseph Starr of the State Department rationalized the abuses, saying, "We must remember that Vietnam is not a country of Anglo-Saxon tradition of personal liberty."[29]

In 1959 Diem passed a law allowing for the execution of opponents within three days of their arrest. This led to the formation of the National Liberation Front, an amalgamation of opposition groups bent on overthrowing his regime and expelling American advisers. Led by a Saigon lawyer, Nguyen Huu Tho, who was subjected to years of torture in Diem's gulag, the NLF derived pronounced support as a result of widespread grievances and its promotion of land reform and literacy campaigns. The CIA's official history acknowledged that villagers paid the NLF a rice tax without coercion. According to the journalist Joseph Buttinger, the organization enlisted people "willing to serve their country in the tens of thousands and extracted from them superhuman efforts and sacrifices in the struggle for independence." The government, meanwhile, attracted "officials with the lowest possible motivation for public service, the only ones fit to serve in a corrupt, inefficient, and despised police-state."[30]

By providing modern weapons and technical support to police and promoting political operations, MSUG was pivotal in contributing to the climate of repression that gave rise to the NLF. Brandstatter wrote to Turner in 1961 to say that he supported Diem's position regarding the role of the Civil Guard in "neutralizing VC activity" and had never agreed with the position that the Americans "should try to help develop a 'democratic police force' under conditions of instability and insurgency. . . . The responsibility for internal security belongs to the police."[31] These comments illustrate how a commitment to civil liberties and humane principles was subordinated to the goal of fighting communism and securing what were perceived as American strategic interests. The Vietnamese people suffered grievously as a result.

The Police in the Counterinsurgency Era: Public Safety Takes Over

As the war expanded, police training became even more central to American "pacification" efforts and contributed to the torture and killing of thousands of revolutionary fighters and civilians. In 1962, as napalm and bombing attacks were launched, the OPS took over from MSUG. A few advisers stayed on. The Kennedy administration viewed Vietnam as a laboratory for new counterinsurgency strategies and valued the police as a substitute for the Vietnamese army, which, Robert H. Johnson of the State Department wrote to Walt W. Rostow, "steals, rapes, and treats the population in a very callous fashion. . . . There are

signs across the countryside: 'why does the government shoot our people.'"
It was hoped that with American training, the police would better ingratiate
themselves with the public through participation in civic action while providing effective security alongside CIA-trained militias. Furthermore, as Jeter
Williamson, head of police training in Danang during the late 1960s and early
1970s, noted, "one or two policemen in each village could get far more intelligence and information than an entire [army] battalion."[32]

From 1962 to 1975, working with several British veterans of the Malayan
campaign, the OPS provided over three hundred advisers and $300 million
(including $26.9 million in 1966 alone) in the attempt to dismantle the NLF.
Police were expanded from 16,000 men to over 122,000. The State Department
funded eight training schools and built five hundred rural police stations and
high-tech urban headquarters equipped with firearms ranges, IBM computers,
and padded interrogation rooms.[33] It outfitted the police with gray and white
uniforms (earning them the nickname "the white mice"); furnished shotguns,
grenades, and radios; and expanded training in explosives and psychological warfare.[34] Police chiefs received two thousand piasters (roughly $25) per
month to pay for information.

Performing duties that would be subcontracted to mercenaries in later wars,
the OPS developed "Tiger Battalions" to escort key government officials and
provide security on American installations. They also mobilized police to protect the Michelin rubber plantation from sabotage and to control labor unrest
against contractors such as the Morrison Knudsen Corporation, which undertook massive infrastructural development and engineering projects reliant on
cheap Vietnamese labor.[35] Police were instructed in modern crowd control
techniques to help quell civil disturbances, which grew in scope as South Vietnamese cities became flooded with refugees from carpet-bombing attacks.[36]

Field reports describe the role of the police in crushing student and Buddhist
protests and demonstrations by disabled veterans against the GVN.[37] In May
1963, as opposition to Diem's rule intensified, police killed nine monks, three
women, and two children at a rally against religious persecution and government violence. In July, according to OPS adviser Ray Landgren, in spite of the
"amazing results" yielded by riot control courses, police displayed "unnecessary
brutality" in suppressing a peaceful Buddhist rally against repeated injustices,
beating monks and other civilians. They then arrested them and herded them
into trucks, which backed into the crowd, running several people over. Police
later scuffled with newsmen trying to report the events.[38] Buddhists responded
by engaging in self-immolation, bringing international attention to their plight
and the crisis enveloping the country.[39]

After Diem was assassinated in November 1963 in a CIA-backed coup, the
OPS tried to rebuild the police intelligence apparatus and reinvigorate counterinsurgency efforts. The director-general of the National Police, Tran Thanh

Ben, was later implicated in an abortive coup against Nguyen Khanh, one of Diem's successors, whose inner circle was "preoccupied with personal vendettas and slander campaigns." The NLF widely infiltrated the government apparatus and controlled much of the countryside. (One report stated that all rural areas were considered "problem areas because none are secure." Once an area was cleared, "the VC just moved in again.")[40]

Working with paid agents and defectors, whose recruitment was often contingent on the fear of being turned over to police, constabulary units launched search and cordons operations, night ambushes, and helicopter missions in adopting what chief adviser Robert Komer termed "an operational and intelligence role against the VC apparatus." William "Pappy" Grieves, head of the Military Assistance Advisory Group (MAAG) in Greece in the mid-1950s who trained the paramilitary National Police Field Force, told reporters that in Vietnam, "in order to walk a beat . . . you had to use military tactics and techniques and formations just for the policeman to survive. . . . So you walk a beat by squads and platoons."[41]

Much as in Laos and Korea, the militarization of U.S. police training spawned high levels of abuse. CIA station chief Douglas Blaufarb rationalized that "it was futile to have expected in the circumstances a punctilious regard in all cases for the niceties of the civil rights of suspected insurgents."[42] John Manopoli and several associates worked with chief of police Nguyen Ngoc Loan, who gained notoriety after being photographed shooting an NLF prisoner in the head. Trained at the French Saint-Cyr military academy, he was the power broker for Vice Premier Nguyen Cao Ky, a Hitler admirer previously removed from a CIA mission for smuggling drugs. An OPS report pointed to Loan's "contempt for individual legal rights" after he had a member of the Constituent Assembly assassinated to break a legislative logjam. Four-star general William Corson wrote in *The Betrayal* that "Loan's National Police methods to enforce the 'laws' make Himmler's Gestapo look like the board of overseers in a Quaker church."[43] Loan epitomized the danger of the police programs in empowering warlords of unsavory character. The Americans put up with his excesses, as they had with "Tiger Kim" in South Korea and Generals Siho and Phao in Laos and Thailand, because he was seen as effective in combating "communist terrorists" and because he was in large part a creation of the United States and the formidable policing apparatus it had built.

"Arresting Anyone under the Suspicion of Being Left-Wing": Agents of Social Control

Seeking to maximize social control in the face of mounting popular resistance, the OPS expanded the identity card program initiated by MSUG and developed a Family Census Program, which enabled police to amass a set of fingerprints, housing information, and data on the political beliefs of nearly 12 million people.[44] Once dissidents were identified, the police undertook village sweeps, usually late at night to catch suspects off guard, "arresting anyone under the remotest suspicion of being left-wing," as one witness put it. "The government has a blacklist of suspects, but I understand that wives, mothers and fathers—anyone with the slimmest association with those on it are being caught in the net."[45] Many of those taken in were peace activists, members of the Cao Dai and Hoa Hao religious sects, students, or politicians. They were easier to apprehend than NLF cadres, who amassed the resources to fight back and sabotaged the identity card program through counterfeiting and by seizing hundreds of thousands of cards.[46] (Moore Business Forms of Green Bay, Wisconsin, subsequently collaborated with the OPS in developing "the Cadillac" of identity cards, which was tamper proof.)

As part of its resource control mandate, the OPS established over 650 police checkpoints to monitor movement and intercept guerrilla supplies. It created a riverboat patrol squad on the Mekong Delta armed with assault rifles, which the NLF got around by using rafts capable of going through rapids that the police boats could not handle.[47] From 1965 to 1969, police confiscated over 22 million kilos of contraband, including foodstuffs, medicine, firearms, and ammunition, and claimed to have detained 458,000 NLF collaborators. Many of those arrested were draft dodgers and ARVN deserters.[48] OPS reports noted that police often stayed by the side of the road to avoid the hot sun and accepted bribes and extorted money from passersby to augment their meager salaries. In one incident in Cu Chi, police searched passengers on a bus twice and forced them to wait for hours on the roadside for little apparent reason. Because it eroded the government's legitimacy, the OPS tried to curtail such practices through instruction in public relations, but without much effect.[49]

Testifying to a lack of cohesion within the GVN, fights broke out between the police and ARVN officers, who committed many crimes, including indiscriminate firing of weapons, smuggling, robbery, stabbings, and running people over with trucks. American troops were little better in their conduct, as police reports reveal, and in one instance shot a member of the national police over cab fare. In a sign of the destructiveness of the war, U.S. jets mistakenly bombed several police headquarters, including in Ban Hai, killing twenty-two officers, and outside Hué, where a former police commander and his pregnant wife and three children were killed.[50]

Between 1967 and 1971, as a result of concerns about drug addiction among American soldiers, the OPS provided over 1,200 police with an eighty-hour course in narcotics enforcement and established a narcotics bureau equipped with boats offshore. Former IPA director Michael McCann ran the $2 million program, which resulted in a 70 percent increase in arrest rates as well as considerable violations of civil liberties.[51] Corruption was pervasive among customs agents, police, prison wardens, and even the head of the narcotics bureau. The *New York Times* tellingly referred to Tan Son Nhut airport as a "drug smugglers' paradise."[52]

As with broader modernization programs, local noncooperation with and resistance to American drug policies were exacerbated by the attempt to impose Western societal standards that were not universal. The massive dislocation bred by the war and the profitability of the black-market economy amidst an influx of luxury goods, as well as low morale and poor pay and recruitment standards, lay at the root of the "legendary" corruption of police, who stole refugee relief supplies, shook down businessmen and farmers, intimidated voters in staged elections, and demanded sex from peasant girls and prostitutes. (One girl was told the way to avoid trouble was to take a police officer as her lover.)[53] A village chief commented, "The police 'protect' the populace the same way that gangsters 'protected' businesses from which they wanted to squeeze a profit."[54]

The enormous scope of police corruption is illuminated in the OPS bureaucratic files at the National Archives. After the press became filled with sensational articles and Alfred W. McCoy published a comprehensive exposé, American officials pressed the GVN to crack down on the problem, though with limited follow-through. The police in concert with local mayors controlled gambling as well as opium dens and brothels which sprang up to service Americans, notably in the resort town of Vung Tau.[55] Because of the pilfering of construction materials, conditions in police precincts and jails were described as "miserable" and "close to barbaric." Police positions were regularly sold, usually for one-third of the graft value of the job. In Quang Tri, police chiefs were charged with selling heroin. They made detainees perform manual labor in their homes for days without sleep as a precondition for release, forcing them to build mansions for their concubines using stolen government construction material and lumber.[56]

The historian Gabriel Kolko provides among the best explanations for the source of corruption and brutality, writing, "The functions, actions, and values of officers and soldiers are the inevitable consequence of the kinds of society they are seeking to create or defend." For Vietnamese, OPS advisers represented foreign coercion and were therefore the target of guerrilla attacks, with the NLF emerging as "heroes" for blowing up police precincts and shelling correctional centers, thus "protecting the people from police abuses."[57]Dolph Owens was the first U.S. adviser to be killed, when his convoy was ambushed en route to the Counter-Guerrilla Training Academy at Cat Lo on November 5, 1960. During the 1968 Tet offensive, where they played a key role in suppressing the joint uprising of the NLF and the North Vietnamese army, field police sustained over three thousand casualties and one thousand deaths. Three U.S. advisers also died. At least twenty-five advisers to the police training program lost their lives during the course of the war, including firearms expert Norman Clowers of the MSU program and Detroit policeman Charlie O'Brien, who had also served in Turkey and Liberia.[58] Rather than fostering order and stability, the training programs fueled internecine hatred and violence and the escalation of conflict.

Quantity of "Neutralizations" High but Quality Low: The Phoenix Program

American-trained police contributed to some of the worst atrocities in Vietnam under the Phoenix program, which was formally inaugurated after the 1968 Tet offensive in response to the failure of police and intelligence agents to warn of the movement of revolutionary forces into Saigon. The central aim of Phoenix was to eliminate the "Vietcong" infrastructure (VCI) through the use of sophisticated computer technology and intelligence-gathering techniques, and improved coordination between military and police intelligence agencies.

Named after a mythical all-seeing bird that selectively snatches its prey, Phoenix had its roots in the Diemist anticommunist campaign overseen by MSUG. The program employed methods such as the use of wanted posters, blacklists, and disguises. Third-country nationals were used for the dirtiest tasks, including South Korean and Filipino mercenaries willing, in the words of one CIA officer, to "slit their grandmother's throat for a dollar eighty-five."[59] Phoenix was headed on the Vietnamese side by General Tran Thien Khiem, Loan's successor, who made a fortune in the narcotics trade. He was loyal to Nguyen Van Thieu, who had ousted Nguyen Cao Ky in a power struggle, centered in part on control of the $88 million heroin trade.[60]

In November 1967, Frank Armbruster of the Hudson Institute drafted a policy brief which provided a blueprint for Phoenix. Written in cold, antiseptic language, the report included a favorable reference to a RAND Corporation study by Chong Sik-Lee on Japanese counterinsurgency during World War II and the U.S.-led anti-Huk campaigns in the Philippines. Armbruster argued that current police operations were too lenient and too poorly organized to succeed at infiltrating the VC apparatus, which had established shadow governments in villages and towns to rival the GVN.

In his view, the police should perform a similar function to the military in depleting enemy forces and weeding out the guerrilla infrastructure through effective intelligence collection, roundups, and interrogations, allowing for a systematic classification of enemy operatives. Photography, ID cards, and fingerprinting, as well as paid informants, were crucial to the identification of VC cadres, who blended easily into the civilian population. Defectors were needed to ensure the success of bounty hunter operations. Effective counterinsurgents were best recruited from among the native population because they knew the terrain. Once identified, he believed, hard-core VC should be isolated and never allowed to return to their communities, or else they should be executed outright. The rest of those detained could be won over through political indoctrination built around a counter-ideology.[61]

Armbruster's essay reflects the embrace of terrorist methods by American counterinsurgency specialists who conceived of Phoenix as a clinically managed operation capable of dismantling the VCI. Unlike military actions resulting in the decimation of the countryside, Phoenix, if carried out correctly, could minimize "collateral damage." The United States could further claim plausible deniability because of the reliance on local Provincial Reconnaissance Units (PRU), or hunter-killer teams, as with the massacres in Indonesia following the 1965 coup.[62]

In practice, Phoenix was anything but methodical and precise in its application of violence, eroding any semblance of government legitimacy. Theodore Shackley, CIA station chief in the late 1960s, wrote in his memoir that CIA officers "found the activity repugnant. They felt that the dossiers were based on dubious information. . . . All too frequently, arrest efforts turned into firefights and more so-called VC were killed than detained for processing."[63] Though initial communications glowed with optimism, claiming that Phoenix was contributing to the "rounding up of large terrorist nets," Thieu used the program to eliminate political rivals, including the noncommunist opposition. Some targets were selected by the NLF, which widely penetrated the state security apparatus. Field reports pointed to the corruption of PRU cadres who used their positions for revenge and extortion, threatening to kill people and count them as VC if they did not pay them huge sums. Atrocities were committed by "VC avenger units" prone to rape, pillage, and mutilation.[64]

While the quantity of "neutralizations" was reported to be high in many districts, the quality was "poor."[65] Public Safety adviser Charles N. Phillips lamented the large number of "phantom kills," which could hamper good "Phung Hoang" ("Phoenix program" in Vietnamese) statistics. There were also "flagrant" cases of report padding, most egregiously in Long An province, where CIA operative Evan Parker Jr. reported that "the numbers just don't add up." Dead bodies were being identified as VC, rightly or wrongly, in the attempt to at least approach an unrealistic quota. The catalogue of agents listed as killed included an inordinate number of "nurses," a convenient way to account for women killed in raids on suspected VC hideouts. PRU disguised as "Vietcong" engaged in search operations in which air support and defoliation were called in to wipe out villages. They also assassinated people in their sleep using silencers on their weapons. A CIA agent commented that when he arrived in his district, he was given a list of 200 people who were to be killed; six months later 260 had been killed—but none of those on the list.[66]

A 1971 Pentagon study found that only 3 percent of "Vietcong" killed, captured, or rallied were full or probationary party members above the district level. Public safety advisers complained that the police Special Branch lacked the "motivation and expertise to properly target actual VCI members," that local village chiefs only paid "lip service" to the program, and that police facilities and equipment remained inadequate.[67] Ralph McGehee, CIA chief in Gia Dinh province, who was nearly driven to commit suicide from guilt, stated in his memoirs that "never in the history of our work in Vietnam did we get one clear-cut, high-ranking Vietcong agent."[68] A key reason for the failure of Phoenix was the wide popular backing for the NLF and fact that PRU were recruited from among unsavory elements. A Phoenix operative noted that they were "a combination of ARVN deserters, VC turncoats, and bad motherfucker criminals the South Vietnamese couldn't deal with in prison, so they turned them over to us. Some actually had an incentive plan: If they killed X number of Commies, they got X number of years off their prison term."[69]

In one well-publicized case, a detainee was kept in an air-conditioned room for four years to exploit his fear of the cold. He was later thrown from a helicopter into the South China Sea from ten thousand feet.[70] Military intelligence specialist K. Barton Osborn told Congress that he had witnessed prisoners being starved or thrown out of helicopters; one woman was prodded in the brain with a six-inch dowel through her ear until she died. In his year and a half with Phoenix, he did not see "a single suspect survive interrogation."[71]Despite later attempts by conservatives to discredit Osborn's character, CIA director William Colby, a graduate of Princeton and Columbia Law School, conceded that much of what Osborn said was likely true.[72] In testimony before Congress, Colby admitted that Phoenix (which he defined as an "attempt to identify the structure of the communist party and go out and capture or shoot them") had led to "unjustifiable abuses" and the death of over twenty thousand people. The GVN placed the total at over forty thousand, and many historians believe even that to be an underestimation. A Phoenix operative who served in Czechoslovakia during World War II commented, "The reports I sent in from my province on the number of communists that were neutralized reminded me of the reports Hitler's concentration camp commanders sent in on how many inmates they had exterminated, each commander lying that he had killed more than the others to please Himmler."[73]

Phoenix epitomizes the way American police training programs have helped facilitate state repression and terror under the rubric of internal security and modernization. The attempt at social control through imposition of an Orwellian regime of mass surveillance and torture led inevitably to humanitarian abuses. In principle, the suppression campaigns were designed to be surgically precise, allowing for a methodical dismantling of the VCI and preservation of village security. Failing to live up to these aims, Phoenix only added to the climate of terror experienced by the Vietnamese.[74]

"The Rats Are as Large as Cats": The OPS and the South Vietnamese Penal Order

The brutal effects of the Phoenix program were compounded by the draconian character of South Vietnam's penal system. Neglected by MSUG, the OPS was given the task of administering and modernizing the prisons, which were seen as venues for winning political converts through reeducation. The State Department sent advisers to improve sanitation, instill a disciplined regimen, and oversee vocational training, reading, and recreation as well as work assignment and release programs, modeled after progressive reforms. A correctional academy was established in Saigon for training guards.

Many of the advisers had experience as correctional officers in American prisons, cauldrons of racial violence and rebellion.[75] The harsh environment carried over into Vietnam, where the political context undercut the reform process further. Owing to massive overcrowding, conditions in most prisons according to OPS surveys were "nightmarish," "appalling," and akin to "hell on earth." Much as in the prisons of the colonial Philippines, garbage was scattered across the floor, and inmates suffered from malnutrition, diarrhea, and diseases such as beriberi caused by a lack of proper sanitation and diet. Ill-maintained kitchen facilities were infested with vermin and flies. One report noted that food was prepared on "primitive stoves" and "cleanliness was unheard of."[76]

Among other indignities, prisoners were forced to use a "honey bucket" as a toilet. Often the only bathing facilities were outdoor wells. CIA agent Orrin DeForest wrote in his memoirs that in one hundred–degree heat, the cells "stank of urine, feces, and the odor of unwashed bodies." Ventilation was poor, and prisoners were deprived of medicine and doctors. Rooms were so overcrowded that prisoners had to sleep standing up or in shifts, and so overrun by cockroaches and rats as to leave observers with the impression that inmates were raising pets.[77] At Kien Tuong provincial prison, just ten kilometers from the seat of government, OPS staffer William C. Benson reported in February 1962 that the cells were "extremely dirty and the stench so nauseating" that it made him sick. Four years later another staffer, Elmer H. Crain, expressed concern about the radicalizing potential of the Binh Duong provincial prison, where most of the prisoners had skin conditions ranging from red sores to large cysts because of a lack of soap with which to bathe and minimal access to medical care.[78]

As under the French occupation, torture of every imaginable technique was widely reported, including sexual abuse. American advisers instructed their protégés in sophisticated psychological methods based on CIA-funded mind-control experiments designed to emphasize the prisoners' helplessness and dependence on their captors.[79] One public safety report acknowledged that there were "sadistic people in authority" who sometimes "beat prisoners to death." A Vietnamese woman recalled: "When you were being interrogated, you could hear the screams of people being tortured. There was a popular saying among the police—*kong danh do co*—If they are innocent, beat them until they become guilty."[80] A Mennonite volunteer told the *Washington Post* that prisoners faced "electroshocks, beatings with pins, water torture and burnings with cigarettes. . . . Of the prisoners I talked with, none had ever had a trial and many had never had a hearing and none knew how long their sentence was."[81]

Forbidden to sing or talk loudly, prisoners were forced to work long hours making uniforms for the ARVN or were employed on labor projects under the surveillance of armed guards. Don Bordenkircher, an OPS adviser who had served as a correctional officer at San Quentin penitentiary in California, stated in his memoirs that inmates remanded to work duty received little or no pay. They were also given courses—or "brainwashed," as OPS personnel conceded—in anticommunist ideology.[82] "Hard-headed inmates" and "communist criminals," as the most recalcitrant were called, faced restrictions on exercise and the right to visitors. They were thrown into solitary confinement for infractions as basic as refusing to salute the GVN flag and were handcuffed permanently, "bolted to the floor," or immobilized by "leg irons," which many advisers claimed was necessary to prevent rioting and escape.[83]

In spite of administrative declarations of improvement, prison conditions only worsened over time. A September 1966 public safety report for Cu Chi district, Hau Nghia Province lamented that since the appearance of the Twenty-fifth Infantry Division, the "influx of VC prisoners has mushroomed out of proportion to the provincial ability to handle them. The problem has been dumped on the national police who are not equipped or trained to handle what amounts to a prisoner of war camp." The report added, "We have 570 prisoners packed into facilities that were overflowing when they had only 120 prisoners. It is an explosive situation that needs immediate attention."[84] Another prisoner surge occurred following the 1968 Tet offensive and again with the growth of the Phoenix program, resulting in serious food shortages and a "lack of adequate confinement space for captured prisoners."[85] Many facilities were operating at seven or eight times capacity. The South Vietnamese Committee to Reform the Prisons calculated that by the early 1970s the system harbored 202,000 political prisoners—six times the number Amnesty International estimated were held in the Soviet Union, East Germany, South Africa, and a half-dozen other authoritarian states combined.[86]

Although this figure is hard to corroborate, American officials conceded that upwards of 70 percent of inmates were political prisoners detained under the An Tri or national security laws outlawing dissent.[87] The lack of legal representation and the shortage of lawyers made efforts to promote due process impossible. The parole system was stymied because many prisoners remained unclassified. Secret reports disclosed that at most three out of ten inmates had access to a trial. When they did take place, legal proceedings were held in closed quarters by the military. Bail was rarely granted. Chief jailers estimated that 61 percent of detainees were innocent.[88]

After a tour of the prison in Chau Doc in November 1968, Bordenkircher, who joined the Foreign Service to avoid sending his kids to school in California with "flower children," noted to his boss Randolph Berkeley that of the 457 prisoners, only twenty-seven had been sentenced and that eleven children under the age of eighteen were currently detained. In Kien Hoa, 606 out of 764 inmates, including twenty-eight children, were being held without trial, while at Phan Ding the total was 2,550 prisoners out of 2,903 in a facility intended for only 440. Inmates had to bathe in shifts and began cooking supper at 4 a.m. to make up for the overcrowding.[89] Public safety officials like Bordenkircher, who three decades later would be appointed to head the Abu Ghraib prison in Iraq, found the situation reprehensible but were powerless to change it. The goal of promoting a tightly disciplined and efficiently managed penal system was impossible in the war climate.

On a November 1968 inspection tour, Bordenkircher found that provincial prisons lacked basic hygiene and were so congested that some prisoners had to sleep in flimsy tents on prison grounds. He commented irately to his superiors that "political reeducation cannot occur until you enable a man to sleep away from his own urine and feces, give him wholesome food and the opportunity for rehabilitation."[90] In Bac Lieu, Bordenkircher recommended the replacement of the entire facility. He observed that prisoners were forced to urinate in jars and that sewage ran loose, even into the parking lot of the Military Assistance Command compound across the street. In Phang Dinh, the overflow of inmates resulted in a water shortage. The latrines were emptied into two ditches and a pond in which prisoners were forced to bathe, and drained into a canal where extra drinking water was obtained. Disease, not surprisingly, ran rampant. The standards in An Xuyen were even more dreadful. Bordenkircher reported that the kitchen was a "shed with four stoves that was also used as a trash dump." The sewage system was broken, and the kitchen was surrounded by "grimy sewage that promotes a very offensive smell throughout the center." The kitchen floor was dirt, and the floor space was shared by the center's animals. "The rats in the kitchen," he proclaimed, "are as large as cats."[91]

These comments provide a vivid indication of the moral decay bred by the U.S. intervention in Vietnam and illustrate how basic standards of human decency break down in war. Between 1967 and 1973, the State Department spent at least $6.5 million for the maintenance and renovation of the forty-two main prisons run by the GVN and built three additional facilities as well as a juvenile reformatory at Dalat. It provided generators and handcuffs, built special isolation cells for hardcore "Vietcong," and oversaw the construction of over thirty state-of-the-art detention centers. Typical of the widespread corruption, many of the supplies were resold on the black market by local authorities, usually cronies of Ky or Thieu, or kept until wardens paid a bribe. William Colby wrote to the director of the agency responsible for pacification that commodities and money destined for correctional centers were "held in Saigon until local authorities were presented with gifts or proper wining and dining." Nguyen Van Thuc, deputy chief jailer of the Kien Phong correctional center, reported that he had had to take "the right people" out to a twenty thousand–piaster ($250) meal and provide them with whiskey and cash gifts to secure access to a generator. Other wardens had to pay two thousand piasters for the use of a forklift and three thousand for a dump truck.[92] No wonder most of the renovations were never completed.

The International Red Cross discovered inmates suffering from scabies and other diseases, as well as food and water shortages, overcrowded and decaying facilities, drinking water contaminated by excrement from the latrines, shackling of prisoners, and the "roughing up" of women in interrogation.[93] OPS advisers described the living conditions of prison staff in at least one institution as being three times worse than those of the inmates. The lack of oversight by chief jailers, who predominantly came from military backgrounds and owed their positions to political favoritism, was another factor accounting for the high level of brutality, as was the internecine hatred engendered by the war and often whipped up by the United States.[94]

Racism and the perceived inferiority of Asians provided a rationalization for human rights violations. OPS reports noted that for cultural reasons, "acceptable standards for prison habitation were far lower in South Vietnam than in the U.S.," and so the conditions were acceptable.[95] Randolph Berkeley, who referred to the South Vietnamese as "babes in the woods" when it came to appreciating the threat posed by the VC, wrote to Ambassador William Colby in September 1971 that the atmosphere was actually "far more relaxed than in American penal institutions. . . . No prison in Vietnam has become a disaster such as San Quentin or Attica."[96] These comments reveal the value placed on social control rather than human rights as a marker of success, both in Vietnam and in the United States. Contrary to Berkeley's depiction, OPS staff conceded that because of arbitrary detention and the degrading treatment of women, the prisons were considered the "Vietnamese equivalent of Dachau and Belsen." General William Corson compared them to Buchenwald, minus the gas chambers.[97]

After a tour of penal facilities in the Mekong Delta, U.S. adviser John Paul Vann commented, "I got the distinct impression that any detainees not previously VC or VC sympathizers would almost assuredly become so after their period of incarceration."[98] Rather than submit to authority, inmates found community in mutual suffering and stiffened their resistance. In an ode to freedom fighters subjected to torture, one incarcerated woman wrote, "But if there were none like you, to bear the suffering to ask for independence, to demand the Vietnamese's right to live a human life, how much longer would our people have to suffer?" Another woman, Nguyen Thi Man, imprisoned at sixteen while helping to care for war orphans, wrote to a friend: "Even if I must die in prison in the end it will be worthwhile. All human beings must die once. But if we have the chance to die for an ideal, I think that we would all choose this kind of death."[99]

In spite of all the publicity it later commanded, the torture in North Vietnam did not approach the scale undertaken by American-backed forces in the South. The office of the army chief of staff acknowledged in 1969 the adoption by the South Vietnamese of "cruel, sophisticated, calculated torture for information," which rendered "hypocritical the pious statements about the treatment of POWs by the President." The *Far Eastern Review* pointed out that "U.S. POW's who talked of oriental torture were all able to stand up and speak into microphones, showing scars here and there, whereas those released from U.S. run jails in Saigon were all incurably crippled. Prolonged malnutrition had turned them into grotesque parodies of humanity."[100]

Some of the worst abuses occurred in Con Son prison, located on an archipelago 180 kilometers off the southern Vietnamese coast, where hardcore "communist criminals" were sent. Prisoner Thep Xanh wrote of his experience: "Deep in my heart I remember nights at Con Son, the echo of the creaking door, the beatings, the crying out at midnight, the shouting of guards, you ask me where is hell; where on earth people cannot live as human beings, where people with heart and soul live like beasts."[101] Con Son, which had been founded as a penal colony by the French in 1862, was plagued, according to the historian Peter Zinoman, by extremely high rates of malaria, cholera, beriberi, and dysentery; physical brutality was rampant, and annual mortality rates ran as high as 13 percent.[102] The conditions during the American war were little better. Inmates reported being worked nearly to death in the fields, severely beaten by trusties, and left on the verge of starvation. Many resorted to quenching their thirst by drinking their own urine.[103]

A December 1969 Red Cross inspection highlighted inadequate sanitary conditions and medical care and found that there had been ten recent escape attempts and a mutiny crushed by Grieves's police field force.[104] In 1970, after veering from the itinerary during a congressional tour, International Voluntary Service employee Don Luce found detainees crammed into six-foot windowless pits, or "tiger cages," where they were forced to subsist on three handfuls of milled white rice and three swallows of water per day. Guards would throw lime into their faces, causing lung disease and tuberculosis. Frank Walton, director of public safety in Vietnam from 1959 to 1961 and 1969 to 1971, sanctioned a report stating that uncooperative prisoners, whom he referred to as "reds who keep preaching the commie line," were "isolated in their cells for months" and "bolted to the floor or handcuffed to leg-irons."[105] Dr. John Champlin of the air force testified before Congress that he had observed paralysis on a large scale, resulting from "severe nutritional deficiency coupled with prolonged immobilization… unique in the history of modern warfare. . . . A computer review of 1200 medical journals and a personal search through medical literature on the health of POW's produced *no* similar descriptions."[106]

Time magazine reported that having been forced into a permanent pretzel-like crouch, tiger cage survivors resembled "grotesque sculptures of scarred flesh and gnarled limbs. . . . They move like crabs, skittering across the floor on buttocks and palms." In a bid to deflect negative publicity, the Department of the Navy gave Morrison Knudson a $400,000 contract to build 384 new isolation cells, dubbed "cow cages" because of their proximity to a cattle-feeding shed. From the available evidence, the conditions appear to have been little better and, as the name suggests, more fit for animals.[107]

On the whole, conditions in South Vietnam's prisons exemplify the violent consequences of the American invasion. Prisoners' diaries and writings provide a testament to the hardship that inmates endured and to the triumph of the human will in the face of state atrocities. Nguyen Lac Le, arrested in November 1968 with his wife, two sisters, and a brother, wrote, "Prison is a place, where we train our wills, it is a battle field, where we need no weapons, our hearts are made of steel which beat down the betrayer, our blood is of bronze, the blood we shed today, will make tomorrow bright."[108] Le's comments demonstrate the dedication of the Vietnamese revolutionaries and the role of the prison in stiffening the spirit of resistance (as under the French occupation). This, more than anything else, contributed to the outcome of the war.

In the 1979 Academy Award–winning film *The Deer Hunter*, the character played by Robert DeNiro and two platoon-mates are tortured in a makeshift POW camp. Submerged underwater, they are subjected to the "water cure" and forced to play Russian roulette before the DeNiro character engineers a miraculous escape. A host of subsequent B-grade movies focused ad nauseam on the plight of American POWs, entirely ignoring the context in which they were detained and the predicament of Vietnamese prisoners. Marred by an underlying racist "Red Peril" subtext, they concealed the dreadful consequences of American police training, prison construction programs, and Phoenix death squad operations, which were suppressed in the public consciousness.[109]

In 1973 Senator Alan Cranston, a California Democrat, told *Time* that USAID had bolstered "a cruel and repressive police apparatus in South Vietnam. A vast surveillance system is in effect, aided by United States communications equipment and personnel. Police torture and inhuman jail conditions, including the notorious tiger cages, await those who criticize the government's policies. That the American taxpayer should subsidize torture is an outrage."[110] Within a generation, this reality had been largely forgotten in the mainstream. Reinforcing the Hollywood revisionism, President Jimmy Carter declared in 1977, "We owe Hanoi no debt because the destruction from the war was mutual."[111] Ronald Reagan went further in asserting, "Ours was in truth a noble cause." By evading responsibility for the atrocities, both leaders helped to pave the way for a revival of American militarism, including the adoption of Phoenix-style operations and torture on a broad scale in Central America and later Iraq. The cycle of imperial manipulation and violence that the seventeen-year-old suicide bomber at the Dalat nightclub warned about would thus continue through the ensuing decades.[112]

Part

The Cold War on the Periphery
Police Training and the Hunt for Subversives in Africa, Latin America, and the Middle East

There are two governments in the United States today. One is visible. The other is invisible. The first is the government that citizens read about in their newspapers and children study about in their civics class. The second is the interlocking, hidden machinery that carries out the policies of the United States in the Cold War. The second invisible government gathers intelligence, conducts espionage, and plans and executes secret operations all over the globe.
—DAVID WISE and THOMAS B. ROSS, *The Invisible Government*, 1964

In 1974, CIA operative Philip Agee published an exposé, Inside the Company, *which rocked the American foreign policy establishment. The book detailed Agee's role in funneling money to centrist, anticommunist candidates in Ecuador and Uruguay, in infiltrating labor unions, and in collaborating with the military and secret police through USAID's Public Safety Division to gain information on leftist groups and contribute to their dismantling. Agee concluded: "American capitalism, based on its exploitation of the poor, with its fundamental motivation in personal greed, cannot survive without force—a secret police force. . . . Now more than ever, exposure of CIA methods could help American people understand how we got into Vietnam and how our other Vietnams are germinating wherever the CIA is at work."[1]*

In Agee's view, the Cold War provided an important pretext for the United States to expand its hegemony, as the "threat" of communism could be invoked to drum up support for intervention. The methods he outlined were employed worldwide, with police training serving as a key means of projecting American power. Staffed by true believers in the American mission, the OPS and its predecessors worked to penetrate and professionalize the internal security apparatus of client regimes as far afield as Africa and the Middle East. CIA agents used the programs to establish police and intelligence liaisons and contributed to the development of mass surveillance states known for terrorizing their own citizens.

After a visit to the Guatemalan police archives, filled with thousands of dossiers on political activists, detailed organizational charts, and information on torture victims and police spies, researcher Kate Doyle commented: "The National Police weren't interested in fighting crime and the files were not organized to support prosecutions. What was important was the hunt for subversives."[2] This emphasis bore the unmistakable stamp of the American training programs, which were designed to expand police intelligence and counterinsurgency capabilities. The architects of U.S. policy were obsessed with countering radical nationalist and guerrilla movements worldwide, the central purpose behind the 1290-d program and the OPS. The hunt for subversives was not unique to Guatemala but part of a global initiative, which spawned myriad abuses and wrought much havoc across the so-called Third World.

Chapter **8**

Arming Tyrants I
American Police Training and the Postcolonial Nightmare in Africa

The neo-colonialism of today represents imperialism in its final and perhaps its most dangerous stage.
—KWAME NKRUMAH, *Neo-Colonialism: The Last Stage of Imperialism,* 1965

Power corrupts, and power corrupts army officers faster than others.
—Public safety review, U.S. Embassy, Rwanda, 1965

In 1961 the State Department issued a report outlining the importance of the police to postcolonial development in Africa. It proclaimed that in many nations, the police "[are] organized under rigid central control, live in barracks, operate in large groups, and make police stations into such formidable spots that any sane citizen wants to avoid them. . . . Public Safety officials believe we should use whatever leverage we have to induce these countries to establish civilian-oriented, western-style police forces. They recognize that this will be a long and difficult process, but the states of Africa that seek our help are probably more amenable to change than the tradition-bound Latin Americans."[1] These comments reveal a great deal about the ideology underlying the police programs. Americans functioning as secular missionaries of modernization were determined to create Western-style police forces, deemed crucial to postcolonial "nation-building." The only barrier they saw was "traditional" attitudes and customs, which they felt could be overcome through proper tutelage and guidance.[2]

The police programs in practice showed much continuity from the colonial period, when the European powers built up indigenous police forces, often along tribal lines, as part of a strategy of divide and conquer, to control unrest and protect vital economic resources for the purpose of exploiting them.[3] An important underlying interest was the containment of radical nationalist movements threatening the Western foothold on the continent. There was little serious effort to promote legislative reforms capable of improving police professionalism and little commitment to human rights (as there had been in Japan prior to the "reverse course").[4]

For all the violence associated with their efforts, European colonial offi-cers often took pride in the professional development of the men under their charge, with whom they forged close bonds over the years.[5] American public safety advisers, by contrast, were frequently rotated in and out of countries and had little knowledge of the local languages and customs and little time to develop the same kinds of relationships. A large degree of cynicism and frustra-tion consequently accompanied the police training programs, on both sides. In the one scholarly study of the programs in Africa, the political scientist Otwin Marenin concludes that police were "not known for their civility" in countries where the United States was most active.[6] The main reason was the emphasis on internal security and social control rather than the protection of civil liberties, and America's alliance with dictatorial rulers who maintained power through police repression.

Training the Emperor's Legions: American Police Training and State Repression in Ethiopia

Between 1953 and 1969, the United States provided $3.3 million in police aid and $147 in military aid—more than in any other country in Africa—to Ethiopia, with the aim of fortifying Emperor Haile Selassie (also known as Ras Tafari). A hero for having mobilized opposition to the 1930s Italian invasion, Selassie had become megalomaniacal, squandering foreign aid on personal monuments as people in the countryside starved. Nevertheless, American policymakers val-ued Selassie as a bulwark against pan-Arab nationalism and for ensuring access to the Kagnew communications facility outside the Eritrean town of Asmara, which transmitted radio signals from the Middle East to the United States.[7]

Under the Overseas Internal Security Program (OISP, formerly 1290-d), the State Department provided police with over $200,000 in equipment, includ-ing Land Rovers, rifles, and radios, and contracted technicians to develop a modern crime lab and record-collection system, allowing for the centraliza-tion of data on dissidents. Dozens of officers were trained in the United States, returning to lead counter-subversive units with several veterans of the Greek civil war.[8] The OISP was headed by Colonel Ralph Selby of the Los Angeles Police Department and Colonel Garland Williams, a Federal Bureau of Narcot-ics (FBN) agent who had apprehended the Jewish mobster Yasha Katzenberg in the 1930s and organized the El Paso border patrol in Texas. A native of Prentiss, Mississippi, Williams was chief of sabotage training with the OSS during World War II and helped form Detachment 101 in Burma, known for trading opium to finance guerrilla activities. He also served with the secret Y Force in Kunming, China, base of the Flying Tigers, who funneled arms to the GMD and ran secret missions into North Korea during the Korean War, supervising POW inter-rogation teams.[9]

In Addis Ababa, Williams worked with Colonel Workneh Gebeyehu, head of the secret police, who committed suicide after being implicated in a failed 1960 coup plot. While still loyal to the emperor, he was involved "not with solving crime," an internal report noted, "but with political intelligence of the type sought after by police in every non-democratic regime," a striking acknowledgment of the connection between American programs and political repression. Williams and Selby assisted Workneh Gebeyehu in cultivating networks of informants. Thousands were placed under surveillance, including opposing politicians. The embassy expressed satisfaction at the effectiveness of the police in the field of political intelligence, commenting favorably that the "emperor keeps opponents under close watch."[10]

As these remarks indicate, the United States contributed to the growth of a modern police state in Ethiopia, resulting in an influx of political prisoners. Inspections revealed that prison accommodations were poor in part because of the lack of a medical budget, minimal standards of due process, and the low caliber of guards. Reforms were proposed, including the development of industrial shops as a mechanism of rehabilitation, though these were slow to get off the ground. Flogging was continuously practiced in many facilities, having been retained in the 1957 penal code.[11]

The Kennedy administration expanded police aid to $1.335 million per year and launched a CIA program to infiltrate the labor movement, similar to the one overseen by Ambassador Edward Korry in Italy and, later, Chile. Over a half-dozen Israelis were subcontracted to train strike force units modeled after the Israeli frontier police. Undersecretary of State George Ball feared that labor organizers, Muslim dissidents, and disaffected university students would unify to overthrow the emperor, playing into Moscow's hands.[12] To prevent this outcome, Kennedy's Special Group on Counter-Insurgency supplied the police with sixty-five General Motors sedans, as well as military helmets, machine guns, M-1 rifles, and laboratory equipment, including polygraph and fingerprint units. The OPS funded a national police academy and trained staff of the Aba Din Imperial Staff College, whose curriculum was based on that of American police academies.[13]

One of the instructors, Ray Foreaker, claimed that the Aba Din College was crucial in contributing to improved professional standards. Fourteen graduates, however, were indicted for burglary and armed robbery, suggesting the broad scale of corruption. A report stated that poor pay left police susceptible to bribery.[14] Clearly the Progressive Era policing paradigm, the reference point for instructors at the academy, was not easily transferable, particularly in the political climate of the Cold War, in which American training was designed to fortify repressive regimes.

In 1968 an OPS-trained unit protected Vice President Hubert Humphrey when students attacked the American embassy with stones during his visit to

Ethiopia. Police subsequently killed three students who were protesting after unions were banned at the main university in Addis Ababa. Epitomizing the lack of regard for human rights, OPS adviser Horton W. Steele congratulated colleague Mitchell Mabardy "on a job well done" in overseeing the suppression of the demonstrations.[15]

The OPS channeled some of its equipment to the military, including fragmentation bombs, considered "ideal for use against dissident bands," namely, Somali-backed rebels led by Muktal Dahir seeking independence in the Ogaden region of southern Somalia. In March 1964, alongside the British and Italians, the OPS expanded advisory support to paramilitary units, which instituted "very severe repressive activity" against the Ogaden Liberation Front, burning villages, killing unarmed civilians, and destroying crops.[16] Selassie also used police brigades to put down a northern uprising by the Eritrean Liberation Front (ELF). Cultivating close ties with Brigadier General Zeremarian Azazzi, commissioner of police for Eritrea, Foreaker, Williams, and Robert Whitmer, a veteran of the anti-Huk campaign in the Philippines, developed a border control service and oversaw "timely and hard-hitting" raids in ELF territory.[17] Airplanes were delivered through a CIA intermediary to counter the Soviet delivery of MiGs to Somalia, which backed the ELF. The American planes were used to strafe villages and machine-gun peasants and their livestock, resulting in mass killings and displacement.[18] In these and other ways, American police aid was used for repressive purposes and helped to aggravate local ethnic conflicts.

The guerrilla movements in Eritrea and Ogaden as well as in the Tigray lands continued resisting Ethiopian encroachment, receiving support from Somalia and other Arab states. In 1974 Selassie was overthrown by the Marxist Mengistu Haile Mariam.[19] In helping prolong the decaying regime of the emperor, American police and military programs radicalized the revolutionary movement and left a legacy of violence.

In Somalia, the United States contributed to the militarization of the police while playing both sides in the Ethiopia-Somalia rivalry. In the late 1950s, on the eve of Somali independence, owing to fears that a "Nasser-like" leader loyal to the Soviet Union might emerge, the United States began providing Somalia with police aid alongside its former colonial overlord, Italy. In a July 1958 police survey, Lieutenant Colonel Russell A. Snook, former superintendent of the New Jersey State Police who had headed police training operations in Italy designed to stabilize the Allied occupation in World War II, concluded that "threats of tribal conflict and foreign subversion make the maintenance of peace and order essential to the development of the country. The Somali government will turn elsewhere for aid if the United States does not provide assistance."[20] Over the next decade, the State Department would spend over $4 million, furnishing helicopters and riot control equipment and financing a training academy, where advisers led by Beryel Pace, former inspector of the Detroit Police Department and a participant in the Phoenix program, served as instructors.

Roger Hilsman, director of the State Department's Bureau of Intelligence and Research during the Kennedy administration, credited the police programs with preventing the spread of a "pseudo populist" revolt thanks to the creation of a small but efficient Western-trained civilian force.[21] These comments reveal the antidemocratic function of the OPS and the elitism of Kennedy administration officials (including the "doves"). In July 1967, coinciding with a $200,000 political action program to foster the election of pro-Western officials, the OPS provided Somalia with emergency communications, small arms, and three Cessna aircraft in response to border violations by Ethiopian troops. Some of the equipment was used in famine relief operations, which had a "salutary effect on police relationships with the people."[22] The State Department and the Pentagon maintained operations in Somalia until 1972, when dictator Siad Barre put the country in the Soviet camp, though they would support Barre during the period of his most brutal repression in the 1980s.[23]

Containing Pan-Arabism and Qaddafi: Police Aid in Northern Africa

Police programs were important to American neocolonial strategy throughout North Africa, which strategic planners viewed as a "rear area for support for military intervention in the Middle East and Persian Gulf."[24] In Libya, after 1290-d architect Henry Villard negotiated a treaty securing base rights in return for technical assistance, advisers such as Frank Walton, Arthur Thurston, and Ray Foreaker developed a crime lab and provided $800,000 in arms, armored cars, handcuffs, and helicopters with machine gun mounts to the civil defense forces of the pro-Western King Idris, before he was overthrown in a 1969 revolution led by Colonel Muammar Quaddafi. Police were trained to protect vital industrial machinery and the country's oil installations, pumping stations, and pipelines.[25]

Elliot B. Hensel, a forensic chemist in Ventura County, California, who later worked in the Philippines, Ethiopia, and Saudi Arabia, wrote in his end-of-tour report:

> It has been a fine experience to start with practically nothing and build an operation entirely with a good future potential. This is particularly satisfying to a law enforcement officer, for in his usual stateside routine, he often feels that he is caught in a revolving door. The same drunk drivers, identical burglars, and the old familiar dope peddlers pass through his laboratory with monstrous regularity; his painstaking work with test tube and microscopes is frequently rejected by clever lawyers and disbelieving juries.... The adviser departs Libya with regret at leaving new friends and colleagues but with the pleasure in having made a small contribution to another country.[26]

These comments provide a window into the motives of public safety officials while playing down the larger strategic purposes for which the programs were designed.

Qaddafi's rise to power was viewed with alarm in Washington, which adopted a containment strategy against him centered on efforts to shore up regional allies.[27] As with the Soviet Union, this approach bore unforeseen costs, particularly in neighboring Chad, where American programs helped to prolong the rule of François Tombalbaye, who remained in power from August 1960 until he was overthrown and killed in a coup d'état in April 1975. The United States viewed Chad as an important "cross-roads between East and Tropical Africa" and a potential base for the spread of pan-Arabist ideals. Tombalbaye dissolved opposing parties, favored his own Sara tribe, and was ruthless in promoting a strong central government, which intelligence reports considered one of his strengths. He was also valued by Washington because he was anti-Arab and pro-French.[28] In 1962, as riots gripped the capital, Fort Lamy (later N'Djamena), U.S. adviser Roger Robinson warned Engle about the inability of the French-backed security forces to meet their "responsibility for controlling dissident elements and to protect [Chad's] frontiers against illegal crossings." He expressed further concern that the adoption of "forceful measures" against Muslims and opposition leaders was creating a political backlash and recommended providing immediate technical assistance and weaponry.[29]

The American ambassador to Chad, John Calhoun, viewed an advisory program as a crucial way to "reduce pressure coming from anti-French elements and young intellectuals" who wanted the country to be "more independent." Operating at a budget of $527,000 per year, the OPS provided modern weapons, telecommunications, and riot control gear and helped to establish an identity card program for social control purposes. It also constructed firearms ranges and created a police mobile strike unit led by a French intelligence officer, Pierre Gabriel, a fifteen-year veteran of the Indochina war.[30]

OPS reports lamented that, owing to a lack of ideological motivation and the corruption of the officer class, in the face of battle the police were "afraid and incompetent, lacked courage, and were prone to defection." Edward Bishop, an army lieutenant from rural Wisconsin with experience in Cambodia, Burma, Vietnam, Turkey, and Japan, proposed stepping up "indoctrination measures" to "alleviate these difficulties."[31] As in many other interventions, the problem persisted, however, as it was contingent on political circumstance. In spite of many shortcomings, the OPS contributed to the prolongation of Tombalbaye's repressive rule and to a vicious cycle of state and anti-state violence which spilled over into neighboring Sudan and exacerbated the war in Darfur. Few people in the United States, meanwhile, could even locate Chad on a map.

During the early 1980s, while undermining peacekeeping efforts by the Organization of African Unity, the Reagan administration funneled Stinger missiles to one of Tombalbaye's main opponents, Hissène Habré, in order to counter Libyan and French influence, and because he supported attacks against Qaddafi. Habré was later accused of some forty thousand political murders and acts of systematic torture, mainly carried out by his political police, whose directors all came from Habré's small Gorane ethnic group.[32] Here again we see the shortsightedness of U.S. policy, which showered weaponry on leaders on the basis of immediate contingencies, without concern for the long-term or human consequences.

Propping Up Dictatorship: American Police Training and Neocolonialism in West Africa

In Liberia, founded as a quasi-colony of the United States, police programs were designed to uphold the power of the African American minority and protect the property of the Firestone rubber corporation, which dominated the economy. Liberia also possessed vital communications facilities off the port of Monrovia. American investments in Liberia totaled over $350 million, second on the continent only to those in South Africa. President William Tubman (1943–1971) was looked on as a "special friend" because of his "commitment to free-enterprise and an open-door economic policy." Firestone executive Byron. H. Larabee viewed him as the "best leader on the African scene."[33]

In 1912 the United States had aided in the creation of Liberia's National Guard. Forty-three years later, in November 1955, the State Department's International Cooperation Administration contracted Richard L. Holcomb, chief of the Bureau of Police Science at the State University of Iowa, to study the six hundred–man police force. Impressed by Firestone's telecommunications and the growth of the capital city, Monrovia, where "people who had never seen a truck three years ago could now operate complex equipment," Holcomb stressed that the police needed to be modernized, emphasizing that the salaries were low and that the force was equipped with only a few shotguns and revolvers. He advocated establishing a radio system and a security detail for the president, who had been the target of a recent assassination attempt.[34]

Between 1955 and 1971, the State Department spent over $3.4 million to implement these goals. The program was headed for a time by Theodore Brown, chief of police in Eugene, Oregon, and director of public safety in Guam, who would become OPS director in Latin America. John Manopoli and Richard Rodgers of the MSU Vietnam project, Edward Payne, a twenty-one-year veteran of the Philadelphia police, and William Cantrell, who helped build an intelligence agency in Uruguay known for torture, were among the other advisers. They provided technical aid and equipment, including airport weapons detectors, military helmets, grenades, and tear gas masks, and developed radio communications, a police academy, and a detective bureau.[35] Over a hundred Liberians were sent for training at the IPA and the New York Police Department (but not in southern police institutions, where Africans were barred). Israeli Mossad and CIA agents such as Cantrell, Brown, and Robert Lowe developed the national intelligence and security services, whose assistant director was an IPA graduate.[36]

Dominated by the Mendes tribe, many of the police were actual security employees of Firestone and served as industrial spies. Prioritizing public security over human rights, the OPS acknowledged the inequitable conditions at Firestone but trained special riot control squads, which in February 1966 killed a labor organizer and wounded several more. In his end-of-tour report, Richard Sutton lamented that the government had an "apathetic attitude" toward curbing social unrest and would wait until a "situation arises." U.S. advisers preferred leaders who promoted aggressive police tactics and cracked down harshly on the left.[37]

The poor human rights climate pervading Liberia was epitomized by wretched prison conditions. Despite President Tubman's provision of $500,000 for modernization, inspections of the Monrovia jail found that the inmates' diet consisted of one pound of rice per day and an occasional piece of dried fish. As in OPS-run facilities in Vietnam, the cells were only two feet by five feet, and plumbing was nonexistent. Prisoners slept on the floors, which were also used as toilets. Other facilities were small huts lacking food distribution or industry, with beatings endemic.[38] Reform was made impossible by overcrowding caused by an influx of political prisoners, resulting from enhanced police surveillance. The OPS reported that persons who made "derogatory remarks against the state" were among those liable to be arrested. An embassy cable stated that President Tubman "rules paternalistically with heavy applications of police power and has indicated a readiness to arrest those suspected of subversion on weak evidence, probably because of his concern that any weakening of his grasp might provoke an attempt to wrest his power from him."[39] These comments provide a clear indication of the repressive ends to which the OPS programs contributed.

In the Ivory Coast, which achieved independence in 1958, American training helped to solidify the rule of Félix Houphouët-Boigny, a conservative autocrat like Selassie who promoted economic privatization and welcomed French engineers in developing the country's infrastructure. Houphouët-Boigny was precisely the type of postcolonial leader Frantz Fanon warned about in *Black Skin, White Masks*—one who sought to emulate European mores, denigrated African culture, and essentially kowtowed to Western interests.[40] He was despised by pan-Africanists like Ghana's Kwame Nkrumah and Sékou Touré of Guinea but was popular in the Western capitals. Public safety reports noted that as a champion of moderate African causes and a strong anticommunist, Houphouët-Boigny provided "strong and acceptable leadership for internal

stability" and warned of the threat of subversive pressure from "radical Ghana-
ians and Guineans . . . subjected to Chicom [Chinese communist] influence."
Dismissing the idea that these "radicals" were motivated by idealism and disil-
lusionment with wide-scale injustice, the reports claimed that the opposition
of students, labor activists, and civil servants was "fanned by anti-government
propaganda put out by pro-communist elements."[41]

These remarks exemplify the conspiratorial theory held by OPS officials and
the American national security bureaucracy, which viewed all popular unrest,
regardless of the circumstances, as being manipulated by communist agents.
As a result, they were able to rationalize heavy-handed police actions even
while acknowledging that many of the governments they were supporting were
autocratic. Through the late 1960s, the OPS provided $389,000 in assistance
to the Ivory Coast, supplying Houphouët-Boigny's internal security forces
with thirty-six transport vehicles as well as revolvers, ammunition, and hand-
cranked generators for use in police precincts. Aided by French advisers in
Senegal, John Manopoli, Garland Williams, and René Tetaz created a riot control force, communications system, and police library stocked with texts used
in American police academies such as O. W. Wilson's *Police Administration* and
J. Edgar Hoover's *Masters of Deceit* on methods of communist subversion. They
also provided training in counterintelligence and FBI-style surveillance.[42] In
this regard, American aid contributed to ample human rights abuses and the
preservation of Houphouët-Boigny's power, which endured into the early 1990s
after he enacted a decree making him president for life.

In Ghana the OPS initiated a $400,000 program after a 1966 CIA-backed
coup overthrew Kwame Nkrumah, the country's first post-independence
leader. Author of an influential book on neocolonialism, Nkrumah took measures beginning in the late 1950s to nationalize key industries, resources, and
crops, including cocoa, and demanded that foreign firms reinvest 60 percent
of their profits in Ghana. The CIA subsequently characterized him as a "vain
opportunist and showboy," and accused him of running up foreign debts for
"unsound state enterprises and political and diplomatic activities designed to
further his own continental ambitions."[43]

The public safety program was designed to shore up the new military-police
junta, dominated by ethnic Ewe and Ashanti, which abandoned Nkrumah's
vision of independent economic development in favor of the model of export-
led growth favored by the West. One of the main coup plotters, John W. K.
Harlley, had been police commissioner of Ghana, subsequently promoted to
inspector general of the Ghana national police. His rise, according to the historian Richard Rathbone, can be attributed to his J. Edgar Hoover–like control of
thick files on political luminaries.[44]

Thomas Finn, an FBI agent from Providence, Rhode Island, who also served
in Thailand and Vietnam, and Harold "Scotty" Caplan, who had experience on

four continents, trained Harlley's men in riot control and counterintelligence and improved records collection and communications. Small arms and over two hundred cameras and die cutters were shipped in to aid in establishing an identity card program, and a dozen Ghanaian police officers were sent to the IPA.[45] One major deficiency, noted by the Ghanaian criminal justice expert Raymond Atuguba, was that there was no serious effort to promote badly needed legislative and judicial reforms. The police were mobilized principally along political lines to suppress pro-Nkrumah elements and a growing labor movement. As in the British colonial era, they served "not the majority of the rural and urban poor, but the elites of the day. . . . They were powerful, brutal and corrupt."[46] Once again, the OPS thus contributed to the spread of considerable repression, as Ghana became marred by instability.

In Nigeria, where police were authorized to shoot robbers on sight, the OPS spent $3.4 million from 1970 to 1972 building a police staff college at Jos. Graduates carried out surveillance on behalf of the reigning military oligarchy and reprisals against the Biafran independence movement. While providing emergency relief to famine victims who captured the world's attention, the Nixon administration refused to recognize the independence movement in order to protect its alliance with Great Britain and because of lobbying by companies such as Gulf Oil, which enjoyed favorable relations with the Nigerian military.[47]

The United States was responsible for abetting repression in several smaller West African nations, including Dahomey (now Benin), the coup capital of Africa in the 1960s, where the OPS provided $266,000 to help reinforce a series of military juntas. Johnson "Jack" Monroe developed a telecommunications system with French advisers and assisted the Sureté in gathering intelligence on opposition party members, potential coup plotters, foreigners, and labor activists. American-trained officers also enforced the censorships of books, newspapers, and movies and rounded up suspected communists in a campaign whose efficiency was enhanced by the importation of modern surveillance and photography equipment.[48]

In Niger, where the French High Command worked to subvert the 1958 elections in favor of pro-French candidate Hamana Diori, who favored the Djerma and Songhay ethnicities, the United States provided over $600,000 in police aid. Much of it went to the French-controlled Sureté, whose agents rounded up members of the leftist Sawaba Party, banned after leader Djibo Bakary unleashed anti-regime propaganda and planned cross-border assaults from exile in Ghana. Some of Bakary's supporters were arrested and hanged in public executions. Field reports noted that through effective cultivation of informants, the Sureté kept abreast of activities within the labor unions, which predominantly supported the Sawaba Party. Arms were funneled through Abidjan in the Ivory Coast with Houphouët-Boigny's collaboration. Respect for civil liberties was not a priority.[49] After meeting with President Diori in June

1965, Thomas Finn and telecommunications specialist Paul Katz recommended expanding support for paramilitary commando units, which were seen as effective in coping with Sawabilt-driven subversion and outside infiltrators.[50] The units, trained in counter-guerrilla tactics, were implicated in serious human rights violations in another dirty war backed by the United States.

In the Central Africa Republic, the OPS provided $241,000 to stabilize the authoritarian rule of David Dacko and his successor Jean-Bédel Bokassa, who declared himself emperor for life in 1966. Internal reports noted that Bokassa was "mentally unstable, prone to erratic behavior," and had aroused "elite and popular discontent with his extravagance" but praised him for opposing all things Islamic and pan-Arabist and for fending off communist infiltrators from Chad and Sudan.[51] Adolphe Bonnefil and Garland Williams were contracted to help solidify his power. Working with French agents, the clandestine Cold Warriors expanded the radio network to aid in intelligence gathering, imported fingerprinting technologies for an identity card program, and developed paramilitary units consisting of tribal minorities to repress the opposition. These units were modeled after the Hmong secret army and the Iranian Gendarmerie (which both men had trained) and were similarly known for their brutality.

In 1962 an OPS survey declared that "only 14 years ago, ordinary police were illiterate people with sack clothing and armed with spears."[52] These remarks provide a window into the ideological underpinning of the programs and the Western "civilizing mission" to uplift supposedly backward African institutions and peoples through the export of modern technology. Other reports emphasized the need to maintain a strong advisory presence because of the careless and shameful treatment of "fine new American material" by local officials. "Experience in other African countries (Upper Volta, Niger) shows that modern American equipment will not be used correctly or well-maintained and will not benefit anyone if there are no 'experts' to advise. . . . The assistance program should thus not simply provide equipment but must include advisory and participant aid."[53] As these comments indicate, Americans felt that they were the only ones capable of ensuring the viability of state-building efforts and denigrated locals for their unfamiliarity with Western weapons and technology. Bokassa meanwhile used the police programs to build up his internal security apparatus and compiled an atrocious human rights record, for which the United States bore partial responsibility. The Ngaragba prison functioned as an "open air theatre," according to historian Florence Bernault, "where torturers and prisoners enacted tragic scenes of power and submission that celebrated Bokassa's personal will and grandeur."[54]

Arming Mobutu's Killers: The OPS and the Postcolonial Nightmare in the Congo

Police training contributed to the highest levels of violence in the Democratic Republic of the Congo (Zaire), where it helped consolidate the power of the notorious dictator Joseph Desiré Mobutu. The motive for the program lay in the Congo's rich mineral wealth and natural resources, which were historically exploited by Western powers.[55] One of the first public safety reports pointed to the Congo's "tremendous possibilities for the future and in economic growth as a producer of copper, tin, uranium, diamonds, palm oil, manganese, great natural wealth." It went on to state, however, that "a comprehensive civil police assistance program was vitally needed with emphasis on increasing disciplinary standards and riot control capabilities."[56]

After the Congo achieved its independence in 1960, the United States collaborated with Belgium in assassinating the country's first prime minister, Patrice Lumumba, a pan-Africanist and socialist characterized by John Foster Dulles as a "Castro or worse." Lumumba's demise was predicated in part on his inability to control the Sureté, built up by the Belgians for internal security purposes. The CIA helped deliver him to rival Moïse Tshombe, a warlord over diamond-rich Katanga province, whose men tortured and killed him.[57]

Rebellions subsequently broke out, led by the Simbas ("lions" in Swahili), a mix of Lumumba supporters and disaffected ethnic groups backed by a delegation of Cuban revolutionaries led by Ernesto "Che" Guevara and by Algerian and Egyptian fighters and other radical African states such as Ghana. The American embassy sought to crush the rebels whom it considered "primitive tribesmen," and provided logistical support and weaponry to the Congolese Army (ANC), including napalm bombs. The CIA trained teams of right-wing Cuban and South African mercenaries headed by Mike Hoare, who was made a lieutenant in the ANC. American pilots flew T-28 bomber missions, which the Special Group on Counter-Insurgency praised for "doing an excellent job in breaking up rebel attacks on ANC positions." Declassified CIA reports, however, show that they missed their target on more than one occasion, including in March 1965, when they bombed a parish church on the Ugandan border and attacked a school, gunning down children.[58]

Robert W. Komer described the covert operation as a "great little exercise in some pretty fancy diplomacy and undercover work to prevent the Congo from going sour."[59] The CIA, however, described towns ravaged by the fighting as "spectacles of misery." And while the Simbas took Western missionaries hostage and were known for practicing ritual cannibalism, American-backed forces carried out horrific atrocities, including spot executions and chaining together suspected guerrillas. An Italian journalist observed of them in 1964 that "occupying a town meant blowing out the doors with rounds of bazooka fire, going into shops and taking anything they wanted. . . . After the looting came the killing. The shooting lasted for three days. Three days of executions, of lynchings, of tortures, of screams, and of terror." The *London Observer* added that the mercenaries not only "shoot and hang their prisoners after torturing them, but use them for target practice and gamble over the number of shots needed to kill them."[60]

The United States eventually consolidated the power of Mobutu, a former Belgian gendarme and ANC chief of staff characterized by the U.S. army attaché as "vain and lazy" and by the State Department as "childish and easily bought off." A Lingala speaker from Equateur, Mobutu went on to rule for thirty years, developing a cult of personality through the media and stealing an estimated $5 billion from the treasury. American policymakers favored strong-armed leaders like Mobutu throughout the Third World because they were seen as capable of containing the threat of regional fragmentation and tribalism and promoting the stability needed to safeguard Western interests and investment.[61]

In September 1963 the United States initiated the public safety program, headed by John Manopoli. The timing was opportune in providing a channel for funneling equipment to the Mobutu regime in the clandestine war against the Simbas. Part of the aim was to relieve the ANC from police duty because it was thought to be near collapse as an organized force. Intelligence reports described it as the equivalent of an "unwanted foreign army" manned by soldiers who "regarded their rifles as meal tickets" and were responsible for widespread "raping and pillaging," smuggling diamonds and gold, and the "cold-blooded murder" of Europeans. The leadership was "immature and dishonest" and "thoroughly disliked."[62]

The police for the most part proved to be little better. Championed by Secretary of State Dean Rusk, Ambassador G. McMurtrie Godley, and Attorney General Robert Kennedy, the OPS program was the largest in Africa at an annual budget of $600,000 (over $5 million in total), with a staff of eleven advisers at its peak. Centralized under Mobutu's command, police were mobilized along military lines to quell "unrest, lawlessness, and banditry" in "problem areas" after the withdrawal of UN forces. Reports lamented its staffing with "any warm body who possessed the required political or tribal affiliation," as well as its poor discipline and its lack of esprit de corps. Investigation of crimes was considered a "farce," and the attitude of the average policeman was "pitiful."[63]

To promote professionalization, the OPS provided uniforms and communications and riot control equipment, tried to screen new recruits, and established a central identification bureau. A Coastal and River Lake Guard and a police motorcycle squad were developed, and over 160 officers were sent to the IPA, one of whom, Bemonatu Mpanga, wrote in a revealing essay: "The use of force or threats during an investigation can be seen as one of our police tactics. . . . Above all, the press should not have the slightest information about our methods of procedure." These comments sum up the undemocratic methods of the police, which U.S. advisers did little to discourage. CIA agents trained the Special Branch, "a power unto themselves" headed by Victor Nendaka, a member of Mobutu's inner circle (known as the Binza group) who kept thick files on political figures (including of their dubious financial transactions) and deployed private bands against rivals. The OPS also developed paramilitary mobile brigades in Kinshasa and Lubumbashi modeled after the one in Indonesia, the pride of the Special Group on Counter-Insurgency.[64]

Because of the enormous task of institution-building, the OPS worked alongside UN and Belgian advisers and nine Israelis who trained the army, including Mobutu himself, in paratrooper skills. They rebuilt the national police school in Kinshasa and developed regional academies with courses in administration, firearms, anticommunism, and jungle warfare. A Nigerian group held sessions in riot control, and Kenyan advisers were sent to Kivi province.[65] In October 1968, after Mobutu passed a law outlawing labor unions, the OPS rushed a shipment of tear gas to quell the protests that broke out. A year later, police killed several hundred demonstrators at the national university in Kinshasa and in Kisangani after the OPS supplied more equipment.[66]

A substantial proportion of police assistance was directed toward protecting Western-owned businesses and securing access to Congo's lucrative mineral wealth. One report advised that because the police were at present incapable of maintaining order, "policing of the diamond mines by private security forces trained by the Belgians was necessary."[67] The OPS devoted considerable energy to reorganizing the police in Katanga province, where Tshombe headed a drive for secession. Known as a "walking museum of colonialism" because of his ties to most of the imperial powers, Tshombe had been supported by the Eisenhower administration in his conflict with Lumumba and received backing from white mercenaries as well as from USAID and the CIA. William F. Buckley and the conservative Young Americans for Freedom were vigorous champions of his cause in the United States. They were part of the so-called Katanga lobby, headed by anticommunist Senator Thomas J. Dodd, a Connecticut Democrat, and the Rockefeller family, which owned a portion of Union Minière, Katanga's largest mining corporation, specializing in the production of copper, cobalt, and zinc.[68]

During the chaos of the post-independence period, OPS reports noted the disintegration and corruption of the Katangan police, led by a Belgian mercenary, Jack Schramme, who disposed of Lumumba's body and were undisciplined and staffed with ex-convicts. Venal officers were accused of stealing uniforms from the USAID warehouse and of killing their concubines if the women refused to accompany them when they were forced to flee. OPS staff worked to mold a new proxy paramilitary force capable of serving as a counterweight to the military and any anti-Western factions that might evolve.[69]

Tshombe eventually made common cause with Mobutu and used the Gendarmerie to help crush political opponents, though Tshombe and regional separatists mounted another rebellion, which the United States was called upon to help suppress. Tshombe subsequently died of a heart attack in exile.[70]

An embassy cable tellingly referred to the "repulsive brutality" of American-backed commando units (in Lubumbashi, capital of Katanga), which created a "difficult moral, human, and public relations position in which the U.S. government has been placed" (on account of its assistance)—comments that go a long way toward explaining why the programs were kept secret.[71] Police aid was on the whole designed to fortify Mobutu's rule and help crush regional revolts linked to the Simbas. The largest was in eastern Kwilu province, led by Pierre Mulele, a minister in Lumumba's deposed government whose followers, consisting primarily of ethnic Mbundu and Pende targeted by ANC repression, embraced a blend of leftist ideology and African magic. Gaining its information from the U.S. embassy, *Time* magazine referred to Mulele's rebellion as "bizarre" and blamed him for wreaking violence across the country, failing to contextualize the rebellion within the larger CIA subversion campaign and the violent takeover of the state by Mobutu. Arguing for expanded support to Tshombe in the *L.A. Times*, the conservative political theorist Russell Kirk claimed that Mulele's followers were "witch doctors indoctrinated in Marxism by the Communist Chinese" and were "fed hemp at breakfast and drugged with Chinese narcotics."[72]

Using psychological warfare tactics developed in the colonial laboratories of the Philippines and Haiti and refined in the jungles of Vietnam and Laos, U.S. advisers sought to intimidate and induce defections among the Mulelists, many of whom were forced to seek asylum in neighboring countries. The OPS provided C-130 helicopters, beefed up border interdiction and worked with the Israeli Mossad in training commandos, who undertook search-and-destroy operations in which they burned villages and shot suspected guerrilla collaborators, facts that went unmentioned in the mainstream press. In Muginda, police organized a punitive expedition to avenge the death of two comrades, killing eighty-seven prisoners through asphyxiation. The CIA reported that "inhabitants favored the rebels" even after government forces took over.[73] In May 1966 the OPS enthused over the capture in Opala of a leader of the "people's army," who was tortured and executed Lumumba-style. In the Stanleyville (Kisangani) area, military and police units opened a drive to seal off commerce in foodstuffs between the population and rebels, who still "infest[ed] the environs of the city," causing much hardship. The rebellion eventually died down after Mulele was lured back from exile by Mobutu and, after being fêted with a caviar dinner, executed by a firing squad.[74]

Many OPS personnel in the Congo (including Manopoli, Jack Ryan, Elmer Adkins, Ray Landgren, Leigh Brilliant, Don Bennett, Roy Hatem, and Charles

Leister) had served in Indochina, where they had also trained police along paramilitary lines. In both settings they contributed to extensive violence, though they were never fully in control of the forces under their guidance. Field reports complained about the misuse of vehicles, the deplorable condition of police academies, and the perpetuation of "tribalism, nepotism, and graft" among American-trained units. Police adviser Robert O'Blake told the State Department in exasperation: "We do not have much leverage to curtail these problems directly. Congo's Minister of the Interior, Etienne Tshisekedi, does not want the advice of foreigners on how to run the police. He is anti-white (and to some extent anti-American) and politically ambitious. The whole team under Mobutu is determined to let the Congolese run their own business."[75]

These comments display the mistrust hampering advisory efforts in the Congo and the tendency of local officials to appropriate equipment for their own ends, without considering the input of Americans. The relationship was one purely of convenience, not mutual respect, reminiscent of the colonial era. Mitchell Mabardy, an air force colonel with the OPS (and CIA), told Byron Engle that the "chronic incompetence of the political leadership was a major barrier to progress."[76] Few would have disagreed, though Mabardy evaded the question of his own responsibility by failing to mention that he and his associates had played a key role in solidifying Mobutu's power.

In a July 1973 report which encapsulated the shortcomings of American training, Jeter Williamson expressed disappointment at a lack of uniformed patrols and emphasized his recommendation that the police develop walking beats or patrol urban areas by bike. Upbeat about the deterioration of rebel activity in the eastern provinces, Williamson also pushed for the delivery of equipment to police in the Shaba province of Katanga, where organized resistance to Mobutu's rule had developed. He warned that new hydroelectric facilities and mines required intensified security because they were vulnerable to sabotage campaigns designed to bring down the government and were attracting the attention of criminal gangs.[77]

Williamson's remarks suggest that the United States continued with the programs for political, economic, and geostrategic reasons. For all his flaws, Mobutu was valued for pacifying the leftist insurgency and for giving Western corporations access to the Congo's rich mineral resources. The OPS was especially influential in providing modern equipment to the police, who operated with a sense of impunity derived from a lack of judicial checks.[78] Mobutu's own actions set the tone. He was prone to "frivolous expenditures," the CIA reported, including the purchase of a luxury villa on the French Riviera. Police routinely enriched themselves through patronage and graft and used a system of *ratissage*, or dragnet operations, to "extort money from and terrorize the population."[79]

In its 1974 termination report, the OPS claimed that its efforts had contributed to the "beginning of an efficient and accountable police force." A more realistic assessment was provided by the scholar Thomas M. Callaghy, who observed in 1985 that the modernized Congolese police remained "ill-disciplined and ill-paid" and had committed a "horror list of crimes," including armed robbery, setting up unauthorized barricades, kidnappings, beatings, rape, forced labor, physical attacks, and extortion in villages and open-air markets; they were guilty of scavenging and pillaging crops, fruit, goats, and chickens and even destroying local fishing grounds with dynamite. Callaghy went on to suggest that the Gendarmerie, one of the creations of the United States' reorganization programs, constituted an "occupying force which lives on the back of the population and has as its major task the muzzling of the people. . . . They consistently leave disorder, unrest, and abused citizens in their wake. They are an organized, free-floating source of coercion in the countryside." Quoting a regional subcommander, he added: "When the population sees a Gendarme it no longer feels safe. In fact quite the contrary."[80]

The OPS helped to arm Mobutu's killers with $2.6 million in advanced weaponry and training, which facilitated the expansion of state terror. Products of the McCarthy era, most of the advisers viewed the world in monolithic terms, interacted mainly with societal elites, and, as with the Michiganders in South Vietnam, were ill-attuned to the social and political realities of the country. They saw themselves as exporting their technical expertise and did not always recognize how their work exacerbated Mobutu's repression, which was gargantuan in scope.

The OPS in the Great Lakes: Support for "Hutu Power" in Rwanda and "Tutsi Power" in Burundi

The war in the Congo led to heightened American intervention throughout the Great Lakes region of East Africa and to the intensification of ethnic violence. In 1965 an advisory mission led by John Manopoli and Adolphe Bonnefil began providing transceivers and communications equipment to the Rwandese police and National Guard. The main aim was to "beef up" Rwanda's predominantly Hutu security forces because "rumors of an invasion by Chicom supported Tutsi elements in Burundi still persist," and because Mulelist rebels in the Congo were using Rwanda as a base to try to overthrow Mobutu. The CIA further warned that an influx of refugees from the Congo fleeing the "depredations of the ANC" were creating instability and food shortages, resulting in explosive conditions that made the country ripe for revolution.[81]

After achieving independence from Belgium in 1959, Rwanda was led by Grégoire Kayabinda, architect of a social revolution bent on reversing the existing class structure, dominated by the Tutsi aristocracy. During the colonial era, the Belgians had stoked ethnic tensions by elevating the Tutsi to a privileged position, sparking a backlash among the majority Hutu, who had been reduced to virtual serfdom and were fighting to obtain political authority under Kayabinda and the Parmehutu Party. Over 150,000 Tutsi subsequently fled to Tanzania, Burundi, the Congo, and Uganda, where diehard elements, as the embassy referred to them, were organizing for reinvasion, making incursions back into Rwanda in the hope of regaining power. They were in turn the victims of reprisal killings. In December 1963 and again in 1966, after a series of cross-border raids, the Parmehutu-controlled National Guard and police shelled refugee huts with mortars and massacred as many as ten thousand Tutsi residents, setting a precedent for the mass killings that would take place in 1994.[82]

Despite the brutality and pervasive corruption of the Kayabinda government, the United States supported the regime because it was "cooperative in the Congo mess," allowing the Americans to use the airfield at Kamembe for air missions against pro-Lumumba rebels in the town of Bakuvu and for flying in supplies. The Tutsi were considered to be left-leaning and were allegedly supported by Cuban advisers and Chinese communists seeking to make inroads into the Great Lakes, although the CIA concluded that there was "no hard evidence of this."[83] The grounds for their rebellion were their political marginalization and persecution, and a desire to reclaim their former status. Revealing the ignorance of U.S. officials, public safety reports referred to Tutsi guerrillas as *inyenzi*, Kinyarwandan for "cockroach," a term used by Hutu hardliners, whom they were relying on for intelligence, to demonize and rally hatred against the Tutsi.[84]

Fearing that Tutsis living in Kigali might assist the "invaders by attempting to disrupt the functioning of the government through demonstrations, strikes, and attacks on key utilities and service installations," the State Department provided $495,000 in technical assistance and riot control equipment to Juvenal Habyarimana, the police minister under Kayabinda. Manopoli told Habyarimana that the "U.S. is sympathetic to the needs of the internal security forces," giving them a green light to carry out their repression. A field report lamented that "the absence of police foot or motorized patrols in Rwanda after dark leaves the population to its own devices for protection from drunken maskers and bandits. . . . As a result, the majority of the sensible citizenry will rarely go forth after dark."[85] Seeking to rectify this problem, and viewing the Sureté as a reliable source of information, the OPS worked with German and Belgian technicians to establish a telecommunications system and training center at Ruhengeri and delivered jeeps, radios, cargo planes, and two light observer aircraft equipped with a public relations/communications system to ease in the tracking of dissidents, both Tutsi rebels and Mulelists. OPS agents trained Habyarimana's men in counterintelligence, border patrol, and psy-war. Tear gas grenades were shipped, and Israeli advisers were subcontracted to train a paramilitary youth organization.[86]

Thanks in part to U.S. and Belgian largesse, Rwanda evolved into a one-party police state dominated by the Hutu caste. An OPS report noted that while the Sureté "investigated" and "flogged the hapless Tutsi around the country," it never "investigated the shady dealings of Rwandan officials," including Isidore Sebazungu, an old-guard Parmehutu who was extremely corrupt and "drove out the Tutsi by widespread intimidation and killing." In 1967 Ambassador Leo Cyr pointed to "the unfortunate process of megalomania creeping up on Habyarimana," who six years later would seize power in coup d'état. This was a natural outcome of the police programs, which helped create a vast policing apparatus that gave great authority to whoever was in command (as in many other cases). The United States generally helped to warp democratic development in Rwanda by flooding the country with advanced weapons and surveillance technologies, to the neglect of needed development aid.[87]

In neighboring Burundi, where power relations were the reverse of those in Rwanda, the United States again allied with the oppressor rather than the oppressed. Between 1964 and 1967, the State Department provided $94,000 in police aid to the Tutsi-dominated regime, which, in the wake of a coup attempt by Hutu in 1965, killed an estimated five thousand civilians, setting the precedent for the slaughter of 100,000 Hutu and Tutsi-Banyarunguru in 1972. (The president, Michel Micombero, was a Tutsi-Hima.) Manopoli, Bonnefil, and Alston Staley worked alongside sixteen Belgians to professionalize the Burundian Gendarmerie and build up its intelligence capabilities. In June 1964 they lauded its role in disarming 1,800 spear-carrying Tutsi refugees congregating near the Rwandan border and escorting them back to their camps. The U.S. embassy, which had sought to discourage raids into Rwanda, claimed that the Tutsi were supported by the Mulelists and also by the Chinese, who were allegedly funneling weapons through a military attaché, Kan Mai, after reopening their embassy, and were behind a newly formed trade union in the capital, Bujumbura. (Mao Zedong is reported to have stated, "Burundi is the way to the Congo and when the Congo falls the whole of Africa will fall.")[88] American policy in the end only helped to aggravate local rivalries and empowered the regime in Burundi, which committed horrific crimes against its people.

The OPS in East Africa: Support for Idi Amin and Resistance by the Socialists

Owing in large part to Kenya's mineral wealth and proximity to the Horn of Africa, it was there that American operations in East Africa were headquartered, and where the United States enacted a $697,000 program from 1965 to 1971. Its main aim was to gain leverage among the security forces and secure the rule of Jomo Kenyatta, an anticommunist, and later of the more autocratic Daniel arap Moi. In May 1964 the Special Group on Counter-Insurgency expressed fear that the "Chicoms" were attempting to assert power through Oginga Odinga, Kenyatta's first vice president and a socialist with ties to the Eastern bloc. Kenyatta placed Odinga under house arrest, fearing a coup plot after discovering a cache of Czech and Bulgarian arms in Odinga's possession. Odinga was subsequently released but replaced by the pro-Western Moi, Washington's favorite.[89]

In 1962, after Byron Engle and Mitchell Mabardy surveyed police operations, an OPS team consisting of several veterans of the Vietnam program established a communications center, coordinated intelligence activities, and set up a police college. Motor vehicles, weapons, and aircraft were provided to the semi-military force (a legacy of the colonial era, when it had been mobilized to crush Mau Mau rebels), staffed by a large number of British expatriates.[90] The government's interests lay in increasing the ability of the police to crack down on radical agitation at the University of Nairobi, keep tabs on the political opposition, and secure the border with Ethiopia and Somalia, where refugees were spilling in because of ongoing wars. The police were also mobilized to enforce strict anti-vagrancy and immigration laws that led to the exclusion of Asian workers and forced the removal of squatters organizing for their rights adjacent to the capital. Paying little heed to the underlying structural roots of the situation, American diplomats expressed fear that the squatter movement would be "captured by trained agitators when they return from their studies in Eastern bloc countries."[91] They in turn prioritized paramilitary-style police training over antipoverty programs capable of easing the squatters' plight.

In Tanzania, the United States sold police helicopters and trained Ranger forces and a riot control unit upon the request of socialist leader Julius Nyerere, who, after leading the independence struggle against Britain in 1964, had helped to put down an army and police mutiny with the aid of British reinforcements, subsequently making it a requirement for officers to be members of his own Tanganyika African National Union Party, known as TANU. The Johnson administration was interested in cultivating Nyerere as an ally and worried about the radicalism in neighboring Zanzibar, a trade center considered to be "communist infested." As diplomats brokered the merger of the two countries, largely as a means of undermining Zanzibar's leftist foreign minister Abdul Rahman Babu, the OPS provided over $640,000 in commodities, including projectiles, guns, walkie-talkies, and tear gas grenades. American funds also helped set up a national police academy, headed by IPA graduate Ephraim P. Temu. Over time, as Nyerere became more radical and began to support agricultural collectivization (Ujamaa) and liberation struggles throughout the continent, relations soured, and American assistance was curtailed.[92]

A similar pattern was seen in Zambia, where police aid was extended alongside British aid to post-independence leader Kenneth Kaunda, a socialist who requested support in putting down a series of regional rebellions and labor disputes in the copper belt. Considering them the "first line of defense" against subversion, U.S. adviser John Lindquist, who held a Ph.D. in criminology from UC Berkeley, provided guns, transceivers, and walkie-talkies to semi-military forces in Lusaka, helped refurbish precincts, and worked with the intelligence service to improve border patrol and surveillance. Informants were cultivated among African National Congress exiles from South Africa whom the CIA was monitoring (considering it a "Marxist terrorist" organization) and leftist free-dom fighters from Angola and Mozambique.[93]

In the late 1960s, after taking steps to nationalize the copper mines, Kaunda came to suspect that CIA agents were using the program to assist South African security forces in repressing the African National Congress and to coordinate attacks on Frelimo, the Liberation Front of Mozambique, whose sanctuaries in the village of Chipatala were decimated by Portuguese planes and American-made weapons.[94] Kaunda also believed that the CIA was plotting a coup against him. He told one of his advisers: "We in Zambia have socialist tendencies, that is, we work for the interests of the common man, and socialism in any form is looked on [by the United States] as the nearest evil to communism. Look at the fate of Nkrumah and [Algerian revolutionary Ahmed] Ben Bella, whose downfall was directly attributed to the work of American secret agents working with the Peace Corps, USIS, CIA and USAID."[95]

Kaunda's comments capture the suspicion and distrust of the motives underlying American technical aid programs widely felt across the developing world. The Zambian cabinet believed that U.S. support for the apartheid regime in South Africa and Southern Rhodesia (now Zimbabwe) and CIA subversion campaigns in Chile, Vietnam, Laos, and Indonesia epitomized the bullying character of American foreign policy. Admiring the Black Power movement, they noted that African Americans were treated as "second-class citizens" in the United States and thought that the government was behind the assassina-tion of Martin Luther King Jr. The Nixon administration was seen as especially insensitive to the plight of minorities and the poor. In 1969 Kaunda cut back on relations with the United States and barred the OPS. He became a leader of the nonaligned movement and struck a deal with Maoist China for the construc-tion of a railway to Tanzania. U.S. ambassador Oliver L. Troxel told departing advisers that "Zambia did not deserve or appreciate United States assistance," comments typical of the patronizing attitude marring American advisory efforts in sub-Saharan Africa.[96]

American programs in East Africa were most damaging in Uganda, where they contributed to the tyranny of Idi Amin. As Mahmood Mamdani recounts in his insightful study *Imperialism and Fascism in Uganda*, sensational popular culture and journalistic depictions have obscured the international context in which Amin's rule took root. Trained by British advisers who considered him "first-rate" and a "good African Sergeant" with a "touch of ruthlessness," he was initially supported by the United States because he was anticommunist and open to foreign investment, in contrast to his predecessor Milton Obote, who had socialist leanings and was critical of America's heavy-handed intervention in the Congo.[97]

During the late 1960s, the OPS conducted surveys of the Ugandan police, which had developed a forensics, fingerprint, and photographic bureau under the British, and trained officers at the IPA. The Israeli Mossad worked with a police paramilitary force, which Obote and later Amin packed with their ethnic kinsmen and directed against their political opponents. State Department planners feared the rise of John Kakonge, secretary-general of the ruling Uganda People's Congress party and "an avowed Marxist" who was attempting to wrest leadership from Obote.[98] After Amin took power in 1971, the Pentagon sold him six Bell helicopters for £700,000, which were used for chasing dissidents and whisking kidnap victims to and from torture sites. (The British provided £1 million in vehicles and equipment and sent seventy Ugandan police for training in Britain.)[99]

When aid was cut in May 1973, two instructors from the Bell Helicopter Company, one of whom was a CIA agent, continued to be attached to the Uganda police air wing.[100] As late as August 1975, the United States provided $287,000 worth of helicopter engines to the regime. Ugandan pilots were trained in the United States along with the chief of intelligence of the Entebbe airport, whose job was to intercept individuals Amin did not want to leave Uganda.[101] At least ten of Amin's secret service men, consisting primarily of ethnic Nubi, received training at the IPA. Three took a postgraduate course at International Police Services, Inc., a CIA-funded academy hidden away in a Washington brownstone mansion. When asked about the usefulness of training Amin's agents, a CIA official explained to the *Washington Post*: "By training Amin's men, we were able to have some influence over Amin. . . . It was also a possibility that we could go back to the trainees later for intelligence operations."[102]

These comments reveal an important rationale underpinning the police programs, namely, the cultivation of reliable intelligence "assets." The scope of Washington's complicity in Amin's reign of terror went further than that, however. A confidential investigation by Representative Donald Pease, an Ohio Democrat, uncovered a $4 million government contract with the Cleveland-based Harris Corporation to train Ugandan technicians and provide Amin with a satellite communications system. These activities, of a kind previously undertaken by the OPS, reflect the privatization of police programs after the OPS was abolished because of the link to extensive human rights violations.[103] U.S. support for Amin was an egregious example of this connection, though other examples abound.

In correspondence with the diplomat Ruben Kamanga, who carefully monitored political developments while stationed at the Zambian embassy in

Washington, D.C, Zambian president Kenneth D. Kaunda lamented the vast American investments in South Africa and the provision of arms to Portugal by the United States to suppress national liberation movements. Weighing whether his administration should accept foreign aid, he commented "The Americans possess technical know-how, but would not give it up without anything in return."[104] Kaunda's comments sum up the bind in which many African leaders found themselves. On one hand, they recognized the need for technical expertise to aid in economic development and the modernization of crucial institutions like the police. On the other hand, they understood the threat to their sovereignty that such aid represented and the potential perils that accompanied it.

Driven in part by an ideology of modernization, American aid indeed usually came with strings attached. It was used to advance an explicitly political agenda, including the desire to access strategic resources, prop up right-wing dictatorships, or gain leverage among security forces in case a leader stepped out of line. Writing about British intervention in the Gold Coast (Ghana), the historian David Killingray notes that "throughout the colonial period, policing was imposed on the people and never enjoyed their consent. . . . [It] had little to do with serving the community and everything to do with upholding the authority of the colonial state."[105] Killingray's comments are equally applicable to the postcolonial period, when the United States empowered forces mobilized to suppress ethnic and regional uprisings and social movements on behalf of leaders who were either imposed from the outside or reliant on foreign aid. Rather than contributing to democratic nation-building, the OPS helped to modernize repression through the importation of sophisticated policing technologies and mechanisms of social control.

During the Cold War, the United States is estimated to have provided over $150 billion in arms to African nations, many of which could not meet the basic needs of their people.[106] Pointing to the Reagan administration's provision of $500 million to the Liberian dictator Samuel K. Doe, whose misrule helped to precipitate a devastating civil war, the political scientist George Klay Kieh Jr. wrote that the behavior of the U.S. government was "analogous to that of a collaborator who supplies a group of arsonists with matches and gasoline and then pretends to be innocent after the fire is set and subsequently destroys life and property."[107] This metaphor applies just as well to the American police programs, which wrought much damage but remained hidden from the public, hence ensuring plausible deniability. And when the fire broke out, the arsonists' collaborators maintained their posture of innocence and righteousness, even claiming the duty of "humanitarian intervention" in order to "save the "backward" natives from the violence and chaos they had helped to sow.[108]

Chapter 9

Arming Tyrants II

Police Training and Neocolonialism in the Mediterranean and Middle East

> We were so obsessed with the communists that we were willing to get into
> bed with anyone who claimed to be anti-communist and this included Nazi
> collaborators, extreme right-wingers, crooks, inept people, etc.
>
> —JAMES KELLIS, U.S. investigator, quoted in Kati Marton, *The Polk Conspiracy,* 1990

In the mid-1950s a reporter asked a member of the Iranian Gendarmerie
why he was shooting at fellow Iranians. "They are your brothers," said the
reporter. The officer replied, "Our shoes are American, our clothes are given by
Americans, and our salaries are paid by them. They instructed us to fire."[1] The
response sums up the devil's bargain local officials worldwide made in allying
with the United States. In return for modern equipment and weapons capable
of securing their power, they in effect gave up their sovereignty and helped to
sow internecine conflict.

As the reconstruction of western Europe proceeded after World War II and
the American war machine grew ever more dependent on oil, a lever of global
domination, State Department planners characterized the Middle East as a "stu-
pendous source of strategic power" and "one of the greatest material prizes in
history." Their greatest fear besides the Soviet Union was that the rise of socialist and pan-Arabist movements would threaten nationalization.[2] Alongside
CIA operations, police modernization and technical aid projects were crucial
in U.S. efforts to thwart these movements and in consolidating pro-Western
regimes open to foreign investment. A State Department envoy stated in a 1951
cable that "stronger police controls could solve most of the internal communist
problems" across the region and thus ensure America's access to oil, which he
called "the single most important factor in American relations with the area."[3]

The United States began implementing this strategy at full strength in 1953
after the overthrow of the secular nationalist Mohammad Mossadegh in Iran.
Through the use of techniques refined in other Cold War hotspots, including
the creation of advanced telecommunications and data management systems,
police were trained in counterintelligence and mobilized for "internal secu-

rity" purposes. Extensive human rights violations ensued. In the short term, the police programs served Washington's interests in helping to fortify client regimes such as that of the Shah and in securing access to oil. Over the long term, however, they fostered a vigorous political backlash and a "blowback" effect, both of which have proved to be cataclysmic.

"Stern Measures to Defeat the Guerrillas": Police Training and the Greek Civil War

Like the U.S. occupations of Japan and Korea, the American intervention in the Greek civil war of 1946–1949 set a precedent for the rest of the Cold War. During the late 1940s, the Truman administration tried to keep indigenous communist movements throughout western Europe in check by means of the Marshall Plan as well as covert methods such as the infiltration of labor unions. In Italy, the military and the CIA equipped the paramilitary Carabinieri to suppress communist demonstrations and to spy on Palmiro Togliatti, the head of the Italian Communist Party, and his associates. In occupied Germany, American advisers reorganized municipal police and established a constabulary responsible for patrolling the border, maintaining order in displaced persons camps, overseeing denazification, and curtailing the black market.[4] American advisers also oversaw the penal system, and according to a secret report, Counter-Intelligence Corps (CIC) agents in some instances obstructed prison management and "interfered with the responsibility of prison wardens by making demands for the release of prisoners," notably Nazi scientists and intelligence agents as part of Operation Paperclip, "contrary to the due process of law."[5]

Denazification, as the historian Carolyn Eisenberg notes, was generally carried out differently in different occupied zones, with U.S. policy contributing to the revival of the old economic order in the belief that the managers of capital would be capable of restoring the country's productivity. Rebuilding the police apparatus was crucial in this context in controlling labor unrest and leftist activists, who, freed from Hitler's concentration camps, were seeking to engender a more sweeping societal transformation.[6] The head of the U.S. police mission in Germany, Colonel Orlando W. Wilson, had been chief of police in Wichita, Kansas, from 1928 to 1939. A protégé of August Vollmer, in the 1950s, he wrote an influential textbook synthesizing many of the progressive ideals in law enforcement. It was used as a blueprint for the international police programs and disseminated in the training academies that were set up worldwide. The central argument, derived from his experiences in the United States and Germany, was that the efficiency of the police could be maximized through the use of up-to date tactical equipment; the scientific deployment of mobile, well-trained troops organized along a hierarchical military model; and the installation of an advanced communications system, comprehensive recordkeeping, and an ongoing public relations program. Supporting the aim of the 1290-d program to "strengthen the resistance of governments against subversion," Wilson reconciled the adoption of political policing operations with a democratic policing model (what he characterized as "Anglo-Saxon concepts"), stating that the "effectiveness of police in dealing with outright subversion and guerrilla activity is directly related to its effectiveness in maintaining law and order."[7]

American policy planners viewed Greece as an important beachhead to the Middle East and its vast oil reserves and thus as a key venue for implementing Wilson's ideals.[8] During World War II, the principal resistance to Nazi occupation had been carried out by the National Liberation Front (better known by its Greek acronym EAM), a coalition of leftist and republican parties led by Ares Velouchiotis and Vaphiadis Markos, of which the communists (KKE, or Communist Party of Greece) were the dominant but not the exclusive element. Emerging as a leading political force, the EAM initiated experiments in communal living and worker-controlled industry, implemented radical land reform and literacy campaigns, and promoted women's rights.[9] In December 1944, Winston Churchill ordered the strafing of Athens by RAF spitfires following an incident in which police were besieged after killing at least ten people and injuring dozens more who were protesting the restoration of German collaborators in the National Guard. Britain subsequently backed royalist forces in a campaign of "white terror" against the EAM, which was accused of instigating the unrest.[10]

Sharing Churchill's fear of radical social movements, the Truman administration channeled nearly $1 billion in emergency aid, including warplanes and stocks of napalm, to fortify the Greek government under Constantin Tsaldaris, who had been a spy for the Nazi regime in Hungary. The American mission under Dwight Griswold, a former Republican governor of Nebraska dubbed by the *New York Times* "the most powerful man in Greece," trained the army and police, which were acknowledged to be "semi-fascist." Secretary of State George C. Marshall, architect of the European recovery plan, wrote to Griswold: "We are aware of the fact that in its efforts to combat the subversive movement, there is a tendency on the part of certain elements in the Greek government to employ strong measures. . . . Stern and determined measures may be necessary to effect the termination of the activities of the guerillas and their supporters as speedily as possible."[11] Marshall's outlook, as these comments reveal, was little different from that of his colonial era predecessors in subordinating human rights to broader geopolitical designs. Those who opposed American power were to be crushed, just like the messianic peasant leaders in the Philippines.

American army advisers worked with the British police mission led by Sir Charles Wickham, the first inspector general of the Royal Ulster Constabulary (a force associated with acts of brutality in Northern Ireland), who trained law enforcement agents throughout the empire, including paramilitary forces in Palestine. According to the historian Georgina Sinclair, while sympathetic to the notion of "policing" rather than "soldiering," Wickham felt that it was a responsibility of the police to fight anyone suspected of being a communist "by an intensification of the normal procedure of operation," a view shared by his American counterparts.[12] Chargé d'affaires James H. Keeley Jr., who kept detailed files of suspected communists while serving as U.S. consul in Salonika from 1936 to 1939, praised Wickham's efforts, writing to Marshall that the British mission had instilled an attitude of professional impartiality in the police of major cities. "It was less successful in this respect with the [Greek] Gendarmerie," he said, "but this is due to circumstances beyond its control, namely the disturbed conditions which have excited passions and required the diversion from its normal peacetime duty of maintaining law and order to that of acting as an auxiliary to the Army in combat against political banditry." Keeley added that without British supervision, "abuse by the Gendarmerie would have reached far more serious proportions," and prison conditions, "bad as they are at present, would have been infinitely worse."[13]

During the reign of proto-fascist General Ioannis Metaxas from 1936 to 1941, the Gendarmerie had been mobilized to dismantle the Communist Party with the aid of U.S. intelligence (as Keeley's activities reveal) and, during World War II, ran death squad operations against EAM partisans in collaboration with the pro-Nazi regime.[14] Afterwards, many of the same individuals continued to command the force, including General Napoleon Zervas, minister of public order, who vowed to answer the terrorism of the guerrillas with "terrorism ten times as strong and slaughter ten times as great." Despite some discomfort with his "violently anticommunist position," the Americans and the British did not purge Zervas, as they had done with war criminals recruited by Reinhard Gehlen's network in Germany, because of his counterintelligence skills and effectiveness against the EAM, and they looked the other way as additional Wehrmacht collaborators were released from prison and restored to positions of prominence.[15]

In the attempt to build an effective internal security apparatus, American and British advisers imparted techniques of data management and population control and supplied Zervas's men with uniforms, Sten guns, mortars, and radios to coordinate patrols. Though conscious of the potential for "right-wing excesses," which were considered to have provoked the civil war, the State Department expanded the Gendarmerie's manpower and encouraged it to attack the guerrillas "aggressively."[16] Soldiers carried out sweep operations, forcibly relocated peasants, and set up checkpoints for resource control purposes, committing abuses such as burning houses as a punitive measure. Peasants accused of supplying food to guerrillas, as well as labor and women's rights activists and other of Tsaldaris's opponents, were among those tortured in underground dungeons or executed by firing squad.[17] Field commanders praised the Gendarmerie for "cleaning up the bandit" situation and countering the "bolshi" presence in Kahenia, Cephalonia, and on the island of Crete. Griswold, who also oversaw police operations in occupied Germany, told the press that those who had been executed were "murderers sentenced by judicial tribunal," while the diplomat Loy Henderson claimed that the elimination of guerrilla warfare was necessary for reconstruction.[18]

Crucial to Anglo-American strategy, advisers worked to modernize urban police forces, including in Athens, where the chief worked closely with the British secret service. They gave lectures at police academies, including in nonlethal riot control and the use of tear gas, distributed literature about the FBI, helped upgrade records collecting and fingerprinting, and initiated a crime-reporting system modeled after the uniform crime report, which was first adopted in the United States in 1930 and exemplified the infatuation of progressive reformers with statistical data in their quest to quantify and then confront social problems. After the formation of the CIA in 1947, the United States developed an intelligence agency in Greece, which carried out photo surveillance, cultivated networks of informants, and became known for "shadowing" Greek political personalities, amassing over 16 million political files.[19]

Among the civilians working with Greek security forces was Theo Hall, administrative officer for the embassy and former chief of police in Wilmette, Illinois. Hall had co-authored an influential text on policing civil disorders and minority relations which advocated for more "preventative police work" and "constant police vigilance over troubled areas" (which became a basis for racial profiling). A liberal internationalist who lamented that the 1943 Detroit race riots had sapped war production and "undermined confidence among our non-white allies," Hall had been a protégé of O. W. Wilson from his days as a beat cop in Wichita and served as his assistant in Germany in reorganizing the police and directing denazification efforts, preparing the way for his tenure in Greece. He had done administrative work alongside Wilson for the Nuremberg Council proceedings and went on to run OPS operations in Guatemala, Bolivia, Ethiopia, and briefly Vietnam after a stint as head of the 1290-d program.[20]

Hall's influence in Greece and that of his contemporaries was hardly positive. The country became the most heavily policed in Europe at a force of over fifty thousand, with a number of museums converted into prisons. Policymakers viewed as their greatest accomplishment the rebuilding of the Gendarmerie, which was crucial to winning the "bandit war." The EAM was gradually decimated, as many of its leaders were exiled or banished into concentration camps such as on the prison island of Makronisis, where conditions resembled those of the Siberian gulag.[21]

The country's authoritarianism was apparent in the investigation of the murder of CBS correspondent George Polk, who had published articles critical of the Truman doctrine and the Tsaldaris government. In a high-level conspiracy, police doctored evidence, accused a dead man of having committed the crime, harassed Polk's wife, and kidnapped and tortured suspected communist ringleader Gregory Stakopolous to force a half-baked confession, even arresting his aged mother. The real killer, Michael Kourtessis, was head of a secret right-wing organization that collaborated with the police in political operations and likely was acting under orders from Tsaldaris.[22]

Through the 1950s, as investment capital from Esso, Dow Chemical, Chrysler and other U.S. corporations poured in, Americans were continuously placed with Greek combat units in preparation for the revival of civil war. Internal reports expressed concerns that the KKE might be restored to legality, about the repatriation of refugees from the Eastern bloc, and by the fact that KKE front organizations won 10 percent of the vote in parliamentary elections in 1952.[23] Operating at an average yearly budget of $300,000, the 1290-d program equipped the Athens police with motor vehicles, radio equipment, IBM computers, and tear gas grenades, which were used to suppress worker and student demonstrations. Advisers such as Miles Furlong of the Detroit Police Department and Theodore Brown, who went on to direct the inter-American police academy in Panama (a precursor to the IPA) and head the OPS in Colombia, El Salvador, and Brazil, worked to establish a central records file and national identification system, contributing to the growth of a mass surveillance state. Modern interrogation and wiretapping techniques were taught. Police arrested people for offenses such as distributing leaflets opposing the establishment of military bases and atomic weapons testing.[24]

In 1963, officers in Salonika were accused of collaborating in the murder of a left-wing deputy, an act that provided the basis for Constantin Costa-Gavras's classic film Z. Political repression peaked during the reign of the colonels, who were later put on trial.[25] Overall, Greece experienced significant disorder in the postwar period, which was exacerbated by American police training programs. Because it evolved as a client state, the country became a model for U.S. policy in the Middle East and the Third World, with Defense Secretary Walt W. Rostow calling for a "Greek solution" in Vietnam.

"Paid For by the USA": Police Aid and the Building of a Client State in Iran

In Iran, police training was integral in stabilizing the power of Shah Mohammad Reza Pahlavi after a 1953 CIA-backed coup overthrew the democratically elected government of Prime Minister Mohammad Mossadegh. The groundwork had been initiated a decade earlier with the advent of a military mission headed by Colonel H. Norman Schwarzkopf, superintendent of the New Jersey

State Police, which modernized the Gendarmerie under the Shah's father, Reza Khan, a Nazi sympathizer who, according to U.S. intelligence, "controlled all phases of public and private life by instilling fear among the people."[26] Schwarzkopf (father of General "Stormin' Norman" Schwarzkopf of Persian Gulf war fame) set up training academies and supplied the Gendarmerie with communications equipment and weapons. His team, which included OSS agent Paul Helliwell, mobilized the Gendarmerie to protect the government against its enemies and set up an intelligence system to keep watch on various political cliques.[27]

In April 1946 the leftist *Rahbar* newspaper, organ of the working-class Tudeh (Masses) Party, characterized the Gendarmerie as a "tool in the hands of the enemies of freedom," which "strangled freedom loving movements."[28] After gendarmes killed one worker and wounded others who were demonstrating for equal wages outside a factory on the border of Azerbaijan, an article posited that the "agents of Mr. Schwarzkopf" were seeking to "help their foreign masters run the country on the principles of capitalism and obtain new zones of influence for obtaining markets and oil." The author, Arman E. Melli, stressed that "the existence of an adviser in the armed forces" of a country is the "beginning of colonization."[29]

Using his contacts in the Gendarmerie, Schwarzkopf (and possibly Helliwell) became part of the group that conspired to overthrow Mossadegh, an "old fashioned liberal . . . and beloved figure of . . . enormous charisma to Iranians of all social classes," according to the political scientist James Bill. The first Iranian to receive a Ph.D. in law from the Sorbonne, Mossadegh had defied American and British interests in nationalizing Iran's oil after his election in 1950. With the fall of Mossadegh, the Shah, formerly a constitutional monarch, became Iran's absolute ruler. Characterized by the CIA as a "devious political practitioner" and a "dangerous megalomaniac," the Shah granted concessions to the Arabian American Oil Company (Aramco) and "ruthlessly eliminated almost all genuine opposition, even of a fairly conservative nature." Reprisals were taken against Mossadegh's supporters and the mass-based Tudeh Party, whose structure was "disrupted by the repressive campaign" and whose leaders were sent into hiding, prison, or exile. Mossadegh himself, spent three years in prison, then remained under house arrest until his death in 1967.[30]

To consolidate the Shah's rule, the United States provided over $240 million in military equipment, including F-84 fighter planes. The Nixon administration allowed the Shah to purchase Maverick missiles and a $500 million IBEX electronic surveillance system as part of what one study has called "the most rapid build-up of military power under peacetime conditions of any nation in the history of the world."[31] In spite of all the resources, the Iranian military was viewed as an inefficient instrument of social control. After five officers were tried for murder, the U.S. embassy reported that the military was hated by the public, a factor that could become "significant if instability should once again come to Iran or various demagogues obtain control of the government."[32]

Under 1290-d, the United States provided over $1 million per year for police training, whose aim was to reduce the "necessity for relying on the armed forces to uphold internal security" and to help the Shah cope with "foreseeable disturbances."[33] The program was headed by Frank Jessup and Michael McCann of the Indiana State Police, a key recruiting ground for the police programs because of the close relationship between Byron Engle and Arthur M. Thurston, chairman of the Farmers National Bank in Shelbyville, who had been superintendent of the Indiana police from 1949 to 1952.[34]

The State Department contracted with professors from the University of Southern California's School of Public Administration, led by John P. Kenney, a former Berkeley patrolman and ICA consultant, to provide courses in police administration at the University of Tehran. FBI agents Carl Betsch and Thomas Finn and Richard Rogers of the MSU Vietnam project rounded out the Iranian advisory team, which established a nationwide telephone and radio network, set up training academies, developed modern photography and crime labs, and brought in IBM computers for the creation of a records management system. The ICA imported tear gas, projectiles, and leg irons through the embassy in Kabul, intensifying the scope of human rights violations.[35]

The national police chief from 1953 to 1960, Alavi Moghaddan, was arrested for extortion and fraud, then briefly promoted to minister of the interior. He was replaced by General Nemattollah Nasiri, the former head of the armed forces, who first came to prominence when he penetrated the guard lines and served Mossadegh the Shah's order of dismissal. According to intelligence reports, the physically large unmarried man slept at the Shah's palace and was his close confidant. His selection provides an example of the direct royal control over the national police and its overt political and military orientation.[36]

In September 1953 a Colonel Giroux, who had a background in police and detective work and had participated in the brutal suppression of a 1932 coal miners' strike in Harlan County, Kentucky, began organizing a national security and intelligence unit, SAVAK, commanded by General Teimur Bakhtiar, who traveled to the United States to take courses from the FBI and the CIA. SAVAK was modeled after the Turkish intelligence agency that was built up under 1290-d. Its mission was to seek out and neutralize threats to the Shah, maintain dossiers on suspicious individuals, and analyze information provided by informants.[37] Kermit Roosevelt, architect of the 1953 coup, and Lucien Conein, an associate of Edward G. Lansdale who played a key role in overthrowing the Ngo brothers in South Vietnam, worked to develop SAVAK into a modern intelligence agency. Officers were taught the tools of spy-craft such as agent recruitment and the use of message drops and safe houses and were trained in psychological warfare and the use of computers to create databases on "subversives." The Israeli Mossad gradually took over training, though the CIA maintained close contacts through the 1970s, when SAVAK was commanded by Nasiri, whom Roosevelt tellingly called "our General."[38]

American police programs on the whole contributed to an expansion of the Shah's social control apparatus and the advent of an Orwellian police state, which many advisers viewed as a marker of Iranian progress. In his end-of-tour report, Frank Jessup recalled that in "the early days, the Shah did not possess the capability of controlling civil disturbances without the use of military force" and had only a loose hold on power, which, thanks to the Americans, had now become more entrenched. Nevertheless, Michael McCann, a professor of police administration at Indiana University who would go on to head the International Police Academy in Washington, noted that problems persisted because "conditions for rapid modernization in the country were not favorable." Police effectiveness was hindered by nepotism, illiteracy, inadequate equipment, and poor pay, which McCann and others felt they could do little to curtail, owing to their being "engrained in Iranian culture."[39] While acknowledging the limits of American power, McCann adopted an Orientalist discourse in linking police shortcomings to cultural backwardness. He overlooked the corrupting political climate bred by the 1953 coup and the misrule of the Shah, who set the benchmark at the top.

Besides molding SAVAK, twenty U.S. advisers, some a remnant from the Schwarzkopf era, assisted the Gendarmerie in breaking up anti-Shah riots and pacifying rebellions by the Baluch, Qashqai, and Kurdish ethnic groups. Under the direction of Colonel Charles Peeke, a former military attaché in Ankara, the ICA developed an intelligence branch and a special strike unit and delivered extensive commodities, including 185 aircraft, 16 Cessna fighters, and CH-I reconnaissance helicopters.[40] The State Department acknowledged that the Gendarmerie was "regarded by the peasants as oppressors," having carried out executions, extortion, and the enforcement of martial law, though it sought to change its image through civic action and rural development programs.[41]

Memorandums from Charles Stelle, the embassy's counselor for political affairs, to the State Department provide insight into the campaign to "hunt down" Dadshah, a Baluch leader seeking to protect tribal lands from encroachment. Characterized by the CIA as a "pocket-sized military genius" and "Robin-Hood type," Dadshah and several comrades were killed in a skirmish after he took down five gendarmes and four pro-government Baluchi. Stelle, a professor of Oriental studies at Harvard and former liaison to Dai Li, and advisers such as Thomas Finn, who trained paramilitary forces in Southeast Asia and Central Africa, instructed the Gendarmerie in surveillance and psychological warfare tactics, leading to Dadshah's downfall. Additional battles were fought in the southwest against antigovernment forces characterized by Stelle as "bandits" and "religious fanatics."[42]

In the late 1950s the Gendarmerie absorbed the Customs Guard and spearheaded opium suppression campaigns in Khorasam province and Azerbaijan. A decade earlier, the widow of anti-drug crusader Hamilton Wright claimed that Iran was a leading global source of opium, in part because of a government monopoly. An American economic mission headed by Arthur Millspaugh even collected opium revenues and directed the royal opium factory, prompting critics to call Millspaugh and his associates "drug sellers."[43] Under American pressure, the Shah passed the first federal anti-opium law in 1955 as part of a drive to clean up vice and legitimate his power. Two FBN agents, Garland Williams and Major McBee, created narcotics squads, which raided opium dens and made use of light aircraft to carry out search-and-destroy campaigns in mountain terrain. Serving at times as a cover for clandestine operations (both Williams and McBee had CIA ties), these initiatives resulted in widely publicized seizures of opium and the destruction of thousands of poppy plants but also caused the displacement of farmers.[44]

Williams and McBee found that opium dens continued to operate clandestinely after the crackdown and were as "difficult to locate as New York speakeasies during prohibition."[45] The Shah allegedly retained a monopoly on all opium plantations. Family members lined their pockets with money from the sale of heroin, which was virtually unknown in Iran prior to the 1953 coup. The Shah's sister Princess Ashraf was arrested by Swiss police for transporting suitcases full of heroin, and his younger brother Mahmoud, who had a reputation as a playboy, trafficked in narcotics between Tehran, Paris, New York, and Detroit. Described by the CIA as possessing a "penchant for danger and cruelty," SAVAK chief Teimur Bakhtiar built a fourteen-story apartment in Tehran, which Tehranis dubbed the "heroin palace." His son was involved in a scheme to import heroin into the United States, ostensibly to fund political policing operations. As with CIA "assets" in Cuba and Thailand who were implicated in the drug trade, the FBI and U.S. Customs were instructed to back off their investigations because the Shah served broader strategic interests, and the United States did not want bad publicity. When Williams raised the subject in a report, he was chewed out by his superiors for "over-stepping his boundaries."[46]

As in Southeast Asia, the cultural acceptance of opium lay at the root of the failure of drug prohibition. In the countryside, excess opium was used in the cultivation of wheat, and peasants used it to fight malaria. In city slums, opium dens served as social clubs where, according to Williams, "men and women sat around on the dirty floor and talked or listened to storytellers recall the ancient glories of Persia." In the capital's great homes, meanwhile, the rich kept expensive and treasured opium pipes for family members and guests.[47] As with other attempts to impose Western mores, most Iranians viewed the new laws as coercive. Criminalization of opium drove prices up and fueled corruption among law enforcement personnel.

Robert R. Schott of the American consulate in Tehran wrote to the State Department in August 1957 that smuggling across the border with Afghanistan was continuing because border guards were taking a cut from the trade. The police chief in Isfahan admitted to Williams: "We've been accepting bribes for so many years that it would be impossible for us to really enforce a law like that. I am a thief and most of my men are thieves."[48] Robert Dreesen, American consul in Azerbaijan reported to the State Department that the police were not even taking "perfunctory action" against the opium houses in Tabriz. "There is serious difficulty encountered in curtailing the consumption of opium because the police force probably has a higher proportion of addicts than any other branch of government service," he explained, adding that the police chief in Tabriz was himself "rumored to be an addict. . . . He constantly wears dark glasses, even when indoors, probably to conceal the dilation of his pupils."[49] These comments all illustrate the paradox of the drug war in Iran, which was a form of neocolonialism in that it was imposed from the outside and its aims were never embraced by local enforcement officials or the civilian population.[50]

In October 1962, Robert W. Komer, a senior staffer on the National Security Council and onetime ambassador to Iraq, drafted an internal defense plan calling for increased assistance to the Gendarmerie, SAVAK, and the national police, partly to obviate the "necessity to use military units to quell demonstrations or riots." Komer observed that Iran remained poor under the Shah despite large foreign exchange revenues from oil. This, he wrote, was breeding public opposition, and the West would be adversely affected by the loss of access to Middle Eastern oil if Iran became dominated by the Soviet bloc. Calling for a "white revolution" to counteract the "red revolution," he expressed concern about the disaffection of students and intellectuals and noted that the loyalty of the Kurdish population, whom the CIA would later recruit to its cause then abandon, was "tenuous."[51]

On the basis of Komer's recommendations, the OPS budget was expanded to $700,000. Advisers such as former Indiana state trooper Walter Weyland oversaw the creation of a firearms range at the police academy and a national identity bureau as well as photography and crime labs and mob control units equipped with water tank sprayers (some sprayed colored water, procured from Rome by Garland Williams). Zoris Wilkins, sheriff of Riverside County, California, installed telecommunications equipment linking remote police outposts to Tehran. Komer wrote enthusiastically to tell Maxwell Taylor, "We've finally gotten [the] Iran special police program out of the bureaucratic quicksand."[52] In June 1963, after demonstrations erupted in Tehran as a result of high unemployment, the OPS provided an emergency shipment of tear gas, police batons, and helmets to militarized riot control units but turned down a request for mounted police advisers because it was felt that "horses would be a liability under conditions of violence." The State Department expressed its gratification to police colonel Abdullah Vasiq for crushing the protests even though at least one major mullah had been killed. In other incidents, the OPS acknowledged the police role in shooting striking teachers and causing "cracked skulls" in suppressing anti-Shah riots.[53]

Police brutality ultimately helped to engender support for Islamist oppositional forces led by Ayatollah Ruhollah Khomeini, who emerged at the forefront of the resistance with the dismantling of the Tudeh Party. Contradicting its human rights rhetoric, the Carter administration expanded arms sales on the eve of the 1979 Islamic revolution and provided riot sticks, tear gas, helmets, and shields, as the Shah's repression intensified.[54] In 1975, Amnesty International had reported that Iran was holding between 25,000 and 100,000 political prisoners. Martin Ennals, secretary-general of Amnesty, noted: "The Shah retains his benevolent image despite the highest rate of death penalties in the world, no valid system of civilian courts, and a history of torture which is beyond belief. . . . No country in the world has a worse record in human rights than Iran."[55]

The police programs played a significant role in facilitating this sorry state of affairs. Making use of sophisticated technology from the United States, SAVAK cultivated networks of informants, spread black propaganda, and, in conjunction with other police units, raided labor and university organizations and kidnapped the Shah's opponents. Many dissidents were hunted down in exile, including Teimur Bakhtiar, who was accused of embezzling $5 million from government coffers and plotting the regime's overthrow from Iraq. SAVAK infiltrated one hundred agents into his network, carried out a fake hijacking to give him a bad name, and then assassinated him in 1970 while he was on a hunting trip.[56]

Within Iran, dissidents were condemned by military tribunals and held in Bagh-e-Mehran and Evin prisons, which contained torture chambers and execution yards. According to CIA analyst Jesse Leaf, agency officials trained SAVAK officers in interrogation methods copied from the Nazis. Although Americans rarely participated in torture, said Leaf, "people who were there saw the rooms and were told of torture. And I know that the torture rooms were toured and it was all paid for by the USA."[57]

The Iranian poet Reza Baraheni, one of many intellectuals detained by the Shah, wrote in *The Nation* that at least "half a million people have been beaten, whipped, or tortured by SAVAK," a cruelty he illustrated with gruesome autopsy photos. In his 1977 book *The Crowned Cannibals*, Baraheni recounted being picked up by SAVAK goon squads and placed in a dark solitary confinement cell, four by eight feet, with nothing but a dirty blanket and no bed. Baraheni noted the tragedy of schoolteachers and doctors being confined when there were shortages of these professionals across the country. Many of his fellow prisoners suffered from dysentery and other diseases and could not stand because of torture injuries such as sore feet, burned backs, or pulled-out toe-nails. Baraheni's beard was ripped out by the head torturer, Hosseinzadeh, and he witnessed others being tortured with snakes.[58]

When the Shah was finally overthrown in 1979, police and SAVAK agents were put on trial, including Colonel Vasiq and General Nematollah Nassiri, who was paraded about on television and subjected to torture before being executed by firing squad. These acts of retribution attest to the depth of public hatred for the policing apparatus built up by the United States, which served as a symbol of the Shah's oppression. The triumph of the Islamic revolution in turn exposed the folly of the modernization theorists and their belief that the United States could manipulate Iranian politics to its liking.

Modernizing Repression in Iraq, Turkey, Lebanon, and Afghanistan

America's heavy-handed influence was widely felt across the Middle East. In Iraq, the United States trained police during the reign of the pro-Western dicta-tor Nuri al-Said, who was overthrown in a 1958 revolution led by Abdul Karim Qasim. The Eisenhower administration intervened out of a desire to tap into the country's oil reserves, developed by British companies receiving lucrative concessions from al-Said.[59] He presided over what British intelligence officers characterized as an "oligarchy of racketeers" who engaged in "shameless land-grabbing" and "tolerated dishonesty and corruption in the police," breeding a widening gulf between the authorities and the majority of the population.[60]

In 1957, fearful that increasing urban discontent, peasant agitation, and military impatience were generating revolutionary conditions, the ICA com-missioned a report on the civil police forces of Iraq, which were at the time heavily subsidized by the British. Under 1290-d, the State Department pledged $1 million in technical aid and equipment to help transform the country from a "semi-feudal" to a "modern civilized state" in which the police would be capa-ble of controlling social unrest driven by "hyper-nationalist" and "anti-colonial elements" opposed to the pro-Hashemite monarchy. The mission of the police would be to protect oil pipelines and Western-owned refineries from sabotage, to infiltrate the communist movement, and to curtail Kurdish uprisings.[61]

Twelve Iraqi officers were sent to the United States for training. Clyde Phelps, veteran of the police programs in Japan, was given an office in the national police headquarters. He introduced the use of tear gas and riot batons to help control demonstrations threatening to bring down al-Said's regime. Police were implicated in the torture and assassination of members of the Iraqi Communist Party, which was outlawed from its inception, and the machine-gunning of civilians, causing the death of hundreds, including teenage girls. Internal reports meanwhile boasted of police success in handling demonstra-tions against British and French plans to seize the Suez Canal and lauded the regime for taking "strong measures to repress and eliminate communist subversive activities."[62]

In December 1957, Theo Hall contracted with the firm of Litchfield, Whiting, Panero, Severud and Associates to draw up plans for a proposed central civil jail at Abu Ghraib in Baghdad West at a cost of $7 million.[63] The deal exemplifies the growth of a police-industrial complex, in which the private sector profited immensely from the expansion of police aid. Construction began right away on the facility and was completed after the 1958 revolution, in which al-Said was killed while trying to flee the country disguised as a woman. The public safety program was closed down at this time because of hostile relations with the new regime, headed by Qasim, who promoted a program of economic nationalism.

In 1963 the Ba'ath Party took power "riding on a CIA train," according to the interior minister, enacting pogroms against suspected communists with the aid of lists provided by U.S. military intelligence. A key source of information was a high-ranking officer of the Baghdad police who served under al-Said and was recruited as a CIA "asset" through the police programs.[64] The 1290-d initiative had paid dividends in this respect. Many Ba'ath victims were tortured at Abu Ghraib, later the site of major human rights violations during the reign of Saddam Hussein and under American military occupation.[65] The central legacy of the police programs was thus the creation of a modern police state apparatus used by different regimes, each for its own ends.

In Lebanon, where the United States feared the growth of pan-Arabism, in 1957 an ICA team headed by Albert DuBois provided $1 million in quasi-military equipment and technical aid to the French-created Gendarmerie to bolster the pro-Western regime of Camille Chamoun, a Maronite Christian who was the subject of a Muslim rebellion after he tried to pass a constitutional amendment allowing him to gain reelection at the end of his six-year term. The marines were eventually sent in to restore order, and Chamoun was replaced by General Fouad Chehab, an anticommunist leader deemed acceptable to American interests.[66] Police training with a heavy emphasis on riot control was conceived of as an alternative to military force, which was applied when covert methods failed to engender the desired results.

Turkey also received over $1 million in police assistance during the 1950s. Internal reports stressed the "authoritarianism" of Prime Minister Adnan Menderes, a wealthy landowner who pushed for the privatization of state industries, and noted that the police were "principally political," which was seen as beneficial in stamping out communist activity. The mission was headed by Charlie O'Brien of the Detroit Police Department (who later died in Vietnam), "Jack" Goin, and Byron Engle, who imported techniques from Japan as director of the national police for a year. Working directly for the CIA, they set up training academies, enhanced surveillance, and instructed the paramilitary Jandarma in riot control. Station wagons, jeeps, and light aircraft were provided, and a radio communication and records system was set up, along with a crime lab equipped with microscopes and field test equipment, in an effort to modernize the repressive state security apparatus. Some CIA "assets" in the police were recruited into secret anticommunist armies, which carried out "black flag operations" and terrorized leftists.[67]

FBN agents Frank Sojat and Garland Williams were attached to the police advisory commission, though their investigations were obstructed by police protecting government officials who sold heroin. Pointing to the case of Ihsan Sekban, a prosperous heroin manufacturer and gang leader who had men in government ministries and the police, Sojat reported to FBN chief Harry J. Anslinger that "important narcotics violators are very wealthy and powerful enough to avoid prosecution and arrest through bribery." Police operations floundered in the early 1960s after a military coup resulted in the hanging of Menderes and the arrest of Kemal Aygun, Istanbul police chief, who worked closely with American intelligence. The unpopularity of the program was reflected in a Turkish newspaper report which declared that American police were teaching their protégés "gangster methods, brutality, and oppression of the people."[68]

The 1290-d program in Afghanistan, a key Cold War battleground and a semi-police state, according to U.S. intelligence, demonstrates the stark limits of American power in the Middle East. The State Department provided $300,000 in police equipment in order to gain leverage among security forces, dominated by ethnic Pashtuns, and help suppress demonstrations against King Zahir Shah and Prime Minister Mohammed Daoud led by pro-communist elements and "religious fanatics" from Kandahar (whom, ironically, the CIA would recruit twenty years later to fight the Soviets).[69]

The principal adviser, Albert Riedel, was a polygraph specialist with the Berkeley Police Department whose experience in Kabul was far from pleasant. He could barely communicate with officers who did not speak English and had difficulty finding a qualified interpreter. While accepting American supplies, including walkie-talkies, cameras, polygraph equipment, tear gas, and leg irons, the Afghan police barely acknowledged Riedel's presence and refused to take any advice on how to manage the police force. Riedel noted to his superiors that he was not even allowed to tag along with police on their patrols and was made to feel like an "old colored gentleman" he once interrogated back in Oregon, "left to sit idly, completely, but however politely ignored." Riedel added that the "Prime Minister never wanted a police adviser. Yes, he would take any free donations of equipment, but they would use it the way they wanted." In his view, the government did not want to be exposed to any new ideas, and the king "could not tolerate any change."[70]

Besides providing insight into existing racial mores, Riedel's comments illustrate the difficulty of trying to impose Western norms in a country where strong nationalist sensibilities prevail and foreigners are viewed with suspicion owing to historical circumstance. They also highlight the dangers of the police programs in providing weaponry to the security forces of authoritarian leaders who invariably appropriate them for their own ends. Unlike many of their counterparts in the developing world desperate for foreign aid, Afghan officials did not pay the usual lip service to the suggestions of American advisers, an attitude resulting in the cutoff of aid and the straining of bilateral relations. The most salient legacy of the 1290-d program in Afghanistan was the identification of the United States with police repression. In a 1959 memo, Arthur Lang of the USOM warned the American embassy in Tehran that it is not "good advertising for the U.S." when prisoners subjected to torture look down at the leg irons and "see the ICA emblem."[71] Indeed, Afghans have remained distrustful of American motives ever since, as we have seen in the scope of resistance to the recent occupation.

Executive Mercenaries: The OPS in Riyadh, Karachi, and Jordan

In Saudi Arabia, where, in the words of CIA agent Robert Baer, Washington sold its soul for access to the country's rich oil fields, police training was designed to fortify the Ibn Saud dynasty, which upheld sharia law and was notorious for adopting strict controls on freedom of expression, repressing women's rights, publicly beheading criminals, and maintaining a fiercely anticommunist, pro-U.S. foreign policy.[72]

America's alliance with Ibn Saud dated to the 1930s, when the king granted oil concessions in return for aid and security assistance. A 1948 CIA report noted that Ibn Saud's power was "so absolute . . . that no problem of internal security really exists. The backwardness of the people precludes organized disaffection."[73] In the late 1950s, the CIA began warning of a growing alliance between communists, Nasserists, Ba'athists, and nationalists which threatened Crown Prince Faisal, a vicious anti-Semite who was seen, according to one report, as the "best representative of our interests in the economic sphere." The Eisenhower administration provided a military grant of $45 million and sold the Saudis $110 million worth of high-tech hardware in return for access to the Dhahran airfield. Police were brought to Michigan State University for training, and a police academy was constructed in Mecca. Great promise was seen in the role of the police in suppressing a strike over segregated living quarters at the Aramco oil conglomerate in 1956, despite the fact that it resulted in public whippings and at least two deaths.[74]

In the early 1960s, after a brief thaw in relations, Faisal sought an increase in military aid owing to his support for the royalists in the civil war in Yemen. Cabinet-level officials were receptive, as they feared that growing internal strife would be an "invitation" for Egyptian president Gamal Abdel Nasser "to re-instigate his activity" on the Arabian peninsula, hence "threatening American economic interests." Saudi Arabia was seen as "key to the entire peninsula," and potentially a "good example for the rest of the Arab world in its promotion of free enterprise."[75] The Johnson administration contracted with Lockheed Martin to provide three squadrons of supersonic aircraft and surface-to-surface missiles and sent a CIA labor attaché to infiltrate oil worker unions. The Americans also built up the intelligence services, the Istikhbarat, whose activities in undermining Nasserist and socialist organizations extended into Egypt, where they sponsored the Muslim Brotherhood.[76]

Between 1968 and 1975, Saudi Arabia deposited $3.3 million in a trust fund with the USAID to pay for police assistance.[77] The program was heavily guarded from the American public and unique in being entirely funded by the Saudis. Several dozen officers were sent to the IPA and to International Police Services, Inc., a CIA front in Washington. In 1971—coinciding with the repression of the Marxist-oriented "Sons of the Arabian Peninsula" allegedly behind a coup attempt—an OPS team headed by Jeter Williamson (who was later presented with a sword and gold scabbard by Faisal's brother) reviewed the surveillance and protection of oil fields for the Ministry of the Interior. He called for improved police coordination and communications to ensure the security of the Arabian American and Getty oil companies. Training and commodities were supplied to help fulfill these ends, including radio transceivers, telephones, vehicles, switchboards, photographic ink, chemical crystals, and other lab equipment.[78]

A major focus of American training was in riot control, the ambassador having lauded the role of the National Guard in suppressing a June 1967 riot outside the headquarters of Aramco, which earned record profits during Faisal's reign and expanded its exploration activities. OPS adviser Edward Bishop, however, lamented the lack of "enthusiasm" of local officials and their "indifference" to technical aid projects, which he felt were being set back by a lack of qualified personnel. The programs nevertheless made significant achievements in frontier defense and in strengthening the security apparatus of the ruling dynasty. Thousands of SAP members were executed or detained in special guard camps under the most inhuman conditions.[79] In 1975, after the OPS disbanded, the Saudi government commissioned a study of internal security organizations and the penal system. The study was directed by Herbert Hardin, former chief of operations in Latin America, and "Jack" Goin, both of whom were paid through private channels. The Vinnell Corporation of Virginia, an engineering firm and mercenary outfit that built military bases in Okinawa during World War II, was subsequently given a $77 million contract to continue training the Saudi police and National Guard, a critical instrument of social control capable of neutralizing the armed forces in the case of a coup.

Staffed predominantly by former Green Berets and OPS officers, Vinnell had a history of serving as a CIA cover. One Pentagon official referred to it as "our own little mercenary army in Vietnam." Some of its men were hired directly by foreign oil companies. A Vinnell staffer and former army officer told *Newsweek*: "We are not mercenaries because we are not pulling triggers. We train people to pull triggers." One of his colleagues added wryly, "Maybe that makes us executive mercenaries."[80] The use of private security contractors enabled the executive branch to get around congressional censure in propping up the House of Saud and securing access to the oil fields after it brokered a secret deal for recycling petrodollars back into the American economy in the wake of the OPEC boycotts.[81] In 2003, Vinnell staffers were targeted in a terrorist attack. By that point the United States had long been identified with political repression and corruption in the country—with much good reason, unfortunately.

In Jordan, the United States adopted a public safety program to fortify King Hussein and to counter the Palestine Liberation Organization (PLO). After the Eisenhower administration established relations with Hussein in the 1950s, the CIA provided cash payments and helped build his intelligence service. The arrival of police advisers such as firearms specialist Elmer Radmer, who had previously served in Cambodia, coincided with Hussein's imposition of martial law, resulting in the outlawing of trade unions and suppression of freedom of speech. The State Department provided revolvers, riot control batons, and shields by way of Lebanon, as well as two DC-3 aircraft. It instructed Jordanians in fingerprint technology and strengthened the curriculum at the Royal Police College, stressing the function of the police as the "first line of defense" against subversion.[82]

Following the 1967 Six-Day War with Israel, the OPS ferreted out $1.1 million in emergency equipment to help Jordan confront Palestinian guerrillas and rioters. CIA agents worked with the secret police in enacting a drive against those who were involved in "political scheming," resulting in a large influx of political prisoners.[83] Raymond W. Meier was assigned to oversee and reform the prison system so that "the Hashemite kingdom of Jordan under the leadership of King Hussein can show the way in the correctional field." Meier inspected jails throughout the country, which he found lacked plumbing, beds, furniture, and proper bathing facilities. (In the Bethlehem jail, inmates had to bathe in their toilets.) Cell doors were often only five feet high, and there were few opportunities for work. Meier lobbied for funding to improve the physical infrastructure and sought to introduce the kinds of correctional innovations that were prevalent in the United States, including juvenile facilities, probation, removal of the mentally ill from the prison population, and vocational training and recreation.

In practice, there is little evidence of improvement. The prison in Amman, for example, continued to house political offenders and remained in "very bad shape," according to internal reports. Inmates were kept in underground cells, and the prison was staffed by officials who "knew how to make people talk," implying a proliferation of torture. The victims of police abuses were characterized as communists, but according to Meier, "other information indicates there were people from several other political groups and students plus the PLO."[84] These comments point to the shortcomings of penal reform and the contributions of the OPS to the suppression of radical nationalist movements, which was a primary aim of the police programs.

Pakistan, valued as a listening post and landing pad for U-2 spy planes, was another authoritarian state receiving police aid: $13 million in this case. The programs were used to funnel weapons to Punjabi general Ayub Khan and his brutal successor Yahya Khan, who courted U.S. support in Pakistan's rivalry with India.[85] American policymakers acknowledged the poor public image of the police, who served as "instruments of the regime in power." They claimed, however, that Chinese and Afghan communists were behind the growing labor and student unrest and rebellions in the northwest among the Baluchi and Pashtuns, necessitating U.S. training for "internal security."[86]

After being transferred from Vietnam, Orval Wooner, who had served as police chief in Bakersfield and Huntington Beach, California, rewrote the detective training and traffic school curriculums and discouraged the "circle of death practice," in which police fired their rifles into a crowd, causing people to be killed in the stampede. Tear gas grenades were shipped to Pakistan, and Pakistani officers were sent to the IPA, the University of Southern California, and American-funded academies in Iran.[87] Peaking at a budget of $1.7 million in 1963, OPS training extended into East Pakistan, where police were involved in suppressing the Bangladeshi independence movement and cooperated with army units who, according to one witness, engaged in some of the "most calculated savagery . . . visited on a civil population in recent times." The Special Group on Counter-Insurgency, fearing that "communist and extreme leftist elements were exploiting the low economic status of the majority of the population," sent Wooner and CIA agents Robert Janus and Robert Nate Bush to Dacca to train police and paramilitary units.[88]

CIA agents operating under the 1290-d program and OPS helped develop Inter-Services Intelligence (ISI), which ran a mass surveillance network rivaling SAVAK. "Jack" Monroe and Charlie Nesbitt, a San Francisco beat cop who served in Indonesia, Jordan, and Saudi Arabia, created an anti-narcotics unit working along the Afghan border. Its effectiveness was hampered by bribery and the corruption of the ISI, which sold heroin to fund clandestine operations. Over time, the police continued to suffer from "low morale and discipline."[89] With an emphasis on internal security, American training contributed to political repression and intensified ethnic divisions that were a legacy of British colonialism and lay at the source of the country's dysfunctionality.

In his book *Sowing Crisis: The Cold War and American Dominance in the Middle East*, Rashid Khalidi traces the impact of the Cold War in exacerbating internecine conflict and facilitating the spread of political authoritarianism and repression in the Middle East. The two superpowers, especially the United States, which enjoyed overwhelming military superiority, focused on achieving strategic advantage and gaining control over vital energy supplies. The region's people became pawns in a larger game of global competition.[90] The police training programs were but one way in which the United States exhibited its influence. Justified under the guise of the Cold War, they strengthened pro-Western despots such as the Shah of Iran and enabled privileged elites to crack down more efficiently on regional minorities and social movements pressing for badly needed social change. American policymakers feared the spread of Arab nationalism and socialism, which threatened Western access to the region's oil. They emphasized the social control function of the police and were influential in importing modern weapons and policing technologies, which enhanced coordination in the hunt for subversives.

During the buildup to the Iraq war and after, Western commentators constantly emphasized a tradition of political authoritarianism and corruption in the Arab states as a marker of their supposed backwardness and need for foreign guidance. Rarely have they acknowledged the role of the United States in propping up dictatorships and contributing to the growth of powerful state security apparatuses mobilized for repression. Doing so would serve to challenge the comforting Orientalist narratives used to rationalize waging the "War on Terror" and might provide the first step toward establishing more harmonious bilateral relations and a peaceful future.

Chapter **10**

The Dark Side of the Alliance for Progress
Police Training and State Terror in Latin America during the Cold War

Only in an atmosphere of public order can the goals of the Alliance be achieved.
—Public Safety Division briefing, Guatemala, 1962

They [police and state security agents] are "trained" to combat "Castro-communist infiltration," as expressed by the hypocritical alienizing language made fashionable by the pro-imperialist dissemination media of the continent.
—Chilean student, April 1965

Murder, torture and mutilation are alright so long as our side is doing it and the victims are communists.
—Viron Vaky, U.S. Deputy Chief of Mission, Guatemala, 1968

In fall 1955 Lee Echols, a national pistol shooting champion and veteran of the police programs in Japan, received a call from his friend Byron Engle asking him to go to Bolivia as part of the 1290-d program. Without hesitation, the forty-nine-year-old customs officer from Calexito, California, accepted and began work setting up training schools and pistol ranges and instructing the secret police in advanced methods of surveillance, interrogation, and infiltration. Fluent in Spanish, Echols subsequently went on to Uruguay and Cuba, where he created a special "traffic squad" (evidently a cover for more secret police operations) under Hernando Hernandez Hernandez, Fulgencio Batista's chief of police, who was later executed by Fidel Castro for alleged crimes against humanity. After a stint as sheriff of Yuma County, Arizona, Echols rounded out his Foreign Service career in the Dominican Republic with the OPS, where he coordinated an elite jungle warfare battalion that was thrust into action in the months preceding the 1965 marine invasion.

Heir to "Chesty" Puller and other Banana War veterans, Echols provides a window into the secret history of American intervention in Latin America during the Cold War. After the 1959 Cuban revolution, police training programs emerged as a crucial dimension of the Alliance for Progress, a Marshall Plan–

type program designed to foster economic development and undercut support for the radical left. The architect of the Alliance, John F. Kennedy, criticized Eisenhower's backing of dictators, which, he said, left the continent ripe for social revolution. In practice, however, his policies displayed more continuity than discontinuity.

Latin American nationalists recognized that an underlying goal of the Alliance was to advance the economic interests of the United States by subsidizing American contractors and improving local infrastructure and transportation to allow for the more efficient extraction of raw materials, while saddling their nations with debt.[1] Although the Alliance brought some benefits, poverty and inequality increased during the 1960s, the "decade of development." Fears about the spread of Cuban-style socialism and an ardent desire to win the Cold War made Kennedy suspicious of even moderate leftist reformers.[2] The majority of Alliance funds were consequently channeled through the CIA to subvert democratic regimes and mount counter-guerrilla operations. Arthur Schlesinger Jr., a Harvard historian and senior Kennedy aide, later lamented that "counterinsurgency was a ghastly illusion which was used cruelly in the hands of its user and distorted and perverted the Alliance's goals."[3]

The Office of Public Safety embodied the imperialistic character of the Alliance. Beneath the humanitarian rhetoric was a continued desire on the part of U.S. officials to mold Latin American societies to their liking and to control political developments. Policymakers saw as a technical problem the need to demilitarize and decentralize the police while at the same time mobilizing them to contain social unrest. They acknowledged that Latin American police forces were repressive but felt this could be overcome through advisory assistance and training. As Roger Hilsman noted in an internal study: "Police cadres [in many Latin American countries] come from the Army and operate as small armies. ... They often function as a means of controlling the populace in the interests of the ruling class. Suspects are addressed imperiously and brusquely. The police are kept in barracks with large numbers on alert status. When disturbances occur, they rush out in large squads. Crowds are met like military opponents with gunfire. Massive fatalities can result."[4]

Hilsman and his colleagues viewed the task of the United States as one of curbing the overtly oppressive character of the police while maintaining their political orientation. Riot control and the suppression of leftist movements were to be accomplished in a more organized and systematic yet humane way. These aims proved to be contradictory and untenable. Advisers could not control or monitor the way weapons and training were adopted. As in other areas, the emphasis placed on counterintelligence and stamping out subversion brought out the most brutal tendencies of the police, while the United States pressed for the passage of national security laws easing legal constraints on police activity. American training programs ultimately contributed to the spread of extensive political violence, which generated resistance and instability rather than stability, in contravention of the Alliance's announced aims. They hindered development and led to a veritable Dark Age in Latin American history, rife with torture and death squads.

"The Cops Were Out-Killing the Communists": Police Training and State Terror in Venezuela and the Dominican Republic

Venezuela exemplifies the diversion of Alliance resources for the purposes of violent social control. The Kennedy administration lavished over $100 million in Alliance funds to President Rómulo Betancourt (1958–1964), a liberal modernizer who replaced dictator Marcos Pérez Jiménez, a favorite of the Eisenhower administration. He promoted technical assistance to industry, public housing, and moderate land reform while accepting the presence of foreign corporations, including Standard Oil, which controlled 95 percent of Venezuela's largest oil company, Creole Petroleum. Although Betancourt was long viewed by the CIA as a progressive capable of preventing the rise of communism, his moderation and acquiescence to foreign oil interests angered young Venezuelans inspired by the Cuban revolution. He cracked down harshly on the left, which resulted in the growth of organizations such as the Movement of the Revolutionary Left and the Armed Forces of National Liberation, led by the anti-imperialist Douglas Bravo.[5]

Peaking at a budget of $460,000 in 1965, police programs were crucial, along with military aid, in the effort to destroy these organizations. Prior to the 1962 elections in Venezuela, at which time half the congress was in prison, the OPS sent John Longan, an Oklahoma City police officer and Texas Border Patrol agent, to train the Caracas police in American-style patrols and in the use of Mace and counterterrorism techniques such as disarming a sniper in a building without harming residents. Drawing on official OPS ideology, Longan emphasized the use of surgical but nonlethal methods of riot control, including the use of tear gas as an alternative to submachine guns, so that "no martyrs were created and the Communists had nothing to exploit."[6]

Paradoxically, the OPS supported a measure eliminating the requirement that a policeman who killed a suspect be arrested, which then spawned death squad activity. The upper-class father of a torture victim wrote the minister of justice that "the goal of defeating communism is not obtained by applying to communists, contrary to Christian ethics, inhuman methods of violence which make us equal to beasts." The Americans saw things differently. The *Los Angeles Times* reported approvingly that as a result of OPS assistance, the "tide of the battle had turned and . . . the cops were out-killing the communists. . . . [E]nemy casualties included a number of red students who hitherto had roamed the city in sports cars and carried on their marauding almost without hindrance."[7]

Showing where their priorities rested, the OPS met monthly with security officers of Creole Petroleum and the major mining companies to discuss insurgency problems. Public safety adviser Clifton Monroe, later chief surveillance officer with the border patrol in Panama, had served for ten years as a Creole supervisor in Caracas. Others such as the Russian Nick Yantsin were affiliated with the Phoenix program in Vietnam. Briefings sent to the embassy expressed satisfaction that the apprehension of top "terrorist commanders" was allowing the OPS mission to change from helping to "put out emergency fires" to the "long, hard business of assisting the Venezuelan government upgrade its police forces."[8] The 1974 phase-out report, co-authored by former Indiana state trooper Stanley Guth, hailed the programs for "meeting the challenges of the 1960s" by confronting "urban terrorism and extremism" and curtailing threats to internal security. The left, however, would reemerge in the 1990s with the revolution of Hugo Chávez, owing to lingering structural inequalities and resentment against the brutality of U.S.-backed regimes.[9]

In the Dominican Republic, where the State Department provided over $4 million in police aid, the Alliance put a similarly benign face on classic imperial policies. In 1962, following the assassination of Rafael Trujillo and the advent of a new government headed by the conservative Joaquín Balaguer, Attorney General Robert Kennedy sent two detectives from the Los Angeles Police Department's "Mexican squad" to train an elite unit, the Cascos Blancos, which helped the government reclaim the streets of Santo Domingo from the revolutionary June 14th movement. Equipped with tear gas, masks, and the white helmets that provided its name, the Cascos Blancos became so hated that in 1965, according to OPS reports, it was the subject of "severe and concentrated attack," effectively "eliminating it as a riot control force."[10]

In April 1965, emergency police aid was delivered to bolster the invasion by U.S. Marines, which was designed to keep out of power the social democrat Juan Bosch, who was seen as a threat to American sugar interests for promoting progressive labor codes.[11] Advisers such as Elmer "Tommy" Adkins and Knute Thorpe were sent from Vietnam to develop telecommunications, modern record keeping, and rural patrol networks. The CIA provided $32.6 million under USAID cover for police intelligence and oversaw "subversive investigations" by the FBI-trained director of national security services and creation of an elite jungle warfare unit. The OPS further subsidized an expansion of the National Police Academy at Boca Chica, built a library specializing in works on communism and counterinsurgency, and imported rifles as well as fingerprinting and ballistics technologies to aid in crowd control. In November 1966 Secretary of State Dean Rusk noted with approval the effective use by Santo Domingo police chief General José Morillo López of "high pressure water vehicles for controlling angry crowds."[12]

As Rusk's comments illustrate, the United States was sanctioning police practices reminiscent of the Jim Crow South. Democrat Wayne Morse of Oregon, one of only two senators to dissent against the Gulf of Tonkin resolution authorizing military intervention in Southeast Asia, was a lone voice of opposition, demanding before the Senate, "Just who are we to think we can teach the Dominican police anything that they did not learn in Trujillo's days." With Belaguer safely reensconced in power, OPS-trained units rounded up sugar union activists, slum community organizers, and Bosch supporters and kept tabs on the Communist Party. Hector Aristy, leader of a constitutionalist party defeated in fraudulent 1966 elections, was among those imprisoned, and two of his bodyguards were killed.[13] Amnesty International called attention to political assassinations, the kidnapping of youth leaders, and the torture of political prisoners. "Jack" Monroe, a veteran of the police programs in Southeast Asia and Africa, lamented that "if [the rumors are] even half-true, it is a sad commentary on the Dominican police that they are involved in official terrorism, assassination, and corruption."[14] Monroe's comments implied that these problems were innate to the Dominican Republic, failing to acknowledge the ways in which American training had contributed to such behavior worldwide.

"Neutralizing" the ELN and FARC: Police Aid and Violence in Colombia

In Colombia, American police programs exacerbated the growth of a vicious civil war rooted in rampant social inequalities and the political marginalization of the poor. During the bloody period of La Violencia (1948–1958), the conservative power structure institutionalized repression and crushed the popular uprising spawned by the assassination of reformist presidential candidate Jorge Eliecer Gaitan. The Eisenhower administration backed General Gustavo Rojas Pinilla, who was favored by the landowning elite.[15] Under the 1290-d program, the National Police were trained in forensics, investigations, and anti-sabotage techniques. A 1958 report by Herbert Hardin, a graduate of the University of California at Berkeley School of Criminology and police administrator in Albuquerque, New Mexico, acknowledged that they were a "repressive type of police organization."[16]

Undeterred, in 1959, after a National Front government led by the liberal Alberto Lleras Camargo took power, a CIA advisory team headed by Hans Tofte and other veterans of the anti-Huk campaign in the Philippines helped build an internal security infrastructure, encouraging improved coordination between the police and military and the establishment of "hunter-killer teams" to defeat loosely organized peasants seeking regional autonomy. In the early 1960s, army and police units launched Plan Lazo ("snare" or "noose"), a clandestine operation to destroy independent self-governing republics. Plan Lazo was followed up by Operation Marquetelia, an aggressive assault on guerrilla-controlled territory using psychological warfare, heavy artillery, and napalm.[17] Reports noted that the casualty rate for security forces went from close to even to a ratio of seven to two. The guerrillas in turn formed the Fuerzas Armadas Revolucionarias de Colombia (FARC), whose leader Manuel Marulanda (known as Tiro Fijo, "Sure Shot") declared the peasantry to be "victims of a policy of fire and sword carried out by oligarchic usurpers of power."[18]

Rooted in peasants' self-defense militias, FARC aimed to promote land reform and nationalize resources controlled by multinational corporations. The Ejército Liberacion Nacional (ELN) was another guerrilla organization supported by the oil workers' union and middle-class students disillusioned by the failure of the National Front of liberals and conservatives to engender sustainable economic development or adopt social programs for the poor. Its most famous recruit was Father Camilo Torres Restrepo, scion of a distinguished Colombian family who believed that Christians had a duty to struggle on behalf of social justice. Speaking to packed crowds about the necessity of expropriating the latifundios, nationalizing natural resources, and forging a people's government, he fused a secular revolutionary Marxism with an intense Roman Catholic faith in an ideology that provided inspiration for liberation theology.[19]

In October 1963, as demonstrations and strikes against conservative president Guillermo León Valencia Muñóz (1962–1968) gripped the capital, the OPS established training schools, set up crime labs, and brought in an intelligence specialist with experience in Malaya. The police, according to one report, "liked to participate in counter-bandit operations with [the] army because of the prospect of better rations, sleeping bags, and raincoats and the issuance of ammunition and grenades." Another report, co-authored by Herbert Hardin, complained that police were handicapped by the judicial system and urged that "bandit gangs are beyond any hope of rehabilitation and therefore should be hunted down through investigative methods with relentless determination." These comments typify the attitude of OPS personnel, who promoted an aggressive Dirty Harry approach to policing that was dismissive of legal controls and led to the spread of human rights violations.[20]

Through the early 1970s, the OPS provided $7.8 million in police aid and sent over 450 Colombians to the International Police Academy. Advisers led by David Laughlin, a retired captain in the Indiana State Police, Theodore Brown, who later defended the OPS before Congress, and John Neeley, a former FBI and CIA agent who had headed the program in Panama, provided canine training and established a civilian registration and identity card program. They imported computers to systematize the collection of information on guerrillas, created a counter-narcotics brigade (whose entire command was implicated in drug crimes in 1976) and a 110-man regiment to protect oil installations vulnerable to sabotage, and provided training in industrial security.[21]

American intervention was motivated largely by geopolitical ambitions, ideology, and economics. American private investment totaled over $700 million, half of it in petroleum, and U.S. exports accounted for 45 percent of the country's imports. A 1963 planning document proclaimed that its rich natural resources, geographic location, and fertile land made Colombia "favorable for rapid economic development. . . . If [foreign aid programs] succeed, then [Colombia] will serve as an outstanding example for other countries and thus demonstrate that firm association with the Western world can offer a path to rapidly increasing living standards."[22]

According to the investigative reporter Gerard Colby, Colombia served as a "pre-Vietnam experiment in [Robert] McNamara's 'systems' approach to integrating communications, rapid air mobility, concentrated firepower, and computer-assisted intelligence for finding and tracking an enemy."[23] The police programs were especially valued in this last context. Reports proudly document the role of the police in "neutralizing leftist and terrorist groups" as a result of expanded telecommunications and "eliminating bandits" loyal to the ELN and FARC. In January 1966 Theodore Brown noted that the "National Police scored well on number of bandits killed, wounded, and captured," and mentioned an incident in which police entered a bar and killed three guerrilla supporters as well as a female employee.[24]

In February 1966 Father Torres was killed by the police, several months after being fired as chaplain of the University of Bogotá for political outspokenness. He had proclaimed: "The people are desperate and ready to stake their lives in order that the next generation may not know slavery, in order that their children . . . may be educated, housed, fed, clothed, and above all that they may have dignity. In order that they may be independent of American power." According to an OPS report, Torres was slain in a jungle firefight along with a female guerrilla, Mona Mariella, as he was bayoneting a felled policeman who had stumbled upon his band while lost.[25]

Sympathetic sources claimed that Torres's band was ambushed and that he was assassinated while tending to a wounded comrade.[26] The exact circumstances are difficult to determine because of the political implications. The OPS reports are highly revealing, nevertheless, of the intimate connection between rural security advisers and the National Police and their monitoring of and direct participation in counter-guerrilla operations. Torres became a martyr to the revolutionary cause, second only to Ernesto "Che" Guevara in the pantheon of leftist heroes of the 1960s. His death ignited demonstrations across the country, which the authorities worked to suppress. Days after his funeral, the OPS established a task force on riot control and shipped 700 shields and fifty megaphones as well as thousands of tear gas grenades and carbines through the army depot.[27]

In October 1968 stepped-up action by police in rural areas dealt damaging blows to FARC, including the death of second-in-command Ciro Trujillo Castano and a high-level cadre, Chone de Humo (meaning "Puff of Smoke"). By May 1970 a full-scale state of siege was in effect, enabling police to justify the abrogation of due process in the name of "national security."[28] Public safety reports noted intensified clashes between guerrillas and police, including members of the ELN's Camilo Torres Front based in Santander, as well as high rates of civilian casualties and deaths totaling over one hundred per month. Bombings and kidnappings in the capital also increased, as did death squad activity and torture by state security forces.[29]

During the mid-1960s, Byron Engle oversaw the reorganization of Colombia's police intelligence organization, the Departamento Administrativo de Seguridad (DAS). An avid hunter and competitive rifle and pistol target shooter whose attention to detail epitomized the professional ethic that the OPS sought to instill in its protégés, Engle had extensive experience working with intelligence services dating from his time in Japan and was fanatically committed to the destruction of "Marxist terrorist" organizations worldwide. Believing that an effective police force should serve as the "eyes and ears of the government," he envisioned that the DAS would spearhead the government's counter-guerrilla war, enabling the police to focus on civilian crimes.[30]

With this goal in mind, the OPS provided hundreds of thousands of dollars in arms and communications equipment and devised index file systems, taught wiretapping techniques, and developed informants in labor and student circles. Leader grants were awarded to DAS chiefs to take courses at the FBI and CIA, including General Jorge Ordóñez Valderrama, who was later indicted on embezzlement and drug trafficking charges.[31] Public safety reports noted a gradual improvement in efficiency and morale at the DAS (whose officers became known for robbing cocaine dealers and reselling their stashes) and heralded its role in "fingering" FARC leaders such as Conrado Salazar (alias "Zarpazo") for the army to kill. During elections, the DAS was devoted to internal security investigations in Bogotá, where it effectively "neutralized [code for longtime confinement or execution] a number of individuals active in the leftist and terrorist organizations."[32]

As in other Cold War "trouble spots," OPS staff imparted novel interrogation methods derived from CIA mind-control experiments, including the use of sodium pentothal and the polygraph to "elicit every shred of information." They brought in telephone wires, electroshock, and polygraph equipment used in torture and set up padded interrogation rooms, which were "proving their worth." One public safety report noted that "in Bogotá and certain other cities throughout Colombia, the necessary interrogation equipment is being installed to provide for modern interrogation procedures." What was meant by the term "modern" is unclear, but it likely implies electronic apparatus and sophisticated methods of psychological coercion designed to facilitate the extraction of information.[33]

The police programs on the whole contributed to the militarization of Colombian society and the spread of vicious cycles of violence. Labor, human rights, and peasant activists were among those rounded up and killed in police sweeps. CIA reports acknowledged that the DAS and other security forces trained by the United States employed "death squad tactics" and had a "history of assassinating civilians in guerrilla areas," cooperating with narcotics-related paramilitary groups in attacks against suspected guerrilla sympathizers, and killing captured combatants.[34] They nevertheless continued to receive lavish funding into the twenty-first century, helping to consolidate the neoliberal order.

"A Counterinsurgency Running Wild": The OPS and Dirty War in Guatemala

As in Colombia, American police training in Guatemala played a key role in converting the national police "from a ramshackle assortment of thugs," as the historian Kirsten Weld puts it, "into a streamlined, professional counter-insurgency apparatus." Valued for its strategic location and proximity to the Panama Canal, Guatemala was heralded as another showpiece for the Alliance and was the site of the largest OPS program in Central America, at a budget over $6 million. American advisers trained 32,000 police, including at least 370 at the IPA, as part of the effort to roll back the 1944 revolution, which overthrew the dictator Jorge Ubico. The revolutionary leaders were seen as dangerously radical, pressing land reform initiatives that threatened the profits of the United Fruit Company. The United States sided with the conservative oligarchy, the clergy, the military, and rabidly anticommunist students who shared in the goal of stamping out the political left and restoring the old social order.[35]

Police aid was first initiated after the 1954 CIA-backed coup against President Jacobo Árbenz, a social democrat who introduced the most progressive labor and land reform laws in Guatemala's history. Intelligence reports characterized him as "brilliant and cultured" and his land reform policy as "moderate, constructive and democratic in its aims." The Dulles brothers nevertheless branded him a communist despite the fact that his ties to the Eastern bloc were limited to accepting arms from Czechoslovakia *after* his regime came under the threat of attack. The CIA adopted a campaign of psychological warfare to create the illusion of widespread opposition and installed in power Carlos Castillo Armas, a right-wing military officer who had been in exile in Honduras.[36]

Once in power, "the liberator" Armas annulled the progressive labor legislation, gave back expropriated land, and allowed plantation owners to cut wages by 30 percent. He jailed Árbenz's supporters, cleaned up the "red-led" unions, in the words of *Time* magazine, and adopted strong-arm tactics to close down newspapers and smash student demonstrations. Up to nine thousand Guatemalans were detained and tortured.[37] In a sign of continuity from the past, Armas appointed José Bernabé Linares to coordinate policing activities and suppress pro- Árbenz activists. Under Ubico during the 1930s, Linares had headed the dreaded secret police, which U.S. intelligence reports had praised for "nipping in the bud" the communist outbreak in the country at that time.[38]

A 1956 ICA report by Fred Fimbres, captain of the vice and narcotics squads in Los Angeles, noted that the operations of the Guatemalan police, controlled by military men loyal to Armas, were "singularly directed towards alertness and preparedness against the threat of communism"—a focus bordering on the "obsessive and neurotic."[39] Embassy cables relayed reports that the police were "trigger happy" with their rifles and submachine guns and committed many "excesses," including incidents in which they beat prison inmates with rubber hoses, persecuted Jews, and fired on crowds. Chief detective Roserdo Perez was a "butcher" notorious for torture, while the chief of special investigations, Jorge Cordova Molina, founder of the Mano Blanco death squad, was described as a "common thug and assassin."[40] The police as a whole suffered from "questionable leadership and administration," and were using equipment that was "barely serviceable." Upon paying a visit to one precinct, advisers were appalled to find police reading comic books and newspapers or resting with their heads on the table.[41]

Operating at a budget of $600,000, the ICA had a mandate to rescue police from their "hopelessness" by reining in egregious abuses while enabling them to control subversion more systematically. Under the 1290-d program, David Laughlin, Rex Morris, Theo Hall, and Desiderio Crisostomo, a police adviser in Laos with six years' experience in Guam, oversaw the renovation of police precincts, developed crime labs and a filing and identity card system, and taught the Henry fingerprinting method. After inspections by James V. Bennett, director of the Federal Bureau of Prisons, the ICA attempted to improve procedures in the central prison by training guards, segregating women and juveniles, and promoting rehabilitation. An investigations bureau was set up under the guidance of CIA agent John Poppa to compile a blacklist of "subversives" targeted for arrest or assassination. The names were culled from the membership rolls of pro-Árbenz parties, teachers' and peasant unions, and the Guatemalan Communist Party (PGT) left behind after the 1954 coup.[42]

Although they were happy to accept equipment, Guatemalan officials, according to internal reports, resented U.S. advisers "showing them what to do and when to do it." The 1290-d planning group lamented that bureaucratic delays were causing the Guatemalans to look to other countries, including France, for police and intelligence training and technical guidance, which it was feared could "lay the groundwork for penetration of the Guatemalan security services by [these] other countries."[43] These comments give a good indication of the imperial rivalries driving American policies, little different from those of the era of the "great game," and reveal how the police programs were designed to enhance U.S. control over subject countries.

In 1955 the International Association of Chiefs of Police, which helped run the 1290-d program, named Armas an honorary police chief for his "unselfish labor for the good of democratic law enforcement in Guatemala." Two years later he was assassinated by a member of his palace guard, whom the embassy characterized as a "communist inspired fanatic" to justify a heightened crackdown on dissent.[44] John P. Longan, later a counterterrorism consultant to the Reagan administration, claimed that as a result of U.S. assistance, police suppressing demonstrations in Guatemala City "did a wonderful job [in mob control] using tear gas and fire hoses and gained prestige in their efforts to avoid violence. . . . They should not be held responsible for the death of six protestors."[45] The families of victims likely felt otherwise.

In 1958 Miguel Ydígoras Fuentes, a former minister in the Ubico regime, became president. The CIA compared him to South Korean president Syngman Rhee in his authoritarianism, noting that he used the police for "personal political advantage." The Kennedy administration nevertheless provided over $27 million in Alliance funds because of his "long record of opposition to communism" and because he provided bases for the Bay of Pigs and Mongoose attacks on Cuba.[46] Intelligence reports warned about the return from exile of communist "big-leaguers" Carlos Manuel Pellecer and Victor Manuel Gutiérrez, who it was rumored were planning on allying with Árbenz and former PGT associates such as José Manuel Fortuny and Che Guevara, a witness to the 1954 coup, to overthrow Ydígoras. According to the embassy, the "internal security situation left little room for complacency" as "retrograde economic and social conditions" were placing the "stability of the country in jeopardy."[47]

In the attempt to save Ydígoras's rule, the State Department established a commodities pipeline and intensified training in surveillance and infiltration tactics, inaugurating an internal security seminar at the National Police Academy. Hundreds were sent to the United States, including ten members of the judicial police, who, in the words of the ambassador, were "employed by the president and other high officials in the investigation and harassment of political opponents and carried out unsavory assignments. . . . This body is feared and despised by virtually everyone in Guatemala except those whom they serve."[48]

Part of the reason for the build-up was that the police were more loyal to Ydígoras than the army, which was gripped by a rebellion led by leftist colonel Marc Antonio Yon Sosa. He found sanctuary in Honduras, where the OPS was administering a $133,000 per year program, and was allegedly teaming up with liberal dissidents to create a powerful "popular front" movement. Assistant Secretary of State Edwin M. Martin testified in February 1963 before the House Foreign Affairs Committee that the OPS was crucial to preserving internal security in Latin America.[49] A month later, with U.S. backing, military officers headed by Enrique Peralta Azurdia overthrew Ydígoras. He had come to be seen as insufficiently anticommunist after inviting Juan José Arévalo back into the country to run for election. Arévalo was the author of *The Shark and the Sardines,* a book critical of U.S policy in Latin America. In April the OPS expedited the shipment of over three thousand batons and hand grenades to assist in suppressing rioters threatening to bring down Peralta's new regime.[50] Through the cultivation of informants and the tapping of telephones and censorship of mail, thousands of dossiers were compiled on suspected radicals. Even U.S. citizens were spied on. Suspicion became sufficient cause for arrest or exile, and cash rewards were provided for the death or arrest of "communist criminals." USAID reports referred to Peralta, who had long-running ties to American intelligence, as a "dictator" and the secret police as "little better than hoodlums," the "lowest dregs in society whom even the army had rejected."[51] When students planned demonstrations at San Carlos University, a hotbed of leftist activism, police were given instructions, with no apparent objections from the OPS, to "shoot if necessary"; there was to be "no mercy" for those who tried to subvert the public order.[52] Democratic policing standards were thus subordinated to the broader Cold War fight.

In November 1965, in reaction to the growth of the Rebel Armed Forces (FAR) and the November 13 Revolutionary Movement, as well as a series of bombings which, according to OPS reports, were predominantly set by state security forces but blamed on the guerrillas in order to preserve a "climate of tension" needed to expand "counter-terror" operations, Longan was brought back from Thailand to set up a rapid response security unit.[53] Within three months it conducted eighty raids and tortured and executed thirty prominent opposition leaders, including Victor Manuel Gutiérrez and Leonard Castillo Flores, leaders of Guatemala's labor and peasant federations during Árbenz's presidency. Their bodies were dumped at sea. Longan told an interviewer in the 1980s that while supportive of the campaign to rid the country of "terrorists," he had little control over the methods employed by police, which he saw as counterproductive. He had, however, provided the killers with high-tech equipment as well as ideological justification and legal cover, so he was deeply complicit.[54]

Operation Limpieza served as the opening salvo in a campaign of "White Terror," as government reports characterized it, in which thousands of regime opponents, including labor and peasant organizers and intellectuals, were rounded up, tortured, and "disappeared." Exemplifying the class dimension of the struggle, the owners and administrators of large plantations were commissioned as members of the National Police.[55] Army commando units and the Fourth Corps of the National Police carried out village sweeps under Director-General Manuel Francisco Sosa Ávila, whom the CIA praised for "forming counter-terrorist squads" which "operate clandestinely against leftist insurgents." This was code for death squad activity carried out by off-duty police officers belonging to front organizations (such as the so-called New Anti-

Communist Organization) which had their headquarters in police precincts and were tacitly supported by the embassy.[56]

In 1967 and 1968 the OPS expanded aid to counterinsurgency operations through contingency funds and funneled weapons in aboard United Fruit Company vessels. Over a thousand Green Berets participated in combat, and twenty-eight were killed. A CIA study noted that "the daily specter of mutilated bodies had created an atmosphere of terror throughout the country." Adviser Mark Seaton was shot at by guerrillas in retaliation for police abuses. A FAR communiqué referred to the National Police as the "den of reaction where most of the 6,000 victims of reactionary violence in Guatemala have been tortured and murdered."[57] Alfred Naurocki of the OPS set up a telecommunications center in the presidential palace, which was used to coordinate policing operations and store information derived from interrogation. The police command structure was militarized, becoming an adjunct of the armed forces, which functioned, internal reports conceded, as "an army of occupation."[58]

In September 1968 the FAR assassinated Colonel John Webber, head of the U.S. military mission, in retaliation for the murder of Rogelia Cruz, a twenty-six-year-old beauty queen with left-wing sympathies. Webber had defended the Guatemalan army's cultivation of hunter-killer squadrons, telling *Time* before his death: "[This is] the way the country is. The communists are using everything they have, including terror, and it must be met." In 1971 Colonel Carlos Arana Osorio declared another state of siege, vowing to eliminate the guerrillas even if it meant "turning the country into a cemetery." American-trained forces proceeded to kill hundreds of "terrorists" and "bandits," mainly in the interior of the country, while continuing raids on private businesses, homes, schools, and even the public zoo.[59]

In a breach of congressional legislation, U.S. advisers participated directly in "anti-hippie patrols" in Guatemala City, in which at least thirty PGT members were "disappeared."[60] Reports claimed that American assistance enabled police to "take the guerrillas by surprise," which led to the "break-up of the FAR, though not as yet elimination of it." The dissemination of black propaganda and recruitment of defectors to penetrate the organization was especially effective. The Nixon administration initiated a crash plan to intensify patrols and improve police communications. Vice President Spiro Agnew gave a special gift of police vehicles to Colonel Arana (the "Butcher of Zacapa"), including Ford Broncos used to transport prisoners.[61]

American officials rationalized acts of state terrorism on the grounds of the Guatemalans' alleged cultural backwardness and innate proclivity for cruelty. Former ambassador to Venezuela C. Allan Stewart claimed that police vigilantism was patterned after "U.S. Far West frontier justice in the days when courtrooms were few and far between."[62] Longan, who, according to the historian Greg Grandin, displayed a "law and order, counter-subversive sensibility similar to that which fueled the growth of domestic anticommunism," blamed the murders on "Guatemala's underlying vein of violence. . . . It's inbred in [the people] and they hate pretty deeply." Showing a poor grasp of history, he later told an interviewer that "under Arbenz—that was the communist regime—they cut off the hands of thieves, so it was traditional, I guess from the time of the Spanish conquest, for some of these countries to react like that to criminals and violence—or overreact, I'd say." Longan added that his job was that of "a technician upgrading the police's capabilities and implementing the policies of our government at that time. . . . If it was to upgrade this or upgrade that, I didn't ask why. If you had a corrupt government or something like that, as long as they were our crooks there wasn't anything I could do about it."[63] These comments shed light on the mentality of police advisers toward the abuse of human rights. Cogs in the machine of empire, they were fulfilling what they saw as their patriotic duty by exporting their technical expertise and professional skills.

Deputy Chief of Mission Viron Vaky provided a lone voice of internal dissent. In a memo to higher-ups, he argued: "[We] have condoned brutal counter-terror operations that led to significant atrocities and encouraged and even blessed them. . . . We suspected that as long as communists are being killed it is alright. . . . After all, hasn't man been a savage from the beginning of time so let us not be too queasy about terror. I have literally heard these arguments from people."[64] Thomas Melville, a priest expelled for sympathizing with the guerrillas and later indicted with Daniel Berrigan for burning draft cards in protest of the Vietnam War, excoriated the role of the United States in keeping the country "terrorized" and empowering an oligarchy in which 2 percent of the Guatemalan people controlled 80 percent of the land and wealth.[65]

The 1975 phase-out report expressed pride that the OPS had helped improve urban patrol and telecommunications, created a dispatch control center, and strengthened riot control capabilities, enabling the police to confront the insurgent threat. Another report concluded that the OPS had helped to "increase police competence and skill in dealing with terrorists by improving mobility and communications." A Senate investigative team found, however, that "the teaching hasn't been absorbed and the U.S. is politically identified with police terrorism. The Guatemalan police operate without any effective judicial restraints."[66]

Human rights activist Holly J. Burkhalter wrote in the *New York Times* that the greatest contribution of the OPS was to "improve military and police intelligence. . . . [W]ith our help, the Guatemalan security forces became a giant computerized death squad."[67] The parallels with Operation Phoenix are striking. During the 1940s, peasant and labor organizations in Guatemala played a key role in ushering in the revolution and creating a climate conducive to the advent of social democracy. With the decimation of these organizations, owing in no small measure to the police programs, Guatemala's future was irrevocably altered. When the formal structure of democracy reemerged in the 1990s after decades of state terror, it was a pale shadow of its former self.[68]

"They See the Motions but Can't Hear the Music": Expanding the Central American Graveyard

The violence and corruption associated with American-trained forces in Guatemala fit a wider regional pattern. In Mexico and Panama, where police were known for repression, the OPS provided vomiting gas, flamethrowers, helicopters, and airplanes, and built up the intelligence services, headed in Panama by drug trafficker Manuel Noriega (who was mentored by OPS adviser Adolph Saenz).[69] In Nicaragua, the programs were initiated to help crush the leftist Sandinista Liberation Front (FSLN) which drew on the anti-imperialist legacy of Augusto César Sandino and the Cuban revolution.

The Kennedy and Johnson administrations kept much of the support secret, training Nicaraguan Guardia Nacional officers clandestinely in El Salvador.[70] The Nixon administration was more open in abetting the tyranny of President Anastasio Somoza, perhaps in return for receiving $1 million in campaign contributions. From 1971 to 1974, under the ambassadorship of Turner Shelton, USAID provided Somoza's regime with over $81,000 in vehicles, radios, and communications and fingerprint equipment to improve coordination in tracking down "subversives."[71] Advisers John Manopoli and Gunther Wagner, the latter a former Nazi soldier and Phoenix program veteran who stayed on afterwards in Nicaragua under private contract, helped rebuild the Guardia following the devastating 1972 earthquake, during which time the force disintegrated into a collection of mobs intent on looting what remained of the capital, Managua. Until the Sandinistas' 1979 revolutionary triumph over Somoza, the Guardia continued to compile an atrocious human rights record, rounding up and torturing Sandinista sympathizers, extorting money from campesinos (farmers), and smashing safe houses. Some of the "disappeared" were dropped from helicopters into live volcanoes.[72]

Police programs in El Salvador resembled those in Guatemala in contributing to the growth of a destructive civil war. In November 1956, under Colonel José Maria Lemus, a representative of the oligarchic elite who won 93 percent of the vote in fixed elections, the ICA initiated a program headed by Roland Kelley, retired chief of police in Fort Lauderdale, Florida. Characterized as "egotistical, aloof, and obstinate," Lemus was given a tickertape parade in Manhattan while his goon squads terrorized opponents and raided the university in San Salvador.[73]

The Kennedy administration encouraged Lemus's successor, Colonel Julio Adalberto Rivera, to implement anticommunist laws mandating sweeping arrests even though it was acknowledged that "influential conservatives in government circles were unwilling to distinguish between members of the small, illegal communist party and less radical leftist, reformist, and opposition elements." Field reports emphasized the need for "accuracy in identifying targets," which required upgraded intelligence so as to avoid popular discrediting of the regime. Reports also pressed for police involvement in civic action programs, including the provision of medical services to help win the war for "hearts and minds."[74]

A September 1965 OPS report noted that the speeches at a union meeting in San Salvador were anti-American and that a U.S. flag was pulled down and burned, remarks showing how the CIA used the police programs to infiltrate and gain information on civic organizations. Providing nearly $2 million in assistance, the OPS constructed a national police school, provided weaponry and riot control training, and built a communications center in police headquarters in San Salvador which housed computerized databanks of "subversives."[75] Advisers such as Theodore Brown helped to professionalize the immigration service and built up paramilitary units, the Salvadoran National Security Agency, and the National Democratic Organization, which evolved into death squads. A result was the development of the Farabundo Martí National Liberation Front (FMLN), an amalgamation of opposition groups led by Caytano Carpio, known as the Ho Chi Minh of Central America.[76]

The 1974 phase-out report claimed that as a result of American tutelage, the police had advanced from a "non-descript group of poorly trained men to a well-disciplined and respected uniformed corps with good riot control and investigative capabilities, good records, and fair communications and mobility."[77] A UN truth commission, however, found that 90 percent of human rights crimes in the 1980s were committed by state security forces, many of them beneficiaries of OPS training or graduates of U.S. military academies such as the School of the Americas. Roberto D'Aubuisson, an IPA graduate who headed the proto-fascist ARENA party, was linked to the 1980 murder of four American nuns and Archbishop Óscar Romero, a liberation theologian who had spoken out against societal injustice.[78]

American officials generally supported a doctrine of counterterror which held that since guerrillas did not typically abide by Western legal norms, neither should the United States or its proxies in dealing with them. Violent psychological warfare techniques were seen to be effective, furthermore, in fostering submission to governmental authority.[79] In practice, state terror produced a popular counterreaction that could be curtailed only through even greater levels of force. Counterinsurgency theorists underestimated the appeal of left-wing guerrilla movements, whose strength was contingent on deep-rooted grievances and long-standing social inequalities and repression, not manipulation by an outside power.[80] The iconoclastic journalist I. F. Stone commented astutely:

In reading the military literature on guerrilla warfare now so fashionable at the Pentagon, one feels that these writers are like men watching a dance from outside through heavy plate glass windows. They see the motions but can't hear the music. They put the mechanical gestures down on paper with pedantic fidelity. But what rarely comes through to them are the injured racial feelings, the misery, the rankling slights . . . the desperation. So they do not really understand what leads men to abandon wife, children, home, career, friends to take to the bush and live gun in hand like a hunted animal; to challenge overwhelming military odds rather than acquiesce any longer in humiliation, injustice, or poverty.[81]

The OPS advisers no doubt fit this paradigm. Subscribing to the simplified ideologies of the Cold War, they lacked empathy for the plight of ordinary people that was breeding a climate of rebellion and failed to understand the causes underlying the growth of leftist movements. They were further disconnected from the human consequences of their work.

Costa Rica: An Exception to the Rule?

Costa Rica was an exception in that American aid did not contribute to the growth of a repressive police state. The reasons have to do with domestic politics and the leadership of José "Don Pepe" Figueres, an anticommunist of social-democratic leanings who maintained a delicate balance between accommodation and resistance to the United States. After coming to power in the late 1940s, Figueres outlawed the Communist Party, abolished the armed forces, and instituted land reform, welfare, and a relatively progressive labor code that resulted in improved living standards but was not so radical as to threaten U.S. business interests. Though pressing him to crack down more stringently on communism, American officials viewed Figueres favorably and did not apply the same stereotypes that they did in other Latin American countries, in part because of Costa Rica's racial homogeneity (including the lack of an Indian population), its parliamentary democracy, and the absence of violent class conflict.[82]

The OPS inaugurated a technical aid program with a budget of $99,000 in 1965 and $327,000 in 1966. A central purpose was to gain leverage among security forces, a pathway toward greater political control. The police were mobilized to contain labor unrest on banana plantations, where minimum wage laws were not enforced, and to suppress urban demonstrations. Workers and students carried massive Che Guevara banners protesting rising costs of living and the spread of American corporate influence.[83] OPS staff led by Jack Ellis, former superintendent of the Kansas City police, trained border patrol units to keep Sandinista guerrillas out of the country. FSLN founder Carlos Fonseca Amador was arrested for crossing the border illegally from Nicaragua and possessing weapons and maps. He was detained at the Alajeula jail, where he spearheaded a riot that was suppressed with the aid of American-imported tear gas.

Police subsequently arrested dozens of students protesting Fonseca's confinement and foiled an attempt by assailants to liberate the "terrorist commander," as he was characterized, in which a prison guard was killed. After he had escaped from a prison bathroom, OPS reports reveal, police intercepted Fonseca's escape car on the outskirts of San José and shot and wounded his comrade, Humberto Ortega. Mrs. Fonseca (Haydee Maria) was also arrested for supporting her husband, who was returned to prison to serve out his term. Fonseca was later killed by the Nicaraguan National Guard.[84]

Thus even in a relatively peaceful country the OPS contributed to the spread of political repression and inequality. The degree of police violence was moderated by the political leadership in Costa Rica, which was largely sympathetic to the anti-Somozan struggle in neighboring Nicaragua and maintained a relatively efficient legal system of checks and balances. The political context and scale in which OPS operations were adopted was ultimately the most decisive factor in determining their outcome.

State Terror in the Southern Cone: Toward Operation Condor

The OPS gained the greatest notoriety in bolstering an assortment of military dictatorships in the Southern Cone of Latin America, particularly Brazil, where it was linked to torture and death squads. Originating in the 1950s, the program grew to a budget of over $1 million per year by 1964, when the CIA backed a coup against democratically elected president João Goulart, who promoted land redistribution and higher wages and developed a plan to force multinationals to invest a portion of their profits back into the Brazilian economy.[85]

Spending over $8 million, the OPS program in Brazil was headed by "Jack" Goin, a forensics expert with long experience in Southeast Asia; Frank Jessup, a counterintelligence specialist who had trained internal security forces on five continents; and Theodore Brown, who had helped run the Phoenix program in Vietnam. The three epitomize the continuity in OPS programs and the way novel techniques were being refined in one place and then redeployed elsewhere in the world. Other advisers included Yale graduate Norman Rosner and Indiana state trooper Albert Bryant, both Vietnam veterans; Fred Zumwalt of the Phoenix Police Department; and Robert L. Barnes, a U.S. Border Patrol agent and police legal affairs officer during the occupation of Japan.[86]

Collectively they helped to set up Brazil's intelligence service and oversaw Operation Bandeirantes, a model for the Phoenix program in its strategy of dismantling the leftist opposition through skilled intelligence work and selective assassination. Supported by the U.S. embassy, Bandeirantes was partially funded by prominent businessmen, including Henning Boileson, president of Ultragas, who sat in on some of the torture sessions and was later gunned down by guerrillas. The OPS worked intimately with death squad operatives, including Amaury Kruel, who first visited Washington in 1958, and Sergio Fleury, head of the secret police in São Paulo, a sadist who tortured victims while high on drugs.[87]

USAID claimed that U.S. training had a "civilizing effect," especially on officers from an Indian background. Declassified reports acknowledge, however, that "police ruled more through fear than respect" and were implicated in off-duty killings in which the corpses of victims were buried in sand or dumped at sea. Investigative scholarship has found that recruits were socialized into a violent masculine subculture in American-funded police academies, where they endured ritualized hazing, accounting in part for the wide scope of brutality. The Brazilian police retain a reputation even today as one of the most violent and militarized police forces in the Western Hemisphere, which is to some extent a legacy of the OPS.[88]

Many of the worst abuses took place after the declaration of martial law in 1968 by General Artur da Costa e Silva and his successor Emilio Garrastazu Medici, who Nixon said he wished were "running the whole continent." American-trained units fired on student demonstrators, seized "subversive literature," infiltrated student and labor organizations, and hunted down leftists, including future presidents Luiz Inácio "Lula" da Silva and Dilma Rousseff and revolutionary theorist Carlos Marighella, who was killed in a police trap. Deploying the kind of rhetoric that was used to justify major human rights abuses, the OPS praised the police for "contributing to the reduction of terrorism" and "driving subversives underground."[89]

The OPS was especially influential in providing riot control training and constructing telecommunications networks and computerized databanks aided by the delivery of IBM equipment. It taught psy-war methods designed to spread disinformation and sow dissension within the ranks of the leftist movements and oversaw the penal system, in which conditions were unsanitary, due process was lacking, and torture, including of women and children, was routine. One of the victims, Flavio Tavares Freitas, a journalist and Christian nationalist, testified that when his jailers jammed electric wires in his ears, teeth, and anus, he saw that the generator producing the shocks had on its side the red, white, and blue shield of USAID, revealing the deep complicity of the United States in the reign of violence being carried out.[90]

In Peru, after a 1962 military coup overthrew the elected leadership, American advisers Dave Laughlin, Clyde Phelps, Cornell graduate Ernest Lancina, and Pennsylvania state trooper George Miller trained rural strike forces in jungle warfare and provided water cannon trucks and telecommunications equipment to police. The police in turn assisted the army in crushing a revolutionary insurrection led by Trotskyite peasant organizer Hugo Blanco and Luis de la Puente Uceda, a leftist intellectual who promoted land reform and literacy campaigns on behalf of the marginalized Quechua population. Police aid spiked to $700,000 in 1965 and $1.1 million in 1966 as the OPS oversaw round-up campaigns and Blanco's capture in Chaupimayo. As in Guatemala, police brutality, including torture and the massacre of Indians occupying large plantations, was magnified by the racism of mestizo officers who sided with landowners in labor disputes. While a few of the advisers were sympathetic to the plight of the Indians, the OPS helped foster their subjugation.[91]

In Bolivia, which State Department planners viewed as vulnerable to the "Communist disease both Stalinist and Trotskyite" because of high poverty rates, the Eisenhower administration introduced police aid in 1956 at a budget of $1.75 million, the highest at the time in Latin America. The operation was run by Lee Echols, who had provided training to OSS operatives during World War II in the use of time detonators, exploding pencils, briefcases with false bottoms, and submachine guns with silencers; skills which made him a valuable asset to the 1290-d program. Bolivian intelligence reports warned that "extreme leftists" might take control of the government, which, after the 1952 revolution, was in the hands of moderate leftists who, "despite their shortcomings," were seen to offer the best hope for "stability and friendship." A central focus of 1290-d was in espionage and riot control training, designed to quell a "mini revolution" of fifteen thousand laid-off tin miners in Santa Cruz who were under the "sway of leftist agitators." The United States further aimed to eliminate the "extreme-left-wing influence" in the civil militia, formed to support the 1952 revolution, by providing indoctrination in the dangers of communism, and to bring it under government control.[92]

The Kennedy administration maintained a budget of $400,000 per year for the program and provided tear gas to help President Paz Estenssoro and his Revolutionary Nationalist Movement crush demonstrations by tin miners and factory workers unsatisfied with the slow pace of reform. Jake Jackson, a former Indiana state trooper and director of Miami civil defense who also served in Brazil, was shot in the back by guerrillas and paralyzed while trying to establish a police post in a remote jungle area while accompanied by the ambassador. Five local police were also killed in the ambush.[93]

After a 1964 coup, which resulted in part from the strengthening of the army through the Alliance for Progress, OPS operations were expanded to counter an insurgency led by Che Guevara. Jake Longan and Adolph Saenz were sent to train police equipped by the United States with machine guns, radios, tear gas, and shields. Field reports noted that the police functioned as a "paramilitary force" acting to "suppress the population" and that "violence to control civil disturbances left many dead." Longan and Saenz's men carried out joint operations with army rangers in hunting down Che, culminating in his schoolhouse assassination in October 1967.[94] In an illustration of the way the War on Drugs was used as a cover for counterintelligence work, Guevara's training camp was discovered by police claiming to be looking for a cocaine processing plant. Walt

W. Rostow viewed Che's death as embodying the "soundness of our preventative medicine assistance to countries facing incipient insurgencies."[95]

In Bolivia, during the 1970s the OPS helped bolster the power of Hugo Banzer, a graduate of the School of the Americas, who is considered the most repressive leader in his country's history, though he received praise from U.S. advisers for "dealing firmly with leftist revolutionaries." The State Department created a narcotics brigade, which developed a reputation for corruption and cruelty. Its first commander took payoffs from cocaine traffickers and tried to overthrow the government.[96]

In Uruguay, the OPS contributed $2 million to the government's "dirty war" against the National Liberation Movement, or Tupamaros, headed by farm labor organizer Raúl Sendic, who, according to the *New York Times*, normally avoided bloodshed but was seeking to create embarrassment for the government and general disorder.[97] In a June 1967 report, Ambassador Henry A. Hoyt lamented the "relaxed attitude" of Uruguayan politicians toward communists, the "arm of a well-organized international subversive movement" that in his view should be systematically dismantled. To help achieve this task, the OPS imported surveillance technologies and submachine guns and cultivated "penetration agents," who infiltrated the Tupamaros and provided detailed information on their leaders, including the writer Eduardo Galeano and José Mujica, who endured over a decade in prison but went on to be elected president of Uruguay in 2009.[98]

Police repression escalated after Jorge Pacheco Areco, who became president in 1967, suspended constitutional rights in response to a growing number of kidnappings and bank robberies. The country that had been known as the "Switzerland of Latin America" came to claim the highest ratio of political prisoners per capita in the world. As in Vietnam, prison administrators worked with behavioral psychologists to design torture techniques tailored to each individual's psychological profile—a method later used at the U.S. military prison in Guantánamo Bay. Mauricio Rosencof, who saw sunlight for a total of eight hours over the eleven years he spent in prison, wrote, "We were beginning to think we were dead, that our cells weren't cells but rather graves, that the outside world didn't exist, that the sun was a myth."[99]

Public safety reports boasted that American training contributed to the intensification "of stake-out operations and raids resulting in the arrest of large numbers of Tupamaro terrorists." Lee Echols and William Cantrell, who was described by the journalist A. J. Langguth as "an orderly, pipe-smoking man devoted to his family," helped develop the dreaded Department of Information and Intelligence, which provided a cover for death squads (among its victims was Fernando Pucurull, the "Uruguayan Che Guevara") and supplied police with voltmeters used for torture. Philip Agee, a CIA liaison with the Montevideo police, resigned from the agency and wrote his exposé *Inside the Company* after hearing the screams of a torture victim in police headquarters where the OPS maintained its offices. He had given the victim's name to police for "preventive detention."[100]

In August 1970, in retaliation for police abuses, the Tupamaros kidnapped and killed Dan Mitrione, head of the OPS in Uruguay. Eulogized in the press as a family man and a victim of communist terror, Mitrione led riot control units in Brazil and the Dominican Republic that were responsible for serious human rights violations. The director of the Uruguayan police stated that he snatched beggars off the streets for Mitrione to use as subjects for teaching interrogation methods; Mitrione brutalized them before his students, torturing four to death. One of the attendees commented that the special horror of the course was "its academic, almost clinical atmosphere. Mitrione's motto was the right pain in the right place at the right time."[101]

According to Langguth, who interviewed members of his family, Mitrione joined the OPS to escape small-town Indiana but also because he had nine children to support and the salary was 10 percent higher than what he received as a beat cop. The son of Italian immigrants, Mitrione was a mediocre but disciplined student at his Catholic high school, where he starred on the football team. His worldview was similar to that of so many of his generation, who embraced what Tom Engelhardt has characterized as the postwar victory culture—an abiding belief in the exceptional nature of the United States and in its overseas mission to export liberal capitalism across the so-called Third World.[102] It was this belief, combined with the conservatism and anticommunism instilled by his small-town upbringing and cultivated institutionally within the OPS, which accounted for the violent methods that Mitrione and his contemporaries employed. For true believers in the Cold War, the ends justified the means.

OPS operations in the Southern Cone paved the way for the rise of Operation Condor, a transnational intelligence operation based in Santiago, Chile, to eliminate leftist dissidents, which led to the kidnapping and death of thousands.[103] Beginning in 1955, the United States helped build the Chilean police and intelligence apparatus under 1290-d. The central aim was to constrain the growth of socialist and communist parties and to suppress labor unrest, which was spreading as a result of unchecked inflation and austerity measures imposed by the conservative military dictator General Carlos Ibáñez del Campo and his successor Jorge Alessandri. Equipped with obsolete European arms and suffering from poor morale, internal security forces did not appear capable of putting down a rebellion by a workers' militia seeking to install a regime of "extreme leftist tendencies." Police were trained in riot control, contra-sabotage, and the protection of strategic industrial installations, including American-run copper refineries. The director-general of the paramilitary Carabineros was sent for instruction at the FBI and then encouraged to travel to other Latin American countries to professionalize their internal security forces. In a sign of continuity from the past, Milton Miles, who trained Dai Li's secret police in China during the 1940s, oversaw the police programs in his capacity as a "naval attaché." One man on whom he started a dossier was a "promising young socialist politician," Salvador Allende.[104]

After the 1962 election of Eduardo Frei, the OPS sent in Reginald Davis, a CIA agent with experience in Indonesia and Vietnam, and Joseph Lingo, director of public safety in Indiana who had served in a half-dozen countries, including Brazil. Forces under their oversight used water hoses and tear gas in suppressing worker and student demonstrations and empowered the centrist Christian Democrats, who, according to one report, "had the police in their bosom."[105] The OPS program was rescinded after Allende's election in 1970 (with Allende dismissing high-ranking police officials trained at the IPA and disbanding the paramilitary riot squad), though the CIA continued to cultivate "assets" in the Carabineros as part of its destabilization campaign. Police aid was revived when Augusto Pinochet took power in a September 1973 coup in which Allende was killed. Pinochet remobilized the police to dismantle the left-ist opposition in a campaign that was extended to neighboring countries under Operation Condor.[106] A substantial number of officers implicated in torture and murder were trained by the OPS. The CIA provided computers to Chile's Direc-torate of Intelligence, a pivotal instrument of state terror headed by Manuel Contreras, a confidant of CIA deputy director Vernon Walters. The directorate was modeled after the Colombian Departamento Administrativo de Seguridad and the Buró de Represión de Actividades Communistas, the secret police of Cuban dictator Fulgencio Batista, established by the CIA in 1955.[107]

The United States played a key role in Condor by providing technical train-ing to police and intelligence services in participant nations, including Argen-tina, Brazil, Bolivia, and Paraguay, which cooperated in hunting down left-wing dissidents. The operation benefited from advanced telecommunications equipment and computerized databanks supplied by the OPS. In an important parallel, the OPS encouraged coordination among Central American police and intelligence agencies in targeting subversives beginning in the early 1960s. American diplomats, CIA agents, and Secretary of State Henry Kissinger all maintained close contact with security forces implicated in terrorist operations and tacitly condoned and helped cover up their actions.[108] Many victims were former government officials and proponents of the pro-democracy left. Con-dor was exposed in the late 1970s after a car bomb killed former Chilean foreign minister Orlando Letelier in Washington, D.C., a month after he published a devastating account of the free-market capitalism being imposed on Chile by the military junta. The United States at this point tried to disassociate itself from the operation, which was funded at least in part by narcotics.[109]

Like the Phoenix program, Condor epitomized the use of American police training to facilitate state repression under the rubric of internal security and modernization. The provision of technical equipment to aid in the hunt for subversives led to considerable abuses across Latin America, as did the inculcation of a national security ideology in which draconian methods were considered necessary to save Judeo-Christian civilization from its internal enemies. Luigi R. Einaudi, a Latin American expert with the RAND Corporation, commented that "a major goal of most—if not all—American sponsored training is to contribute to actively anticommunist and openly pro-American attitudes."[110] This focus was perhaps most damaging from a human rights vantage point, as it led to the demonizing of social movements, which were subjected to systematic campaigns of harassment and terror.

In *Political Policing*, Martha K. Huggins argues persuasively that the police programs strengthened a host of bureaucratic authoritarian regimes, whose internal security apparatus gained the capacity to penetrate more deeply than ever before into civil society and thereby stifle citizen participation. The ratcheting up of repression was rationalized by technocratic elites and their American backers as part of an ideology linking national security to economic development.[111] For all the lofty rhetoric, the Alliance for Progress played a key role in stifling democratic development and suppressing social reform. Leftist movements, the backbone of civil society, which drew strength from oppressed sectors, were driven underground, resulting in vicious cycles of terror and counterterror. The abuses spawned by the OPS were rational in that they contributed to the empowerment of regimes that served American interests, not least in providing a favorable investment climate contingent on keeping organized labor in check.[112] But the legacy of surveillance, torture, and violence would, in the end, be difficult to overcome.

Conclusion
The Violence Comes Full Circle—From the Cold War to the War on Terror

In his trilogy on the American empire, Chalmers Johnson demonstrates how the United States has historically projected its power through a variety of means, including economic blackmail and the manipulation of financial institutions, covert operations, propaganda, arms sales, and, most important, the development of a network of military bases whose scale dwarfs that of all previous empires, including Rome.[1] This book has sought to examine another important structural dimension of U.S. power, namely, the training of police and paramilitary units under the guise of humanitarian assistance, which preceded and continued through the era of global military bases. The central aim of the police programs was to promote the social stability deemed necessary for liberal capitalist development and to strengthen the power of local elites serving American geostrategic interests. Driven by the Progressive Era emphasis on professionalization and modernization, the programs were critical in recruiting local intelligence "assets" and in establishing sophisticated surveillance apparatuses to monitor and destroy social movements deemed threatening to the United States. Police were valued more than the military as the "first line of defense" against subversion and were seen as best capable of implementing "civic action" programs designed to "win hearts and minds." They were trained in riot control and counterinsurgency and even taught bomb making.

Because of the emphasis on political policing and militarization and America's penchant for supporting right-wing dictators out of geopolitical and economic expediency, the police programs contributed to the growth of repression and violence. They helped to perpetuate and even create particular types of authoritarian regimes that were dependent on foreign aid for their survival and developed repressive surveillance and internal security apparatuses to quash dissent. The political scientist Thomas Lobe concluded in a 1977 study that the achievements of the OPS were "like massage parlor transactions—seedy and degrading . . . foreboding ill for civil liberties and human rights."[2] The OPS and its predecessor agencies were especially influential in providing modern weapons, building advanced telecommunications networks to aid in the tracking

232

of subversives, and providing ideological conditioning to state security forces which established a rationale for major human rights violations. The empowerment of paramilitary forces skilled in the black arts of psychological warfare fueled the growth of deadly internecine conflict and death squad activity, which the United States supported under programs like Phoenix and Operation Bandeirantes.

Many of the originators of the OPS recognized that police modernization could contribute to the warping of democratic development in countries lacking an independent legal system and a judiciary capable of reigning in abuses. Roger Hilsman wrote in a secret report that in Asia, "the danger of counterguerrilla police becoming a 'pocket army' is well recognized. Once a police unit attains a separate identity [from the police chain of command] and administrative autonomy, the problem of militarization arises." Pointing to the growth of a repressive internal security apparatus in South Vietnam under Diem and the advent of a coup d'état in Honduras owing to U.S. training of the paramilitary civil guard, General Maxwell Taylor cautioned that the OPS was creating rival power centers to the army, inimical at times to American interests.[3] Hell-bent on stopping communism and asserting U.S. hegemony, the "best and the brightest" in Washington did not heed their own warnings, with profound consequences.

The police programs exemplify the dark side of American empire. As Alfred W. McCoy has noted, while previous colonial powers developed elaborate foreign services and cultivated Orientalist intellectuals to help them better understand the cultures they were bent on subordinating, the United States during the long American century placed special emphasis on exporting new technologies to gain and systemize statistical information for purposes of social control, an inclination that grew out of corporate, bureaucratic culture and the domestic initiatives of the Progressive Era and accounted in large part for the importance of the police programs. The vast statistical charts and mass of raw data (much of it inaccurate) on the NLF hierarchy in Vietnam and the numbers of enemies reportedly captured and killed under Operation Phoenix took this inclination to absurd levels, though it had many precedents.[4]

The obsession among leading intellectuals with order and stability as a precondition for development was another key factor underlying the growth of the police programs. Rooted, again, in Progressive Era ideologies, it led the United States to embrace despotic leaders who, ironically, provoked the rise of insurgency and thus the very instability that threatened the ability of their countries to integrate into the global economy, which the "new mandarins" saw as crucial to their progress. From the conquest of the Philippines through the Cold War era, those at the wrong end of U.S. guns were primarily supporters of radical nationalist, socialist, and reformist movements seeking badly needed social change. A consistent goal of American foreign policy was to gain access to strategic resources and military bases and to empower proxy regimes eager to open up their economies to foreign investment, thus ensuring collaboration with illiberal forces dedicated to keeping organized labor and the political left in check. Those who resisted U.S. intervention were thoroughly dehumanized, and this paved the way for their violent repression.[5]

Despite its forceful reach, American power is not omnipotent. Cultural arrogance and an inability to understand the complexities of local politics hampered efforts to expand American influence and manipulate political developments. Although policymakers were convinced that the application of new technologies could facilitate the control of populations, in numerous interventions this proved to be a chimera. The police programs often empowered strong-armed leaders and corrupt police chiefs who used the weaponry to advance their own agendas and to wipe out personal enemies. They further spawned endless cycles of violence and contributed to the delegitimizing of American client regimes and the strengthening of resistance movements because of the abuses they inflicted. In this respect, the police programs epitomize the limits of American social engineering efforts and power.[6]

After World War II, American police training programs were implemented almost exclusively by proxy, exposing the gap between the rhetorical anti-imperialism employed by government officials and the reality of American global ambitions. The power of the United States was advanced in a more clandestine but no less heavy-handed fashion than in the past and in comparison to that of its European predecessors. The secret farming out of police and security work was politically expedient and cost effective, and could allow for plausible deniability if violence got out of hand. In this respect, the programs embody what Noam Chomsky has characterized as the "democratic deficit" in the United States, and what Johnson calls the dangerous growth of unchecked executive power.[7] The public was constantly deceived about the functions of the police programs, which were rarely discussed in the press, and had little way of knowing that their tax dollars were contributing to police repression around the world. Even Congress was at times kept in the dark, particularly with regard to the clandestine cold war in Southeast Asia, which was funded partially through the trade in narcotics.[8]

The OPS was abolished in 1974 owing to pressure from peace and human rights activists. Senator James Abourezk, a South Dakota Democrat, spearheaded passage of the bill cutting off police aid after receiving a visit from a Brazilian delegation detailing the role of American assistance in contributing to "disappearances" and torture on a broad scale. He proclaimed before the Senate that in providing millions of dollars' worth of fragmentation grenades, machine guns, riot batons, rocket mortars, and antipersonnel mines to repressive police forces, the United States had "helped consolidate the power of dictators" and enabled them to "squash their opposition. . . . One would be hard pressed to find the American humanitarian spirit in furnishing grenades and isolation cells."[9]

Although participants staunchly defended its record and claimed that host country leaders begged them to stay on, the OPS and the worldview from which it derived were publicly repudiated. The legacy of the organization, however, would live on, embodying the resilience of the American commitment to empire. Governments had become dependent on imported policing technologies, which they continued to employ even after U.S. advisory support was cut. Many OPS staffers, including John P. Longan in Venezuela, stayed on as private consultants. Commercial arms sales to traditional U.S. clients continued unabated in spite of President Carter's human rights rhetoric. Between 1976 and 1979, American firms acquired export licenses for the sale to Third World police of 126,622 pistols and revolvers, 51,906 rifles and submachine guns, 615,612 tear gas grenades, 8,870 canisters of chemical Mace, and 55.8 million rounds of small ammunition, which were often used to suppress dissent and support authoritarian regimes such as those in Chile and South Africa.[10]

As these figures suggest, the OPS spawned the growth of a formidable police-industrial complex, which contributed to the spread of political repression globally. A 1970 report boasted that the OPS had been instrumental in "stimulating U.S. industry to develop new and improved police equipment" such as tear gas, munitions with a nine-year shelf life, a police baton with a marking dye feature, a riot helmet with a built-in radio receiver, lightweight body armor that floats, and communication devices operating on solar cells instead of batteries. George Orwell's *1984* nightmare was coming to pass as new technologies allowed for ever greater sophistication in social control techniques all over the world.[11]

In August 1970 the Associated Press reported that the New York Police Department had been able to catch jewel thieves by using an electronic device developed for night fighting in Vietnam which magnifies light more than one hundred times. Remote-controlled airplanes receiving signals from ground sensors used in Operation Igloo-White in Laos were adopted for narcotics interdiction along the Mexican border. Byron Engle, who became a private consultant to police organizations after the OPS disbanded, as well as director of the National Rifle Association, testified before the Kerner Commission on civilian disorder in the 1960s: "In working with the police in various countries we have acquired a great deal of experience in dealing with violence ranging from demonstrations and riots to guerrilla warfare. Much of this experience may be useful in the U.S."[12]

Thus the national security establishment sought to reimport the novel police techniques promoted by the OPS back into the United States to contain societal unrest. American police consequently became more militarized, as with the creation of SWAT teams, and more sophisticated in using computerized databanks, tear gas, and wiretaps. Prison environments became harsher, and the black radical movement and the student left were effectively pacified as the empire's techniques were turned against its own citizens.[13]

Many 1290-d and OPS veterans were appointed to head law enforcement organizations, where they continued to advance methods honed on the peripheries of the Cold War. While dodging protesters outside his office at MSU (which must have been a strange experience for a former football star), Art Brandstatter advised the Detroit Police Department on riot control formation during the 1967 ghetto uprising, in which rioters were treated as "insurgents"; he later became director of the Federal Law Enforcement Center in Fort Glynn, Georgia. In 1980 Adolph Saenz, who had helped track Che Guevara in Bolivia and was Dan Mitrione's predecessor in Uruguay, was appointed director of corrections in his home state of New Mexico, where the prisons were characterized by a Department of Justice report as among the harshest and most punitive in the nation. Two days into his tenure he helped suppress an inmate takeover in Santa Fe and kept a veil of secrecy over the penitentiary in its aftermath, branding critical journalists "Marxists." He was soon forced to resign when the conditions underlying the riot, including kitchens full of rat droppings and a culture of violence in which gang rape was routine, did not change.[14]

In August 1969, after People's Park demonstrators in Berkeley were subjected to beatings and torture, the sheriff of Alameda County defended the brutality in a telling statement: "We have a bunch of young deputies back from Vietnam who tend to treat prisoners like Vietcong."[15] Such remarks reveal the direct link between repression overseas and at home. In 2009, Chicago police officer Jon Burge was accused of hundreds of acts of torture, including the use of electroshock and cattle prods, placing bags over suspects' heads, and staging mock executions to extort confessions, tactics he learned as a military police officer in Vietnam and through the Phoenix program.[16]

Abolishing the OPS did not mean the end of the global police programs. As traditional elites and neoconservatives mobilized to restore American power in the wake of Vietnam, the Ford, Carter, and Reagan administrations subcontracted police training and other security assistance to private firms such as the Vinnell Corporation, which secretly worked with the Saudi National Guard.[17] They also farmed out these tasks to foreign intelligence services such as the Israeli Mossad, which provided weapons and training to the military and police of a number of repressive regimes, including apartheid South Africa, the Congo under Mobutu, and Iran under the Shah. In Guatemala, after President Carter cut aid on human rights grounds, Israeli advisers worked with the feared G-2 intelligence and sold police equipment, including electronic technology and computers used in a vicious campaign against the leftist Guerrilla Army of the Poor and the Mayan Indian population.[18]

The Foreign Assistance Act of 1974 included a stipulation allowing for the continuation of police aid for counter-narcotics purposes. Many OPS and CIA agents, including Lucien Conein, Edward Lansdale's top assistant (or consigliere, as some historians characterize him because of the mafia-style tactics he employed), found jobs with the State Department's International Narcotics Matters Division and the Drug Enforcement Administration (DEA), which provided training and equipment to police along the OPS model.[19] In Argentina, between 1973 and 1974 President Richard M. Nixon increased the counter-narcotics budget from $3,000 to $347,000—the same amount, not coincidentally, that Congress cut from police programs because of their support for methods of "selective torture" and "assassination." Social Welfare Minister José López Rega, who was later charged with funding death squads through cocaine trafficking, proclaimed on television that drug war aid would "be used in the anti-guerrilla campaign as well."[20] Stan Goff, a Special Forces officer in Colombia who headed a counter-narcotics team, remarked that the training he conducted was anything but counter-narcotics: "It was . . . updated Vietnam-style counter-insurgency, but we were advised to refer to it as counter-narcotics should anyone ask."[21]

Beginning in 1983, the Reagan administration urged Congress to formally reinstitute OPS-style training. Elliot Abrams, assistant secretary of state for human rights and humanitarian affairs, argued: "There are still a large number of police forces in the world where they simply don't understand that they can effectively do their work without indiscriminate violence and brutality. Perhaps if they learned a little bit more about modern professional police tactics, they would be more effective and more compassionate."[22] Congress subsequently enacted waivers allowing for the training of foreign police in counterterrorism by the FBI and CIA, specifically in Central America, where it contributed to considerable repression. In El Salvador, the State Department, FBI, and USAID created a forensics laboratory and police investigative unit whose members were implicated in political murders, and in Guatemala they provided vehicles and mobile radios and created an elite counter-narcotics brigade linked to serious human rights abuses.[23]

In January 1986 the Department of Justice established the International Criminal Investigative Training Assistance Program (ICITAP), headed by former FBI inspector David J. Kriskovich, which assumed many of the former functions of the OPS, though with stricter limitations. Its mission was to assist in the development of the investigative and forensics functions of police, academic curricula, and administrative and management capabilities. It was not authorized to provide lethal equipment or assistance that related to arrest or the use of force.[24]

In December 1989, after the administration of George H. W. Bush overthrew Panamanian strongman Manuel Noriega, a onetime protégé of Adolph Saenz, the ICITAP provided training in counterintelligence and riot control with the aim of suppressing a low-level insurgency against his replacement, Guillermo Endara, a neoliberal banker who was nearly as corrupt.[25] Operating on a budget of $13.2 million, American advisers created two police training academies, upgraded crime laboratory equipment and forensics capabilities, and supplied new uniforms. Psychological warfare techniques were promoted for use against resistance forces as union leaders and newspaper editors were detained and the offices of politicians opposed to the invasion were ransacked.[26]

The head of the police operation, James Steele, was a Purple Heart recipient who had served under George Patton Jr. in Vietnam and coordinated the U.S. military advisory group in El Salvador, supervising hunter-killer commando squads which battled the leftist FMLN. After an all-night hostage standoff, he helped thwart a coup plot by chief of police Colonel Eduardo Herrera Hassan, a School of the Americas graduate known for directing the repression of demonstrators under Noriega.[27] This incident exemplifies the long-standing tendency of American programs to foster a climate of instability and violence, owing largely to the military thrust of the training. (Hassan had initially been empowered under the ICITAP programs.) A year after the invasion, polls revealed that 64 percent of Panamanians distrusted the police, while only 26 percent expressed any confidence in them.[28]

Police training remained a feature of U.S. foreign policy throughout the 1990s, when Washington retained its propensity for intervention despite the collapse of its major imperial rival. With the Clinton administration emphasizing multilateralism, police advisory missions were carried out in conjunction with the United Nations to assist in post-conflict nation-building and included lectures on human and civil rights. While having some positive impact, this emphasis was largely mitigated by the political context in which the ICITAP was implemented and the failure to promote effective judicial and prison reform.[29] The programs were further tarnished by the contracting with private security firms such as DynCorp International of Falls Church, Virginia (formerly Eastern California Airways), whose employees were involved in the child sex-slave trade in Bosnia and illegal arms sales.[30]

In Egypt, dictator Hosni Mubarak's secret police were supplied with tear gas and other repressive instruments and schooled at FBI headquarters in Quantico, Virginia. In Peru, the CIA trained paramilitary units under war criminal Vladimir Montesinos in a Phoenix-style operation against the leftist Sendero Luminoso which spun out of control.[31] In Haiti, American-financed police contributed to the violence after the 1991 coup against Jean-Bertrand Aristide, a liberation theologian committed to land and wealth redistribution. After he reassumed the presidency under the condition that he promote fiscal austerity, the ICITAP incorporated former military and paramilitary officers into the police force, which was built up as a check on his power. Extrajudicial killings and torture remained endemic.[32] As these cases reveal, despite claims that the end of the Cold War spawned a new era of humanitarian intervention, the police programs showed a strong continuity with the past. The ongoing politicization and militarization of police and CIA infiltration of the programs contributed to the growth of repression, as did support for corrupt and authoritarian leaders out of geopolitical expediency.[33]

The destructive impact of police training is most acutely felt today in the Middle East, where any pretense of promoting democratic police standards has been subordinated to larger military goals. The September 11 terrorist attacks created a climate ripe for the Bush administration to carry out the neoconservative agenda of expanding the American "empire of liberty" to all corners of the globe, including "failed states" such as Afghanistan and Iraq, where intervention was designed to flex U.S. muscle and control Middle East and Central Asian energy resources.[34] As in the past, police training and financing were conceived as a key covert mechanism for establishing pro-Western bulwarks committed to a neoliberal economic vision and a global Pax Americana. In practice, however, these efforts helped unleash violent social forces which the United States could not ultimately control, exposing once again the limits of American power.

In Afghanistan, after nine years and over $7 billion spent on training and salaries, American advisers could not say in 2010 how many officers were on duty or where thousands of trucks and other equipment issued to police had gone. A government report concluded that "nepotism, financial improprieties, and unethical recruitment practices were commonplace" among U.S.-backed forces, which engaged in widespread criminal activity and bribery and were "overmatched in counter-insurgency and counter-narcotics operations." Less than 20 percent of the population in the eastern and southern provinces trusted the police, who were frequently stationed in territories distant from their own homes, making them appear an occupying force. A taxi driver told RAND analyst Seth G. Jones, "Forget about the Taliban, it is the police we worry about."[35]

Superficially invoking the post–World War II occupation of Japan, American policymakers and pro-war intellectuals have long emphasized the importance of effective policing in providing the security needed for economic development and the entrenchment of the new social order. In his influential *Learning How to Eat Soup with a Knife: CI Lessons from Malaya and Vietnam*, Lieutenant Colonel John Nagl writes: "Local forces have inherent advantages over outsiders in a CI [counterinsurgency] campaign. They can more easily gain intelligence. They don't need to hire translators to run patrols and understand local behavioral patterns and the local terrain."[36] Repeating the mantras of Vietnam-era modernization theorists, Nagl and his contemporaries overlooked the contempt for the State Department advisers shown by local officials in Afghanistan during the 1950s and the appropriation of police equipment for repressive ends in a pattern that has repeated itself.

After the 2001 invasion of Afghanistan, Germany was given the task of rebuilding the Afghan National Police (ANP) as a means of consolidating the power of U.S.-NATO client Hamid Karzai, a former deputy foreign minister, whose father was assassinated by Taliban agents in 1999. Born to a distinguished Pashtun family of the Popalzai clan in Kandahar, Karzai ran an NGO in Pakistan during the 1980s assisting the anti-Soviet mujahidin, earning the nickname the "Gucci guerrilla" for spending most of his time networking in the lobby of the Islamabad Holiday Inn. According to Meena Siddiqui, a human rights attorney in Kabul, "Karzai had a good past, a good life, and ate well but he cannot do good for his people because he did not come from the people." Many ANP officers were Karzai cronies drawn from warlord militias and hardened by years of fighting against the Soviets and in the subsequent civil wars. Western intervention helped to stoke ethnic rivalries between the Tajik, Uzbek, Hazara, and Pashtun, bringing out their most violent tendencies.[37]

In 2003, criticizing Germany for its focus on community policing over counterinsurgency, the State Department gave DynCorp, which had airlifted supplies to U.S. troops during the Korean War, a $1.1 billion contract for modernizing the ANP. Advisers traveled around the country seeking to upgrade record keeping, communications, and riot control capabilities. New precincts were constructed, shoddily in a number of cases owing to cost-cutting measures by private contractors, forcing police at times to interrogate people in their private residences. Training centers were set up, offering courses in handcuffing, weapons maintenance, constitutional procedure, and guerrilla warfare. British and Canadian trainers gave lectures on crime scene investigation, evidence collection, and dismantling IEDs. Many of the recruits were illiterate. Much as with the ill-fated police academy in Laos, they sat in classrooms that baked in summer and froze in winter, listening to English-speaking instructors through poorly trained translators who were unfamiliar with police terminology. The journalist Ann Jones noted that the exercises looked like military maneuvers.[38]

The establishment of an identity card system and a biometric archive of fingerprints and headshots reflected the deep mistrust of the population inherent in counterinsurgency operations and an imperial drive for control reminiscent of previous U.S. interventions. The sophistication of new technology did not translate into greater efficiency, however, owing largely to the political context and excessive firepower employed by U.S. and NATO troops, which drove ordinary Afghans into the resistance, a "mélange of nationalists and Islamists, shadowy kohl-eyed mullahs and head-bobbing religious students," according to the journalist Anand Gopal, "as well as erudite university students, poor illiterate farmers and veteran anti-Soviet commanders."[39]

Drawn primarily from low-paid police forces in Texas, South Carolina, Georgia, and Florida, DynCorp employees made between $75,000 and $153,000 per year (compared to $20,000 to $30,000 for OPS officers), fifty times more than their Afghan counterparts, who resented their presence. Attrition rates among Afghan recruits exceeded 20 percent. Loyal primarily to regional warlords, police slept at checkpoints, shook down villagers, shot unarmed demonstrators, terrorized people in house-to-house raids, and intimidated journalists and voters during fraudulent elections. In Babaji north of Lashkar Gah, officers bent on taking revenge against clan rivals abducted and raped preteen girls and boys. In 2006 the Kabul chief of police, Jamil Jumbish, was implicated in murder, torture, and bribery, and his replacement, Amanullah Guzar, in extortion, land grabbing, and the kidnapping of three UN workers.[40] These abuses fit the historical pattern and are partly a product of the social polarizations and corruption bred by the U.S.-NATO intervention and mobilization of police for military and political ends.

WikiLeaks documents confirm wide-scale police brutality and its cover-up. In one case, the chief of police in Balkh province raped a sixteen-year-old girl and ordered his bodyguard to fire on a civilian who tried to report the incident. When the bodyguard refused, he was shot dead.[41] In a sign the war was being lost, after a U.S. Army tank smashed into a traffic jam in May 2006, police threw off their uniforms and joined protesters looting buildings, vehicles, and police posts, denouncing the occupation.[42]

The absence of an effective legal or judicial system and the Bush administration's support for torture increased the lawlessness of the ANP. The Red Cross reported massive prison overcrowding, "harsh" conditions, and a lack of clarity about the legal basis for detention, and found that inmates were being subjected to "cruel" treatment in violation of the Geneva Conventions, including sexual abuse of women and juveniles incarcerated for escaping bad marriages. Many were held for lengthy periods without charges or lawyers in facilities lacking even rudimentary toilets. An undisclosed number died in custody, including hundreds transported by the Uzbek warlord Rashid Dostum in unventilated containers, where they suffocated to death or were shot.[43]

General Stanley A. McChrystal reported in 2009 that Afghan prisons served as a key recruiting base and "sanctuary [for Islamic militants] to conduct lethal operations" against government and coalition forces, including the 2008 bombing of the Serena Hotel in Kabul, which was allegedly planned from prison without interference. In Kandahar in 2011, prison guards were stoned on drugs when five hundred inmates escaped.[44]

Although there was limited evidence of Taliban involvement, the United States has supported leading narcotics traffickers such as Hezb-Y-Islami commander Hajji Juma Khan and his son Abdul Khalil Andarabi, head of the Northeast Highway Police, causing production to escalate to over eight thousand tons per annum by 2010.[45] According to WikiLeaks documents, Hamid Karzai pardoned five border police officers caught with 124 kilograms (273 pounds) of heroin and intervened in a drug case involving the son of a wealthy supporter. The president's half-brother Ahmed Wali, who was assassinated in July 2011 by a member of his own inner circle, was a CIA "asset" who headed a paramilitary group that targeted top Taliban commanders and used drug proceeds to fund state terror operations. Izzatullah Wasifi, Hamid Karzai's 2007 appointment as anticorruption chief, spent almost four years in a Nevada prison for selling heroin to an undercover cop. Vice President Ahmed Zia Massood meanwhile was caught entering Dubai with $52 million in cash. A CIA officer commented: "Virtually every significant Afghan figure has had brushes with the drug trade. If you are looking for Mother Teresa, she doesn't live in Afghanistan."[46]

Cheryl Bernard, a RAND analyst and wife of Zalmay Khalilzad, U.S. ambassador to the UN during the George W. Bush administration, explained one of the key reasons for the lack of good governance: "[To defeat the Soviets] we threw the worst crazies against them that we could find and there was a lot of collateral damage. . . . Then we allowed them to get rid of, just kill all the moderate leaders. The reason we don't have moderate leaders in Afghanistan today is because we let the nuts kill them all. They killed all the leftists, the moderates, the middle-of-the-roaders. They were just eliminated, during the 1980s and afterwards." The United States continues to tolerate a high level of corruption out of perceived geopolitical expediency, claiming that it is ingrained within the political culture of Afghanistan. In reality, however, it is a product of historical contingencies, the breakdown of social mores caused by the war climate, and the need among officials who lack popular legitimacy to obtain money for counterinsurgency.[47]

Similar factors were at play during the 1960s, when Vietnam and Laos were at the center of the world drug trade, benefiting from American backing of corrupt officials who controlled the traffic, with the CIA overseeing the production and sale of opium by Hmong guerrillas in order to finance the secret war against the Pathet Lao. History is thus coming full circle in Afghanistan, which produces over 90 percent of the world's heroin and has been widely characterized as a "narco-state."[48] Drug money has corrupted all facets of society, crippled the legal economy, and made it nearly impossible to carry out the simplest development projects. As in South Vietnam under U.S. occupation, the main airport has become a major transshipment point for heroin, and the position of police chief in many provinces is auctioned off to the highest bidder because of its enormous graft value. By 2009, the price for a job as chief of police on the border was rumored to be upwards of $150,000.[49]

Richard Holbrooke, who served as special envoy to Afghanistan from 2009 until his death in December 2010, described the $800 million counter-narcotics campaign run by DynCorp as "the most wasteful" government program he had seen in forty years. Frequently targeting competitors of U.S.-backed warlords, police counter-narcotics teams armed with hoes, sticks, and weed whackers eradicated a paltry 2,373 acres of poppies in raids that killed or wounded dozens of Afghans and were met with stones, snipers, roadside bombs, and angry mobs. Many farmers contracted with militiamen equipped with state-of-the-art satellite phones, semiautomatic weapons, and Toyota pickups to protect their fields. Aerial defoliation destroyed crops of watermelons and wheat, which was unsurprising, as DynCorp was at the time facing a class-action suit by Ecuadorian peasants for spraying herbicides in Colombia that drifted across the border, resulting in the destruction of food crops and the death of several children.[50]

In 2007 the U.S. military took over police training and tried to clean up corruption by raising salaries and implementing electronic pay. Little changed apart from further militarization. The journalist Nir Rosen overheard one sergeant tell his men, "Throw some fuckin' grenades, we're not there to arrest people, just fuckin' kill people."[51] Through the police programs, CIA agents worked with the National Security Directorate, staffed with many former KGB "assets" who cultivated informants and carried out assassinations in a program frequently exploited by agents pursuing personal feuds.[52] In November 2009, five British soldiers were assassinated by the policemen they were training, and nine ANP were killed by a coalition bomb while trying to rescue American soldiers. In February 2010, American Special Forces mistakenly killed a local police chief and a prosecutor in a nighttime raid. An ANP officer subsequently killed six American advisers.[53] These incidents epitomized the growing chaos in Afghanistan, whose people have suffered greatly under the U.S.-NATO occupation.

In Pakistan in 2004, in addition to $15 billion in military aid, which President Pervez Musharraf diverted to bolster the Taliban's insurgent network and prepare for war with India, the Bush administration began providing tens of millions of dollars to the Pakistani police through the ICITAP and DEA. American advisers introduced a computerized security system to monitor movement across the border and created counter-narcotics units and a police air wing equipped with three Caravan spotter planes and eight Huey helicopters to aid in counterinsurgency. Replicating the role played by auto-defense units during the Lao secret war and "Chesty" Puller's men in Nicaragua nearly a century ago, police performed a vital role alongside private security firms such as Xe (formerly Blackwater) identifying targets for Predator drone attacks which killed hundreds of civilians, including seventy-three children in the village of Bala Boluk in Afghanistan's Western Farah province.[54] U.S.-trained forces were meanwhile implicated in "large-scale enforced disappearances," primarily of "activists pushing for greater regional and ethnic rights . . . in Baluchistan and Sindh," while the government used the "rhetoric of fighting terrorism to attack its internal critics."[55]

In Iraq, police programs typify the fiasco of American state-building efforts there. Using the pretext of 9/11 to launch a preemptive invasion, the Bush administration aimed to turn Iraq into a showplace for free-market ideals and a base for the projection of American power in the Middle East. It instead created a violent dystopia by exploiting ethnic fault lines in the society, turning Iraq into a modern-day killing field. The United States initially planned to empower exiled politicians associated with the Iraqi National Congress, notably Ahmad Chalabi, a CIA "asset" implicated in a banking scandal in Jordan, who fed the Americans misinformation in support of the invasion. The Coalition Provisional Authority (CPA) under L. Paul Bremer III, former assistant to Secretary of State Henry Kissinger, ignited wide-scale resistance as a result of troop brutality and privatization schemes that led to brazen corruption and a decline in social services. With reluctance, the United States eventually backed the Islamist Shia Dawa Party, headed by former Syrian secret police sergeant Nouri al-Maliki, which had ties to Iran and had suffered repression under Saddam Hussein.[56]

As in past interventions, police programs in Iraq were designed to establish an effective intelligence and social control apparatus, considered vital for stabilizing the occupation. After the "shock and awe" campaign of March 2003, looters destroyed police stations and equipment, and police abandoned their posts as American military officers stood by. Kidnappings and criminal activity proliferated. Police training, however, did not begin until November. The mission was headed by Bernard B. Kerik, former New York City police commissioner, who had won fame in leading rescue efforts at ground zero on 9/11 and notoriety when he was sentenced in 2010 to four years in prison after being found guilty of tax fraud and public corruption. Kerik told reporters that he had been given only ten days to prepare for his post in Iraq, which he did by watching A&E documentaries on Saddam Hussein. A high school dropout, Kerik had previously been expelled from Saudi Arabia for illegally spying on the medical staff at a hospital where he directed the security detail.[57]

With scant knowledge of the country's history and culture, Kerik and two dozen other retired law enforcement agents met with local police officials and oversaw the rebuilding of new police precincts and training facilities. Gruff and muscle-bound, Kerik took part in nighttime raids with paramilitary rangers headed by his protégé Ahmed Kadhim Ibrahim, who was accused of torturing prostitutes with electroshocks. The Pentagon issued Taser guns (used by American law enforcement agencies to incapacitate suspects through the release of twenty-six watts of electrical energy) and provided high-tech radio, computer, and surveillance equipment, which enabled the Iraqi police to collect over a million fingerprints, which were scanned through satellite link to Washington.[58]

The major training academy for Iraqi police was built outside Amman,

Jordan. Here, three thousand cadets were given an eight-week course in techniques such as immobilizing suspects, using handcuffs, and carrying out counter-guerrilla warfare. Translating instruction from English to Arabic ate up 50 percent of the time. Under the de-Ba'athification policy (a departure from the practice of recruiting from the ancien régime), Saddamist officers were deprived of their positions and often took up arms with the insurgency. Many enlistees were criminals or insurgents using the program to get weapons. Bremer complained to Secretary of State Condoleezza Rice that the Americans "were just pulling kids off the streets and handing them badges and AK-47s. . . . [T]he most fundamental role of any government is law and order. The fact that we didn't crack down on it right from the start sent a message that we were not prepared."[59]

In March 2004, DynCorp was awarded a $750 million contract to professionalize the Iraqi National Police (INP). Operating with few legal restrictions, contractors alienated the population through such practices as "driving through the streets fast and furious without regard for the locals," public drunkenness, whoring, and torturing and shooting civilians. One of their slogans was "I do this job for the opportunity to kill the enemies of my country and also to get that boat I always wanted. . . . [W]hen engaged I will lay waste to everything around me." The company angered the CPA when it raided Ahmad Chalabi's home, overcharged on fuel, and wasted money building an Olympic-size swimming pool for the use of its employees. CNN anchor Tucker Carlson reported that contractors with whom he was embedded beat a suspected kidnapper "into a bloody mound" before turning what was left of him "over to the Iraqi police."[60]

Under DynCorp's oversight, the INP remained riddled with cronyism, drug abuse, and corruption, its payrolls padded with phantom employees.[61] Historically, the forces trained by the United States to subdue their own countrymen have taken on the character of paid mercenaries with little loyalty to the cause they purportedly represent. Iraq is no exception—except that they were now being trained by mercenaries. Asked by a Wall Street reporter about America's stated goal of bringing democracy to Iraq, cadets giggled and pointed to the nearby Ministry of Oil, the only major ministerial building U.S. troops saved from looters during the invasion. "They want our oil," said twenty-year-old Hassan Muhned. "We have no democracy now. Maybe we will have it if the Americans leave." But, he added, they should not leave until he was paid.[62]

WikiLeaks documents demonstrate the centrality of police to counterinsurgency efforts in Iraq, including mounting raids, dispersing crowds, capturing weapons, guarding strategic installations, providing intelligence to marines, and cleaning up IED sites. Once U.S. troops cleared a village or town, the place was usually turned over to the police. Several reports point to civilian killings in shootouts amidst a general climate of lawlessness.[63] As the country descended into civil war, Shiite militias loyal to the Dawa Party and cleric Moqtada al-Sadr used American weapons to engage in ethnic cleansing operations. Driving through city streets with dead bodies in the backs of their trucks, they made forays into Sunni neighborhoods targeting Saddam loyalists and also killed Palestinians and anyone with the Sunni name Omar. Investigative journalists and two hundred academics opposed to the U.S. invasion were among those assassinated, including Abdul Latif al-Mayah, the director of the Baghdad Center for Human Rights, who denounced the corruption of the Iraqi Governing Council on Al-Jazeera television twelve hours before he was killed. According to the *New Statesman*, al-Mayah "spoke for people on the street and made some politicians quite jealous." Jerry Burke, a police trainer from Massachusetts who served two tours in Iraq, told reporters in 2007 that the INP was unsalvageable as an institution; he believed that many of its members should be prosecuted for human rights violations, war crimes, and death squad activities.[64]

Some of Burke's colleagues worked with special police commandos, recruited from Saddam's Special Forces after the reversal of the de-Ba'athification policy, whose mission was to "neutralize" high-level insurgents. American strategy in this respect was modeled after the Phoenix program in Vietnam, of which Vice President Dick Cheney was enamored, and also Ronald Reagan's terrorist wars in Central America during the 1980s. In 2004 Cheney called for the "Salvador option," referring to the U.S. role in training paramilitaries to assassinate left-wing guerrillas during El Salvador's "dirty war," largely with the aim of intimidating the population.[65] James Steele, who commanded Salvadoran forces responsible for "disappearances," torture, and the massacre of civilians, was appointed chief adviser to the Iraqi police commandos.[66]

An executive with Enron who lied to Congress about smuggling weapons to the contras, Steele worked under Ambassador John Negroponte, who, during the 1980s, covered up extrajudicial killings in Honduras, a staging base for attacks on Nicaragua. With such men in charge, the journalist Dahr Jamail wrote, it was no coincidence that daily life in Iraq came to resemble "what the death squads generated in Central America. . . . Hundreds of dead lay unclaimed at the morgue—blood-caked men who had been shot, knifed, garroted or apparently suffocated by the plastic bag still over their heads. Many of the bodies were sprawled with their hands still bound."[67]

By training and arming Iraqi police officials who became notorious for corruption, beatings, kidnappings, and executions, American advisers contributed immeasurably to the bloodbath in Iraq. Fitting a long-standing precedent, the United States favored hard-liners like Adnan Thabit, head of the police commandos, whom close aides compared to the Godfather and who hosted a grotesque "reality" show on U.S.-backed Al-Iraqiya television which displayed badly beaten Iraqis confessing to resistance activities. The head of the Ministry of the Interior in 2005–6, Bayan Jabr, a former high-ranking member of the

Iranian-backed Badr Brigade, the military arm of the fundamentalist Shiite Supreme Council for the Islamic Revolution, which he incorporated into the INP, oversaw a torture chamber beneath his offices in which survivors were left with drill marks on their skulls. Serving later as finance minister, Jabr worked with General David Petraeus, who ran the military police training program in 2005, and Steven Casteel of the CPA, who as DEA intelligence chief in the 1990s oversaw the killing of drug lord Pablo Escobar and trained Andean security forces known for "disappearing" peasant leaders and union activists.[68]

In December 2006 the Iraq Study Group portrayed a grave and deteriorating state of affairs, noting: The Shiite dominated police units "cannot control crime and . . . routinely engage in sectarian violence, including the unnecessary detention, torture, and targeted execution of Sunni Arab civilians. . . . Many police participated in training in order to obtain a weapon, uniform, and ammunition for use in sectarian violence."[69] A Human Rights Watch report around the same time detailed police methods of interrogation in which prisoners were beaten with cables and pipes, shocked, or suspended from their wrists for prolonged periods. One interviewee commented, "This isn't a police force, it's a bunch of thugs." What such reports ignore is the systematic U.S. responsibility. When an earnest army captain, Phil Carter, complained to Major General Ghassan Adnan al-Bawi, the police chief in Diyala province, about torture, al-Bawi tellingly responded, "I only do what you do," citing Guantánamo Bay and Abu Ghraib.[70]

As in Afghanistan, the INP was a frequent target of insurgent attacks, 43 percent of which, according to one study, were directed against U.S.-backed security forces. Nearly three thousand police were killed and over five thousand injured between September 2005 and April 2006 alone. Two DynCorp employees and military advisers died in the same period. In a reflection of the violent climate bred by the occupation, several high-ranking officers, including the head of the serious crimes unit in Baghdad, were shot dead by U.S. soldiers who thought they were suicide bombers.[71] Iraqi police expressed resentment toward Americans and rarely acknowledged their advice, condemning them as cowardly and hypocritical for not taking the same risks to their lives and for being better protected from attack. Many felt that they were being set up to be killed. A police lieutenant in Baghdad complained, "The [Americans] hide behind the barricades while we are here in the streets without even guns to protect ourselves."[72]

As in the Philippines and Vietnam earlier, American advisers harbored racial stereotypes of Iraqis and had a paternalistic and colonial mindset that bred further resentment. In a memoir of his year in Iraq, Robert Cole, a police officer from East Palo Alto, California, and a DynCorp employee, explains that these attitudes were ingrained in a mini–boot camp training session, where he was "brainwashed, reprogrammed, and desensitized" and "morphed" into a "trained professional killer." One of the major lessons taught was that Iraqis understand only force. Cole was told to shoot first and think later and to instruct police to do the same. "If you see a suspicious Iraqi civilian, pull your weapon and gun him down," he was instructed. "You don't fire one . . . or two shots. . . . You riddle his sorry ass with bullets until you're sure he's dead as a doorknob."[73]

This is an inversion not just of democratic police methods but even of Western counterinsurgency doctrine, which, at least in theory, advocates moderation in the use of force in order to avoid antagonizing the population and creating martyrs.[74] No wonder the scope of violence has been so vast. Nevertheless, despite all the bloodshed and all the negative reports, the Iraq Study Group recommended expanding police training. Efforts were made to include Sunnis and purge corrupt elements.[75] Extrajudicial violence remained endemic, however, in spite of a decline in ethnic killings resulting from the exhaustion of the warring parties and the triumph of the Shia. On March 16, 2009, the *New York Times* reported that police continuously linked to torture had abducted and killed six prisoners released from Camp Bucca in retribution for their days as insurgents. In spring 2011 they shot unarmed civilians demonstrating in sympathy with the Egyptian revolution.[76]

During the 2007-8 "surge," heavy responsibility was delegated to the police for manning checkpoints and aiding in combat operations against Muqtada al-Sadr's Mahdi Army, Al-Qaeda, and other resistance forces, intensifying opportunities for extortion and abuse. The long-term consequences remain uncertain. Robert M. Witajewski, director of the U.S. embassy's Law Enforcement and Correctional Affairs program, expressed concern that in "over-militarizing the police," the United States was potentially "creating an entity that could cause a coup down the road."[77] There are plenty of historical examples of such fears being borne out. Few in Washington, however, appeared to acknowledge them, as was evident in the Obama administration's provision of over $2 billion for police and security assistance as the U.S. troop presence was scaled down.

American mismanagement of the Iraqi correctional system compounded the negative effects of the police programs and helped catalyze opposition to the occupation. Like police precincts, Iraq's prisons and courthouses were badly looted in the aftermath of the invasion. Prisoner records went missing, and inmates escaped or were released by Saddam before he fled into hiding. In May 2003, Attorney General John Ashcroft contracted with ICITAP to restore law and order by rebuilding the prisons. Structural repairs were undertaken and a guard training course was initiated. Ashcroft pointed to the new prison system as a shining example of the freedom that the United States was supposedly spreading in Iraq.

According to a RAND Corporation study, however, nearly 90 percent of detainees were innocent of any charge and were often held for long periods without trial. (By 2011 the court system remained nonfunctional, with one-sixth of judges accused of corruption.) As in Vietnam, sweeping arrests led to rampant overcrowding, resulting in outbreaks of tuberculosis, scabies, and other diseases. Inmates had to sleep standing up and were subjected to sensory deprivation, beatings, and other forms of psychological torture long promoted by the CIA. Guards provided condoms and medical care in return for cash rewards or sexual favors. Male and female prisoners, including juveniles, were raped. Riots, hunger strikes, and attacks by insurgents were common. The Pentagon claimed that those who died in custody were "shot while trying to escape." One American officer stated that six years was a life sentence in an Iraqi prison because that was the estimated lifespan there.[78]

A far cry from the Ph.D.s in occupied Japan, many of the Americans selected to oversee the prison system had checkered pasts when it came to prisoners' rights, having been accused of malfeasance as correctional executives in the United States. The assistant director of prisons, John J. Armstrong, for example, had been forced to resign as head of the Department of Corrections in Connecticut after settling a lawsuit brought by the American Civil Liberties Union and the families of two inmates who died in a supermax facility which the National Prison Project referred to as a "high-tech dungeon." One of the victims died of heart failure after going into diabetic shock and then being hit with a fifty thousand–volt electric charge by a guard wielding a stun gun. Armstrong also ignored complaints of sexual abuse of female guards on his watch. He was appointed by the since disgraced Republican governor John G. Rowland, who once complained that prisons in Connecticut resembled "Club Med–style resorts."[79] These comments reflected the tough-on-crime attitude prevalent among conservatives that led to deteriorating conditions and a decline in concern for prisoners' rights, which spilled over into America's international practices.[80]

ICITAP staff member Terry Deland faced lawsuits while serving as director of corrections in Utah for subjecting prisoners to cruel and unusual punishment after a rebellion over unacceptable conditions, including forcing them to lie facedown outdoors for days on end and leaving them to urinate and defecate on themselves. Deland further refused to discipline guards who had kept a non-violent offender naked for fifty-six days in a "strip cell," which was described in court documents as having "no windows, no interior lights, no bunk, no floor covering, and no toilet except for a hole in the concrete floor which was flushed irregularly from outside the cell." Another ICITAP staffer, Colonel Lane McCotter, as director of the Texas Department of Corrections had forced thousands of inmates into tiny isolation chambers for record periods in response to gang violence. He had also been forced to resign as corrections director in Utah in 1997 when a mentally ill inmate died after guards left him shackled naked to a restraining chair for sixteen hours. McCotter then became an executive of a private prison company whose jails were strongly criticized in a Justice Department report just a month before the department sent him to Iraq. One of the company's facilities in Santa Fe, New Mexico, lacked adequate medical and mental health care and had no suicide prevention plan, which contributed to an inmate's hanging himself.[81]

McCotter first identified Abu Ghraib as the best site for America's main civilian prison and helped to rebuild the facility and train guards after the U.S. invasion. Many of the torture techniques employed there which first came to light in 2004, including sexual humiliation and sensory deprivation, had long been used in American prisons where a number of the guards previously worked. Julian Bond, chairman of the NAACP, commented: "Sadly, there is no surprise in the horrific photos from Iraq. Americans of color are all too familiar with incidents of prisoner abuse stretching from the distant past to the present day. It begins when the person held prisoner is considered less 'human' than the prison guard." Senator Charles Schumer, a New York Democrat, agreed: "When you ask yourself why there is a mess in Iraqi prisons, just look at the kind of oversight and checking that was done with the people that were put in charge. With these kinds of people, was there any doubt that the prison system would be run in a decent way? Absolutely not."[82]

In 2006 the Department of Justice appointed OPS veteran Donald Bordenkircher to repair the public relations damage caused by the Abu Ghraib scandal and improve conditions for the eighty thousand civilian prisoners in Iraqi facilities overseen by the United States—a similar task to the one he had been given after the exposure of the "tiger cages" in Vietnam. In the intervening years, Bordenkircher had done consulting work in Saudi Arabia and was warden of the federal penitentiary in Moundsville, West Virginia, which a Chicago-based prison reform association characterized as among the worst in the country: it was infested with cockroaches and fleas, there was a stench from bad plumbing and the leaking of raw sewage, the cells were less than half the recommended size, and there were no rehabilitation programs.

Known as tough-talking and a stern disciplinarian, Bordenkircher would lock down the whole facility even for relatively minor infractions by a few inmates and force those inmates to spend months in solitary confinement. He once stated that if a hostage situation occurred, after one warning the hostage-taker would be executed, regardless of his demands. In 1986, after his election as town sheriff in Moundsville, Bordenkircher oversaw the crushing of an inmate rebellion that arose as a result of wretched prison conditions not far removed from those he had overseen a decade and a half earlier in South Vietnam. The warden at the time was one of Bordenkircher's protégés who had been his deputy and was also known for his authoritarian style.[83]

A product of the post–World War II "victory culture" who grew up in an impoverished Ohio steel town during the depression, Bordenkircher subscribed throughout his career to a fundamentally conservative outlook, characterized by a disdain for any kind of dissent against the status quo, regardless of the circumstances. In this respect he resembled contemporaries such as Byron Engle, who believed that the "left-wing" press and "limousine liberals" in Congress had conspired to destroy the OPS. Engle championed neoconservative causes in retirement, including pressing for an end to congressional sanctions against the white supremacist government of Ian Smith in Southern Rhodesia (Zimbabwe) and for more aggressive measures to combat "Marxist terrorism" worldwide.[84] Another example is Jeter Williamson, who at age eighty-eight wrote a letter to the editor of the Greensboro, North Carolina, *News and Record* on the eve of the 2004 election criticizing Democratic candidate John F. Kerry's "vicious defamation" of U.S. troops during the war in Vietnam, stating that he himself was not aware of any atrocities except for "terrorist action" committed by the "Vietcong" against civilians and police whom he had trained, fifteen of whom were killed each month.[85]

As his memoirs relate, Bordenkircher viewed those who helped to expose the use of tiger cages, including in an odd pairing Donald Luce and William Colby, as dupes of Hanoi propaganda. He first joined the OPS, he writes, to avoid raising his children in California at a time when antiwar activism proliferated. Considering the abuse at Abu Ghraib to have been nothing more than "serious college hazing," he claims that in Iraq, prisoners told him that Al-Qaeda received assistance from one of Saddam's sons before 9/11 and that weapons of mass destruction existed, vindicating the decision to go to war.[86] Bordenkircher serves as an interesting bridge figure who exemplifies the continuity in policies from Vietnam to Iraq to the United States itself, where harsh measures are continuously justified on "security" grounds and by the demonization of various social groups. He further embodies the paradoxes of the police programs by promoting the professionalization and modernization of criminal justice institutions in the service of U.S. global hegemony, the kind of thinking that has led to considerable excesses and violence.

Since the Nixon and Reagan eras, with the decline of the rehabilitative ideal, the American criminal justice system has been marred by systematic abuse, making its representatives ill-suited for the task of rebuilding the Iraqi system, or that of any other country. In 2001, Human Rights Watch reported that prisoners in the United States were "beaten with fists and batons, stomped on, kicked, shot, stunned with electronic devices, doused with chemical sprays, choked, and slammed face first into concrete floors by the officers whose job it is to guard them. Inmates have ended up with broken jaws, smashed ribs, perforated eardrums, missing teeth, burn scars—not to mention psychological scars and emotional pain. Some have died." A disproportionate amount of the cruelty took place during George W. Bush's tenure as governor of Texas, where a judge concluded that "the prisons had become a culture of sadistic and malicious violence."[87] Much as with the OPS, modern-day police advisers have helped transfer to other countries some of the worst aspects of the American criminal justice system, contributing to extensive human rights violations. Their role in exporting repression encapsulates the dark side of the American empire, which has been sustained through the decades, like all other empires, by violence and coercion. The Iraqi and Afghan people are but the latest to bear its wrath.

Abbreviations Used in Notes

AFHRA	Air Force Historical Research Agency, Maxwell Air Force Base, Montgomery, Ala.
AIDNC	Development Project Files Related to Narcotics Control, Office of Public Safety, NARA
AMAG	American Military Assistance Greece
AMHI	U.S. Army Military History Institute, Carlisle Barracks Military History Research Institute, Carlisle, Pa.
ASJ	Arthur Schlesinger Jr. Papers, White House Files, John F. Kennedy Presidential Library, Boston
BFEA	U.S. State Department, Bureau of Far Eastern Affairs
BIA	Records of the Bureau of Insular Affairs, NARA
BNDD	Records of the Bureau of Narcotics and Dangerous Drugs (formerly FBN), NARA
CI	Special Group on Counter-Insurgency, John F. Kennedy cabinet
CIA	Central Intelligence Agency, Center for the Study of Intelligence, Washington, D.C.
CIB	Criminal Investigation Branch, U.S. Army
CIC	Counter-Intelligence Corps, U.S. Army
CORDS	Records of the Office of Civil Operations for Rural Development Support, NARA
DDEL	Dwight D. Eisenhower Presidential Library, Abilene, Kans.
GHQ SCAP	Records of the General Headquarters, Supreme Commander for the Allied Powers, NARA
GAO	U.S. Government Accountability Office, Washington, D.C.
GPO	U.S. Government Printing Office
HLHU	Houghton Library, Harvard University
HQ MACV	Headquarters, Records of U.S. Military Assistance Command, Vietnam
HQ USAV	Headquarters, Records of U.S. Army, Vietnam
HSTL	Harry S. Truman Presidential Library, Independence, Mo.
HTA	Henry T. Allen Papers, Manuscript Division, Library of Congress, Washington, D.C.

ICA	Records of the International Cooperation Administration, U.S. Department of State, NARA
IPA	International Police Academy, Washington, D.C.
IPS	Internal Defense and Public Safety
JFKL	John F. Kennedy Presidential Library, Boston
KUBARK	*Counterintelligence Interrogation and Human Resource Exploitation Training Manual*, George Washington University, Washington, D.C.
LBJL	Lyndon Baines Johnson Library & Museum, Austin, Tex.
MAAG	Military Assistance Advisory Group
MSUA	Michigan State University Archives
MSUG	Michigan State University Vietnam Advisory Group
NARA	National Archives and Records Administration, College Park, Md.
NACLA	North American Congress on Latin America
NSA	National Security Archive, George Washington University, Washington, D.C.
NSCF	National Security Council Files, Harry S. Truman Presidential Library, Independence, Mo.
NSF	National Security Files
OCB	Operations Coordinating Board
OCMH	Office of the Chief of Military History, Department of the U.S. Army, Washington, D.C.
OISP	Overseas Internal Security Program
OMGUS	Records of the Office of Military Government for Germany, NARA
OPS	Records of the Office of Public Safety, NARA
OSS	Records of the Office of Strategic Services, NARA
POF	President's Office Files, Counterinsurgency, JFKL
PSD	Records of the Public Safety Division, NARA
PSF	President's Secretary's Files
RAFSEA	Records of U.S. Armed Forces in Southeast Asia, NARA
RAOOH	Records of Allied Operations and Occupation Headquarters, World War II, NARA
RDEA	Records of the Drug Enforcement Administration, NARA
RDS	Records of the Department of State, NARA
RFAA	Records of the U.S. Foreign Assistance Agencies, NARA
RFAK	Records of the U.S. Foreign Assistance Mission to Korea, National Archives, College, Park, Md.
RG	Record Group
RWK	Robert W. Komer Papers, John F. Kennedy Presidential Library, Boston

SCAP	Records of the Supreme Commander for the Allied Powers, Washington National Records Center, Suitland, Md.
SHAEF	Records of Supreme Headquarters Allied Expeditionary Force, National Archives, Washington, D.C.
TTU	Texas Tech University, the Vietnam Center and Archive, Lubbock
USAFIK	Records of U.S. Army Forces in Korea, NARA
USAID	Records of the U.S. Agency for International Development, Washington, D.C.
USOM	Records of the United States Operations Mission, NARA
WCF	William Cameron Forbes Papers, Houghton Library, Harvard University
ZNA	Zambian National Archives, Lusaka

Notes

Introduction

1. Mark Hosenball, Ron Moreau, and T. Christian Miller, "The Gang That Couldn't Shoot Straight: Six Billion Dollars Later, the Afghan National Police Can't Begin to Do Their Jobs Right—Never Mind Relieve American Forces," *Newsweek*, March 19, 2010, 29.

2. See Martha K. Huggins, *Political Policing: The United States and Latin America* (Durham: Duke University Press, 1998); Michael T. Klare and Cynthia Aronson, *Supplying Repression: U.S. Support for Authoritarian Regimes Abroad* (Washington, D.C.: Institute for Policy Studies, 1981); A. J. Langguth, *Hidden Terrors: The Truth about U.S. Police Operations in Latin America* (New York: Pantheon Books, 1978), 120.

3. George Orwell, *Shooting an Elephant and Other Essays* (New York: Harcourt Brace and Company, 1945), 3–4.

4. See Lesley Gill, *The School of the Americas: Military Training and Political Violence in the Americas* (Durham: Duke University Press, 2004), for a parallel.

5. See Robert Wiebe, *The Search for Order 1877–1920* (New York: Hill and Wang, 1966); Tony Platt, ed., *The Iron Fist and the Velvet Glove: An Analysis of the U.S. Police* (Berkeley: Center for Research on Criminal Justice, 1975).

6. See William E. Leuchtenburg, "Progressivism and Imperialism: The Progressive Movement and American Foreign Policy, 1898–1916," *Mississippi Valley Historical Review* 39 (December 1952): 500; Alan Dawley, *Changing the World: American Progressives in War and Revolution* (Princeton: Princeton University Press, 2003). For insights into the ideological vision of policy elites, see Michael H. Hunt, *Ideology and U.S. Foreign Policy* (New Haven: Yale University Press, 1987); Gabriel Kolko, *The Roots of American Foreign Policy: An Analysis of Power and Purpose* (Boston: Beacon Press, 1969); Michael Latham, *The Right Kind of Revolution: Modernization, Development, and U.S. Foreign Policy from the Cold War to the Present* (Ithaca: Cornell University Press, 2011).

7. On this point, see Alfred W. McCoy, *Policing America's Empire: The United States, the Philippines, and the Rise of the Surveillance State* (Madison: University of Wisconsin Press, 2009).

8. Mark H. Haller, "Historical Roots of Police Behavior: Chicago, 1890–1925," *Law and Society Review* 10 (Winter 1976): 308.

9. Frank J. Donner, *Protectors of Privilege: Red Squads and Police Repression in Urban America* (Berkeley: University of California Press, 1991); Samuel Walker, *Popular Justice: A History of American Criminal Justice,* 2nd ed. (New York: Oxford University Press, 1998), 62.

10. Lincoln Steffens, *The Autobiography of Lincoln Steffens,* vol. 1 (New York: Harcourt Brace, 1931), 207.

11. Simon A. Cole, *Suspect Identities: A History of Fingerprinting and Criminal Identification* (Cambridge: Harvard University Press, 2001); Samuel Walker, *A Critical History of Police Reform* (Washington, D.C.: Lexington Books, 1977).

12. Marilynn S. Johnson, *Street Justice: A History of Police Violence in New York City* (Boston: Beacon Press, 2003), 9; Donner, *Protectors of Privilege*, 44–64; Sydney Harring, *Policing a Class Society: The Experience of American Cities, 1865–1915* (New Brunswick: Rutgers University Press, 1983).

13. Richard A. Leo, *Police Interrogation and American Justice* (Cambridge: Harvard University Press, 2008), 24; National Commission on Law Observance and Enforcement, *Report on Lawlessness in Law Enforcement*, no. 11 (Washington, D.C.: GPO, 1931), 38, 173; National Commission on Law Observance and Enforcement, *Report on Police*, no. 14 (Washington, D.C.: GPO, 1931), 17; Gene E. Carte and Elaine H. Carte, *Police Reform in the United States: The Era of August Vollmer, 1905–1932* (Berkeley: University of California Press, 1974), 66–67; Emmanuel H. Lavine, *The Third Degree: A Detailed and Appalling Exposé of Police Brutality* (New York: Vanguard Press, 1930); Platt, *The Iron Fist and the Velvet Glove*, 32–41; Joe Domanick, *To Protect and to Serve: The LAPD's Century of War in the City of Dreams* (New York: Figueroa, 2003), 49. For more on the problems associated with police "professionalization" in the Progressive Era, see Thomas A. Reppetto, *The Blue Parade* (New York: Free Press, 1978); and William Turner, *The Police Establishment* (New York: G. P. Putnam, 1968).

14. See David Rothman, *Conscience and Convenience: The Asylum and Its Alternatives in Progressive America* (Boston: Little, Brown, 1980); Rebecca M. McLennan, *The Crisis of Imprisonment: Protest, Politics, and the Making of the American Penal State, 1776–1941* (New York: Cambridge University Press, 2008).

15. See Donald L. Garrity, "The Prison as Rehabilitative Agency," in *The Prison: Studies in Institutional Organization and Change*, ed. Donald Cressey (New York: Holt, Rinehart & Winston, 1961), 358–81; Frank Tannenbaum, *Crime and the Community* (Boston: Ginn, 1939), 71; Mabel Elliott, *Coercion in Penal Treatment: Past and Present* (Ithaca, N.Y.: Pacifist Research Bureau, 1947), 38, 41; James V. Bennett, with Rodney Campbell, *I Chose Prison* (New York: Knopf, 1970), 25; Eric Cummins, *The Rise and Fall of California's Radical Prison Movement* (Palo Alto: Stanford University Press, 1994); Kenyon J. Scudder, *Prisoners Are People* (New York: Doubleday, 1952).

16. John L. Gillin, *Taming the Criminal: Adventures in Penology* (New York: Macmillan, 1931), 295–96.

17. David M. Oshinsky, *"Worse Than Slavery": Parchman Farm and the Ordeal of Jim Crow Justice* (New York: Free Press, 1997); Gillin, *Taming the Criminal*, 263; Robert Perkinson, *Texas Tough: The Rise of America's Prison Empire* (New York: Metropolitan Books, 2010). Mortality rates not surprisingly were extraordinarily high.

18. Kate Richards O'Hare, *In Prison* (New York: Knopf, 1923), 63, 65, 67; Edgardo Rotman, "The Failure of Reform: United States, 1865 to 1965," in *The Oxford History of the Prison*, ed. Norval Morris and David Rothman (New York: Oxford University Press, 1995), 177. Joseph Fishman, the U.S inspector for prisons, referred to county jails in this period as a "debauch of dirt, disease, and degeneracy" (quoted in Rotman, 177). See also Joseph F. Fishman with Vee Perlman, *Crucibles of Crime* (New York: Cosmopolis Press, 1923).

19. George Jackson, *Soledad Brother: The Prison Letters of George Jackson*, rev. ed. (New York: Lawrence Hill Books, 1994).

20. Ben H. Bagdikian and Leon Dash, *The Shame of the Prisons* (New York: Pocket Books, 1972), 3. See also Leonard Orlando, *Prisons: Houses of Darkness* (New York: Free Press, 1975); Editors of Ramparts and Frank Browning, *Prison Life: A Study of the Explosive Conditions in America's Prisons* (New York: Harper & Row, 1972).

21. See Sasha Abramsky, *American Furies: Crime, Punishment, and Vengeance in the Age*

of Mass Imprisonment (Boston: Beacon Press, 2007); James Austin and John Irwin, *It's About Time: America's Imprisonment Binge,* rev. ed. (Belmont, Calif.: Wadsworth, 1996); Christian Parenti, *Lockdown America: Police and Prisons in the Age of Crisis* (London: Verso, 1999); Hanna Holleman, Robert W. McChesney, John Bellamy Foster, and R. Jamil Jonna, "The Penal State in an Age of Crisis," *Monthly Review* 61 (June 2009): 1–16.

22. Studs Terkel, "Servants of the State: A Conversation with Daniel Ellsberg," *Harper's,* February 1972, 56.

23. See Charles DeBenedetti, ed., *Peace Heroes in Twentieth-Century America* (Bloomington: Indiana University Press, 1986), 6, 7; Ellen Schrecker, *Many Are the Crimes: McCarthyism in America* (Boston: Little, Brown, 1998); William W. Turner, *Power on the Right* (Berkeley: Ramparts Press, 1971).

24. Robert H. Holden, *Armies without Nations: Public Violence and State Formation in Central America, 1821–1960* (New York: Oxford University Press, 2004), 156. A source of information on the backgrounds of police advisers which I rely on throughout the book is Reg Davis and Harry James, *The Public Safety Story: An Informal Recollection of Events and Individuals Leading to the Formation of the AID Office of Public Safety,* April 2001; RG 286, Records Relating to the International Association of Chiefs of Police, box 5. The political scientist Thomas Lobe estimates that half the Office of Public Safety (OPS) officers took the job "for the money, for adventure, to escape bad marriages, or to shack up with Asian women." Thomas D. Lobe, "U.S. Police Assistance For the Third World," Ph.D. diss., University of Michigan, 1975, 390.

25. Police expert David Bayley defines a democratic police force as one that is accountable to the public in whose name its powers are authorized. See David H. Bayley, *Patterns of Policing: A Comparative International Analysis* (New Brunswick, N.J.: Rutgers University Press, 1985); and George E. Berkeley, *The Democratic Policeman* (Boston: Beacon Press, 1969).

26. O. W. Wilson, "Report on Public Safety Training Program of ICA," July 21–27, 1958, MSU Vietnam Project, box 679, MSUA; Lauren J. Goin, memoir, April 1991, Institute of Inter-American Affairs Collection, University of Illinois at Springfield, Archives, Special Collections; Colonel Virgil Ney, "Guerrilla Warfare and Modern Strategy," in *Modern Guerrilla Warfare: Fighting Communist Guerrilla Movements, 1941–1961,* ed. F. M. Osanka, introduction by Samuel Huntington (New York: Free Press, 1962), 25–38. Wilson, the dean of the Berkeley School of Criminal Justice, provided key intellectual support for the programs as a State Department consultant.

27. Hoover quoted in R. Andrew Kiel, *J. Edgar Hoover: The Father of the Cold War; How His Obsession with Communism Led to the Warren Commission Coverup and Escalation of the Vietnam War,* foreword by Carl Oglesby (Lanham, Md.: University Press of America, 2000), 27. See also J. Edgar Hoover, *Masters of Deceit: The Story of Communism in America and How to Fight It* (New York: Pocket Books, 1959); Melvyn Dubofsky, *We Shall Be All: A History of the Industrial Workers of the World* (Chicago: Quadrangle Books, 1969).

28. Kiel, *J. Edgar Hoover,* 26; Regin Schmidt, *Red Scare: FBI and the Origins of Anticommunism in the U.S., 1919–1943* (Copenhagen: Museum Tusculanum Press, University of Copenhagen, 2000), 20, 53; Kenneth D. Ackerman, *Young J. Edgar Hoover: Hoover, the Red Scare, and the Assault on Civil Liberties* (New York: Carroll & Graf, 2007).

29. Cecilia Menjívar and Néstor P. Rodríguez, "State Terror in the U.S.–Latin American Interstate Regime," in *When States Kill: Latin America, the U.S., and Technologies of Terror,* ed. Cecilia Menjívar and Néstor P. Rodríguez (Austin: University of Texas Press, 2005), 10; Max Paul Friedman, *Nazis and Good Neighbors: The United States Campaign against the Germans of Latin America in World War II* (New York: Cambridge University Press, 2003),

ix, 66. On FBI programs in China, see Frederic Wakeman Jr., "American Police Advisers and the Nationalist Chinese Secret Service, 1930–1937," *Modern China* 18 (April 1992): 107–37.

30. Athan G. Theoharis, *The FBI and American Democracy: A Critical History* (Lawrence: University of Kansas Press, 2004); Frank J. Donner, *The Age of Surveillance: The Aims and Methods of America's Political Intelligence System* (New York: Knopf, 1980), 4; Fred J. Cook, *The FBI Nobody Knows* (New York: Macmillan, 1964); Schrecker, *Many Are the Crimes.*

31. Hardy quoted in David Wise, *The American Police State: Government against the People* (New York: Random House, 1976), 311; David Cunningham, *There's Something Happening Here: The New Left, The Klan, and FBI Counterintelligence* (Berkeley: University of California Press, 2004); Nelson Blackstock, *COINTELPRO: The FBI's Secret War on Political Freedom,* introduction by Noam Chomsky (New York: Vintage, 1975). New evidence reveals that the "people's historian" Howard Zinn was among those subjected to extensive spying and harassment. Cunningham shows how the FBI focused almost exclusively on the New Left and not extreme right-wing and genuine terrorist organizations such as the Klan.

32. See Huey P. Newton, *War against the Panthers: A Study of Repression in America* (New York: Harlem River Press, 2000); Ward Churchill and Jim Vander Wall, *Agents of Repression: The FBI's Secret Wars against the Black Panther Party and the American Indian Movement* (Boston: South End Press, 1988); Jeffrey Haas, *The Assassination of Fred Hampton: How the FBI and Chicago Police Murdered a Black Panther* (New York: Lawrence Hill Books, 2010). Some Panthers remain in solitary confinement today, having been driven to insanity through prolonged isolation.

33. See Michael T. Klare, "Policing the Empire," *Commonweal,* September 18, 1970, 455–61.

34. See Martha K. Huggins, Mika Haritos-Fatouros, and Philip G. Zimbardo, *Violence Workers: Police Torturers and Murderers Reconstruct Brazilian Atrocities* (Berkeley: University of California Press, 2002), 68, 74; Huggins, *Political Policing.*

35. E. H. Adkins Jr., "Resources Control, National Police of Vietnam," PSD, USOM, March 1965, 23.

36. Arthur M. Thurston, "Survey of the Training Activities of the A.I.D. Police Assistance Program," November 1962, USAID, OPS, Papers of President Kennedy, NSF, box 338, folder NSAM 177, Police Assistance Programs; William J. Bopp, *O.W.: O.W. Wilson and the Search for a Police Profession* (Port Washington, N.Y.: Kennikat Press, 1977), 72, 136; Monthly Report, April 1966, RG 286, USAID, OPS, Technical Services Division, Colombia, box 4. Parker quoted in William W. Turner, *Invisible Witness: The Use and Abuse of the New Technology of Crime Investigation* (Indianapolis: Bobbs-Merrill, 1968), 196.

37. "Minutes of Meeting, OCB Working Group on NSC Action 1290-d," January 18, 1955, DDEL, White House Office Files, NSC Staff Papers, OCB, Central File, box 16, folder Internal Security; Eric Pace, "Douglas MacArthur II, 88, Former Ambassador to Japan," *New York Times,* November 17, 1997; Wolfgang Saxon, "Henry S. Villard, 95, Diplomat Who Wrote Books in Retirement," *New York Times,* January 25, 1996. After his retirement from the Foreign Service, Villard moved to Los Angeles and wrote books on birds and about his encounters with Ernest Hemingway during World War I in Italy, where he served as an ambulance driver. Possessing a purely colonialist view of Africa, he was the heir to a New York fortune (his father was a railroad tycoon) and editor of the *Harvard Crimson* in the early 1920s. MacArthur escaped a kidnapping attempt in Iran in 1972 by militants opposed to the Shah.

38. Albert R. Haney, "Observations and Suggestions Concerning OISP," January 30, 1957, OCB, DDEL, box 18, folder Internal Security. Haney's tenure in Korea is discussed in Tim Weiner, *Legacy of Ashes: The History of the CIA* (New York: Doubleday, 2007), 56, 57. He ran

covert teams into North Korea that were infiltrated by double agents, leading to the deaths of many.

39. See Noam Chomsky, *Rethinking Camelot: JFK, the Vietnam War, and U.S. Political Culture* (Boston: South End Press, 1993); Robert Dean, *Imperial Brotherhood: Gender and the Making of Cold War Foreign Policy* (Amherst: University of Massachusetts Press, 2001); Bruce Miroff, *Pragmatic Illusions: The Presidential Politics of John F. Kennedy* (New York: David McKay, 1976). For the Camelot view, see Arthur M. Schlesinger Jr., *A Thousand Days: John F. Kennedy in the White House* (Boston: Houghton Mifflin, 1965); Roger F. Hilsman, *To Move a Nation: The Politics of Foreign Policy in the Administration of John F. Kennedy* (New York: Doubleday, 1967); Theodore C. Sorenson, *Kennedy* (New York: Harper & Row, 1965).

40. Robert W. Komer, "Memo for Members of Study Groups on Deterrence of Guerrilla Warfare, Revised Draft Outline," March 8, 1961, JFKL, RWK, box 414, folder 1, Special Group. For the aggressiveness of Kennedy's inner circle, see also Michael McClintock, "The Kennedy Crusade," in *Instruments of Statecraft: U.S. Guerilla Warfare, Counterinsurgency, and Counterterrorism, 1940–1990* (New York: Pantheon Books, 1992), 161–79.

41. Chester Bowles, "Memo for the President on Counter-Subversion Training for Latin American Police Forces," September 30, 1961," JFKL, NSF, box 331; Charles Maechling Jr., "Proposed Plan of Operations for Interdepartmental Police Committee (NSAM 146)," April 27, 1962, JFKL, NSF, RWK, box 413, folder Counter-Insurgency: Police Program, 1961–1963. See also David Halberstam's landmark book *The Best and the Brightest*, rev. ed. (New York: Ballantine Books, 1993).

42. "Policy Research Study: Internal Warfare and the Security of the Underdeveloped States," Department of State, November 20, 1961, JFKL, POF, box 98; David G. Epstein, "The Police Role in Counterinsurgency Efforts," *Journal of Criminal Law, Criminology, and Police Science* 58 (March 1968): 148–51; Nancy Stein, "Policing the Empire," in *The Iron Fist and the Velvet Glove: An Analysis of the U.S. Police,* ed. Tony Platt, 2nd ed. (Berkeley: Center for Research on Criminal Justice, 1977), 42.

43. Don Bordenkircher, as told to Shirley Bordenkircher, *Tiger Cage: An Untold Story* (Cameron, W.Va.: Abby Publishing, 1998), 26; memorandum, Bernard G. Brannon, Chief of KCPD, to Sgt. G. E. Squires, "Captain Byron Engle: Age 42, on Leave," October 7, 1952, courtesy of the Kansas City Police Department Historical Branch; Lobe, "U.S. Police Assistance for the Third World," 57–58; William Rosenau, "The Kennedy Administration, U.S. Foreign Internal Security and the Challenge of Subterranean War, 1961–1963," *Small Wars and Insurgencies* 13 (Autumn 2003): 85.

44. Arthur M. Thurston, "Survey of the Training Activities of the A.I.D. Police Assistance Program," November 1962, JFKL, Papers of President Kennedy, NSF, box 338, folder NSAM 177, Police Assistance Programs; A. J. Langguth, *Hidden Terrors: The Truth about U.S. Police Operations in Latin America* (New York: Pantheon, 1978), 242; Jack Anderson, "CIA Teaches Terrorism to Friends," *Washington Post,* October 8, 1973; Michael T. Klare and Nancy Stein, "Police Terrorism in Latin America: Secret U.S. Bomb School Exposed," NACLA, January 1972, https://nacla.org; Michael McCann to Byron Engle, November 7, 1966, "Training of Foreign Police Personnel in Bomb Disposal," RG 286, USAID, OPS, IPS, box 8, folder 1.

45. Robert W. Komer to Walt Rostow, "Let's Not Forget the OISP," May 4, 1961, RWK, box 413, folder Counter-Insurgency Police Programs.

46. Robert W. Komer to McGeorge Bundy and Maxwell Taylor, "Cutbacks in Police Programs Overseas" May 5, 1962, RWK, box 413, folder Counter-Insurgency Police Programs. Also RWK to Carl Kaysen, June 22, 1962, ibid.

47. Charles Maechling Jr., "Camelot, Robert Kennedy, and Counter-Insurgency: A Memoir," *Virginia Quarterly Review* (Summer 1999): 438–58; Charles Maechling Jr., "Counterinsurgency: The First Ordeal by Fire," in *Low Intensity Warfare: Counterinsurgency, Proinsurgency, and Antiterrorism in the Eighties,* ed. Michael T. Klare and Peter Kornbluh (New York: Pantheon Books, 1988), 33. On Maechling's earlier role in support of the programs, see his "Proposed Plan of Operations for Interdepartmental Police Committee (NSAM 146)," April 27, 1962, RWK, box 413, folder Counter-Insurgency: Police Program, 1961–1963. Churchill quoted in Georgina Sinclair, *At the End of the Line: Colonial Policing and the Imperial Endgame, 1945–1980* (Manchester: Manchester University Press, 2006), 189.

48. See Nils Gilman, *Mandarins of the Future: Modernization Theory in Cold War America* (Baltimore: Johns Hopkins University Press, 2003); John J. Johnson, ed., *The Role of the Military in Underdeveloped Countries* (Princeton: Princeton University Press, 1962); Robert A. Packenham, *Liberal America and the Third World: Political Development Ideas in Foreign Aid and Social Science* (Princeton: Princeton University Press, 1973).

49. See Walt W. Rostow, "Guerrilla Warfare in Underdeveloped Areas," in *The Vietnam Reader,* ed. Marcus G. Raskin and Bernard B. Fall (New York: Vintage Books, 1967), 108–16.

50. Kennan quoted in Noam Chomsky, *Turning the Tide: The U.S. in Latin America* (Montreal: Black Rose, 1987), 57; and David Schmitz, *Thank God They're on Our Side: The United States and Right-Wing Dictatorships, 1921–1965* (Chapel Hill: University of North Carolina Press, 1999), 149. On Kennan's political outlook, see Walter L. Hixson, *George F. Kennan: Cold War Iconoclast* (New York: Columbia University Press, 1989).

51. Kennan quoted in James Peck, *Washington's China: The National Security World, the Cold War, and the Origins of Globalism* (Amherst: University of Massachusetts Press, 2006), 70; Takemae Eiji, *Inside GHQ: The Allied Occupation of Japan,* trans. Robert Ricketts and Sebastien Swann (New York: Continuum, 2002), 555; Kate Doyle, "Human Rights and the Dirty War," confidential airgram, U.S. embassy in Mexico City, March 24, 1976, NSA, document 6.

52. See Alfred W. McCoy, *A Question of Torture: CIA Interrogation, from the Cold War to the War on Terror* (New York: Metropolitan Books, 2006), 62; "CIA, KUBARK Counterintelligence Interrogation," July 1963, NSA, 87; Michael T. Klare, *War without End: American Planning for the Next Vietnams* (New York: Knopf, 1972), 382–83; William Blum, *Killing Hope: U.S. Military and CIA Interventions since World War II* (Monroe, Me.: Common Courage Press, 2004), 202; "Testimony of Master Sergeant Donald Duncan," in *Against the Crime of Silence: Proceedings of the Bertrand Russell International War Crimes Tribunal,* ed. John Duffet (New York: O'Hare Books, 1968), 461.

53. See Gabriel Kolko, *Confronting the Third World: United States Foreign Policy 1945–1980* (New York: Pantheon, 1988); William Appleman Williams, *The Tragedy of American Diplomacy* (Cleveland: World Publishing, 1959); Harry Magdoff, *The Age of Imperialism* (New York: Monthly Review Press, 1968). For analysis of the importance of secrecy and U.S. foreign policy, see Ola Tunander, "Democratic State versus Deep State: Approaching the Dual State of the West," in *Government of the Shadows: Parapolitics and Criminal Sovereignty,* ed. Eric Wilson (London: Pluto Press, 2009), and Peter Dale Scott, *The War Conspiracy: The Secret Road to the Second Indochina War* (Indianapolis: Bobbs-Merrill, 1972).

54. Charles Maechling Jr., "Camelot, Robert Kennedy, and Counter-Insurgency: A Memoir," *Virginia Quarterly Review* (Summer 1999): 438–58; Thomas Lobe, *United States National Security Police and Aid to the Thailand Police* (Denver: University of Denver Graduate School of International Studies, 1977), 106. European scholars studying the history of police training in colonial settings have found similarly poor relations. See, e.g., Marieke

Bloembergen, "Between Public Safety and Political Control: Modern Colonial Policing in Surabaya (1911–1919)" (unpublished paper in author's possession).

55. Huggins, *Political Policing*; Klare, *War without End*; Langguth, *Hidden Terrors*; Michael McClintock, *The American Connection: State Terrorism and Popular Resistance in Guatemala and El Salvador*, 2 vols. (London: Zed Books, 1985); McClintock, *Instruments of Statecraft*; Noam Chomsky and Edward S. Herman, *The Political Economy of Human Rights: The Washington Connection and Third World Fascism* (Boston: South End Press, 1979); Kolko, *Confronting the Third World*; McCoy, *A Question of Torture*; McCoy, *Policing America's Empire*.

56. For a synthesis of scholarly debates over empire, see Alfred W. McCoy and Francisco A. Sarano, eds., *Colonial Crucible: Empire and the Making of the Modern American State* (Madison: University of Wisconsin Press, 2009).

57. See Michael E. Latham, *Modernization as Ideology: American Social Science and "Nation-Building" in the Kennedy Era* (Chapel Hill: University of North Carolina Press, 2000); David Engerman et al., eds., *Staging Growth: Modernization, Development, and the Global Cold War* (Amherst: University of Massachusetts Press, 2003); David Ekbladh, *The Great American Mission: Modernization and the Construction of an American World Order* (Princeton: Princeton University Press, 2010). An example of imperial denial, Ekbladh's study is especially limited in ignoring political economy entirely (a shortcoming of much of this literature), failing to discuss the larger geostrategic context in which development programs were implemented, and failing to discuss the consequences of these programs, including the link to environmental degradation and displacement of peasants.

58. Michel Foucault, *Discipline and Punish: The Birth of the Prison*, trans. Alan Sheridan (New York: Vintage, 1977); Thomas G. Blomberg and Karol Lucken, *American Penology: A History of Control* (Hawthorne, N.Y.: Aldine de Gruyter, 2000); David J. Rothman, *The Discovery of the Asylum: Social Order and Disorder in the New Republic*, rev. ed. (Boston: Little, Brown, 1990), ix.

Part I: Taking Up the "White Man's Burden"

1. See Matthew Frye Jacobson, *Barbarian Virtues: The United States Encounters Foreign Peoples at Home and Abroad* (New York: Hill and Wang, 2000), 7; Walter LaFeber, *The New Empire: An Interpretation of American Expansion* (Ithaca: Cornell University Press, 1963).

2. Alfred W. McCoy, *Policing America's Empire: The United States, the Philippines, and the Rise of the Surveillance State* (Madison: University of Wisconsin Press, 2009).

1. The First Operation Phoenix

1. John R. White, *Bullets and Bolos: Fifteen Years in the Philippine Islands* (New York: Century Company, 1928), 74.

2. See Luzviminda Francisco, "The First Vietnam: The Philippines-American War, 1899–1902," in *The Philippines: End of an Illusion* (London: Association for Radical East Asian Studies [AREAS], 1973), 106–45; Paul A. Kramer, *The Blood of Government: Race, Empire, the United States, and the Philippines* (Chapel Hill: University of North Carolina Press, 2006), quotation 145.

3. William Cameron Forbes, *The Philippine Islands* (Boston: Houghton Mifflin, 1928), 188. On the distinctive imperial anticolonialism practiced by the United States, see William A. Williams, *The Tragedy of American Diplomacy*, rev. ed. (New York: Norton, 2009).

4. Richard W. Smith, "The Philippine Constabulary," *Military Review* 48 (May 1968): 73–80; M. Dean Havron et al., *Constabulary Capabilities for Low-Level Conflict* (McLean, Va.: Human Science Research, 1969), 1–2.

5. Roger Hilsman, "Internal War: The New Communist Tactic," in *The Guerrilla and How to Fight Him*, ed. Lieutenant Colonel T. N. Greene (New York: Praeger, 1965), 26, 27. For Hilsman's ideas on unconventional warfare, see his *American Guerrilla: My War behind Japanese Lines* (Washington, D.C.: Potomac Books, 2007).

6. Michael H. Hunt, *The American Ascendancy: How the United States Gained and Wielded Global Dominance* (Chapel Hill: University of North Carolina Press, 2007); R. W. Van Alstyne, *The Rising American Empire* (Cleveland: World Publishing, 1960); Thomas J. McCormick, *China Market: America's Quest for Informal Empire, 1893–1901* (Chicago: Quadrangle Books, 1967); Albert J. Beveridge, "In Support of an American Empire," *Congressional Record*, 56th Congress, 1st sess., 1899–1900 (Washington, D.C.: GPO, 1900), 704. See also his "The March of the Flag," in *The Meaning of the Times, and Other Speeches* (Indianapolis: Bobbs-Merrill, 1908), 47–57.

7. See Peter W. Stanley, *A Nation in the Making: The Philippines and the United States, 1899–1921* (Cambridge: Harvard University Press, 1974); and his "William Cameron Forbes: Proconsul in the Philippines," *Pacific Historical Review* 35 (May 1966): 285–301; Forbes, *The Philippine Islands*; Warwick Anderson, *Colonial Pathologies: American Tropical Medicine, Race, and Hygiene in the Philippines* (Durham: Duke University Press, 2006).

8. Glen Anthony May, *Social Engineering in the Philippines: The Aims, Execution, and Impact of American Colonial Policy, 1900–1913* (New York: Greenwood Press, 1980); H. W. Brands, *Bound to Empire: The United States and the Philippines* (New York: Oxford University Press, 1992), 61; Scott Nearing and Joseph Freeman, *Dollar Diplomacy: A Study in American Imperialism* (New York: Viking Press, 1925). By the 1920s, over 120 U.S. companies were operating in the Philippines.

9. William Cameron Forbes, Journal, vol. 1, 4, WCF; Joan Jensen, *Army Surveillance in America, 1775–1980* (New Haven: Yale University Press, 1991), 100; H. T. Allen, memo for General Wright, October 1, 1902, HTA.

10. U.S. Department of War, *Third Annual Report of the Philippines Commission*, pt. 1, 2 vols., BIA (Washington, D.C.: GPO, 1902), 1:3, 33; Lebbeus R. Wilfley, *The Peace Problem in the Philippines*, address delivered by the Honorable L. R. Wilfley, Attorney General, Philippines, before the YMCA, July 11, 1905 2 vols. (Manila: E. C. McCullough, 1905), 4; H. T. Allen, letter to William H. Taft, October 1, 1902, HTA.

11. Richard W. Smith, "Philippine Constabulary," *Military Review* (May 1968): 75; Alfred W. McCoy, *Policing America's Empire: The United States, the Philippines, and the Rise of the Surveillance State* (Madison: University of Wisconsin Press, 2009), 46.

12. U.S. Department of War, *Third Annual Report of the Philippines Commission*, 1:108, 114; McCoy, *Policing America's Empire*, 109.

13. Alfred W. McCoy, "Policing the Imperial Periphery: Philippine Pacification and the Rise of the U.S. National Security State," in *Colonial Crucible: Empire in the Making of the Modern American State*, ed. Alfred W. McCoy and Francisco A. Scarano (Madison: University of Wisconsin Press, 2009), 114.

14. McCoy, *Policing America's Empire*, 107.

15. U.S. Department of War, *Third Annual Report of the Philippines Commission*, 1:107.

16. Harold Hanne Elarth, *The Story of the Philippine Constabulary* (Los Angeles: Globe Print Co., 1949), 2; Charles B. Elliot, *The Philippines: To the End of the Military Regime, with a Prefatory Note by Elihu Root* (Indianapolis: Bobbs-Merrill, 1917), 177; Major Emmanuel Baja, *Philippine Police System and Its Problems* (Manila: Pobre's Press, 1933), 102–3.

17. Baja, *Philippine Police System and Its Problems,* 331; Anne L. Foster, "Models for Governing: Opium and Colonial Policies, 1898–1910," in *The American Colonial State in the Philippines: Global Perspectives,* ed. Julian Go and Anne L. Foster (Durham: Duke University Press, 2003); David F. Musto, *The American Disease: Origins of Narcotics Control,* 3rd ed. (New York: Oxford University Press, 1973), 28; McCoy, *Policing America's Empire,* 150–51, 246.

18. U.S. Department of War, *Reports of the Acting Director of Constabulary, Annual Reports, Report of the Philippines Commission,* June 30, 1908 (Washington, D.C.: GPO, 1909), 373.

19. See William E. Leuchtenburg, "Progressivism and Imperialism: The Progressive Movement and American Foreign Policy, 1898–1916," *Mississippi Valley Historical Review* 39 (December 1952): 483–504.

20. McCoy, *Policing America's Empire,* 320, 321, 337; Jensen, *Army Surveillance in America, 1775–1980,* 163–67. Herbert Yardley of the State Department commented of Van Deman: "His heavily lined face reminded me of Lincoln's. . . . He appeared old and terribly tired, but when he turned his deep eyes towards me I sensed his power" (McCoy, *Policing America's Empire,* 298).

21. Elarth, *The Story of the Philippine Constabulary,* 2; Thomas A. Reppetto, *The Blue Parade* (New York: Free Press, 1978), 129.

22. Vic Hurley, *Jungle Patrol: The Story of the Philippine Constabulary* (New York: Dutton, 1938), 30; McCoy, *Policing America's Empire,* 6, 222, 231. William Cameron Forbes acknowledged in his diary that junior army officers had been "arrogant" and "rude," as a consequence of their excessive authority, though he claimed that there was excellent machinery in place for making complaints. Forbes, Journal, vol. 1, January 1905.

23. Forbes, Journal, vol. 1, 49. Echoes of Forbes's remarks could be heard nearly a hundred years later in mainstream debates about U.S. troop withdrawals from Afghanistan and Iraq.

24. Hurley, *Jungle Patrol,* 89; *The Constabulary Story,* prepared by the Public Information Office, headquarters Philippine Constabulary (Manila: Bustamante Press, 1978), 97.

25. For a profile of Allen, see McCoy, *Policing America's Empire,* 86–91; quot. 89. On his earlier career, see Robert L. Bullard, *Fighting Generals: Illustrated Biographical Sketches of Seven Major Generals in World War I* (Ann Arbor: J. W. Edwards, 1944), 87–95.

26. Letter to General Hughes, September 12, 1901, HTA, box 7.

27. Henry Allen to William H. Taft, November 19, 1902, HTA, box 7.

28. Letter to Simeon Spina, Esquire, February 17, 1902, HTA, box 7.

29. See Robert Gellately and Ben Kiernan, eds., *The Specter of Genocide: Mass Murder in Historical Perspective* (New York: Cambridge University Press, 2003); Matthew Frye Jacobson, *Barbarian Virtues: The United States Encounters Foreign Peoples at Home and Abroad* (New York: Hill and Wang, 2000).

30. Henry T. Allen, "Report to the Secretary of Commerce and Police," August 31, 1902, Reports of the Chief of the Philippines Constabulary, Manila; Vince Boudreau, "Methods of Domination and Modes of Resistance: The U.S. Colonial State and Philippines Mobilization in Comparative Perspective," in Go and Foster, *The American Colonial State in the Philippines,* 256–91; Hurley, *Jungle Patrol,* 115.

31. Coats, "The Philippine Constabulary," 205; Elarth, *The Story of the Philippine Constabulary,* 109; Wilfley, *The Peace Problem in the Philippines,* 4; McCoy, *Policing America's Empire,* 130, 189–90. Aurelio Tolentino, an anticolonialist playwright and gifted orator, led an uprising alongside General Artemio Ricarte. Threatened with long-term incarceration, he began promoting American-Filipino cooperation and became a constabulary informant.

32. Allen, "Report to the Secretary of Commerce and Police"; Renato Constantino and Letizio R. Constantino, *A History of the Philippines: From the Spanish Colonization to the Second World War* (New York: Monthly Review Press, 1975), 261; Hurley, *Jungle Patrol,* 118.

33. Coats, "The Philippine Constabulary," 242; White, *Bullets and Bolos,* 152; Hurley, *Jungle Patrol,* 120; McCoy, *Policing America's Empire,* 147; Francisco, "The First Vietnam," 13–14. Eluding capture for over a decade, Salvador was assassinated after the constabulary penetrated his inner circle. Colonel Bandholtz, who oversaw the campaign, admitted that Salvador "treats the barrio people well and . . . prays with them and asks for contributions which they usually give" (Francisco, "The First Vietnam," 13–14).

34. Elarth, *The Story of the Philippines Constabulary,* 125; McCoy, *Policing America's Empire,* 221.

35. Jack C. Lane, *Armed Progressive: General Leonard Wood* (San Rafael: Presidio Press, 1978), 120; Andrew J. Bacevich Jr., "Disagreeable Work: Pacifying the Moros, 1903–1906," *Military Review* 62 (June 1982): 50–51; John G. Holme, *The Life of Leonard Wood* (New York: Doubleday, 1920), 136. In Cuba, Wood established a Rural Guard under the premise that "the Cubans should kill their own rats." See Louis A. Pérez Jr., "The Pursuit of Pacification: Banditry and the U.S. Occupation of Cuba, 1899–1902," *Journal of Latin American Studies,* 18, 2 (November 1986): 313–32.

36. Constantino and Constantino, *A History of the Philippines,* 245; Kramer, *The Blood of Government,* 293.

37. White, *Bullets and Bolos,* 106–7; Donald Smythe, *Guerrilla Warrior: The Early Life of John J. Pershing* (New York: Charles Scribner & Sons, 1973), 162.

38. Lane, *Armed Progressive,* 128.

39. William J. Pomeroy, *American Neo-colonialism: Its Emergence in the Philippines and Asia* (New York: International Publishers, 1970), 98; Peter G. Gowing, *Mandate in Moroland: The American Government of Muslim Filipinos, 1899–1920* (Quezon City: Philippines Center for Advanced Studies, 1977), 240. Gowing notes that strict censorship of the press was imposed by Pershing. Reporters who approached the scene were arrested.

40. White, *Bullets and Bolos,* 196, 202; Elarth, *The Story of the Philippines Constabulary,* 132; Holme, *The Life of Leonard Wood,* 137; Donald Smythe, "Pershing and the Disarmament of the Moro," *Pacific Historical Review* 31 (August 1962): 242. As the historian Martin Thomas points out, these characterizations were typical of colonial discourse; see his *Empires of Intelligence: Security Services and Colonial Disorder after 1914* (Berkeley: University of California Press, 2008).

41. Coats, "The Philippines Constabulary," 240; Hurley, *Jungle Patrol,* 99, 131.

42. White, *Bullets and Bolos,* 157; Hurley, *Jungle Patrol,* 73.

43. Hurley, *Jungle Patrol,* 31, 146.

44. U.S. Department of War, *Third Annual Report of the Philippines Commission,* 1:110.

45. Allen, letter to J. Franklin Bell, April 19, 1902; letter to Albert Beveridge, May 3, 1902, HTA, box 7.

46. White, *Bullets and Bolos,* 137.

47. See Kristin L. Hoganson, *Fighting for American Manhood: How Gender Politics Provoked the Spanish-American and Philippine-American Wars* (New Haven: Yale University Press, 1998); Susan Jeffords, *The Remasculinization of America: Gender and the Vietnam War* (Bloomington: Indiana University Press, 1989).

48. Bullard, *Fighting Generals,* 91. On Pershing's career, see Smythe, *Guerrilla Warrior.*

49. See McCoy, *Policing America's Empire.* On Shanton, see "Col. George R. Shanton," April 19, 1919, RDS, Related to the Internal Affairs of the Dominican Republic, 1910–1929,

M626-839.01, roll 35; Julie Greene, *Canal Builders: Making America's Empire in the Panama Canal* (New York: Penguin Books, 2009), 85, 87, 88.

50. Baja, *Philippines Police Systems and Its Problems,* 128; Kramer, *The Blood of Government,* 292; Forbes, *The Philippine Islands,* 493; Gowing, *Mandate in Moroland,* 171.

51. Forbes, Journal, vol. 1, January 31, 1905, WCF. See also Stanley, *A Nation in the Making,* 122.

52. Michael Salman, "'Nothing Without Labor' Penology, Discipline, and Independence in the Philippines under United States Rule," in *Discrepant Histories: Translocal Essays on Filipino Cultures,* ed. Vicente L. Rafael (Philadelphia: Temple University Press, 1995), 113–14.

53. See, e.g., Peter Zinoman, *The Colonial Bastille: A History of Imprisonment in Vietnam, 1862–1940* (Berkeley: University of California Press, 2001), 37; Ann Laura Stoler, "In Cold Blood: Hierarchies of Credibility and the Politics of Colonial Narratives," *Representations* 37 (Winter 1992): 178.

54. U.S. Department of War, *Third Annual Report of the Philippines Commission,* 1:110.

55. Constantino and Constantino, *A History of the Philippine,* 246; Forbes, *The Philippine Islands,* 489; U.S. Department of War, Annual Reports, Fiscal Year Ending 1908, "Report to the Philippine Commission to the Secretary of War, 1908," pt. 1 (Washington, D.C.: GPO, 1909), 54; U.S. Department of Justice, Ramon Victorio, "Prison System in the Philippine Islands," speech before the American Prison Congress, Salt Lake City, August 15, 1921, in Government of the Philippine Islands, Department of Justice, *Catalogue of Products of the Industrial Division of Bilibid Prison* (Manila: Bureau of Printing, 1924), 3–5.

56. Salman, "Nothing Without Labor," 117–18; Kramer, *The Blood of Government,* 317; Francisco, "The First Vietnam," 16.

57. Victorio, "Prison System in the Philippine Islands," 3–5; Forbes, *The Philippine Islands,* 490; John Lewis Gillin, *Taming the Criminal: Adventures in Penology* (New York: Macmillan, 1931), 44; Victor G. Heiser, *Annual Report of the Bureau of Health for the Philippine Islands, 1906* (Manila: Bureau of Printing, 1906).

58. See Rodney J. Sullivan, *Exemplar of Americanism: The Philippines Career of Dean C. Worcester* (Ann Arbor: University of Michigan Center for Southeast Asian Studies, 1991), 112.

59. "Annual Report of the Director of Prisons for 1928," WCF, Annual Reports; Nathaniel Lee Smith, "Cured of the Habit by Force: The U.S. and the Global Campaign to Punish Drug Consumers, 1898–1970" (Ph.D. diss., University of North Carolina, 2007), 50–51.

60. "Annual Report of the Director of Prisons for 1928"; Forbes, *The Philippine Islands,* 495, 497; Manuel A. Alzate, *Convict Labor in the Philippine Islands: Presented at the Ninth International Prison Congress Held in London, August 1925* (Manila: Bureau of Printing, 1926), 57; U.S. Department of Justice, Government of the Philippine Islands, Bureau of Prisons, *General Information Relative to the Bureau of Prisons* (Manila: Bureau of Printing, 1924), 46.

61. *Going to Jail in Manila,* directed by Burton Holmes (Paramount, 1921), cited in Emily S. Rosenberg, *Financial Missionaries to the World: The Politics and Culture of Dollar Diplomacy, 1900–1930* (Cambridge: Harvard University Press, 1999), 203.

62. Gillin, *Taming the Criminal,* 45.

63. Ibid., 52.

64. Erving Goffman, *Asylums: Essays on the Social Situation of Mental Patients and Other Inmates* (Chicago: Aldine, 1962). See also David J. Rothman, *Conscience and Convenience: The Asylum and Its Alternatives in Progressive America* (Boston: Little, Brown, 1980).

65. Forbes, *The Philippine Islands,* 492; U.S. Department of War, *Report of the Special Mission on Investigations to the Philippine Islands, to the Secretary of War* (Washington, D.C.: GPO, 1921); Alzate, *Convict Labor in the Philippine Islands,* 43.

66. William Cameron Forbes, *Reports of Inspection of the Provincial Jails*, March 29, 1928, WCF.

67. Ibid., December 2, 1927.

68. On the pitfalls of the Filipinization program, see Kramer, *The Blood of Government*, 216.

69. William Cameron Forbes, *1928 Report, San Ramon Prison*, WCF, Annual Reports.

70. William R. George, *The Junior Republic: Its History and Ideals* (New York: Appleton, 1910); Rebecca McLennan, *The Crisis of Imprisonment: Protest, Politics, and the Making of the American Penal State, 1776–1941* (New York: Cambridge University Press, 2008), 331.

71. White, *Bullets and Bolos*, 316. Returning the praise, Forbes referred to White in his memoirs as a man of "sterling character, great vision, splendid enthusiasm, and boundless energy. [He] infused a life and spirit into the colony which up until that time had been lacking." Forbes, *The Philippine Islands*, 505.

72. White, *Bullets and Bolos*, 317.

73. Forbes, *The Philippine Islands*, 509.

74. *Manila Times*, June 12, 1909; see also Lyman Beecher Stowe, "A Prison That Makes Men Free," *The World's Work* 27 (April 1914): 626–28; Jesus C. Legazpi, *The Iwahig Penal Colony: A Study* (University of Manila, 1953), 16, 27.

75. Gillin, *Taming the Criminal*.

76. Michael Salman, "'The Prison That Makes Men Free': The Iwahig Penal Colony and the Simulacra of the American State in the Philippines," in McCoy and Scarano, *Colonial Crucible*, 116–26.

77. Legazpi, *The Iwahig Penal Colony*, 27; William Cameron Forbes, *Reports of Inspection of the Iwahig Prison, 1928*, WCF, Annual Reports.

78. Salman, "Nothing Without Labor," 120.

79. Chalmers Johnson, *Nemesis: The Last Days of the American Republic* (New York: Metropolitan Books, 2006), 75, 76; Eric Foner, "The Lie That Empire Tells Itself," *London Review of Books* May 19, 2005, 16.

80. McCoy, *Policing America's Empire*, 61; Stephen R. Shalom, *The United States and the Philippines: A Study in Neocolonialism* (Philadelphia: Institute for the Study of Human Issues, 1981).

2. "Popping Off" Sandinistas and Cacos

1. Smedley D. Butler *Old Gimlet Eye: The Adventures of Smedley D. Butler.* as told to Lowell Thomas (New York: Farrar & Rinehart, 1933), 210; James H. McCrocklin, *Garde d'Haiti, 1915–1934: Twenty Years of Organization and Training by the U.S. Marine Corps* (Annapolis: Naval Institute Press, 1956), 67.

2. Hans Schmidt, *Maverick Marine: General Smedley D. Butler and the Contradictions of American Military History* (Lexington: University Press of Kentucky, 1987), 231, 237; Smedley D. Butler, *War Is a Racket: The Antiwar Classic by America's Most Decorated Soldier* (New York: Feral, 2003).

3. Root quoted in Martha Huggins, *Political Policing: The United States and Latin America* (Durham: Duke University Press, 1998), 25; Walter LaFeber, *Inevitable Revolutions: The United States in Central America* (New York: Norton, 1984); Scott Nearing and Joseph Freeman, *Dollar Diplomacy: A Study in American Imperialism* (New York: Viking Press, 1925); Louis A. Pérez Jr., "Intervention, Hegemony, and Dependency: The United States in the Circum-Caribbean, 1898–1980," *Pacific Historical Review* 51, 2 (May 1982): 168.

4. Richard Millett, *Guardians of the Dynasty: A History of the U.S. Created Guardia Nacional de Nicaragua and the Somoza Family* (New York: Orbis Books, 1977), 41.

5. Hans Schmidt, *The United States Occupation of Haiti, 1915–1934* (New Brunswick: Rutgers University Press, 1971), 71, 210; Butler, *Old Gimlet Eye*, 211; Ernest H. Gruening, "The Conquest of Haiti and Santo Domingo," in *New York Times Current History: A Monthly Magazine* 15 (October–March 1922): 885–96. As a leader, Bobo bore a strong resemblance to the populist priest Jean-Bertrand Aristide, a victim of CIA subversion campaigns in the 1990s and 2000s.

6. Franklin D. Roosevelt, Acting Secretary of the Navy, to Secretary of State, December 14, 1915, and Alexander S. Williams to Secretary of State, "Weekly Report," May 7, 1918, both RDS, Related to Internal Affairs of Haiti, 1910–1929, 838.105 (hereafter RDS, Haiti); Glen Fowler, "Lemuel Shepherd Jr., Ex-Chief of Marines Who Served in Three Wars," *New York Times*, August 8, 1990.

7. Colonel Orval Townshend to Walter O'Bowell, August 15, 1925, RG 165, War Department, General and Special Staffs, M1488 (hereafter RG 165, M1488). On the New Jersey and Pennsylvania constabularies, see Thomas A. Reppetto, *The Blue Parade* (New York: Free Press, 1978), 130–31; David R. Johnson, *American Law Enforcement: A History* (St. Louis: Forum Press, 1981), 158–61.

8. Fred Baldwin, "Smedley Butler and Prohibition Enforcement in Philadelphia, 1924–1925," *Pennsylvania Magazine of History and Biography* 84 (July 1960): 352–68; Schmidt, *Maverick Marine*, 149.

9. Mary A. Renda, *Taking Haiti: Military Occupation and the Culture of U.S. Imperialism, 1915–1940* (Chapel Hill: University of North Carolina Press, 2001), 147; Schmidt, *The United States Occupation of Haiti*, 90, 91; Samuel G. Inman, *Through Santo Domingo and Haiti: A Cruise with the Marines* (New York: Committee on Cooperation in Latin America, 1919), 68, 69.

10. Faustin Wirkus and Taney Dudley, *The White King of La Gonave* (Garden City, N.Y.: Garden City Publishers, 1931), 68; "Marine King," *Time*, January 26, 1931, 15; William Seabrook, *The Magic Island* (New York: Harcourt Brace, 1929), 171–84.

11. U.S. Congress, Senate, *Inquiry into Occupation and Administration of Haiti and Santo Domingo*, 77th Cong., 1st and 2nd sess., vol. 1 (Washington, D.C.: GPO, 1922), 163–69; *Occupied Haiti: Being the Report of a Committee of Six Disinterested Americans Representing Organizations Exclusively American, Who, Having Personally Studied Conditions in Haiti in 1926, Favor the Restoration of the Independence of the Negro Republic*, ed. Emily Greene Balch (New York: Writers Publishing, 1927).

12. Alexander S. Williams to Secretary of State, "Weekly Report," July 22, 1918, RDS, Haiti; Renda, *Taking Haiti*, 150, 162.

13. Schmidt, *Maverick Marine*, 163; "Czar of Tenderloin Left Only $14 Estate," *New York Times*, January 30, 1918; Marilynn S. Johnson, *Street Justice: A History of Police Violence in New York City* (Boston: Beacon Press, 2003), 41, 43. According to a naval investigation, Williams instructed at least one Gendarmerie officer to avoid taking prisoners and, if "any of the prisoners were Cacos and had arms in their possession, to do away with them." Renda, *Taking Haiti*, 340.

14. "Report of Activities," July 1, 1920–June 30, 1921, RDS, Haiti.

15. "Haiti: Summary of Intelligence," February 1921, May 26, 1926, "Bolshevik Activities in Haiti," RG 165, War Department, M1507.

16. John H. Craige, *Cannibal Cousins* (New York: Minton, Balch, 1934), 58–59; Grace D. Watson and Emily Greene Balch, "The Press and the Prisons," in Balch, *Occupied Haiti*, 144–45.

17. Alexander S. Williams to Secretary of State, "Weekly Report," January 28, 1919, RDS, Haiti.

18. Frederic M. Wise, *A Marine Tells It to You,* as told to Meigs O. Frost (New York: J. H. Sears, 1929), 309.

19. "Report of the President's Commission for the Study and Review of Conditions in the Republic of Haiti," March 26, 1930 (Washington, D.C.: GPO, 1930), 4; John H. Craige, *Black Baghdad* (New York: Minton, Balch, 1933), 161; Balch, *Occupied Haiti,* 134; Renda, *Taking Haiti;* Harry A. Franck, *Roaming through the West Indies* (New York: Blue Ribbon Books, 1920), 149; Allan R. Millett, *Semper Fidelis: The History of the United States Marine Corps* (New York: Free Press, 1980), 199.

20. Alexander S. Williams to Secretary of State, "Weekly Report," May 28, 1918, RDS, Haiti; Craige, *Black Baghdad,* 132, 133; Irwin R. Franklyn, *Knights of the Cockpit: A Romantic Epic of the Flying Marines in Haiti* (New York: Dial Press, 1931), 66, 67.

21. "Report of Activities," July 1, 1920–June 30, 1921, RDS, Haiti. One Gendarmerie officer named Williston stacked all the hats of those he'd killed on a pole as a visible body count.

22. Alexander S. Williams to Secretary of State, "Weekly Report," November 6, 1918, RDS, Haiti. Peralte was a French-trained lawyer characterized by one marine as "handsome, brave and intelligent" and by another as having a "gift for flamboyant proclamations and the more inflaming brands of oratory." See Max Boot, *The Savage Wars of Peace: Small Wars and the Rise of American Power* (New York: Basic Books, 2003), 175.

23. Lester Langley, *The Banana Wars: United States Intervention in the Caribbean, 1898– 1934* (Wilmington, Del.: Scholarly Resources, 2002), 155–56; R. H. Greathouse, "King of the Banana Wars," *Marine Corps Gazette* 44 (June 1960): 29–33; Craige, *Cannibal Cousins,* 93. Craige referred to Hanneken as a "magnificent soldier." He was assisted by another Medal of Honor winner, Lieutenant William R. Button, who spoke Creole fluently and adopted camouflage techniques.

24. Commanding Officer to Brigade Commander, July 15, 1921, RDS, Haiti; McCrocklin, *Garde d'Haiti,* 115; Craige, *Cannibal Cousins,* 72, 92. Craige records these comments from captured supporters of Batraville who were allegedly with him prior to Murth's death.

25. "Haiti: Summary of Intelligence," March, April, May, July, October 1921, RG 165, War Department, M1507.

26. "Report of Activities," July 1, 1920–June 30, 1921, RDS, Haiti; Franklyn, *Knights of the Cockpit,* 227, 228. On the terrible history of air power in the twentieth century, see Michael Sherry, *The Rise of American Air Power: The Creation of Armageddon* (New Haven: Yale University Press, 1995); Beau Grosscup, *Strategic Terror: The Politics and Ethics of Aerial Bombardment* (London: Zed Press, 2006).

27. American Legation to the President, September 11, 1919, RDS, Haiti; Carl Kelsey, "The American Intervention in Haiti and the Dominican Republic," *Annals of the American Academy of Political and Social Science* 100, no. 1 (March 1922): 137; McCrocklin, *Garde d'Haiti,* 100.

28. Grace D. Watson and Emily Greene Balch, "Judiciary and Civil Liberties," in Balch, *Occupied Haiti,* 138; Robert Heinl Jr. and Nancy Heinl, *Written in Blood: The Story of the Haitian People, 1492-1995,* rev. ed. (New York: University Press of America, 1996), 484.

29. Alexander S. Williams to Secretary of State, "Weekly Report," September 3 and 19, 1918, RDS, Haiti.

30. Ibid., September 19, 1918; Helena Hill Weed, "Hearing the Truth about Haiti," *The Nation,* November 9, 1921, 533–35.

31. U.S. Congress, *Inquiry into Occupation and Administration of Haiti and Santo Domingo,* 1:517, 556; Lars Schoultz, *Beneath the United States: A History of U.S. Policy toward Latin America* (Cambridge: Harvard University Press, 1998), 256–57.

32. Schmidt, *The United States Occupation of Haiti*, 80, 147. Butler was apparently fond of his "ape man" black servant Antoine, who was a "faithful slave" to the Butler children (ibid., 147).Those who sought equality and power, however, were viewed differently.

33. U.S. Congress, *Inquiry into Occupation and Administration of Haiti and Santo Domingo*, 1:516–18; Gendarmerie, Expeditionary Commander, to Major General Commandant, February 12, 1916, RDS, Haiti; Balch, *Occupied Haiti*, 125; Kelsey, "The American Intervention in Haiti and the Dominican Republic," 137. Supporting U.S. efforts to "Christianize" the "backward" Haitians, Evans argued that the atrocities committed by U.S. forces and their proxies belied the missionary spirit of the church and warranted the removal of the Americans.

34. Balch, *Occupied Haiti*, 131; Schmidt, *The United States Occupation of Haiti, 1916–1934*; Michel-Rolph Trouillot, *Haiti, State against Nation: The Origins and Legacy of Duvalierism* (New York: Monthly Review Press, 1990), 106–7.

35. Michael S. Laguerre, *The Military and Society in Haiti* (Knoxville: University of Tennessee Press, 1993), 77–78; Robert Fatton Jr., *The Roots of Haitian Despotism* (New York: Lynne Rienner, 2007), 175.

36. American Ambassador, Port-au-Prince, to Department of State, May 15, 1959, RG 286, USAID, OPS, Latin America Branch (hereafter RG 286, LAB), Haiti, box 77. See also Bernard Diederich and Al Burt, *Papa Doc and the Tonton Macoutes*, foreword by Graham Greene, 2nd ed. (Princeton: Marcus Wiener, 2005).

37. John Gerassi, *The Great Fear in Latin America* (New York: David McKay, 1965), 194.

38. "Marine Unit Going to Haiti," *Washington Post Times Herald*, March 1959; Heinl and Heinl, *Written in Blood*, 618; Charles T. Williamson, *The U.S. Naval Mission to Haiti, 1959–1963* (Annapolis, Md.: U.S. Naval Institute Press, 1999), 12, 19; Herbert Hardin, OPS, to Secretary of State, Haiti, May 15, 1963, RG 286, LAB, Haiti, box 77.

39. American embassy, Port-au-Prince, to Secretary of State, "Revolvers for the Haitian Police," October 1970, RG 286, LAB, Haiti, box 77.

40. Bruce J. Calder, *The Impact of Intervention: The Dominican Republic during the U.S. Occupation of 1916–1924* (Austin: University of Texas Press, 1984), 115, 116; Rayford Logan, *Haiti and the Dominican Republic* (New York: Oxford University Press, 1968), 61; Alvey Adee to Secretary of State (Charles Hughes), October 13, 1922, RDS, Records Related to the Internal Affairs of the Dominican Republic, 1910–1929, M626-839.01, roll 35 (hereafter RDS, DR). For policy background, see David Healy, *Drive to Hegemony: The United States in the Caribbean, 1898–1917* (Madison: University of Wisconsin Press, 1988); Melvin M. Knight, *The Americans in Santo Domingo* (New York: Vanguard Press, 1928).

41. William W. Russell, "Guardia, Santa Domingo," April 19, 1921, and "Effectiveness of Guardia Nacional Dominicana," April 24, 1923, RDS, DR; Alvey Adee to Secretary of State, October 13, 1922.

42. Calder, *The Impact of Intervention*, 56, 58; Knight, *The Americans in Santo Domingo*, 118; G. Pope Atkins and Larman C. Wilson, *The United States and the Trujillo Regime* (New Brunswick: Rutgers University Press, 1972), 32; Millett, *Semper Fidelis*, 197. One of Shanton's successors, Colonel Presley M. Rixey, had been physician to Theodore Roosevelt.

43. Calder, *The Impact of Intervention*, 61; William W. Russell to Secretary of State, December 10, 1924, RDS, DR.

44. Franklin Frost to Secretary of State, July 12, 1927, RDS, DR; Langley, *The Banana Wars*, 152–54; Sumner Welles, *Naboth's Vineyard: The Dominican Republic, 1844–1924*, vol. 2 (New York: Payson & Clarke, 1928), 805–10.

45. See Eric Paul Roorda, *The Dictator Next Door: The Good Neighbor Policy and the Trujillo Regime in the Dominican Republic, 1930–1945* (Durham: Duke University Press, 1998); Jesús de Galindez, *The Era of Trujillo: Dominican Dictator* (New York: Columbia University

Press, 1958). On the Haitian massacre, see Eric Paul Roorda, "Genocide Next Door: The Good Neighbor Policy, the Trujillo Regime, and the Haitian Massacre of 1937," *Diplomatic History* 20, no. 3 (June 2007): 301–19.

46. See Thomas W. Walker, *Nicaragua: The Land of Sandino* (Boulder: Westview Press, 1986); Juan José Arevalo, *The Shark and the Sardines* (New York: L. Stuart, 1961), 25; Schmidt, *Maverick Marine*, 54. According to *The Nation*, Nicaraguan mothers were still warning their children a decade later, "Hush, Major Butler will get you," if they did not go to sleep. Butler wrote to his wife, "It is terrible we should be losing so many men fighting all because Brown brothers [the bankers] may have some money down there." Schmidt, *Maverick Marine*, 54.

47. Franklin Gunther to Secretary of State, January 10, 1912, RDS, Records Related to the Internal Affairs of Nicaragua, 1910–1929, 817.05 (hereafter RDS, Nicaragua).

48. Harold Norman Denny, *Dollars for Bullets: The Story of American Rule in Nicaragua* (New York: Dial Press, 1929). Butler described marine-sponsored elections in Nicaragua as follows: "The opposition candidates were declared bandits when it became necessary to elect our man to office. Our candidates always win. In one election, nobody liked the fellow; . . . the district was canvassed and 400 were found who would vote for the proper candidate. Notice of the opening of the polls was given five minutes beforehand, the 400 voters were assembled in a line and when they had voted, in about two hours, the polls were closed." In Schmidt, *The United States Occupation of Haiti, 1915–1934*, 99.

49. Ralph S. Keyser, "Plan for the Establishment of a Constabulary in Nicaragua," December 13, 1924, RDS, Nicaragua; David Schmitz, *Henry L. Stimson: The First Wise Man* (Wilmington, Del.: Scholarly Resources, 2001), 58.

50. Ralph S. Keyser, "Constabularies for Central America," *Marine Corps Gazette* 11 (June 1926): 88. See also Emily S. Rosenberg, *Financial Missionaries to the World: The Politics and Culture of Dollar Diplomacy, 1900–1930* (Cambridge: Harvard University Press, 1999).

51. Ralph S. Keyser, "Plan for the Establishment of a Constabulary in Nicaragua," RDS, Nicaragua.

52. Calvin B. Carter to the Honorable Charles Eberhardt, "Guardia Nacional," October 1, 1925; and Arthur Harris, "Discipline in Guardia," G-2 Intelligence Report, August 24, 1934, RG 165, M1488; Michel Gobat, *Confronting the American Dream: Nicaragua under U.S. Imperial Rule* (Durham: Duke University Press, 2005), 218–19.

53. "Nicaragua: Loyalty and Discipline," G-2 Report, June 8, 1933, and Alex A. Cohen, "Activity in Guardia Nacional," G-2 Intelligence Report, June 2, 1934, RG 165, M1488; Richard Grossman, "The Blood of the People," in *When States Kill: Latin America, the U.S., and Technologies of Terror*, ed. Cecilia Menjívar and Néstor Rodríguez (Austin: University of Texas Press, 2005), 65; Neill Macaulay, *The Sandino Affair* (Chicago: Quadrangle Books, 1967), 178.

54. Evans F. Carlson, "The Guardia Nacional de Nicaragua," *Marine Corps Gazette* 21 (August 1937): 15; Alex A. Cohen, "Friction between Guardia and Civilians," G-2 Intelligence Report, February 14, 1934, RG 165, M1488; Gobat, *Confronting the American Dream*; M. Dean Havron et al., *Constabulary Capabilities for Low-Level Conflict* (McLean, Va.: Human Science Research, 1969), 67.

55. Gobat, *Confronting the American Dream*, 217; Langley, *The Banana Wars*, 211.

56. Fred T. Cruse, "Honduras: Political," May 15, 1929, RG 165, M1488. Turcios, a noted poet and journalist, was Sandino's representative in Tegucigulpa and helped gain recruits by disseminating Sandino's writings and communiqués.

57. On Sandino's worldview and guerrilla operations, see Robert Edgar Conrad, ed., *Sandino: The Testimony of a Nicaraguan Patriot, 1921–1934* (Princeton: Princeton University

Press, 1990); Michael J. Schroeder, "The Sandino Rebellion Revisited: Civil War, Imperialism, Popular Nationalism, and State Formation Muddled Up Together in the Segovias of Nicaragua, 1926–1934," in *Close Encounters of Empire: Writing the Cultural History of U.S.–Latin American Relations,* ed. Gilbert Joseph et al. (Durham: Duke University Press, 1998), 222.

58. Conrad, *Sandino,* 16; Van Gosse, *Where the Boys Are: Cuba, Cold War America and the Making of the New Left* (London: Verso, 1993), 17; Carleton Beals, "With Sandino in Nicaragua," *The Nation,* February 22 and 29, 1928, 204–5; 232–33.

59. Schmitz, *Henry L. Stimson,* 57.

60. LaFeber, *Inevitable Revolutions,* 26; Greg Grandin, *Empire's Workshop: Latin America, the United States, and the Rise of the New Imperialism* (New York: Metropolitan Books, 2006), 22.

61. Carlson, "The Guardia Nacional de Nicaragua," 18; Langley, *The Banana Wars,* 212; George B. Clark, *With the Old Corps in Nicaragua* (San Francisco: Presidio Press, 2001), 105; Harold Denny, "Marines Push Drive in Nicaragua Wilds," *New York Times,* June 21, 1928.

62. Smith quoted in Burke Davis, *Marine! The Life of Lieutenant General Lewis (Chesty) Puller* (Boston: Little, Brown, 1962), 65.

63. Ibid., 3, 376; Lewis B. Puller Jr., *Fortunate Son* (New York: Grove Press, 1991), 20; Jon Hoffman, *Chesty: The Story of Lieutenant General Lewis B. Puller* (New York: Random House, 2003).

64. Carlson, "The Guardia Nacional de Nicaragua," 10, 15; Gregorio Selser, *Sandino* (New York: Monthly Review Press, 1981), 82; Grossman, "The Blood of the People," 70–71; Macaulay, *The Sandino Affair,* 116.

65. Major Julian C. Smith, USMC, et al., *A Review of the Organization and Operations of the Guardia Nacional de Nicaragua* (Quantico: Marine Corps, 1937), 25; McCauley, *The Sandino Affair,* 100.

66. Millett, *Guardians of the Dynasty,* 156.

67. Schmitz, *Henry L. Stimson,* 60; Tim Merrill, ed., *Nicaragua: A Country Study* (Washington, D.C.: GPO, 1993); Alex A. Cohen, Military Attaché, "Who's Who: General Anastasio Somoza, Commander of the Guardia Nacional," G-2 Intelligence Report, February 13, 1934, RG 165, M1488. The G-2 report noted that he "possessed a pleasing personality and likes to ingratiate himself with Americans."

68. J. Edgar Hoover, G-2 Assistant Chief of Staff, to Adolf A. Berle Jr., Assistant Secretary of State, June 17, 1941, RG 165, M1488; Alex Cohen, "5 Privates Shot for Treason," G-2 Intelligence Report, June 6, 1936, RG 165, M1488; Millett, *Guardians of the Dynasty,* 184; Michael D. Gambone, *Eisenhower, Somoza, and the Cold War in Nicaragua, 1953–1961* (Westport, Conn.: Praeger, 1997), 110.

69. Suzanne Jonas, "Nicaragua," full issue of NACLA (North American Congress on Latin America), *North American and Empire Report* (February 1976): 24; Jack Anderson and Les Whitten, "Somoza: Caricature of a Dictator," *Washington Post,* September 29, 1977; Grossman, "The Blood of the People," 65. For the larger pattern of U.S. support for right-wing dictatorship, see David F. Schmitz, *Thank God They're on Our Side: The United States and Right-Wing Dictatorships, 1921–1965* (Chapel Hill: University of North Carolina Press, 1999).

70. Luis Napoli to Herbert Hardin, September 12, 1958, RG 286, LAB, Nicaragua, box 90, folder 1; "Nicaragua: The Champ Is Dead," *Time,* October 8, 1956, 43.

71. David M. Anderson and David Killingray, eds., *Policing the Empire: Government, Authority and Control, 1830–1940* (Manchester: Manchester University Press, 1991); David M. Anderson and David Killingray, eds., *Policing and Decolonisation: Nationalism, Politics*

and the Police, 1917–1965 (Manchester: Manchester University Press, 1991). See also Martin Thomas, *Empires of Intelligence: Security Services and Colonial Disorder after 1914* (Berkeley: University of California Press, 2008); Georgina Sinclair, *At the End of the Line: Colonial Policing and the Imperial Endgame, 1945–1980* (London: Ashgate, 2006); David Killingray "Securing the British Empire: Policing and Colonial Order, 1920–1960," in *The Policing of Politics in the Twentieth Century: Historical Perspectives,* ed. Mark Mazower (Providence: Berghahn Books, 1997), 167–91.

72. Marvin Goldwert, *The Constabulary in the Dominican Republic and Nicaragua: Progeny and Legacy of United States Intervention* (Gainesville: University of Florida Press, 1962), 62.

73. Managua to Secretary of State, October 20, 1962, RG 286, LAB, Nicaragua, box 90, folder 1.

74. Herbert O. Hardin to the Files, "Visit to Embassy, USOM Managua," September 12, 1958, RG 286, LAB, Nicaragua, box 90, folder 1.

Part II: Under the Facade of Benevolence

1. See Tom Engelhardt, *The End of Victory Culture: Cold War America and the Disillusioning of a Generation,* rev. ed. (Amherst: University of Massachusetts Press, 2007); Noam Chomsky, *For Reasons of State* (New York: Pantheon, 1973); Gabriel Kolko, *The Politics of War: The World and U.S. Foreign Policy, 1943–1945* (New York: Random House, 1968).

2. This point is not always well recognized by mainstream historians writing in the United States today, whose viewpoint continues to be warped by the stultifying ideologies of American exceptionalism and the Cold War. While at times overly romanticizing them, New Left scholars were better able to empathize with the social origins and appeal of the communist revolutionary movements, largely because they were able to transcend the ideological dogma of the times. For an outstanding analysis, see Mark Selden, *China in Revolution: The Yenan Way Revisited* (Armonk, N.Y.: M. E. Sharpe, 1995).

3. Quoted in Laurence H. Shoup and William Minter, *Imperial Brain Trust: The Council on Foreign Relations and United States Foreign Policy* (New York: Authors Choice Press, 1977), 228; MacArthur quoted in John Dower, "The U.S.-Japan Military Relationship," in *Postwar Japan, 1945 to the Present,* ed. Jon Livingstone, Joe Moore, and Felicia Oldfather (New York: Pantheon, 1973), 236. On the long-standing U.S. drive for hegemony in the Asia-Pacific, see Bruce Cumings, *Dominion from Sea to Sea: Pacific Ascendancy and American Power* (New Haven: Yale University Press, 2009); Richard Drinnon, *Facing West: The Metaphysics of Indian-Hating and Empire-Building* (Norman: University of Oklahoma Press, 1980). For strategic planning after World War II, see also Chomsky, *For Reasons of State.*

4. See Frederic Wakeman Jr., *Spymaster: Dai Li and the Chinese Secret Service* (Berkeley: University of California Press, 2003), 192–205, 305; Michael Schaller, *The U.S. Crusade in China, 1938–1945* (New York: Columbia University Press, 1979), 247; Milton E. Miles, *A Different Kind of War: The Little-Known Story of the Combined Guerrilla Forces Created in China by the U.S. Navy and the Chinese during World War II* (Garden City, N.Y.: Doubleday, 1967), 434, 474–75. On connections with the Green Gang and the opium trade, see Jonathan Marshall, "Opium and the Politics of Gangsterism in Nationalist China," *Bulletin of Concerned Asian Scholars* 8 (August 1976): 19–48; Edward R. Slack Jr., *Opium, State, and Society: China's Narco-Economy and the Guomindang, 1924–1937* (Honolulu: University of Hawai'i Press, 2001); William O. Walker III, *Opium and Foreign Policy: The Anglo-American Search for Order in Asia, 1912–1954* (Chapel Hill: University of North Carolina Press, 1991), 151.

5. William L. Neumann, *America Encounters Japan: From Perry to MacArthur* (Baltimore: Johns Hopkins University Press, 1969), 2. On the hysterical response to the Chinese revolution among U.S. policy elites, see James Peck, *Washington's China: The National Security World, the Cold War, and the Origins of Globalism* (Amherst: University of Massachusetts Press, 2006).

6. See Alfred W. McCoy, *Policing America's Empire: The United States, the Philippines, and the Rise of the Surveillance State* (Madison: University of Wisconsin Press, 2009); Bruce Cumings, *The Origins of the Korean War: The Roaring of the Cataract, 1947–1950,* vol. 2 (Princeton: Princeton University Press, 1990), 31.

7. See Mark Selden and Alvin Y. So, eds., *War and State Terrorism: The U.S., Japan, and the Asia-Pacific in the Long Twentieth Century* (New York: Rowman and Littlefield, 2004); Noam Chomsky, *Failed States: The Abuse of Power and Assault on Democracy* (New York: Metropolitan Books, 2006), among other works by this gifted scholar; Alfred W. McCoy, *A Question of Torture: CIA Interrogation from the Cold War to the War on Terror* (New York: Metropolitan Books, 2005); and Adam West, ed., *Genocide, War Crimes and the West: History and Complicity* (London: Zed Books, 2002).

8. Drinnon, *Facing West,* xiv; Sir Robert Thompson, *Defeating Communist Insurgency: The Lessons of Malaya and Vietnam* (New York: Praeger, 1966), 103; Sir Robert Thompson, *Make for the Hills* (London: Leo Cooper, 1989), 128. See also Marc Curtis, *Unpeople: Britain's Secret Human Rights Abuses* (London: Vintage 2004), 211; Robert W. Komer, *The Malayan Emergency in Retrospect: Organization of a Successful Counter-insurgency Effort* (Santa Monica: RAND Corporation, 1972); A. J. Stockwell, "Police during the Malayan Emergency, 1948–1960," in *Policing and Decolonization: Nationalism, Politics and the Police, 1917–1965,* ed. David M. Anderson and David Killingray (Manchester: Manchester University Press, 1992), 105–27; Roger Hilsman, *To Move a Nation: The Politics of Foreign Policy in the Administration of John F. Kennedy* (New York: Doubleday, 1967), 431. Drawing on Thompson's ideas, the U.S. Army counterinsurgency manual relates that "[local] police are often the best force for countering small insurgent bands supported by the local population [as a result of their frequent contact with the population]. In COIN [counterintelligence] operations, special police strike units may move to different AOs [areas of operation] while patrol police remain in the local area on a daily basis and build a detailed intelligence picture of the insurgent strength, organization and support." *U.S. Army/Marine Corps Counterinsurgency Field Manual (U.S. Army Field Manual No. 3-24, Marine Corps War Fighting Publication No. 3-33.5)* (Chicago: University of Chicago Press, 2007), 231.

3. "Their Goal Was Nothing Less than Total Knowledge"

1. "Midnight in a Great City Plot," RDS, Office of Research Intelligence, Relating to the Internal Affairs of Japan (1945–1949), decimal file 894 (hereafter RDS, Japan).

2. John W. Dower, "Occupied Japan and the American Lake, 1945–1950," in *America's Asia: Dissenting Essays on Asian-American Relations,* ed. Edward Friedman and Mark Selden (New York: Vintage Books, 1971), 186–207; Noam Chomsky, *Deterring Democracy* (New York: Hill and Wang, 1991), 52; Gar Alperovitz, *Atomic Diplomacy: Hiroshima and Potsdam; The Use of the Atomic Bomb and the American Confrontation with Soviet Power,* rev. ed. (New York: Pluto Press, 1994); Walter LaFeber, *The Clash: U.S.-Japanese Relations throughout History* (New York: Norton, 1997), 256.

3. See Christopher Aldous, *The Police in Occupation Japan: Control, Corruption, and Resistance to Reform* (New York: Routledge, 1997); Howard B. Schonberger, *Aftermath of*

War: Americans and the Remaking of Japan, 1945–1952 (Kent, Ohio: Kent State University Press, 1989). Drawing on Edward W. Said's *Orientalism,* Naoko Shibusawa points out in *America's Geisha Ally: Reimagining the Japanese Enemy* (Cambridge: Harvard University Press, 2006) that in popular discourse, Japan's image shifted from that of hated and barbaric enemy to one of a passive, childlike people ripe for the exportation of alleged American beneficence and consumerist values, which it was believed were needed to lead the country into maturity.

4. "Japanese Opinions on Future of National Police Reserve," *Japan Review,* August 30, 1950, and American embassy, Tokyo, to Department of State, September 8, 1950, both RDS, Japan; "Political Reorientation of Japan, September 1945–September 1948," Report of the Government Section, Supreme Commander for the Allied Powers, 292–93, RG 331, Records of the General Headquarters Supreme Commander for the Allied Powers (GHQ SCAP), G-2, RAOOH, Public Safety Division, Police Branch (1945–1952) (hereafter Police Branch), box 332; D. Eleanor Westney, *Imitation and Innovation: The Transfer of Western Organizational Patterns to Meiji Japan* (Cambridge: Harvard University Press, 1987), 33–99; Elise K. Tipton, *The Japanese Police State: The Tokkô in Interwar Japan* (Honolulu: University of Hawai'i Press, 1990). Police repression against the Japanese Communist Party and labor movement started right from their inception in the early twentieth century.

5. See William S. Borden, *The Pacific Alliance: United States Foreign Economic Policy and Japanese Trade Recovery, 1947–1955* (Madison: University of Wisconsin Press, 1984); Noam Chomsky, *For Reasons of State* (New York: Pantheon Books, 1973); John W. Dower, "Asia and the Nixon Doctrine: The New Face of Empire," in *Open Secrets: The Kissinger-Nixon Doctrine in Asia,* ed. Mark Selden and Virginia Brodine, foreword by Noam Chomsky (New York: Harper & Row, 1972), 144–45.

6. Aldous, *The Police in Occupation Japan,* 9; Michael Schaller, *Douglas MacArthur: The Far Eastern General* (New York: Oxford University Press, 1989), 121; Takemae Eiji, *Inside GHQ: The Allied Occupation of Japan,* trans. Robert Ricketts and Sebastien Swann (New York: Continuum, 2002), 161; Bruce Cumings, *The Origins of the Korean War: The Roaring of the Cataract, 1947–1950,* vol. 2 (Princeton: Princeton University Press, 1990), 104–5. The Prussian-born Willoughby maintained clandestine ties to right-wing militarists, including the bacteriological war criminal General Shiro Ishii. After MacArthur was fired in Korea, Willoughby became an adviser to Francisco Franco's government in Spain and wrote an intelligence digest for the right-wing evangelist Billy James Hargis, serving as an honorary member of the John Birch Society. He also set up an "anti-communist international" using money from the Hunt brothers in Texas and ex-Nazis to whom he was connected. In 1971, still up to his old tricks, he accused the CIA-connected MIT Center for International Studies of being infiltrated by communists.

7. John W. Dower, *Embracing Defeat: Japan in the Wake of World War II* (New York: Norton, 1999); Colonel H. E. Pulliam, "Democratic Stable Government and Internal Security Power Implements," August 5, 1947, RG 331, GHQ SCAP, Far East Command, Military Intelligence Section, PSD, box 283; Aldous, *The Police in Occupation Japan,* 166, 167. Pulliam went on to head the police administration program at Washington State University.

8. Bernard G. Brannon, Chief of Kansas City Police Department, to Sgt. G. E. Squires, "Captain Byron Engle—Age 42, on Leave," October 7, 1952, courtesy of the Kansas City Police Department Historical Branch; Galen I. Johnson, "Policing in Kansas City: Reform, Reorganization, and the Crime-Fighting Image, 1939–1961" (M.A. thesis, University of Missouri–Kansas City, 1991); Lear B. Reed, *Human Wolves: Seventeen Years of War on Crime* (Kansas City: Brown-White, Lowell Press, 1941), 383, 384. Described by a colleague as an

"extrovert impatient for action, quick to anger, and a man of strong likes and dislikes," Reed was a minister's son who, during a stint with the FBI, was indicted though never convicted for manslaughter in the death of a woman in St. Louis. As the chief of the Kansas City Police, he wrote that when "Uncle Sam is ready to put up the barbed wire, we'll be the first to help him string it up." See Thomas A. Reppetto, *The Blue Parade* (New York: Free Press, 1978), 288–93, quote on 289.

9. Reppetto, *The Blue Parade;* Don Bordenkircher, *Tiger Cage: An Untold Story* (New York: Abby Publishing, 1998), 26; Robert H. Bruce, "Impact of the Occupation of Japan on American Notions about U.S.-Induced Reform in the Third World," *Indian Journal of American Studies* 75, no. 2 (1985): 124–25.

10. Oscar G. Olander, *Michigan State Police: A Twenty-five-Year History* (East Lansing: Michigan Police Journal Press, 1942), 104; Harold Mulbar, *Interrogation* (Springfield, Ill.: Charles C. Thomas, 1951); "Testimony of Harold Mulbar," in *Investigation of Un-American Propaganda Activities in the United States, Hearings before a Special Committee on Un-American Activities, House of Representatives,* 75th Cong., 3rd sess., on House Resolution 282, vol. 2, October 11, 12, 13, 1938, Flint, Michigan (Washington, D.C.: GPO, 1938), 1709; Sidney Fine, *Sit-Down: The General Motors Strike of 1936–1937* (Ann Arbor: University of Michigan Press, 1969), 238.

11. On the limits of New Deal liberalism, see Barton J. Bernstein, "The New Deal: The Conservative Achievements of Liberal Reform," in *Towards a New Past: Dissenting Essays in American History,* ed. Barton J. Bernstein (New York: Knopf, 1968), 263–88. Also Chris Hedges, *Death of the Liberal Class* (New York: Nation Books, 2010).

12. "Police Branch Weekly Staff Conference," November 21, 1950, Police Branch, box 332; "The Status of Police Reorganization in Japan," Department of State, Division of Research for Far East, April 22, 1949, RG 59, RDS, Division of Research for Far East Reports, 1946–1952, box 4; Johnson F. Monroe, Police Administrator, to David S. Arnold, August 25, 1950, Police Branch, box 328; Bruce, "Impact of the Occupation in Japan," 124.

13. See Aldous, *The Police in Occupation Japan,* 51; Joe Moore, *Japanese Workers and the Struggle for Power, 1945–1947* (Madison: University of Wisconsin Press, 1983), 12–13; Herbert Bix, *Hirohito and the Making of Modern Japan* (New York: Harper, 2001).

14. Aldous, *The Police in Occupation Japan,* 51; Hans Baerwald, *The Purge of Japanese Leaders under the Occupation,* rev. ed. (New York: Greenwood Press, 1977), 71, 76; Eiji, *Inside GHQ,* 479; Ralph J. Braibanti, "Administration of Occupied Areas," RDS, Japan.

15. Edward R. Bishop to PSD Division, "Report About 1st Phase In-Service Training," May 31, 1951, Police Branch, box 334, folder Reports.

16. On the innovations pioneered at Berkeley, see Gene Carte and Elaine H. Carte, *Police Reform in the United States: The Era of August Vollmer, 1905–1932* (Berkeley: University of California Press, 1975). Records of the correspondence have been preserved in the August Vollmer Papers at the Bancroft Library, Berkeley. See, e.g., Eiji Suzuki, Osaka Metropolitan Police Department, to August Vollmer, October 7, 1950; Yusai Takahashi to August Vollmer, March 30, 1947.

17. See Frederic Wakeman Jr., *Spymaster: Dai Li and the Chinese Secret Service* (Berkeley: University of California Press, 2003), 192–205; Frederic Wakeman Jr., *Policing Shanghai, 1927–1937* (Berkeley: University of California Press, 1995), 74; Oliver J. Caldwell, *A Secret War: Americans in China, 1944–1945* (Carbondale: Southern Illinois University Press, 1971), 73. The brutality of the Machado regime and its secret police is documented in Carleton Beals, *The Crime of Cuba* (Philadelphia: J. B. Lippincott, 1933).

18. Johnson F. Monroe, Police Administrator, to David S. Arnold, August 25, 1950, Police Branch, box 328; Chief CID to Chief of CID National Rural Police Headquarters, "On the

Promotion of Scientific Investigation," April 19, 1950, Police Branch, box 332. The budget for 1949 and 1950 alone was 30 billion yen and 10 billion for 1951 and 1952.

19. Calvin H. Goddard, "The Bureau of Forensics Ballistics" and "The Northwestern Crime Detection Laboratory," in *Silent Witness: The Emergence of Scientific Criminal Investigations* (Gaithersburg, Md.: International Association of Police Chiefs, 1977), 68–72, 77–82; "Milestones," *Time,* March 7, 1955; C. W. Muehlberger, "Col. Calvin Hooker Goddard, 1891–1955," *Journal of Criminal Law, Criminology, and Police Science* 46 (May–June 1955): 103–4.

20. "Police Branch Weekly Staff Conference," November 21, 1950, Police Branch, box 332; "The Problem of Civil Liberties in Japan," April 1, 1946, RDS, Japan; "Monthly Report: Police Project," March 3, 1951, Police Branch, box 332.

21. "The Problem of Civil Liberties in Japan"; Henry Oinas-Kukkonen, *Tolerance, Suspicion, and Hostility: Changing U.S. Attitudes towards the Japanese Communist Movement, 1944–1947* (Westport, Conn.: Greenwood Press, 2003), 24; Alfred Oppler, *Legal Reform in Occupied Japan: A Participant Looks Back* (Princeton: Princeton University Press, 1976).

22. Civil Information and Education Section, October 5, 1948, SCAP, RDS, Japan; also R. F. Malburg to Chief, Public Safety Division, Attn. Mr. Kimberling, "Police and Jails," June 28, 1947, courtesy Douglas MacArthur Research Center, Norfolk, Va., Robert F. Malburg Papers.

23. Olander, *Michigan State Police,* 14–15, 36, 90; Earl H. De Long and Fred E. Inabu, "A Law Enforcement Program for the State of Illinois," *Journal of Criminal Law and Criminology* 26 (January-February 1936): 741–51; M. J. Heale, "The Triumph of Liberalism? Red Scare Politics in Michigan, 1938–1945," *Proceedings of the American Philosophical Society* 139 (March 1995): 44–66; James B. Jacobs, "The Conduct of Local Political Intelligence" (Ph.D. diss., Princeton University, 1977). On the history of U.S. red squads, see Frank Donner, *Protectors of Privilege: Red Squads and Police Repression in Urban America* (Berkeley: University of California Press, 1991).

24. A. G. Sulzberger, "La Guardia's Tough and Incorruptible Police Commissioner," *New York Times,* November 11, 2009; Marilynn S. Johnson, *Street Justice: A History of Police Violence in New York City* (Boston: Beacon Press, 2003), 177, 179; Lewis J. Valentine, with Fiorello La Guardia, *Night Stick: The Autobiography of Lewis J. Valentine* (New York: Dial Press, 1947); James Lardner and Thomas Reppetto, *NYPD: A City and Its Police* (New York: Henry Holt, 2000), 233.

25. Oscar Olander, "Special Report, Rural Police Planning Group," June 1946, Police Branch (1945–1952), box 336, folder Reports; "Political Reorientation of Japan," Report of the Government Section, Supreme Commander for the Allied Powers, September 1945–September 1948 (Washington, D.C.: GPO, 1948), 293.

26. Lewis Valentine, "Valentine Report," Police Branch, box 335, folder Reports; Valentine, *Nightstick,* 296; "Valentine Is Likely to Go to Japan; Wants 10 Police Experts as Aides," *New York Times,* February 1, 1946; Lindesay Parrott, "Valentine Amused by Japan's Police," *New York Times,* March 14, 1946.

27. Paul Harrison to Joseph Hawthorne, Tokyo, March 7, 1950, Police Branch, box 328; Alfred C. Oppler, *Legal Reform in Occupied Japan: A Participant Looks Back* (Princeton: Princeton University Press, 1976), 171; Ralph J. D. Braibanti, "Japan's New Police Law," *Far Eastern Survey* 18 (January 24, 1949): 19.

28. "Summation of Non-Military Activities, Japan," GHQ-SCAP (April 1948), 56.

29. See John Lewis Gillin, *Taming the Criminal: Adventures in Penology* (New York: Macmillan, 1931), 26.

30. "Detention of Prisoners, Valentine Report" and Monthly Report, April 26, 1946, Police Branch, box 335, folder Reports; "Civil Report of Police Forces under Militarists," RG 331, SCAP, GHQ, Far East Command, PSD, box 283; Valentine, *Nightstick,* 306; Aldous, *The Police in Occupation Japan,* 82.

31. Burdette G. Lewis, *The Offender and His Relation to Law and Society,* introduction by George Wickersham (New York: Harper & Brothers, 1921). Lewis obtained his Ph.D. from Cornell University, where he heard Osborne give a speech about the innovative penal reforms he had adopted at Sing Sing prison in New York. He criticized the Auburn model of solitary confinement as "utterly contrary to every modern principle of psychology. . . . The old dungeons and cave-like coolers are relics of barbarism which have survived because those who built correctional institutions and the institutional officials never had the advantage of training and discipline acquired in the modern psychological labs and public schools" (9).

32. "Summation of Non-military Activities, Japan," GHQ-SCAP (April 1948), 56; "Detention of Prisoners, Valentine Report," Police Branch, box 335, folder Reports.

33. "Public Safety Report, Amori Main Prison," Prison Branch, box 339, folder Amori P. Arakawa Village; "Summation of Non-military Activities, Japan," GHQ-SCAP (March 1948), 64.

34. Interview with G. C. Kimmel, November 15, 1946, RG 331, GHQ-SCAP, G-2, PSD, RAOOH, Prison Branch (1945–1952), box 339, folder Amori P. Arakawa Village (hereafter Prison Branch); "Public Safety Report, Amori Main Prison," Prison Branch, box 339, folder Amori P. Arakawa Village.

35. "Public Safety Report, Abashira Main Prison," August 31, 1950, Prison Branch, box 339, folder Abashiri Main Prison.

36. "Fuchu: The Model Prison That Hasn't Been Copied," *Japan News,* October 28, 1950, 5, Prison Branch, box 340.

37. "Summary Report on the Real State of Fuchu Prisons" by Kazuo Murai, April 26, 1948; Burdett Lewis to H. E. Pulliam, Chief PSD, GHQ, April 29, 1948; and Dr. Burdett Lewis, Lloyd McCorkle, and George Kimmel, "Inspection Report Fuchu Prison," November 12, 1946, Prison Branch, box 340.

38. Maj. Reed, Maxwell, Lt. George Cornelius, "Report on Hiroshima Main Prison," November 1, 1950; George W. Cornelius, "Report on Fukushima Prisons" and "Group Escapes Tokyo Detention House," February 24, 1949; and Captain Fomenko, "Report on Hachinoke Branch Prison, November 17, 1947, Prison Branch, box 341; R. F. Malburg to Chief, Public Safety Division, Attention: Mr. Kimberling, "Police and Jails" June 28, 1947; and "Marunouchi Police Station Jail," June 10, 1947, RG 99, Papers of Robert Malburg, Douglas MacArthur Research Center, Norfolk, Va., box 1. For analysis of the racial stereotypes guiding U.S. foreign policy in Japan, see Shibusawa, *America's Geisha Ally.*

39. H. E. Pulliam to Dr. Burdett Lewis, April 27, 1949, Prison Branch, box 315; "Lloyd McCorkle, Prison Aide," *New York Times,* May 17, 1984; Lloyd W. McCorkle, "Guided Group Interaction in a Correctional Setting," *International Journal of Group Therapy* 4 (April 1954): 199–203; Richard R. Korn and Lloyd W. McCorkle, *Criminology and Penology* (New York: Holt, 1959). McCorkle promoted a critical view of the dehumanizing effects of prison life and, like Lewis, believed in the importance of addressing the root causes of crime. He was later appointed New Jersey's commissioner of corrections and went on to chair the law department at John Jay School of Criminal Justice.

40. "Public Safety Report, Chiba Main Prison," March 27, 1951, Prison Branch, box 339, folder Chiba Main Prison; Chief, Public Safety Division, "Report Covering TDY, Kobe, Kyoto, Maisuru, Higashimaizuru, Miyazu, 12–21 September 1949," October 4, 1949, Prison

Branch, box 348, folder Taira Branch Detention House; "Jail Guards Suspected of Cooperating in Red Activities with Prisoners," Osaka, February 9, 1951, Police Branch, box 351.

41. Burdett Lewis to H. E. Pulliam, Chief, Public Safety Division, September 24, 1947, Prison Branch, box 281. On Dowd's career, see Victoria Graham, "Executioner: Ex-Warden Pulled Lever 13 Times, Has No Guilt Feelings," *Bowling Green Daily News,* April 24, 1973.

42. Alfred W. Dowd, Acting Chief Prison Administrator, to Chief, Public Safety Division, February 12, 1949, Prison Branch, box 339, folder Communism; Graham, "Executioner."

43. Paul Harrison to Chief Police Administrator, "Custody of Prisoners," October 6, 1950, Police Branch, box 334, folder Reports.

44. George F. Kennan, *Memoirs: 1925–1950* (Boston: Little, Brown, 1967), 390; LaFeber, *The Clash,* 272; George F. Kennan to Dean Acheson, memorandum, August 23, 1950, Secretary of State File, Acheson Papers, Truman Presidential Library (online archive). On Kennan's fundamentally antidemocratic political outlook, see Walter L. Hixson, *George F. Kennan: Cold War Iconoclast* (New York: Columbia University Press, 1989).

45. "Recommendations Concerning the Japanese Police System" October 19, 1948, RG 59, RDS, Bureau of Far Eastern Affairs (1946–1952) (hereafter Far Eastern Affairs), box 4, folder Reports; Philip Jessup, memo for Dean Rusk, July 20, 1950, RDS, Japan.

46. Joyce Kolko and Gabriel Kolko, *The Limits of Power: The World and United States Foreign Policy, 1945–1954* (New York: Harper & Row, 1972), 525; Shigeru Yoshida, *The Yoshida Memoirs: The Story of Japan in Crisis,* trans. Kenichi Yoshida (Boston: Houghton Mifflin, 1962), 176–77; John W. Dower, *Empire and Aftermath: Yoshida Shigeru and the Japanese Experience, 1878–1954* (Cambridge: Harvard University Press, 1979).

47. "Summation of Non-Military Activities," GHQ-SCAP (April 1948), 55; Shuichi Sugai, "The Japanese Police System," in *Five Studies in Japanese Politics,* ed. Robert E. Ward (Ann Arbor: University of Michigan Press, 1957), 7; Chalmers Johnson, *Conspiracy at Matsukawa* (Berkeley: University of California Press, 1972), 101; Aldous, *The Police in Occupation Japan,* 203.

48. "Soviet Propaganda Concerning the Japanese Police Force," January 4, 1948, RDS, Far Eastern Affairs, box 4, folder Reports.

49. On the savagery of the bombings, see Michael S. Sherry, *The Rise of American Air Power: The Creation of Armageddon* (New Haven: Yale University Press, 1987), 23–28, 57–59; John W. Dower, *War without Mercy: Race and Power in the Pacific War* (New York: Pantheon Books, 1986), 294–300.

50. Moore, *Japanese Workers and the Struggle for Power,* 189; Dower, *Embracing Defeat,* 270.

51. Robert B. Textor, *Failure in Japan with Keystones for a Positive Policy,* foreword by Owen Lattimore (New York: John Day, 1951), 100; Gary D. Allinson, *Japan's Postwar History* (Ithaca: Cornell University Press, 1997), 72.

52. Kolko and Kolko, *The Limits of Power,* 524; Schonberger, *Aftermath of War,* 145; Glenn Davis and John G. Roberts, *An Occupation without Troops: Wall Street's Half-Century Domination of Japanese Politics* (Tokyo: Yen Books, 1996); Herbert P. Bix, "American Labor and Japanese Unionists," in *Postwar Japan: 1945 to the Present,* ed. Jon Livingston, Joe Moore, and Felicia Oldfather (New York: Random House), 1973, 173; Dower, *Embracing Defeat,* 544. Dodge was referred to as an "economic czar." Chalmers Johnson concludes that the Dodge plan cut inflation but "at the cost of a recession in Japan, a sharp rise in unemployment, and some of the harshest working conditions since the end of the war years. . . . Thousands of workers were fired." Johnson, *Conspiracy at Matsukawa,* 68.

53. Oinas-Kukkonen, *Tolerance, Suspicion, and Hostility;* Schonberger, *Aftermath of War;*

Moore, *Japanese Workers and the Struggle for Power*, 116; Robert Scalapino, *The Japanese Communist Movement, 1920–1966* (Berkeley: University of California Press, 1967), 76.

54. Oinas-Kukkonen, *Tolerance, Suspicion, and Hostility*; Yoneyuki Sugita, *Pitfall or Panacea: The Irony of U.S. Power in Occupied Japan, 1945–1952* (New York: Routledge, 2003); "Nagoya Municipal Office District Plastered with Communist Handbills," *Yukan Chubu Nihon Shimbun* (Nagoya), March 21, 1951, Police Branch, box 351, folder Press; Textor, *Failure in Japan*, 104; Johnson, *Conspiracy at Matsukawa*, 60, 61. On MacArthur's ultraconservatism, see Schaller, *Douglas MacArthur*. In 1949 the journalist Mark Gayn wrote on the restoration of former war criminals: "The purge, as of this date, has become a sham. War criminals sit in the Diet, the Cabinet and the imperial court, draw new 'democratic' legislation and administrate the purges to fit their political ends. War criminals are 'revising' the textbooks, running the press, dominate the radio and moving picture industries. Thought control agents, purged and purged again, keep reappearing in positions of responsibility— often with American encouragement." Gayn, *Japan Diary*, 494.

55. "The Status of Police Reorganization in Japan," April 22, 1949; "Nagoya Municipal Office District Plastered with Communist Handbills"; "Police Reports to Be Screened," *Nippon Times*, August 13, 1950, and "National Police Reserve Order," *Nippon Times*, August 10, 1950, Police Branch, box 328; "Are There Still Some Red Policemen? Performance of Duty Is Excellent, Difficult to Identify 'Secret Faction,'" March 25, 1951, Police Branch, box 351, folder Press; "Subversive Activity," March 15, 1951, RG 331, SCAP, G-2, PSD, General File (hereafter PSD General File), box 282; "Warrants of Arrest for Tokuda and Eight Top-Level JCP Members," CIC Report, June 15, 1951, PSD General File, box 314; "Discharge of Communists from Japan Government Ministries," November 3, 1950, CIC Report, PSD General File, box 316; John M. Steeves, "The Japanese Police System," December 17, 1952, RDS, Japan; Dower, *Embracing Defeat*, 271, 272; "Japan Puts Curb on Yokosuka Reds," *New York Times*, June 11, 1950; Lindesay Parrott, "Japan Acts to Bar Workers Disorder: Orders Police to Crack Down on Communist Inspired Strikes and Rioting," *New York Times*, June 17, 1949.

56. *Nippon Times*, July 19, 1950, Police Branch, box 328, folder Press. MacArthur's views on communism are articulated in Major General Courtney Whitney, *MacArthur: His Rendezvous with History* (New York: Knopf, 1956), 308–9.

57. Byron Engle to Chief, PSD, "Report on Communist Demonstrations," June 3, 1950, Police Branch, box 332; "Communist Spy Nabbed after Getting Information Re Anti Red Police Tactics," *Mainichi News*, December 13, 1950; "Tokuda Kyuchi," CIC Report, July 1950, June 15, 1951, PSD General File, box 314; Harold Mulbar, "Fired Communist Agitators," October 20, 1950, and "Arrest of Communists," November 9, 1950, Police Branch, box 329; Lt. Arthur McCaslin Thurston, RG 226, Records of OSS Personnel File, 1941–1945, box 77; "Personality Sketch" May 23, 1944; and Ezra Shine, "Report on Interrogation of Student Lee," Philadelphia, May 17 and 18, 1944, RG 226, Records of OSS Personnel File, box 211. According to documents I've seen at the Truman Presidential Library, Thurston also spent time as an OSS agent in Bolivia, possibly tracking down Nazis. He was also a liaison to British intelligence. On FBI wiretapping practices, see William W. Turner, "I Was a Burglar, Wiretapper, Bugger and Spy for the FBI," *Ramparts* (November 1966): 51–55, and his *Invisible Witness: The Use and Abuse of the New Technology of Crime Investigation* (Indianapolis: Bobbs-Merrill, 1968). During the 1930s, Congress outlawed wiretapping. Franklin Roosevelt, however, who admired J. Edgar Hoover's tough posture, gave executive authority for the attorney general to approve it "when necessarily involving the defense of the nation." Turner, "I Was a Burgler," 52. The OSS and CIA regularly employed it under the same

pretext. Yoshikawa was credited with breaking the Sorge spy case involving a Soviet agent in 1941 and loyally served the Tojo order.

58. Orrin DeForest with David Chanoff, *Slow Burn: The Rise and Bitter Fall of American Intelligence in Vietnam* (New York: Simon & Schuster, 1990), 76.

59. Harry Emerson Wildes, *Typhoon in Tokyo: The Occupation and Its Aftermath* (New York: Macmillan, 1954), 24; Chalmers Johnson, ed., *Okinawa: Cold War Island* (San Francisco: University of San Francisco Japan Policy Research Institute, 1999), 5; Eiji, *Inside GHQ,* 162, 163, 165; David E. Kaplan and Alec Dubro, *Yakuza: Japan's Criminal Underworld* (Berkeley: University of California Press, 2003), 45, 48; "Subversive Activity," February 15, 1951, CIC Report, March 15, 1951, PSD General File, box 282. The Special Z Unit was headed by a Lieutenant Jack Y. Cannon, who later penetrated Castro's guerrilla operation against Batista in Cuba. See Peter Dale Scott, *Deep Politics and the Death of JFK* (Berkeley: University of California Press, 1993), 178.

60. Kaplan and Dubro, *Yakuza,* 45, 46.

61. Eiji, *Inside GHQ,* 164, 165.

62. Johnson, *Street Justice,* 177; August Vollmer, *The Police and Modern Society,* reprinted with a new introduction by James Q. Wilson (Montclair, N.J.: Patterson Smith, 1971), xi.

63. Byron Engle to Chief, Public Safety Division, "Shigeo Shindo," and "Control of Disturbances in the Tokyo Area," Police Branch, box 330, folder Demonstrations. On the use of tear gas against the Bonus marchers, see Howard Zinn, *A People's History of the United States: The Twentieth Century* (New York: Perennial, 2003), 117.

64. Prison Branch, PSD, to William A. Downs, Memo, Chief Public Safety, and "Test Results of Riot Type Shot-Gun," Prison Branch, box 339, folder Current Prisons; Joe Williams report, "Control of Parades and Mass Demonstrations," June 1952, Police Branch, box 332.

65. Interview with Byron Engle, in William D. Steeves Jr., "The U.S. Public Safety Program, Its Evolution and Demise" (master's thesis, George Washington University School of Public and International Affairs, 1975) 36; Robert H. Bruce, "Human Rights and U.S. Training of Third World Police," *Conflict Quarterly* 8 (Winter 1988): 53. For a description of police brutality during the 1952 May Day demonstrations, see Dower, *Embracing Defeat,* 554.

66. Johnson, *Conspiracy at Matsukawa,* 43. Although the supposition is impossible to prove because Willoughby destroyed all his secret files, the murders at Matsukawa could have been an early example of the kind of black propaganda operation documented in Graham Greene's novel *The Quiet American.* See Kaplan and Dubro, *Yakuza,* 46.

67. Paul M. Harrison to Byron Engle, "Hiroshima Demonstration," August 8, 1950; and "Report on Eight Communists Arrested for Anti–Atomic Bomb Propaganda," Police Branch, box 330, folder Demonstrations; "Summation of Non-Military Activities in Japan," April 1946, GHQ-SCAP (Washington, D.C.: GPO, 1946), 51; Johnson F. Monroe to H. Matsumoto, "On a Korean School and Its Korean Teachers," May 10, 1951; and Harold Mulbar to Chief, Police Administration, "Moves among the Korean Communists in Japan," March 2, 1951, Police Branch, box 329; Burton Crane, "16 Korean Rebels Arrested in Tokyo," *New York Times,* April 28, 1946. According to U.S. Army Counter-Intelligence Corps (CIC) files, an American missionary, Neal Hartman, a conscientious objector in World War II, was among those subjected to police surveillance and harassment after giving a speech advocating pacifism.

68. Textor, *Failure in Japan,* 105.

69. Press Reports, January 1949, RDS, Japan; Paul Harrison to Chief Police Administra-

tor, "Custody of Prisoners," October 6, 1950, Police Branch, box 334, folder Reports; Tsumeo Saito, "GI Hurt by Reds at Tokyo Rally," *Nippon Times,* May 31, 1950; Theodore Cohen, *Remaking Japan: The American Occupation as New Deal* (New York: Free Press, 1987), 255; CIC Report, April 15, 1951, PSD General File, box 282.

70. Scalapino, *The Japanese Communist Movement,* 86; Harold Mulbar, "Arrest of Communist," November 9, 1950, March 2, 1951, Police Branch, box 329; "Subversive Activity," February 15, 1951, CIC Field Reports, Japan, PSD General File, box 282; "Bomb Explosion Kills One Japanese," *Migagi,* August 28, 1950, CIC Report, PSD General File, box 314. Yennan was the base of the Chinese Communist Party during China's civil war, in which they pioneered various reforms to win over the population while establishing an effective guerrilla army.

71. Press Reports, January 1949, RDS, Japan; "Report from Mr. Kurai, Chief of the Guard Section, MPD," June 4, 1950, Police Branch, box 330, folder Demonstrations; "Nagoya Municipal Office District Plastered with Communist Handbills."

72. Johnson F. Monroe to Harold Mulbar, "Purging of Leaders and Confiscation of Assets," August 30, 1950, Police Branch, box 330. Monroe later worked for the OPS in Pakistan, Africa, Vietnam, and the Dominican Republic.

73. "Communist Activities in Speech-Making by Candidates Running for Metropolitan Governorship," Police Branch, box 329; CIC Field Reports, Japan, March 15, 1951, PSD General File, box 282; Dower, *Embracing Defeat,* 414.

74. Harold Mulbar, "Communist Publications Seized,"Police Branch, box 329; CIC Report, March 15, 1951, PSD General File, box 282.

75. Aldous, *The Police in Occupation Japan,* 101; Virgil Kilgore to Chief, Public Safety Division, "Progress Report on Prisoner Conveyance," March 30, 1951, Police Branch, box 334; Textor, *Failure in Japan,* 101; "Police Third Degree Methods Lead to Suicide," *Jiman Shimbun,* January 29, 1951, Police Branch, box 351, folder Press; Robert Whiting, *Tokyo Underworld: The Fast Times and Hard Life of an American Gangster in Japan* (New York: Pantheon Books, 1999), 62.

76. Takeo Takagi, "Why Japan's Police Is Dreaded," *Nippon Times,* March 21, 1954; "Police Third Degree Methods Lead to Suicide."

77. "Summation of Non-Military Activities in Japan, October 1947," GHQ, Supreme Allied Command (Washington, D.C.: GPO, 1947), 31; "Swindle by Former Chairman of Public Safety Commission," February 26, 1950, Police Branch, box 332; "Satagaya Police Station, Chief Ken Maejima, RG 99, Papers of Robert Malburg, Douglas MacArthur Research Center, Norfolk, Va., box 1, folder 2; Wildes, *Typhoon in Tokyo,* 188.

78. Whiting, *Tokyo Underworld,* 85, 86; "Summation of Non-Military Activities in Japan, October 1947," 31. Known for his street-fighting prowess, including an incident in which he knocked out an American black belt in a barroom fight with one punch, the Korean-born Machii became close with the head of the Korean CIA. In western Europe, the CIA analogously employed French and Corsican narcotics traffickers and gangsters to break dockworkers' strikes in Marseilles and to kill communists.

79. Kaplan and Dubro, *Yakuza,* 48, 49; Davis and Roberts, *An Occupation without Troops.*

80. Whiting, *Tokyo Underworld,* 17; "Summation No. 7, Non-Military Activities in Japan, April 1946," GHQ, Supreme Allied Command (Washington, D.C.: GPO, 1946), 52; "Summation of Non-Military Activities in Japan, January 1948," GHQ, Supreme Allied Command (Washington, D.C.: GPO, 1948), 53. In some cases, GIs were punished. One report notes the breaking up of a smuggling ring for clothing and PX supplies, in which a soldier was killed while resisting arrest.

81. Aldous, *The Police in Occupation Japan,* 183, 103; Textor, *Failure in Japan,* 101; Yuki Tanaka, *Japan's Comfort Women: Sexual Slavery and Prostitution during World War II and the U.S. Occupation* (New York: Routledge, 2001), 123. Many of the worst abuses took place in Okinawa, where prostitution around U.S. military bases and sexual abuse are still a problem.

82. Robert E. Kuhnle to Army Criminal Investigations Division, "Opium Raid," October 30, 1952; and William H. Sullivan, 2nd Secretary of the embassy, to Robert Murphy, American Consul to the Department of State, November 24, 1952, RDS, LA90 44, folder Japan.

83. Japanese Liaison Section, G-2, Johnson Monroe, "Hostile Action against Chinese Residents Alleged," Radio Press, April 10, 1951, Police Branch, box 351, folder Press; Wildes, *Typhoon in Tokyo,* 197. Speer, a Texan, later worked for the Federal Bureau of Narcotics (FBN) in Thailand and Indochina.

84. Callum A. MacDonald, *Korea: The War before Vietnam* (New York: Free Press, 1986), 224; Christopher Robbins, *The Invisible Air Force: The Story of the CIA's Secret Airlines* (London: Macmillan, 1979), 228–45.

85. See Alfred W. McCoy, *The Politics of Heroin: CIA Complicity in the Global Drug Trade* (New York: Lawrence Hill, 1991); Tim Weiner, *Legacy of Ashes: The History of the CIA* (New York: Doubleday, 2007), 117; Jonathan Marshall, *Drug Wars: Drug Enforcement as Counterinsurgency* (San Francisco: Cohan and Cohen Publishers, 1987), 54; Scott Anderson and Jon Lee Anderson, *Inside the League: The Shocking Exposé of How Terrorists, Nazis, and Latin American Death Squads Have Infiltrated the World Anti-Communist League* (New York: Dodd, Mead, 1986), 62; Whiting, *Tokyo Underworld,* 83–84. In the 1970s, as the Japanese and Korean agent for Lockheed Aircraft Corporation, Kodama bribed the Prime Minister Kakuei Tanaka, forcing his resignation. During the Japanese occupation of China, one of his methods was to enter a village and have the mayor shot to ensure the villagers' full cooperation in donating supplies. The CIA was generally known to recruit gangsters to carry out some of its more unsavory operations.

86. Aldous, *The Police in Occupation Japan,* 223; Dower, *Empire and Aftermath,* 347; Dower, "The U.S.-Japan Military Relationship," in Livingston, Moore, and Oldfather, *Postwar Japan,* 240.

87. Michael Schaller, *Altered States: The United States and Japan since the Occupation* (New York: Oxford University Press, 1997), 45; William McDougall, "Vulnerable but Valuable: General Eichelberger Urges Strong Police to Japan—Stresses Red Danger," *Nippon Times,* February 1949; Eiji, *Inside GHQ,* 488; Hanson Baldwin, "Japan's Army Starts: National Police, While Not a Military Force, Provides Potential Cadres for New Army," *New York Times,* December 25, 1950; "Japanese Opinion on Future National Police Reserve," *Japan Review,* August 30, 1950, and J. Owen Zurheller, American Vice Consul to Tokyo, "National Police Reserve," January 24, 1951, both RDS, Japan.

88. "Leaflet Issued by the Communist Party, Chitose Cell," October 1952, RDS (1950–1954), folder Japan.

89. McDougall, "Vulnerable but Valuable"; Omar Bradley to the President, January 24; James Webb to Robert Lovett, Secretary of Defense, September 28, 1951, RDS, Japan.

90. David Cortright, *Peace: A History of Movements and Ideas* (New York: Cambridge University Press, 2008), 120; M. E. Weinstein, "The Evolution of the Japanese Self-Defense Forces," in *The Modern Japanese Military System,* ed. J. H. Buck (London: Sage, 1975); Weiner, *Legacy of Ashes,* 120, 121; "OCB Report Pursuant to NSC Action 1290-d," August 4, 1955, DDEL, box 17, folder Internal Security.

91. "OCB Report Pursuant to NSC Action 1290-d," January 3, 1957, DDEL, box 18. Kaya's career and CIA ties are discussed in Weiner, *Legacy of Ashes,* 121. The prime minister in the

late 1950s, Nobusuke Kishi, was a member of the war cabinet during World War II and a Class-A war criminal. His career was bankrolled by Yoshio Kodama, who assisted him in suppressing leftist demonstrations against the signing of a base treaty with the Eisenhower administration, supported by members of the Japan lobby such as *Newsweek* foreign affairs editor Harry Kern and ex-ambassador Joseph Grew.

92. Sugai, "The Japanese Police System," 1. For a similar conclusion, see also Walter Ames, *Police and Community in Japan* (Berkeley: University of California Press, 1981).

93. See LaFeber, *The Clash;* Chalmers Johnson, *Blowback: The Costs and Consequences of the American Empire* (New York: Owl Books, 2000), 35; Johnson, *Okinawa.*

94. James Dobbins et al., *America's Role in Nation-Building: From Germany to Iraq* (Santa Monica, Calif.: RAND Corporation, 2003). For an analysis of how false historical analogies from the occupation of Japan were used in support of the war in Iraq, see John Dower, *Cultures of War: Pearl Harbor/Hiroshima/9-11/Iraq* (New York: Norton, 2010). David Bayley, in *Forces of Order: Police Behavior in Japan and the United States* (Berkeley: University of California Press, 1976), praises the Japanese police for their professionalism in combating crime in the 1970s while ignoring their involvement in political operations. A similar lack of critical perspective is evident in Bayley's later work on police training programs in Afghanistan and Iraq, which he championed.

95. Dower's book is also significant in retrieving Japanese agency. See also Schaller, *Altered States;* Schonberger, *Aftermath of War;* Moore, *Japanese Workers and the Struggle for Power.*

96. See Chomsky, *Deterring Democracy;* Gavan McCormack, *Client State: Japan in the American Embrace* (London: Verso, 2007); Weiner, *Legacy of Ashes,* 121. While the United States after 1952 obviously did not control every decision made by the Japanese government, it helped to ensure the preservation of one-party LDP rule and the suppression of leftist movements pushing for a more independent course, including nonalignment in the Cold War (or closer alliance with the PRC and/or Soviet Union). In return for continued foreign aid, Japan was compliant, furthermore, with larger U.S. foreign policy goals in Southeast Asia, providing an important base for American aggression in Indochina. Horace Feldman, CIA station chief in Japan in the late 1950s, tellingly informed *New York Times* journalist Tim Weiner: "We ran Japan during the occupation and we ran it in a different way in these years after the occupation. General MacArthur had his ways, we had ours." Weiner, *Legacy of Ashes,* 121.

4. "Law in Whose Name, Order for Whose Benefit?"

1. Headquarters, U.S. Army Military Government in Korea, to All Concerned, "Investigation of the Police," July 30, 1946, RG 554, United States Army Forces in Korea, Records Regarding the Okinawa Campaign (1945-1948), United States Military Government, Korean Political Affairs, box 25 (hereafter USAFIK Okinawa).

2. Bruce Cumings, *The Origins of the Korean War,* vol. 1, *Liberation and the Emergence of Separate Regimes, 1945-1947* (Princeton: Princeton University Press, 1981); Callum A. McDonald, *Korea: The War before Vietnam* (New York: Free Press, 1986), 11. On Syngman Rhee's background, see Robert T. Oliver, *Syngman Rhee: The Man behind the Myth* (New York: Dodd & Mead, 1960); and on Kim Il Sung and the North Korean revolution, see Dae Sook-Suh, *Kim Il Sung: The North Korean Leader* (New York: Columbia University Press, 1988); and especially Charles K. Armstrong, *The North Korean Revolution, 1945–1950* (Ithaca: Cornell University Press, 2004), which stresses the revolution's indigenous roots.

3. Bruce Cumings, *Korea's Place in the Sun: A Modern History* (New York: Norton, 1997), 210.

4. Cumings, *The Origins of the Korean War;* "The Position of the U.S. with Respect to Korea," National Security Council Report 8, April 2, 1948, PSF, Truman Papers, HSTL.

5. Jon Halliday and Bruce Cumings, *Korea: The Unknown War* (New York: Pantheon, 1988), 23; Dong-Choon Kim, *The Unending Korean War: A Social History,* trans. Sung-ok Kim (Larkspur, Calif.: Tamal Vista Publications, 2000), 80. When asked by the journalist Mark Gayn whether Rhee was a fascist, Lieutenant Leonard Bertsch, an adviser to General John R. Hodge, head of the American occupation, responded, "He is two centuries before fascism—a true Bourbon." Mark Gayn, *Japan Diary* (New York: William Sloane, 1948), 352.

6. "A History of the Korean National Police (KNP)," August 7, 1948, USAFIK Okinawa, box 25.

7. Bruce Cumings, *The Origins of the Korean War,* vol. 2, *The Roaring of the Cataract, 1947–1950,* rev. ed. (Ithaca: Cornell University Press, 2004), 186, 187; Gregory Henderson, *Korea: The Politics of the Vortex* (Cambridge: Harvard University Press, 1968), 143.

8. Roy C. Stiles and Albert Lyman, "The Administration of Justice in Korea under the Japanese and in South Korea under the U.S. Army Military Government in Korea to August 15, 1958: Paper by American Advisory Staff," Department of Justice, RDS, Records Related to the Internal Affairs of Korea, 1945–1949, decimal file 895 (hereafter cited RDS, Korea).

9. Harry Maglin, "Organization of National Police of Korea," December 27, 1945, USAFIK Okinawa, box 25; Everett F. Drumright to Secretary of State, "FBI Training," December 22, 1948, RDS, Korea; Philip H. Taylor, "Military Government Experience in Korea," in *American Experiences in Military Government in World War II,* ed. Carl J. Friederich (New York: Rinehart, 1948), 377; Harold Larsen, *U.S. Army History of the United States Armed Forces in Korea,* pt. 3, chap. 4, "Police and Public Security" (Seoul and Tokyo, manuscript in the Office of the Chief of Military History, 1947–48).

10. Gayn, *Japan Diary,* 390; Cumings, *The Origins of the Korean War,* 1:164; Col. William H. Maglin, "Looking Back in History: . . . The Korean National Police" *Military Police Professional Bulletin* (Winter 1999): 67–69; John Muccio to Secretary of State, August 13, 1949, Department of Justice, RDS, Korea. Ch'oe Nûng-jin ("Danny Choy"), chief of the KNP Detective Bureau, called the KNP "the refuge home for Japanese-trained police and traitors," including "corrupt police who were chased out of North Korea by the communists." Cumings, *The Origins of the Korean War,* 1:166, 167. Maglin, who rose to provost marshal, was the son of a New York police captain. He had been a parole officer in New York State; had experience training the French, Italian, and Mexican police; and commanded military police training in Fort Riley, Kansas, during World War II. In North Korea, by contrast, police officers during the colonial period were purged, and authorities worked to rebuild a new police force of people without collaborationist backgrounds. This was a factor accounting for the legitimacy of the revolutionary government, Charles Armstrong notes, although the security structure still built on the foundations of the old in its striving for total information control. Armstrong, *The North Korean Revolution,* 205.

11. Edward Wismer, Police Adviser, to Director of National Police, June 6, 1947, USAFIK, RG 554, Records Regarding Korean Political Affairs (1945–1948), box 26; Kim, *The Unending Korean War,* 185; Cumings, *The Origins of the Korean War,* 1:502. An American police supervisor commented that there was enough evidence on both Chang and Chough to "hang them several times over" (ibid.). Hodge justified their appointment by pointing to their fierce anticommunism and loyalty to the American command. The CIA characterized

Chang, managing director of the bank of Taegu in the 1940s who heralded from one of Korea's oldest and wealthiest families, as "an intelligent, ambitious opportunist who, while basically friendly to the United States, is erratic and unreliable when excited." NSCF, CIA, box 4, HSTL.

12. Stiles and Lyman, "The Administration of Justice in Korea under the Japanese and in South Korea under the U.S. Army Military Government in Korea to August 15, 1958" RDS, Korea; "History of the Korean National Police," August 7, 1948, USAFIK Okinawa, box 25; ; Larsen, "Police and Public Security," 5, 6.

13. "Interview with Lt. Col. Earle L. Miller, Chief of Police of Kyonggi-do, 15 Nov. 1945 to 29 Dec. 1945," February 3, 1946; Harry S. Maglin, "Organization of National Police of Korea," December 27, 1945, USAFIK Okinawa, box 25; "Summation of Non-Military Activities in Korea," September 1946, GHQ-SCAP, 18; "Summation of Non-Military Activities in Korea," February 1948, GHQ-SCAP, 187; Arthur F. Brandstatter, Personnel File, Michigan State University Archives. Beginning his career in 1919, Miller was a patrolman, detective, and head of police training with the Chicago Police Department, teaching courses in pistol firing and ordnance use.

14. "Interview with Major Arthur F. Brandstatter, Police Bureau, 7 December 1945," USAFIK Okinawa, box 25.

15. "Summation of Non-Military Activities in Korea," November 13, 1945, GHQ-SCAP; "History of the Korean National Police," August 7, 1948; "Police Bureau Renovates Good But Wrecked System," The Corps Courieur, February 12, 1946, USAFIK Okinawa, box 26; "Summation of Non-Military Activities in Korea," September 1946, GHQ-SCAP, 18; "Summation of Non-Military Activities in Korea," February 1948, GHQ-SCAP, 187; "Chief of Korean Uniformed Police Visits U.S. Provost Marshall," Journal of Criminal Law, Criminology and Police Science 44 (July–August 1953): 220.

16. "Summation of Non-Military Activities in Korea," November 13, 1945, USAFIK Okinawa, box 26; J. H. Berrean to Major Millard Shaw, Acting Advisor, Department of Police, July 27, 1948, USAFIK Okinawa, box 25; D. L. Nicolson to J. Edgar Hoover, March 29, 1949, RDS, Korea, file 895; Henderson, Korea, 142–43. On the Chinese precedent, see Mary Miles, "The Navy Launched a Dragon," unpublished manuscript, Naval War College, Newport, R.I., chap. 28, "Unit Nine, School of Intelligence and Counter-Espionage."

17. Major Robert K. Sawyer, Military Advisers in Korea: KMAG in Peace and War, The United States Army Historical Series, ed. Walter G. Hermes (Washington, D.C.: OCMH, GPO, 1962), 13; Bruce Cumings, The Korean War: A History (New York: Random House, 2010), 134; Peter Clemens, "Captain James Hausman, U.S. Military Adviser to Korea, 1946–1948: The Intelligence Man on the Spot," Journal of Strategic Studies 25, no. 1 (2002): 184; John Merrill, Korea: The Peninsular Origins of the War (Newark: University of Delaware Press, 1989), 100. Cumings characterized Hausman, who enlisted in the army at the age of sixteen to escape the depression, as the Korean Edward Lansdale (a legendary CIA agent), minus the concern for civic action.

18. Allan R. Millett, "Captain James R. Hausman and the Formation of the Korean Army, 1945–1950," Armed Forces and Society 23 (Summer 1997): 503–37; Clemens, "Captain James Hausman," 170; Allan R. Millett, The War for Korea, 1945–1950: A House Burning (Lawrence: University Press of Kansas, 2005), 173.

19. Joyce Kolko and Gabriel Kolko, The Limits of Power: The World and United States Foreign Policy, 1945–1954 (New York: Harper & Row, 1972), 290; Richard D. Robinson, "A Personal Journey through Time and Space," Journal of International Business Studies 25, no. 3 (1994): 436.

20. Cumings, *The Origins of the Korean War,* 1:267; Henderson, *Korea,* 145; Richard C. Allen, *Korea's Syngman Rhee: An Unauthorized Portrait* (Rutland, Vt.: Charles E. Tuttle, 1960).

21. Max Bishop to Charles Stelle, "Answers to Questions on the Korean Situation in Light of the Withdrawal of Soviet Troops," February 10, 1949, RG 59, RDS, Records of the Division of Research for Far East Reports (1946–1952), box 4, folder 1.

22. Armstrong, *The North Korean Revolution;* Cumings, *The Origins of the Korean War,* 1:267; Donald Nichol, *How Many Times Can I Die?* (Brooksville, Fla.: Vanity Press, 1981), 119; John Reed Hodge to Douglas MacArthur, September 27, 1946, USAFIK Okinawa, box 25; "Communist Capabilities in South Korea," Office of Reports and Estimates, CIA, February 21, 1949, PSF, Truman Papers, HSTL.

23. "Summation of Non-Military Activities in Korea," September 1946, GHQ-SCAP, 18; "Strikes/Riots," September 1946–May 1947, USAFIK Okinawa, box 25, folder 3; "Summation of Non-Military Activities in Korea," September 1946, GHQ-SCAP, 17; 27; Everett F. Drumright to Secretary of State, "Amending of Organization of National Traitors Acts," December 22, 1948, RDS, Korea, file 895; Henderson, *Korea,* 146; Richard D. Robinson, "Betrayal of a Nation," unpublished manuscript, 1960, 147 (courtesy of Harvard Yenching Library); Daily Korean Bulletin, June 14, 1952, NSCF, CIA, box 4, HSTL. Lee Sang Ho, editor of the suspended *Chung Ang Shin Mun,* and Kwang Tai Hyuk, chief of the newspaper's administrative section, were characteristically sentenced to eighteen months' hard labor for printing "inflammatory articles." For harsh police repression of the labor movement, see Hugh Deane, *The Korean War, 1945–1953* (San Francisco: China Books, 1999), 40.

24. Millard Shaw, "Police Comments on Guerrilla Situation," August 6, 1948, USAFIK Okinawa, box 26; George M. McCune, *Korea Today* (Cambridge: Harvard University Press, 1950), 88; Kim, *The Unending Korean War,* 186; Cumings, *The Origins of the Korean War,* 2:207. Yo's daughter suspects that Chang T'aek-sang was the culprit in her father's murder. U.S. military intelligence may have collaborated in the assassination of another of Rhee's rivals, Kim Ku, who was opposed to American intervention. Ku's assassin, An Tu-hui, was released from Taejon penitentiary after a visit by a U.S. Army counterintelligence officer and was afterwards promoted to army major.

25. Nichol, *How Many Times Can I Die,* 135; "Summary Conditions in Korea," November 1–15, 1946, USAFIK Okinawa, box 25; "Summation of Non-Military Activities in Korea," June 1947, GHQ-SCAP, 26. Some of these rackets involved U.S. soldiers. An army colonel, for example, looted over four thousand cases of precious artworks from museums, shrines, and temples. After he was caught, he was sent home on "sick leave." Robinson, "Betrayal of a Nation," 290.

26. Cumings, *The Origins of the Korean War,* 2:188.

27. "History of the Police Department," USAFIK Okinawa, box 25; Robinson, "A Personal Journey through Time and Space," 437; Robinson, "Betrayal of a Nation," 155. Robinson subsequently resigned from the army and became a professor of management at MIT. He wrote some of the first articles in the U.S. press on Palestinian refugees. In North Korea, while dissidents were sent to labor and "re-education" camps, the use of torture to extract confessions was abolished and according to the leading authority on the revolution, rarely practiced. Armstrong, *The North Korean Revolution,* 208.

28. "Korean-American Conference," October 29, 1946; and "Report Special Agent Wittmer, G-2,Summary," November 3, 1946, USAFIK Okinawa, boxes 25 and 26.

29. "Korean-American Conference"; Robinson, "Betrayal of a Nation," 151; "South Korea: A Police State?" February 16, 1948, RDS, Division of Research for Far East Reports (1946–1952), box 3; "Communist Capabilities in South Korea."

30. Kim, *The Unending Korean War*, 123.

31. James I. Matray, *The Reluctant Crusade: American Foreign Policy in Korea, 1941–1950* (Honolulu: University of Hawaii Press, 1985), 77; Gayn, *Japan Diary*, 371. Yi Pom Sok's OSS connections are revealed in Robert John Myers, *Korea in the Cross Currents: A Century of Struggle and the Crisis of Reunification* (New York: Palgrave Macmillan, 2001), 74. Lee's associate An Ho-Sang apparently served in the Hitler jugend for three years. Voss, an OSS agent and fascist admirer, was a council member of the Boy Scouts of America and founder of the Boy Scouts in the Philippines.

32. Adviser Millard Shaw considered the cross-border operations acts "bordering on terrorism" which "precipitate retaliatory raids . . . from the North." Report, Major Millard Shaw, Acting Advisor, "Guard of the 38th Parallel by the National Police," November 1946, USAFIK Okinawa, box 25, folder 3; Cumings, *The Origins of the Korean War*, 2:195. The first to challenge the standard interpretation was I. F. Stone in *The Hidden History of the Korean War* (New York: Monthly Review Press, 1969), originally published in 1952. New evidence from Soviet archives about Stalin's reluctant backing of the North Korean invasion does not contradict the point that the Rhee regime and the United States were at least equally responsible for the outbreak of the war.

33. "Police Fraternization Or Being Bribed by Prisoners," August 28, 1946, USAFIK Okinawa, box 26, folder 10; G-2 Periodic Report, "Civil Disturbances," Seoul, Korea, September 1947, USAFIK Okinawa, box 25; Henderson, *Korea*, 144.

34. Kolko and Kolko, *The Limits of Power*, 288; John Caldwell, with Lesley Frost, *The Korea Story* (Chicago: Henry Regnery Co., 1952), 8; Robinson, "Betrayal of a Nation," 156.

35. Roy C. Stiles and Albert Lyman, "The Administration of Justice in Korea under the Japanese and in South Korea under the U.S. Army Military Government in Korea to August 15, 1948," paper by American Advisory Staff, Department of Justice, RDS, Korea, file 895; "Joint Korean-American Conference," October 1946, USAFIK Okinawa, box 26; Gayn, *Japan Diary*, 423.

36. "South Korea: A Police State?" February 16, 1948, RDS, Division of Research for Far East Reports, 1946–1952, box 3.

37. Larsen, "Police and Public Security," 60.

38. "A History of the Korean National Police (KNP)," August 7, 1948, USAFIK Okinawa, box 25; "Let Us Avenge the Victims of Kwanju," People's Committee pamphlet. August 25, 1946, USAFIK Okinawa, box 25; Cumings, *Origins of the Korean War*, 1:364–66, 550.

39. George E. Ogle, *South Korea: Dissent within the Economic Miracle* (London: Zed Books, 1990), 12; Henderson, *Korea*, 147; Cumings, *The Origins of the Korean War*, 1:356–57. At Yongchon, 350 kilometers from Seoul, a mob of ten thousand disarmed and kidnapped forty policemen after ambushing the police station and burned the homes of rightist backers of the police.

40. John R. Hodge to Douglas MacArthur, SCAP, April 17, 1948; Police Diary, Major Albert Brown, Survey, October 1946, and "Korean-American Conference," USAFIK, Okinawa, box 26; "Summation of Non-Military Activities in Korea," July 1947, GHQ-SCAP, 34; Henderson, *Korea*, 146; Cumings, *The Origins of the Korean War*, 1:357. Henderson notes that not one identifiable North Korean agent was involved in the protests, which leftists claimed exceeded anything that had taken place under the Japanese.

41. "Summation of Non-Military Activities," February 1948, GHQ-SCAP, 182; Richard J. Johnston, "Political Jailing in Korea Denied: Authorities Say 17,867 Held Are Accused of Theft, Riot, Murder and Other Crimes," *New York Times*, November 26, 1947; Richard J. Johnston, "Seoul Aids Police in Checking Reds," *New York Times*, September 6, 1949; Richard J. Johnston, "Korean Reds Fight Police and Others," *New York Times*, July 29, 1947;

"Summation of Non-Military Activities in Korea," September 1946, GHQ-SCAP, 22; "Summation of Non-Military Activities in Korea," December 1947, GHQ-SCAP, 165; Henderson, *Korea,* 167; Maglin, "Looking Back in History," 69. A conservative Korean newspaper proclaimed, "Sometimes even those known as passionate patriots are accused as leftist subversive elements without sufficient material evidence." Captain Richard D. Robinson details a case in which the mother of one of the Taegu rioters was tortured to death by police. Robinson, "Betrayal of a Nation," 156.

42. "History of the Police Department" and "Investigation of the Police," July 30, 1946, USAFIK Okinawa, box 25; "Visit to Wanju Jail," August 1, 1946, USAFIK Okinawa, box 27, folder 1; "Sanitary Inspection of Jails," USAFIK Okinawa, box 26, folder 4; Gayn, *Japan Diary,* 406, 407; Robinson, "Betrayal of a Nation," 152.

43. Major General W. F. Dean to Lt. Commander John R. Hodge, "Review by the Department of Justice of Persons Confined to Prisons or Police Jails Who Might Be Considered Political Prisoners," April 5, 1948, USAFIK, Records of the General Headquarters, Far East Command, General Correspondences (1943–1946), AI 1370, box 1.

44. "Summation of Non-Military Activities," April 1948, GHQ-SCAP, 170; "Summation of Non-Military Activities in Korea," July 1947, GHQ-SCAP, 22.

45. "Summation of Non-Military Activities," January 1948, GHQ-SCAP, 181; "Report of Daily Police Activities," USAFIK Okinawa, box 27, folder Civil Police; "Summation of Non-Military Activities in Korea," August 1947, GHQ-SCAP, 196; Larsen, "Police and Public Security," 133, 145; Bertrand M. Roehner, "Relations between Allied Forces and the Population of Korea," Working Report, Institute for Theoretical and High Energy Physics, University of Paris, 2010, 168.

46. Cumings, *The Origins of the Korean War,* 2:252.

47. Cumings, *The Korean War,* 122; Millett, "Captain James R. Hausman and the Formation of the Korean Army," 503.

48. "Cheju-do: Summation of Non-Military Activities," June 1948, GHQ-SCAP, 160; Merrill, *Korea,* 66.

49. "Field Report, Mission to Korea, U.S. Military Advisory Group to ROK," RG 469, Mission to Korea, U.S. Military Advisory Group to the ROK, Records Related to the KNP (1948–1961) (hereafter KNP), box 4, folder Cheju-do; Cumings, *The Origins of the Korean War,* 2:250–59; Merrill, *Korea,* 125. My thanks to Cheju-do native Sinae Hyun for providing me with a better understanding of the internal dynamics fueling the violence there during this period. After the massacre, the U.S. military command oversaw an increased police presence and stepped up local training efforts at the Cheju-do police school, which they financed. William F. Dean to Director of National Police, July 30, 1948, USAFIK Okinawa, box 26, folder Cheju-do.

50. Merrill, *Korea,* 113; *Time,* November 14, 1948, 6.

51. "Award of UN Service Medal to the National Police, Mission to Korea, Office of Government Services, Senior Adviser to KNP," February 10, 1954, PSD, GHQ-SCAP (1955–1957), box 1, folder Awards and Decorations; "Policy Research Study: Internal Warfare and the Security of the Underdeveloped States," November 20, 1961, JFKL, POF, box 98; Kim, *The Unending Korean War,* 122; Tim Weiner, *Legacy of Ashes: The History of the CIA* (New York: Doubleday, 2007), 56, 57. Haney's career was saved because he assisted Allen Dulles's son, who had been wounded in combat. Future OPS staffer Garland Williams was also affiliated with the clandestine operations in North Korea.

52. Charles J. Hanley and Jae-Soon Chang, "Summer of Terror: At Least 100,000 Said Executed by Korean Ally of US in 1950," *Japan Focus,* July 23, 2008.

53. James Cameron, *Point of Departure* (London: Oriel Press, 1978), 131–32; McDonald,

Korea, 42; also Nichol, *How Many Times Can I Die,* 128. CIC agent Donald Nichol, a confidant of Rhee, reported that he stood by helplessly in Suwan as "the condemned were hastily pushed into line along the edge of the newly opened grave. They were quickly shot in the head and pushed in the grave. . . . I tried to stop this from happening, however, I gave up when I saw I was wasting my time" (ibid.)

54. Hanley and Chang, "Summer of Terror"; Bruce Cumings, "The South Korean Massacre at Taejon: New Evidence on U.S. Responsibility and Cover-Up," *Japan Focus,* July 23, 2008; Bruce Cumings, *Korea's Place in the Sun: A Modern* History (New York: Norton, 1997), 25; Kim, *The Unending Korean War;* Halliday and Cumings, *Korea;* Charles J. Hanley, Sang-Hun Choe, and Martha Mendoza, *The Bridge at No Gun Ri: A Hidden Nightmare from the Korean War* (New York: Holt, 2000). Reflecting the barbarity of U.S. wartime conduct, General Curtis LeMay boasted, "We burned just about every town in North Korea—and South Korea too." Cumings, *Korea's Place in the Sun,* 298.

55. On U.S. strategic designs in Southeast Asia, see Chalmers Johnson, *Blowback: The Costs and Consequences of American Empire* (New York: Henry Holt, 2000); Gabriel Kolko, *Confronting the Third World: United States Foreign Policy, 1945–1980* (New York: Pantheon, 1990); John W. Dower, "Occupied Japan and the American Lake, 1945–1950," in *America's Asia: Dissenting Essays on Asian-American Relations,* ed. Edward Friedman and Mark Selden (New York: Vintage Books, 1971), 186–207.

56. Colonel Albert Haney, "OCB Report Pursuant to NSC Action 1290-d," August 5, 1955, DDEL, OCB, box 17, folder Internal Security; "Analysis of Internal Security Situation in ROK Pursuant to Recommended Action for 1290-d," in *Foreign Relations of the United States, 1955–1957,* pt. 2, *Korea,* ed. Louis Smith (Washington, D.C.: GPO, 1993), 183.

57. "Bandit Activity Report," May 1, 1954, KNP (1953–1955), box 4; Park Byong Bae, Chief, Security Division, "Operation Report," July 1, 1954, and "Periodic Operations Report," May 27, 1954, KNP (1953–1955), box 4; "Results of Police Operations," July 15, 1954, KNP (1953–1955), box 2; "Summary of NSC Action 1290-d Report on Korea," DDEL, OCB, box 17, folder Internal Security.

58. "G-2 Section Report," February 2, 1954, KNP (1953–1955), box 4.

59. "Quarterly Historical Report," July 10, 1954, KNP (1953–1955), box 4; also "G-2 Section Report," March 25; May 2, 1954.

60. "Johnny" to Police Adviser, "Bandit Activity Report," May 1, 1954, KNP (1953–1955), box 4.

61. "Police Wipe Out Last Known Guerrilla Band and "Red Bandit Chief Slain, Two Killed," *Korea Times,* December 1956, NA.

62. Henderson, *Korea,* 173.

63. William Maxfield to Director, NP [National Police], ROK, February 16, 1954, KNP (1953–1955), box 1; Gregg Brazinsky, *Nation Building in South Korea: Koreans, Americans, and the Making of a Democracy* (Chapel Hill: University of North Carolina Press, 2007), 28–30; *Report of an Amnesty International Mission to the Republic of Korea, March 27–April 9, 1975* (London: Amnesty International, 1977), 29; William J. Lederer, *A Nation of Sheep* (New York: Norton, 1961), 79; "Combined Korean Communities in USA Picket White House to Protest Carnage of Korean Youth," April 22, 1960, DDEL, OCB, White House Office, Central Files, General File, Korea, box 821; Peer De Silva, *Sub Rosa: The CIA and the Uses of Intelligence* (New York: Times Books, 1978), 163.

64. "Solon Alleges Police Attack," *Korea Times,* October 26, 1956; "Captain Warren S. Olin: Chungmu Distinguished Military Service Medal with Silver Star," March 1, 1955, Republic of Korea, courtesy National Archives and Records Administration, St. Louis; see also "Culprit Charges Police Plotted Murder," *Korea Times,* December 15, 1956; "May 5 Riot

Nets Prison Term for 14," *Korea Times,* May 14, 1956. A Pacific war veteran from New Jersey, Olin won a Bronze Star and a Silver Star and went on to head the army's Criminal Investigation Branch in Vietnam, retiring in 1973.

65. Kim, *The Unending Korean War,* 201–2; Cumings, *The Origins of the Korean War,* 2:265. For eight months in 1947, Kim was Chang Taek-sang's personal bodyguard.

66. Muccio, quoted in Cumings, *The Korean War,* 183. One document preserved at the National Archives which points to the close symbiotic relationship between U.S. advisers and General Kim was a letter from Colonel Joseph Pettet of the Public Safety Branch thanking him for "the wonderful party you gave us on October 29, 1954. The food and entertainment was superb as always at a 'Tiger' Kim party." Joseph Pettet to Chief Kim, November 1, 1954, KNP (1953–1955), box 1.

67. "Quarterly Historical Report," July 10, 1954, KNP (1953–1955), box 4, folder 3; Albert R. Haney, "Observations and Suggestions Concerning OISP," January 30, 1957, DDEL, OCB, box 18, folder Internal Security.

68. Lyman Lemnitzer to Thomas Wilson, Assistant Chief of Public Safety Division, Senior Adviser to KNP, USOM Mission to Korea, June 5, 1956, KNP (1955–1957), box 4, folder 3; "Periodic Operations Report," May 27, 1954, KNP (1955–1957), box 4; "1956 Guide," KNP (1955–1957), box 1, folder National Police Laboratory File. On Goin, see Lauren J. Goin, "Details Reproduced by Metal Casting," *Journal of Criminal Law, Criminology, and Police Science* 43 (July–August 1952): 250–55; Lauren J. Goin, William H. McKee, and Paul L. Kirk, "Human Hair Studies: Application of the Micro-determinant of Comparative Density," *Journal of Criminal Law, Criminology, and Police Science* 43 (July–August 1952): 263–73. Goin served in the navy during the Pacific war and was for five years chief micro-analyst at the Wisconsin State Crime Lab before becoming director at Allegheny. He wrote his master's thesis at Berkeley under Paul Kirk, who was well known in the field of criminalistics and worked on the Manhattan Project in World War II.

69. MSUG Monthly Report, October 1960, MSUA, Vietnam Project, box 679. On the repressive nature of Chiang's secret police apparatus in Taiwan, see Jay Taylor, *The Generalissimo's Son: Chiang Ching-kuo and the Revolutions in China and Taiwan* (Cambridge: Harvard University Press, 2000). Taylor quotes a CIA operative who reported hearing executions being carried out in a soccer stadium: "Ching-kuo got all the communists but also a lot of others" (211).

70. Gene E. Carte and Elaine Carte, *Police Reform in the United States: The Era of August Vollmer, 1905–1932* (Berkeley: University of California Press, 1975), 49; Nathan Douthit, "August Vollmer, Berkeley's First Chief of Police, and the Emergence of Police Professionalism," *California Historical Review* 54 (Summer 1975): 101–24; O. W. Wilson, "August Vollmer," *Journal of Criminal Law, Criminology, and Police Science* 44 (May–June 1953): 95. Speaking out in 1936 against the War on Drugs, Vollmer presciently stated, "Stringent laws, spectacular police drives, vigorous prosecution, and imprisonment of addicts and peddlers have proved not only useless and enormously expensive but they are also unjustifiably and unbelievably cruel in their application." August Vollmer, *The Police and Modern Society* (Berkeley: University of California Press, 1936), 117.

71. Ray Foreaker to Michigan State College, East Lansing, March 9, 1956; "National Police Advisors Have Varied Assignments," USIS Seoul, February 15, 1956, KNP (1955–1957), box 1, folder 3. Marc Logie, who fought with the GMD and French foreign legion, succeeded Foreaker as PSD chief.

72. See William Turner, *The Police Establishment* (New York: G. P. Putnam's Sons, 1968), 170. Many of the Berkeley criminologists who advised the Oakland police went on to act as consultants with problem-ridden police departments across the United States. John Ingersoll,

for example, rose to become director of the Bureau of Narcotics and Dangerous Drugs, spearheading drug war programs in Southeast Asia. Charles Gain, chief of police during the 1960s and villain to the New Left and the Black Panthers, was also a Vollmer student and protégé who served with the Berkeley Police Department. Some of his recollections are available at the Vollmer oral history project on UC Berkeley Bancroft Library's website. On racial problems, see Edward Keating, *Free Huey!* (San Francisco: Ramparts Press, 1971), and the memoirs of Black Panther leaders.

73. "List of Police Officers Who Have Been to the United States," KNP (1948–1961), box 3, folder Korean Student Records; "Chief of Korean Uniformed Police Visits U.S. Provost Marshall," *Journal of Criminal Law, Criminology, and Police Science* 44 (July–August 1953): 220.

74. Turner, *The Police Establishment*, 72; Joseph G. Woods, "The Progressives and the Police: Urban Reform and the Professionalization of the Los Angeles Police" (Ph.D. diss., UCLA, 1973). After their training was complete, the KNP officers were taken to Disneyland. Howard K. Smith of ABC commented after Parker's death from a heart attack that "his policemen won a reputation for efficiency but also for implacable enmity toward the lower strata of society, the poor, the ignorant, the unemployed." Turner, *The Police Establishment*, 84. His bigotry was evident when, after the Watts uprising, he told reporters that somebody had thrown a rock and, "like monkeys in a zoo," others followed. Alisa S. Kramer, "William H. Parker and the Thin Blue Line: Politics, Public Relations, and Policing in Postwar Los Angeles" (Ph.D. diss., American University, 2007), 290.

75. "Juvenile Reformatories," September 23, 1955, KNP (1953–1955), box 1, folder 3; "Information Related to the Establishment of a Reformatory," KNP (1953–1955), box 2.

76. American embassy, Tehran, to Secretary of State, "Use of Light Aircraft in Opium Eradication Campaign," September 26, 1969, RG 286, USAID, Operations Division, Africa and the Near East and South Asia Branch, box 62, folder 2.

77. J. P Anninos, "Narrative Report of Korean Gangster Operations in Pusan," February 11, 1954; and "Operations of Gangsters," KNP (1953–1955), box 1, folder 3; "Narcotic Trade and Black-Marketing," July 2, 1955, KNP (1953–1955), box 1, folder Monthly Narcotics Reports; "Black Market," June 20, 1955, KNP (1953–1955), box 1, folder Black Market Activities.

78. "Report on Conduct of Korean Military Police Personnel," June 27, 1955, KNP (1953–1955), box 1, folder 3; "Report of Accident with Fatality," March 16, 1955; and "Summary of UN-ROK Incidents Reported by the KNP," May 1955, KNP (1953–1955), box 1, folder 2; "Summary of US-ROK Offenses and Incidents," KNP (1953–1955), box 1, folder Coordinating Committee Law and Order; "Demonstrations at Inchon," August 18, 1955, KNP (1953–1955), box 3.

79. "Policy Research Study: Internal Warfare and the Security of the Underdeveloped States," November 20, 1961, POF, box 98.

80. See Byong Kook-Kim and Ezra Vogel, eds., *The Park Chung-Hee Era: The Transformation of South Korea* (Cambridge: Harvard University Press, 2011); Scott Anderson and Jon Lee Anderson, *Inside the League: The Shocking Exposé of How Terrorists, Nazis, and Latin American Death Squads Have Infiltrated the World Anti-Communist League* (New York: Dodd, Mead, 1986), 52; Cumings, *The Origins of the Korean War,* 2:266. Park's treachery after the Yosu rebellion resulted in the purge of hundreds of constabulary officers and the death of many former friends. Hausman's involvement in the coup is acknowledged in Clemons, "Captain James Hausman," 193.

81. Current Foreign Relations, "Korea Purifies Political Activities," March 21, 1962, JFKL, NSF, box 431; Ogle, *South Korea,* 23.

82. Lauren J. Goin, Lt. Shannon, and Arthur M. Thurston, "Survey of Civil Internal Security Forces, Republic of Korea," May 1966, RG 286, USAID, OPS, Programs, Surveys, and

Evaluations, box 6; Johnson, *Blowback*, 107; De Silva, *Sub Rosa*, xi. De Silva incidentally helped recruit Nazi spy Reinhard Gehlen after World War II and was involved with the Phoenix program in Vietnam. Information on Thurston was provided by Sergeant Gary Wilkinson of the Indiana State Police Department, an acquaintance of some of Thurston's former colleagues. Thurston, who also served with the police programs in Indonesia, Libya, and Somalia, died in the early 2000s.

83. "Korea: A Political-Military Study of South Korean Forces, Intelligence Annex to Study on Korea, Prepared by Defense Intelligence Agency," April 1962, JFKL, NSF, box 431; Thomas A. Finn and James A. Cretecos, "Evaluation of the Public Safety Program, USAID, Korea, June 28, 1971–July 18, 1971," http://pdf.usaid.gov/pdf_docs/PDABZ913.pdf; Goin, Shannon, and Thurston, "Survey of Civil Internal Security Forces, Republic of Korea." On Jessup's tenure in Indiana, see Marilyn S. Olsen, *Gangsters, Gunfire, and Political Intrigue: The Story of the Indiana State Police* (Indianapolis: .38 Special Press), 2001, 75; Julien Mader, *Who's Who in the CIA* (Berlin: J. Mader, 1968), 261.

84. "Korea: A Political-Military Study of South Korean Forces," April 1962, JFKL, NSC, box 431; Byron Engle to Frank Kolnacki, December 13, 1968, TSD, box 5, folder Korea; Lauren J. Goin, Memoir, April 1991, Institute of Inter-American Affairs Collection, Courtesy of University of Illinois at Springfield Archives, Special Collections. CIA agent George "Speedy" Gaspard stated that police under his command "killed 119 [North Korean] agents . . . . We didn't take any prisoners, that was difficult to do. They wouldn't just surrender." In George Schultz Jr., *The Secret War against Hanoi* (New York: Harper Collins, 1999), 58.

85. "Alleged ROK Massacres," RG 472, Records of the Armed Forces in South East Asia (RAFSEA), Criminal Investigations Branch, boxes 34–36; Noam Chomsky and Edward S. Herman, *The Political Economy of Human Rights: The Washington Connection and Third World Fascism* (Boston: South End Press, 1979), 313; Frank Baldwin, Diane Jones, and Michael Jones, *America's Rented Troops: South Koreans in Vietnam* (Philadelphia: American Friends Services Committee, 1975); Bernd Greiner, *War without Fronts: The USA in Vietnam* (New Haven: Yale University Press, 2009), 190.

86. Interview with Jack Goin, December 9, 1975, and Byron Engle, January 27, 1976, in William D. Steeves Jr., "The U.S. Public Safety Program, Its Evolution and Demise" (master's thesis, George Washington University, School of International Affairs, 1975), 9; Brazinsky, *Nation Building in South Korea*. Many ideologically driven scholars adopt the same perspective in presenting Korea as a successful case of U.S. foreign policy, Brazinsky included. Paul Wolfowitz argued in a 2009 *New York Times* editorial that South Korea should serve as a model for U.S. "nation-building" in Iraq.

87. *Report of an Amnesty International Mission to the Republic of Korea, 27 March–9 April 1975*, 8–9, 37. See also "New Repression in South Korea," *New York Times*, May 29, 1980; Suh Sung, *Unbroken Spirits: Nineteen Years in South Korea's Gulag*, trans. Jean Ingles (New York: Rowman and Littlefield, 2001).

88. See Henry Scott-Stokes and Jai-Eui Lee, eds., *The Kwangju Uprising: Eyewitness Press Accounts of Korea's Tiananmen*, foreword by Kim Dae Jung (New York: M. E. Sharpe, 2000); Timothy Shorrock, "The U.S. Role in Korea in 1979–1980," *Sisa Journal*, February 28, 1996, www.kimsoft.com/Korea/Kwangju3.htm; Kim, *The Unending Korean War*, ix; Johnson, *Blowback*, 116. Richard Holbrooke, who later served as special envoy to Afghanistan, was among the State Department officials who gave a green light for and then covered up the atrocity.

89. Martha K. Huggins, Mika Haritos-Fatouros, and Philip Zimbardo, *Violence Workers: Police Torturers and Murderers Reconstruct Brazilian Atrocities* (Berkeley: University of California Press, 2002), 8.

5. "Free Government Cannot Exist without Safeguards against Subversion"

1. Joseph Knox, "Former Greensboro Police Chief Now Taking 'Home Leave' in City," *Greensboro Daily News,* December 12, 1960. This information was also conveyed to me in a phone conversation with Williamson's daughter Virginia "Patsy" Harrington, a retired journalist who spent time in the Far East as a teenager when her father was serving there.

2. "Philippines' Police Work Appraised: Williamson Points to Shortcomings," *Greensboro Daily News,* July 1956 (courtesy of Patsy Harrington, Jeter Williamson family collection). On Lansdale, see Richard Drinnon, *Facing West: The Metaphysics of Indian-Hating and Empire-Building* (Norman: Oklahoma University Press, 1980), 392; Jonathan Nashel, *Edward Lansdale's Cold War* (Amherst: University of Massachusetts Press, 2006).

3. Noam Chomsky, "Vietnam and United States Global Strategy," in *The Chomsky Reader,* ed. James Peck (New York: Pantheon Books, 1987), 231; Walt W. Rostow and Richard V. Hatch, *An American Policy in Asia* (Cambridge: MIT Press, 1955), 7.

4. See Richard J. Aldrich, Gary D. Rawnsley, and Ming-Yeh Rawnsley, eds., *The Clandestine Cold War in Asia, 1945–65: Western Intelligence, Propaganda and Special Operations* (London: Frank Cass, 2000); Peter Dale Scott, *The War Conspiracy: The Secret Road to the Second Indochina War* (New York: Bobbs-Merrill, 1972).

5. Dean Acheson, memo for the President [Harry S. Truman], "Allocation of Section 303 Funds to Provide Police Equipment for the Indonesian Constabulary," January 9, 1950, RG 59, RDS, Bureau of Far Eastern Affairs, Records Relating to Economic Aid, box 3, and RDS, Bureau of Far Eastern Affairs, Indonesia (hereafter RDS, Indonesia), box 5106, folder 1; also *Foreign Relations of the United States, 1950: East Asia and the Pacific,* vol. 6 (Washington, D.C.: GPO, 1976), 964–66; Gabriel Kolko, *Confronting the Third World: United States Foreign Policy, 1945–1980* (New York: Pantheon, 1988).

6. Said Soekanto, Chief of State Police, Republic of Indonesia, to Secretary of State, June 2, 1949, RDS, Indonesia, box 5106, folder 1; Audrey R. Kahin and George McT. Kahin, *Subversion as Foreign Policy: The Secret Eisenhower and Dulles Debacle in Indonesia* (New York: New Press, 1995), 31; Robert J. McMahon, *Colonialism and Cold War: The United States and the Struggle for Indonesian Independence, 1945–49* (Ithaca: Cornell University Press, 1981), 280. My thanks to Marieke Bloembergen for providing me with information on Soekanto.

7. "Analysis of the Internal Security Situation in Indonesia and Recommended Action," Operations Coordinating Board, Washington, D.C., November 16, 1955, Papers of LBJ, NSF, White House Office, National Security Council Staff, Operations Coordinating Board, Washington, D.C., box 43, folder Indonesia; George McT. Kahin, *Nationalism and Revolution in Indonesia* (Ithaca: Cornell University Press, 1952).

8. William Lacey to Louise Page Morris, January 5, 1950, RDS, Indonesia, box 5106, folder 1. For a portrait of Page Morris, see Michael Holzman, *James Jesus Angleton, the CIA, and the Craft of Counterintelligence* (Amherst: University of Massachusetts Press, 2008), 146–47; Ted Morgan, *A Covert Life: Jay Lovestone, Anti-communist and Spymaster* (New York: Random House, 1999), 259–80. "Pagie," as she was known, carried on a twenty-five-year affair with Lovestone and was the mistress of "Wild Bill" Donovan during her days in the OSS. Her brother Edward was also in the CIA.

9. Matthew Fox to American embassy, Djakarta, and Raden Soekanto to William Lacey, May 11, 1949, both RDS, Indonesia, box 5106, folder 1. On Fox's political connections and business dealings, see Peter Dale Scott, "Exporting Military-Economic Development: America and the Overthrow of Sukarno, 1965–1967," in *Ten Years' Military Terror in Indonesia,* ed. Malcolm Caldwell (Nottingham: Bertrand Russell Peace Foundation, 1975), 213; Gerlof D.

Horman, "American Business Interests in the Indonesian Republic, 1946–1949," *Indonesia* 35 (April 1983): 125–32. Fox was a onetime executive of Universal International Pictures who had served on the war planning board and in the U.S. Army during World War II.

10. Acheson, "Allocation of Section 303 Funds," RDS, Indonesia, box 5106.

11. R. E. Murphy to John Peurifoy, "Training and Indoctrination in the U.S. of Certain Indonesian Police Officials," January 26, 1950, RDS, Indonesia, box 5106.

12. Mr. Merchant to Mr. Peurifoy, "Training and Indoctrination in the U.S. of Certain Indonesian Police Officials," January 27, 1950, RDS, Indonesia, box 5106.

13. William Lacy to Dean Rusk, "Regarding Indonesian Police Trainee Program," March 14, 1951; Louise Morris to William B. Lacey, January 18, 1950; H. Merle Cochran to Lt. Col. Beach, "U.S. Training Aids for the Indonesian Police," December 8, 1950; R. E. Murphy to John Peurifoy, January 26, 1950; William O. Hall to Mr. Merchant, February 6, 1950; American embassy, Djakarta, to Soekanto, April 19, 1950, all RDS, Indonesia, box 5106; Joseph Burkholder Smith, *Portrait of a Cold Warrior* (New York: G. P. Putnam, 1976), 221.

14. R. H. Ingersoll to James O'Sullivan, "Indonesian Police Intelligence," April 28, 1950, RDS, Indonesia, box 5106; Louis Kubler to Merle Cochran, April 18, 1951, RDS, Indonesia, box 5106; "Commendation for Lt. Col. Louis Kubler," August 30, 1946, RG 226, OSS Personnel Files, box 423.

15. "Committee to Strengthen the Security of the Free World," January 26, 1963, RWK, box 412, folder 1; American embassy, Djakarta, to Secretary of State, December 11, 1964, Papers of LBJ, NSF, Asia and the Pacific, box 246, folder Indonesia; intelligence memo, HSTL, NSCF, CIA, box 2.

16. "Analysis of the Internal Security Situation in Indonesia and Recommended Action," Operations Coordinating Board, Washington, D.C., November 16, 1955, DDEL, OCB, box 43, folder Indonesia; Vijay Prashad, *The Darker Nations: A People's History of the Third World* (New York: New Press, 2007); Kahin and Kahin, *Subversion as Foreign Policy.*

17. John Foster Dulles to American embassy, Djakarta, June 3, 1955, RDS, box 4681, Hugh Cumming, Djakarta, to Secretary of State, June 10, 1955, RDS, Indonesia, box 4681.

18. American embassy to Secretary of State, September 13, 1958, RDS, Indonesia, box 4681; Howard Jones to Secretary of State, December 19, 1959, RDS, Indonesia, box 4681; Joseph J. Lingo and Melville M. "Buck" Fruit, "Confidential Program Evaluation: Study Report of Police Assistance Project in Indonesia," March 1963, RG 286, Records of the USAID, OPS, Internal Defense and Public Safety, Office of the Director (hereafter IPS), box 8, folder Indonesia; Michael McClintock, *Instruments of Statecraft: U.S. Guerrilla Warfare, Counterinsurgency, and Counter-Terrorism, 1940–1990* (New York: Pantheon Books, 1992), 44. Another adviser, Bob Brougham, was a former navy pilot and bush pilot for missionaries in Borneo.

19. "Analysis of the Internal Security Situation in Indonesia and Recommended Action," Operations Coordinating Board, Washington, D.C., November 16, 1955, DDEL, OCB, box 43, folder Indonesia; "OCB Report Pursuant to NSC Action 1290-d," September 12, 1955, DDEL, OCB, box 17, folder Internal Security; American embassy, Manila, to American embassy, Djakarta, February 25, 1955, RDS, Indonesia, box 5106.

20. William Blum, *Killing Hope: United States Military and CIA Interventions since World War II* (Monroe, Me.: Common Courage Press, 1998), 102; Smith, *Portrait of a Cold Warrior,* 240. Liberal support for the repression of communists is outlined in Arthur Schlesinger Jr., *The Vital Center: The Politics of Freedom* (1949), rev. ed. (Boston: Houghton Mifflin, 1962), 135.

21. Seymour Weiss to Mr. Wilson, Indonesian Police, April 17, 1959, American embassy,

Djakarta, to Department of State, RDS, Indonesia, box 4681; American embassy, Djakarta, to Department of State, "Indonesian Prisons at Cheribon and Tjilatjap (Nusa Kanbargon)," August 1, 1959, RDS, Indonesia, box 4681. Much as in Castro's Cuba, foreign interference caused Sukarno to crack down more harshly on dissenters and led him to initiate a system of "guided democracy" in which state power was centralized.

22. American embassy, Djakarta, to Secretary of State, March 3, 1953, RDS, Indonesia, box 5106; American embassy, Manila, to American embassy, Djakarta, February 25, 1955, RDS, Indonesia, box 4681.

23. Bob Fruit, "Indonesian Police Training Project," from James Galbraith to Mr. Day, August 6, 1954, RDS, Indonesia, box 5106.

24. "Policy of RI Police," April 2, 1958, American embassy, Djakarta, to Department of State, RDS, Indonesia, box 4681; Kahin and Kahin, *Subversion as Foreign Policy*, 120; Kenneth J. Conboy and James Morrison, *Feet to the Fire: Covert Operations in Indonesia, 1957–1958* (Annapolis: Naval Institute Press, 1998).

25. Kahin and Kahin, *Subversion as Foreign Policy*, 180; Blum, *Killing Hope*, 103; Tim Weiner, *Legacy of Ashes: The History of the CIA* (New York: Anchor, 2008), 175, 176. After securing his release in 1962, Attorney General Robert Kennedy allegedly told Pope, who had dropped supplies for the French at Dienbienphu, to "lose himself in the United States" and never speak of his experience again. In 2005 he told a reporter: "I enjoyed killing Communists. I liked to kill Communists any way I could get them." Weiner, *Legacy of Ashes*, 175.

26. Howard Jones to Secretary of State, December 19, 1959, RDS, Indonesia, box 4681.

27. Bradley R. Simpson, *Economists with Guns: Authoritarian Development and U.S.-Indonesian Relations, 1960–1968* (Palo Alto: Stanford University Press, 2008), 81, 82; Robert Komer to Mr. Davis, "Indonesian Civic Action and Mobrig," July 19, 1962; "Committee to Strengthen the Security of the Free World," RWK, box 412, folder 1.

28. Byron Engle to Robert Lowe, April 1963; also Paul H. Skuse, "Public Safety Monthly Report," December 6, 1962; "Public Safety Monthly Report," April 1963, all TSD, box 9, folder Indonesia.

29. Henry M. Samoriski, "Mobrig Training Programs," February 21, 1963, TSD, box 9, folder Indonesia; "Memo for the President: Assistance Program in Indonesia, 1964," RG 286, USAID, OPS, East Asia Branch, Records Relating to Indonesia (1963–1966), box 1, folder Advisory Training and Assistance; "Public Safety Program Summary, Indonesia," May 13, 1963, IPS, box 8; George Ball to Secretary of State, December 11, 1964, Papers of LBJ, NSF, Country File, box 246, folder Indonesia. Background on Robert Lowe was found in his OSS file, RG 266, Records of the OSS, box 464. Lowe was trained at the secret Camp X in Oshawa, Ontario, where agents were taught the art of silent killing, among other clandestine skills.

30. Director of Intelligence, "Indonesian Communist Party," April 27, 1966; and "The Upheaval of Indonesia," October 8, 1965, Papers of LBJ, NSF, Country File, box 246, folder Indonesia; Kathy Kadane, "Ex-Agents Say CIA Compiled Death Lists for Indonesia, *San Francisco Examiner*, May 20, 1990; David Ransom, "The Berkeley Mafia and the Indonesia Massacre," in *Two, Three . . . Many Vietnams: A Radical Reader on the Wars in Southeast Asia and the Conflicts at Home*, ed. the Editors of *Ramparts* with Banning Garrett and Katherine Barkley (San Francisco: Canfield Press, 1971), 144, 145. On the circumstances surrounding the coup, see John Roosa, *Pretext for Mass Murder: The September 30th Movement and Suharto's Coup d'État in Indonesia* (Madison: University of Wisconsin Press, 2006); Ralph W. McGehee, "The Indonesian Massacre and the CIA," *Covert Action Quarterly* 35 (Fall 1990): 57.

31. Howard Jones to Secretary of State, "Transshipment of Public Safety Commodities," April 9, 1965, and Howard Jones to Secretary of State, "Termination of Public Safety Project," February–March 1965, both TSD, box 9, folder Indonesia.

32. Robert Amory, oral history interview, JFKL; Lingo and Fruit, "Confidential Program Evaluation: Study Report of Police Assistance Project in Indonesia"; "Public Safety Program Summary, Indonesia," May 13, 1963, IPS, box 8.

33. *Indonesia: An Amnesty International Report* (London: Amnesty International, 1977), 2; Richard Tanter, "The Totalitarian Ambition: Intelligence and Security Agencies in Indonesia," in *State and Civil Society in Indonesia,* ed. Arief Budiman (Clayton, Victoria: Centre of Southeast Asian Studies, Monash University, 1999), 215–89; Joshua Barker, "State of Fear: Controlling the Criminal Contagion in Suharto's New Order," in *Violence and the State in Suharto's Indonesia,* ed. Benedict Anderson (Ithaca: Southeast Asia Program Publications, Southeast Asia Program, Cornell University, 1999), 20–54.

34. Carmel Budiardjo, "Repression and Political Imprisonment," in Caldwell, *Ten Years' Military Terror in Indonesia,* 95–105; Director of Intelligence, "The Upheaval in Indonesia," CIA Report, October 8, 1965, Papers of LBJ, NSF, Country File, Asia and the Pacific, box 246; Daniel S. Lev, "The Criminal Regime: Criminal Process in Indonesia," in *Figures of Criminality in Indonesia, the Philippines, and Colonial Vietnam,* ed. Vicente L. Rafael, Ithaca: Southeast Asia Program Publications, Southeast Asia Program, Cornell University, 1999), 183; Justus M. Van der Kroel, "Indonesia's Political Prisoners," *Pacific Affairs* 49 (Winter 1976–77): 625–47.

35. CIA Director of Intelligence, memo, April 29, 1966, and "Indonesia: Prospects for Economic Stability," Papers of LBJ, NSF, Country File, July 1968, box 249; Rob Barnett to Charles Mann, Indonesia, April 21, 1966, RG 286, USAID, OPS, East Asia Branch (hereafter East Asia Branch), Records Relating to Indonesia (1963–1966), box 2. See also Kolko, *Confronting the Third World,* 182; Noam Chomsky and Edward S. Herman, *The Political Economy of Human Rights: The Washington Connection and Third World Fascism* (Boston: South End Press, 1979), 154, 155.

36. James L. McMahon, Chief of Technical Services Division, OPS, to Dr. Soebianto, Brigadier General of Police, Negara Djakarta, January 27, 1971, TSD, box 4, folder Indonesia; "Biographic Information of Key Indonesian Personalities," Southeast Asia Report, March 10, 1983, Foreign Broadcast Information Service, 15. McMahon, who held a degree in police administration from Michigan State University, served as a police adviser (under CIA cover) in South Korea, the Philippines, Thailand, and Vietnam.

37. "Biographic Information of Key Indonesian Personalities," 14.

38. Peter Dale Scott, *American War Machine: Deep Politics, the CIA Global Drug Connection, and the Road to Afghanistan* (New York: Rowman and Littlefield, 2010), 89. On the interests of the American oil companies Shell-Stanvac and Standard Oil in Thailand, see American embassy, Bangkok, to Secretary of State, "Shell-Stanvac Proposal for Oil Refinery," June 18, 1959, RG 59, RDS BFEA, Thailand Files (hereafter RDS, Thailand), box 5068, folder 1.

39. Daniel Fineman, *A Special Relationship: The United States and Military Government in Thailand, 1947–1958* (Honolulu: University of Hawaii Press, 1997), 123, 133; W. H. Godel to William Donovan, 1953, AMHI, the Papers of William Donovan, box 9, document 4058; Brigadier General Elliott R. Thorpe, *East Wind, Rain: The Intimate Account of an Intelligence Officer in the Pacific, 1939–1949* (Boston: Gambit, 1949), 268, 269.

40. "Private Training Venture," *New York Times,* September 20, 1957; "Lt. Col. Paul Lionel Helliwell"; and Hunter Fulford to Colonel E. F. Connely, "Major Willis H. Bird," January 24, 1944, RG 226, Records of the OSS, Personnel Files, box 57; R. Harris Smith, *OSS: The*

Secret History of America's First Central Intelligence Agency (Berkeley: University of California Press, 1972), 273, 330; Douglas Valentine, *The Strength of the Wolf: The Secret History of America's War on Drugs* (London: Verso, 2004), 155; Peter Dale Scott, "Drugs and Oil: The Deep Politics of U.S. Asian Wars," in *War and State Terrorism: The United States, Japan, and the Asia-Pacific in the Long Twentieth Century,* ed. Mark Selden and Alvin Y. So (New York: Rowman and Littlefield, 2004), 187; Penny Lernoux, *In Banks We Trust* (New York: Doubleday, 1984), 77; "Officials Involved in Opium Running," American embassy, Bangkok, to Department of State, July 7, 1958, RDS, Thailand box 1, folder 5. After World War II, Helliwell was Far East division chief of the Strategic Service Unit, the successor to OSS, charged with controlling the pipeline of covert funds for secret operations throughout East Asia. A close colleague of Helliwell and Bird, Princeton grad Sherman Joost led Kachin guerrillas in Burma during World War II as commander of OSS Detachment 101, known for trading in opium.

41. William Turner to Mr. Robert Joyce, Policy Planning Staff, Bangkok, November 7, 1951, in Classen et al., *Foreign Relations of the United States, 1951: Asia and the Pacific,* pt. 2, vol. 6, ed. Paul Classen et al. (Washington, D.C.: GPO, 1977), 1633; Fineman, *A Special Relationship,* 135; Scott, *American War Machine,* 86. Bird's close relationship to Phao stemmed in part from his marriage to the sister of Thai air force officer Sitthi Sawetsila, one of Phao's cronies.

42. Fineman, *A Special Relationship,* 143; Garland Williams to American embassy, Tehran, "Narcotics Situation in Southeast Asia and the Far East," August 4, 1959, RG 286, USAID, OPS, Africa and Near East and South Asia Branch (hereafter Africa and Near East and South Asia Branch), box 62, folder Narcotics; Alfred W. McCoy, *The Politics of Heroin: CIA Complicity in the Global Drug Trade* (New York: Lawrence Hill, 1991), 175–76; Bertil Lintner, *Burma in Revolt: Opium and Insurgency since 1948* (Bangkok: White Lotus, 1994), 106.

43. Fineman, *A Special Relationship,* 135.

44. McCoy, *The Politics of Heroin,* 185; *New York Times,* November 6, 1957.

45. Richard K. Stewart to Mr. Rockwood Fester, October 27, 1955, RDS, Thailand, box 5068; Sinae Hyun, "Cold Warriors on the Margins: Thai-U.S. Relations and the Emergence of the Border Patrol Police, 1947–1965" (master's thesis, University of Wisconsin, Madison, 2009), 54; Surachert Bamrungsuk, "United States Foreign Policy and Thai Military Rule, 1947–1977" (master's thesis, Cornell University, 1985).

46. Thomas Lobe, *U.S. National Security Policy and Aid to the Thailand Police* (Denver: University of Denver Graduate School of International Studies, 1977), 27; Darrell Berrigan, "They Smuggle Dope by the Ton," *Saturday Evening Post,* May 5, 1956, 42, 156–57.

47. American embassy, Bangkok, to Department of State, "The Narcotic Situation in Thailand," June 29, 1955, RDS, Thailand, box 5068; American embassy to Secretary of State, October 19, 1956, RDS, Thailand, box 5068.

48. Garland Williams to American embassy, Tehran, "Narcotics Situation in Southeast Asia and the Far East," August 4, 1959, Africa and Near East and South Asia Branch, box 62, folder Narcotics. Government records point to Willis Bird's having been arrested for smuggling opium via Air America planes in the early 1960s. His cousin William Bird was also involved in covert operations and illegal activity in Southeast Asia. See also Harry J. Anslinger to Gilbert Yates, February 25, 1959, RDEA, BNDD, box 164, file Vietnam; M. J. W. Pevoy and J. M. Wilkinson, "References to Thailand in Mr. McCoy's Book," 1972, RG 59, RDS, Offices of Thai and Burma Affairs (1963–1975), box 5, folder Narcotics.

49. Fineman, *A Special Relationship,* 150–51; McCoy, *The Politics of Heroin,* 185; Peter Dale Scott, *Drugs, Oil, and War: The United States in Afghanistan, Colombia, and Indochina* (New York: Rowman and Littlefield, 2003), 191.

50. Fineman, *A Special Relationship,* 135.

51. Ibid., 172–73; Banning Garrett, "Thailand: The Next Domino," in Editors of *Ramparts, Two, Three . . . Many Vietnams,* 125; Ralph Thaxton, "Modernization and Counter-Revolution in Thailand," in *Remaking Asia: Essays on the American Uses of Power,* ed. Mark Selden (New York: Pantheon Books, 1974), 247–79. One of the anthropologists was the racial theorist Carleton Coon, formerly of the OSS.

52. Anthony Cave Brown, *The Last Hero: Wild Bill Donovan* (New York: Times Books, 1982), 822–23. See also Douglas Waller, *Wild Bill Donovan: The Spymaster Who Created the OSS and Modern American Espionage* (New York: Free Press, 2011).

53. F. G. Robertson to the Secretary, "Possible Designation of General William Donovan as Ambassador to Thailand," June 2, 1953; and Bill Donovan to President Eisenhower, May 7, 1954, DDEL, OCB, John Foster Dulles Papers, Personnel Series, box 1, folder Donovan. Interestingly, the principal reservation the State Department had over Donovan's appointment involved his old contacts with Pridi and the Free Thai movement during World War II. Since U.S. policy shifted after the war and many of the Free Thai were now dissidents, Donovan was urged to downplay his prior relationship and keep select OSS colleagues away from Pridi, and preferably out of the country.

54. Fineman, *A Special Relationship,* 181; W. H. Godel to William Donovan, [n.d.], 1953, Papers of William Donovan, AMHI, box 9, document 4058.

55. Raymond R. Coffey and Joseph Z. Taylor, *Thailand Public Safety/Border Patrol Police, Remote Area Security Development: An Approach to Counter-Insurgency by the Border Patrol Police,* USOM, USAID (Bangkok, 1971), 2; Betty DuMaine to Richard M. Nixon, March 15, 1969, IPS, box 9.

56. *Brief History of Camp Narasuan: Police Aerial Reinforcement Unit,* USOM, USAID (Bangkok, 1968); "Interview with Bill Lair, Conducted by Steve Maxner," December 11, 2001, TTU. On the eastern European precedent, see Peter Grose, *Operation Rollback: America's Secret War behind the Iron Curtain* (Boston: Houghton Mifflin, 2000). Lair, who was Willis Bird's brother-in-law, helped organize the clandestine Hmong army in Laos. He candidly notes how his men obtained a percentage of the money from drug seizures, to which they were entitled by law.

57. "OCB Report Pursuant to NSC Action 1290-d," September 12, 1955, DDEL, OCB, box 17, folder Internal Security.

58. Jeffrey Race, "The War in Northern Thailand," *Modern Asian Studies* 8 (January 1974): 90; Fineman, *A Special Relationship,* 206–7; Waller, *Wild Bill Donovan,* 373.

59. Ralph White, "Observations on Hill Tribes and the Security of Thailand"; and J. Marsh Thompson to Ambassador Ralph Ungar, January 30, 1962, RDS, Thailand (1960–1963), box 3. See also Seth S. King, "Thai Village Winks at Opium Traffic," *New York Times,* August 1, 1965; Maxner, "Interview with Bill Lair.".

60. *The Civic Action Program of the Border Patrol Police and the USOM Public Safety Division* (Bangkok, 1962), 46; Coffey and Taylor, *Thailand Public Safety/Border Patrol Police,* 2; Douglas Blaufarb, *The Counter-Insurgency Era: U.S. Doctrine and Performance* (New York: Free Press, 1977), 194; Hyun, "Cold Warriors on the Margins."

61. Lobe, *U.S. National Security Police and Aid to the Thailand Police,* 82; White, "Observations on Hill Tribes and the Security of Thailand"; J. Marsh Thompson to Ambassador Ralph Ungar, January 30, 1962, RDS, Thailand, box 3.

62. Pevoy and Wilkinson, "References to Thailand in Mr. McCoy's Book"; Robert Lowe, "Observations on Thai National Police–USAID Police Project," RDS, Thailand, box 6; Ralph McGehee, *Deadly Deceits: My Twenty-five Years in the CIA* (New York: Ocean Press, 1999),

80; Al McCoy, "Subcontracting Counter-Insurgency," *Bulletin of Concerned Asian Scholars* (December 1970): 156; Race, "The War in Northern Thailand." As Hyun notes ("Cold Warriors on the Margins"), Thai officials had similarly patronizing views of the hill tribespeople.

63. Bob Lowe, OPS Far-East, to Jeter Williamson, "Observations on the Thai National Police," June 25, 1963, RDS, Thailand, box 6, folder Thailand; K. S. Masterson, "Counter-Insurgency in Thailand," vol. 1, "Summary and Evaluation," Weapons System Evaluation Group, June 1968, Papers of LBJ, NSF, Country Files, Pacific Branch, box 286, Thailand.

64. Lobe, *U.S. National Security Policy and Aid to the Thailand Police*, 76.

65. Kevin J. Hewison, "The State and Capitalist Development in Thailand," in *Essays in the Political Economy of Structural Change*, ed. Richard A. Higgott and Richard Robison (London: Routledge, 1985), 278.

66. Marvin J. Jones and Philip Batson, *A Brief History of USOM Support to the Thai National Police Department*, USAID, OPS (Bangkok, 1969), 12; Task Force Southeast Asia, Department of State, "Status Report of Counter-Insurgency Projects in Thailand, Vietnam, and Cambodia," 1962, RG 59, RDS BFEA, Office of the Country Director for Laos, box 1; Coffey and Taylor, *Thailand Public Safety/Border Patrol Police*, appendix 3; E. H. Adkins Jr., "A Survey Report of the National Identity Card Program, Royal Government of Thailand, Bangkok," December 20, 1963, RG 286, USAID, OPS, Office of the Director, Programs, Surveys, and Evaluations, Thailand, box 11.

67. "Public Safety Program, USOM/Thailand, 1957–1963" (Bangkok, 1963), 2; Jones and Batson, *A Brief History of USOM Support to the Thai National Police Department*, 1–2.

68. Bob Lowe, "Observations on the Thai National Police," RDS, Thailand, box 6, folder Thailand; Haney, "OCB Report Pursuant to NSC Action 1290-d," September 12, 1955, DDEL.

69. "Public Safety Program, USOM/Thailand" (1957–1963), 4.

70. Personal interview with Walter "Sticky" Burch, former deputy chief of police, Greensboro, N.C., April 27, 2010; Eugene Miller, "A Real Man: New Chief of Police Came Up Hard Way," *Greensboro Record*, October 1951; "Captain Williamson Heads Class at FBI School," [*Richmond (Va.) Times-Dispatch*], January–March 1948 (both clippings courtesy of Patricia "Patsy" Harrington); Jerry Bledsoe, "Cops in Black & White," *Rhinotimes.com*, February 12, 2010; "Retired Cop Lauded for Outstanding Service," Greensboro Police, www.greensboro-nc.gov. On racial and economic discrimination in Greensboro in the 1950s and the reluctance of the white elite to move against Jim Crow in spite of their claims to be less bigoted than poor white "rednecks," see William Chafe, *Civilities and Civil Rights: Greensboro, North Carolina, and the Black Struggle for Freedom* (New York: Oxford University Press, 1980), 51.

71. "Ex-Police Chief Describes Subversion in Thailand," *Greensboro Daily News*, July 25, 1965; Hutter Williams, "Warning Issued on Red Takeover in Vietnam," *Lynchburg (Va.) Daily Advance*, July 29, 1965; "Former Chief Tells of Thai Police Work," *Greensboro Record*, December 12, 1960; Jim Schlosser, "Ex-Chief of Police Remembered," *Greensboro Daily News*, June 3, 2005.

72. See James V. Bennett with Rodney Campbell, *I Chose Prison* (New York: Knopf, 1970); Robert M. Freeman, *Correctional Organization and Management: Public Policy Challenges, Behavior, and Structure* (Woburn, Mass.: Butterworth, Heinemann, 1999), 218.

73. U.S. Department of Justice, *Report on the Prisons of Thailand: James V. Bennett, Director Federal Bureau of Prisons*, October 26, 1960, International Cooperation Administration, East Asia Branch, Thailand, box 213, Thai Penology.

74. Bennett quoted in Andrew E. Hunt, *David Dellinger: The Life and Times of a Nonviolent Revolutionary* (New York: New York University Press, 2006), 58–59. On the oppressive

climate in U.S. prisons around this time, see Ben H. Bagdikian, *Caged: Eight Prisoners and Their Keepers* (New York: Harper & Row, 1976), xii, xiii.

75. Seymour J. Jones to John C. Evar and Kenneth Kugel, "Bowen Report," April 25, 1962, RDS, Thailand (1960–1963), box 3; "Policy Research Study: Internal Warfare and the Security of the Underdeveloped States," November 20, 1961, POF, box 98.

76. Robert C. Lowe to Kenneth Kugel, May 2, 1962, RDS, Thailand, box 3; Bob Lowe to Jeter Williamson, June 25, 1963, RDS, Thailand, box 6, folder Thailand; Seymour J. Janow to Johnson Monroe, Director OPS, "Counter-Insurgency Training Program for Provincial Police," March 18, 1963, RDS, Thailand; Byron Engle to Hamilton Fowler, January 2, 1963, RDS, Thailand, box 6; "Program Assessment: Thailand, 1963," RG 286, USAID, OPS, Office of the Director, International Police Academy, box 4; General Saiyud Kerdphol, *The Struggle for Thailand: Counter-Insurgency, 1965–1985* (Bangkok: Southern Research Center, 1986), 25; "Reds Reported Stepping Up Infiltration," November 23, 1963, in *Survey Report of National Identity Card Program, Royal Government of Thailand* (Washington, D.C.: State Department, 1963).

77. Jones and Batson, *A Brief History of USOM Support to the Thai National Police Department*, 1–2; Jeter Williamson, Chief Public Safety Division, to Tracey Park, "Ad Hoc Village Security Committee," September 1, 1965, OPS, East Asia Branch, Thailand, box 211, Special Police Problems, folder 1; "Village Police Program," December 21, 1965, OPS, East Asia Branch, Thailand, box 211, Special Police Problems, folder 1; Voice of the People of Thailand, March 2, 1965 (clandestine), TTU, Vietnam Center, Virtual Archive, www.virtualvietnam.ttu.edu.

78. Katherine A. Bowie, *Rituals of National Loyalty: An Anthropology of the State and the Village Scout Movement in Thailand* (New York: Columbia University Press, 1997), 66.

79. American embassy to Secretary of State, "Helicopter Requirements, Roles, and Missions," November 1967, TSD, box 21, folder Thailand: General Helicopters; Martin Gleason to Jeter Williamson, June 20, 1967, TSD, box 22; John W. Henderson, "Thailand National Defense and Internal Security," Area Handbook (Washington, D.C.: Department of the Army, 1971); American embassy Bangkok to Secretary of State, November 1973, RG 472, U.S. Forces in Southeast Asia, Thailand, Joint U.S. Military Advisory Group, box 2.

80. Jones and Batson, *A Brief History of USOM Support to the Thai National Police Department*, 3.

81. Bowie, *Rituals of National Loyalty,* 102–3; Thomas Lobe and David Morrell, "Thailand's Border Patrol Police: Paramilitary Political Power," in *Supplementary Military Forces: Reserves, Militias, Auxiliaries,* ed. Louis Zurcher and Gwyn Harries-Jenkins (Beverly Hills: Sage, 1978), 153–78; Michael T. Klare, *American Arms Supermarket* (Austin: University of Texas Press, 1984), 196; E. Thadeus Flood, *The United States and the Military Coup in Thailand: A Background Study* (Washington, D.C.: Indochina Resource Center, 1976); Scott, *American War Machine,* 127; Tyrell Haberkorn, *Revolution Interrupted: Farmers, Students, Law, and Violence in Northern Thailand* (Madison: University of Wisconsin Press, 2011). Lao mercenaries formerly in the pay of the CIA were also involved in the massacre, which was rationalized in part by false claims of a planned Vietnamese invasion, similar to the claims initiated by the CIA to justify its escalation of the secret war in Laos (see chapter 6).

82. Jeremy Kuzmarov, *The Myth of the Addicted Army: Vietnam and the Modern War on Drugs* (Amherst: University of Massachusetts Press, 2009), 142; Alfred W. McCoy, *Drug Traffic: Narcotics and Organized Crime in Australia* (Sydney: Harper & Row, 1980); Roger Ernst, Director, U.S. Operations Mission, Bangkok, to Joe W. Johnson, Audit Manager, Bangkok Office, Far East Bureau, October 3, 1973, East Asia Branch, Thailand, box 212, folder 1, 346.

83. "Pramual Case Linked to Foreign Aid Bill," Department of State telegram, American embassy, Bangkok, to Secretary of State, November 15, 1972, East Asia Branch, Thailand, box 212, folder 3; "Summaries of Recent Thai Language Press," American embassy, Bangkok, to Secretary of State, October 5, 1972, East Asia Branch, Thailand, box 212, folder 3; "Thanom: Why I Jailed Pramual," *Bangkok Post,* April 27, 1973; "Pramual: It Could Have Been 40 Years," *Bangkok Post,* April 25, 1973; "Drug Car Belonged to Narcotics Chief," *Bangkok Post,* August 27, 1973; McCoy, *The Politics of Heroin,* 581; Douglas Valentine, *The Strength of the Pack: The Personalities, Politics, and Espionage Intrigues That Shaped the DEA* (Walterville, Ore.: Trine Day, 2009), 255–56. In another case exposing the broad scale of corruption, the car carrying a 125-kilogram haul of morphine on the Lampong highway was found to belong to Lampong's deputy superintendent for narcotics suppression, Police Lieutenant Narong Rergitthikorn.

84. McCoy, *The Politics of Heroin,* 191. For the larger pattern, see Odd Arne Westad, *The Global Cold War: Third World Intervention and the Making of Our Times* (New York: Cambridge University Press, 2005). For a claim of success, see George K. Tanham, *Trial in Thailand* (New York: Crane Russak, 1974).

85. "From Special Agents to Gestapo," *Manila Chronicle,* October 8, 1946; Nathaniel P. Davis to Secretary of State, October 30, 1946; and Richard Ely to John Howard, "Status of Philippines Constabulary," November 25, 1949, Philippines Republic, RDS Internal Affairs (1945–1949), decimal file 894. On the continuities from the colonial era, see Alfred W. McCoy's masterpiece *Policing America's Empire: The United States, the Philippines, and the Rise of the Surveillance State* (Madison: University of Wisconsin Press, 2009).

86. Benedict J. Tria Kerkvliet, *The Huk Rebellion: A Study of Peasant Revolt in the Philippines* (Quezon City: New Day Publishers, 1979), 147; George McGehee to Mac Bundy, "Counter-Guerrilla Campaigns in Greece, Malaya, and the Philippines," November 21, 1961, JFKL, NSF. On the influence of women in the Huk movement, see Vina A. Lanzona, *Amazons of the Huk Rebellion: Gender, Sex, and Revolution in the Philippines* (Madison: University of Wisconsin Press, 2009).

87. Philippines, Country Paper, April 28, 1953, RG 469, RFAA, Records Related to MSA Program in Thailand, 1952, 1953, box 1.

88. Nathaniel P. Davis to Secretary of State, June 28, 1947, Philippines Republic, RDS, Department of State, Internal Affairs (1945–1949), decimal file 894; "Military Estimate of the Situation in Philippines," June 1, 1948, HTSL, Papers of Harry S. Truman, PSF, Intelligence Files, 1946–1953, Internal Reports File, box 217.

89. See Drinnon, *Facing West,* 392; Nashel, *Edward Lansdale's Cold War.* One technique that Lansdale recounts in his autobiography *In The Midst of Wars: An American's Mission to Southeast Asia* (New York: Harper & Row, 1972) was the "vampire trick," whereby a Huk soldier was kidnapped, killed, and drained of blood and his atrophied corpse hung on a wire in the middle of a Huk village to strike fear into the villagers. Lansdale's sidekick Colonel Charles Bohannen was a former ethnographer at the Smithsonian Institution and a specialist in Navajo folklore who applied the study of culture, particularly folk superstition, to the war on the Huk guerrilla army.

90. Napoleon D. Valeriano and Charles T. R. Bohannen, *Counter-Guerilla Operations: The Philippine Experience* (New York: Praeger, 1962), 97; Edward Lansdale to Walt W. Rostow, August 10, 1961, JFKL, NSF, Meetings and Memoranda, box 327A; McCoy, *Policing America's Empire,* 375; Kerkvliet, *The Huk Rebellion,* 196; Roger Hilsman, report to John F. Kennedy, "Role and Mission of Rural Police in South Vietnam," 55, JFKL, Hilsman Papers, box 332; "Policy Research Study: Internal Warfare and the Security of the Underdeveloped States, Department of State," November 20, 1961, POF, box 98. Another internal study of

the constabulary concluded that "considerable numbers of alleged dissidents were killed in operations" but that the efforts of the constabulary had been "unsuccessful." "Military Estimate of the Situation in Philippines," June 1, 1948, Papers of Harry S. Truman, PSF, Intelligence Files, 1946–1953, HSTL, Internal Reports file, box 217.

91. "Philippines: Shored Up Defenses," *Newsweek*, July 10, 1950, 34; *Soldier Heroes: A Handbook of the Major Medals Awarded by the Philippines Constabulary and Armed Forces*, foreword by Ferdinand Marcos (Manila: National Media Production Center, 1981), 30.

92. "Annual Status Report on Operations Pursuant to NSC Action 1290-d to Operations Coordinating Board for the National Security Council," January 3, 1957, Country Report, Philippines, DDEL, OCB, Central File Series, box 18, folder Internal Security; Fidel Ramos, *The Constabulary Story* (Quezon City: Bustamante Press, 1978), 303; draft paper by Deputy Director, Office of Philippines and Southeast Asian Affairs, NSC 84/2, January 15, 1951, in Classen et al., *Foreign Relations of the United States, Asia and the Pacific*, pt. 2, 6:1510.

93. Jeter L. Williamson, *A Survey of Police Services and Problems in the Philippines* (Manila: Institute of Public Administration, University of the Philippines, 1955), 17–31; "Annual Status Report on Operations Pursuant to NSC Action 1290-d to Operations Coordinating Board for the National Security Council," December 1955–November 1956, Country Report, Philippines, DDEL, OCB, Central File Series, box 18, folder Internal Security; "Philippines' Police Work Appraised: Williamson Points to Shortcomings," *Greensboro Daily Record*, June 1956 (approximate date; from records of Patsy Harrington).

94. Conversation with Patsy Harrington; ICA Newsletter, February 1957, MSUA Vietnam Project, box 679. Wilson ran the Los Angeles Police Department crime lab for a number of years and was an internationally recognized authority in criminalistics.

95. Gene Blake, "Deputy Chief of Police to Take Vietnam Post," *Los Angeles Times*, July 6, 1969; George C. Wilson, "South Vietnam Police Advisor from L.A. Assailed," *Los Angeles Times*, July 9, 1970; Frank E. Walton, "Selective Distribution of Police Patrol Force: History, Current Practices, Recommendations," *Journal of Law, Criminology, and Police Science* 49 (July–August 1958): 167; Frank Donner, *Protectors of Privilege: Red Squads and Police Repression in Urban America* (Berkeley: University of California Press, 1990), 245–55; Joe Domanick, *To Protect and to Serve: The LAPD's Century of War in the City of Dreams* (New York: Figueroa, 2003), 109; "Invasion from Within," September 1952, in *Parker on Police*, ed. O. W. Wilson (Springfield, Ill.: C. C. Thomas, 1957), 49–66. On the World War II exploits of the Black Sheep, see Frank E. Walton, *Once They Were Eagles: The Men of Black Sheep Squadron* (Lexington: University Press of Kentucky, 1986). "Pappy" Boyington was a flying ace who survived twenty months in a Japanese POW camp.

96. Frank E. Walton to James E. Ingersoll, USOM, Philippines, October 1, 1964, IPS, box 9, folder Philippines.

97. Ramos, *The Constabulary Story*, 317, 320; Special Group on Counter-Insurgency to American embassy, Manila, "Medical Activity by Police and Paramilitary Forces in the Philippines," September 14, 1962, IPS, box 11; John Sidel, "The Usual Suspects: Nardong Putik, Don Pepe Oyson, and Robin Hood," in Rafael, *Figures of Criminality in Indonesia, the Philippines, and Colonial Vietnam*, 74; Alfred W. McCoy, "Covert Netherworld: Clandestine Services and Criminal Syndicates in Shaping the Philippine State," in *Government of the Shadows: Parapolitics and Criminal Sovereignty*, ed. Eric Wilson (London: Pluto Press, 2009), 232.

98. Ramos, *The Constabulary Story*, 54; James C. Scott, *Moral Economy of the Peasant: Rebellion and Subsistence in Southeast Asia* (New Haven: Yale University Press, 1976), 1–12, 225–40; Stephen R. Shalom, *The United States and the Philippines: A Study in Neo-Colonialism* (Philadelphia: Institute for the Study of Human Issues, 1981), 115.

99. Shalom, *The United States and the Philippines,* 69; Raymond Bonner, *Waltzing with a Dictator* (New York: Vintage Books, 1988); Chomsky and Herman, *The Political Economy of Human Rights,* 218; Thomas Finn and James L. McMahon, *Evaluation Public Safety Program,* USAID Philippines, April 1972. This last report concluded that maintaining rights to the bases and promoting American enterprise represented the primary U.S. interests in the Philippines.

100. Richard P. Claude, "Human Rights in the Philippines and United States Responsibility," Boston University School of Theology, Working Paper, February 3, 1978, 4; Chomsky and Herman, *The Washington Connection and Third World Fascism,* 241.

101. Jeter L. Williamson and Paul Katz, "Philippines Termination Phase-Out Report, 1974," USAID, OPS, 1975, 3; Finn and McMahon, *Evaluation Public Safety Program.*

102. Walden Bello and Severina Rivera, eds., *The Logistics of Repression and Other Essays: The Role of U.S. Assistance in Consolidating the Martial Law Regime in the Philippines* (Washington, D.C.: Friends of the Filipino People, 1977), 30; Alfred W. McCoy, *A Question of Torture: CIA Interrogation from the Cold War to the War on Terror* (New York: Metropolitan Books, 2006), 82; Jeter L. Williamson and Paul Katz, "Evaluation Team, Termination Phase-Out Study, Public Safety Project, Philippines," USAID, 1974, 52–55. Geraldine Jelsch, Byron Engle's wife, was also part of the OPS team.

103. Bello and Rivera, *Logistics of Repression,* 30; McCoy, *Policing America's Empire,* 403. See also U.S. House, Committee on the Judiciary, *Testimony of Benedict J. Kerkvliet, Woodrow Wilson International Center for Scholars,* in *Political Prisoners in South Vietnam and the Philippines,* Hearings before the Subcommittee on Asian and Pacific Affairs, 93rd Cong., 2nd sess., June 1974 (Washington, D.C.: GPO, 1974), 74; McCoy, *A Question of Torture,* 91; Williamson and Katz, "Philippines Termination Phase-Out Report, 1974," 34.

104. "Constabulary," Anti-Narcotics Unit, June 9, 1972, IPS, Philippines, box 9, folder 1.

105. Comptroller General of the United States, "Report to the Congress: Stopping U.S. Assistance to Foreign Police and Prisons" (Washington, D.C.: GAO, 1976), 22, 25; American embassy, Manila, to Secretary of State, Washington D.C., "Narcotics Control," February 1974, IPS, box 10, folder Narcotics; Frank E. Walton to Mr. James H. Ingersoll, Chief Survey Team, Director USOM, Philippines, USAID, October 1964, IPS, Philippines, box 9; Alfred W. McCoy, "The New Politics of Heroin in Southeast Asia" *Oui Magazine,* December 1976, 154; Sidel, "The Usual Suspects."

106. Bello and Rivera, *Logistics of Repression,* 31; McCoy, *Policing America's Empire,* 387.

107. Editors of *Ramparts* and Frank Browning, *Smack!* (New York: Harper & Row, 1972), 15.

108. Quoted in Naomi Klein, *The Shock Doctrine: The Rise of Disaster Capitalism* (New York: Metropolitan Books, 2007), 69; McGehee, *Deadly Deceits.*

109. See Westad, *The Global Cold War.*

6. The Secret War in Laos and Other Vietnam Sideshows

1. Willard O. Brown, "Memo for Ambassador, Report by Mr. Paul Skuse," August 28, 1959, and "Monthly Public Safety Report," March 4, 1959, RG 469, RFAA, USOM, Laos, General Records (1957–1960) (hereafter USOM Laos), box 1, folder Special Commando Units

2. Quoted in William Blum, *Killing Hope: U.S. Military and CIA Interventions since World War II* (Monroe, Me.: Common Courage Press, 2002), 140.

3. Len E. Ackland, "No Place for Neutralism: The Eisenhower Administration and Laos," in *Laos: War and Revolution,* ed. Nina S. Adams and Alfred W. McCoy (New York: Harper

& Row, 1970), 139–40; Charles A. Stevenson, *The End of Nowhere: American Policy toward Laos since 1954* (Boston: Beacon Press, 1972), 1, 29. An influential book on counterinsurgency at the time was David Galula, *Counterinsurgency Warfare: Theory and Practice* (St. Petersburg, Fla.: Hailer Publishing, 1964).

4. Internal Security Police Program, NSC 1290-d, Laos, February 19, 1957, DDEL, OCB, box 40, folder Laos.

5. USAID, *United States Agency for International Development, Termination Report, Vientiane, Laos, 1975* (Washington, D.C.: GPO, 1975), 10. This viewpoint has been advanced convincingly by Noam Chomsky in numerous books and articles, most notably *For Reasons of State* (New York: Pantheon, 1973). He incorporates analysis from the so-called Wisconsin school, including William A. Williams, *The Tragedy of American Diplomacy*, rev. ed. (New York: Norton, 1988). On the historical attachment of U.S. empire-builders to the Asia-Pacific, which they viewed as an extension of the western frontier, see Bruce Cumings, *Dominion from Sea to Sea: Pacific Ascendancy and American Power* (New Haven: Yale University Press, 2009); and Richard Drinnon, *Facing West: The Metaphysics of Indian-Hating and Empire-Building* (Norman: University of Oklahoma Press, 1980).

6. Martin Stuart-Fox, *A History of Laos* (New York: Cambridge University Press, 1997), 101; Horace Smith, "Significant Developments in Laos, 1958–1960," July 29, 1966, Papers of LBJ, NSF, Country File, Pacific Branch, box 268, folder Laos; Mervyn Brown, *The War in Shangri-la: A Memoir of Civil War in Laos* (London: Radcliffe, 2001), 212.

7. *Causes, Origins, and Lessons of the Vietnam War: Hearings before the Committee on Foreign Relations,* U.S. Senate, 92nd Cong., 2nd sess., May 9, 10, 1972 (Washington, D.C.: GPO, 1972), 198. The CIA characterized Souphanouvong's wife, who was Vietnamese, as "highly intelligent and charming." "Political Situation in Laos," August 21, 1958, USOM Laos, box 1. For a critical view of the Pathet Lao which recognizes their organizational strength, see Bernard B. Fall, "The Pathet Lao: A 'Liberation' Party" in *The Communist Revolution in Asia: Tactics, Goals, and Achievements,* ed. Robert A Scalapino (Englewood Cliffs, N.J.: Prentice Hall, 1965), 180–82. On Souphanouvong's background, see *Autobiography of Prince Souphanouvong* (Kuala Lampur: Malaysia Mining Corporation Berhad, 1989).

8. U.S. Congress, House, Committee of on Government Operations, *United States Aid Operations in Laos: Hearings, March 11–June 1, 1959, Seventh Report,* 86th Cong., 1st sess., June 1959 (Washington, D.C.: GPO, 1959), 3.

9. Ibid.; Arthur Schlesinger Jr., *A Thousand Days: John F. Kennedy in the White House* (Boston: Beacon Press, 1957), 325; Bernard B. Fall, *Anatomy of a Crisis: The Laotian Crisis of 1960–1961* (New York: Doubleday, 1969), 164. Vinnell funded clandestine activities such as police training in Saudi Arabia and Vietnam. The vice president of Universal Construction Co. was Willis Bird.

10. Oudone Sananikone, *The Royal Lao Army and U.S. Army Advice and Support* (Washington, D.C.: U.S. Army Center of for Military History, 1981), 46; Stevenson, *The End of Nowhere,* 38–39; Rufus Phillips, "Laos—The Critical Years from 1956–1959—A First-Hand Account," CIA, Conference on Laos, Cambodia, and Thailand, Texas Tech University, Vietnam Center, March 13, 2009. One CIA agent, Dick Holm, reflected years later on the "arrogance and ignorance of Americans serving in Laos . . . . We had only minimal understanding of the history, culture, and politics of the people we wanted to aid. . . . Our strategic interests were superimposed onto a region where our president had decided to 'draw the line' against communism. And we would do it our way." Richard L. Holm, *The American Agent: My Life in the CIA* (London: St. Ermin's Press, 2003), 178.

11. Victor B. Anthony and Richard R. Sexton, "The U.S. Air Force in Southeast Asia: The War in Northern Laos," 1954–1973, AFHRA, 1993, 26; Thomas L. Ahern Jr., *Undercover Armies: CIA and Surrogate Warfare in Laos, 1961–1973* (Washington, D.C.: CIA, Center for the Study of Intelligence, 2006); Seth Jacobs, "'No Place to Fight a War': Laos and the Evolution of U.S. Policy toward Vietnam, 1954–1963," in *Making Sense of the Vietnam Wars: Local, National, and Transnational Perspectives,* ed. Mark P. Bradley and Marilyn B. Young (New York: Oxford University Press, 2008), 49. Reflecting the prejudices of the time, Eisenhower referred to the RLA as "a bunch of homosexuals" (ibid.)

12. Jacques Nevard, "Reverses in Laos Laid to 'Myth of Invasion' by Powerful Foes," *New York Times,* April 23, 1961; Roger Hilsman, *To Move a Nation: The Politics of Foreign Policy in the Administration of John F. Kennedy* (New York: Doubleday, 1967), 113. The pacifist tendencies of the 1960s New Left were similarly derided by the "newspaper of record," which has a long history of warmongering, evident recently in the debacle over Iraq and its supposed weapons of mass destruction. See Edward S. Herman, *The Myth of the Liberal Media* (New York: Peter Lang, 1999).

13. "Internal Warfare and the Security of Underdeveloped States," Department of State, November 20, 1961, POF, box 98; "History of the Office of Public Safety," RG 286, Records of the USAID, PSD, OPS, Southeast Asia Branch, Laos (hereafter OPS Laos), box 4; Stuart-Fox, *A History of Laos,* 105.

14. Frank Walton, Paul Skuse, and Wendell Motter, *A Survey of the Laos National Police,* Vientiane, USAID, OPS, 1965, 28. On Skuse's CIA connections, see Julius Mader, *Who's Who in CIA* (Berlin: J. Mader, 1968), 481; John D. Marks, "How to Spot a Spook," *Washington Monthly* (November 1974): 5–11.

15. U.S. Congress, House, Committee of on Government Operations, *United States Aid Operations in Laos: Hearings, March 11–June 1, 1959, Seventh Report,* 32.

16. Elmer B. Staats, "Operations Plans for Laos, Operations Coordinating Board," June 4, 1958, TTU; American embassy in Laos to Department of State, May 22, 1956, telegram, in *Foreign Relations of the United States, 1955–1957,* ed. John P. Glennon, vol. 21, *East Asian Security: Cambodia and Laos,* ed. Edward C. Keefer and David W. Mabon (Washington, D.C.: GPO, 1990), 763.

17. G. B. Erskine, Assistant Secretary of Defense for Special Operations, to Assistant Secretary of Defense for International Security Affairs, "Military Equipment for the National Army," April 18, 1956, in *Foreign Relations of the United States, 1955–1957,* 21:759.

18. Byron Engle and Louise Page, *Report on the Internal Security Services of Laos: National Police and Royal Gendarmerie,* Foreign Operations Division, USAID, OPS, Laos, May 1955; Walton, Skuse, and Motter, *A Survey of the Laos National Police,* 25, 33.

19. "Civil Police Administration," December 30, 1955, USOM Laos (1955–1959), box 1, file Police Program.

20. Paul Skuse to Soukan Vilayrsarn and Willard Brown to John Tobler, November 23, 1959, RFAA, USOM Laos, Cables and Airgrams (1955–1958) (hereafter USOM Laos, Cables), box 1; "Paper Prepared by the Operations Coordinating Board: Analysis of Internal Security Situation in Laos (Pursuant to NSC Action 1290-d) and Recommended to Action," December 21, 1955, in Keefer and Mabon, *East Asian Security,* 718–23.

21. Paul Skuse to Daly Lavergne, October 4, 1958, USOM Laos, Cables, box 1.

22. USOM Manila to Theo Hall, chief PSD, Civilian Police Administration, November 19, 1958, USOM Laos, Cables, box 1.

23. Ibid.; Lauren J. Goin and Charles Leister, "Evaluation of the Public Safety Program," USAID, OPS, Laos, November 1969. Chai held a B.A. and an M.A. in public administration from Washington University.

24. "General Outline of the Police Training Project" and "ICA Public Safety Program in Laos," May 18, 1959, Vincent Cillis, Public Safety Division, "Terminal Report," April 23, 1958, all PSD, USOM Laos, box 1, Police Programs.

25. U.S. Congress, House, Committee of on Government Operations, *United States Aid Operations in Laos: Hearings, March 11–June 1, 1959, Seventh Report,* 2; "ICA Annual Status Report on Operations Pursuant to NSC Action 1290-d to Operations Coordinating Board for the National Security Council," December 1955–November 1956, DDEL, OCB, box 18, folder Internal Security.

26. "Conversation with Khouranhok Souvannavong," March 16, 1959, USOM Laos, box 1. On rising costs of living and corruption, see Noam Chomsky, "A Visit to Laos," *New York Review of Books,* July 23, 1970, 21–33; Alfred W. McCoy, *The Politics of Heroin: CIA Complicity in the Global Drug Trade,* rev. ed. (New York: Lawrence Hill, 1991).

27. Nikolas Perazic to Vincent Cillis, "Visit to Sayaboury," March 7, 1958, and Nikolas Perazic to Vincent Cillis, "Re: Sam Neua," March 13, 1958, both USOM Laos, box 1, Police Programs; Ahern, *Undercover Armies,* 552.

28. Paul Skuse to Nikolas Perazic, Public Safety Division, April 2, 1959, USOM Laos, box 1, Police Programs; Walton, Skuse, and Motter, *A Survey of the Laos National Police,* 30–34.

29. Perazic to Cillis, "Visit to Sayaboury; Henry D. Hecksher to Hank Miller and Paul Skuse, "Police Information," USOM Laos, box 1, Police Programs; Jacobs, "No Place to Fight a War," 49.

30. Perazic to Cillis, "Re: Sam Neua."

31. "Police Civic Action Activities," May 18, 1964, RG 286, Records of USAID, OPS, Office of the Director, IPS, (hereafter IPS), box 6, folder 3; "Conversation with Khouranhok Souvannavong."

32. Anthony and Sexton, "The U.S. Air Force in Southeast Asia," 26; Walter S. Robertson to the Secretary, "Preliminary Analysis of Lao Election Results," May 17, 1958; and Henry T. Koren to Department of State, June 23, 1958, RG 59, RDS, box 3362; Stevenson, *The End of Nowhere,* 96; Peter Dale Scott, "Laos: The Story Nixon Won't Tell," *New York Review of Books,* April 9, 1970, 35–45; Brown, *War in Shangri-la,* 212; Paul F. Langer and Joseph Zasloff, *North Vietnam and the Pathet Lao: Partners in the Struggle for Laos* (Cambridge: Harvard University Press, 1970), 66.

33. Sananikone may have also ordered the assassination in 1954 of Defense Minister Kou Voravong, who had promoted conciliation with the Pathet Lao. See "The Murder of Kou Voravong, Defense Minister of Laos" in "3349," *Iron Man of Laos: Prince Phetsarath Ratanavongsa,* ed. David K. Wyatt, trans. John B. Murdoch (Ithaca, N.Y.: Southeast Asia Program, Department of Asian Studies, Cornell University, 1978), 86–89. Some scholars believe, alternatively, that the murder was ordered by Thai police chief Phao Sinyanon, who was seeking to expand Thai hegemony in Laos. See, e.g., Arthur Dommen, *The Indochinese Experience of the French and the Americans: Nationalism and Communism in Cambodia, Laos, and Vietnam* (Bloomington: University of Indiana Press, 2001), 306–7.

34. William Lederer, *A Nation of Sheep* (New York: Fawcett Crest, 1967), 12–13; Fall, *Anatomy of a Crisis,* 137; Sananikone, *The Royal Lao Army and U.S. Army Advice and Support,* 51; Brown, *War in Shangri-la,* 25; Peter Dale Scott, *American War Machine: Deep Politics, the CIA Global Drug Connection, and the Road to Afghanistan* (New York: Rowman and Littlefield, 2010), 99; "Question of Vietminh Presence," American embassy, Vientiane, to Secretary of State, February 10, 1964, LBJL, NSF, box 265. Paul Langer and Joseph Zasloff of RAND, both dogmatically anticommunist, concede in *North Vietnam and the Pathet Lao* that there was no evidence that North Vietnamese units crossed the border. Internal docu-

ments show that there was no proof of an invasion as late as 1964. Bernard Fall characterized the claims advanced in the media by CIA-connected *Washington Post* columnist Joseph Alsop as "nonsense." Fall, *Anatomy of a Crisis,* 135, 138

35. Wilfred G. Burchett, T*he Furtive War: The United States in Vietnam and Laos* (New York: International Publishers, 1963), 173–74; Phoumi Vongvichit, *Laos and the Victorious Struggle of the Lao People against U.S. Neo-Colonialism* (Hanoi: Neo Lao Haksat Publications, 1969), 118. A note on Burchett: In my view, Burchett's pro-communist and anti-imperialist sensibilities do not make him any less credible a reporter than pro-Western journalists who display their own bias. And while it is true that Burchett often accepted government proclamations in communist countries uncritically (his book *China: The Quality of Life* is a particular embarrassment), on the whole, his work is very valuable in documenting the war from the "other side," in relaying its human consequences, and in presenting the worldview of the guerrilla fighters and revolutionary nationalists which is not chronicled or even acknowledged by many Western commentators (including some historians today). Nevertheless, if available, other sources should be used in weighing his claims. For a fair and generally favorable assessment of his life's work, see Ben Kiernan, ed., *Burchett: Reporting the Other Side of the World* (London: Quartet Books, 1987).

36. Sananikone, *The Royal Lao Army and U.S. Army Advice and Support,* 52.

37. Ibid., 106; McCoy, *The Politics of Heroin,* 333; Vongvichit, *Laos and the Victorious Struggle of the Lao People against U.S. Neo-Colonialism,* 199; Ahern, *Undercover Armies,* 49; American embassy, Vientiane, to Secretary of State, December 9, 1963, LBJL, NSF, Laos, box 265; "Political Situation in Laos," August 21, 1958, USOM, Laos, box 1.

38. Mr. Rice to Henry L. T. Koren, "Phoumi's Sins and Blunders," May 4, 1962, RG 59, RDS, Bureau of Far Eastern Affairs, General Records, Office of the Country Director for Laos, box 1 (hereafter Office of the Country Director for Laos); Anthony and Sexton, "The U.S. Air Force in Southeast Asia," 35; Ahern, *Undercover Armies,* 11; Stuart E. Methven, *Laughter in the Shadows: A CIA Memoir* (Annapolis: Naval Institute Press, 2008), 77; Arthur J. Dommen, *Conflict in Laos: The Politics of Neutralization,* rev. ed. (New York: Praeger, 1971), 134. Methven claims that the figure was 3,927 votes, a number derived from his birth date, September 3, 1927.

39. Burchett, *The Furtive War,* 175–76; Philippe Devillers, "The Laotian Conflict in Perspective," in Adams and McCoy, *Laos: War and Revolution,* 44–45; Stuart-Fox, *A History of Laos,* 111–12; Sananikone, *The Royal Lao Army and U.S. Army Advice and Support,* 60. Sananikone claims that Phoumi set Souphanouvong free to avoid a political backlash.

40. American embassy to Secretary of State, "Question of Vietminh Presence," February 10, 1964, LBJL, NSF, Laos, box 265. It was not until later that PAVN (People's Army of Vietnam) involvement became more wide-scale. The manner in which the U.S. government distorted the facts before the public and sold the war by claiming North Vietnamese "aggression" is similar to that regarding the conflict in South Vietnam, where PAVN units did not cross the Seventeenth Parallel systematically until *after* the U.S. invasion. As a reference point, see George McT. Kahin, *Intervention: How America Became Involved in Vietnam* (New York: Knopf, 1986).

41. Anthony and Sexton, "The U.S. Air Force in Southeast Asia," 35; Sananikone, *The Royal Lao Army and U.S. Army Advice and Support,* 77.

42. Wilfred G. Burchett, *The Second Indochina War: Laos and Cambodia* (New York: International Publishers, 1970), 169; Douglas S. Blaufarb, *Organizing and Managing Unconventional War in Laos, 1962–1970* (McLean, Va.: Human Resources Research Organization, 1972), 41; American embassy, Vientiane, to Secretary of State, August 4, 1964, LBJL, Laos,

box 268; Dean Rusk to American embassy, Vientiane, and American embassy to Secretary of State, August 18, 1964, both LBJL, NSF, box 265; Bromley Smith to President, December 14, 1964; and George Denney Jr., U.S. Department of State, to Secretary of State, January 27, 1965, LBJL, NSF, box 269. With regard to the sanctioning of the T-28s, Ambassador Leonard Ungar pledged in a memo to Dean Rusk, "We will keep the U.S. entirely out of this matter with the press, indicating if pressed, that the bombs were in the FAR [Laotian army] arsenal and they apparently have taken the decision if necessary to use them." American embassy, Vientiane, to Secretary of State, March 20, 1964, LBJL, NSF, Country File Asia and the Pacific, Laos, box 265. In May 1964, American aircraft began carrying out operations against strategic Pathet Lao encampments and road networks.

43. Paul H. Skuse to Mr. Daly Lavergne, Director USOM, "Weapons and Ammo for the Lao Police," August 7, 1959, USOM Laos, box 1, Police Programs.

44. Mr. Alden C. Gillchrist, Procurement Officer, USOM Laos, to Mr. John P. Duke, USOM Thailand, radiogram, October 6, 1959, USOM Laos, box 1, Police Programs.

45. USOM Vietnam to USOM Laos, "Buildings for Lao National Police," August 6, 1959, USOM Laos, box 1.

46. Public Safety Division to Mr. Paul Skuse, "Firearms Training," December 15, 1959, USOM Laos, box 1, Police Programs.

47. Walton, Skuse, and Motter, *A Survey of the Laos National Police,* 28. Ryan, a graduate of the University of Minnesota, had spent seven years in Vietnam. He was later murdered by police adviser Robert Kimball for having an affair with Kimball's Vietnamese mistress. On Ryan's background, see Jack E. Ryan, personnel file, Michigan State University archives. Kimball was acquitted in Ryan's murder but sentenced to five years for killing Nguyen Thi Hai, his mistress. He was granted amnesty after a year and returned to the United States.

48. Hugh Toye, *Laos: Buffer State or Battleground* (London: Oxford University Press, 1968), 141; Ahern, *Undercover Armies,* 49.

49. "Summary of Public Safety Employees Wounded and/or Killed in the Line of Duty," IPS, box 10, folder OPS Casualties. Skuse survived and went on to serve in Vietnam. USAR-MACV to Washington, D.C., "Laos," April 18, 1964, LBJL, NSF, box 266, folder Laos; CIA Report, October 18, 1964, LBJL, NSF, box 269.

50. Lansdale memo, July 1961, TTU; Brown, *War in Shangri-la,* 73.

51. Seymour Topping, "Laotians Trace Coup to the Ambitions of a General," *New York Times,* April 27, 1964; D. Gareth Porter, "After Geneva: Subverting Laotian Neutrality," in Adams and McCoy, *Laos: War and Revolution,* 202; Burchett, *The Second Indochina War,* 156; Sananikone, *The Royal Lao Army and U.S. Army Advice and Support,* 73, 79; CIA Intelligence Report, "Decision at Military Officers Meeting Concerning the Reorganization of the Lao Government," April 26, 1964, LBJL, NSF, box 266, folder Laos. Chiang Ching-kuo's background and political activities are described in Scott Anderson and Jon Lee Anderson, *Inside the League: The Shocking Exposé of How Terrorists, Nazis, and Latin American Death Squads Have Infiltrated the World Anticommunist League* (New York: Dodd, Mead, 1986), 56. See also Joseph J. Heinlein Jr., "Political Warfare: The Nationalist Chinese Model" (Ph.D. diss., American University, 1974); and Jay Taylor, *The Generalissimo's Son: Chiang Ching-kuo and the Revolutions in China and Taiwan* (Cambridge: Harvard University Press, 2000), 206–22.

52. Walton, Skuse, and Motter, *A Survey of the Laos National Police,* 34.

53. "Battle of the Neckerchiefs," *Time,* February 12, 1965, 20, 21; Topping, "Laotians Trace Coup to the Ambitions of a General"; William H. Sullivan, U.S. Mission to Laos, 1968, "Post Report," TTU; CIA Intelligence Report, "Decision at Military Officers Meeting Concerning the Reorganization of the Lao Government."

54. Walton, Skuse, and Motter, *A Survey of the Laos National Police,* vi, 1; "Battle of the Neckerchiefs"; U.S. Army Vietnam to Bundy, July 20, 1964, LBJL, NSF, box 268, Laos.

55. Walton, Skuse, and Motter, *A Survey of the Laos National Police,* vi, 1.

56. Sananikone, *The Royal Lao Army and U.S. Army Advice and Support,* 125. The intrigues of plotting the coup and its failure are chronicled in a series of memos in the Laos country files at LBJL, box 269; see, e.g., CIA Information Cable, "Departure of Phoumi-Siho Party for Bangkok," February 11, 1965; and William Sullivan, American embassy, Vientiane, to Secretary of State, March 29, 1965, LBJL, NSF, Laos, box 269. According to former USAID official Loring Waggoner, as reported by Alfred McCoy, Kouprasith's right-hand man, General Thonglith Chokbengboung, told him at a funeral several years after the incident that "Siho was dirty and corrupt" and that he was "glad" that he had had a hand in eliminating him (*The Politics of Heroin,* 605).

57. CIA Info Cable, April 19, 1964; Situation Report, April, 18, 1964; CIA, Office of Current Intelligence, "Background of April 19 Rightist Coup in Laos," April 22, 1964, LBJL, NSF, Laos, box 266.

58. Michael Forrestal to John F. Kennedy, April 9, 1962, Office of the Country Director for Laos, box 1; "Never Were So Many Warnings Ignored as in Laos" and "Dulles Didn't Want Peace in Indochina," *I. F. Stone Weekly,* January 9, 1961, LBJL, NSF, box 266, folder Laos; D. Gareth Porter, "After Geneva: Subverting Laotian Neutrality," in Adams and McCoy, *Laos: War and Revolution,* 179–213.

59. Adolphe Bonnefil, "Plans for Incorporation of Special Commando Units in the LNP," April 23, 1959, RFAA, USOM Laos, box 1, folder Special Commando Units.

60. Charles Maechling Jr., "Development of Indigenous Police and Paramilitary Resources, Department of State, Organization for Internal Defense Matters," JFKL, NSF, box 338.

61. Bonnefil, "Plans for Incorporation of Special Commando Units in the LNP"; L. B. Swick to Jack H. Tobler, dictated by Paul Skuse, October 13, 1959, USOM Laos, box 1, folder Special Commando Units; Henry D. Hecksher, CIA Station Chief, to Henry Miller," November 2, 1959, ibid.; Colonel Virgil Ney, "Guerrilla Warfare and Modern Strategy," in *Modern Guerrilla Warfare: Fighting Communist Guerrilla Movements, 1941–1961,* ed. F. M. Osanka, introduction by Samuel Huntington (New York: Free Press, 1962), 25–38; Drinnon, *Facing West.* There is only limited evidence from the archives (from the material I have gone through) of Pathet Lao assassinations of public officials. In one documented incident, a police master sergeant and a corporal were shot to death by Pathet Lao cadres while riding their bicycles to work in March 1965. Ralph Johnson went on to participate in the Phoenix program in Vietnam.

62. Bonnefil, "Plans for Incorporation of Special Commando Units in the LNP"; Hon. Leonard Ungar, U.S. embassy, Laos, to Department of State, "Commando Units to Operate against PL-Held Route 7," December 11, 1963, LBJL, NSF, Laos, box 265.

63. "A History of PSD in Laos," USOM Laos, box 1, folder Special Commando Units; "Situation at Xieng Khouang," August 27, 1958.

64. L. B. Swick to Paul H. Skuse, "Auto-Defense," December 14, 1959, USOM Laos (1955–1959), box 1, folder Special Commando Units.

65. See Nicholas Evan Sarantakes, *Keystone: The American Occupation of Okinawa and U.S.-Japanese Relations* (College Station: Texas A&M Press, 2000), 38.

66. Walton, Skuse, and Motter, *A Survey of the Laos National Police,* vi, 1; Willard O. Brown, memo for Ambassador, "Report by Mr. Paul Skuse," USOM, Laos, box 1, folder Special Commando Units; Burchett, *The Second Indochina War,* 161; Fred Branfman, "The Secret Wars of the CIA," in *Uncloaking the CIA: Conference on the CIA and World Peace,* ed. Howard E. Frazier (New York: Free Press, 1978), 92.

67. "OCB Report Pursuant to NSC Action 1290-d," August 4, 1955, DDEL, OCB, box 17, folder Internal Security; G. Linwood Barney, "The Meo of Xieng Khouang Province, Laos," in *Southeast Asian Tribes, Minorities, and Nations,* ed. Peter Kunstadter (Princeton: Princeton University Press, 1967), 275.

68. U.S. Army, Laos, to Department of State, Washington, D.C., April 1964, LBJL, NSF, Country File, Asia Pacific, box 266, folder Laos; Sananikone, *The Royal Lao Army and U.S. Army Advice and Support,* 78. On Vang's background, see Ahern, *Undercover Armies,* 29; Timothy Castle, *At War in the Shadow of Vietnam: U.S. Military Aid to the Royal Lao Government, 1955–1975* (New York: Columbia University Press, 1997), 155, 156.

69. Willard O. Brown, memo for Ambassador, "Report by Mr. Paul Skuse"; "Monthly Public Safety Report, Paul Skuse," March 4, 1959, USOM Laos, box 1, folder Special Commando Units.

70. Ahern, *Undercover Armies,* 150; Methven, *Laughter in the Shadows,* 72.

71. CIA to McGeorge Bundy, September 2, 1964, LBJL, NSF, box 268, folder Laos. Route 7 was a heavily bombed area northeast of Phonsavan, the capital of Xieng Khouang province, running from the North Vietnamese border through the Plain of Jars.

72. Douglas S. Blaufarb, *The Counterinsurgency Era: U.S. Doctrine and Performance, 1950 to the Present* (New York: Free Press, 1977), 138; Andrew Tully, *CIA: The Inside Story* (New York: William Morrow, 1962), 217.

73. Ahern, *Undercover Armies,* 213. See also Robert Dean, *Imperial Brotherhood: Gender and the Making of Cold War Foreign Policy* (Amherst: University of Massachusetts Press, 2001), 61.

74. Ahern, *Undercover Armies,* 241, 254.

75. Fred Branfman, *Voices from the Plain of Jars: Life under an Air War* (New York: Harper & Row, 1972), 22.

76. Ahern, *Undercover Armies,* 458; McCoy, *The Politics of Heroin,* 318; Joseph J. Trento, *Prelude to Terror: The Rogue CIA and the Legacy of America's Private Intelligence Network* (New York: Carroll and Graf, 2005), 38. In the National Archives, I found a document pointing to the arrest of Alan Jack Rommel, a twenty-eight-year-old medical technician in Laos, on narcotics violations in Hong Kong. The arrest report mentioned that he was "an associate of the late Tom Dooley in Burma," a known CIA agent. Whether Rommel was dabbling in drugs on the side or was part of something more systematic is not clear. "Alan Jack Rommel," January 24, 1961, RG 170, Records of the DEA, box 160, folder Laos.

77. McCoy, "The Secret War in Laos, 1955–1975," 195; Perry L. Lamy, "Barrel Roll, 1968–1973: An Air Campaign in Support of National Policy," Maxwell Air Force Base, May 10, 1995; Bromley Smith to President, December 14, 1964, LBJL, NSF, Laos, box 269. Operation Barrel Roll focused on northern Laos, while Operation Steel Tiger took place in the eastern portion of the country along the Ho Chi Minh Trail.

78. Ambassador Sullivan to Secretary of State, May 13, 1964, U.S. embassy to USAID; and "Accidental Air Strike," January 21, 1965, LBJL, NSF, box 269, folder Laos. In the errant strike in Khang Khay, on November 22, 1965, the embassy reported that "although 6–8 bombs landed on target, an overwhelming proportion of the ordnance was delivered on Khang Khay [town] itself and considerable destruction was achieved. . . . Most sorties clearly hit the wrong target despite such features as a lake and road network which to a layman's eye, would seem to have made target identification feasible." William Sullivan to Secretary of State, November 24, 1965, LBJL, NSF, box 269, folder Laos.

79. Noam Chomsky, introduction to Adams and McCoy, *Laos: War and Revolution,* xviii; Branfman, *Voices from the Plain of Jars,* 23; Stuart-Fox, *A History of Laos,* 144.

80. Branfman, *Voices from the Plain of Jars,* 38–39.

81. T. D. Allman, "Ruined Town a Vignette of War in Laos," *New York Times,* October 17, 1969; T. D. Allman, "The War in Laos: Plain Facts," *Far Eastern Economic Review,* January 8, 1972, 16; Fred Branfman, "A Lake of Blood," *New York Times,* April 7, 1971; Branfman, *Voices from the Plain of Jars,* 4.

82. Ahern, *Unconventional Armies,* 181; Branfman, *Voices from the Plain of Jars,* 48–49, 81; Burchett, *The Second Indochina War;* Garrett, "Subversion and Revolution in Laos," 97.

83. Robert Shaplen, *Time Out of Hand: Revolution and Reaction in Southeast Asia* (New York: Harper & Row, 1969), 348; Ahern, *Unconventional Armies,* 327; McCoy, *The Politics of Heroin,* 436.

84. Walton, Skuse, and Motter, *A Survey of the Laos National Police,* vi, 1. Information on Gordon Young is drawn from McCoy, *The Politics of Heroin,* 339, and Young, *Journey from Banna* (Indianapolis: Xilibris, 2011). McBee's shadowy background is detailed in Douglas Valentine, *The Strength of the Pack: The Personalities, Politics, and Espionage Intrigues That Shaped the DEA* (Walterville, Ore.: Trine Day, 2009), 64, 166–67. John Doney was another adviser with CIA connections who trained paramilitary "hunter-killer" squads in Colombia.

85. Walton, Skuse, and Motter, *A Survey of the Laos National Police,* 6, 7, 9.

86. Ibid., 35. Trained at a French Gendarmerie school and with the police Special Branch in Malaya, Pradichit, a member of the national Olympic committee, was a military attaché to Thailand from 1962 to 1964 serving in Bangkok, where he coordinated BPP and Police Aerial Reconnaissance Unit support for the RLA and the Hmong army in the secret war.

87. Peter Ellena, John Means, and Paul Katz, "Laos, Termination Phase-Out Study by the Public Safety Project," May 1974, RG 286, USAID, OPS, Office of the Director of Program Surveys and Evaluation, Technical Services Division (hereafter TSD), box 6, folder Laos.

88. Paul H. Skuse, Chief Public Safety Advisor, USAID Laos, to Leonard Friesz, "Public Safety Reloading," December 18, 1968, TSD, box 6, folder Laos.

89. "Public Safety Project Laos, Phase-Out," May 1974, TSD box 6, folder Laos; Lauren J. Goin and Charles Leister, "Evaluation of the Public Safety Program, USAID Laos," November 1969. On OPS counter-narcotics efforts during the early 1970s, see Jeremy Kuzmarov, *The Myth of the Addicted Army: Vietnam and the Modern War on Drugs* (Amherst: University of Massachusetts Press, 2009), 140–43. Pathet Lao leader Phoumi Vongvichit commented accurately that "anti-opium measures in Vientiane" served as a "camouflage for CIA" activities. American embassy Manila, to Secretary of State, Washington, D.C., February 1974, IPS, box 10.

90. The term "sideshow" derives from William Shawcross's important study *Sideshow: Kissinger, Nixon, and the Destruction of Cambodia* (New York: Pocket Books, 1979).

91. Edward P. Lilly to Mr. Satterthwaite, "Comments on Report to NSC Pursuant to NSC Action 1290-d," September 26, 1955, DDEL, OCB, box 17, folder Internal Security; Report of 1290-d Working Group, February 16, 1955; Byron Engle and Louis [*sic*] Page, "Secret Report on Internal Security Services of Cambodia: National Police, Municipal Police, Surface Defense Forces," Foreign Operations Administration, Phnom Penh, April 1, 1955, MSUA, Vietnam Project. Louise Page is listed as "Louis" Page on this report and also in official OPS employment records. She was said to be affiliated with International Police Equipment Corporation, a known CIA front. This was evidently part of her cover.

92. T. C. Niblock to Byron Engle, Cambodia, "Monthly Report, 8-13-1963," November 18, 1963; "Monthly Public Safety Report," September 19, 1963, TSD, box Cambodia, folder 3; Ben Kiernan, *How Pol Pot Came to Power: Colonialism, Nationalism, and Communism in Cambodia, 1930–1975* (London: Verso, 1985), 216.

93. Robert W. Komer, "Memo for Members of Study Groups on Deterrence of Guerrilla Warfare, Revised Draft Outline," March 8, 1961, RWK, box 414, folder 1, Special Group. On U.S. strategic and economic interests in Burma, see Jonathan Marshall, "Opium, Tungsten, and the Search for National Security, 1940–1952," in *Drug Control Policy: Essays in Historical and Comparative Perspective,* ed. William O. Walker III (University Park: Pennsylvania University Press, 1992). On how the War on Drugs was later used to perpetuate support for Ne Win's forces, see Bertil Lintner, "Heroin and Highland Insurgency in the Golden Triangle," in *War on Drugs: Studies in the Failure of U.S. Narcotics Policy,* ed. Alfred W. McCoy and Alan A. Block (Boulder: Westview Press, 1992), 274; and Kuzmarov, *Myth of the Addicted Army,* chap. 6.

94. See Wilfred Burchett and Norodom Siahnouk, *My War with the CIA: The Memoirs of Prince Norodom Sihanouk as Related to Wilfred Burchett* (New York: International Publishers, 1962); "Records of the Third Meeting of the Inter-Agency Police Group," February 18, 1963, RG 286, USAID, OPS, International Police Academy, box 8, folder 1.

95. Kiernan, *How Pol Pot Came to Power,* 252; Peter Dale Scott, *Drugs, Oil, and War* (New York: Rowman and Littlefield, 2004), 167–70; Douglas Valentine, *The Phoenix Program* (New York: Morrow, 1991), 328.

96. Red Sutton to James Cretecos, "Narcotics Enforcement in Cambodia," June 14, 1971, RG 286, USAID, OPS, Thailand, Narcotics, box 19, folder 4; American embassy, Phnom Penh, to Department of State, "Cambodian Drug Suppression Report no. 1," January 27, 1972, "Trafficking in Illicit Narcotics by Air in Southeast Asia," May 28, 1972, and "Narcotics Training Customs," June 1973, all RDS, BFEA, Cambodia (1970–1973), box 3057.

97. See Mark Selden and Alvin Y. So, eds., *War and State Terrorism: The United States, Japan, and the Asia-Pacific in the Long Twentieth Century* (New York: Rowman & Littlefield, 2004); Noam Chomsky and Edward S. Herman, *The Political Economy of Human Rights,* vol. 1, *The Washington Connection and Third World Fascism* (Boston: South End Press, 1979), 240; Anthony Lewis, "Another Senate Test," *New York Times,* July 9, 1973, 33.

98. Quoted in Cumings, *Dominion from Sea to Sea,* 471.

99. See especially Mahmood Mamdani, "The Cold War after Indochina," in *Good Muslim, Bad Muslim: America, the Cold War, and the Roots of Terror* (New York: Pantheon, 2005); Chalmers Johnson, *Blowback: The Costs and Consequences of the American Empire* (New York: Metropolitan Books, 2002).

7. "As I Recall the Many Tortures"

1. Quoted in James Bower to Jack Ryan, PSD, "Grenade Incident at Banmethuot," April 19, 1965, RG 472, RAFSEA, HQ MACV, CORDS, Public Safety Directorate, Field Operations (hereafter CORDS Public Safety), Director General Records, box 2.

2. Warren Hinckle, Robert Scheer, and Sol Stern, "Michigan State: The University on the Make," introduction by Stanley K. Scheinbaum, *Ramparts,* April 1966, 80–97.

3. Statement by John Hannah, president, Michigan State University, April 22, 1966, Hannah Papers, MSUA; "With the CIA in Vietnam: Campus Cloaks a 'Spy' Operation, Raises a Dispute in the Midwest," *Lansing State Journal,* April 18, 1966, article in Hannah Papers. In response to the *Ramparts* article, Wesley Fishel commented in a veiled substantiation of its charges, "There was no secret about intelligence agents' presence on the project's payroll and they performed no cloak and dagger work—they were simply there to train the Vietnamese civil police in countersubversive activities." Hannah himself acknowledged the employment of individuals with intelligence backgrounds to work in the field of "countersubversion."

4. Seth Jacobs, *Cold War Mandarin: Ngo Dinh Diem and the Origins of America's War in Vietnam, 1950–1963* (New York: Rowman & Littlefield, 2006), 7, 17, 21; U.S. Congress, Senate, *Causes, Origins, and Lessons of the Vietnam War: Hearings before the Committee on ForeignRelations*, 92nd Cong., 2nd sess., May 9, 10, 1972 (Washington, D.C.: GPO, 1972), 198. When asked at the hearing whether it was true that Ho Chi Minh would have received 80 percent of the popular vote in an election, OSS agent Frank White responded, "certainly yes" (198).

5. Jacobs, *Cold War Mandarin*, 26, 85.

6. Dr. Wesley R. Fishel, "Remarks to the Rotary Club of Saigon: The Role of the Michigan State University Group in Vietnam," September 12, 1957, *Vietmy*, February 1957, 41; Robert Scigliano and Guy H. Fox, *Technical Assistance in Vietnam: The Michigan State University Experience* (New York: Praeger, 1965), 2; Joseph Starr, "Civil Police Administration Program," October 18, 1956, RG 469, RFAA, 1948–1961, Office of Public Services, box 1.

7. Quoted in Marc Curtis, *Unpeople: Britain's Secret Human Rights Abuses* (London: Vintage, 2004), 203.

8. See John Ernst, *Forging a Fateful Alliance: Michigan State University and the Vietnam War* (East Lansing: Michigan State University Press, 1998), 13, 14; ICA, "Annual Status Report on Operations Pursuant to NSC Action 1290-d to Operations Coordinating Board for the National Security Council," December 1955–November 1956, DDEL, White House Office, NSC, OCB, Central File Series, box 18, folder Internal Security; Howard Hoyt, Chief of Police, Kalamazoo, Mich., and Coordinator, German police training program, to Albert Scheiern, Grand Rapids, Mich., Turner Papers. Internal records show, for example, that MSU sponsored Heinz Gutadel, age thirty, a member of the Frankfurt police department who had been drafted into the Wehrmacht in World War II, became a fighter pilot, and was shot down over Dunkirk. He was later sent to Russia and served in the Nazi army in Normandy, where he was captured and released after two years in a POW camp. Another of the invitees was Karl Meyer, age twenty-six, a German naval officer captured in the Mediterranean. No one at MSU appeared to express any consternation about their backgrounds.

9. Arthur F. Brandstatter, Personnel File, MSUA. In 1961 Brandstatter was named a Silver Anniversary All-American by *Sports Illustrated*, an honor he shared with Green Bay Packers coach Vince Lombardi and Oklahoma coach Charles "Bud" Wilkinson. Robert Kennedy and Richard Nixon were among the judges. Brandstatter retired from the U.S. military in 1969 with the rank of brigadier general after thirty-two years' service. Born in McKee Rock, Pennsylvania, he earned both B.A. and M.SC degrees from MSU in police administration.

10. Personnel File, Howard G. Hoyt, MSUA. During World War II, Hoyt was director of security for Gopher ordnance works in St. Paul, Minnesota, possibly engaging in industrial surveillance. His son, a Korean War veteran, was also in police administration at MSU.

11. Jack Ryan to Howard Hoyt, "General Nguyen Van La," April 1, 1958, MSUA Vietnam Project, box 683; "Sureté or VBI and Municipal Police in Brief," MSUA Vietnam Project, box 679; Jack E. Ryan to Howard Hoyt, "General Information Regarding the VBI and Its General Headquarters," April 17, 1956, 4, TTU; Ernst, *Forging a Fateful Alliance*, 65–66. Le was later promoted to the Defense Department.

12. Jack E. Ryan, "Brief History of the Sureté in Indochina," MSUG, January 19, 1956, 7; Arthur Brandstatter et al., "Field Trip Report: Police and Security Services," May 9–11, 1960; and "Field Trip Report VBI (Cong An), Long An, Kien Hoa, and Binh Duong Provinces," December 10–11, 1959, MSUA Vietnam Project, box 684; Ralph H. Smuckler and members of the police team, "Report on the Police of Vietnam" MSUG, Technical Assistance Project, December 1, 1955; "Public Safety Assistance: Vietnam, Historical Background," CORDS,

PSD, Public Safety Program, Information Handbook; Maxwell Taylor, "Memo for Members of the Special Group: U.S. Support of Foreign Paramilitary Forces," RG 286, Records of the USAID, OPS, Program Surveys and Evaluations, box 5, folder 1.

13. Noam Chomsky and Ngo Vinh Long, "Thirty-Year Retrospective on the Fall of Saigon," public forum held at Massachusetts Institute of Technology, Boston, on the thirtieth anniversary of the end of the Vietnam War, April 30, 2005; John McCabe to Martin L. Gross, "Monthly Activity Report," December 1961, RG 286, Records of the USAID, OPS, Operations Division, East Asia Branch, Vietnam, Police Operations (hereafter OPS East Asia Branch), folder 1.

14. "Report of NSC 1290-D Working Group, Summary of Status of Internal Security Forces Prepared by the Pentagon," Appendix B,"Survey of the Vulnerability of Various Countries to Communist Subversion," February 16, 1955, DDEL, OCB, box 16, folder Internal Security; Albert Haney, "OCB Report Pursuant to NSC Action 1290-d, "August 5, 1955, DDEL, OCB, box 17, folder Internal Security.

15. The strength of the Vietminh and the dependency of the Vietnamese government on foreign patronage are misrepresented by the so-called revisionists or neo-orthodox historians such as Mark Moyar (in *Triumph Forsaken* [New York: Cambridge University Press, 2008]) and Edward Miller (in "Vision, Power, and Agency: The Ascent of Ngo Dinh Diem, 1945–1954," *Journal of Southeast Asian Studies* 35 [2004]: 433–58), who ignore considerable evidence and documentation in their efforts to rehabilitate Diem and rationalize the U.S. intervention.

16. "Personnel," MSUA Vietnam Project, box 679. Some of the CIA men assigned to the VBI were listed under generic names in the MSU records (Arthur Stein, William A. K. Jones, and Dan Smith) in order to hide their real identities. George Kimball, a twenty-five-year year veteran of the Detroit police who trained radio technicians, died suddenly from illness during his tour.

17. Jack Ryan, Personnel File, MSUA; Margaret Lauterbach, "MSU-Trained Vietnamese Praised by U.S. Adviser," *East Lansing Town Courier,* June 30, 1965; "VBI Detention Center," October 7, 1958, MSUA Vietnam Project, box 684; Ryan and Manopoli to Hoyt, "Gia Dinh Detention Center," August 21, 1958, MSUA Vietnam Project, box 684. Ryan officially served as a lecturer on the MSU faculty for a year before going to Vietnam, though it is not clear if he ever taught any classes. Howard Hoyt characterized Boudrias as "undependable, dishonest and vicious," an example of the internal dissension among the MSU advisers.

18. MSUG September Monthly Reports, October 8, 1957; "Civil Guard in Brief," MSUA Vietnam Project, box 679; Howard Hoyt to USOM Saigon, "Monthly Civil Police Report, November"; and "Semi-Annual Report," July 1957, MSUA Vietnam Project, box 679; *The PentagonPapers:The Senator Gravel Edition,* vol. 1 (Boston: Beacon Press, 1971), 314, quoted in John A. Nagl, *Learning to Eat Soup with a Knife: Counterinsurgency Lessons from Malaya and Vietnam* (Chicago: University of Chicago Press, 2007), 121. Walton was also at the time a lieutenant colonel in the Marine Reserve. Updike told a British official that he sought to mold the civil guard after police forces in New York which fought the "Red Indians," reading books about those forces in preparation. See William Rosenau, *US Internal Security Assistance to South Vietnam: Insurgency, Subversion, and Public Order* (London: Routledge, 2005), 133.

19. Edward W. Weidner, Chief Adviser National Institute of Administration, Saigon, "Second Report of the MSUG in Public Administration to the Government of Vietnam," December 31, 1955; and Howard W. Hoyt, "Training Plan for Assisting the Government of Vietnam in the Training of Their Civil Police Force, MSUG, Police Division, Saigon," November 1957, MSUG, 15; Ernst, *Forging a Fateful Alliance,* 65.

20. The correspondence is scattered throughout the records of the MSUA Vietnam Project. Hoyt also relished the opportunity to travel in Europe on his journey home. His wife, Blanche, was perceptive in criticizing the fawning media depictions of Mme. Nhu, noting that she was "hated and feared by the people" and that the Nhus had become millionaires, with property in many parts of the world, including huge homes built for them in England. For the ugly American reference, see William J. Lederer and Eugene Burdick, *The Ugly American* (New York: Norton, 1962). The colorful novel criticizes Americans for living like colonials in Southeast Asia while the communists were out in the field "winning hearts and minds."

21. "Confidential Memo: Interview with Returning Vietnam Staff Members," Ralph Turner Papers, MSUA Vietnam Project, box 1694 (hereafter Turner Papers); Scigliano and Fox, *Technical Assistance in Vietnam*, 18–19.

22. "Confidential Memo: Interview with Returning Vietnam Staff Members." After ending his tenure with the Vietnam project in September 1960, along with his wife Hoyt bought a travel lodge in Oklahoma City, where he had grown up, and became a consultant to the Oklahoma City police force. In letters to former colleagues he expressed his desire to return to Vietnam, though it does not appear that he ever served with the OPS.

23. Jack E. Ryan to Howard Hoyt, "General Information Regarding the VBI and Its General Headquarters," April 17, 1956, TTU; "Ryan Interview with Mr. Phan Van Son, Study of the VBI in the Field, Tanan Province," April 23, 1956, MSUA Vietnam Project, box 681; E. C. Updike, "Field Trip to Binh-Dinh, Phu-Yen, Khanh Hoa, Ninh Tuan Province with Director General of the Civil Guard," March 19–22, 1958, MSUA Vietnam Project, box 681.

24. Wesley R. Fishel, Howard W. Hoyt, and Ralph Turner, "Preliminary Report of a Central Record Bureau Service, MSUG," August 1957, MSUG; Ryan to Hoyt, "General Information Regarding the VBI and Its General Headquarters"; "Seventh Report of the MSUG in Public Administration to the Government of Vietnam, Saigon," June 39, 1958, MSUG, 9.

25. Ralph F. Turner, Personnel File, MSUA Vietnam Project; Daniel Behringer, "Old-Time Touch: He's a Crime, Nostalgia Buff," *Lansing State Journal,* July 18, 1977. In 1973 Turner received the Bruce Smith Award from the American Academy of Forensics Sciences and in 1981 was given distinguished faculty honors by MSU on the occasion of his retirement.

26. "September Monthly Report," MSUG, October 8, 1957; "August Monthly Report," September 8, 1958; "November Monthly Report on Civil Police Administration Program for Republic of Vietnam," December 3, 1957; and "February Monthly Report," March 12, 1958, MSUA Vietnam Project, box 679; Shields, Wiener, Siemek, "Field Trip Report, VBI, Long An, Kien Hoa, Binh Duong," December 10–11, 1959, MSUA Vietnam Project, box 681; "Field Trip Report, VBI (Cong An), Darlac, Pleiku, Kontum," October 12–17, 1959; and "Field Trip Report, VBI, Vinh Long," November 17–20, 1959, MSUA Vietnam Project, box 684.

27. "Ryan Interview with Mr. Phan Van Son"; "Ryan Interview with Mr. Hyunh, Quang Phuoc, Can Tho Province," April 19, 1956, TTU Virtual Vietnam Archive; Thomas L. Ahern Jr., *The CIA and the House of Ngo: Covert Action in South Vietnam, 1954–1963* (Washington, D.C.: CIA, Center for the Study of Intelligence, 1999), 95; Nguyen Thi Dinh, *No Other Road to Take,* trans. Mai V. Elliot (Ithaca: Cornell Southeast Asia Program, 1976), 56–58; Martin A. Nicolaus, *The Professors, the Policemen, and the Peasants: The Sociology of the Michigan State University Group Vietnam Project, 1955–1962* (Burnaby, B.C.: Simon Fraser University, 1966), 1.

28. James M. Carter, *Inventing Vietnam: The United States and State Building, 1954–1968* (New York: Cambridge University Press, 2008), 68; Douglas Valentine, *The Phoenix Program* (New York: William Morrow, 1991), 32; William Benson to John F. McCabe, "Visit to Chi Hoa Prison," May 4, 1961, RG 286, USAID, OPS, Vietnam, box 287, Penology; "The

Prison of Chi Hoa," MSUA Vietnam Project, box 680; Wilfred G. Burchett, *The Furtive War: The United States in Vietnam and Laos* (New York: International Publishers, 1963), 49.

29. Ahern Jr., *The CIA and the House of Ngo,* 95; Marilyn B. Young, *The Vietnam Wars, 1945–1990* (New York: HarperPerennial, 1991), 339; Jack Ryan to Ralph Turner, February 8, 1961, Turner Papers; Joseph Starr, "Civil Police Administration Program," October 18, 1956, RG 469, RFAA, 1948–1961, OPS, box 1. OPS adviser Frank Walton similarly wrote in a secret memo that the Diem regime employed the police in "Gestapo-like operation[s] with midnight arrests, holding without charge, brutality and detentions in secret locations." Rosenau, *US Internal Security Assistance to South Vietnam,* 125.

30. Joseph Buttinger, *Vietnam: A Dragon Embattled,* vol. 2 (New York: Frederick A. Praeger, 1967), 952–53; Jeffrey Race, *War Comes to Long An: Revolutionary Conflict in a Vietnamese Province* (Berkeley: University of California Press, 1972), 197; David Hunt, *Vietnam's Southern Revolution: From Peasant Insurrection to Total War, 1959–1968* (Amherst: University of Massachusetts Press, 2009); Truong Nhu Tang, *A Vietcong Memoir: An Inside Account of the Vietnam War and Its Aftermath* (New York: Harcourt Brace Jovanovich, 1985); Pham Van Bach, ed., *Fascist Terror in South Vietnam: Law 10/59* (Hanoi: Gioi, 1961). See also George McT. Kahin, *Intervention: How America Became Involved in Vietnam* (New York: Knopf, 1986), 155; Bernard B. Fall, *The Two Vietnams: A Political and Military Analysis,* 2nd ed. (Boulder: Westview Press, 1984), 272

31. Art Brandstatter to Ralph Turner, "Analysis of Role of Security Services," February 3, 1961, Turner Papers, MSUA. As a postscript, in 1965, members of the MSUG still on the faculty, including Brandstatter, Turner, and Fishel, signed a petition that appeared in the *New York Times* condemning the academic teach-in movement, supported by their former colleague Stan Sheinbaum, for perpetuating "numerous falsehoods" and a naïveté about the character of the "Vietcong." Later, after the political winds shifted, many MSUG personnel claimed to be against the war, placing much of the blame for the failure of state-building projects on the South Vietnamese.

32. Robert H. Johnson, "Memo for Walt Rostow, Subject Civic Action in Vietnam," October 6, 1961, JFKL, NSF, box 113; Michael McClintock, *Instruments of Statecraft: U.S. Guerrilla Warfare, Counterinsurgency, and Counterterrorism, 1940–1990* (New York: Pantheon, 1992); Stan Swofford, "Law Enforcement Expert Home Now," *Greensboro Daily News,* [n.d.] 1974 (courtesy of Patsy Harrington, family collection).

33. "The Role of Public Safety in Support of the National Police of Vietnam," April 1, 1969, USAID, OPS (Washington, D.C.: GPO, 1969); Ngo Vinh Long, "The CIA and the Vietnam Debacle," in *Uncloaking the CIA,* ed. Howard Frazier (New York: Free Press, 1978), 71; "Public Safety Assistance: Vietnam, Historical Background," CORDS, Public Safety Program, Information Handbook, RG 286, USAID, OPS, Office of the Director of Programs, Surveys, and Evaluations (hereafter Programs, Surveys, and Evaluations), box 5.

34. Arthur Shively to Charles Sloane, "Requisition for Weapons," September 1, 1965, CORDS Public Safety, box 1; "Public Safety Assistance: Vietnam, Historical Background," CORDS, Public Safety Program, Information Handbook; Frank Walton to Arthur Z. Gardiner, "MAAG Coastal Surveillance Concept," OPS East Asia Branch box 278, folder 2 ; "Resources Control by the National Police of Vietnam," July 1966 (Washington, D.C.: GPO, 1966); Robert Lowe to Col. Pham Van Lieu, Director General of National Police, Police HQ, Saigon, CORDS Public Safety, box 1, Vietnam; Thomas L. Ahern Jr., *The CIA and Rural Pacification in South Vietnam* (Washington, D.C.: CIA, Center for the Study of Intelligence, 2006), 279–88; John F. Sullivan, *Of Spies and Lies: A CIA Lie Detector Remembers Vietnam* (Lawrence: University Press of Kansas, 2002).

35. "Required Arms for Presidential Guard," July 20, 1961, OPS East Asia Branch, box 278, folder Police Operations; James Bower to Charlie O'Brien, "Labor Strike at RMK Projects in Cam Ranh Bay Area," November 15, 1965, CORDS Public Safety, box 2; "November Monthly Report on Civil Police Administration Program for Republic of Vietnam, "December 3, 1957, MSUA Vietnam Project, box 679; Captain Horner to Howard Hoyt, "Security for Johnson, Drake and Paper of Vietnam Inc.," April 10, 1958, MSUA Vietnam Project, box 690; Carter, *Inventing Vietnam,* 185.

36. Thomas Finn to John F. Manopoli, Chief of Public Safety, April 29, 1968, RG 286, USAID, OPS, Technical Services Division, General Correspondences, box 13, folder Vietnam.

37. Byron Engle to Frank Walton, "Police Attack on Buddhist Demonstrations," July 1963, CORDS Public Safety, box 5; Otto Ludwig, PSD, to Robert Lowe, "Buddhist Demonstration," March 23, 1966, CORDS Public Safety, box 5.

38. Ray Landgren to Frank Walton, "Observations of Buddhist Police Incident 17 July 1963 at 582 Pham Tranh Gien Near the Ginc Minh Pagoda," July 17, 1963, OPS East Asia Branch, box 286. These actions seem to have been typical; police later murdered the French correspondent Paul Léandri for reporting facts that challenged the official view of a North Vietnamese takeover of the South. For reports on another incident of police harassment of reporters, see U.S. Congress, Senate, Committee on Foreign Relations, "Ambassador Durbrow's Press Relations, Situation in Vietnam," Hearings, 86th Cong., 1st sess. (Washington, D.C.: GPO, 1959), 25 and Wilfred Burchett, *Grasshoppers and Elephants: Why Vietnam Fell* (New York: Urizen Books, 1977), 16.

39. Buttinger, *Vietnam,* 996; Jacobs, *Cold War Mandarin,* 154.

40. Tang, *A Vietcong Memoir,* 90; CIA Report, October 1, 1964, LBJL, NSF, box 269, folder Laos; Shively to Sloane, "Requisition for Weapons" "Briefing for Mr. McNamara, Weekly Report," July 1965, CORDS Public Safety, box 1.

41. Robert W. Komer, "The Other War in Vietnam: A Progress Report" (USAID 1966), 14, Ogden Williams Papers, TTU; David Welch, "Pacification in Vietnam," *Ramparts,* October 1967, 61–79; Orrin DeForest, "Endless War," *New York Times,* August 16, 1990. On the Malayan precedent, see Leon Comber, *Malaya's Secret Police, 1945-1960: The Role of the Special Branch in the Malayan Emergency* (Singapore: ISEAS/Monash University Press, 1997); Valentine, *The Phoenix Program,* 92. Grieves had a reputation for being uncouth and an alcoholic. In 1972 he became deputy to public safety chief Byron Engle after a stint as deputy commander of the Special Warfare Center at Fort Bragg under General William Yarborough.

42. Douglas Blaufarb, *The Counterinsurgency Era: U.S. Doctrine and Performance, 1950 to the Present* (New York: Free Press, 1977), 216.

43. William Corson, *The Betrayal* (New York: Norton, 1968), 92; Thomas L. Ahern Jr., *CIA and the Generals: Covert Support to Military Government in South Vietnam* (Washington, D.C.: CIA, 2006), 46; Leigh Brilliant to John Manopoli, "Monthly Report," April 1968, CORDS Public Safety, General Records, box 9; Tom Buckley, "Portrait of an Aging Despot," *Harper'sMagazine,* April 1972, 68–72. William J. Lederer characteristically wrote in the introduction to *Our Own Worst Enemy* (New York: Norton, 1968) that he could not thank his Vietnamese friends by name because if he did, "they might receive a midnight visit from General Loan's men, or Vice President Ky's secret police" (7). Ky was characterized by Diem as a "cowboy," a term usually reserved for flamboyant Cholon gangsters.

44. "National Identity Registration Project: ID Card, Public Safety Division, Office of Civil Operation," June 8, 1966, Programs, Surveys, and Evaluations, Thailand, box 11, folder 4; "Resources Control, National Police of Vietnam," March 1965, PSD, USOM, Saigon, 23;

E. H. Adkins Jr., "The Police and Resource Control in Counter-Insurgency," January 1964, PSD, USOM, Saigon, 76; Orrin DeForest with David Chanoff, *Slow Burn: The Rise and Bitter Fall of American Intelligence in Vietnam* (New York: Simon & Schuster, 1990), 76. The OPS replicated this system in the Philippines, Thailand, and worldwide.

45. Noam Chomsky and Edward S. Herman, *The Political Economy of Human Rights: The Washington Connection and Third World Fascism* (Boston: South End Press, 1979), 331–32; Tang, *A Vietcong Memoir*, 81, 102–16; Sandra C. Taylor, *Vietnamese Women at War: Fighting for Ho Chi Minh and the Revolution* (Lawrence: University Press of Kansas, 1999). Training manuals stressed the importance of carrying out arrests late at night or in the dawn hours to catch suspects unaware.

46. "Monthly Report, Long Xuyen, An Giang Province," June 1967, CORDS Public Safety, box 1; Amnesty International, *Political Prisoners in South Vietnam* (London: Amnesty International Publications, Indochina Resource Center, 1973), 36; Tang, *A Vietcong Memoir*, 81; "Saigon Peace Candidate Released after 5 Years," *New York Times*, March 27, 1973.

47. "Resources Control, National Police of Vietnam," March 1965, PSD, USOM, 40–41; "Monthly Report: Tuyen Duc Province," December 15, 1965, CORDS Public Safety, box 1.

48. "The Role of Public Safety in Support of the National Police of Vietnam," April 1, 1969, OPS, USAID (Washington, D.C.: GPO, 1969); L. J. Chapman to Glenn Dodge, "Increased Reporting and Apprehension of ARVN Deserters," April 18, 1966, RG 472, RAFSEA, HQ USAV, Provost Marshall, Protective Services Division, Criminal Investigations Branch (1972) (hereafter CIB), box 1, folder 1; Robert K. Brigham, *ARVN: Life and Death in the South Vietnamese Army* (Lawrence: University Press of Kansas, 2006).

49. E. H. Adkins Jr., "The Police and Resource Control in Counter-Insurgency," January 1964, PSD, USOM, Saigon, 42; Robert Lowe, Memo for the Senior Adviser, "Resources Control Survey of Hau Nghia Province," September 13, 1966, CORDS Public Safety, General Records, box 4; Jacob Harris to Marcus J. Gordon, "Resource Control, Hué," December 7, 1965, CORDS Public Safety, General Records, box 4.

50. "Excerpt from "Goin's Monthly Arrest Report," October 1965, CORDS Public Safety, box 1; Collier, Marion, to Sloane, "Incident Involving Military and NP," March 15, 1966, CORDS Public Safety, box 5; Ken Cox to Robert Lowe, "Monthly Report, Bien Hoa," April 1966, February 1976; Stephen J. Ledogar, "Monthly Report," September 19, 1966, CORDS Public Safety, box 5; A.M. Craig, Beryel J. Pace, "Monthly Report, Precinct no. 1," December 4, 1968, CORDS Public Safety, box 14, folder Phuong Hoang; Jacob Harris to Robert Lowe, "Bombing Demilitarized Zone Police Compound," September 27, 1965; Monthly Report, Central Lowlands Hué, September 1965, CORDS Public Safety, box 2.

51. Michael G. McCann, Director, OPS, Bureau, to John Manopoli, Chief, Vietnam Division, "Historical Narrative: PSD Support of Narcotic Control," Personnel Policy Division, Drug Abuse Programs, box 286, folder 2; U.S. embassy, Saigon, to Secretary of State, OPS, Vietnam Division, "Narcotics Control," November 11, 1972, box 112, folder 3; "Updating of Narcotics Control Action Program, Office of Public Safety to American embassy, Saigon," July 1971, RG 286, USAID, OPS, East Asia Branch, Narcotics Control, Vietnam (hereafter Narcotics Control Vietnam), box 113, folder 6; Howard Groom to Frank Walton, Monthly Narcotics Bureau Report, June 1969, CORDS Public Safety, Monthly Reports, box 2. For further details, see my *Myth of the Addicted Army: Vietnam and the Modern War on Drugs* (Amherst: University of Massachusetts Press, 2009), chap. 6. Manopoli, Frank Walton, and Jon Weiss, a Las Vegas police officer who assisted in the overthrow of Cheddi Jagan in Guyana, also ran the program.

52. Holmes Brown and Don Luce, "The Present Situation of Chi Hoa Prison," in *Hostages of War: Saigon's Political Prisoners*, ed. Brown and Luce (Washington, D.C.: Indochina

Mobile Education Project, 1973), 56; Frank Walton to Charles Vopat, "Alleged Corrupt Practices of Nguyen Huy Thong, Chief, Narcotics Bureau," March 31, 1971, Narcotics Control, Vietnam, box 112, folder 4; Henry Kamm, "Drive Fails to Halt Drug Sale in Vietnam," *New York Times,* August 30, 1971; Alfred W. McCoy, *The Politics of Heroin: CIA Complicity in the Global Drug Trade,* rev. ed. (New York: Lawrence Hill, 2004), 255–56.

53. "Alleged National Police Misconduct (Shakedown)," March 18, 1972, RG 286, USAID, OPS, Office of the Assistant Chief of Staff, CORDS, box 278, folder 2; "PSD Survey of Black Market Activities," April 16, 1964, OPS East Asia Branch, box 285, folder Black Market.

54. William J. Lederer, *The Anguished American* (London: Victor Gollancz, 1968), 120; Corson, *The Betrayal,* 93–94; U.S. Congress, Senate, Committee on the Judiciary, "Testimony of Frederick P. Herter, War Related Civilian Problems in Indochina," pt. 3, "Vietnam," 92nd Cong., 1st sess., April 21, 1971 (Washington, D.C.: GPO, 1971), 24; Don Luce and John Sommer, *Vietnam: The Unheard Voices* (Ithaca: Cornell University Press, 1969), 96; Noam Chomsky and Edward S. Herman, "Saigon's Corruption Crisis: The Search for an Honest Quisling," *Ramparts* (December 1975): 22.

55. Richard D. Braaten to Charles Sloane, "Weekly Highlight Report," December 22, 1965, CORDS Public Safety, box 1; Chester C. Jew to John Manopoli, "CORDS Monthly Report," July 5, 1968, CORDS Public Safety, box 14, folder Phuong Hoang; Kuzmarov, *Myth of the Addicted Army;* Theodore Brown to Deputy, CORDS, "Allegations of Corruption in Vung Tau," October 12, 1967, CORDS Public Safety, box 21.

56. James McMahon to Bob Lowe, "Quang Tri NP/Charges of Misconduct," September 19, 1966, CORDS Public Safety, box 5; Elmer Brick, Senior Adviser, Quang Tri, to David Lazar, Deputy, June 17, 1970, CORDS Public Safety, box 5; William Colby to CORDS, "Corruption in Bien Hoa," July 2, 1970, CORDS Public Safety, Phung Hoang, box 21, folder Corrupt Practices; Charles Whitehouse, Deputy, CORDS, to Ambassador William Colby, "Shakedowns," June 22, 1970, CORDS Public Safety, box 21, folder Corrupt Practices; MAC-CORDS to George S. Eckhardt, "Alleged National Police Misconduct (Shakedown)," March 18, 1972; William Colby to Tran Van Khiem, "Illegal Movement of Goods and Corruption of Certain GVN Personnel," December 15, 1969, CORDS Public Safety, Phung Hoang, box 21, folder Corrupt Practices.

57. Lederer, *The Anguished American,* 120; Gabriel Kolko, *Anatomy of a War: Vietnam, the United States, and the Modern Historical Experience* (New York: Pantheon, 1985); Kurt Jacobsen, *Pacification and Its Discontents* (Chicago: Prickly Paradigm Press, 2009), 48.

58. "The Role of Public Safety in Support of the National Police of Vietnam," April 1, 1969, USAID, OPS (Washington, D.C.: GPO, 1969), 6. Clowers's background was with the Tacoma, Washington, Police Department. John McCabe, a Berkeley graduate who served three tours in Korea, was among the others killed.

59. Valentine, *The Phoenix Program,* 25; Ahern, *The CIA and Rural Pacification in Vietnam,* 58.

60. Valentine, *The Phoenix Program;* 262; McCoy, *The Politics of Heroin,* 216–22.

61. Frank Armbruster, *A Military and Police Security Program for South Vietnam* (Hudson, N.Y.: Hudson Institute, August 10, 1967), HI-881-RR, DOD.

62. See McClintock, *Instruments of Statecraft.* Another model was the OPS and CIA-organized "hunter-killer" teams, which contributed to the demise of FARC (Fuerzas Armadas Revolucionario de Colombia) and other guerrilla organizations in Colombia. See chapter 10.

63. Theodore Shackley with Richard A. Finney, *Spymaster: My Life in the CIA* (Dulles, Va.: Potomac Books, 2005), 233; Blaufarb, *The Counterinsurgency Era,* 247.

64. "Phung Hoang, Monthly Report," April 29, 1971, CORDS Public Safety, box 13; Tang, *A Vietcong Memoir,* 210; Ahern, *The CIA and Rural Pacification,* 309; Michael T. Klare,

"Operation Phoenix and the Failure of Pacification in South Vietnam," *Liberation* 17 (May 1973): 21–27; Al Santoli, *Everything We Had: An Oral History of the Vietnam War by Thirty-three Americans Soldiers Who Fought It* (New York: Random House, 1981), 204–5.

65. "Monthly Report," October 24, 1971, CORDS Public Safety, box 14, folder Quality Neutralizations; "Monthly Report," June 2, 1971, CORDS Public Safety, box 10; Monthly Report, Chung Thien, November 18, 1969, CORDS Public Safety, Phung Hoang, box 3; Martin E. Pierce, "Consolidated VCI Infrastructure Neutralization Report," April 1–30, 1969, CORDS Public Safety, box 4.

66. "Monthly Report," December 30, 1970 and "Monthly Report," April 29, 1971, CORDS Public Safety, box 13, folder Monthly Consolidated Reports; "Minutes of Phung Hoang Advisor's Monthly Confirmation," December 10, 1971, CORDS Public Safety, box 10; Evan Parker Jr. to Tucker Gougleman, "VCI Neutralizations," January 18, 1969, CORDS Public Safety, Phung Hoang, box 1; "Phung Hoang Herbicide Operation," June 17, 1972, CORDS Public Safety, Phung Hoang, box 6; Iver Peterson, "Vietnam: This Phoenix Is a Bird of Death" *New York Times,* July 25, 1971; Robert Komer, "The Phung Hoang Fiasco," CORDS, Public Safety, Phung Hoang, box 21.

67. "Monthly Report," October 24, 1971, CORDS Public Safety, box 14, folder Quality Neutralizations; "Minutes of Phung Hoang Advisor's Monthly Confirmation," December 10, 1971, CORDS Public Safety, box 10; Alfred W. McCoy, "Torture in the Crucible of Counterinsurgency," in *Iraq and the Lessons of Vietnam: Or, How Not to Learn from the Past,* ed. Marilyn B. Young and Lloyd C. Gardner (New York: New Press, 2007), 241.

68. Ralph W. McGehee, *Deadly Deceits: My Twenty-five Years in the CIA* (New York: Sheridan Square Publications, 1983), 156.

69. Valentine, *The Phoenix Program,* 61. See also Tang, *A Vietcong Memoir.*

70. Frank Snepp, *Decent Interval: An Insider's Account of Saigon's Indecent End Told by the CIA's Chief Strategy Analyst in Vietnam,* rev. ed. (Lawrence: University Press of Kansas, 2002), 31, 38.

71. U.S. Congress, House, Committee on Armed Services, Hearings, July 2, 20, 25, 1973, "U.S. Assistance Programs in Vietnam," 93rd Cong., 1st sess. (Washington, D.C.: GPO, 1973), 319–21; Frank Browning and Dorothy Forman, eds., *The Wasted Nations: Report of the International Commission of the Enquiry into United States Crimes in Indochina* (New York: Harper, 1972), 203.

72. McCoy, "Torture in the Crucible of Counterinsurgency," 243. In his book *Phoenix and the Birds of Prey* (Annapolis: Naval Institute Press, 1997), Mark Moyar, a right-wing apologist for the Phoenix program and the Vietnam War (as well as the Indonesian genocide of 1965), tries to discredit Osborn's character as a means of invalidating his testimony. A few other historians, some quite well respected, have also adopted this spurious claim.

73. Valentine, *The Phoenix Program,* 192; Bernd Greiner, *War without Fronts: The USA in Vietnam* (New Haven: Yale University Press, 2009), 62.

74. "Summary of Problems of Phung Hoang Program: Recommendation for Turning It Over to the National Police," Secretary of State to American embassy, OPS East Asia Branch (1971–1973), box 280; McLintock, *Instruments of Statecraft,* 190–92.

75. See, for example, Burt Useem and Peter Kimball, *States of Siege: U.S. Prison Riots, 1971–1986* (New York: Oxford University Press, 1986).

76. Frank Walton to William C. Benson, "Visit to Vung Tau Prison," July 8, 1961, OPS East Asia Branch, box 287 (penology), folder 2; William C. Benson to John F, McCabe, "Preliminary Survey of Central Prison, Chi Hoa," Ibid, folder 2; "Debrief of a Prison Advisor," OPS East Asia Branch, box 287 (penology), folder 1; Phuoc Thuy and Gia Dinh, *Vietnam,*

1960-1967 (Honolulu: Asian Training Center, 1967), 14; Don Bordenkircher, as told to Shirley Bordenkircher, *Tiger Cage: An Untold Story* (Cameron, W. Va.: Abby Publishing, 1998), 54; Burchett, *The Furtive War*, 47; "The Rehabilitation System of Vietnam," PSD, USOM to Vietnam, foreword by Frank Walton, January 1961, OPS East Asia Branch, box 287 (penology), page 29 of report.

77. William C. Benson to Frank E. Walton, "Visit to Bien Hoa Provincial Prison," June 1, 1961, OPS East Asia Branch, box 287 (penology), Penology; Thomas Lippman, "Clandestine Document Assails South Vietnam on Prisoners," *Washington Post,* July 27, 1973; DeForest, *Slow Burn,* 31, 32, 55.

78. "Visit to Kien Tuong Provincial Rehabilitation Center," *Moc Hoa,* February 19, 1962; William C. Benson to Frank E. Walton, Visit to Bien Hoa Prison," June 1, 1961, OPS East Asia Branch, box 287 (penology), folder 2 ; Elmer H. Crain to Bob French, "Binh Duong Prison Inspection," October 29, 1966, OPS East Asia, box 287 (penology).

79. L. J. Cipriani to William R. Wagner, April 1972, CIB, box 1, folder 1; U.S. Congress, House, Subcommittee on Asian and Pacific Affairs, Hearings, *Testimony of David and Jane Barton: The Treatment of Political Prisoners in South Vietnam by the Government of the Republic of South Vietnam,* 93rd Cong., 1st sess., September 13, 1973 (Washington, D.C.: GPO, 1973), 50–51; Amnesty International, *Political Prisoners in South Vietnam* (London: Amnesty International Publications, 1973), 36; "Letter Charges Torture at Second Vietnamese Prison," *New York Times,* July 17, 1970; Holmes Brown and Don Luce, *Hostages of War: Saigon's Political Prisoners* (Washington, D.C.: Indochina Mobile Education Project, 1973), 71; Chomsky and Herman, *The Washington Connection and Third World Fascism,* 333; Alfred W. McCoy, *A Question of Torture: CIA Interrogation from the Cold War to the War on Terror* (New York: Metropolitan Books, 2005).

80. "Debrief of a Prison Adviser (Public Safety), Phuoc Thuy and Gia Dinh, Vietnam," 1960–1967 (Honolulu: Asian Training Center, 1967), 10–11; Brown and Luce, *Hostages of Wars,* 14.

81. Jack Anderson, "Prisoners Tortured in South Vietnamese Jails," *Washington Post,* August 31, 1970; Young, *The Vietnam Wars, 1945–1990,* 61. See also Dennis Neeld, "South Vietnam's Non-Persons," *Washington Post,* June 24, 1973; "Letter Charges Torture at Second Vietnamese Prison," *New York Times,* July 17, 1970.

82. William C. Benson to John F. McCabe, "Visit to Pleiku Rehabilitation Center," December 12, 1961, also "Visit to Darlac Rehabilitation Center," "Chi Hoa," and "Nhan Vi (Con Son)," in same report, OPS East Asia Branch, box 287, folder 1, Penology; Fred Branfman, "South Vietnam's Police and Prison System: The U.S. Connection," in *Uncloaking the CIA,* ed. Howard Frazier (New York: Free Press, 1978), 114; Bordenkircher, *Tiger Cage,* 59.

83. William Benson to John F. McCabe, "Nhan Vi (Con Son)"; OPS East Asia Branch, Penology, folder 1; William C. Benson to Frank Walton, "Visit to Bien Hoa Prison," June 1, 1961, July 14, 1961, OPS East Asia Branch, box 287, folder 1; "The Rehabilitation System of Vietnam," PSD, USOM to Vietnam, 29.

84. Robert Lowe, Memo for Senior Adviser, "Resources Control Survey of the Hau Nghia Province," September 13, 1966, CORDS Public Safety, General Records, box 5, Cu Chi.

85. "Monthly Report, Correction and Detention," October–November 1968, CORDS Public Safety, Monthly Reports (July–November 1968), box 2.

86. "After the Signing of the Paris Agreements: Documents on South Vietnam's Political Prisoners," *Narmic-VRC* (June 1973): 27; Chomsky and Herman, *The Washington Connection and Third World Fascism,* 330.

87. "South Vietnam's Prisons," *Washington Post,* July 20, 1973; Madelaine Reberioux, *The Forgotten Prisoners of Nguyen Van Thieu by A Group of French University Professors,* trans. John Atherton et al. (Paris: RP Books, 1973), also available on-line at TTU; Bordenkircher, *Tiger Cage,* 180.

88. Randolph Berkeley to William Colby, September 15, 1971, HQ MAVC, Vietnam, TTU, 4; memo for Randolph Berkeley, Branch Chief, C & D Branch, PSD, "Results of Joint US/GVN Survey of 14 Correctional Centers of IV CTZ," November 25, 1968, CORDS Public Safety, Phung Hoang, box 14, folder Correctional Centers; "The Rehabilitation System of Vietnam," PSD, USOM to Vietnam, OPS East Asia Branch, box 287 (penology).

89. D. E. Bordenkircher to Randolph Berkeley, "Capacity of Correctional Centers" and "Survey of Chau Doc Prison," November 25, 1968, CORDS Public Safety, Phung Hoang, box 14, folder Correctional Centers. Berkeley had a background in military counterintelligence. When he worked in an official capacity for the OPS, his office was located next to William Colby's.

90. D. E. Bordenkircher, memo for Randolph Berkeley, Public Safety Division, November 25, 1968, CORDS Public Safety, Phung Hoang, box 14, folder Correctional Centers.

91. D. E. Bordenkircher to Randolph Berkeley, "An Xuyen Prison," November 11, 1968, CORDS Public Safety, Phung Hoang, box 14, folder Correctional Centers.

92. William Colby to CORDS, "Allegations of Extortion," April 24, 1970, CORDS, Public Safety, box 21.

93. "ICRC Visits to GVN Correctional Facilities," November 2, 1970, OPS East Asia Branch, box 287, folder 1, Penology; Greiner, *War without Fronts,* 78.

94. "Kien Tuong," CORDS Public Safety, Phung Hoang, box 2, folder Correctional Centers; "The Rehabilitation System of Vietnam, PSD, USOM to Vietnam, 12.

95. Robert Lowe to Wade Lathram, "GVN Prison System and Related Problems," July 13, 1966 CORDS Public Safety, General Records, box 5.

96. Randolph Berkeley to William E. Colby, MACV, September 15, 1971, TTU. On the volatile prison conditions in Attica and San Quentin and throughout the United States, see Ben H. Bagdikian and Leon Dash, *The Shame of the Prisons* (New York: Pocket Books, 1972); Frank Browning and The Editors of *Ramparts,* eds., *Prison Life: A Study of the Explosive Conditions in America's Prisons* (New York: Harper & Row, 1972).

97. Armbruster, *A Military and Police Security Program for South Vietnam;* Corson, *The Betrayal,* 92, 93.

98. Richard A. Hunt, *Pacification: The American Struggle for Vietnam's Hearts and Minds* (Boulder: Westview Press, 1995), 239; also "Thieu's Political Prisoners," *Newsweek,* December 18, 1972, 61; Bernard Fall, "Unrepentant, Unyielding: An Interview with Vietcong Prisoners," *New Republic,* February 4, 1967, 19–24; "Monthly Report: Corrections and Detention," November 14, 1968, CORDS Public Safety, Monthly Reports (July–November 1968), box 1; Donald Duncan, "The Prisoner," *Ramparts,* September 1969, 51–56. An inmate at Chi Hoa told *Newsweek* that on arrival "only two out of every ten prisoners in the communist cell block were real communists, but you can be sure that ten out of ten will leave as communists." "Thieu's Political Prisoners," *Newsweek,* December 18, 1972, 61.

99. Doris Longacre and Max Ediger, eds., *Release Us from Bondage: Six Days in a Vietnamese Prison* (Akron: Mennonite Central Committee Peace Section, July 1974), 2; Fred Branfman, "Vietnam: The POW's We Left Behind," *Ramparts* (December 1973): 14.

100. Noam Chomsky, *Towards a New Cold War: U.S. Foreign Policy from Vietnam to Reagan,* rev. ed. (New York: Free Press, 2003), 170; Greiner, *War without Fronts,* 79. For

evidence that the claims of torture and mistreatment of U.S. POWs were exaggerated in the United States, see Jerry Lembcke, *Hanoi Jane: War, Sex, and Fantasies of Betrayal* (Amherst: University of Massachusetts Press, 2010), 54–61.

101. Longacre and Ediger, *Release Us from Bondage,* 9–10.

102. Peter Zinoman, *The Colonial Bastille: A History of Imprisonment in Vietnam, 1862-1940* (Berkeley: University of California Press, 2001), 29, 94–97. A flaw of Zinoman's otherwise excellent book is its failure to identify the continuity between French and American penal practice in Indochina.

103. Bordenkircher, *Tiger Cage,* 199; Longacre and Ediger, *Release Us from Bondage,* 7; William C. Benson to John F. McCabe, "Visit to 'Nhan Vi (Con Son),'" December 1961, PSD, OPS East Asia Branch, box 287, folder 1, Penology.

104. "ICRC Visits to GVN Correctional Facilities Public Safety Review," November 2, 1970, OPS East Asia Branch, box 287, folder 1, Penology, 12; William "Pappy" Grieves to Frank Walton, Monthly Report, October 1970, CORDS Public Safety, Monthly Reports, box 10.

105. "The Rehabilitation System of Vietnam," PSD, USOM, 29; Sylvan Fox, "4 South Vietnamese Describe Torture in Prison 'Tiger Cage,'" *New York Times,* March 3, 1973; Bordenkircher, *Tiger Cage,* 180. Bordenkircher, who worked at Con Son, claims that prisoners were shackled only at night to prevent them from escaping because the doors were easy to pry open. He admits that some inmates were paralyzed but remains proud of his involvement.

106. U.S. Congress, House, Committee on Foreign Affairs, Subcommittee on Asian and Pacific Affairs, *The Treatment of Political Prisoners in South Vietnam by the Government of the Republic of South Vietnam,* 93rd Cong., 1st sess., September 13, 1973 (Washington, D.C.: GPO, 1973), 20; Lars Schoultz, *Human Rights and United States Policy toward Latin America* (Princeton: Princeton University Press, 1981), 181.

107. Brown and Luce, *Hostages of War,* app. B, 43; Anthony Lewis, "Whom We Welcome," *New York Times,* March 31, 1973; Gordon Young, *Journey from Banna* (Indianapolis: Xilibris, 2011), 269. Young was sent to Con Son after the "tiger cages" were exposed and pushed for the replacement of warden Nguyen Van Ve.

108. Longacre and Ediger, *Release Us from Bondage,* 11.

109. See H. Bruce Franklin, *M.I.A. or Mythmaking in America: How and Why Belief in Live POWs Has Possessed a Nation* (New Brunswick: Rutgers University Press, 1989), and his *Vietnam and Other American Fantasies* (Amherst: University of Massachusetts Press, 2000), 15.

110. "Paying for Thieu's Police," *Time,* September 17, 1973, 26.

111. Don Irwin, "U.S. Owes No Debt to Hanoi, Carter Says," *Los Angeles Times,* March 5, 1977.

112. For a prescient analysis, see Noam Chomsky and Edward S. Herman, *The Political Economy of Human Rights,* vol. 2, *After the Cataclysm: Postwar Indochina and the Reconstruction of Imperial Ideology* (Boston: South End Press, 1979).

Part III: The Cold War on the Periphery

1. Philip Agee, *Inside the Company: CIA Diary* (Harmondsworth: Penguin Books, 1974), 563, 597.

2. Kate Doyle, "The Atrocity Files: Deciphering the Archives of Guatemala's Dirty War," *Harper's Magazine,* December 2007, 52–62.

1. Department of State, "Policy Research Study: Internal Warfare and the Security of the Underdeveloped States," November 20, 1961, JFKL, POF, box 98.

2. On the ethnocentrism and paternalism underpinning U.S. involvement in Africa, see George White Jr., *Holding the Line: Race, Racism, and American Foreign Policy towards Africa, 1953–1961* (New York: Rowman & Littlefield, 2005); and Larry Grubbs, *Secular Missionaries: Americans and African Development in the 1960s* (Amherst: University of Massachusetts Press, 2009).

3. See David M. Anderson and David Killingray, eds., *Policing the Empire: Government, Authority and Control, 1830–1940* (Manchester: Manchester University Press, 1991); Georgina Sinclair, *At the End of the Line: Colonial Policing and the Imperial Endgame 1945–1980* (Manchester: Manchester University Press, 2006); Anthony Clayton and David M. Killingray, *Khaki and Blue: Military and Police in British Colonial Africa* (Athens, Ohio: University Center for International Studies, 1989).

4. Raymond Atuguba, "Ghana: Changing Our Inherited Police Institutions," in *Africa's Challenge: Using Law for Good Governance and Development,* ed. Ann Seidman et al. (Trenton: Africa World Press, 2007), 64.

5. See, e.g., Clayton and Killingray, *Khaki and Blue,* 141.

6. Otwin Marenin, "United States Aid to African Police Forces: The Experience and Impact of the Public Safety Assistance Program," *African Affairs* 84 (Fall 1986): 541.

7. Harold Marcus, *Ethiopia, Great Britain, and the United States, 1941–1974: The Politics of Empire* (Berkeley: University of California Press, 1983), 90; White, *Holding the Line,* 52; Jeffrey A. Lefebvre, *Arms for the Horn: U.S. Security Policy in Ethiopia and Somalia, 1953–1991* (Pittsburgh: University of Pittsburgh Press, 1991), 75; Ryszard Kapuscinski, *The Emperor: The Downfall of an Autocrat* (New York: Vintage, 1978).

8. Theo Hall, ICA, to Leo Cyr, American embassy, Addis Ababa, March 13, 1956; and Elbert C. Haney to Ambassador James P. Richards, April 15, 1957, RG 59, RDS, North Africa, 1955–1959, box 4881; American embassy, Addis Ababa, to Secretary of State, "Development of Mutual Security Program and Long-Range Country Plan for Ethiopia," October 29, 1956, RG 286, USAID, OPS, Operations Division, Africa and Near East and South Asia Branch, box 10, Ethiopia (hereafter Africa and Near East and South Asia Branch).

9. Details of Williams's career can be found in Douglas Valentine, *The Strength of the Wolf: The Secret History of America's War on Drugs* (London: Verso, 2004), 28, 44; and John C. McWilliams, *The Protectors: Harry J. Anslinger and the Federal Bureau of Narcotics, 1930–1962* (Newark: University of Delaware Press, 1990). Before organizing the border patrol, in 1936 Williams was selected to negotiate an anti-smuggling agreement with Mexican president Lázaro Cárdenas that allowed Treasury agents to operate inside Mexico. In El Paso he came in contact with Carl Eiffler, legendary head of OSS Detachment 101, and Lee Echols, a police adviser in Japan and Bolivia (see chapter 10). Peter Dale Scott, in *Deep Politics and the Death of JFK* (Berkeley: University of California Press, 1996), 168, notes Williams's propensity to recruit underworld informants such as "Sonny" Fassoulis as strategic assets for the CIA in deep-cover work. This is among the reasons why narcotics agents were so valued by "the Agency."

10. Ralph Selby, "Imperial Ethiopian Police Survey and End of Tour Report," August 1, 1959, Africa and Near East and South Asia Branch, box 11, Ethiopia; American embassy, Addis Ababa, to Department of State, Washington, D.C., "Internal Security in Ethiopia," March 20, 1958, Africa and Near East and South Asia Branch, box 12, folder Ethiopia. See

also Christopher Clapham, "The December 1960 Ethiopian Coup d'État," *Journal of African Affairs* (December 1968): 495–507. According to his biographer Ryszard Kapuscinski, Selassie had aides read him the intelligence reports every morning at breakfast. Chief of police Tsigue Dibon was also implicated in the 1960 coup and was killed.

11. Selby, "Imperial Ethiopian Police Survey and End of Tour Report"; Steven Lowenstein, "Ethiopia," in *African Penal Systems,* ed. Alan Milner (London: Routledge & Kegan Paul, 1969), 47. In another archaic practice, family members of victims were allowed to pull the trigger in cases of capital punishment.

12. "Ethiopia: Key Sectors and Description of U.S. Programs Bearing on Counter-Insurgency," RG 286, USAID, OPS, Internal Defense and Public Safety, Office of the Director (hereafter IPS), box 6, folder 3. Korry discusses both programs in Patricio Guzman's documentary *Salvador Allende* (2007); David Stout, "Edward Korry, 81, Is Dead; Falsely Tied to Chile Coup," *New York Times,* January 20, 2003.

13. George Ball from Washington to Addis, "Delivery of Military Helmets," November 8, 1965; and Edward Korry to Secretary of State, "Request for Police Equipment," May 31, 1964, RG 286, USAID, OPS, Technical Services Division, General Correspondence (hereafter TSD), Ethiopia; Ray Foreaker, "End of Tour Report for Ethiopia," March 18, 1964, TSD, Ethiopia; Elliot Hensel, "End of Tour Report;" "Israeli Activities with African Civil Security Forces," Africa and Near East and South Asia Branch, box 4, folder Chad, and box 10, folder Ethiopia.

14. Ray Foreaker, "End of Tour Report for Ethiopia," March 18, 1964, TSD, Ethiopia; "Public Safety Monthly Report," January 23, 1968, TSD, Ethiopia.

15. "Public Safety Monthly Report," March 1969, Africa and Near East and South Asia Branch, box 1, Ethiopia; Horton Steele to Colonel Mitchell Mabardy, "USAID Mission to Ethiopia," August 2, 1969; and "Public Safety Monthly Report," April 1969, Africa and Near East and South Asia, box 10, folder Ethiopia.

16. Ray Foreaker, "End of Tour Report for Ethiopia," March 18, 1964, TSD, Ethiopia; "Assessment of Insurgency Threat in the Ogaden," Africa and Near East and South Asia Branch, box 10, folder Ethiopia; Ernest Lefever, *Spear and Scepter: Army, Police, and Politics in Tropical Africa* (Washington, D.C.: Brookings Institute, 1970), 169.

17. "Public Safety Monthly Report," February 1968, Africa and Near East and South Asia Branch, box 10, folder Ethiopia; Horton Steele, "Public Safety Monthly Report," July 1969, ibid., box 11; Horton Steele, "Public Safety Monthly Report, November 9, 1967, ibid., box 12.

18. Ray Foreaker, "Public Safety Monthly Report," October–November, 1963, TSD, Ethiopia; Mary Dines, "Ethiopian Violation of Human Rights in Eritrea," in *The Long Struggle of Eritrea for Independence and Constructive Peace,* ed. Lionel Cliffe and Basil Davidson (Trenton: Red Sea Press, 1988), 149.

19. Christopher Clapham, *African Guerrillas* (London: James Currey, 1998); Andargachew Tiruneh, *The Ethiopian Revolution, 1974–1987: Transformation from an Aristocratic to a Totalitarian Autocracy* (Cambridge: Cambridge University Press, 1993); Odd Arne Westad, *The Global Cold War: Third World Intervention and the Making of Our Times* (New York: Cambridge University Press, 2007), 270.

20. Russell A. Snook and William M. McGhee, "Report of Survey of the Police Corps of Somalia," July 1958, North Africa, 1958, IPS, box 11, folder Somalia. On Snook's involvement in Italy, see, e.g., Russell A. Snook to Commissioner of Public Safety, October 19, 1943, "Organization of Training Battalion," RG 331, Records of the Allied Operations and Occupation Headquarters, Allied Control, Italy, box 1314.

21. Roger Hilsman, "Internal War: The New Communist Tactic," in *The Guerrilla and How to Fight Him,* ed. T. N. Green (New York: Praeger, 1965), 31.

22. "Monthly Report, Somalia," February 1966, RG 286, USAID, OPS, Geographic Files, box 20 (hereafter Geographic Files); American embassy, Mogadishu, "Public Safety Procurement," July 17, 1967, TSD, box 9, folder Somalia; "Monthly Report, Somalia," April 1965, Geographic Files, box 20; "Editorial Note," *Foreign Relations of the United States, 1964–1968,* vol. 24, *Africa,* ed. Nina Davis Howland (Washington, D.C.: GPO, 1999), 495.

23. See Mohammed Diriye Abdullahi, "In the Name of the Cold War: How the West Aided and Abetted the Barre Dictatorship of Somalia," in *Genocide, War Crimes, and the West: History and Complicity,* ed. Adam Jones (London: Zed Books, 2004), 241–60. After Barre took over, many U.S.-supported police commanders were jailed or exiled.

24. Lefebvre, *Arms for the Horn,* 15.

25. George C. Miller, "Report of Consultation to U.S. Embassy: Industrial Security and the Libyan Police," November 1965, Africa and Near East and South Asia Branch, box 1, folder Libya; Frank Walton to Byron Engle, "Arming of Defense Forces," March 11, 1968, Africa and Near East and South Asia Branch, box 30, folder Libya. On U.S. interests in Libya in the 1950s, see Wilbur Eveland, *Ropes of Sand: America's Failure in the Middle East* (New York: Norton, 1980), 316; Henry Villard, *Libya* (Ithaca: Cornell University Press, 1956).

26. Elliott B. Hensel, "End of Tour Report," October 1, 1963, Africa and Near East and South Asia Branch, box 30, folder Libya.

27. Geoff Simmons, *Libya and the West: From Independence to Lockerbie* (London: I. B. Tauris, 2003). Frank Walton characterized the revolution as a damaging blow to U.S. interests.

28. Adolph Bonnefil, Garland Williams, and Sydney Wagoner, "Public Safety Report of Civil Police Forces of Chad," TSD, box 1, folder Chad. See also Karl Van Meter, "The French Role in Africa," in *Dirty Work,* vol. 2, *The CIA in Africa,* ed. Ellen Ray, Karl Van Meter, and Louis Wolf (New York: Pantheon Books, 2009), 209.

29. Roger Robinson to Byron Engle, November 21, 1967, Africa and Near East and South Asia Branch, box 4, Chad.

30. "Monthly Report," December 1965, and "Rebel Activity, December 1–31, 1967," Africa and Near East and South Asia Branch, box 12, folder Chad; John F. Manopoli and Sydney Wagoner, "Supplementary Survey of the Civil police Forces of the Republic fo Chad," January 1966, OPS, USAID, 1966; Edward R. Bishop, "Monthly Public Safety Report," June 1968, Africa and Near East and South Asia Branch, box 4, folder Chad.

31. Edward R. Bishop, "Monthly Public Safety Report," May 1968, Africa and Near East and South Asia Branch, box 4, folder Chad.

32. "Government Anti-rebel Activity," December 26, 1967, Africa and Near East and South Asia Branch, box 12, folder Chad; René Lemarchand, "The Crisis in Chad," in *African Crisis Areas and U.S. Foreign Policy,* ed. Gerald J. Bender, James S. Coleman, and Richard L. Sklar (Berkeley: University of California Press, 1985), 239–56; Mahmood Mamdani, *Saviors and Survivors: Darfur, Politics, and the War on Terror* (New York: Pantheon, 2009), 215. As Mamdani notes, the connections between the Chadian civil war and the crisis in Darfur are not well understood by student and celebrity anti-genocide activists, who are often ignorant of the broader geopolitical context.

33. Benjamin Read, memo for McGeorge Bundy, March 24, 1965, LBJL, NSF, Country File, Africa, box 92, Liberia; B. H. Larabee to Joseph Palmer, Deputy Assistant Secretary of State, May 2, 1958, OCB, Central Files, box 821. See also D. Elwood Dunn, *Liberia and the United States during the Cold War: Limits of Reciprocity* (New York: Palgrave Macmillan,

2009), 42; Richard P. Tucker, *Insatiable Appetite: The United States and the Ecological Degradation of the Tropical World,* rev. ed. (New York: Rowman and Littlefield, 2007), 133–34, 145. An American official told future president Ellen Johnson-Sirleaf, who was a dissident at the time, "Our strategic interests are more important than democracy." Noam Chomsky, *Deterring Democracy* (New York: Hill & Wang, 1991), 240.

34. "Survey of the Liberian National Police Force," ICA, Department of State, October–November 1955, Africa and Near East and South Asia Branch, box 1, folder Liberia.

35. "Commodity Supplies," TSD, box 14, Liberia; "Israeli Activities with African Civil Security Forces," Africa and Near East and South Asia Branch, box 4, folder Chad; Frank A. Jessup, "Manpower Analysis of the Liberian National Police, Report to the Secretary of State by the U.S. Survey Mission to Liberia," April 11, 1966, TSD, box 1, Liberia. Jim Lewis of the Indiana State Police and James L. McCarthy, deputy sheriff in Ontario County, New York, and graduate of the FBI training academy, were other advisers in Liberia who went on to serve in Vietnam, as did Bob Lowe and Charlie O'Brien.

36. John Manopoli and Frederick C. Hubig Jr., "Evaluation Public Safety Program for the Republic of Liberia," October 1972, Africa and Near East and South Asia Branch, box 22, Liberia.

37. Joe Stork, "World Cop: How America Builds the Global Police State," in *Policing America,* ed. Anthony Platt and Lynn Cooper (Englewood Cliffs, N.J.: Prentice Hall, 1974), 66; Richard Sutton, "End of Tour Report," September 1, 1965, Africa and Near East and South Asia Branch, box 22, Liberia. "A Nationwide Broadcast on the Firestone Strike," Monrovia, February 12, 1966, in *The Official Papers of William V. S. Tubman, President of the Republic of Liberia: Covering Addresses, Messages, Speeches, and Statements 1960–1967,* ed. E. Reginald Townsend and Abeodu Bowen Jones (London: Longmans, for the Department of Information and Cultural Affairs, Monrovia, Liberia, 1968), 375–77. Tubman attributed the strike to the "mysticism of unrealistic ideologies that are illusions." For more on Firestone's exploitative practices and U.S. interests in Liberia, see Arthur I. Hayman and Harold Preece, *Lighting Up Liberia* (New York: Creative Age Press, 1943); and Penny Von Eschen, *Race against Empire: Black Americans and Anticolonialism, 1937–1957* (Ithaca: Cornell University Press, 1997), 39.

38. Frank Loveland, "Report on the Prison System of the Republic of Liberia," May 1962, Africa and Near East and South Asia Branch, box 22, Liberia; Gerald H. Zarr, "Liberia," in Milner, *African Penal Systems,* 197.

39. Joint Team of Government of Liberia and U.S. Agency for International Development, *Report on Evaluation of U.S. Public Safety Assistance to Liberia as Related to Law Enforcement Agencies* (Washington, D.C., October 16, 1972), 3; Jerry Knoll to Hendrik Van Oss, "Liberia Internal Security Survey," June 9, 1966, Africa and Near East and South Asia Branch, box 25, Liberia.

40. See Virginia Thompson, "The Ivory Coast," in *African One-Party States,* ed. Gwendolyn M. Carter (Ithaca: Cornell University Press, 1962) and Frantz Fanon, *Black Skin, White Masks,* trans. Charles Lam Markmann (New York: Grove Press, 1967). Boigny tellingly described colonialism as "a necessary evil if it was an evil."

41. Mitchell A. Mabardy to Byron Engle, Director OPS, February 4, 1966, TSD, box 9; John Manopoli and René Tetaz, "Supplementary Survey of National Police Forces, Republic of the Ivory Coast," Abidjan, USAID, OPS, 1966; Norman Schonoover, "End of Tour Report," September 16, 1969, TSD, box 9, Ivory Coast.

42. John Manopoli and René Tetaz, "Public Safety Monthly Report, January–February 1966," Africa and Near East and South Asia Branch, box 9.

43. "Ghana's Political and Economic Malaise: Special Memorandum Prepared in the Central Intelligence Agency," July 19, 1962, in Howland, *Foreign Relations of the United States, 1964–1968*, 24:468; Michael Latham, *The Right Kind of Revolution: Modernization, Development, and U.S. Foreign Policy from the Cold War to the Present* (Ithaca: Cornell University Press, 2011), 87, 89. On U.S. support for the coup, see John Stockwell, *In Search of Enemies: A CIA Story* (New York: Norton, 1978), 201; Seymour Hersh, "CIA Said to Have Aided Plotters Who Overthrew Nkrumah in Ghana," in Ray, Van Meter, and Wolf, *Dirty Work*, 2:159–63.

44. Richard Rathbone, "Political Intelligence and Policing in Ghana in the Late 1940s and 1950s," in *Policing and Decolonisation: Politics, Nationalism and the Police, 1917–1965*, ed. David Anderson and David Killlingray (Manchester: Manchester University Press, 1992), 101–2. See also Simon Baynham, *The Military and Police in Nkrumah's Ghana* (Boulder: Westview, 1988); Ahmad Rahman, *The Regime Change of Kwame Nkrumah* (New York: Palgrave Macmillan, 2007); Ruth First, *Power in Africa* (New York: Pantheon, 1970), 387. First details how the military junta imposed privatization and austerity measures at the behest of the World Bank and IMF.

45. Thomas Finn to Byron Engle, "ID Cards for Ghana," November 26, 1968, TSD, box 2. Caplan served in South Korea, Indonesia, Vietnam, Turkey, and Uruguay.

46. Atuguba, "Ghana: Changing Our Inherited Police Institutions," 64. Ghanaian prisons were marred by "animal overcrowding" and "severe and dehumanizing regimes."

47. "Statement on Biafra, Honorable Elliot Richardson," July 15, 1969, American Report, June 16–31, 1969, ZNA; "Robbers to Be Shot on Sight in Nigeria," *Zambia Times,* January 27, 1967; Michael T. Klare and Cynthia Aronson, *Supplying Repression: U.S. Support for Authoritarian Regimes Abroad* (Washington, D.C.: Institute for Policy Studies, 1981); Melvin Gurtov, *The United States against the Third World* (New York: Praeger, 1974), 70. For a history of the Nigerian police, see Tekena N. Tamuno, *The Police in Modern Nigeria, 1861–1965* (Lagos: Ibadan University Press, 1970).

48. Johnson F. Monroe, Dahomey, September 1, 1961, TSD, box 12, folder Dahomey (Benin); "PS Monthly Report," December 6, 1965, Africa and Near East and South Asia Branch, box 12, Monthly Reports. On political developments, see Samuel Decalo, *Coups and Army Rule in Africa: Motivations and Constraints*, rev. ed. (New Haven: Yale University Press, 1990), 22, 89; A. B. Assenson and Yvette M. Alex-Assenson, *African Military History and Politics: Coups, Ideological Incursions, 1900–Present* (New York: Palgrave Macmillan, 2001), 89. Between 1963 and 1972 there were six coups in Benin. In 1972 a young leftist army officer named Matthieu Kérékou seized power, sweeping away forever what Decalo describes as the "old political and military establishment" (117).

49. Johnson Monroe, "ICA Survey Report on the Civil Police Forces of the Republic of Upper Volta, Niger, Dahomey, and Togo," September 1, 1961, Africa and Near East and South Asia Branch, box 5, folder Niger; Decalo, *Coups and Army Rule in Africa*, 253, 255.

50. Thomas Finn and Paul Katz, "Trip Report on Niger Security Forces," May 31–June 11, 1965, TSD, box 15, folder Niger.

51. American embassy, Bangui, to Secretary of State, "U.S. Policy Assessment for Central African Republic," June 15, 1968; Charles Gordon to Rob Forsberg, December 7, 1968, TSD, Central African Republic; Central Africa General Situation, LBJL, NSF, Country Files, Africa, box 80. See also, Brian Titley, *Dark Age: The Political Odyssey of Emperor Bokassa* (Montreal: McGill-Queens University Press, 1997).

52. Garland Williams and Sydney Wagoner, "Report of the Security Forces, Central Africa Republic," May 5, 1962, TSD, box 1, folder Central African Republic.

53. Ibid. For critical analysis of the racial stereotypes and ethnocentrism underlying American policy, see White, *Holding the Line;* and Grubbs, *Secular Missionaries.*

54. Florence Bernault, "The Politics of Enclosure in Colonial and Post-Colonial Africa," in *A History of Prison and Confinement in Africa,* ed. Florence Bernault, trans. Janet Roitman (Portsmouth, N.H.: Heinemann, 2003), 33; Didier Bigo, "Ngaraba, L'impossible Prison," *Revue Française de Science Politique* 39, no. 6 (1989), 867–85.

55. See Adam Hochschild, *King Leopold's Ghost: A Story of Greed, Terror, and Heroism in Colonial Africa* (Boston: Houghton Mifflin, 1998).

56. "Police Survey Mission to the Congo," June 1963, TSD, box 1, folder Congo. On U.S. economic interests in the Congo, see David N. Gibbs, *The Political Economy of Third World Intervention* (Chicago: University of Chicago Press, 1991).

57. See George Nzongala-Ntalaja, *The Congo from Leopold to Kabila: A People's History* (London: Zed Books, 2003), 107; Sean Kelley, *America's Tyrant: The CIA and Mobutu of Zaire* (Washington, D.C.: American University Press, 1993), 37; Ludo De Witte, *The Assassination of Lumumba* (London: Verso, 2002); Crawford Young, *Politics in the Congo: Decolonization and Independence* (Princeton: Princeton University Press, 1965), 467.

58. "CIA Situation Report: The Congo," March 3, 1965, LBJL, NSF, box 87, Congo. They also bombed a customs post. Donald Rickard was the CIA case officer for Hoare and assisted in the arrest of Nelson Mandela in South Africa. Laurent Kabila, future president of the Congo, was a key Simba leader.

59. Oral history interview, Robert W. Komer, April 9, 1973, JFKL, RWK; "Minutes of CI," June 18, 1964, RG 286, USAID, OPS, Office of the Director, IPS, box 6, folder 4.

60. Piero Gleijeses, *Conflicting Missions: Havana, Washington, and Africa, 1959–1976* (Chapel Hill: University of North Carolina Press, 2002), 72–73; "CIA Intelligence Memorandum: The Situation in Congo," March 1965, LBJL, NSF, box 87, Congo. Ernest Lefever, a political scientist with the Brookings Institute who was Ronald Reagan's first choice for assistant secretary of state, commented in his book *Spear and Scepter* that the "English unit under Hoare was widely respected for its discipline and civility" (112). Perhaps this was true among the white Westerners, but not among the Congolese. CIA agent Richard Holm characterized Hoare's unit as "the toughest, nastiest bunch of men" he had ever seen, who kept scorecards on the number of blacks they killed. Richard L. Holm, *The American Agent: My Life in the CIA* (London: St. Ermin's Press, 2003), 16.

61. See George Nzongala-Ntalaja, "United States Policy towards Zaire," in *African Crisis Areas and U.S. Foreign Policy,* ed. Gerald J. Bender, James S. Coleman, and Richard L. Sklar (Berkeley: University of California Press, 1985), 233; Crawford Young and Thomas Turner, *The Rise and Decline of the Zairian State* (Madison: University of Wisconsin Press, 1985), 180–81; David F. Schmitz, *Thank God They're on Our Side: The United States and Right-Wing Dictatorships, 1921–1965* (Chapel Hill: University of North Carolina Press, 1999).

62. "CIA Intelligence Memorandum: The Security Situation in Congo," June 17, 1964, LBJL, NSF, box 81, Congo; see also Marenin, "United States Aid to African Police Forces," 525; "Public Safety Monthly Report," September 1965, IPS, box 5, folder Congo.

63. "Police Survey Mission to the Congo," June 1963; "Public Safety Monthly Report, July 1965," and John F. Manopoli, "End of Tour Report," April 1966, TSD, Congo.

64. "Public Safety Monthly Report," December 1965, Africa and Near East and South Asia Branch, box 4, Congo; "Public Safety Monthly Report," May/June 1966, "Public Safety Monthly Report," July 7, 1966, TSD, Congo, Box 5; and "Termination Phase-Out Study, Zaire," Public Safety Project, USAID, OPS, 1974; Michael G. Schatzberg, *The Dialectic of Oppression in Zaire* (Bloomington: Indiana University Press, 1988), 39, 41; Lorrin Rosenbaum,

"Government by Torture," *Worldview* (April 1975): 26; Young, *Politics in the Congo,* 469. Nendaka was vice president of Lumumba's MNC party prior to his defection.

65. Zach Levey, "Israel and the Congo," talk at the Annual Conference of the Society for Historians of American Foreign Relations, Falls Church, Va., June 27, 2009; "Israeli Activities with African Civil Security Forces," Africa and Near East and South Asia Branch, box 4, folder Chad; "Public Safety Program in DRC," June 17, 1969, Africa and Near East and South Asia Branch, box 4, Congo; Lefever, *Spear and Scepter,* 129; Sinclair, *At the End of the Line,* 63.

66. "Public Safety Report," April 1968, Africa and Near East and South Asia Branch, box 4; Mitchell Mabardy to Byron Engle, June 16, 1969, Africa and Near East and South Asia Branch, box 22; Jonathan Kwitny, *Endless Enemies: The Making of an Unfriendly World* (New York: Penguin Books, 1986), 90.

67. "Public Safety Report," April 1968, Africa and Near East and South Asia Branch, box 22.

68. Gleijeses, *Conflicting Missions,* 65; Gurtov, *The United States against the Third World,* 62–63; Young Americans for Freedom poster, Zambian National Archives, Lusaka. Dodd, incidentally, was also a major backer of Phoumi Nosavan in Laos.

69. "Public Safety Monthly Report," July 7, 1966; May 12, 1966, TSD, Congo, box 5; Edgar O'Ballance, *The Congo-Zaire Experience, 1960–1998* (New York: Palgrave Macmillan, 2005), 128. Tshombe's mercenaries were referred to in U.S. internal reports as "rabble." After the killing of Lumumba (with associates Maurice Mpolo and Joseph Okite), the Belgian Gerard Soete recounted that Gendarmerie agents chopped up the corpses before dissolving them in acid. They were drunk for the two days because "we did things an animal wouldn't do."

70. "CIA Intelligence Memorandum: The Mercenary Mutiny and the Tshombe Plot," July 25, 1967, LBJL, NSF, box 87, folder Congo.

71. Robert H. McBride, American embassy to Secretary of State, July 15, 1967, LBJL, NSF, box 80, Chad/Congo.

72. "The Congo: Death of a Rebel," *Time,* October 18, 1968, 40. Benoît Verhaegen, *Rebellions au Congo* (Brussels: Centre de Recherche et d'Information Socio-politiques, 1966), 64; Russell Kirk, "U.S. Hesitant to Help Tshombe against Marxist Witch Doctors," *Los Angeles Times,* September 7, 1964. Verhaegen's careful study points to the deterioration of living conditions, lack of basic services including schools, and misery of the population as breeding support for the Mulelists. For the general pattern of media bias and propaganda, see Noam Chomsky and Edward S. Herman, *Manufacturing Consent: The Political Economy of the Mass Media* (New York: Pantheon, 1989); and on Orientalist stereotypes of Third World peoples, see Edward W. Said, *Culture and Imperialism* (New York: Vintage, 1994).

73. "Public Safety Monthly Report," May 12, 1966, TSD, box 5, folder Congo; CIA report, "The Congo: Assessment and Prospects," December 31, 1964, LBJL, NSF, box 87, Congo; Verhaegen, *Rebellions au Congo,* 78.

74. "Public Safety Monthly Report," May 12, 1966, TSD, box 5; American embassy to Secretary of State, July 15, 1967, LBJL, NSF, box 98, Congo; "The Congo: Death of a Rebel," *Time,* October 18, 1968, 40.

75. Robert O'Blake to Herman Klein, April 13, 1967, Africa and Near East and South Asia Branch, box 4, folder Congo; Ray Landgren, "Police Problems," Africa and Near East and South Asia Branch, box 4, folder Congo. On poor prison conditions in the Congo which failed to provide even a minimum of services, see C. Reuben, "Footnotes by a Visiting Sociologist," in Milner, *African Penal Systems,* 31.

76. Mitchell Mabardy to Byron Engle, "Briefing on Congo Program," June 6, 1966, Africa and Near East and South Asia Branch, box 5, folder Congo.

77. Jeter Williamson with R. H. Robinson and H. D. Miller, "Evaluation: Public Safety Program, Zaire," July–August 1973, TSD, box 12, folder Congo.

78. Ibid.; see also Stuart Methven, *Laughter in the Shadows: A CIA Memoir* (Annapolis: Naval Institute Press, 2008), 139. Mobutu did ultimately nationalize certain industries to bolster his Pan-African credentials, placing them in the hands of personal cronies.

79. T. M. Callaghy, *The State-Society Struggle: Zaire in Comparative Perspective* (New York: Columbia University Press, 1985), 295; Charles Leister Jr. to Byron Engle, "Gendarmerie Running Amuck [*sic*] in Kinshasa," August 2, 1972, Africa and Near East and South Asia Branch, box 4, folder Congo; CIA Special Report, "The Congo: A Political Assessment," June 28, 1968, LBJL, NSF, box 98, folder Congo.

80. Callaghy, *The State-Society Struggle,* 294–98. See also Schatzberg, *The Dialectics of Oppression,* 63–65; Thomas Plate and Andrea Darvi, *Secret Police: The Inside Story of a Network of Terror* (New York: Doubleday, 1981), 181.

81. "Public Safety Monthly Report," February 1966; May 12, 1966, TSD, Congo, box 5, "Rwanda Public Safety Program, 1967," TSD, box 19, folder Rwanda.

82. Ed Hamilton to Walt W. Rostow, "Possible Points for Discussion with the Rwandan Ambassador," July 18, 1967, LBJL, NSF, Country File, Africa, box 98, folder Rwanda; Nicholas Katzenbach, memo for the president, August 11, 1967, LBJL, NSF, box 98, Rwanda; Mahmood Mamdani, *When Victims Become Killers: Colonialism, Nativism, and the Genocide in Rwanda* (Princeton: Princeton University Press, 2001).

83. "Police Survey Mission to the Republic of Rwanda," May 1964, IPS, box 11, folder Rwanda; Hamilton to Rostow, "Possible Points for Discussion with New Rwandan Ambassador; Alston Staley, "Monthly Report, Public Safety Program," January 13, 1967, Africa and Near East and South Asia branch, box 39, folder Rwanda.

84. "Rwanda, FY 1966," TSD, box 8, folder Rwanda; Leo Cyr to Department of State, April 28, 1967, Africa and Near East and South Asia Branch, box 39. British intelligence officers in Uganda, where Tutsi refugees came to be seen as a security threat used the same term.

85. Leigh Brilliant to Mitchell A. Mabardy, "Vehicles and Communications Equipment for Rwanda"; John Manopoli, "Monthly Report, Public Safety Program," September 1965, and "Monthly Report, Public Safety Program," July 1966, all Africa and Near East and South Asia Branch, box 39, Rwanda.

86. Dean Rusk to American embassy, Kigali, March 23, 31, 1966, TSD, box 8, folder Rwanda; Monthly Report, Public Safety Program, July/August 1967," TSD, box 19, Rwanda.

87. Bob DuBose to Ed Hamilton, March 8, 1966; and Ambassador Leo Cyr to Department of State, April 28, 1967, Africa and Near East and South Asia branch, box 39, folder Rwanda. As a postscript, by 1990, after Habyarimana refused to acquiesce to an invasion of the Congo to unseat Mobutu, who had become a political embarrassment, the United States switched allegiances, backing an invasion from Uganda by the Tutsi-Rwandan Patriotic Front, which precipitated the vicious civil war that culminated in the 1994 mass killings and the Congo war of the late 1990s.

88. "Police Survey Mission to the Kingdom of Burundi," May–June 1964, RG 286, USAID, OPS, Surveys and Evaluations, box 1, folder Burundi; René Lemarchand, *Burundi: Ethnic Conflict and Genocide* (New York: Cambridge University Press, 1995); Thomas P. Melady, *Burundi: The Tragic Years (An Eyewitness Account)* (New York: Orbis Books, 1974). On Chinese influence in the region, which appears to have been quite limited but was used as an excuse to upgrade U.S. arms supplies and covert action, see Frank R. Vilafana, *Cold War in the Congo: The Confrontation of Cuban Military Forces, 1960–1967* (New Brunswick, N.J.: Transaction, 2009), 76; David Wise and Thomas B. Ross, *The Espionage Establishment* (New York: Random House, 1967), 190.

89. "Minutes from CI Meeting," October 29, 1964, IPS, box 6, folder 7; Charles Maechling Jr., "Memo for CI: East Africa: Current Internal Security Situation," IPS, box 6. See also *Not Yet Uhuru: The Autobiography of Oginga Odinga* (New York: Hill & Wang, 1967).

90. Byron Engle, Office of Public Safety, and Colonel Mitchell A. Mabardy, "Summary Report, Kenya National Police, Special Assessment," Africa and Near East and South Asia Branch, box 8, Kenya.

91. Ferguson, Nairobi embassy, to USAID, "Public Safety Report for April–May 1968," TSD, box 13, folder Kenya; Seth Singleton, "Supplementary Military Forces in Sub-Saharan Africa: The Congo, Kenya, Tanzania, and Zaire," in *Supplementary Military Forces: Reserves, Militias, Auxiliaries*, ed. Louis A. Zurcher and Gwyn Harries-Jenkins (Beverly Hills: Sage Publications, 1978), 231.

92. Johnson F. Monroe to Byron Engle, "Report on the Public Safety Activities in East Africa," March 27, 1964; Byron Engle to Jack Goin, April 30, 1964; and Lauren J. Goin and Beryel Price, "The Relationship of the Police Force to the Security Service, United Republic of Tanganyika and Zanzibar," June 1964, TSD, box 21, folder Tanganyika; Gleijeses, *Conflicting Missions*, 246; Amrit Wilson, *U.S. Foreign Policy and Revolution: The Creation of Tanzania* (London: Pluto Press, 1989).

93. John Lindquist, "Survey of the Zambian Police," October 16–November 7, 1969, Africa and Near East and South Asia Branch, box 57, folder Zambia (also TSD, box 12, Zambia); "Police Complete British Course," *Zambia Times*, January 27, 1967, 1. On American support for the apartheid regime in South Africa and the underlying geostrategic and economic interests driving U.S. policy in the region, see Thomas Borstelmann, *Apartheid's Reluctant Uncle: The United States and Southern Africa in the Early Cold War* (New York: Oxford University Press, 1993); William Minter, *King Solomon's Mines Revisited: Western Interests and the Burdened History of South Africa* (New York: Basic Books, 1986). On CIA involvement, see Stockwell, *In Search of Enemies*.

94. Kenneth Kaunda to Manda, February 23, 1967, ZNA; reports, S. C. Mbilishi from Simon Kapwepwe, June 16–31, 1967, ZNA; personal conversation with Kenneth Kaunda, March 22, 2003. I had the opportunity to visit Zambia and spoke with residents of Lusaka who still remember the planes flying overhead.

95. Kenneth Kaunda to Ruben Kamenga, June 9, 1968, ZNA, Relations with the USA, MFA 101/3/108.

96. Ibid.; Michael Sata, "Chinese Investment in Africa: The Case of Zambia," paper presented to the Committee on Human Rights Studies, Harvard University, October 24, 2007; John Lindquist, "Conversation with the U.S. Ambassador to Zambia," May 26, 1970, Africa and Near East and South Asia Branch, box 57, folder Zambia.

97. Mahmood Mamdani, *Imperialism and Fascism in Uganda* (Trenton, N.J.: Africa World Press, 1984), 78; Clayton and Killingray, *Khaki and Blue*, 266. See also Pat Hutton and Jonathan Bloch, "How the West Established Idi Amin and Kept Him There," in Ray, Van Meter, and Wolf, *Dirty Work*, 2:171–80; and Marc Curtis, *Unpeople: Britain's Secret History of Human Rights Abuses* (London: Vintage, 2004), 245–61.

98. Johnson F. Monroe to Byron Engle, "Report on Public Safety Activities in East Africa," March 27, 1964, Geographic Files, box 20, folder Tanganyika; "Israeli Activities with African Civil Security Forces," Africa and Near East and South Asia Branch, box 4, folder Chad; Decalo, *Coups and Army Rule in Africa*, 163.

99. Clayton and Killingray, *Khaki and Blue*, 104.

100. Jack Anderson, "U.S. Helped to Train Amin Henchmen," *Washington Post*, July 12, 1978; Jack Anderson and Les Whitten, "Ugandans Get Pilot Training in U.S.," *Washington Post*, November 7, 1977.

101. Jack Anderson and Les Whitten, "Ugandans Get Pilot Training in U.S." *Washington Post,* November 7, 1977; Jack Anderson, "Idi Amin of Uganda Still Flying High," *Washington Post,* April 27, 1978.

102. Mamdani, *Imperialism and Fascism in Uganda,* 79. See Singleton, "Supplementary Military Forces in Sub-Saharan Africa," 214–16.

103. See Jeremy Scahill, *Blackwater: The Rise of the World's Most Powerful Mercenary Army* (New York: Nation Books, 2007). Staying on illegally under private contract, CIA agent Frank Terpil became a personal assistant to Amin, directing some of his executions. Joseph C. Goulden, *The Death Merchant: The Brutal True Story of Edwin P. Wilson* (New York: Bantam, 1985).

104. Kaunda to Kamanga, June 9, 1968.

105. David Killingray, "Guarding the Extending Frontier: Policing the Gold Coast, 1865–1913," in Anderson and Killingray, *Policing the Empire,* 123.

106. William D. Hartung and Bridget Moix, *Deadly Legacy: U.S. Arms to Africa and the Congo War* (New York: Arms Trade Resource Center, World Policy Institute, 2000), 4.

107. In Assenson and Alex-Assenson, *African Military History and Politics,* 107.

108. For an effective critique of the concept of "humanitarian intervention," see Jean Bricmont, *Humanitarian Imperialism* (New York: Monthly Review Press, 2006); Edward S. Herman and David Peterson, *The Politics of Genocide,* foreword by Noam Chomsky (New York: Monthly Review Press, 2010).

9. Arming Tyrants II

1. "Arman E. Melli, *Rahbar,*" May 5, 1946, RG 59 (1945–1949), RDS, box 7329, folder Iran.

2. See Lloyd C. Gardner, *Three Kings: The Rise of an American Empire in the Middle East after World War II* (New York: New Press, 2009); Melvyn P. Leffler, *A Preponderance of Power: National Security, the Truman Administration, and the Cold War* (Stanford: Stanford University Press, 1992), 79–80; Noam Chomsky, *Deterring Democracy* (New York: Hill and Wang, 1991), 53; Salim Yaqub, *Containing Arab Nationalism: The Eisenhower Doctrine and the Middle East* (Chapel Hill: University of North Carolina Press, 2004); "Strategic Significance of Iran" and "Statement of Policy by the NSC on U.S. Policy towards Iran," December 30, 1954, DDEL, OCB, box 8.

3. Gabriel Kolko, *Confronting the Third World: United States Foreign Policy 1945–1980* (New York: Pantheon, 1988), 70.

4. Jonathan Dunnage, "Continuity in Policing Politics in Italy, 1920–1960," in *The Policing of Politics in the Twentieth Century: Historical Perspectives,* ed. Mark Mazower (Providence: Berghahn Books, 1997), 80; O. W. Wilson to Office of Military Government, "Requests for Arms and Ammunition for Issue to German Police," November 16, 1946; and Theo Hall to Director, Office of Military Government, "Police Raids in Prevention of Black Market Activities," April 24, 1947, RG 260, U.S. Occupation Headquarters, OMGUS, Public Safety Branch, Records Related to German Police, 1945–1949 (hereafter OMGUS Public Safety Branch), box 274; Robert Murphy, "Report on Special Branch and Public Safety Organization and Operations in Cologne, with an Emphasis on Denazification Program," May 24, 1945, RG 84, Foreign Service Posts, Office of the U.S. Political Adviser to Germany, Berlin, 1945, box 18; Kendall D. Gott, *Mobility, Vigilance, and Justice: The U.S. Army Constabulary in Germany, 1946–1953* (Fort Leavenworth, Kans.: Combat Studies Institute Press, 2005), 20–31; Brian A. Libby, "Policing Germany: The U.S. Constabulary, 1946–1952" (Ph.D. diss., Purdue University, 1977); Robert M. W. Kempner, "Police Administration," in *Governing Postwar Germany,* ed. Edward H. Litchfield et al. (Port Washington, N.Y.: Kennikat Press, 1953), 403–18.

5. "Monthly Report of Prison Branch Activities," September 6, 1946, OMGUS Public Safety Branch, box 274. On the recruitment of former Nazis, see Christopher Simpson, *Blowback: The First Full Account of America's Recruitment of Nazis and Its Disastrous Effect on the Cold War, Our Domestic and Foreign* Policy, 2nd ed. (New York: Collier Books, 1989). The prison branch in Germany was run by T. Wade Markley, who went on to run the federal penitentiary in Terre Haute, Indiana, and by Wade Gerlach, a social worker.

6. Carolyn W. Eisenberg, *Drawing the Line: The American Decision to Divide Germany, 1944-1949* (New York: Cambridge University Press, 1996). For a sample of public safety activities, see, e.g., "Report from Public Safety Offices in Stuttgart," October 28, 1948, OMGUS Public Safety Branch, box 278; "Semi-Monthly Report," August 28, 1947, OMGUS Public Safety Branch, box 277; O. W. Wilson to chief PSD, "Comments Regarding Public Safety Matters in Bavaria," December 26, 1946, OMGUS Public Safety Branch, box 274; O. W. Wilson, "Removal of Nazis in the German Reichpost," September 23, 1945, RG 84, Foreign Service Posts, Office of the United States Political Adviser to Germany, Berlin, 1945, box 18. The military historian George F. Hofmann has stressed the importance of the G-2 intelligence function of the U.S.-trained constabulary and its function in spying on the communist and socialist parties and gaining advanced information on strikes. See George F. Hofmann, "Cold War Mounted Warriors: U.S. Constabulary in Occupied Germany," *Armor Magazine* 116 (September–October 2007), www.usconstabulary.com/armor_mag-con_occup_germ.html.

7. William J. Bopp, *O. W.: O. W. Wilson and the Search for a Police Profession* (Port Washington, N.Y.: Kennikat Press, 1977), 5; O. W. Wilson, "Report on Public Safety Training Program of ICA," July 21–27, 1958, MSU Vietnam Project, box 679. James L. McCraw, a U.S. Border Patrol agent, and Major Ulrich Urton, who had experience in police work in Europe and the United States, were among the other key advisers serving with the police programs in Germany.

8. See Lawrence S. Wittner, *American Intervention in Greece, 1943-1949* (New York: Columbia University Press, 1982); Bruce R. Kuniholm, *The Origins of the Cold War in the Near East: Great Power Conflict and Diplomacy in Iran, Turkey, and Greece* (Princeton: Princeton University Press, 1980).

9. U.S. intelligence noted that local leaders of the organization were soldiers, tobacco workers, schoolteachers, and lawyers. "Greece" situation report, Papers of Harry S. Truman, PSF, Intelligence Files, 1946–1953, Central Intelligence Reports File, Situation Reports, box 217; Wittner, *American Intervention in Greece, 1943-1949*, 3; Dominique Eudes, *The Kapetanios: Partisans and Civil War in Greece, 1943-1949*, trans. John Howe (New York: Monthly Review Press, 1970). Echoing official propaganda, many today continue to mischaracterize the leftist movement in Greece as a proxy of the Soviet Union; see, e.g., Walter Russell Mead, "A Hegemon Comes of Age," *Foreign Affairs* July–August 2009, 142. For a well-researched account emphasizing the nationalism and idealism underlying the movement, based on extensive interviews with female guerrillas, see Janet Hart, *New Voices in the Nation: Women and the Greek Resistance, 1941–1964* (Ithaca: Cornell University Press. 1996).

10. Wittner, *The American Intervention in Greece, 1943-1949*, 141; "Royal Greek Embassy," March 23, 1948, RG 59, RDS, Near East, Internal Affairs of Greece (1945–1949), 868 (hereafter RDS, Greece); Mark Mazower, "Policing the Anti-Communist State in Greece, 1922–1974: 'Law in whose name; order for whose benefit?'" in Mazower, *The Policing of Politics in the Twentieth Century*, 130–31; Col. William R. Needham, "Paramilitary Forces in Greece, 1946–1949" (Carlisle Barracks, Pa.: Army War College, 1971), 60; Joyce Kolko and Gabriel Kolko, *The Limits of Power: The World and United States Foreign Policy, 1945-1954* (New York: Harper & Row, 1972), 225.

11. Robert Coe to Secretary of State, June 13, 1945, RDS, Greece; Dana Adams Schmidt, "Griswold—'Most Powerful Man in Greece,'" *New York Times Sunday Magazine,* October 12, 1947, 10; George C. Marshall to Dwight Griswold, July 11, 1947, Papers of Dwight P. Griswold, HSTL, AMAG Correspondence, box 1 (hereafter GP AMAG). Griswold, who was repudiated by Nebraska voters for saddling the state with the largest appropriations and taxes in its history, told reporters: "I hold the cards. . . . When you've got a lot of money to spend, you're in a strong position." Schmidt, "Griswold," 10; also "Griswold Accepts Greek Mission Job: Appointment Protested by Democrats," *Lincoln Star,* GP AMAG.

12. Georgina Sinclair, "The 'Irish' Policeman and the Empire: Influencing the Policing of the British Commonwealth," *Irish Historical Studies* 36, no. 142 (November 2008): 181. Nearly seventy at the time, Wickham was a distinguished alumnus of Harrow and the Royal Military College at Sandhurst and holder of the French Légion d'Honneur. In London, one outraged constituent wrote to his MP: "The sending of members of the Ulster Constabulary to Greece can be interpreted in only one way. This police force is trained in the use of firearms and is associated with many acts of brutality in N. Ireland; its chief was associated with the discreditable episode of the 'Black and Tans.' . . . In his latest speeches, Mr. Churchill . . . underlined the necessity of maintaining 'law and order' in the confusion that has followed the collapse of the Nazi 'New Order.' One asks 'Law in whose name, order for whose benefit'? Greece has become nothing short of a police state." Mazower, "Policing the Anti-Communist State in Greece, 1922-1974," 144.

13. Robert Coe to Secretary of State, June 13, 1945, RDS, Greece; James Hugh Keeley, Chargé d'Affaires, to Secretary of State, "Extension until January 11, 1948, of British Police and Prison Mission in Greece," March 26, 1947; and "Extension until December 11, 1948, of British Police and Prison Mission," RDS, Greece. In the late 1940s, as ambassador to Syria, Keeley sponsored a right-wing coup.

14. Jack C. Davis, "The Role of the Greek Police during the Conflict of 1946–1949," March 8, 1971, AMHI, 34; Department of State Biographical Information, Napoleon Zervas, GP AMAG. Keeley's papers at Princeton University's Mudd Library contain information he compiled as consul in Salonika on communists which he derived from U.S. intelligence contacts with the Gendarmerie and secret police of the Metaxas regime. Keeley's role in using the Gendarmerie to gain intelligence on communist activity is typical of the U.S. collusion with Metaxas's anticommunist campaign. For the pattern of U.S. support for rightist dictators in the 1930s, see David F. Schmitz, *Thank God They're on Our Side: The United States and Right-Wing Dictatorships, 1921–1965* (Chapel Hill: University of North Carolina Press, 1999).

15. Zervas quoted in Kolko and Kolko, *The Limits of Power,* 405; Mazower, "Policing the Anti-Communist State in Greece, 1922–1974," 117; Olive Sutton, *Murder Inc. in Greece* (New York: New Century Publishers, 1948); Department of State Biographical Information, Napoleon Zervas; Loy Henderson to Gov. Griswold, "Skouras Memo," July 1, 1947, GP AMAG; "Report by Chief Legal Advisor of a Visit to the Courts in the Peloponnese," June 30–July 5, 1945, Military Liaison Branch, Greece, Legal Branch, Police Mission, 298-A, NARA. In an interrogation report made known to U.S. intelligence, Herman Neubacher, a former German official in the Balkans, declared that Zervas, as head of the major noncommunist resistance group in World War II, had agreed to an "unofficial truce with the Germans which lasted until the summer of 1944 and took no action against the Germans, probably because of the absence of pressure from the British. . . . He was always against the communists however." Department of State Biographical Information, Napoleon Zervas, GP AMAG. Gehlen was a Nazi war criminal recruited by the OSS and CIA under Operation Paper to provide intelligence on the Soviet Union for rollback operations behind the Iron Curtain.

16. "Notes on Meeting Held on 3rd September 1947 to Discuss the Future of the British Police and Prison Mission," September 10, 1947; Douglas Dillon to Secretary of State, October 24, 1947, RDS, Greece; J. C. Murray, "The Anti-Bandit War," *Marine Corps Gazette,* 38 (January–May 1954): 60–69; Michael McClintock, *Instruments of Statecraft: U.S. Guerilla Warfare, Counterinsurgency, and Counterterrorism, 1940–1980* (New York: Pantheon Books, 1992), 14–16.

17. "By the Women Kept in Prison" to Embassies of Great Britain, U.S., France, and Chief, Soviet Military Mission, May 1945; and "By Those Kept in Prison at the State Factory for Cutting Tobacco" to public prosecutor at Athens, Minister of Interior and Justice, Military Liaison Branch (Greece), Legal Branch, Police Mission, 298-A, NARA; UN Investigative Commission Report, June 26, 1947, GP AMAG; Sutton, *Murder Inc. in Greece;* Kati Marton, *The Polk Conspiracy: Murder and Cover-Up in the Case of CBS News Correspondent George Polk* (New York: Farrar, Straus and Giroux, 1990), 145; Davis, "The Role of the Greek Police during the Conflict of 1946–1949"; Edgar O' Ballance, *The Greek Civil War, 1944–1949* (New York: Praeger, 1966), 214.

18. "Notes on Meeting Held on 3rd September 1947 to Discuss the Future of the British Police and Prison Mission"; L. Pittman Springs, American Consul General, to Secretary of State, May 24, 1946, RDS, Greece; Major General Katambis, Supreme Command, "Report to the American Embassy," April 15, 1949, RDS, Greece; correspondence of Dwight Griswold and George C. Marshall, and Loy Henderson to Governor Griswold, "Skouras Memo," July 1, 1947, GP AMAG.

19. Clifford Norton to Colleague, March 19, 1947, RDS, Greece; Wittner, *The American Intervention in Greece, 1943–1949,* 150; Theo Hall, "Report on the Internal Security Services of Greece, ICA," April 1956, RG 286, USAID, OPS, Operations Division, Africa and Near East and South Asia Branch, box 60, folder Greece (hereafter Africa and Near East and South Asia Branch); Daniele Ganser, *NATO's Secret Armies: Operation Gladio and Terrorism in Western Europe* (London: Frank Cass, 2005), 215, 216.

20. "Wilmette Chief of Police to Aid in German Rule," *Chicago Tribune,* June 24, 1945; Reg Davis and Harry James, *The Public Safety Story: An Informal Recollection of Events and Individuals Leading to the Formation of the AID Office of Public Safety,* April 2001, http://pdf.usaid.gov/pdf_docs/; Theo Hall, "Berlin District Public Safety Weekly Report," August 6, 1946, OMGUS Public Safety Branch, box 277; Joseph E. Wechler and Theodore Hall, *The Police and Minority Groups: A Program to Prevent Disorders and to Increase Relations between Opposite Racial, Religious, and National Groups* (Chicago: International City Managers Association, 1944), 1, 3.

21. Hall, "Report on the Internal Security Services of Greece"; H. J. Clay, "Use of Museum as a Prison," May 1945, Military Liaison Branch, Greece, Legal Branch, Police Mission, 298-A; Wittner, *The American Intervention in Greece 1943–1949,* 143–45; Nicos C. Alivizatos, "The 'Emergency Regime' and Civil Liberties, 1946–1949," in *Greece in the 1940s: A Nation in Crisis,* ed. John O. Iatrides (Hanover, N.H.: University Press of New England, 1981), 222; Sutton, *Murder Inc. in Greece.*

22. Marton, *The Polk Conspiracy,* 221, 273, 283. "Wild Bill" Donovan and the influential columnist Walter Lippmann participated in the cover-up by championing the official government claims about the murder. Donovan fired investigator James Kellis, an OSS war hero in China, after he raised critical questions. The British police mission was also involved in the cover-up and may have directly colluded in the murder (which had all the markings of a black operation) with Tsaldaris, whose political career was eventually brought down by a corruption scandal.

23. "Report to NSC Pursuant to NSC Action 1290-d," September 12, 1955, DDEL, OCB (Overseas Coordinating Board), White House Office, National Security Council Staff, box 17, folder Internal Security.

24. George McGehee to Mac Bundy, "Counter-Guerrilla Campaigns in Greece, Malaya, and the Philippines," November 21, 1961, JFKL, RWK, box 414, folder 1, Special Group; "Greek Police Records," American Embassy, Athens, to Secretary of State, June 25, 1958; and Edward Kennelly, "Public Safety Program in Greece," Africa and Near East and South Asia Branch, box 60, folder 2; Monthly Public Safety Report, December 17, 1960; "Lamination of ID Cards for Greece," April 4, 1960; and "Monthly Public Safety Report, July 1958," Africa and Near East and South Asia Branch, box 61, folder 1. On Theodore Brown's record as police chief in Eugene, see "City's Police Traffic Safety Mark Praised," *Eugene Register Guard,* August 25, 1954. Brown claimed that the programs enabled Greek police to "combat underground communistic activities more effectively."

25. See James Beckett, *Barbarism in Greece: A Young American Lawyer's Inquiry into the Use of Torture in Contemporary Greece, with Case Histories and Documents,* foreword by Senator Claiborne Pell (New York: Walker, 1970); Christopher Montague Woodhouse, *The Rise and Fall of the Greek Colonels* (New York: Franklin Watts, 1985); Mazower, "Policing the Anti-Communist State in Greece, 1922–1974," 148; Peter Murtagh, *The Rape of Greece: The King, the Colonels, and the Resistance* (London: Simon & Schuster, 1994).

26. James A. Bill, *The Eagle and the Lion: The Tragedy of American-Iranian Relations* (New Haven: Yale University Press, 1988), 41; Victor J. Croizat, "Imperial Iranian Gendarmerie," *Marine Corps Gazette* (October 1975): 29; "Iran" situation report, Papers of Harry S. Truman, PSF, Intelligence Files, 1946–1953, Central Intelligence Reports File, Situation Reports, box 217. In an earlier era, in 1911, an American economist, W. Morgan Shuster, was invited by the monarch, Mohammad Ali Shah, to reorganize the country's finances. Finding the country plagued by "banditry," which made it impossible for taxes to be collected in the hinterland, he recommended the formation of an 8,400-man rural constabulary under the Ministry of Finance to address the problem. Although Shuster was expelled from Iran at the urging of the Russians, the Gendarmerie was eventually formed under the command of Swedish officers.

27. F. L. Satton to Secretary of State, "Suggested Reforms in Iranian Police Organization," April 26, 1946, RG 59 (1945–1949), RDS, box 7329, folder Iran; Andrew Tully, *CIA: The Inside Story* (New York: William Morrow, 1962), 94; Steven R. Ward, *Immortal: A Military History of Iran and Its Armed Forces* (Washington, D.C.: Georgetown University Press, 2009), 172; Croizat, "Imperial Iranian Gendarmerie," 29; "Lt. Col. Paul Lionel Helliwell," RG 226, Records of the OSS, Personnel Files, box 0326. Schwarzkopf, a captain in the army in World War I, was a West Point classmate of Matthew Ridgway and of "Lightning Joe" Collins, famous for investigating the Lindbergh kidnapping. His background is traced in Leo J. Coakley, *Jersey Troopers: A Fifty-Year History of the New Jersey State Police* (New Brunswick: Rutgers University Press, 1971). At one point Schwarzkopf boasted of controlling the Iranian parliament (*majlis*).

28. "Arman E. Melli, *Rahbar,*" May 5, 1946.

29. Ibid.

30. "Report to NSC Pursuant to NSC Action 1290-d," DDEL, OCB, box 17; Stephen Kinzer, *All the Shah's Men: The American Coup and the Roots of Middle East Terror* (New York: Wiley, 2003); Tully, *CIA,* 97; Ward, *Immortal,* 195; Juan Cole, *Engaging the Muslim World* (New York: Palgrave Macmillan, 2009), 214; Bill, *The Eagle and the Lion,* 55.

31. Mark J. Gasiorowski, *U.S. Foreign Policy and the Shah: Building a Client State in Iran* (Ithaca: Cornell University Press, 1991), 113; Michael T. Klare, *American Arms Supermarket*

(Austin: University of Texas Press, 1984), 108, 116; Thomas M. Ricks, "U.S. Military Missions to Iran, 1943–1978: The Political Economy of Military Assistance," *Iranian Studies* 12 (Summer–Autumn 1979): 163–93.

32. "Murder Trial of 5 Army Officers in Isfahan and Implications," June 19, 1955, RDS, Related to the Internal Affairs of Iran (1955–1959), decimal file 894.

33. James P. Grant to Special Group on Counter-Insurgency, "Subject: Status Report on Police Gendarmerie and Civic Action Program in Iran," April 30, 1963, JFKL, NSF, box 4.

34. See Marilyn Olsen, *Gangsters, Gunfire, and Political Intrigues: The Story of the Indiana State Police* (Indianapolis: .38 Special Press, 2001), 69–70; "Lt. Arthur McCaslin Thurston," RG 226, Records of OSS, Personnel File, 1941–1945, box 77; Maochun Yu, *OSS in China: Prelude to Cold War* (New Haven: Yale University Press, 1996), 226.

35. Michael G. McCann, "Completion of Tour Report," September 12, 1959, ICA; Colonel Charles Peeke, "End of Tour Report," July 1, 1963; and Miles J. Furlong, "End of Tour Report," June 27, 1963, Africa and Near East and South Asia Branch, box 61; Arthur Lang, USOM Afghanistan, to American embassy, Tehran, "Marking Requirements," April 23, 1959, Africa and Near East and South Asia Branch, box 60, folder Afghanistan; "Monthly Report, Iran," September 1961, Africa and Near East and South Asia Branch, box 62, folder 5. Kenney, an associate professor and coordinator of police administration programs at USC, was later appointed president of the American Society of Criminology. In 1960 he coauthored an influential book on policing; see John P. Kenney, "An Evaluation of the Training of Foreign Police Officers in the United States," Civil Police Administration, Office of Public Services, International Cooperation Administration (September 1957). Betsch later served in the Philippines.

36. "Monthly Report, Iran," December 1960, Africa and Near East and South Asia Branch, box 62, folder 5.

37. Gasiorowski, *U.S. Foreign Policy and the Shah*, 91; Gholam Reza Afkhami, *The Life and Times of the Shah* (Berkeley: University of California Press, 2009), 381, 384; James P. Grant to Special Group on Counter-Insurgency, "Status Report on Police Gendarmerie and Civic Action Program in Iran," April 30, 1963, JFKL, NSF, box 4; "Analysis of Internal Security Situation in Iran and Recommended Action," NSC Action no. 1290-d, December 22, 1954, DDEL, OCB, box 43, folder Iran.

38. Gasiorowski, *U.S. Foreign Policy and the Shah*, 118; Wilbur Crane Eveland, *Ropes of Sand: America's Failure in the Middle East* (New York: W. W. Norton, 1980), 95; Bill, *The Eagle and the Lion*, 100. Some CIA covert action specialists such as Edwin Wilson worked under the cover of private security companies, while others such as Thomas L. Ahern Jr., who was later taken captive in the 1979–1981 Iranian hostage crisis, worked under the cover of the narcotics control program.

39. Frank Jessup, "Completion of Tour Report," February 10, 1960; and Michael McCann, "End of Tour Report," April 25, 1962, Africa and Near East and South Asia Branch, box 61, folder 4.

40. Colonel Charles Peeke, "End of Tour Report," July 1, 1963, and Furlong, "End of Tour Report," June 27, 1963, both Africa and Near East and South Asia Branch, box 61; "Outline of Country Internal Defense Plan," October 30, 1962, JFKL, RWK, box 424; American embassy, Tehran, to Department of State, "Strengthening of Police Functions of the Imperial Iranian Gendarmerie," May 29, 1963, RG 286, USAID, OPS, Office of the Director, Internal Defense and Public Safety (hereafter IPS), box 8.

41. Grant to Special Group, "Status Report on Police Gendarmerie and Civic Action Program in Iran," April 30, 1963; Iran Situation Report, Papers of Harry S. Truman, PSF,

Intelligence Files, 1946–1953, Central Intelligence Reports File, Situation Reports, box 217; Croizat, "Imperial Iranian Gendarmerie," 28.

42. American embassy to Department of State, "Hunt for Dadshah; Charles C. Stelle to Department of State, "Death of Bandit Dadshah" January 14, 1958, RDS, Related to the Internal Affairs of Iran (1955–1959), decimal file 894. Stelle, formerly a member of OSS Detachment 101 in Burma, went on to become deputy director of State Department intelligence. His career in the OSS and its background are discussed in R. Harris Smith, *OSS: The Secret History of America's First Intelligence Agency* (Berkeley: University of California Press, 1972), 264. Information is also available in his OSS personnel file at the National Archives (RG 226, box 743).

43. Colonel Charles Peeke, "End of Tour Report," July 1, 1963, Africa and Near East and South Asia Branch, box 61; Harry J. Anslinger to George McGehee," August 4, 1949, RG 59 (1945–1949), RDS, box 7329, folder Iran; Douglas Valentine, *The Strength of the Wolf: The Secret History of America's War on Drugs* (London: Verso, 2004), 169–70.

44. McBee was African American, a rarity among CIA agents of the period. "Remarks, Garland H. Williams, Narcotics Adviser," April 21, 1957; and American embassy, Tehran, to Department of State, "Control of Narcotics Drugs," October 22, 1959, RDS, Related to the Internal Affairs of Iran (1955–1959), decimal file 894; Garland Williams, "Completion of Tour Report," April 9, 1959, American embassy, Tehran, to Secretary of State, July 21, 1961, Africa and Near East and South Asia Branch, box 61. Williams received praise from CIA deputy chief Desmond Fitzgerald for his "outstanding service." On the long-standing links between U.S. counter-narcotics and clandestine operations, see Alan A. Block, "Anti-Communism and the War on Drugs," in *Perspectives on Organizing Crime,* ed. Block (London: Kluwer Academic Publishers, 1991), 209–26. Michael McCann and Charles Peeke, a known CIA agent, were also involved in the counter-narcotics programs.

45. Wiley for Secretary of State and Commissioner Anslinger, May 2, 1948, RG 59 (1945–1949), RDS, box 7329, folder Iran.

46. Michael Parrish, "Iran: The Portrait of a U.S. Ally," *Christian Science Monitor,* May 29, 1963; Iran Report, the Documentation Centre of Confederation of Iranian Students, *Documents on the Pahlavi Reign of Terror in Iran: Eyewitness Reports and Newspaper Articles* (Frankfurt: Centre of Confederation of Iranian Students, 1977), 19; Garland Williams to American embassy, Tehran, "Narcotics Situation in Southeast Asia and the Far East," August 4, 1959, Africa and Near East and South Asia Branch, box 62, folder Narcotics; Valentine, *The Strength of the Wolf,* 117. For the broader historical pattern, see Peter Dale Scott, *Drugs, Oil, and War: The United States in Indochina, Colombia, and Afghanistan* (New York: Rowman & Littlefield, 2003).

47. Alfred W. McCoy, *The Politics of Heroin: CIA Complicity in the Global Drug Trade,* rev. ed. (New York: Lawrence Hill, 2004), 125. Williams's experience in Turkey is documented by Matthew Pembleton in his unpublished paper "Istanbul and the Knights Errant of the Federal Bureau of Narcotics, 1948–1960." Williams was also in Greece around this time.

48. Robert R. Schott, "American Consulate to Department of State," August 24, 1957, RDS, Related to the Internal Affairs of Iran (1955–1959), decimal file 894; Darius M. Rejali, *Torture and Modernity: Self, Society, and State in Modern Iran* (Boulder: Westview Press, 1994), 77; McCoy, *The Politics of Heroin,* 468.

49. Robert Dreesen, American Consul, to Department of State, "Anti-Opium Campaign in Azerbaijan," April 17, 1956, RDS, Related to the Internal Affairs of Iran (1955–1959), decimal file 894.

50. For a critique of the international drug war as a form of neocolonialism, see Thomas Szasz, *Ceremonial Chemistry: The Ritual Persecution of Drugs, Addicts, and Pushers* (New York: Anchor Books, 1975).

51. "Outline of Country Internal Defense Plan, Iran," October 30, 1962, JFKL, RWK, box 424; Robert W. Komer to Ralph Dungan, "Sense of Disquietude about Iran," October 23, 1962, JFKL, RWK; Bill, *The Eagle and the Lion,* 192.

52. Robert W. Komer to Max Taylor, July 7, 1962, JFKL, RWK, box 413; Leonard Friesz to Thomas Finn, June 4, 1968, RG 286, USAID, OPS, Technical Services Division (hereafter TSD), box 9, folder Iran; "Monthly Report, September 1961, Iran," Africa and Near East and South Asia Branch, box 62, folder 5; Records of the Third Meeting of the Interagency Police Group, February 18, 1963, IPS, box 8, folder 1; Charles Siragusa to Garland Williams, Rome, July 14, 1958, BNDD files. Frank Walton served for a period as one of the OPS advisers after being transferred from Vietnam.

53. "Outline of Country Internal Defense Plan, Iran," October 30, 1962, JFKL, RWK, box 424; Stuart W. Rockwell to Ambassador, "Riot Control Equipment," July 12, 1963; "Performance of the National Police in the Tehran Riots, June 5–6, 1963," IPS, box 8, folder 3; "Monthly Report," September and May 1961, Africa and Near East and South Asia Branch box 62, folder 5.

54. Earnest R. Oney, "The Eyes and Ears of the Shah," *Intelligence Quarterly* 1 (February 1986): 3; Klare, *American Arms Supermarket,* 124; Bill, *The Eagle and the Lion,* 192; Baqer Moin, *Khomeini: The Life of the Ayatollah* (London: I. B. Tauris, 1999).

55. Amnesty International, *Annual Report, 1974–1975* (London: Amnesty International Publications, 1975), 129.

56. Gasiorowski, *U.S. Foreign Policy and the Shah,* 157; Joseph Trento, *Prelude to Terror: The Rogue CIA; The Legacy of America's Private Intelligence Network and the Compromising of American Intelligence* (New York: Basic Books, 2005), 56.

57. Alfred W. McCoy, *A Question of Torture: CIA Interrogation from the Cold War to the War on Terror* (New York: Metropolitan Books, 2006), 74–75; A. J. Langguth, "Torture's Teachers," *New York Times,* June 11, 1979; Rejali, *Torture and Modernity,* 78–79.

58. Reza Baraheni, *The Crowned Cannibals: Writings on Repression in Iran,* introduction by E. L. Doctorow (New York: Vintage Books, 1977), 7, 133, 149; Reza Baraheni, "The SAVAK Documents," *The Nation,* February 23, 1980, 198–202. See also Jalal Al-i-Ahmad, *Occidentosis: A Plague from the West,* trans. and ed. R. Campbell, introduction by Hamid Algar, Contemporary Islamic Thought Persian Series (Berkeley: Mizan Press, 1984).

59. See Christopher Sullivan and Manaf Damluji, "The Origins of American Power in Iraq, 1941–1945," *Peace and Change* 34 (July 2009): 238–60.

60. Tariq Ali, *Bush in Babylon: The Recolonisation of Iraq* (London: Verso, 2003), 61; Hanna Batatu, *The Old Social Classes and the Revolutionary Movements of Iraq: A Study of Iraq's Old Landed and Commercial Classes and of Its Communists, Ba'athists, and Free Officers* (New Jersey: Princeton University Press, 1978), 342–44.

61. "Report on the Civil Police Forces of Iraq," May 1957; and George Denney Jr. to Acting Secretary, April 5, 1965, Africa and Near East and South Asia Branch, box 62, folder Iraq; "Appendix B: Survey of Various Countries to Communist Subversion, Report of NSC 1290-d Working Group," February 16, 1955, DDEL, OCB, box 16, folder Internal Security; Douglas Little, *American Orientalism: The United States and the Middle East since 1945* (Chapel Hill: University of North Carolina Press, 2002), 201.

62. "Report on the Civil Police Forces of Iraq," May 1957, Africa and Near-East and South Asia Branch, box 62, folder Iraq; George Deney Jr. to Acting Secretary, April 5, 1965; "OCB Report Pursuant to NSC Action 1290-d," August 5, 1955, DDEL, OCB, box 17, folder Internal

Security. On the systematic campaign of repression against the communists, which was supported by the United States, see Batatu, *The Old Social Classes and the Revolutionary Movements of Iraq;* and Ilario Salucci, *A People's History of Iraq: The Iraqi Communist Party, Workers' Movements, and the Left, 1924–2004* (Chicago: Haymarket Books, 2003), 23–34. In 1949 the labor leader Yusuf Salman Yusuf ("Fahd") was publicly hanged and his body was left in a public square as a warning to Baghdad's workers not to organize against the regime. Phelps later served with the OPS in Brazil and Peru.

63. Theo Hall to Clyde Phelps, "Abu Ghraib," December 2, 1957, Africa and Near East and South Asia Branch, box 62, folder Iraq.

64. See Saïd K. Aburish, *A Brutal Friendship: The West and the Arab Elite* (New York: St. Martin's 1997), 140; Tim Weiner, *Legacy of Ashes: The History of the CIA* (New York: Doubleday, 2007), 141; Weldon C. Matthews, "The Kennedy Administration, Counterinsurgency, and Iraq's First Ba'thist Regime," *International Journal of Middle East Studies:* 43,4 (2011), 646–647.

65. For interesting insights on this history, see Ali, *Bush in Babylon.*

66. Theo Hall, "Report on the Gendarmerie of Lebanon," ICA, October 1957; Edwin H. Arnold to J. H. Smith, from Robert Rupard, "Assistance to the Gendarmerie of Lebanon: Status Report," May 1958, Africa and Near East and South Asia Branch, box 64, Lebanon; Albert DuBois, Chief Public Safety Adviser, memo for the record, June 27, 1961, RG 469, Records of the U.S. Foreign Assistance Agencies, 1948–1961, ICA, USOM, Lebanon, Public Safety Division, box 1; Irene L. Gendzier, *Notes from the Minefield: United States Intervention in Lebanon and the Middle East, 1945–1958* (New York: Columbia University Press, 1997); Melvin Gurtov, *The United States against the Third World* (New York: Praeger, 1974), 36.

67. Edward Vinson to Wade Fleetwood, "Report on the Internal Security Services of Turkey," March 1957; "Monthly Report, Civil Police Forces of Turkey," November 1957, June 14, 1958, July 16, 1959; Edward R. Bishop, "End of Tour Report, Ankara"; and James McGregor, "End of Tour Report," April 17, 1962, all Africa and Near East and South Asia Branch, box 66, Turkey. The secret armies included neo-fascist elements who helped orchestrate a coup in 1980 and spearheaded the brutal repression of Kurdish uprisings. Ganser, *NATO's Secret Armies,* 230, 31. Black flag operations are designed to deceive the public in such a way that the operations appear as though they are being carried out by other entities. On Turkish politics, see Andrew Mango, *Turkey: A Delicately Poised Ally* (Beverly Hills: Sage Publications, 1975); Carter Vaughn Findley, *Turkey, Islam, Nationalism, Modernity: A History, 1789–2007* (New Haven: Yale University Press, 2009).

68. Frank Sojat to Mr. H. J. Anslinger, "Progress Report no. 3," October 1, 1951; Frank Sojat to Mr. H. J. Anslinger, "Progress Report no. 4," November 5, 1951; and "Former Istanbul Customs Chief Caught with 15 Kilos of Heroin," Istanbul, September 2, 1951, Records of the Drug Enforcement Administration, RG 170, BNDD, 1916–1970, Turkey Special Files, box 25; Pembleton, "Istanbul and the Knights Errant of the Federal Bureau of Narcotics, 1948–1960." Before buying his way out of murder and drug trafficking charges, Sekban was regularly allowed to leave prison and visit his family.

69. American embassy, Kabul, to Department of State, "Kandahar Unrest: Situation after December 1959 Riots"; and Arthur Lang, "End of Tour Report," February 1959 to March 1961, Africa and Near East and South Asia Branch, box 60, folder Afghanistan. On larger development programs, see Nick Cullather, "Damming Afghanistan: Modernization in a Buffer State," *Journal of American History* 89 (September 2002): 512–37.

70. Albert E. Riedel, "Monthly Report on Civil Police Program for Afghanistan," January 29, 1958, Africa and Near East and South Asia Branch, box 60, folder Afghanistan.

71. Arthur Lang, USOM Afghanistan to American embassy, Tehran, "Marking Requirements," April 23, 1959, Africa and Near East and South Asia Branch, box 60, folder Afghanistan.

72. See, e.g., David E. Long, *The United States and Saudi Arabia: Ambivalent Allies* (Boulder: Westview Press, 1985); Saïd K. Aburish, *The Rise, Corruption, and Coming Fall of the House of Saud* (New York: St. Martin's Press 1994); Robert Baer, *Sleeping with the Devil: How Washington Sold Our Soul for Saudi Crude* (New York: Crown, 2003).

73. "Arab States: Saudi Arabia," situation report, Papers of Harry S. Truman, PSF, Intelligence Files, 1946–1953, Central Intelligence Reports File, Situation Reports, box 217.

74. See Nathan Citino, *From Arab Nationalism to OPEC: Eisenhower, King Saud, and the Making of U.S.-Saudi Relations* (Bloomington: Indiana University Press, 2002); Mordechai Abir, *Oil, Power, and Politics: Conflict in Arabia, the Red Sea, and the Gulf* (London: Frank Cass, 1974); Dean Rusk to American embassy, Jidda, "Internal Defense Plan, Saudi Arabia," June 16, 1964, IPS, box 6, folder 2; Robert Vitalis, *America's Kingdom: Mythmaking on the Saudi Oil Frontier* (Palo Alto: Stanford University Press, 2007), 159, 160. Faisal described Marxism as a "subversive creed originated by a vile Jew." Robert Dreyfuss, *Devil's Game: How the United States Helped to Unleash Fundamentalist Islam* (New York: Metropolitan Books, 2005), 142. Hitler felt the same way. Abir describes Faisal as an evolutionary modernizer who adopted a modern education system and transport and communications infrastructure. "While he may have seemed an anachronism to the sophisticated intelligentsia of the Arab countries, he nevertheless had some attraction for the orthodox, uneducated Arab masses and especially Puritan Saudi tribesmen and farmers" (35).

75. Rusk to American embassy, Jidda, "Internal Defense Plan, Saudi Arabia;" "Minutes of Meeting of CI," August 13, 1964, IPS, box 6.

76. Long, *The United States and Saudi Arabia,* 45; Robert Dreyfuss, *Devil's Game,* 142.

77. U.S. Congress, House, Government Accountability Office, "Stopping U.S. Assistance to Foreign Police and Prisons," February 19, 1976, GAO, ID-76-517; "Saudi Arabia, Public Safety Program Overview," Africa and Near East and South Asia Branch, box 4, folder Reports.

78. E. H. Adkins and George Miller, "Survey Report of the Surveillance and Protection of the Saudi Arabian Oil Fields and Installations for the Ministry of the Interior, Kingdom of Saudi Arabia," December 1971, TSD, box 4, Saudi Arabia; Jeter Williamson, Chief Public Safety Adviser, AID Riyadh, "Monthly Report," American embassy, Jidda, to Department of State, June 1968, TSD, box 4, Saudi Arabia; Michael McCann and John Means, "Report of Survey of Public Security Forces of Kingdom of Saudi Arabia" (USAID, August 1966); Department of State, "Annual U.S. Policy Assessment: Saudi Arabia," March 30, 1966, LBJL, National Security File, Country File, Middle East, box 155, Saudi Arabia.

79. American embassy, Saudi Arabia, to American embassy, Tehran, Africa and Near East and South Asia Branch, box 66, folder Saudi Arabia; Edward R. Bishop, "Report of the Study of the Saudi Security Forces Riot Control Capabilities," June 7, 1967, Africa and Near East and South Asia Branch, box 65, folder Saudi Arabia. On the repression of the SAP, see Abir, *Oil, Power, and Politics,* 54.

80. William D. Hartung, "Mercenaries Inc.: How a U.S. Company Props Up the House of Saud," *The Progressive* 60 (April 1996): 26–28; Kim Willenson, "This Gun for Hire," *Newsweek,* February 24, 1975, 30; U.S. Congress, House, Committee on International Relations, *Defense Contractors' Training of Foreign Military Forces,* Hearings before the Subcommittee on International Political and Military, 94th Cong., 1st sess., 1976 (Washington, D.C.: GPO, 1976), 11; "Executive Mercenaries: The Case of Saudi Arabia," in *The Iron Fist and the Velvet Glove: An Analysis of the U.S. Police,* ed. Tony Platt (Berkeley: Center for Research

on Criminal Justice, 1975), 171; Pratap Chatterjee, *Iraq, Inc.: A Profitable Occupation* (New York: Seven Stories Press, 2004), 127.

81. See Peter Dale Scott, "Drugs and Oil: The Deep Politics of U.S. Asian Wars," in *War and State Terrorism: The United States, Japan, and the Asia-Pacific in the Long Twentieth Century,* ed. Mark Selden and Alvin Y. So (New York: Rowman and Littlefield, 2004), 175; David E. Shapiro, *The Hidden Hand of American Hegemony: Petrodollar Recycling and International Markets* (Ithaca: Cornell University Press, 1999).

82. Dean Rusk to Amman USAID, June 24, 1966, TSD, box 11, folder Jordan Reports; "Public Safety Reports," June 1966; "Amman, Jordan," July 15, 1966, TSD, box 11, folder Jordan Reports; Avi Shlaim, *Lion of Jordan: The Life of King Hussein in War and Peace* (New York: Alfred A. Knopf, 2008), 150, 151; Bob Woodward, "CIA Paid Millions to Jordan's King Hussein," *Washington Post,* February 18, 1977; Douglas Little, "Mission Impossible: The CIA and the Cult of Covert Action in the Middle East," *Diplomatic History* 28 (November 2004): 663–701.

83. Rusk to Amman USAID, June 24, 1966; "Public Safety Reports," June 1966, TSD, box 11, folder Jordan Reports; "Amman, Jordan," July 15, 1966; Thomas Lobe, "U.S. Police Assistance for the Third World" (Ph.D. diss., University of Michigan, 1975), 85. Several thousand Palestinians are estimated to have been killed in this period. PLO founder Ahmed al-Shuqairy, an outspoken critic of King Hussein, was long a target of police surveillance in Jordan.

84. Raymond W. Meier, "A Recommended Correctional System for the Hashemite Kingdom of Jordan," USAID, PSD, Amman, Africa and Near East and South Asia Branch, box 63, Survey of Jordan Prisons; Raymond W. Meier, Prison Consultant, "Final Report, Amman, Jordan," August, 1966, TSD, box 11, folder Jordan Reports.

85. "OCB Report Pursuant to NSC Action 1290-d," Country Report, Pakistan, August 4, 1955, DDEL, OCB, box 17, folder Internal Security; Robert J. McMahon, *The Cold War on the Periphery: The United States, India, and Pakistan* (New York: Columbia University Press, 1994); Saeed Shafqat, *Civil-Military Relations in Pakistan: From Zulfikar Ali Bhutto to Benazir Bhutto* (Boulder: Westview Press, 1997), 184.

86. Johnson Monroe and Mitchell Mabardy, "Evaluation Report, Public Safety Program for Provincial Police and Civil Armed Forces," August–September 1968, Africa and Near East and South Asia Branch, box 65, folder Pakistan; W. Paul Kelley, "Public Safety, Monthly Report, January 1960," Africa and Near East and South Asia Branch, box 64, Tariq Ali, *Can Pakistan Survive? The Death of a State* (London: Verso, 1983), 109.

87. Joseph J. Corr to Johnson F. Munroe, "Report on Police Reforms," July 1963, IPS, box 3, folder Pakistan; U.S. embassy, Karachi, to AID, "Public Safety Program for Pakistan: Joint Embassy/AID/Country Team Message," April 26, 1963, IPS, box 3, folder Pakistan.

88. "USAID in East Pakistan," May 1967, State Department, USAID, 24; U.S. embassy, Karachi, to AID, "Public Safety Program for Pakistan: Joint Embassy/AID/Country Team Message" April 26, 1963, IPS, box 8; Pakistan; Gurtov, *The United States against the Third World,* 170; Noam Chomsky and Edward S. Herman, *The Political Economy of Human Rights: The Washington Connection and Third World Fascism* (Boston: South End Press, 1979), 106; "Bio-Data Information: Robert N. Bush," July 12, 1971, and Colonel Dao Quan Hien, "Security Protection Plan for Lower House, Presidential, and Vice-Presidential Elections," Bien Hoa, Republic of Vietnam, August 1971, both courtesy Sgt. Gary Wilkinson, Indiana State Police, Ret. A captain in the Indiana State Police and a decorated World War II combat veteran with experience in South Korea and Vietnam, Bush received a Purple Heart and Silver Star for combat exploits in Europe during World War II. He graduated from Purdue University in the 1930s, where he starred on the football team. He had a twenty-year police career, which included a stint as chief of internal and external security for the

Cumins engine company. In the early 1970s he worked with the police Special Branch in Bien Hoa as part of the Phoenix program.

89. "Report to NSC OCB Board Pursuant to NSC Action 1290-d," September 12, 1955, DDEL, OCB, box 17; Ahmed Rashid, *Descent into Chaos: The United States and the Failure of Nation Building in Pakistan, Afghanistan, and Central Asia* (New York: Viking, 2008), 36; Eqbal Ahmad, "Pakistan Signposts to a Police State," *Journal of Contemporary Asia* 4 (April 1974): 423–38. On the corruption of the ISI, see Lawrence Lifschultz, "Pakistan: The Empire of Heroin," in *War on Drugs: Studies in the Failure of U.S. Narcotics Policy,* ed. Alfred W. McCoy and Alan A. Block (Boulder: Westview Press, 1992), 319–52.

90. Rashid Khalidi, *Sowing Crisis: The Cold War and American Dominance in the Middle East* (Boston: Beacon Press, 2009). See also Aburish, *A Brutal Friendship;* Little, *American Orientalism.*

10. The Dark Side of the Alliance for Progress

1. See Lee Echols, *Hilarious High-Jinks and Dangerous Assignments* (Washington, D.C.: National Rifle Association, 1990); David Tobis, "The Alliance for Progress: Development Program for the United States," in *Guatemalan Rebellion: Unfinished History,* ed. Jonathan L. Fried et al. (New York: Grove Press, 1983), 92–97; Richard P. Tucker, *Insatiable Appetite: The United States and the Ecological Degradation of the Tropical World* (New York: Rowman & Littlefield, 2007).

2. Arthur M. Schlesinger Jr., *Robert Kennedy and His Times* (New York: Mariner Books, 2002), 467; Stephen G. Rabe, *The Most Dangerous Area in the World: John F. Kennedy Confronts Communist Revolution in Latin America* (Chapel Hill: University of North Carolina Press, 1999); Bruce Miroff, *Pragmatic Illusions: The Presidential Politics of John F. Kennedy* (New York: David McKay, 1976), 124.

3. Arthur M. Schlesinger Jr., "The Alliance for Progress: A Retrospective," in *Latin America: The Search for a New International Role,* ed. Ronald G. Hellman and H. Jon Rosenbaum (New York: John Wiley & Sons, 1975), 83; Noam Chomsky, *Turning the Tide: U.S. Intervention in Central America and the Struggle for Peace* (Montreal: Black Rose Books, 1987), 12; Charles Maechling Jr., "Counterinsurgency: The First Ordeal by Fire," in *Low Intensity Warfare: Counter-Insurgency, Pro-Insurgency, and Anti-terrorism in the Eighties,* ed. Michael T. Klare and Peter Kornbluh (New York: Pantheon Books, 1988), 26–27.

4. "Internal Warfare and the Security of Underdeveloped States," POF, box 98.

5. See Stephen G. Rabe, *The Road to OPEC: United States Relations with Venezuela, 1919–1976* (Austin: University of Texas Press, 1982), 146; Richard Gott, *Guerrilla Movements in Latin America* (London: Nelson, 1970), 151; John Gerassi, *The Great Fear in Latin America* (New York: Collier, 1965), 159; Steven Schwartzberg, "Rómulo Betancourt: From a Communist Anti-Imperialist to a Social Democrat with U.S. Support," *Journal of Latin American Studies* 29 (October 1997): 613–65.

6. "Public Safety Report," November and December 1965, RG 286, USAID, OPS Technical Services Division, box 24 (hereafter TSD), Venezuela; "Records of the 4th Meeting, Interagency Group," April 30, 1963, RG 286, USAID, OPS, Internal Defense and Public Safety, Office of the Director, box 8 (hereafter IPS); Peter T. Chew, "America's Global Peace Officers," *Kiwanis Magazine* (April 1969): 24; Michael T. Klare, *The Mercenarization of the Third World: U.S. Military and Police Assistance Programs* (New York: North American Congress on North America, 1970), 11; John P. Longan, "Memoir," with James D. Williams (January 1986), 34, Courtesy of University of Illinois at Springfield Archives, Special Collections.

7. Martha K. Huggins, *Political Policing: The United States and Latin America* (Durham: Duke University Press, 1998), 113; Amnesty International, *Venezuela Report, 1998* (London: Amnesty International, 1998), 2; James D. Cockcroft, *Latin America: History, Politics, and U.S. Policy,* 2nd ed. (Chicago: Nelson-Hall Publishers, 1996), 389. Communist Party leader Alberto Lovera was among those killed.

8. "John P. Longan, "Monthly Reports, Venezuela," April and May–June 1966, TSD, box 24, folder Venezuela; Michael T. Klare, *War without End: American Planning for the Next Vietnams* (New York: Knopf, 1972), 252.

9. Stanley W. Guth and Bryan L. Quick, "Venezuela Termination Phase-Out Report," April 1974, RG 286, USAID, OPS, Geographic Files, box 12, folder Venezuela (hereafter Geographic Files); Nikolas Kozloff, *Hugo Chávez: Oil, Politics, and the Challenge to the U.S.* (New York: Palgrave Macmillan, 2006).

10. Klare, *War without End,* 253; José Moreno, *Barrios in Arms: Revolution in Santo Domingo* (Pittsburgh: University of Pittsburgh Press, 1970). One of the heads of the Cascos Blancos, Col. Francisco Caamaño Deñó, was a son of Trujillo's chief torturer. In 1965 he defected to the revolutionaries and was later groomed as Che Guevara's successor in Bolivia. For the role of the OPS programs in contributing to the entrenchment of dictator Forbes Burnham in Guiana after the CIA-backed ouster of democratic socialist Cheddi Jagan, see Stephen G. Rabe, *U.S. Intervention in British Guiana: A Cold War Story* (Chapel Hill: University of North Carolina Press, 2009).

11. Eric Thomas Chester, *Rag-Tags, Scum, Riff-Raff, and Commies: The U.S. Intervention in the Dominican Republic, 1965–1966* (New York: Monthly Review Press, 2001); Rabe, *The Most Dangerous Area in the World,* 48. Thomas Mann, Johnson's chief adviser on Latin America, called Bosch an "impractical fellow" and "idealist who writes books. . . . We don't think that he is a communist [but we] don't think that [he] understands that the communists are dangerous."

12. Dean Rusk to USAID Santo Domingo, "Police Civic Action," May 11, 1966; "Public Safety Report, Santo Domingo," November–December 1965, May 1966; and "Public Safety Monthly Report, Santo Domingo," April 1966, Geographic Files, box 19, folder Santo Domingo, Monthly Reports; American Embassy to Secretary of State, "Shipment Arrival in Santo Domingo," May 31, 1966, TSD, box 12, folder Dominican Republic, Weapons and Tear Gas. A CIA "asset" recruited through the police programs, Morillo was involved in a 1963 coup against Bosch, who served briefly in the presidency.

13. "Public Safety Monthly Report, Santo Domingo," May 1966, Geographic Files, box 19, folder Santo Domingo, Monthly Reports; Lauren J. Goin, William Broe, and LT. [his first name is never given, a sign he is CIA] Shannon, "Dominican Republic: The Civil Security Force Development Plan," September 13, 1965, USAID, OPS, http://pdf.usaid.gov/pdf_docs/PNADN991.pdf; Noam Chomsky and Edward S. Herman, *The Political Economy of Human Rights: The Washington Connection and Third World Fascism,* vol. 1 (Boston: South End Press, 1979), 244, 246; Norman Gall, "Santo Domingo: The Politics of Terror," *New York Review of Books,* July 22, 1971, 15–19; Morse quoted in Thomas D. Lobe, "U.S. Police Assistance For the Third World" (Ph.D. diss., University of Michigan, 1975), 123.

14. Johnson Monroe to American embassy, La Banda, September 2, 1971; and "Political Evaluation," October 7, 1971, IPS, box 4, folder Dominican Republic.

15. See Mary Roldán, *Blood and Fire: La Violencia in Antioquia, Colombia, 1946–1953* (Durham: Duke University Press, 2002); David Bushnell, *The Making of Modern Colombia: A Nation in Spite of Itself* (Berkeley: University of California Press, 1993), 231

16. Herbert O. Hardin to American embassy, June 19, 1958, RG 286, USAID, OPS, Latin America Branch, box 23, folder Colombia (hereafter OPS Latin America Branch).

17. Dennis M. Rempe, "Guerrillas, Bandits, and Independent Republics: U.S. Counter-Insurgency Efforts in Colombia, 1959–1965," *Small Wars and Insurgencies* 6 (Winter 1995): 304–27; Michael McClintock, *Instruments of Statecraft: U.S. Guerrilla Warfare, Counterinsurgency, Counter-terrorism, 1940–1990* (New York: Pantheon Books, 1992), 222–23; "Strategic Study of Colombia," April 4, 1963, ASJ, White House Files, WLT 29, folder Colombia; William P. Yarborough, "U.S. Special Warfare Center," in *U.S. Department of the Army, Office of the Chief of Information, Special Warfare, U.S. Army: An Army Specialty* (Washington, D.C.: GPO, 1963). Arthur M. Schlesinger Jr., senior aide to President Kennedy, recommended that the United States keep its support secret in order to avoid any bad publicity. Hans Tofte served in the anti-Nazi underground in Denmark and was credited by General Matthew Ridgway with the "collection of vital intelligence on North Korea." Tofte went on to serve in the Philippines and across Latin America as an unconventional warfare specialist. In 1966 he was dismissed by the CIA for having classified documents in his Washington apartment. See James Barron, "Hans Tofte, World War II Spy Later Dismissed by the CIA," *New York Times*, August 28, 1987.

18. McClintock, *Instruments of Statecraft*, 222–23; "Strategic Study of Colombia," April 4, 1963. See also Geoff Simmons, *Colombia: A Brutal History* (London: Saqi Books, 2004), 48.

19. See Eduardo Pizarro Leongómez, "Revolutionary Guerrilla Groups in Colombia," in *Violence in Colombia: The Contemporary Crisis in Historical Perspective*, ed. Charles Bergquist, Ricardo Peñaranda, and Gonzalo Sánchez. (Wilmington, Del.: Scholarly Resources, 1992), 180; Walter J. Broderick, *Camilo Torres: A Biography of the Priest-Guerrillero* (New York: Doubleday, 1975); Gott, *Guerrilla Movements in Latin America*, 220–21.

20. David Laughlin, Robert Bowling, and Herbert Hardin, "Report on the Police in the Republic of Colombia," December 1962, OPS, Latin America Branch, box 5, Colombia; "Monthly Report," February 1966, TSD, box 4, Colombia. The Clint Eastwood *Dirty Harry* films, in which Eastwood's character, a San Francisco detective, adopts extralegal vigilante methods to get the "bad guys," was a cult hit among conservatives and encouraged the law and order movement.

21. David Laughlin to Byron Engle, "Visit to Chile and Colombia," October 8, 1963, OPS, Latin America Branch, box 235, folder Colombia; "Republic of Colombia Police Communications Survey Report," 1963, TSD, box 1, folder Colombia; Clifton Monroe, "Survey of the Industrial Security Operations of Empresa Colombia de Petroleas," November 1969, and Arlen Jee et al., "Termination Phase-Out Study," Public Safety Project, April 1974, all three TSD, box 1, folder Colombia; Jonathan Marshall, *Drug Wars: Corruption, Counterinsurgency, and Covert Operations in the Third World* (San Francisco: Cohan and Cohen, 1991), 5. Neeley served with the FBI in Argentina before World War II. Other advisers included Roy Driggers of the New Mexico State police and Peter Ellena of Pasadena, California, who also served in Brazil, Uruguay, and Laos.

22. "Termination Phase-Out, Public Safety Project, of Colombia," April 1974, TSD, box 14, "Strategic Study of Colombia," April 4, 1963, JFKL, Country File Colombia, box 29, folder Colombia; Jeffrey F. Taffet, *Foreign Aid as Foreign Policy: The Alliance for Progress in Latin America* (New York: Routledge, 2007), 155. Taffet provides some useful data but underplays the violent side of the Alliance and how it was used to support U.S. economic interests.

23. In Greg Grandin, *Empire's Workshop: Latin America, the United States, and the Rise of the New Imperialism* (New York: Metropolitan Books, 2006), 98.

24. "Public Safety Monthly Report," January and February 1966, and Theodore Brown, "Public Safety Monthly Report," April 18, 1966, both TSD, Colombia, box 4, Colombia. Also, "Public Safety Monthly Report" January 1967, OPS Latin America Branch, box 32. On

the Colombian counterinsurgency, see Douglas Stokes, *America's Other War: Terrorizing Colombia* (London: Zed Books, 2005), 57; Nazih Richani, *Systems of Violence: The Political Economy of War and Peace in Colombia* (Albany: State University of New York Press, 2002); Adolph Saenz, *The OPS Story: A True Story of Tupamaro, Terrorists, Assassinations, Kidnappings in Colombia, and Communist Subversion and Insurgency* (San Francisco: Robert Reed, 2002), 279. Cash rewards were offered for the assassination of guerrilla leaders, in a forerunner of the Vietnam Phoenix program.

25. Gérard Chaliand, *Revolution in the Third World,* rev. ed., trans. Diana Johnstone (New York: Viking, 1989), 64–65; "Public Safety Monthly Report," February 1966, TSD, box 4, Colombia.

26. Broderick, *Camilo Torres,* 332–23; Gott, *Guerrilla Movements in Latin America,* 223.

27. Theodore Brown to Byron Engle, April 22, 1966, TSD, box 4, Monthly Reports 1966; American embassy, Bogotá, to Dean Rusk, "Emergency Procurement," March 10, 1966; Geoffrey Oberdich, Federal Laboratories Inc. Washington Office to Mr. Pat Connelly, USAID, February 14, 1966 TSD, box 4, Colombia.

28. "Public Safety Monthly Report," October 1968, December 1968, and May 1970," all OPS Latin America, box 32; Saenz, *The OPS Story,* 22.

29. "Public Safety, Monthly Report, January 1967," OPS Latin America branch, Box 32. Recently declassified documents on the National Security Archive website paint a grim picture of the abuses. See, for example, "Colombia CI: Steps in the Right Direction," February 2, 1994, Director of Intelligence, NSA; Rempe, "Guerrillas, Bandits, and Independent Republics," 304–27; J. Patrice McSherry, *Predatory States: Operation Condor and Covert War in Latin America* (New York: Rowman & Littlefield, 2005), 19.

30. Saenz, *The OPS Story,* 272; "AID Official Byron Engle Dies at 79," *Washington Post,* January 12, 1990.

31. "Public Safety Monthly Report," October 1966, OPS Latin America Branch, Colombia, box 30, folder Monthly Public Safety Reports; "Public Safety Monthly Report," February 1968, OPS Latin America Branch, Colombia, box 30, folder Monthly Public Safety Reports.

32. "Public Safety Monthly Report," December 1968, OPS Latin America Branch, Colombia, box 32, folder Monthly Public Safety Reports; Peter Ellena, "Evaluation of AID Public Safety Program in Colombia," July 1969, USAID, OPS, http://pdf.usaid.gov/pdf_docs/PDACM630.pdf; Marshall, *Drug Wars.*

33. "Public Safety Monthly Report," February and April 1966, TSD, box 4; December 1968, OPS Latin America Branch, Colombia, box 32, folder Monthly Public Safety Reports; Alfred W. McCoy, *A Question of Torture: CIA Interrogation, from the Cold War to the War on Terror* (New York: Metropolitan Books, 2006); A. J. Langguth, *Hidden Terrors: The Truth about U.S. Police Operations in Latin America* (New York: Pantheon, 1978), 85; Philip Agee, *Inside the Company: A CIA Diary* (New York: Simon & Schuster, 1975).

34. "CIA Intelligence Report," 1994, www.gwu.edu/~nsarchiv/colombia/19940126.pdf; American embassy, Bogotá, to Secretary of State, "General Ramirez Lashes Out at State Department Report: More Generals under Investigation for Paramilitary Links," August 1998, www.gwu.edu/~nsarchiv/NSAEBB/NSAEBB327/doc01_19980813.pdf; "Trujillo Declassified: Documenting Colombia's Tragedy without End," October 5, 2008, NSA; Javier Giraldo, *Colombia: The Genocidal Democracy,* foreword by Noam Chomsky (Monroe, Me.: Common Courage Press, 2002); Forrest Hylton, *Evil Hour in Colombia* (London: Verso, 2006).

35. "Briefing, Public Safety Division," OPS Latin America Branch, box 65, folder Guatemala; Kirsten Weld, "Reading the Politics of History in Guatemala's National Police Archives" (Ph.D. diss., Yale University, 2010); Stephen Schlesinger and Stephen Kinzer,

Bitter Fruit: The Story of the American Coup in Guatemala, 2nd ed. (Cambridge: David Rockefeller Center for Latin American Studies, Harvard University, 1999); Greg Grandin, *The Last Colonial Massacre: Latin America in the Cold War* (Chicago: University of Chicago Press, 2004).

36. Nick Cullather, *Secret History: The CIA's Classified Account of Its Operations in Guatemala, 1952–1954* (Palo Alto: Stanford University Press, 1999), 12, 20, 22; Stephen M. Streeter, *Managing the Counterrevolution: The United States and Guatemala, 1954–1961* (Athens: Ohio University Center for International Studies, 2000), 93; American embassy, Guatemala, to Department of State, "Mutual Security Program in Guatemala," September 21, 1959, RDS, RG 59, RDS, box 4215, folder Guatemala (hereafter RDS, Guatemala).

37. "Fighter's End," *Time,* August 5, 1957, 23; Thomas Melville and Marjorie Melville, *Guatemala: Another Vietnam?* (New York: Penguin Books, 1971), 120–21; Gerassi, *The Great Fear in Latin America,* 182.

38. Cullather, *Secret History,* 113; Michael McClintock, *The American Connection: State Terror and Popular Resistance in Guatemala,* 2 vols. (London: Zed Books, 1985), 2:18; Stephen G. Rabe, *The Killing Zone: The United States Wages Cold War in Latin America* (New York: Oxford University Press, 2011), 53; Linares was known for torturing prisoners with electric-shock baths and head-shrinking steel skullcaps,

39. Fred Fimbres, "Report on the National Police in the Republic of Guatemala," 1956, RDS, RG 59, box 4215, folder Guatemala; Kate Doyle, "The Atrocity Files: Deciphering the Archives of Guatemala's Dirty War," *Harper's,* December 2007, 52–62.

40. Joint State ICA to American embassy, Guatemala, December 12, 1955, and American embassy to Department of State, July 13, 1956, both RDS, RG 59, box 4215, folder Guatemala; Herbert Hardin, "Use of Firearms by National Police of Guatemala," March 28, 1962, OPS Latin American Branch, box 65, folder Guatemala.

41. Arlen Jee, "Criminalistics Operations of the National Police, Republic of Guatemala, Summary and Follow-Up," November 19, 1970, IPS, International Police Academy, box 4; American embassy, Guatemala, to Department of State, "Law on Organizing the National Police," July 5, 1955, RDS, RG 59, box 4215, Guatemala.

42. McClintock, *The American Connection,* 2:33; "Report to NSC Pursuant to NSC Action 1290-d," September 12, 1955, DDEL, OCB, White House Office, National Security Council Staff, Overseas Coordinating Board, box 17, folder Internal Security; David Atlee Phillips, *The Night Watch* (London: Robert Hale, 1978), 52. Poppa could be a code name for Phillips and/or Lee Echols, who spent time in Guatemala.

43. "Report to NSC Pursuant to NSC Action 1290-d," September 12, 1955; January 3, 1957.

44. "Fighter's End."

45. William B. Connett Jr., Secretary of Embassy, "Report on National Police," October 1, 1958; and Smith to Guatemala City, October 10, 1958, RDS, RG 59, box 4215, folder Guatemala; Streeter, *Managing the Counterrevolution,* 93. After large anticorruption protests at Las Jornadas were violently broken up, Herbert Hardin similarly claimed that the reliance by the National Police on depressed fire from riot guns instead of rifle firearms probably "lowered the number of casualties considerably." Weld, "Reading the Politics of History in Guatemala's National Police Archives," 148.

46. American embassy to the Department of State, "Internal Security Situation and Needs," April 6, 1961, OPS Latin America Branch, box 65, folder Guatemala; John P. Longan, "Tour Report," May 24, 1960, OPS Latin America Branch, box 65, folder Guatemala; Lauren J. Goin and S. Morey Bell, "Evaluation, Public Safety Program USAID Guatemala," December 1971, 58; Rabe, *The Most Dangerous Area in the World,* 72.

47. American embassy, Guatemala City, to Secretary of State," July 24, 1960, OPS Latin America Branch, box 65, folder Guatemala; American embassy to the Department of State, "Internal Security Situation and Needs," April 6, 1961.

48. American embassy to the Department of State, "Internal Security Situation and Needs," April 6, 1961; Robert H. Holden, "Securing Central America against Communism: The United States and the Modernization of Surveillance in the Cold War," *Journal of Inter-American Studies and World Affairs* 41 (Spring 1999): 16. Nevertheless, the OPS continued over time to work closely with the Judicial police, even setting up a special academy. See, for example, Herbert O. Hardin to D. L. Crisostomo, September 11, 1961, OPS Latin America Branch, box 65, folder Guatemala.

49. U.S. Congress, House, Committee on Foreign Affairs, Hearings, *Statement by Assistant Secretary Edwin M. Martin before the Latin American Subcommittee on the Subject of Communist Subversion in the Hemisphere,* 89th Cong., 2nd sess., February 18, 1963 (Washington: D.C.: GPO, 1963); "For Robert W. Komer: Guatemala Internal Security Situation," May 8, 1962, JFKL, NSC, folder Guatemala; "Public Safety Monthly Report, Tegucigalpa," August 11, 1965, Latin America Branch, box 9, folder Honduras; "Minutes of the CI Meeting," April 8, 1965, IPS, box 6, folder 3.

50. Memorandum for the President from Deputy Secretary of Defense, "Capability of the Guatemalan Government to Control Riots," JFKL, POF, box 118; "Inventory of Riot Control Equipment," JFKL, POF, box 118; Rabe, *The Most Dangerous Area in the World,* 75–76.

51. McClintock, *The American Connection,* 2:52; "Meeting PSD Guatemala," October 9, 1963, and Herbert Hardin to Byron Engle, "Proper Management of Program, Guatemala," September 18, 1963, both Latin America Branch, box 65, folder 3; Doyle, "The Atrocity Files."

52. CIA information cable, "Planned Government Measures to Counter the Communist and Student Plans for Possible Violence on March 20, 1964," LBJL, National Security Files, Country File, Latin America, box 54, folder Guatemala.

53. Byron Engle, Director OPS, to John P. Longan, Chief Public Safety Advisor, Venezuela, "Plans to Counter Extortion/Kidnappings in Guatemala," June 4, 1966, NSA.

54. Guatemala to USAID, "Public Safety Monthly Report," October 1964, Latin America Branch, Country File, box 65, folder Guatemala; Grandin, *The Last Colonial Massacre,* 36; Longan, "Memoir."

55. Melville and Melville, *Guatemala: Another Vietnam?,* 267; Adolfo Gilly, "The Guerrilla Movement in Guatemala," *Monthly Review* 17 (May 1965): 9–40.

56. Thomas Hughes, INR [Intelligence and Research, State Department], to the Secretary, "A Counter-Insurgency Running Wild?" October 23, 1967, NSA; Weld, "Reading the Politics of History in Guatemala's National Police Archives," 161; Norman Gall, "Slaughter in Guatemala," *New York Review of Books,* May 20, 1971, 14.

57. Gott, *Guerrilla Movements in Latin America,* 87.

58. McClintock, *The American Connection,* 2:59, 84; CIA Special Reports, "Guatemalan Communists Take a Hard Line on Insurgency," August 6, 1965, LBJL, National Security File, Country File, Latin America, box 154, folder Guatemala; CIA internal memo, "Guatemala after the Military Shake-Up," May 13, 1968, LBJL, National Security File, Country File, Latin America, box 54, folder Guatemala; Eduardo Galeano, *Guatemala: Occupied Country* (New York: Monthly Review Press, 1968), 71.

59. "Guatemala: Caught in the Crossfire," September 6, 1968, 42; Walter LaFeber, *Inevitable Revolutions: The United States in Central America* (New York: Norton, 1984), 257; Doyle, "The Atrocity File," 61.

60. "Guatemalan Anti-Terrorist Campaign," *Defense Intelligence Agency, Secret Intelligence Bulletin,* January 12, 1971, NSA.

61. McClintock, *The American Connection,* 2:107; Penny Lernoux, *Cry of the People: United States Involvement in the Rise of Fascism, Torture, and Murder and the Persecution of the Catholic Church in Latin America* (New York: Doubleday, 1980), 186; "Public Safety Program in Guatemala" and "Public Safety in Guatemala: A Useful Program," IPS, box 1, folder Guatemala.

62. Ambassador C. Allan Stewart, "Report on Visit to Central America and Panama to Study AID Public Safety Programs," May 18–June 14, 1967, NSA; Hughes to the Secretary, "A Counter-Insurgency Running Wild?"

63. Grandin, *The Last Colonial Massacre,* 73; Greg Grandin, "Off the Beach: The United States, Latin America, and the Cold War," in *A Companion to Post-1945 America,* ed. Jean-Christophe Agnew and Roy Rosenzweig (London: Blackwell, 2002), 493.

64. Viron Vaky to Mr. Oliver, "Guatemala and Counter-Terror," March 29, 1968, www.gwu.edu/~nsarchiv/NSAEBB/NSAEBB11/docs/05-04.htm.

65. U.S. Congress, Senate, Committee on Foreign Relations, Hearings, *The Nature of the Revolution,* 90th Cong., 2nd sess., February 26, 1968 (Washington, D.C.: GPO, 1968); Melville and Melville, *Guatemala: Another Vietnam?* See also Thomas Melville, *Through the Glass Darkly: The American Holocaust in Central America* (Philadelphia: Xlibris, 2005).

66. "Public Safety in Guatemala: A Useful Program"; also Lauren J. Goin and S. Morey Bell, "Evaluation Public Safety Program, OPS Latin America Branch, Guatemala," December 1971; Huggins, *Political Policing,* 191.

67. Holly J. Burkhalter, "Guatemala Asks the U.S. for Trouble," *New York Times,* March 30, 1987.

68. Grandin, *The Last Colonial Massacre,* 1; Jennifer Schirmer, *The Guatemalan Military Project: A Violence Called Democracy* (Philadelphia: University of Pennsylvania Press, 1998); Piero Gleijeses, "Afterword: A Culture of Fear," in Cullather, *Secret History.* Police brutality and corruption remain endemic, exemplified by the fact that at this writing, two former police chiefs were on trial for narcotics trafficking.

69. American consulate, Mexico, to Department of State, "Narcotics: Illegal Flow in the U.S. from Mexico," January 25, 1960, and David Rowell to Max Chaplin, February 18, 1969, both OPS Latin America Branch, box 88, folder Mexico; "Monthly Reports, Panama," April 1965–June 1966, TSD, box 21, folder Panama; Saenz, *The OPS Story.* On corruption in the Mexican police and intelligence services and their involvement in political "disappearances," see Peter Dale Scott, *American War Machine: Deep Politics, the CIA Global Drug Connection, and the Road to Afghanistan* (New York: Rowman & Littlefield, 2010), 46.

70. Matilde Zimmermann, *Sandinista: Carlos Fonseca and the Nicaraguan Revolution* (Durham: Duke University Press, 2001), 53; Richard Grossman, "The Blood of the People: The Guardia Nacional's Fifty-Year War against the People of Nicaragua, 1927–1979," in *When States Kill: Latin America, the U.S., and Technologies of Terror,* ed. Cecilia Menjívar and Néstor Rodríguez (Austin: University of Texas Press, 2005), 67; "Monthly Public Safety Report," May 1968, El Salvador, OPS Latin America Branch, box 60, folder Monthly Reports.

71. Elmer H. Adkins Jr. and Morris Grodsky, "Office of Public Safety, Nicaragua, Termination Phase-Out," 1975, OPS Latin America Branch, Nicaragua, box 90, folder 1.

72. Amnesty International, *The Republic of Nicaragua: An Amnesty International Report Including the Findings of a Mission to Nicaragua,* May 10–15, 1976 (London: Amnesty

International Publications, 1977), 15, 23, 25, 26; Zimmermann, *Sandinista,* 94, 119. During Wagner's tenure in South Vietnam, his home was attacked by the "VC" in retaliation for his involvement in clandestine operations. Two OPS advisers, Al Farkas and James McCarthy, were killed defending it. Another OPS adviser in Nicaragua, Lucien Gormont, was a tele-communications specialist who had previously worked in South Korea.

73. Gerassi, *The Great Fear in Latin America,* 178; "President and Foreign Minister on Current Situation in El Salvador," October 20, 1960, OPS Latin America Branch, Box 59, El Salvador.

74. William Brubeck to McGeorge Bundy, "El Salvador," November 30, 1962; Department of State to American embassy, "El Salvador Plan of Action to July 1, 1963," December 20, 1962, and CIA telegram, "Salvadoran Police Anticipation of Communist Violence," July 3, 1962, both JFKL, NSF, box 69, El Salvador; Earl Searle, "Public Safety Report, El Salvador," October 1963, OPS Latin America Branch, box 59, El Salvador; Holden, "Securing Central America against Communism," 7.

75. "Public Safety Report," September 1965; and "Monthly Reports," April 1962, El Salvador, IPS, box 10, El Salvador; "Monthly Report," June 1966, El Salvador, TSD, box 16, folder El Salvador.

76. McClintock, *The American Connection,* 1:216–18; Theodore Brown, "End of Tour Summary Report, Chief Public Safety Advisor, USAID San Salvador," December 14, 1962, OPS Latin America Branch, box 59, El Salvador; Cynthia J. Aronson, "Window on the Past: A Declassified History of Death Squads in El Salvador," in *Death Squads in Global Perspective: Murder with Deniability,* ed. Bruce B. Campbell and Arthur D. Brenner (New York: St. Martin's Press, 2000), 92.

77. "Termination Phase-Out Report, Public Safety Project," May 1974, El Salvador, TSD, box 16, folder El Salvador.

78. Lesley Gill, *The School of the Americas: Military Training and Political Violence in the Americas* (Durham: Duke University Press, 2004); Mark Danner, *The Massacre at El Mozote: A Parable of the Cold War* (New York: Vintage Books, 1993); Chomsky, *Turning the Tide;* Grandin, *Empire's Workshop,* 131.

79. McClintock, *The American Connection,* 1:218.

80. See Timothy Wickham-Crowley, *Guerrillas and Revolution in Latin America: A Comparative Study of Insurgents and Regimes since 1956* (Princeton: Princeton University Press, 1992); Greg Grandin, "Living in Revolutionary Time: Coming to Terms with the Violence of Latin America's Long Cold War," in *A Century of Revolution: Insurgent and Counterinsurgent Violence during Latin America's Long Cold War,* ed. Greg Grandin and Gilbert M. Joseph (Durham: Duke University Press, 2010), 1–45. The essays in the latter volume serve as an important corrective to neoliberal scholars such as Jorge Castañeda who dehistoricize the guerrilla warfare of the Cold War by blaming it on the "revolutionary romanticism" of the New Left. Rehashing the viewpoint of liberal and conservative Cold Warriors, they ignore the deep-rooted structural variables shaping its genesis and the role of ferocious state repression in radicalizing opposition movements.

81. I. F. Stone, "Anti-Guerrilla War: The Dazzling New Military Toothpaste for Social Decay," in *In a Time of Torment: 1961–1967* (Boston: Little, Brown, 1967), 173–74.

82. See Kyle Longley, *The Sparrow and the Hawk: Costa Rica and the United States during the Rise of José Figueres* (Tuscaloosa: University of Alabama Press, 1997); Charles D. Ameringer, *Don Pepe: A Political Biography of José Figueres of Costa Rica* (Albuquerque: University of New Mexico Press, 1978). Figueres had long collaborated with the CIA, although he was also allegedly the target of at least one assassination plot.

83. "Public Safety Program Summary, Costa Rica," 1970, OPS Latin America Branch, box 8. For a discussion of the limits of Don Pepe's reforms, see Noam Chomsky, *Necessary Illusions: Thought Control in Democratic Societies* (Boston: South End Press, 1989), 111–12; LaFeber, *Inevitable Revolutions,* 105, 106.

84. "Public Safety Monthly Report," December 1969, November 1970, and September 1970, Costa Rica, IPS, box 39, folder Costa Rica. On Fonseca, see Zimmermann, *Sandinista.*

85. Rabe, *The Most Dangerous Area in the World,* 144; Naomi Klein, *The Shock Doctrine: The Rise of Disaster Capitalism* (New York: Metropolitan Books, 2007), 63.

86. Capsule biographies of these individuals can be found in Saenz, *The OPS Story,* 426–27; "Testimony of Theodore Brown, Chief Public Safety Adviser, USAID Brazil," in *United States Policies and Programs in Brazil, Hearings before the Subcommittee on Western Hemisphere Affairs of the Committee on Foreign Relations, United States Senate,* 92nd Cong., 1st sess., May 4, 1971 (Washington, D.C.: GPO, 1971), 3–51. A devout Christian who, according to a former colleague, did not drink, smoke, or even cuss, Brown was deputy to chief of mission Michael McCann in Vietnam from 1969 to 1973. McCann also served a stint in Brazil.

87. Huggins, *Political Policing,* 151; Chaim Litewski, dir., *Citizen Boileson* (NTSC, 2010). Boileson originally hailed from the Netherlands.

88. See Martha K. Huggins, Mika Haritos-Fatouros, and Philip G. Zimbardo, *Violence Workers: Police Torturers and Murderers Reconstruct Brazilian Atrocities* (Berkeley: University of California Press, 2002); "Monthly Report," September 1970, OPS Latin America Branch, box 17, folder Brazil.

89. "Monthly Report," March, September, October, November 1968, OPS Latin America Branch, box 17, folder Brazil. Nixon quoted in Hal Brands, *Latin America's Cold War* (Cambridge: Harvard University Press, 2010), 129. On Carlos Marighella, see his *Minimanual of the Urban Guerrilla* (Chapel Hill: University of North Carolina Press, 1985).

90. Dan Mitrione, "End of Tour Report," June 11, 1965; "Monthly Report," October 1971, OPS Latin America Branch, box 17, folder Brazil; George Miller, "Public Safety Survey Report, State of Paraiba," February 1967, OPS Latin America Branch, box 11; Lernoux, *Cry of the People,* 23; Langguth, *Hidden Terrors,* 193; Amnesty International, *Report on Allegations of Torture in Brazil* (London: Amnesty International, 1976), 49. In 1967, the commander of the Gendarmerie in Serrado Caparao province wrote a letter thanking USAID for communications equipment, which he said was decisive in anti-guerrilla operations. Rodrigo Patto Sa Motta, "Modernizing Repression: USAID and the Brazilian Police," *Revista Braziliera de Historia* 30, no. 59 (June 2010).

91. Gott, *Guerrilla Movements in Latin America,* 271; Hugo Blanco, *Land or Death: The Peasant Struggle in Peru* (New York: Pathfinder Press, 1972), 11, 14; "Monthly Report of Public Safety Program, Lima," May 1963, IPS, box 102, folder Peru; "Monthly Reports of Public Safety Program, Lima," June 1966, TSD, box 18, folder 2: Peru; American embassy, Lima, to Department of State, "Agrarian Violence at Hacienda Huapra: Eyewitness Accounts Incriminate Police," August 23, 1960, IPS, box 100, folder Peru; American embassy, Lima, to Department of State, "Plantation Labor Conditions," December 16, 1960, OPS Latin America Branch, box 100, folder Peru. Blanco was later released from jail after an international campaign led by human rights activists. Another rebel group promoting indigenous rights emerged in the mid-1960s: Túpac Amaru, named after an eighteenth-century Indian leader and headed by Guillermo Lobatón. The left was repressed but would resume armed struggle in the 1980s under the banner of the more violent Sendero Luminoso. George Miller also served in Libya and the Philippines; he would die in Vietnam.

92. Lee Echols to Theo Hall, November 7, 1957, OPS Latin America Branch, box 4, folder Bolivia; Echols, *Hilarious High-Jinks and Dangerous Assignments,* 168, 174; "OCB Report

Pursuant to NSC Action 1290-d," August 4, 1955, DDEL, OCB, box 17, folder Internal Security. For insight into the 1952 revolution and Bolivian politics, see James Dunkerley, *Rebellion in the Veins: Political Struggle in Bolivia, 1952–1982* (London: Verso, 1984); and Laurence Whitehead, *The United States and Bolivia: A Case of Neo-Colonialism* (London: Haslemere, 1969). On Echols's OSS experience, see Diane L. Hamm, *Military Intelligence: Its Heroes and Legends* (Honolulu: University Press of the Pacific, 2001), 88.

93. John Doney and Richard Frederick, "Evaluation of Public Safety Project," March 1973, OPS Latin America Branch, box 5, folder Bolivia; Saenz, *The OPS Story,* 203; Thomas Field, "Ideology as Strategy: Military-Led Modernization and the Origins of the Alliance for Progress in Bolivia," *Diplomatic History* 36.1 (January 2012): 147–83. Saenz reports that Jackson became suicidal while living out his days in Panama. To add insult to injury, Bob Clark, superintendent of the Nevada Highway Patrol, died from pneumonia during the evacuation of Jackson as a result of the high altitude.

94. Adolph Saenz, "Study and Report of Police Organization and Operations in Bolivia," June 1967, USAID, OPS, RG 286, Latin America, box 5, folder Bolivia; Saenz, *The OPS Story,* 204, 212.

95. Walt W. Rostow to the President, "Death of Che Guevara," October 17, 1967, NSA, Che Guevara Collection; Douglas Valentine, *The Strength of the Wolf: The Secret History of America's War on Drugs* (London: Verso, 2004), 386. For new evidence on the killing, see Michael Ratner and Michael Smith, *Who Killed Che? How the CIA Got Away with Murder* (New York: Orbis Books, 2011).

96. John Doney and Richard Frederick, "Evaluation of Public Safety Project," March 1973, OPS Latin America Branch, box 5, folder Bolivia; Jaime Malamud Goti, "Reinforcing Poverty: The Bolivian War on Cocaine," in *War on Drugs: Studies in the Failure of U.S. Narcotics Policy,* ed. Alfred W. McCoy and Alan Block (Boulder: Westview Press, 1992), 67, 81; Kathryn Lebedur, "Bolivia: Clear Consequences," in *Drugs and Democracy in Latin America: The Impact of U.S. Policy,* ed. Colletta A. Youngers and Eileen Rosin (Boulder: Lynne Rienner, 2005); Marshall, *Drug Wars,* 4. Nazi Klaus "The Butcher of Lyon" Barbie was head of Bolivia's secret police for a period under Banzer.

97. "Guerrillas Seize 2 in Uruguay," *New York Times,* August 1, 1970; Alain Labrousse, *The Tupamaros: Urban Guerrillas in Uruguay,* trans. Dinah Livingstone (Harmondsworth: Penguin, 1973). The Tupamaros were named after Inca leader Túpac Amaru, who staged an unsuccessful rebellion against Spanish forces in 1780 and was captured and executed. They also drew inspiration from José Artigas, the "father of Uruguayan independence," and, according to the CIA, did not associate with the Uruguayan Communist Party, which followed the Soviet line of peaceful coexistence and a parliamentary approach to power.

98. OPS, "Study of Uruguayan Tupamaros National Liberation Movement (MLN)," July 1, 1971, IPS, box 10, folder Uruguay; and CIA report, "The Tupamaros: Portrait of the Urban Guerrilla in Uruguay," RG 286, USAID, IPS, box 10, folder Uruguay; American embassy, Montevideo, to Secretary of State, "Internal Security: Alertness to Political Insurgency," LBJL, National Security Files, Country Files, Latin American Branch, box 74, folder Uruguay. Galeano was referred to as a bright young intellectual of the movement and a talented writer.

99. American embassy, Montevideo, to Secretary of State, "Internal Security: Alertness to Political Insurgency"; Klein, *The Shock Doctrine,* 93; "Death of a Policeman: Unanswered Questions About a Tragedy," *Commonweal,* September 18, 1970, 456, 457; Jeffrey Ryan, "Turning on Their Masters: State Terrorism and Unlearning Democracy in Uruguay," in Menjívar and Rodríguez, *When States Kill,* 279, 284; unpublished letter on police brutality, in Labrousse, *The Tupamaros,* 152–54. Thousands of trade union activists and students were among those tortured.

100. "Public Safety Report, February 1974," April 1974, OPS Latin America Branch, box 4, folder Uruguay; Agee, *Inside the Company*, 445–46, 461–68; Saenz, *The OPS Story*, 124; Albert L. Bryant and Lucien V. Gormont, "Termination Phase-Out Study, Public Safety Project, Uruguay," April–May 1974, OPS Latin America Branch, box 4, folder 20.

101. Langguth, *Hidden Terrors*, 312; McCoy, *A Question of Torture*, 72; Wolfgang S. Heinz and Hugo Fruhling, *Determinants of Gross Human Rights Violations by State and State-Sponsored Actors in Brazil, Uruguay, Chile, and Argentina: 1960–1990* (The Hague: Martinus Nijhoff Publishers, 1999), 101.

102. Tom Engelhardt, *The End of Victory Culture: Cold War America and the Disillusioning of a Generation* (Amherst: University of Massachusetts Press, 2007); Langguth, *Hidden Terrors*, 42.

103. McSherry, *Predatory States*; John Dinges, *The Condor Years: How Pinochet and His Allies Brought Terrorism to Three Continents* (New York: New Press, 2002).

104. "OCB Report Pursuant to NSC Action 1290-d," Country Report, Chile, August 4, 1955, DDEL, OCB, box 17, folder Internal Security. On Miles's role, see Frederic Wakeman Jr., *Spymaster: Dai Li and the Chinese Secret Service* (Berkeley: University of California Press, 2003), 506. Miles was commander of the Panama Canal Zone in the mid-1950s, when the first public safety programs were launched.

105. American embassy, Chile, to Secretary of State, "Internal Security Program," January 6, 1958, OPS Latin America Branch, box 23; "Public Safety Monthly Report," April and July 1965; and "Puntillazo, El Siglo," April 25, 1965, OPS TSD, box 2, folder Chile. Lingo was also on the faculty of the Northwestern Traffic Institute and served in Indonesia, Thailand, and Argentina.

106. For an insider's perspective, see Theodore Shackley with Richard A. Finney, *Spymaster: My Life in the CIA* (Washington, D.C.: Potomac Books, 2006), 270.

107. J. Patrice McSherry, "Operation Condor: Hemispheric 'Counter-Terror,'" in Menjívar and Rodríguez, *When States Kill*, 35; Ralph W. McGehee, *Deadly Deceits: My Twenty-five Years in the CIA* (New York: Ocean Press, 1999), 27; Jonathan Franklin, "Ex-Spy Chief Says CIA Helped Him Set Up Pinochet's Secret Police," *Guardian*, September 23, 2000, 17; "Chilean Police Plan to Patrol Streets with 120-Car Fleet," *New York Times*, October 9, 1973.

108. McSherry, *Predatory States*, 36; Dinges, *The Condor Years*, 65, 71; Byron Engle through William S. Gaud, "Measures to Control Travel of Subversives from the OAS States and Cuba," August 11, 1964; and "Minutes of Meeting of CI," August 13, 1964, IPS box 6.

109. See Saul Landau and John Dinges, *Assassination on Embassy Row* (New York: Pantheon Books, 1980); Peter Kornbluh, *The Pinochet File: A Declassified Dossier on Atrocity and Accountability* (New York: New Press, 2003); Scott, *American War Machine*, 37–38. Letelier had been in charge of negotiating the terms of expropriation with corporations such as the International Telephone and Telegraph company involved in the plotting to sabotage Allende's government. The car bomb was allegedly set by Contreras, ex-CIA agent Michael Townley, and Bay of Pigs veterans linked to the narcotics trade and terrorist crimes such as the blowing up of a Venezuelan airplane. On "security" cooperation in Central America, see Robert Holden, "Securing Central America against Communism: The United States and the Modernization of Surveillance in the Cold War," *Journal of Inter-American Studies and World Affairs* 41 (Spring 1999): 1–30; Paul Katz, Central America Telecommunications Report, February 1964, TSD, box 1.

110. Luigi R. Einaudi and Alfred Stepan, *Latin American Institutional Development: Changing Military Perspectives in Peru and Brazil* (Santa Monica: RAND Corporation, 1971), 108–9.

111. Huggins, *Political Policing*, 117.

112. This point has been very well documented in the important though often neglected works of Noam Chomsky and Edward S. Herman, including *The Political Economy of Human Rights: The Washington Connection and Third World Fascism*, and Herman's *The Real Terror Network: Terrorism in Fact and Propaganda* (Boston: South End Press, 1982). See also Klein, *The Shock Doctrine*, and Rabe, *The Killing Zone*.

Conclusion

1. In this Johnson builds on a corpus of previous work, including most notably the seminal contributions of the so-called Wisconsin school. See Chalmers Johnson, *Blowback: The Costs and Consequences of the American Empire* (New York: Owl Books, 2000); *The Sorrows of Empire: Militarism, Secrecy, and the End of the Republic* (New York: Metropolitan Books, 2004), and *Nemesis: The Last Days of the American Republic* (New York: Metropolitan, 2008).

2. Thomas Lobe, *U.S. National Security Policy and Aid to the Thailand Police* (Denver: Graduate School of International Studies, University of Denver, 1977), 112.

3. "Policy Research Study: Internal Warfare and the Security of the Underdeveloped States, Department of State," November 20, 1961, POF, box 98; Maxwell Taylor, "Memo for Members of the Special Group: U.S. Support of Foreign Paramilitary Forces," RG 286, USAID, OPS, Program Surveys and Evaluations, box 5, folder 1.

4. See Alfred W. McCoy, *Policing America's Empire: The United States, the Philippines, and the Rise of the Surveillance State* (Madison: University of Wisconsin Press, 2009); James W. Gibson, *The Perfect War: Technowar in Vietnam* (New York: Atlantic Monthly Press, 1986); Kurt Jacobsen, *Pacification and Its Discontents* (Chicago: Prickly Paradigm Press, 2009).

5. See Noam Chomsky and Edward S. Herman, *The Political Economy of Human Rights: The Washington Connection and Third World Fascism* (Boston: South End Press, 1979); Gabriel Kolko, *Confronting the Third World: United States Foreign Policy, 1945–1980* (New York: Pantheon, 1989); Noam Chomsky, "The Responsibility of Intellectuals," in *American Power and the New Mandarins* (New York: Pantheon, 1967), 323–66. There is a lot of recent literature on the influence of social scientists and the making of U.S. foreign policy; see, e.g., Michael Latham, *Modernization as Ideology: American Social Science and "Nation-Building" in the Kennedy Era* (Chapel Hill: University of North Carolina Press, 2000).

6. See Andrew Bacevich, *The Limits of Power: The End of American Exceptionalism* (New York: Metropolitan Books, 2008); Michael Adas, *Dominance by Design: Technological Imperatives and America's Civilizing Mission* (Cambridge: Harvard University Press, 2006).

7. See Noam Chomsky, *Failed States: The Abuse of Power and the Assault on Democracy* (New York: Metropolitan Books, 2007). See also Peter Dale Scott, *The Road to 9/11: Wealth, Empire, and the Future of America* (Berkeley: University of California Press, 2007); Sheldon Wolin, *Democracy Incorporated: Managed Democracy and the Specter of Inverted Totalitarianism* (Princeton: Princeton University Press, 2008).

8. See Peter Dale Scott, *Drugs, Oil, and War: The United States in Afghanistan, Colombia, and Indochina* (New York: Rowman & Littlefield, 2003); Alexander Cockburn and Jeffrey St. Clair, *Whiteout: The CIA, Drugs, and the Press* (London: Verso, 1998).

9. "Testimony of James Abourezk," *Congressional Record*, October 1, 1973, 32259; "Testimony of George McGovern," *Congressional Record*, March 27, 1974, 8423; telephone interview with James Abourezk, December 2007. Abourezk told me that the OPS was dedicated to "teaching dictators how to torture." He added, "Now, we are the lead torturers."

10. Michael T. Klare, *American Arms Supermarket* (Austin: University of Texas Press, 1984), 22.

11. See Vince Pinto, "Weapons for the Home-Front," and Lee Webb, "Repression: A New Growth Industry," in *Policing America*, ed. Anthony M. Platt and Lynn B. Cooper (Englewood Cliffs, N.J.: Prentice Hall, 1974); "OPS Processing and Developing of Public Safety Equipment," RG 286, USAID, OPS, TSD, box 4, folder 3. See also William W. Turner, *Invisible Witness: The Use and Abuse of the New Technology of Crime Investigation* (Indianapolis: Bobbs-Merrill, 1968), 275–89.

12. Michael T. Klare, "Policing the Empire," in Platt and Cooper, *Policing America*, 64; *Police on the Homefront: They're Bringing It All Back* (Philadelphia: National Action Research on the Military-Industrial Complex, American Friends Service Committee, 1971), 16–17; Richard Kunnes, *The American Heroin Empire: Power, Profits, and Politics* (New York: Dodd, Mead, 1972), 34.

13. Edward J. Epstein, *Agency of Fear: Opiates and Political Power in America* (New York: Putnam, 1977); Frank Browning, "They Shoot Hippies Don't They?," *Ramparts*, November 1970, 14–23; Radley Balko, *Overkill: The Rise of Paramilitary Police Raids in America* (Washington, D.C.: Cato Institute, 2006); Peter B. Kraska and Victor E. Kappler, "Militarizing American Police: The Rise and Normalization of Paramilitary Units," *Social Problems* 44 (February 1997): 1–18; Michael Klare, "Bringing It Back: Planning for the City," in Platt and Cooper, *Policing America*, 97–104; Douglas Valentine, "Homeland Insecurity," in *Police State America: U.S. Military and "Civil Disturbance" Planning*, ed. Tom Burghardt (Montreal: Arm the Spirit Solidarity, 2002), 141–89.

14. Brandstatter, Personnel File, MSUA; Joan Jenson, *Army Surveillance in America, 1775–1980* (New Haven: Yale University Press, 1991), 241; Bert Useem and Peter Kimball, eds., *States of Siege: U.S. Prison Riots, 1971–1986* (New York: Oxford University Press, 1989), 97; Roger Morris, *The Devil's Butcher Shop: The New Mexico Prison Uprising* (Albuquerque: University of New Mexico Press, 1983), 47, 194. Many OPS veterans served as consultants to local police organizations. O. W. Wilson, whose textbooks were used in police academies worldwide, capped off his distinguished career as chief of the Chicago police, retiring just before the brutal suppression of the demonstrations during the 1968 Democratic Party convention.

15. Quoted in Eqbal Ahmed, "Revolutionary Warfare and Counterinsurgency," in *National Liberation: Revolution in the Third World*, ed. Norman Miller and Roderick Aya (New York: Free Press, 1971), 213. See also Alan Wolfe, *The Seamy Side of Democracy: Repression in America* (New York: David McKay, 1973); Nelson Blackstone, *COINTELPRO: The FBI's Secret War on Political Freedom*, introduction by Noam Chomsky (New York: Vintage, 1975); Tracy Tullis, "A Vietnam at Home: Policing the Ghettos in the Counterinsurgency Era" (Ph.D. diss., New York University, 1999).

16. See John Conroy, *Unspeakable Acts, Ordinary People: The Dynamics of Torture* (New York: Knopf, 2000); Tonya McClary and Andrea Ritchie, *In the Shadows of the War on Terror: Persistent Police Brutality and Abuse of People of Color in the United States* (New York: UN Human Rights Committee, December 2007); Jullily Kohler-Hausmann, "Militarizing the Police: Officer Jon Burge, Torture and War in the 'Urban Jungle,'" in *Challenging the Prison-Industrial Complex: Activism, Arts, and Educational Alternatives*, ed. Stephen John Hartnett (Urbana: University of Illinois Press, 2011), 43–72.

17. See Jeremy Scahill, *Blackwater: The Rise of the World's Most Powerful Mercenary Army* (New York: Nation Books, 2007); Ken Silverstein, *Private Warriors* (London: Verso, 2000); Naomi Klein, *The Shock Doctrine: The Rise of Disaster Capitalism* (New York: Metropolitan Books, 2007).

18. Jane Hunter, *Israeli Foreign Policy: South Africa and Central America* (Boston: South End Press, 1987); 116–17; Noam Chomsky, *Turning the Tide: U. S. Intervention in Central America and the Struggle for Peace* (Montreal: Black Rose, 1987).

19. Lars Schoultz, *Human Rights and United States Policy toward Latin America* (Princeton: Princeton University Press, 1981), 182–83; Michael T. Klare and Cynthia Aronson, *Supplying Repression: U.S. Support for Authoritarian Regimes Abroad* (Washington, D.C.: Institute for Policy Studies, 1981), 28. Mitchell Mabardy (Congo, Kenya, Vietnam), Chester Jew (Vietnam), Anthony Ruiz (Dominican Republic and Latin America), and Cesar Bernal (Latin America) were among the OPS advisers employed by the DEA.

20. J. Patrice McSherry, *Predatory States: Operation Condor and Covert War in Latin America* (New York: Rowman & Littlefield, 2004), 74–75; Penny Lernoux, *Cry of the People: United States Involvement in the Rise of Fascism, Torture, and Murder and the Persecution of the Catholic Church in Latin America* (New York: Doubleday, 1980), 338–39; Peter Dale Scott and Jonathan Marshall, *Cocaine Politics: Drugs, Armies, and the CIA in Central America* (Berkeley: University of California Press, 1991), 44.

21. Douglas Stokes, *America's Other War: Terrorizing Colombia* (London: Zed Press, 2005), 90; *The Colombian National Police, Human Rights, and U.S. Drug Policy* (Washington, D.C.: Washington Office on Latin America, May 1993), 24; Jonathan Marshall, *Drug Wars: Corruption, Counterinsurgency, and Covert Operations in the Third World* (San Francisco: Cohan & Cohan, 1991), 22.

22. Ethan A. Nadelmann, *Cops across Borders: The Internationalization of U.S. Criminal Law Enforcement* (University Park: Pennsylvania State University Press, 1993), 120.

23. Ibid., 122; Shirley Christian, "Congress Is Asked for $54 Million to Aid Latin American Antiterrorist Efforts," *New York Times,* November 6, 1985; Martha Doggett, *Underwriting Injustice: AID and El Salvador's Judicial Reform Program* (New York: Lawyers' Committee for Human Rights, 1989); Kirsten Weld, "Reading the Politics of History in Guatemala's National Police Archives" (Ph.D. diss., Yale University, 2010), 234.

24. U.S. Department of State, Bureau of Public Affairs, *Criminal Justice and Democracy in the Western Hemisphere* (Washington, D.C.: GPO, April 1989); Adolph Saenz, *The OPS Story* (San Francisco: Robert D. Reed, 2002), 12.

25. On the political circumstances surrounding this intervention and the pretexts used to sell it to a gullible public, see Noam Chomsky, *Deterring Democracy* (London: Verso, 1991), 150; and Christina J. Johns, *State Crime, the Media, and the Invasion of Panama* (Boulder: Westview Press, 1991).

26. Anthony Gray and Maxwell Manwaring, "Panama: Operation Just Cause," in *Policing the New World Disorder: Peace Operations and Public Security,* ed. Robert B. Oakley, Michael J. Dziedzic, and Eliot M. Goldberg (Washington, D.C.: National Defense University Press, 1998), 57; Richard H. Shultz Jr., *In the Aftermath of War: U.S. Support for Reconstruction and Nation-Building in Panama Following Just Cause* (Montgomery, Ala.: Air Force University Press, 1993), 80–81, 99.

27. Chomsky, *Deterring Democracy,* 156; Eric Schmitt, "U.S. Helps Quell Revolt in Panama," *New York Times,* December 6, 1990. On Steele, see Scahill, *Blackwater,* 354.

28. Shultz, *In the Aftermath of War,* 106–7.

29. See Michael Bailey, Robert Maguire, and J. O'Neil Pouilot, "Haiti: Military Police Partnership for Public Security," in *Policing the New World Disorder: Peace Operations and Public Security,* ed. Robert B. Oakley, Michael J. Dziedzic, and Eliot M. Goldberg (Washington, D.C.: National Defense University Press, 1988), 242. For analysis of the limits of the human rights curriculum in military training academies, see Lesley Gill, *The School of the*

Americas: Military Training and Political Violence in the Americas (Durham: Duke University Press, 2005). There is no comparable study for the police programs.

30. Robert Capps, "Outside the Law," *Salon,* June 25, 2002, http://dir.salon.com/story/news/feature/2002/08/06/dyncorp/index.html; "Sex Slave Whistle-Blowers Vindicated," *Salon,* August 6, 2002, http://dir.salon.com/story/news/feature/2002/08/06/dyncorp/index.html; Pratap Chatterjee, *Iraq, Inc.: A Profitable Occupation* (New York: Seven Stories Press, 2004), 111. DynCorp tried to cover up the crimes, which included contracting by its employees of personal sex slaves as young as twelve years old, and then fired two employees who spoke out about the abuses. They were later vindicated in court. None of the DynCorp employees involved in the sex trade were ever prosecuted.

31. Robert Dreyfuss, *Devil's Game: How the United States Helped Unleash Fundamentalist Islam* (New York: Metropolitan Books, 2005), 320; "Ambassador Margaret Scobey, Egyptian Government Struggling to Address Police Brutality," www.wikileaks.de; Abderrahman Beggar, "The Path of State Terror in Peru," in *When States Kill: Latin America, the U.S., and Technologies of Terror,* ed. Cecilia Menjívar and Néstor Rodríguez (Austin: University of Texas Press, 2005), 266–67; Gill, *The School of the Americas,* 163–97; Stokes, *America's Other War.* Montesinos was also deeply implicated in the narcotics traffic.

32. Peter Hallward, *Damming the Flood: Haiti, Aristide and the Politics of Containment* (London: Verso, 2007), 67; Rachel Neild, "The Haitian National Police," Washington Office on Latin America Briefing Paper, March 18, 1996, 1; "Haiti: Security Compromised Recycled Haitian Soldiers on the Police Front Line," *Human Rights Watch Americas* 7 (March 1995): 1–27; Tim Weiner, "CIA Formed Haitian Unit Later Tied to Narcotics Trade," *New York Times,* November 14, 1993; Paul Farmer, *The Uses of Haiti,* foreword by Noam Chomsky (Monroe, Me.: Common Courage Press, 1994), 34. Emmanuel Constant, head of the Front for the Advancement and Progress of Haiti, a brutal paramilitary militia, was among those to receive CIA funding, along with Guy Philippe, who in 2004 led a successful coup against Aristide after returning from exile in the Dominican Republic. What role the police programs played remains in question, though it is clear they were used to cultivate contacts within the national security establishment. Rwanda, led by Paul Kagame, was another authoritarian state where U.S. advisers trained the National Police. See Filip Reyntjens, *The Great African War: Congo and Regional Geopolitics, 1996–2006* (New York: Cambridge University Press, 2009), 72.

33. On the continued imperial motives driving U.S. foreign policy in this period, see Stephen R. Shalom, *Imperial Alibis: Rationalizing U.S. Intervention after the Cold War* (Boston: South End Press, 1993); Noam Chomsky, *A New Generation Draws the Line: Kosovo, East Timor, and the Standards of the West* (London: Verso, 2000); David Gibbs, *First Do No Harm: Humanitarian Intervention and the Destruction of Yugoslavia* (Nashville: Vanderbilt University Press, 2009).

34. See, e.g., Noam Chomsky, *Hegemony or Survival: America's Quest for Global Dominance* (New York: Metropolitan, 2004); Michael T. Klare, *Blood and Oil: The Dangers and Consequences of America's Growing Petroleum Dependency* (New York: Metropolitan, 2004).

35. James Glanz, "The Reach of War: U.S. Report Finds Dismal Training of Afghan Police," *New York Times,* March 30, 2006; Ahmed Rashid, *Descent into Chaos: The United States and the Failure of Nation Building in Pakistan, Afghanistan, and Central Asia* (New York: Viking, 2008), 204–5; Matthew Hoh, talk delivered to the Tulsa Council on Foreign Relations, December 7, 2010; Seth G. Jones, *In the Graveyard of Empires: America's War in Afghanistan* (New York: Norton, 2009), 172.

36. See James Dobbins et al., *America's Role in Nation-Building: From Germany to Iraq* (Santa Monica: RAND Corporation, 2002); John A. Nagl, *Learning to Eat Soup with a*

Knife: Counterinsurgency Lessons from Malaya and Vietnam (Chicago: University of Chicago Press, 2007), 3; Seth G. Jones et al., *Establishing Law and Order after Conflict* (Santa Monica: RAND Corporation, 2005); *The U.S. Army–Marine Corps Counter-Insurgency Field Manual,* U.S. Army Field Manual no. 3-24, Marine Corps War Fighting Publication no. 3-33.5, foreword by Gen. David H. Petraeus and James F. Amos, foreword to the University of Chicago Press edition by Lt. Col. John A. Nagl with a new introduction by Sarah Sewall (Chicago: University of Chicago Press, 2007), 231; David H. Bayley and Robert Perito, *The Police in War: Fighting Insurgency, Terrorism, and Violent Crime* (Boulder: Lynn Riener, 2010). Bayley and Perito argue that poor managerial oversight compromised police training programs, which the authors deem crucial in "stabilizing" countries occupied by the United States. While managerial oversight was indeed poor, the authors fail to question the larger imperial agenda to which the programs were attached and provide only a cursory examination of the history of police programs, glossing over their link to torture and state repression. For a critique that still resonates, see Chomsky, "The Responsibility of Intellectuals." John Dower critiques the superficiality of comparisons with Japan in his thoughtful book *Cultures of War: Pearl Harbor/Hiroshima/9–11/Iraq* (New York: Norton, 2010).

37. See Tariq Ali, "Mirage of the Good War," in *The Case for Withdrawal from Afghanistan,* ed. Nick Turse (London: Verso, 2010), 51; Nick Mills, *Karzai: The Failing American Intervention and the Struggle for Afghanistan* (Hoboken: Wiley, 2007); Marc Herold, "An Excess of Corruption and a Deficit of Toilets: America and Karzai's Success in Afghanistan," *RAWA* (Revolutionary Association of Women of Afghanistan) *News,* September 28, 2010; Ahmed Rashid, *Taliban* (New Haven: Yale University Press, 2000). A 2011 study found longstanding friction in the relationship between the Taliban and Al-Qaeda; see Carlotta Gall, "NYU Report Casts Doubt on Taliban's Ties with Al Qaeda" *New York Times,* February 6, 2011.

38. Ann Jones, "Meet the Afghan Army: Is It a Figment of Washington's Imagination," in Turse, *The Case for Withdrawal from Afghanistan,* 76; Bayley and Perito, *The Police in War,* 21; Rashid, *Descent into Chaos,* 205; Tim Bird and Alex Marshall, *Afghanistan: How the West Lost Its Way* (New Haven: Yale University Press, 2011), 123; Judy Dempsey, "Germany Criticized for Its Training of Afghan Police," *New York Times,* October 15, 2006; U.S. Government Accounting Office, *Afghanistan Security: Efforts to Establish Army and Police Have Made Progress, but Future Plans Need to Be Better Defined* (Washington, D.C.: GAO, June 2005), 23–25; "Training" October 3, November 3, 2006, www.wikileaks.de; "Watchdog Company Botched Afghan Police Stations," Associated Press, October 26, 2010.

39. Vikash Yadav, "Animalizing Afghans: Biometrics and Biopolitics in an Occupied Zone," Panel on Policies and Practices of Intervention in South Asia: Afghanistan and Pakistan, Association for Asian Studies Conference, Honolulu, April 1, 2011; Anand Gopal, "Who Are the Taliban? The Afghan War Deciphered," December 4, 2008, www.tomdispatch.com.

40. D. Gareth Porter, "A Bigger Problem than the Taliban? Afghanistan's U.S.-Backed Child Raping Police," *Counterpunch,* July 30, 2009, www.counterpunch.org/porter07302009.html; Nir Rosen, *Aftermath: Following the Bloodshed of America's Wars in the Muslim World* (New York: Nation Books, 2010), 465; Jones, *In the Graveyard of Empires,* 172; Marc Herold, "Afghanistan: Terror U.S. Style," *Frontline,* March 11, 2009, www.rawa.org/temp/runews/2009/03/11/terror-u-s-style.html; Carlotta Gall, "Afghans Raise Toll of Dead from May Riots in Kabul to 17," *New York Times,* June 8, 2006; Douglas Valentine, "Provincial Reconstruction Teams and the CIA's Dirty War in Afghanistan," *Z Magazine,* February 2010, 31–35; Sayed Yaqub Ibrahimi, "Afghan Police Part of the Problem," *Institute for War and Peace Reporting,* RAWA News, June 6, 2006, www.rawa.org/police-3.htm.

41. "Unvarnished Look at Hamstrung Fight," *New York Times,* July 25, 2010; Rosen, *Aftermath,* 465; "'Killing You Is a Very Easy Thing for Us': Human Rights Abuses in Southeast Afghanistan," *Human Rights Watch,* July 2003, 20–44; Pratap Chatterjee, "Afghan Police Still Out of Step," *Asia Times,* March 2, 2010; "Kunduz Politics of Corruption in the Baghlan Police Forces," December 5, 2005, http://wikileaks.k-5.su/cable/2005/12/05KABUL5181. html.

42. Tonita Murray, "Police Building in Afghanistan: A Case Study in Civil Security Reform," *International Peacekeeping* (January 2007), 108–26.

43. William Fischer, "Rights: Afghan Prison Looks Like Another Guantánamo," *IPS News,* January 15, 2008; Makia Monir, "Pul-e-Charkhi Jail Inmates Face Awful Life," *RAWA News,* August 13, 2008, www.rawa.org/temp/runews/2008/08/13/pul-e-charkhi-jail-inmates-face-awful-life.html; Deepa Babington, "Sold, Raped and Jailed: A Girl Faces Afghan Justice," Reuters, March 31, 2010; Paul Fitzgerald and Elizabeth Gould, *Invisible History: Afghanistan's Untold Story* (San Francisco: City Lights Books, 2009), 317. On the deteriorating conditions for women in Afghanistan, in spite of claims by leading liberal intellectuals that the mission was undertaken for their benefit, see Malalai Joya with Derrick O'Keefe, *A Woman among Warlords: The Extraordinary Story of an Afghan Who Dared to Raise Her Voice* (New York: Scribner, 2009).

44. Bob Woodward, "McChrystal: More Forces or Mission Failure," *Washington Post,* September 21, 2009; Rod Nordland and Sharifullah Sahak, "Afghan Government Says Prisoner Directed Attacks," *New York Times,* February 11, 2011; "Break for the Hills," *The Economist,* April 28, 2011.

45. James Risen, "Propping Up a Drug Lord, Then Charging Him," *New York Times,* December 12, 2010; Pierre-Arnaud Chouvy, *Opium: Uncovering the Politics of the Poppy* (Cambridge: Harvard University Press, 2010; Julien Mercille, "The U.S. 'War on Drugs' in Afghanistan: Reality or Pretext?" *Critical Asian Studies* 43, no. 2 (2011): 285-309. Gretchen Peters's book *Seeds of Terror: How Heroin Is Bankrolling the Taliban and Al Qaeda* (New York: St. Martin's Press, 2009) exemplifies the long-standing practice among U.S. government officials and journalists of blaming U.S. enemies for trafficking in drugs when it is U.S. allies and proxies who are the principal players. The seasoned Afghan scholar Antonio Giustozzi writes in *Koran, Kalashnikov, and Laptop: The Neo-Taliban Insurgency in Afghanistan* (New York: Columbia University Press, 2008), "There is little evidence of the Taliban encouraging the farmers to grow poppies and of their involvement in the trade" (88).

46. Dexter Filkins, Mark Mazetti, and James Risen, "Brother of Afghan Leader Said to Be Paid by CIA," *New York Times,* October 27, 2009; Joya, *A Woman among Warlords,* 205; "Cables Cite Pervasive Afghan Corruption, Starting at the Top," *New York Times,* December 3, 2010; Peter Dale Scott, *American War Machine: Deep Politics, the CIA Global Drug Connection, and the Road to Afghanistan* (New York: Rowman and Littlefield, 2010), 234–35.

47. Fitzgerald and Gould, *Invisible History,* 285. See also Sonali Kolkhatkar and James Ingalls, *Bleeding Afghanistan: Washington, Warlords, and the Propaganda of Silence* (New York: Seven Stories Press, 2006); Pratap Chatterjee, "Paying Off the Warlords: Anatomy of a Culture of Corruption," in Turse, *The Case for Withdrawal from Afghanistan,* 81–86.

48. Dana Lewis, "Dangerous Ride: Training Afghanistan's Police," Fox News blog, October 14, 2008, http://onthescene.blogs.foxnews.com/2008/10/14/dangerous-ride; Carlotta Gall, "Opium Harvest at Record Level in Afghanistan," *New York Times,* September 3, 2006; Alfred W. McCoy, "Can Anybody Pacify the World's No. 1 Narco-State?," March 30, 2010, www.tomdispatch.com.

49. Barnett R. Rubin, *Road to Ruin: Afghanistan's Booming Opium Industry* (Washington, D.C.: Center for American Progress, 2004); Patrick Cockburn, "Afghans to Obama: Get

Out, Take Karzai with You," *Counterpunch,* May 6, 2009, www.counterpunch.org; Rashid, *Descent into Chaos,* 326–27; "Wedded to the Warlords: NATO's Unholy Afghan Alliance," *Globe and Mail,* June 3, 2011. Brigadier General Abdul Razik, a brutal NATO-backed warlord who bragged about not taking prisoners alive, pulled in $5 million a month as chief of the counter-narcotics police in Kandahar (he subsequently became police chief).

50. "Holbrooke Calls Afghan Anti-Drug Policy Most Wasteful Ever Seen," *Progressive Review,* March 23, 2009, http://prorev.com/2009/03/holbrooke-calls-afghan-anti-drug-policy.html; Chouvy, *Opium,* 113; "Farmers Attack Anti-Drug Police, Afghanistan, Four Hurt," February 2, 2007, www.wikileaks.de; James Nathan, "The Folly of Afghan Opium Eradication," *USA Today Magazine,* March 2009, 26–30. On the War on Drugs in Latin America, see Ted G. Carpenter, *Bad Neighbor Policy: Washington's Futile War on Drugs in Latin America* (New York: Palgrave Macmillan, 2006); and for parallels with Vietnam, where farmers fired at planes overhead sent to defoliate their fields, see my *Myth of the Addicted Army: Vietnam and the Modern War on Drugs* (Amherst: University of Massachusetts Press, 2009).

51. Nir Rosen, "Something from Nothing: U.S. Strategy in Afghanistan," *Boston Review,* January–February 2010, 10.

52. See, e.g., "State to AID, Kunduz Authorities Turn to Militias as Security Deteriorates," October 9, 2010; "Unconventional Security Forces: What's Out There?," November 11, 2009; and "Afghan Police Training: Shift to Focused District Development," November 15, 2007, www.wikileaks.ch; "Militias in Kunduz: A Tale of Two Districts," January 10, 2010, www.wikileaks.ch/cable/2010/01/10KABUL12.html; Giustozzi, *Koran, Kalashnikov, and Laptop,* 162. On the CIA's involvement in the war, see Tom Engelhardt and Nick Turse, "The Shadow War: Making Sense of the New CIA Battlefield," in Turse, *The Case for Withdrawal from Afghanistan,* 127–35.

53. Fisnik Abrashi, "Nine Police Officers Killed in Southern Afghanistan," *Toronto Globe and Mail,* March 26, 2009; Rory Stewart, "Afghanistan: What Could Work," *New York Review of Books,* January 14, 2010, 60; Richard A. Oppel Jr. and Abdul Waheed Wafa, "Afghan Investigators Say U.S. Troops Tried to Cover Up Evidence in Botched Raid," *New York Times,* April 6, 2010; Alissa J. Rubin, "Afghan Killer of Six Americans Was Trusted Police Officer," *New York Times,* November 30, 2010; Brian Brady, "Drugs and Desertion: How the UK Really Rates Afghan Police," *The Independent,* March 28, 2010.

54. C. Christine Fair and Peter Chalk, eds., *Fortifying Pakistan: The Role of U.S. Internal Security Assistance* (Washington, D.C.: United States Institute of Peace Press, 2006), 51; Jeremy Scahill, "The Secret U.S. War in Pakistan," *The Nation,* December 21–28, 2009, 11; Patrick Cockburn, "Who Killed 120 Civilians? The U.S. Says It's Not a Story," *Counterpunch,* May 11, 2009, www.counterpunch.org/whitney05152009.html.

55. Tariq Ali, *The Duel: Pakistan on the Flight Path of American Power* (New York: Scribner, 2008); Seth Jones and Christine Fair, *Counterinsurgency in Pakistan* (Santa Monica: RAND Corporation, 2010), 97; Elizabeth Gould and Paul Fitzgerald, *Crossing Zero: The AfPak War at the Turning Point of American Empire* (San Francisco: City Lights Books, 2011), 62; Amnesty International, *Denying the Undeniable: Enforced Disappearances in Pakistan* (London: Amnesty International, July 2008), 9. On the long-standing involvement of the Pakistani military and intelligence services in the drug trade, see Lawrence Lifschultz, "Pakistan: The Empire of Heroin," in *War on Drugs: Studies in the Failure of U.S. Narcotics Policy,* ed. Alfred W. McCoy and Alan A. Block (Boulder: Westview Press, 1992), 319–52. Facing impeachment, Musharraf resigned in August 2008.

56. See Michael Schwartz, *War without End: The Iraq War in Context* (Chicago: Haymarket Books, 2008); Thomas E. Ricks, *Fiasco: The American Military Adventure in Iraq* (New York: Penguin, 2006); Patrick Cockburn, *Muqtada: Muqtada al-Sadr, the Shia Revival, and*

the Struggle for Iraq (London: Scribner, 2008); Aram Roston, *The Man Who Pushed America to War: The Extraordinary Life, Adventures, and Obsessions of Ahmad Chalabi* (New York: Nation Books, 2008); Rosen, *Aftermath;* David Bacon, "Union-Busting, Iraqi-Style," *The Nation,* October 6, 2010. Neurosurgeon Iyad Allawi, who had ties to American and British intelligence, was another of the key politicians in exile.

57. Sam Dolnick, "Kerik Is Sentenced in Corruption Case," *New York Times,* February 18, 2010; Benjamin Weiser, "Kerik Pleads Not Guilty to a Revised Indictment," *New York Times,* December 29, 2008. Kerik was found guilty of accepting a free renovation of his home from a firm with ties to the mafia which was hoping to receive a lucrative contract and of failing to disclose a $250,000 loan to White House officials who were vetting him for the job of heading the Department of Homeland Security. His ouster from Saudi Arabia raises unanswered questions about what his true purposes were and who he was working for.

58. Rajiv Chandrasekaran, *Imperial Life in the Emerald City: Inside Iraq's Green Zone* (New York: Knopf, 2006), 84–89; Lt. Col. Bo Barbour, "The Taser M26 in Operation Iraqi Freedom," *Military Police: The Professional Bulletin of the Military Police Corps,* HQ, Department of the Army, April 2004, 47–49; Capt. Jason Burke, "Standing Up: The Iraqi Police Force," ibid., 40–41; Alfred W. McCoy, "Imperial Illusions: Information Infrastructure and U.S. Global Power," in *Endless Empires: Spain's Retreat, Europe's Eclipse, and America's Decline,* ed. Alfred W. McCoy, Joseph M. Fradera, and Stephen Jacobson (Madison: University of Wisconsin Press, forthcoming 2012).

59. Chandrasekaran, *Imperial Life in the Emerald City,* 84–89; Ali Allawi, *The Occupation of Iraq: Winning the War, Losing the Peace* (New Haven: Yale University Press, 2007), 188–89. See also Michael Moss, "How Iraq Police Reform Became Casualty of War," *New York Times,* May 22, 2006; and Mathieu Deflem and Suzanne Sutphin, "Policing Post-War Iraq: Insurgency, Civilian Police, and the Reconstruction of Society," *Sociological Focus* 39, no. 4 (November 2006): 265–283.

60. Ken Isenberg, *Shadow Force: Private Security Contractors in Iraq* (Westport: Praeger, 2009), 91–94; Robert Y. Pelton, *Licensed to Kill: Hired Guns in the War on Terror* (New York: Crown, 2006); Renae Merle, "Coming under Fire: DynCorp Defends Its Work in Training Foreign Police Forces," *Washington Post,* March 19, 2007; Nir Rosen, "Security Contractors: Riding Shotgun with Our Shadow Army in Iraq," *Mother Jones,* April 24, 2007, http://motherjones.com/politics/2007/04/security-contractors-riding-shotgun-our-shadow-army-iraq; Tucker Carlson, "Hired Guns," *Esquire,* March 2004, www.bravocompanyusa.com/Articles.asp?ID=143; Anna Mulrine, "Rogue Security Companies Threaten U.S. Gains in Afghan War," *Christian Science Monitor,* October 21, 2010; Chatterjee, *Iraq, Inc.,* 111, 112, 150. Carlson also mentions an incident in which contractors cut in a mile-long gas line by waving their guns at motorists.

61. Jill Carroll, "Old Brutality among New Iraqi Forces," *Christian Science Monitor,* May 4, 2005; Nir Rosen, "The Myth of the Surge," *Rolling Stone,* March 6, 2008, www.rollingstone.com/politics/story/18722376/the_myth_of_the_surge; Timothy Williams and Omar Al-Jawoshy, "Drug and Alcohol Abuse Growing in Iraqi Forces," *New York Times,* October 25, 2010; "[stricken] Detains [stricken] Police Chief for Corruption," January 24, 2004, www.wikileaks.org.

62. Andrew Higgins, "As It Wields Power Abroad, U.S. Outsources Law and Order Work," *Wall Street Journal,* February 2, 2004.

63. Detain By_Police Support Unit,_IP, And TF_LAR IVO (Route):_AIF DET, August 15, 2007; Demonstration IVO AS:_INJ/Damage, August 8, 2005; Police Actions by Hit IVO HIT (Route):_CIV KIA, September 25, 2007; Weapons/Ammo Confiscated BY [stricken] in

Mosul: [stricken] INJ/Damage, April 4, 2005; and "Dead Body Found," June 12, 2005, www.wikileaks.org.

64. Spencer Ackerman, "Training Iraq's Death Squads," *The Nation*, June 4, 2007, 20–26; Ken Silverstein, "Jerry Burke on Iraq's Corrupt Police Force," *Harper's*, September 11, 2007, http://harpers.org/archive/2007/09/hbc-90001180; Christopher Allbritton, "Why Iraq's Police Are a Menace," *Time*, March 20, 2006, www.time.com/time/world/article/0,8599,1175055,00.html; Patrick Cockburn, *The Occupation: War and Resistance in Iraq* (London: Verso, 2006), 123; Nicolas J. S. Davies, *Blood on Our Hands: The American Invasion and Destruction of Iraq* (Ann Arbor: Nimble Books, 2010), 244–316.

65. See Greg Grandin, *Empire's Workshop: Latin America, the United States, and the Rise of the New Imperialism* (New York: Metropolitan Books, 2005), 1; Robert Dreyfuss, "Phoenix Rising," *American Prospect*, January 1, 2004, 11; Jane Mayer, *The Dark Side: The Inside Story of How the War on Terror Turned into a War on American Ideals* (New York, Doubleday, 2008), 144; Shane Bauer, "Iraq's New Death Squads," *The Nation*, June 22, 2009, 11–25.

66. Peter Maas, "The Salvadorization of Iraq: The Way of the Commandos," *New York Times Magazine*, May 1, 2005, 1; David Corn, "From Iran-Contra to Iraq," *The Nation*, May 7, 2005, www.thenation.com/blog/156167/iran-contra-iraq. Steele also worked closely with the right-wing Cuban terrorist Luis Posada Carriles. His business career is profiled on http://premierespeakers.com/jim_steele/bio. At this writing Steele owns a private security firm (likely a CIA front) and consults for the Pentagon.

67. Dahr Jamail, "Managing Escalation: Negroponte and Bush's New Iraq Team," January 9, 2007, http://antiwar.com/jamail/?articleid=10289.

68. Maas, "The Salvadorization of Iraq," 1; Klein, *The Shock Doctrine*, 371; Solomon Moore, "Killings Linked to Shiite Squads in Iraqi Police Force," *Los Angeles Times*, November 29, 2005; Davies, *Blood on Our Hands*, 253–54; Ken Silverstein, "The Minister of Civil War: Bayan Jabr, Paul Bremer, and the Rise of the Iraqi Death Squads," *Harper's*, August 2006, 67–73. The CIA characterized Jabr, known for dressing in fancy Western suits, as "corrupt and thuggish" (Silverstein, 67).

69. James A. Baker III and Lee H. Hamilton, *The Iraq Study Group Report* (Washington, D.C.: United States Institute of Peace, 2006), 13.

70. Ahmed S. Hashim, *Insurgency and Counter-Insurgency in Iraq* (Ithaca: Cornell University Press, 2006), 330; Carroll, "Old Brutality among New Iraqi Forces"; Rod Nordland, "With Local Control, New Troubles in Iraq," *New York Times*, March 16, 2009; Rosen, *Aftermath*, 70; "Murder of Civilian," June 2, 2006; "IZ Detainee Abuse Summary at IP Station," August 2, 2005; and "Alleged Detainee Abuse at Diyala Jail," May 25, 2006, www.wikileaks.org.

71. Cockburn, *The Occupation*, 194; Robert Cole, *Under the Gun in Iraq: My Year Training the Iraqi Police*, as told to Jan Hogan (Amherst, N.Y.: Prometheus Books, 2007), 60–61; (Enemy Action) Direct Fire RPT (Small Arms)_West/SE_IP:_ISF KIA_CIV KIA_UE KIA; "Drive By Shooting on Police, Vic Ar Ramadi," January 3, 2004; "Attack on Police Chief and Bodyguard," January 17, 2004; and "Attack on Haditha Police Station," January 27, 2004, www.wikileaks.org.

72. Hashim, *Insurgency and Counter-Insurgency*, 25.

73. Cole, *Under the Gun in Iraq*, 60–61. See also Mark R. Depue, *Patrolling Baghdad: A Military Police Company and the War in Iraq* (Lawrence: University Press of Kansas, 2007).

74. A classic work on Western counterinsurgency doctrine, recently reissued, is David Galula, *Counterinsurgency Warfare: Theory and Practice* (New York: Hailer, 2005).

75. See Thomas E. Ricks, *The Gamble: General David Petraeus and the American Military Adventure in Iraq, 2006-2008* (New York: Penguin, 2009), 166. While presenting some

valuable information, this book is written as a panegyric to the U.S. military and David Petraeus, typical of mainstream media coverage.

76. Nordland, "With Local Control, New Troubles in Iraq"; Rosen, "The Myth of the Surge"; "Iraqi Police Said to Fire on Protest, Striking 7," *New York Times,* April 17, 2011.

77. Solomon Moore, "U.S. Expands Training to Address Iraqi Police Woes," *Los Angeles Times,* March 9, 2006.

78. Alfred W. McCoy, *A Question of Torture: CIA Interrogation from the Cold War to the War on Terror* (New York: Metropolitan Books, 2006); "Commando Guards Kill Prison Inmate, Wound Two in Escape Attempt," Associated Press, September 18, 2008; Davies, *Blood on Our Hands,* 285; Rosen, *Aftermath,* 284, 300; Amnesty International, *New Order, Same Abuses: Unlawful Detentions and Torture in Iraq* (London: Amnesty International, 2010); "IZ Prison Riot," February 2, 2004; "Prisoners Escape from Tikrit Jail," March 25, 2004; "RPG Attack on Abu Ghraib Prison," April 17, 2004; "Riot at Prison, Detainee Killed," April 10, 2004; "IZ Run Prison Uprising," June 21, 2004; and "(Criminal Event) Murder RPT:_ISF KIA" May 7, 2009; www.wikileaks.org.

79. Fox Butterfield and Eric Lichtblau, "The Reach of War: The Congress, Screening of Prison Officials Is Faulted by Lawmakers," *New York Times,* May 21, 2004; Fox Butterfield, "Justice Dept. Report Shows Trouble in Private U.S. Jails Preceded Job Fixing Iraq's," *New York Times,* June 6, 2004; Leah Caldwell, "Iraqi Dungeons and Torture Chambers under New American Trained Management," *Prison Legal News,* September 2004, www.november.org/stayinfo/breaking2/PLN9-04.html.

80. See Christian Parenti, *Lockdown America: Police and Prisons in the Age of Crisis* (New York: Verso, 1999); Elliot Currie, *Crime and Punishment in America* (New York: Metropolitan Books, 1998).

81. Butterfield, "Trouble in Private U.S. Jails Preceded Job Fixing Iraqis'"; Caldwell, "Iraqi Dungeons and Torture Chambers under New American Trained Management"; Robert Perkinson, *Texas Tough: The Rise of America's Prison Empire* (New York: Nation Books, 2010), 314. McCotter, a Green Beret in Vietnam, was a protégé of law-and-order hawk George Belo, who in the 1960s presided over a harsh and racist penal order as director of the Texas Department of Corrections, which became the target of landmark prisoner rights lawsuits.

82. Sasha Abramsky, *American Furies: Crime, Punishment, and Vengeance in the Age of Mass Imprisonment* (Boston: Beacon Press, 2007), 156; Caldwell, "Iraqi Dungeons and Torture Chambers under New American Trained Management"; Bond quoted in Timothy Black, *When Heart Turns Rock Solid: The Lives of Three Puerto Rican Brothers On and Off the Streets* (New York: Pantheon Books, 2009), 260.

83. See Useem and Kimball, *States of Siege,* 167.

84. See Byron Engle et al., *The Rhodesian Election: An Eye-Witness Account* (Washington, D.C.: American Conservative Union, 1979), 5. Engle supported Smith's bombings of the "terrorist sanctuaries" of "Marxist" guerrillas Joshua Nkomo and Robert Mugabe, widely considered at the time in Zimbabwe to be freedom fighters.

85. Letter to the editor, *Greensboro News and Record,* October 10, 2004. Williamson intended to vote for George W. Bush, stating in the letter, "I could never support for commander-in-chief of our armed forces someone who had vilified [our troops] as reminiscent of Genghis Khan." Recent scholarship making use of newly declassified records has shown that atrocities were in fact committed systematically by U.S. forces in Vietnam, no surprise given the abundance of evidence put forward at the time by the antiwar movement, journalistic exposés, and antiwar GIs.

86. Don Bordenkircher, *Tiger Cage: An Untold Story* (New York: Abby Publishing, 1998), 96; Ryan Mauro, "U.S. Official: Iraqis Told Me WMDs Sent to Syria," *World Net Daily,* July 30, 2008, www.wnd.com/index.php?fa=PAGE.view&pageId=71076. Adolph Saenz was another OPSer who worked in Iraq, serving as a senior State Department consultant and adviser to border patrol units.

87. Quoted in Black, *When Heart Turns Rock Solid,* 259; see also Abramsky, *American Furies;* Perkinson, *Texas Tough,* 340–43; Anne Marie Cusack, *Cruel and Unusual: The Culture of Punishment in America* (New Haven: Yale University Press, 2009); McClary and Ritchie, *In the Shadow of the War on Terror;* Hanna Holleman, Robert W. McChesney, John Bellamy Foster, and R. Jamil Jonna, "The Penal State in an Age of Crisis," *Monthly Review* 61 (June 2009): 1–16.

Index

1290-d program (Overseas Internal Security Program), 60–61, 73, 77–78, 129, 130, 138, 142–47, 166, 169, 190, 192–93, 202–3, 212, 227, 229, 236; and Eisenhower administration, 9–10; and Guatemala, 217–18; and Indonesia, 102–3; and Iran, 195–96, 200; and Iraq, 200; and Korea, 93–96; and Laos, 124, 132–33; and Thailand, 109, 111; and Vietnam, 143–44

Abourezk, James, 234–35, 357
Abrams, Elliot, 237
Abu Ghraib prison, 156, 201, 247, 250
Abu-Jamal, Mumia, 5
Acheson, Dean, 80, 100
Adkins, Elmer H., Jr., 146, 179, 211
Afghanistan, 1, 16, 202–3, 239–43
Afghanistan National Police, 240–41, 243
African National Congress (ANC), 185
Agee, Philip, 163, 228–29
Aglipay, Bishop Gregorio, 24
Agnew, Spiro, 220
Aguinaldo, Emiliano, 23
Ahern, Thomas L., Jr., 137, 340
Al-Bawi, Adnan, 247
Alcatraz Prison, 113
Aldous, Christopher, 78
Alessandri, Jorge, 229
Allen, Henry T., 26, 27, 29
Allende, Salvador, 230
Alliance for Progress, 208, 210, 216, 231
Allman, T. D., 136
al-Maliki, Nouri, 244
al-Mayah, Abdul Latif, 246
Altamirano, Pedro, 49
al-Sadr, Moqtada, 246, 248
al-Said, Nuri, 200–201
Al-Qaeda, 248, 251

American Indians (Native Americans), 21, 28, 49, 99, 110, 133, 316
American Civil Liberties Union (ACLU), 25, 86, 249
American Communist Party, suppression of, 7, 25
Amin, Idi, 185–86
Amnesty International, 13, 97, 199, 212
Amory, Robert, Jr., 105
Andarabi, Abdul Khalil, 241
Anderson, David, 51
Angleton, James Jesus, 101
Anslinger, Harry J., 202
Anton Sudjarwo, 106
An Tu-hui, 288
Arabian American Oil Company (ARAMCO), 12, 194, 203, 204
arap Moi, Daniel, 183–84
Árbenz, President Jacobo, 216–17, 221
Areco, Jorge Pacheco, 228
Arévalo, Juan José, 218
Aristide, Jean-Bertrand, 238, 360
Aristy, Hector, 212
Armas, Carlos Castillo, 216–17, 218
Armbruster, Frank, 152, 153
Armstrong, John J., 249
Ashcroft, John, 248
Ashida, Hitoshi, 72
Attica Prison, 158
Atuguba, Raymond, 174
Ávila, General Manuel Francisco Sosa, 219
Aygun, Kemal, 202
Azazzi, Zeremarian, 168
Azurdia, Enrique Peralta, 218–19

Babineau, Ray, 139, 144
Babu, Abdul Rahman, 184
Baer, Robert, 204

12, 100, 101, 103, 104, 105, 178; and OPS, 104; and prisons, 103

Industrial Workers of the World (IWW; Wobblies), 7, 25, 63

Ingersoll, John, 292

Inman, Samuel Guy, 40

International Association of Chiefs of Police, 61, 218

International Cooperation Administration (ICA). *See* 1290-d program

International Criminal Investigative Training Assistance Program (ICITAP), 237–38, 243, 248

International Monetary Fund (IMF), 105

International Police Academy (IPA), 11, 12, 97, 114, 116, 118, 137, 138, 150, 172, 174, 177, 186, 206, 213, 216, 230

International Red Cross, 158, 159

International Voluntary Service (IVS), 136, 159

Iran: 1290-d program and SAVAK, 195–96, 200; 1953 CIA coup, 193–94; 1979 revolution, 199–200; anti-opium campaign, 197–98; Gendarmerie, 188, 339; support for the Shah, 194; torture in, 199–200; Tudeh Party, 194, 199

Iraq: and 1290-d program, 200; Abu Ghraib prison, 156, 201, 247, 250; Ba'ath party, 201; correctional system and abuses, 248–51; Iraqi National Police (INP), 245–47; sectarian violence and civil war, 246–47; suppression of communists, 200, 201, 343; "surge," 248; U.S. invasion of, 244

Israel, 178, 182, 205; and Mossad, 172, 179, 186, 236

Italian Carabinieri, 101, 189

Ivory Coast, 172–73

Iwahig penal colony, 34–35, 66

Jabr, Bayan, 246–47, 365

Jackson, George, 5

Jackson, Jake, 227, 355

Janus, Robert, 103, 206

Japan: and Japan lobby, 69; Japanese Communist Party (JCP), 9, 58, 69–71; Liberal Democratic Party (LDP), 76, 77; Matsukawa incident, 73; National Police Reserve (NPR), 76–77; occupation of Korea, 80–81; Okinawa, 77, 124, 284;

police corruption, 75; penal reform, 65–68; police suppression of May Day demonstrations, 72; police training, 9, 57–78; police use of torture, 74; and Public Safety Division Z Unit, 71, 282; Rural Guard, 65, 76; seizure of newspapers, 74; Tokkô (special higher police), 58, 71, 74

Jeansonne, Tracy, 1

Jessup, Frank, 96–97, 196, 225

Jew, Chester, 359

Jiang Jieshi (Chiang Kai-Shek), 54, 61, 80, 131

Jimenez, Marcos Pérez, 210

Joedodihardjo, Soetjipto, 104

Johnson, Chalmers, 35, 69, 232, 234, 280

Johnson, Marilynn S., 63

Johnson, Ralph, 133, 311

Johnson, Robert H., 147

Johnson, U. Alexis, 122

Johnson administration, 132

Jones, Howard P., 104–5

Jones, Seth G., 239

Joost, Sherman, 299

Jordan, and King Hussein, 205–6

Jos, Nigeria, police college, 174

Jumbish, Jamil, 241

juvenile facilities, 4, 95

Kades, Charles, 59

Kahin, George McT., 100

Kaji, Wataru, 71

Kakonge, John, 186

Kamanga, Ruben, 186

Kan Mai, 183

Kansas City Police Department, 57, 59–60, 125, 146, 224

Karzai, Ahmed Wali, 242

Karzai, Hamid, 240–41

Katay Don Sasorith, 123, 125

Katz, Paul, 118, 175

Katzenberg, Yasha, 166

Kaunda, Kenneth, 184, 186, 187

Kaun Soo Pak, 92

Kaya, Okinori, 77

Kayabinda, Grégoire, 181, 182

Keely, James H., Jr., 191, 337

Kelley, Roland, 222

Kellis, James, 188, 338

Kendrick, W. Freeland, 39

Kennan, George F., 13, 68, 78

Kennedy, John F., 10, 209
Kennedy, Robert, 10, 104, 146, 177, 211
Kennedy administration, 132, 135, 147, 167, 169, 222; and Bolivia, 227; and El Salvador, 222–23; and Ethiopia, 167; and Indonesia, 104; and South Korea, 95; and Special Group on Counter-Insurgency, 10–12, 104, 114, 132, 176, 178, 183, 209; and Thailand, 111, 113; and Venezuela, 210; and Vietnam, 147–48
Kenney, John P., 195, 340
Kenya, 183–84
Kenyatta, Jomo, 183, 184
Kérékou, Mathieu, 330
Kerik, Bernard B., 244, 364
Kerry, John F., 251
Key, David, 107
Keyser, Ralph, 47, 48
khaki and red. *See* Philippines: and development of constabulary
Khalidi, Rashid, 206
Khan, Hajji Juma, 241
Khmer Rouge, 138
Khoranhok Souvannavong, 127
Kieh, George Klay, Jr., 187
Kikunami, Katsumi, 75
Killingray, David, 51, 187
Kimball, George, 316
Kimball, Robert, 310
Kimberling Arthur, 62
Kim Chong-Won ("Tiger Kim"), 92–93, 108, 149, 292
Kim Dong-Choon, 91
Kim Il Sung, 79, 90
Kim Ku, 288
Kim Tu-Han, 86
King, Martin Luther, Jr., 8, 185
King Idris. *See* Libya
Kipling, Rudyard, 18, 25
Kirk, Russell, 179
Kissinger, Henry, 230
Klare, Michael T., 14
Klusman, Charles F., 135
Knapp, Harry S., 46
Knowles, H. H., 37
Knox, Philander, 49
Kolko, Gabriel, 14, 151
Komer, Robert W., 10, 12, 99, 113, 149, 176, 198
Kong Le, 130, 131

Korea (Republic of Korea): and 1290-d program, 93–96; and American Military Government and U.S. Military Advisory Group, 79–89; Cheju-do uprising, 83, 89–90, 290; constabulary, 80, 83; Inchon Boys Prison, 89; Korean Central intelligence Agency (KCIA), 96; and Korean War, 90–92, 98, 103, 166; Kwanju uprising, 97; National Police and U.S. training programs, 9, 79–98; October 1946 Revolts, 87–88; and Office of Public Safety (OPS), 96–97; Republic of Korea Army (ROKA), 83; retention of pro-Japanese officers, 82, 83; Seoul, 82; South Korean Labor Party (SKLP), 84, 89; Truth and Reconciliation Commission, 90; Wanju Jail, 88; Yosu rebellion, 90, 93, 293
Korry, Edward, 167
Kouprasith Abhay, 131, 132, 311
Kourtessis, Michael, 193
Kowalski, Frank, 77
Kriangsak Chamanand, 114
Kriskovich, David J., 237
Kubler, Louis E., 102
Kusomoto, J., 66, 67

Lacey, William, 101
Lair, James "Bill," 109
Lamb, Carroll H., 35
Lancina, Ernest, 226
Landgren, Ray, 137, 148, 179
Lane, Arthur Bliss, 51
Langguth, A. J., 14, 228
Lansdale, Edward, 99, 109–10, 116, 195, 237, 303
Lansing, Robert, 44
Laos: and 1290-d program, 124, 132–33; auto-defense units, 132–34; bombing of, 136, 310, 312; Done Noune Academy, 126; and Geneva Accords, 122, 135; Hmong clandestine army, 121, 134–36, 175, 242; National Police (LNP), 124–38; and OPS, 137–38; Pathet Lao (Neo Lao Hak Xat), 122, 127–28, 129, 132–34, 137–38, 242, 311; Plain of Jars (Sam Neua and Phong Saly provinces), 122, 129, 133, 134, 136; and police training, 121–38; Royal Lao Government (RLG), 122, 123; Royal Lao Army (RLA), 123–24, 129, 133; and War on Drugs, 138, 313

Turkey, 201–2
Turner, Ralph, 93, 146–48, 317, 318
Turner, William, 107

Ubico, Jorge, 216, 217
Uganda, 185–86
Ungar, Leonard, 114, 310
Uniform Crime Report (UCR), 192
United Fruit Company, 49, 216, 220
United States Army Counter-Intelligence Corps (CIC), 72, 84, 86, 108, 189, 288
United States Army Criminal Investigations Division (CID), 84
Universal Construction Company, 123, 306
University of Southern California, 195, 206
Unocal, 139
Untung, Colonel, 104
Updike, Everett, 144, 316
Urton, Ulrich, 336

Vaccaro Brothers Fruit Company, 48
Vaky, Viron, 208, 221
Valderrama, General Jorge Ordóñez, 215
Valentine, Lewis, 63–65, 72, 82
Valeriano, Napoleon, 116
Van Deman, Ralph, 25, 265
Vang Pao, 134–36, 139
Van Houth, 139
Vann, John Paul, 158
Vasiq, Abdullah, 199, 200
Vásquez, Horacio, 46
Vattah Phankam, 127, 130, 134, 137
Velouchiotis, Ares, 190
Venezuela, 210–11
Vernon, Wyman, 94
Vietnam: and 1290-d program, 143–44; Army of the Republic of Vietnam (ARVN), 144, 150, 156; Buddhist protests, 148; Bureau of Investigations (VBI), 143, 145, 146; Civil Guard, 144–45, 147; French Sureté, 141, 143; and Geneva Accords, 142, 144; Hoa Hao and Cao Dai religious sects, 143, 150; National Police Field Force, 149; and OPS, 148; penal system administration, 155–60; police training, 141–61; Provincial Reconnaissance Units (PRUs), 153–55
Villamor, Ignacio, 30
Villard, Henry S., 10, 169, 260
Vincent, Stenio, 45

Vinnell Corporation, 123, 204–5, 236, 306
Vithoon Yasawasdi, 114
Vollmer, August, 4, 61, 94, 143, 189, 292
Voss, Ernest, 86, 289
Vung Tau, 151

Wagner, Gunther, 222, 353
Walters, Vernon, 230
Walton, Frank, 117, 131, 137, 145, 159, 169, 316, 318, 320, 342
War on Drugs, 5, 75–76, 95, 115, 119, 138, 139, 150, 197, 227, 237, 242–43, 313. *See also* Drug Enforcement Administration; Federal Bureau of Narcotics
Wasifi, Izzatullah, 242
Webber, Colonel John, 220
Wedemeyer, Albert, 85
Weiss, Jon, 320
Weld, Kirsten, 216
Welles, Sumner, 46
Weyland, Walter, 198
White, Frank, 123, 315
White, John R., 21, 27, 28, 29, 34, 268
Whitmer, Robert, 116, 168
Wickham, Charles, 190–91, 337
Wickersham Report, 4
Wikileaks, 241, 242, 245
Wilkins, Zoris, 198
Williams, Alexander S., 41–44, 269
Williams, Alexander S. "Clubber," 41
Williams, Garland, 108, 166–67, 168, 173, 175, 197, 198, 202, 290, 326, 341
Williamson, Jeter, 99, 111–12, 116, 126, 148, 180, 204, 251, 366
Willoughby, Gen. Charles, 59, 71, 72, 276, 282
Wilson, Charles M., 117, 304
Wilson, Edwin, 340
Wilson, Orlando W., 112, 143, 173, 189–90, 192, 259, 358
Wirkus, Faustin E., 40
Wise, Frederic M., 42
Witajewski, Robert M., 248
Wood, Leonard, 28, 266
Wooner, Orvall, 206
Worcester, Dean, 28, 132
Wright, Luke E., 23
Wu Han Chai, 85

Xe (Blackwater), 243

Jeremy Kuzmarov received his PhD in history from Brandeis University in 2006 and holds BA and MA degrees from McGill University. He has taught at Bucknell University and Emmanuel College and is J. P. Walker Assistant Professor of History at the University of Tulsa. He is the author of *The Myth of the Addicted Army: Vietnam and the Modern War on Drugs* (University of Massachusetts Press, 2009). In 2010, Kuzmarov was named a Top Young Historian by History News Network. He lives in Tulsa with his wife, Ngosa, and daughter, Chanda.